The Law Code of Hammurabi

Transliterated and Literally Translated from its Early Classical Arabic Language

Arabic Transliteration, Arabic and English Translations, Introduction, and Critique by

Saad D. Abulhab

Blautopf Publishing

B l a u t o p f Publishing
blautopfpublishing.com
New York

Colophon
English text set in *Cambria*, *Calibri* and *Arial*
Arabic text set in *PF NuyorkArabic* and *Arial*

Publisher's Cataloging-in-Publication Data

The Law Code of Hammurabi: Transliterated and Literally Translated from its Early Classical Arabic Language/ [Editor] Saad D. Abulhab
p. cm.
1. Hammurabi, King of Babylonia. 2. Code of Hammurabi.
3. Law -- Iraq -- Babylonia – Sources. 4. Arabic Language – History.
5. Cuneiform inscriptions, Akkadian.
6. Law, Assyro-Babylonian -- Translations into English.
7. Law, Assyro-Babylonian -- Translations into Arabic.
I. Title. II. Hammurabi. Akkadian. III. Hammurabi. English.
IV. Hammurabi. Arabic. V. Abulhab, Saad D.

PJ3771.G6 A235 2017
892.119–dc22
Library of Congress Control Number: 2017962789
CIP

ISBN: 978-0998172705 (hardcover)
ISBN: 978-1981340903 (paperback)
Google Play: 1981340904 (ebook)

First Edition

Printed by Lightning Source©, an INGRAM© company

25 23 21 19 17 8 7 6 5 4 3 2 1

DEDICATION

To the early scholars of the Islamic Arab civilization whose unparalleled, unbiased, and truly scientific linguistic research had produced the many incredible historical Arabic etymological references that have preserved the substantial facts about the grammar, usage, and history of the Arabic language, the undisputed language of the people of the greater Arabian Peninsula, including Iraq and the Levant, past and present, without their magnificent manuscripts, I could not have done my pioneering research.

To my wife, Sabine, and my daughters, Yasmine and Zena, whose genuine caring and integrity, and inspiring hard work and accomplishments, provide me with the peace of mind I need to continue my research work.

TABLE OF CONTENTS

An Introduction to the Language and Script of the Hammurabi Stele

The translation work herein presented is my second major work on an important ancient Mesopotamian document, since the early 2011. It involves a new translation and Arabic transliteration of a non-literary text written in an old Akkadian language. Namely, the old Babylonian law code inscribed in cuneiform on the well-preserved stele of King Hammurabi (1810-1750 BCE) of Babylonia, which is the earliest known law code in the world. My first translation work involved a breakthrough Arabic transliteration and translation of about 800 text lines of a late Akkadian language literary work from the standard edition of the Epic of Gilgamesh, and about 100 corresponding lines from the old Babylonian and Ugaritic editions. This work was published in 2016 as a book titled "The Epic of Gilgamesh: Selected Readings from its Original Early Arabic Language".

In this current translation I employed the same decipherment methodology I used in the first one. Specifically, I deciphered all Latin transliterated cuneiform words, whether Sumerian or Akkadian, utilizing the historical Arabic etymological references as primary tools, and the modern Assyriology references as secondary tools. Using this approach, the resulting translation is therefore a translation based on *actual* documented word meanings and usages, rather than *speculated* ones. As with my first work, to ensure wider accessibility and critical feedback to the working details of my developing but proven metodology, this second translation work was also openly shared with students and scholars of Arabic and Assyriology, ahead of the book publication of the completed work.

The methodology I employed to uncover the underlying Arabic root words is time-consuming but simple. For each so-called Akkadian and Sumerian word, I first checked the meanings it was assigned in modern western dictionaries, namely, the Chicago Assyrian Dictionary (CAD)* and the electronic version of the Pennsylvania Sumerian Dictionary (ePSD). I then used a self-compiled master Latin-Arabic letter substitution table (provided in the Part 2.1) in order to arrive to the

* Instead of CAD I used the Akkadian-Arabic Language Dictionary (AALD) by Ali Y. al-Jubouri, professor of the Akkadian and Cuneiform studies in the University of Mosul, a value-added concise Arabic translation of CAD published by the Abu Dhabi Culture and Heritage Council in 2009, which included an expanded introduction of the Akkadian language and marked more than 1700 Arabic words in CAD still in use today.

possible phonetically equivalent Arabic root word(s). This table is based on my research notes about the Sumerian-Akkadian and Akkadian-Akkadian letter substitutions in the ancient inscriptions, and the Arabic-Arabic letters substitutions confirmed by the old Arabic manuscripts. Root word(s) with identical or logically close meanings in both the historical Arabic manuscripts (i.e. Lisan al-Arab) and the modern western Akkadian dictionaries, were then thoroughly examined in the Arabic references to pinpoint the most likely root(s) and to select the actual historically-confirmed meaning(s). In the few cases where no identical or close meaning(s) were found, I used the best possible meaning(s) from either the Arabic or the western references.

To compare my work withprior work done on the Hammurabi code, I consulted with seven previous translations. Five from the early 20th century and two from after the mid-20th century. The first was in English by H. Otto Sommer in 1903, but it was adapted from the German translation by Hugo Winckler (1863-1913) in 1902. The second was by Claude Hermann Walter Johns (1857-1920) in 1903. The third was by Robert Francis Harper (1864-1914) in 1904. The fourth was by W. W. Davies in 1905. The fifth was by Leonard William King (1869-1919) in 1910. The sixth was in Arabic by Maḥmūd al-Amīn (d. 1980) in 1961. The last one was by Mervyn E. J. Richardson (1943-) in 2000. For my translation, I used the cuneiform Latin transliterations provided by Harper as my primary text. However, I have also consulted with the transliterations offered by Richardson, and used his transliterations of the recovered fragments corresponding to the erased 33 laws on the main Hammurabi stele in the Louvre.

With the publication of this book, exactly one year after the publication of my translation of three key tablets from the epic of Gilgamesh, I hope the two books combined will serve as a unique textbook and reference tool to study from an Arabic prespective the language of the ancient Akkadians for a time period extending over two millennia, from about 2200 BCE onward. This book, when used in conjunction with the author's previous Epic of Gilgamesh book, provides the open-minded students and scholars of both Arabic and Assyriology a detailed insight into the pioneering methodology employed by the author to decipher old Mesopotamian texts. Namely, using the historical etymological Arabic manuscripts which were written by hundreds of accomplished scholars more than a thousand years ago as the authorotative references.*

The result of using this new methodology does not only provide more accurate, non-speculated, translations, and preserve the spirit and linguistic style of the original texts, but also provide more realistic phonetic values of the cuneiform signs, which in turn produce far more realistic readings and understanding of the overall text. The old Arabic linguistic tools provide us the opportunity to correct the many awkward translations currently presumed for key lines in both of texts. Just to mention few, the reader can compare this new translation of the following laws to other translations: §58, §64, §65 §66, §70, §71, §73, §102, §126, §132, §142, §172, §181, §191, §202, §221, §226, §227, §233, §235, §246, §248, §251. Additionally, reading the Hammurabi code through Arabic makes it very clear that many of its laws were written intentionally to reference previous ones, a standard way in writing laws even today.

* Part 2.2 include a list of these references which were written between 905 CE and 1790, well the before modern discoveries in Mesopotamia.

Naturally, no translation of any ancient text can be proclaimed 100% accurate, let alone a translation utilizing a new and developing methodology. However, in this new translation of the Hammurabi law code, I have gained far more experience in deciphering ancient Mesopotamian texts using my own approach, and I therefore hope I have made far less mistakes. In fact, I would not exaggerate to proclaim that after 11 months working on this fascinating project, I feel as if I am able to read aloud the text of the code of Hammurabi in its own exact old Arabic sentences!

The text of the Hammurabi stele offers students of both Arabic and Assyriology a perfect and unique opportunity to accurately study the language and grammar of its ancient Arabic language. To offer a textbook reference value and ease of use, the numbered phonetic transcription for each law is offered right above its corresponding numbered Arabic transcription. The text of each law is literally translated into Arabic and English in order to illustrate to students how the translation was concluded, to account for each and every word in the original law text, and to preserve its actual overall writing style. A detailed subject guide to the laws of Hammurabi is also given in the beginning of Part 1, to illustrate the well-thought organization of the codex and to facilitate easier reading experience. Finally, all relevant reference entries from both the historical Arabic manuscripts and the modern linguistic tools of Assyriology are provided as author's referenced words index in the Part 2.3. Next in this expanded introduction, I will briefly discuss three important topics. The identity of the ancient language of Mesopotamia, the layout and script of the Hammurabi stele, and the meaning of the nickname Hammurabi according to the evidence of his own words in a key paragraph of his prologue on the stele.

The One Language of Ancient Mesopotamia

Six years ago, following several years of extensive work on major Arabic Nabataean and Musnad inscriptions, I stumbled upon an eye-opening fact regarding the Nabataeans, pointed out more than a thousand years ago by the accomplished scholars of the Islamic Arab civilizations. They said the Nabataeans of Iraq (old Mesopotamians) were *much* older than the Nabataeans of the Levant and Northern Hijaz, whom most scholars today refer to *exclusively* as "the Nabataeans". In contrast to the misleading claim by western scholars that the origin of the Nabataeans is "unknown"*, scholars of the old Islamic Arab civilizations defined the Nabataeans as those who settled in cities and farmed lands, clearly to differentiate them from the nomad Arabs. Even the people of ancient Oman were referred to as the Nabataeans of Oman by the early Islamic Arab scholars. In their definition, these scholars were classifying the Arabs exclusively, since they have never called the Persian or Roman farmers and settlers of cities, Nabataeans! In fact, the people of the prominent tribe of Quraysh in Makkah, the tribe of prophet Muhammad, have historically prided themselves as being "part of the Nabataeans of Kūtha Rabba (i. e. Ur), which was said to be the birthplace of Abraham"†

---

* Jane Taylor. Petra and the Lost Kingdom of the Nabataeans. 2001.

† "They are the Nabataeans and one who belongs to them is Nabataean. In al-Ṣaḥḥāḥ: they were settling in al-Baṭā'iḥ among Iraqis. *Ayyūb bin al-Qaryah* said: the people of ʿUmān are Arabs who were Nabatized, and the people of Baḥrayn were Nabataeans who were Arabized. *Ibn al-ʿAbbās* said: we the people of *Quraysh* are part of the Nabataeans of *Kūtha Rabba* (i. e. Ur), which was said to be the birthplace of Abraham and the Nabataeans were its

Clearly, the Nabataeans (i.e. the Canaanites of the Levant and the Akkadians of Mesopotamia) did not speak a foreign, non-Arabic language, nor were they of a foreign race. Since they were basically classified only as land and city dwellers, they must have spoken the language of their nomad ancestors, with a variety of localized dialects not worthy of classification as "different languages". Just as it was and still is the case with their descendants of the Fertile Crescent, thousands of years later, before and after Islam! This is not a speculation: it was not a coincidence that the language of the Ugaritic version of the Epic of Gilgamesh from northwestern Syria was linguistically identical to that of the Babylonian edition! The above conclusions about the language of the ancient people of the Fertile Crescent are the only scientifically feasible ones. The nomad Arabs must have predated the absolute majority of the settled populations in the northern Arabian Peninsula. City folks do not evolve to or choose to become Bedouins!

The "Epic of Gilgamesh" and the "Code of Hammurabi" were *very clearly* written in a formal, early Arabic language, not a local dialect of the Arabic language. That formal language could not have been the daily spoken language of any particular local group. It must have been only a written language, just like the more developed formal Arabic language of the Quran and pre-Islamic poetry, or the modern classical Arabic that was subsequently developed and is still being used even today. If one can read any document *literally* through classical Arabic, then it is Arabic document. It is that clear and that simple! After all, the formal language documented in the Quran could not have been a result of only hundreds of years of evolution, but thousands of years.

The overwhelming evidence of an early classical Arabic identity of the language of both Gilgamish and Hammurabi texts can not only be seen through its words, but also in the grammar of its sentences. All root word derivations are either identical or slightly different from the derivations used in classical Arabic. The vocalizations of subjects, objects, verbs, and genitives in the Akkadian sentences are astonishingly identical to that of formal Arabic. The loose and sometimes "chaotic" placement of words in sentences is strikingly identical to that of pre-Islamic old Arabic. In my observation, the older the formal Akkadian language was the clearer in its formal Arabic identity! The fascinating language of the code of Hammurabi, compared to that of the Epic of Gilgamesh, is a definite example of that.

Despite the incredible, technical accomplishments of the field of Assyriology, to an outsider, this field seems overly close-minded and politicized. Dealing with scholars in this field frequently feels like dealing with members of a fanatic cult. The founding fathers laid out key groundless assumptions and their future students keep on "chanting"! Even though the overwhelming majority of scholars and students of Assyriology lack any suitable knowledge of the Arabic language, past or present, they would immediately theorize that the Akkadian language could not be early Arabic. Those few, who are willing to accept an Arabic connection, would rush to explain

---

inhabitants. *'Amru bin Ma'ad Yakrub* said that *'Umar* told him through *Sa'd bin Abī Waqqās* and said: 'he is an Arab in his giving and Nabataean in his collection'. He wanted to say he was skillful in his construction and taxing practices like the Nabataeans, because they were the prominent people of Iraq. *Ibn Awfá* said: 'we were before the Nabataeans of the Levant', and in other sources: 'we were Nabataeans from the Levant'". Ibn Mandhūr (d. 1311). *Lisan al-'Arab*. Root word entry: nbṭ.

that the languages of the greater Arabian Peninsula were all derived from a presumed mother "Semitic" language. Except that, after more than two centuries since the invention of this unsubstantiated, biblically-inspired "Semitic" classification, by western scholars in the early 19th century, we are yet to find a single inscription of this *never-existing* mother language!* In fact, the name *Shem* (Arabic: *Sām*) did not even make it to the Quran, the most important textbook of the Arabic language, the language of 90% of the people of the greater Arabian Peninsula, past and present.

Andrew George wrote *"I find translations of Babylonian poems more satisfactory when they treat the text as Akkadian (a fully deciphered east Semitic language), rather than classical Arabic (a west Semitic language). West and East Semitic have different morphology, especially of the verb, and that makes a big difference to parsing the verb forms"*†. He further explained that *"Features of Akkadians that distinguish it from most other Semitic: (a) the range of consonants is sharply reduced, probably under influence of Sumerian, (b) word order in prose is subject-object-verb (SOV) as in Sumerian (Semitic is usually VSO), and (c) the verbal conjugations are put to uses different from their counterparts in other Semitic."*‡ George is right, treating a Babylonian text as ancient Akkadian rather than relatively modern, classical Arabic is far more satisfactory. However, let alone Semitic is a purely coined language, the Akkadian language is not *"fully deciphered"* nor the classical Arabic language is geographically-confined. We do not know *exactly* how the Akkadian or Sumerian words *actually* pronounced or sounded through the imperfect "Latinized" cuneiform script (i.e. *ša* could be *sha, dha, tha, ta*, or *sa*). Nor do we know for sure how many current Arabic consonants were used in either Akkadian or Sumerian. The word order in prose in old Arabic was never strictly VSO, nor was it strictly SOV in Akkadian. Even if classical Arabic, which is a formal written-only language, was first evolved in western Arabia, and was different in its linguistic style than Akkadian, it needs not be morphologically or characteristically identical to an ancestral formal language, to qualify as a substantially same language. Old English and Shakespearian English are both English even though they don't share exact characteristics. Having *"different morphology"* is more a byproduct of an evolution process of a language, writing methodology, and script, than an indication that early classical Arabic is a different language than formal Akkadian.

Following the publication of my unique translation of three tablets of the Epic of Gilgamesh, I sent several proposals via email to major American universities to present my findings in an open forum. The responses I received were the usual and expected responses I became accustomed to over the years. A prominent Yale professor of Assyriology quickly proclaimed: *"this member of the assyriology section will pass. this man thinks that the epic was originally in arabic, and, evidently, that akkadian is a dialect of 'old arabic'"*. Another one from New York University wrote after couple days: *"the author's work appears not to share some of the most basic commonly agreed*

* "The name Semite, or Shemite, means a descendant of Shem, one of the sons of Noah, whose ancestors are listed most prominently in the Table of Nations (Gen. 10:21–31). August Ludwig von Schlözer is generally credited with the origin of the name Semite in 1781. Von Schlözer derived the term from Shem, the eldest son of Noah (Gen. 5:32; 6:10; 9:18; 10:1; 1 Chron. 1:4), to describe a family of related languages". Bigalke, Ron J. Jr., *Anti-Semitism*. Article Abstract. The Encyclopedia of Christian Civilization. November 25 2011. DOI: 10.1002/9780470670606.wbecc0054

† Personal email exchange with Prof. Andrew George of the SOAS, the University of London, on October 25th, 2014.

‡ Andrew George, Babylonian and Assyrians: a History of Akkadian. *https://eprints.soas.ac.uk/3139/1/PAGE_31-71.pdf*

analytical categories for interpretation of Gilgamesh, and I would not recommend my Department as a venue for any proposed talk". Reading through the above hasty and readily dismissive answers, with meaningless phrases like "*commonly agreed analytical categories for interpretation*", I am not sure where to classify them. Surely, they belong somewhere between ignorance and "scholarly censorship".

Early on, the founding fathers of Assyriology* proclaimed the origin of the Sumerians, the people and their language, is "unknown". Two hundred years later, their faithful students/scholars in universities around the world continue in their footsteps, struggling to solve this "mysterious" puzzle! Sounds familiar? Recall, western scholars also theorized that the exact origin of the Nabataeans is "unknown". The hypothesis of an "unknown" Sumerian origin should, therefore, raise a red flag, and be worthy of further investigation. In my fairly thorough examination, coming across hundreds of presumed Sumerian words within the Akkadian inscriptions, I have not encountered any Sumerian word that could not be explained fully using the historical Arabic manuscripts. The common claim that the Arabic and Sumerian languages are fundamentally different languages because the Sumerian words consisted of two syllables only, and the Arabic root words consist of three, is a baseless claim. Arabic has plenty of two-letter root words, and the Sumerian language has plenty of multiple-syllable (or consonant letters) words†.

German scholar and historian Kurt W. Marek (C. W. Ceram) wrote, "*The existence of the Sumerians was originally assumed on the basis of scientific deductions. Today their existence is no longer doubted; too many examples of their art and handicrafts are on exhibit in our museums.*" He continued saying "*one fact is beyond doubt: the Sumerians, a non-Semitic, dark-haired people—"black-headed" is the term for them in the inscriptions—were the last to enter the great delta of the Tigris and Euphrates. Before their arrival the land had been settled by two, probably different, Semitic tribes. But the Sumerians brought with them a superior culture, some of its basic elements already developed to their final form, which they imposed upon the barbaric Semites. Where was the Sumerian homeland? Archeology has yet to answer this question. The Sumerian language is somewhat similar to the ancient Turkish, or Turanian. That is all that is known about them, and everything else is pure hypothesis. People who habitually represented their gods as standing on mountains, who prayed to them from high places and who for this purpose even built artificial hills or ziggurats, on the plains of their adopted land, could not, it seems, have come from flat country.*"‡ Marek summarized very precisely and eloquently western scholar's point of view regarding the Sumerians.

Before discussing the above hypotheses which were not "scientific deductions" at all, it should be pointed out first, that the term "black-headed", which was explained as "black-haired", is fully based on the translation of the Sumerian word *SAG.GIG* and its Akkadian equivalent. However,

---

* Sir Austen Henry Layard is generally considered the Father of Assyriology, "though he himself would probably have applied the epithet to Sir Henry Rawlinson", according to the Cambridge Library Collection Blog, for example, https://cambridgelibrarycollection.wordpress.com/2014/05/27/the-father-of-assyriology/

† Many examples of such two-letter Arabic words, usually represented as root words with last letter repeated (i.e. مدّ؛ مدد), and of multiple consonant letters Sumerian words can be found in Section 2.3, "Referenced Words Index".

‡ Kurt W. Marek (C. W. Ceram). Gods, Graves, and Scholars: the Story of Archeology. 1951.

this translation is a purely speculated one! The Akkadian equivalent, *ṣalmat qaqqadi* ظلمة قَقَدِ, relates to head darkness (i.e. mind cluelessness), not blackness as color. Just as the Akkadian equivalent of the Sumerian word *utu'e* for sunrise, ṣīt šamši ضِيةً\ضِحْية شمسِ, relates to sun lightness /rising, not whiteness as color. Even modern Sumerian dictionaries stayed away from this "black-haired" notion and offered meanings like "headache" or "humankind". Luckily, the word *SAG.GIG* appeared in an important paragraph of Hammurabi's prologue in the stele. I translated the word there according to old Arabic language analysis as "pitch darkness of mind" (i.e. ignorance and cluelessness). The reader will have a chance to decide later if the current circulated translations of this paragraph, where Hammurabi supposedly said he came out like the god Shamash (or the sun) over the black-headed people (or race), makes any sense. If indeed this word means "black-haired" people, referring to the foreign Sumerian elite minority, then Hammurabi's sentence would be excluding the majority of his subjects, the Akkadians! Besides, the ancient Arabs (or so-called Semites) are even more black-haired than the Turkic or any other presumed Asian group coming from the east. Why would these Sumerian "outsiders" be nicknamed "black-haired" in a land where everyone is black-haired?

Second, if before the arrival of the Sumerians, Sumer was settled by "two, probably different, Semitic tribes" (i.e. Arabs), then the early language of the land was indeed the language of the Akkadian Arabs. Assuming the ruling Sumerian elite were of foreign origin does not change this fact, unless one would claim that they forced their "new" language on the people. By large, foreign occupiers communicate in their subjects' language. Of course, western scholar's claim that the Sumerian rulers were outsiders is not supported by any scholarly evidence. Unless one would count as scholarly evidence the racist and inaccurate assertion that the Sumerians who had "a superior culture", "which they imposed upon the barbaric Semites", "could not, it seems, have come from flat country". The early scholars, it seems, were not aware of the geography of Arabia which has plenty of hills and mountains, and by no means a "flat country". In fact, the ancient heart of Arabia and the source of its successive migrations, Yemen, "carved" superior civilizations in their high mountains. The above ridicules notion of "barbaric Semites" reminds one with the racist assertions of the known Oxford-trained archeologist, T. E. Lawrence, who claimed the Arabs, *"were a limited, narrow-minded people, whose inert intellects lay fallow in incurious resignation." "Their imaginations were vivid, but not creative." "They have no organizations of mind or body. They invented no systems of philosophy, no complex mythologies".*[*]

The common notion that the Sumerian language has sounds and letters not existing in Akkadian or Arabic is another incorrect hypothesis. No one can be certain how the Sumerian words actually sounded. Transliterating these words from their early primitive cuneiform symbols into Latin words have surely complicated and blurred the picture even further. It is my observation though, that the early Sumerian writing system was possibly seen as an inadequate system to represent the spoken and formal languages of the land and therefore needed to be replaced. The more developed and precise Akkadian cuneiform writing system was not "borrowing" the writing system of an independent language, but reforming the earlier highly-limited Sumerian writing

---

[*] Saad D. Abulhab. DeArabyzing Arabia: Tracing Western Scholarship on the History of the Arabs and Arabic Language and Script. 2011.

system for a single evolving language. The words and sentence structures of the so-called Sumerian language clearly confirm that. One cannot conclude with any certainty that the peculiar structure of the written Sumerian sentences was mimicking the actually-spoken sentences, or it was just an abstract writing methodology to record a language. I think it was a mixture of both.

Earlier this year, a scholar of Assyriology and a good friend of mine sent me a Sumerian sentence side by side it's completely different-sounding equivalent Akkadian sentence, to illustrate that the two languages are completely different languages. He also pointed out to the modern discoveries of many Akkadian tablets used by scribes as Akkadian-Sumerian language lexicons, to further support his point. Of course, having same language dictionaries is quite normal and does not prove the two languages are different (i. e. Lisan al-Arab is a same language dictionary). With an open mind, I examined the two sentences for a couple days, only to conclude that the so-called Sumerian sentence was a clear and sound Arabic sentence, written in a beautiful southern Iraqi slang flavor. Even today, the southern Iraqi dialect is closely related to the dialects of the Bedouin Arabs and the people of Yemen.

The fact that the two Akkadian and Sumerian sentences were different does not indicate they were from two different languages. In Arabic, as in all other languages, one can easily identify different sentences having identical meanings during any one historical time period, and particularly during two different historical time periods. In the given sentences I examined, the Sumerian sentence clearly utilized word usages that were gradually replaced over a long period of language evolution. The identical meanings of the corresponding words in both sentences, as documented in the neutral Arabic historical manuscripts, clearly indicate that the two sentences belong to one language. To conclude, there is no concrete evidence that the Sumerian language was substantially different than the Akkadian language and could not been a proto Arabic language in its very early stages or just a written form of an early southern Iraqi Arabic dialect.

Below are the Latin transliterations of both sentences in question, followed by my Arabic transliterations, and my modern Arabic and English translations. Also provided below are entries from the Arabic historical references.

<u>Sumerian version:</u>

im.nu.te.en diĝir.ra.na gi-gim in.ša$_5$.ša$_5$

إمْنُؤ تعِنْ [طعِنْ] دِجرَّنَة غِيْ-جيمَ ينشَعْشَعْ

الواحد اللاخائف [اللامطيع] إلاهِه، مثل قصبة، يتشعشع (يتكسَّر ويتطاير)

The one (who is) not weary (fearful) [not obeying] of his god, like a reed, he shall be shattered

<u>Akkadian version:</u>

la pa-li-iḫ DINGIR-šú ki-ma qa-né-e uḫ-ta-aṣ-ṣi-iṣ

لا فَلِه دِنْجِرْ ذو كيمَ قَنَئ يُحْتَصِص

اللامُبارِك [اللامُتقي (اللاخائف)] إلاهِه، مثل قصبة، يتناثَرْ

The not weary (fearful) of his god, like a reed, he shall be scattered

Referenced Words:

te

تعع \ تعا (لسان العرب) ووقع القومُ في تَعاتِعَ إذا وقعوا في أراجيف وتخليط. التَّعُّ: الاسْتِرْخاء. تَعَّ تَعًا وأَتَعَّ: قاء كَثَعَّ؛ والتعْتعةُ: الحركة العَنيفة، وقد تَعْتَعه إذا عتَله وأقْلقه. أبو عمرو: تَعْتَعْتُ الرجلَ وتَلْتَلْتُه: وهو أن تُقْبِلَ به وتُدْبِرَ به وتُعنِفَ عليه في ذلك، وهي التعتعة والتَّلْتلةُ أيضاً. وفي الحديث: حتى يؤخَذَ للضعيف حقُّه غير مُتعتَع، بفتح التاء، أي من غير أن يُصيبه أذى يُقْلِقه ويُزعجه. والتَّاعي اللِّبأُ المسترخي،

طعع \ طعا (لسان العرب) حكى الأزهري عن ابن الأعرابي: طَعَا إذا تباعد. غيره: طعَا إذا ذلَّ. أبو عمرو: الطاعي بمعنى الطائع إذا ذلَّ. قال ابن الأعرابي: الإطْعاءُ: الطَّاعةُ. والطَّعْطَعُ من الأرض: المطمئن.

nu

نأي (لسان العرب) النَّأْيُ: البُعدُ. نأى يَنأى: بَعُد، بوزن نعى ينْعى. ونأوْتُ: بَعُدْت، لغة في نأيْتُ. والنَّأْيُ المُفارقة؛ قال المنذري: أنشدني المبرد: أعاذِلَ، إنْ يُصْبِحْ صَدايَ بقَفْرةٍ بَعِيداً، نآني زائري وقريبي قال المبرد: قوله نآني فيه وجهان: أحدهما أنه بمعنى أبعدني كقولك زِدْته فزاد ونقصته فنقص، والوجه الآخر في نآني أنه بمعنى نأى عني، والنُّؤْي والنِّئْي والنَّأْيُ والنُّؤى، بفتح الهمزة على مثال النُّفى؛

gi

غيي \ غيا (لسان العرب) الغايةُ: مدى الشيء. والغايةُ أقْصى الشيء. اللَّيْثُ : الغايةُ مدى كلِّ شيءٍ وألِفُه ياءٌ، وهو من تأْليف غَيْنٍ وياءين، وتَصْغيرُها غُيَيَّة، تقول: غَيَّيْت غاية. وغايةُ الخمّار: رايتُه. وغيّاها: عملها، وأَغْياها: نصبها. والغاية القَصَبة التي يُصادُ بها العصافيرُ. والغياية: السحابة المُنفردة، وقيل: الواقفة؛ عن ابن الأعرابي.

ša

شعع \ شعا (لسان العرب) وتطايرَت العَصا والقَصَبةُ شعاعاً إذا ضربت بها على حائط فتكسَّرتْ وتطايرت قِصَداً وقطعاً. وأشَعَّ البعيرُ بَوْله أي فرَّقه وقطَّعه، وكذلك شَعَّ بوله يَشُعُّه أي فرّقه أيضاً فشعَّ يَشِعُّ إذا انتشر وأوْزَع به مثله. ابن الأعرابي: شَعَّ القومُ إذا تفرَّقوا؛ قال الأخطل: عِصابةُ سَبْيٍ شَعَّ أنْ يُتَقَسَّما أي تفرَّقوا حِذارَ أن يُتقسَّموا. قال ابن المبارك: شَعْشَعها خلط بعضها ببعض كما يُشَعْشَعُ الشرابُ بالماء إذا مُزِجَ به، ورُوِيتْ هذه اللفظةُ سَغْسَغها، بالسين المهملة والغين المعجمة، وغارةٌ شَعْواءُ: فاشيةٌ متفرّقة؛

diĝir; dingir

دجر (لسان العرب) الدَّجرُ: الحَيْرةُ، الدال والجيم والراء أصلٌ يدلُّ على لُبْس. فالدَّيجور: الظَّلام؛

دجج (القاموس المحيط) والدُّجُجُ، بضمتينِ: شدةُ الظُّلْمَةِ، كالدُّجَة، والجبالُ السُّودُ. وأسْودُ دُجْدُجٌ ودُجاجِيٌّ، بضمهما: حالكٌ. ولَيْلَةٌ دَيْجوجٌ ودَجْداجةٌ: مُظْلِمةٌ.

دنج (لسان العرب) الدُّنُجُ: العُقلاءُ من الرجال.

دجا (الصّحاح في اللغة) الدُجى: الظلمة. يقال: دجا الليل يدْجو دُجْوًا. وليلةٌ داجيةٌ. وكذا أدجى الليلُ وتَدجّى. ودياجي الليل: حنادسُه، كأنّه جمع ديْجاةٍ. قال الأصمعيّ: دَجا الليل إنّما هو ألبسَ كلَّ شيء، وليس هو من الظُلمة. قال: ومنه قولهم: دجا الإسلامُ، أي قويَ وألبس كلَّ شيء.

pa-li-iḫ

فَلَّهُ (القاموس المحيط) فلَّهُ وفلَّلَهُ: ثلَمه فتفلَّلَ وانفلَّ وافتَلَّ، و~ القومَ: هزَمهُم، فانفَلُّوا وتَفَلَّلوا. وقومٌ فَلٌّ: مُنْهزِمون

qa-né-e

قنا (لسان العرب) وقيل: كل عصا مستوية فهي قناة، وقيل: كل عصا مُستوية أو مُعْوجَّة فهي قناة، والجمع كالجمع؛ التهذيب: أبو بكر وكلُّ خشبة عند العرب قَناةٌ وعَصا ، والرُّمح عصاً ؛ قال أبو منصور: القناة من الرماح ما كان أجوف كالقَصبة، ولذلك قيل للكظائم التي تجري تحتَ الأرض قنوات، واحدتها قناة، ويقال لمجارِي مائها قصَبٌ تشبيها بالقَصَب الأجوف، وقناةُ الظهر: التي تنتظم الفقار.

uḫ-ta-aṣ-ṣi-iṣ

حصص (لسان العرب) وحصَّ شعرَهُ وانْحصَّ: انجرَدَ وتناثرَ. وانْحصَّ ورَقُ الشجر وانْحتَّ إذا تناثر. ويقال: حَصْحَصْتُ التراب وغيره إذا حرَّكْته وفحصْته يميناً وشمالاً.

The Layout and Script of the Hammurabi Stele

Before proceeding into the translation of the Hammurabi law code on the stele in the Louvre museum, it is important to share with the reader how this stele was organized, how it should be read, and what exact cuneiform script it utilized. This may seem like an unnecessary topic to discuss, but following several in-depth discussions with even scholars of Assyriology, I concluded that there are wide misconceptions about the crucial technical details of this stele and its script, that need to be clarified.

Students of Assyriology are taught that cuneiform is a strictly right-to-left script. Here is how this script was described to me by an excellent student of Assyriology: *"Sumerian, Babylonian and*

Assyrian cuneiform wedges were always written pointing left to right or top to bottom. Wedges written diagonally follow the same rule, left to right. There is not a single sign written with the wedge pointing to the left or bottom to top." An accomplished scholar of Assyriology wrote me: *"the direction of cuneiform writing is always from left to right, the reason being that when a scribe places the tablet in his left hand to mark the cuneiform signs on it with his right hand, using a reed pen, he would not be able to see the line of writing clearly if he goes right-to-left".* His last point is widely emphasized in practical workshops teaching cuneiform writing in schools and museums. Supporting the above explanations further, all transcriptions and fonts of the cuneiform script follow this strict left-to-right order.

It is true that the cuneiform script seen on many thousands of tablets produced in the first millennium BC were strictly left-to-right. However, the earliest forms of a relatively matured cuneiform script started as a monumental (top-to-bottom) script with wedges always written pointing right-to-left or top to bottom. In other words, it started as a strictly right-to-left script. Some refer to this script as "proto cuneiform". Except that this so-called "proto cuneiform" was in use for thousands of years, and even during the time periods when the left-to-right script was in use! The Hammurabi stele, one the most important Akkadian documents, is a good example! A reasonable directionality classification of the cuneiform script should therefore be, multi-directional script. In fact, the ancient cuneiform script behaves exactly like the prominent Arabic Musnad script, which was used for more than 2000 years in Arabia before its replacement by the modern Arabic script after Islam. In both scripts, the signs or letters changed their orientations (i. e. flipped) according to their ordering direction.

To understand how the cuneiform script was written on the stele, one must understand its layout first. The Hammurabi stele is 2.25 m (7.4 ft.) tall. The bottom third of it, about 0.7 m (2.25 ft.), has no writing. About half of this unwritten area was buried to anchor the stone in its upright position, which was its position for writing and reading. Both, the engraving of the Hammurabi and Shamash image and the chiseling of the cuneiform signs were clearly done on the stone in this upright position. The cylinder-like stele was divided into 44 horizontal bands (row fields), which were in turn cross-divided by thin columns, extending from the top of the written area to its bottom, going around the stone. Within each of these bands the scribe placed the cuneiform signs top-to-bottom in the enclosed mini columns, moving right-to-left. This would ensure that the text of each law will be placed together in a specific area of a specific band and these laws will be ordered top-to-bottom along the written area. In other words, law #1 will be in an upper band, while law #282 will be in a bottom band. Unfortunately, 5 horizontal bands in the stele, assumed to contain 33 laws, were intentionally erased. However, scholars recovered tablet fragments elsewhere containing some of these lost laws.

For the sake of simplifying the reading of the cuneiform script on the stele, Bergmann "opened" all bands from top to bottom and "stitched" them together into one long horizontal strip. He then inverted it 90 degrees counterclockwise and divided it into pieces, placing them as equal columns on paper to achieve a strict left-to-right reading order. Furthermore, he marked the start of each

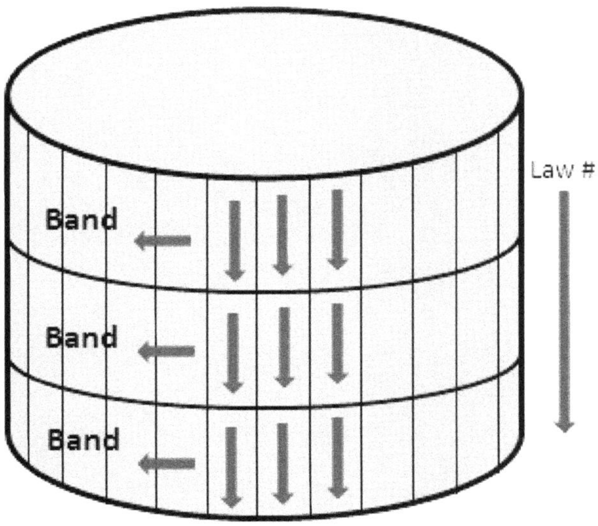

Figure (1) (left) A full image of the 2.25 m (7.4 ft.) tall Hammurabi basalt stele kept today in the Louvre Museum, Paris. Notice that the bottom third of the index finger like stone, about 0.7 m (2.25 ft.), has no writing. Also notice the many horizontal bands around the stone, cross-divided by thin columns stretching over the full length of the writing area. (Above) A cross-section diagram of the stele demonstrating the right-to-left, top-to-bottom direction of cuneiform signs writing in a mini column within the boundary of each band to form a band area for each specific law. The same direction is followed for reading, and law numbers increase downwards.

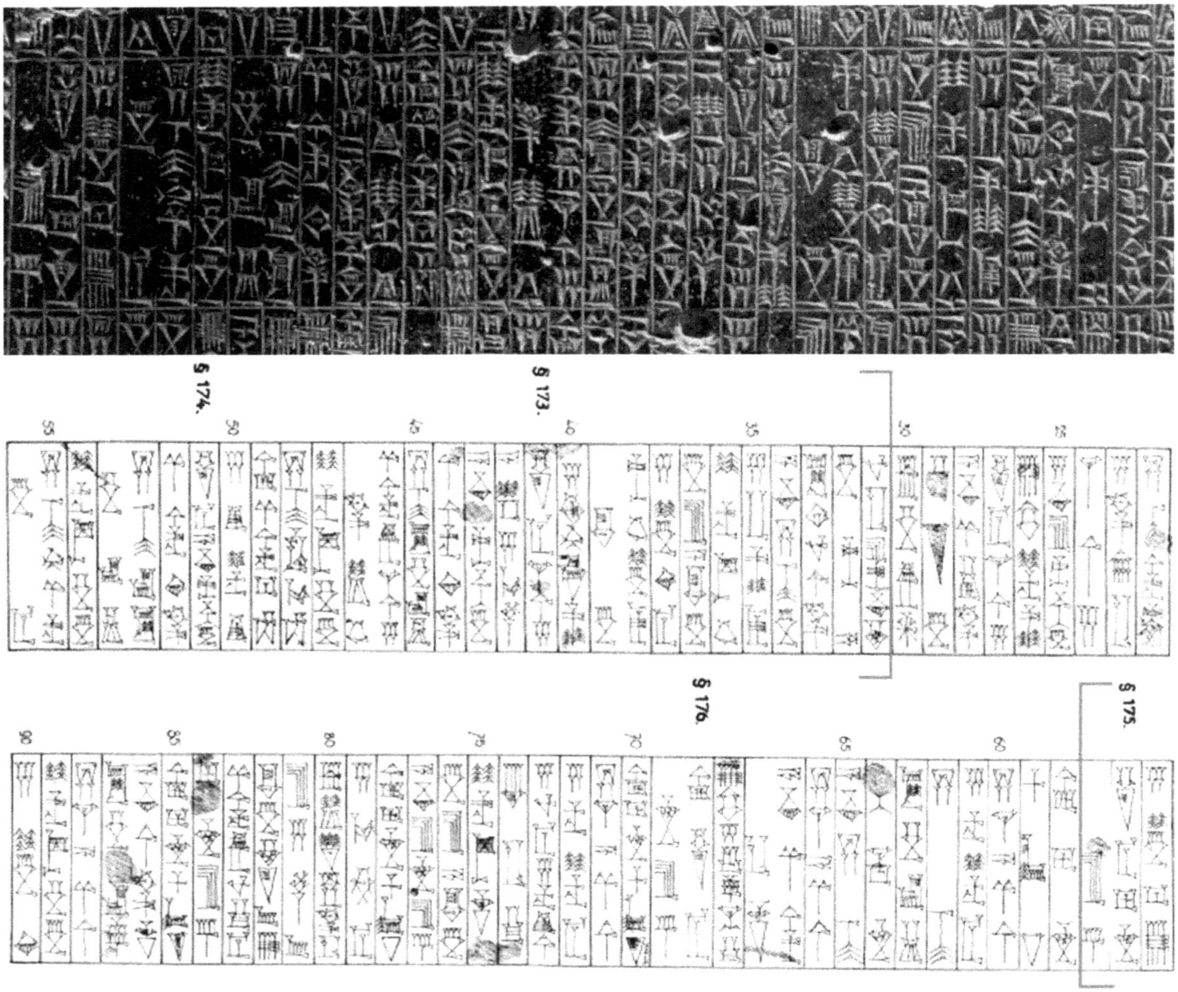

Figure (2) An actual sample of a horizontal band (row) area from the Hammurabi stele in its normal vertical reading position, including part of §172, §173, §174, and the first line of §175 (above), compared to the corresponding text area from the cuneiform transcription produced by Bergmann, who divided each band into multiple areas and flipped them 90 degrees counterclockwise forming numbered columns, to simplify reading the actual right-to-left pointing, top-to-bottom traditional cuneiform signs as left-to-right pointing cuneiform band as a new column number with a total of 39 columns (i.e. row fields) excluding the five lost ones. This unfortunate approach did not only distort the actual orientation characteristics of the cuneiform signs on the stele, but with his use of the word "column" for the actual row fields, he confused many into believing that these so-called columns referred to the thin columns seen on the stone in its normal upright position!*

The misunderstanding of how the Hammurabi stele is organized, combined with the misconception that the cuneiform script is a strictly left-to-right, led many of those interested in the stele to come up with all sort of strange scenarios. I was told in an email that "*the scribe must*

* E. Bergman S. J. Codex Hammurabi: Textus primigenius. Editio Tertia. 1953.

have had the stele lying horizontally on the ground with the illustration to his left. There he first marked out the parallel circles to give him his columns, then he chiseled out the signs in the usual left-to-right starting with the first "strip" to his left, being column 1 and so on". Another colleague wrote me that the scribe "*wrote the left-to-right pointing cuneiform signs within each long vertical thin column, starting from the top of the stone to its bottom, then he continued writing in the same manner, moving left-to-right, in the next long column*". This last scenario would make the ordering of the laws on the stone so chaotic that it would be impossible to read them!

To clarify any misconception regarding the cuneiform script directionality, I would like to share Andrew George's explanation as stated in his usual precise and scholarly style*:

"for stone inscriptions the Babylonians used an archaic monumental script. Until about 1200 BC, they also retained the very ancient orientation of cuneiform signs, which compared with later scripts (after 2000 BC at latest), was rotated 90 degrees clockwise. What you see on the CH stele are columns of writing in which the signs in each line are read from top to bottom, and the lines themselves from right to left. If you rotate everything 90 degrees to the left, the writing is set out in the same way as on clay tablets of the period: signs read left to right, lines in a column read top to bottom."

In other words, the cuneiform script started as a right-to-left script, with signs having wedges pointing either right-to-left or top-to-bottom, then these signs were later flipped 90 degrees counterclockwise to allow the new left-to-right ordering, making it a rich multi-directional script, not a left-to-right script. Just for philosophical comparison, the historically top-to-down, right-to-left Chinese script became mostly left-to-right script in modern times, but this does not make it a strictly left-to-right script.

Syrian scholar M. A. Mādūn theorized that the Musnad script was derived from the cuneiform script.† He was completely right in his linking of the two scripts. The fact that both scripts were used simultaneously during a long historical time period, extending more than a thousand years, should not be arbitrarily overlooked. Back in 2011, I read a Musnad inscription (dated about 300 CE) following a request from its owner whose father bought that inscription stone from southern Yemen in the early 1960s. The inscription, which I named the Saʿad Ta'lib inscription, contained a typical right-to-left Musnad writing. I would like to invite the readers to examine the full image of that stone, which I have published in a previous book‡, to realize that most of its letters were indeed chiseled as cuneiform wedges! Below, the image of the the top two lines of the inscription.

Notice that the Musnad letter Alif (shown in two examples on the right side of the image) is almost identical to the cuneiform sign A --for Alif-- (shown below them) in its late flipped, left-to-right orientated, which was consisting of two main parallel downward pointing wedges (i.e. nails) and a third small vertical wedge on top of the right one. It seems that the Musnad Alif shape was created by cutting the left main wedge of the cuneiform A shape into two wedges, and tilting

* Personal email exchange on December 3rd, 2017.

† Muḥammad ʿAlī Mādūn. Khaṭṭ al-Jazm ibn al-Khaṭṭ al-Musnad. 1989.

‡ Saad D. Abulhab. Inscriptional Evidence of Pre-Islamic Classical Arabic: Selected Readings in The Nabataean, Musnad, and Akkadian Inscriptions. 2013

the small right wedge towards them. This slight alteration may explain the future shape of Arabic Hamzah ء and its optional placement on the top of the modern Arabic Alif أ.

Figure (3) Top two lines of the Saʿad Taʾlib Musnad stone. Notice the chiseled cuneiform wedges all over. On the right, two images of the Musnad letter *Alif* on the stone compared to an image of the same letter, cuneiform sign *A*, in its late flipped, left-to-right orientation.

A final note regarding the numbering of the Hammurabi laws on the stele. Even though laws are numbered, these numbers were only concluded after reading the text of the laws. The text of the code itself did not include any numbering system. In fact, the lost 5 bands of text area which are presumed to include the missing 66-99 laws may have included even more than 33 laws, which would mean the total number of laws on the stele could have been more than the official 282 laws. German trained Iraqi scholar, al-Amīn, thought the total number of laws was a little more than 300 laws.*

The fact that law numbers on the Hammurabi stele where suggested based on scholars' readings of the continuous text around the stele means the total number of laws is dependent on a specific reading. Many laws currently given specific numbers were in fact referencing immediately preceding laws. Some of these dependent laws could have been part the preceding laws, which will make the total number of laws smaller. In my translation, I chose to keep the numbers of all laws consistent with the numbers used by all other translations, because the language of these addendum seem to be intentionally used to make these dependent laws independent laws referencing previous ones, but also can be cited without them.

The Meaning of the Nickname Hammurabi

It is commonly believed today that the name Hummurabi or *ẖam-mu-ra-bi*, was derived from a presumed Amorite name *'am-mu-ra-pi*, meaning "the kinsman is a healer." Accordingly, the first part *'ammu* (عمو) means "paternal kinsman" and the second part *ra-pi* (رافِ) means "healer". Although the above English nickname "the kinsman is a healer" sounds more like a Native American name than Mesopotamian, it is acceptable, provided that the word "healer" was used in the meaning of "reformer", "fixer" or "mender", not a medical healer!

Note that the words *'ammu* (عمّو) and *ẖammu* (حمّو) have similar meanings in the historical Arabic references, including the meaning "paternal kinsman", and the meaning "the ordinary people" or

* Maḥmūd al-Amīn. Sharīʿat Ḥammūrābī. 2nd Edition. 2005.

"the masses". Additionally, the letters *bā'* (ب) and *fā'* (ف) are interchangeable in Arabic, making the Latin transliterated words *ra-bi* and *ra-pi* interchangeable. In the Latin transliterations of Akkadian, the letter *p* mostly stands for *f* (ف), but can also be the letter *b* (ب). This can explain why in the Nabataean script, developed many centuries later, these two letters were almost identical! Therefore, the two words above can be transliterated in Arabic *ra'bi* (رأب) or *rab'i* (ربئ) and *ra'fi* (رأف) or *rap'i* (رفئ), respectively. According to the historical Arabic references, the word *ra-bi* is possibly derived from the root word *ra'aba* (رأب) meaning "to fix by uniting the parts", "to reform", or "to mend". Alternatively, this word could be derived from the Arabic root words *rababa* (ربب) or *rabba* (ربّ), in the same meaning. Meanwhile, the word *ra-pi* could also be derived from the Arabic root words *rafa'a* (رفأ) in the same exact meaning, or from *ra'afa* (رأف) or *rafafa* (رفف), meaning "to be extra compassionate", a very similar meaning. A better translation, therefore, should be either "the (unifying) reformer kinsman" or "the compassionate kinsman".

However, one should consider the case where the Latin transliterated word *ra-bi* could be *rab'i* (ربئ) from the Arabic root word (ربأ), meaning "to guard", "to oversee", or "to look ahead for". Then, alternatively and more likely, the meaning of the nickname Hammurabi can be, "the father of the masses", "the leader of the masses", or "the guardian of the masses". This alternative translation is not an arbitrary one. In fact, in paragraph #3 of Hammurabi's introduction to his laws, he specifically listed the personal qualifications that led the God (i.e. god Anu) and god Enlil to name him *ḫa-am-mu-ra-bi* or *'am-mu-ra-bi*. This paragraph indirectly, eloquently, and adequately explained the meaning of his nickname. Listed below are five translations of paragraph #3 according to the translations I referenced. Following a brief discussion, I will offer my own, Arabic-based, translation. According to Winckler translation of paragraph #3 of the prologue, Hammurabi said:

*"at that time Anu and Bêl called me, Hammurabi, the great prince, who fears God, to give justice a status in the country, to destroy the wicked and bad, that the strong should not overcome the weak, that I might rise over the black-headed ones; like Shamash, to illuminate the land and to further the welfare of humanity"**

According to Harber translation of paragraph #3 of the prologue, Hammurabi said:
"At that time, Anu and Bel called me Hammurabi, the exalted prince, the worshiper of the gods, to cause justice to prevail in the land, to destroy the wicked and the evil, to prevent the strong from oppressing the weak, to go forth like the Sun over the Black Head Race, to enlighten the land and to further the welfare of the people"†

According to Davies translation of paragraph #3 of the prologue, Hammurabi said:
"it was then that Anu and Bel called me, Hammurabi, the exalted prince, a God-fearing man, by name, to cause justice to be practiced in the land, to destroy the wicked and the evil [alike], to prevent the strong from oppressing the weak, so that I might go forth like Shamash' to rule over the Black-haired people, to give light to the land, and, like Anu and Bel, promote the welfare of mankind."‡

* H. Otto Sommer. Records of the Past: The laws of Hammurabi, King of Babylonia. Volume II, Part III. 1903. Adapted from the German translation by Hugo Winckler. Die Gesetze Hammurabis. 1902.

† Robert Francis Harper. The Code of Hammurabi, King of Babylon, about 2250 BC. 1904.

‡ W. W. Davies. The Codes of Hammurabi and Moses. 1905

Aaccording to King translation of paragraph #3 of the prologue, Hammurabi said:
"Then Anu and Bel called by name me, Hammurabi, the exalted prince, who feared God, to bring about the rule of righteousness in the land, to destroy the wicked and the evil-doers; so that the strong should not harm the weak; so that I should rule over the black-headed people like Shamash, and enlighten the land, to further the well-being of mankind."[*]

And according to Richardson translation of paragraph #3 of the prologue, Hammurabi said:
"It was then that Anu and Enlil ordained Hammurabi, a devout prince who fears the gods, to demonstrate justice within the land,to destroy evil and wickedness, to stop the mighty exploiting the weak, to rise like Shamash over the mass of humanity, illuminating the land; they ordained me, to improve the welfare of my people." [†]

Unfortunately, neither Johns nor al-Amīn provided their translations of the above paragraph. Nevertheless, according to all five translations, none of the attributes and personal qualifications that Hammurabi used in this paragraph to describe himself had anything to do with being a "healer". On the other hand, they all emphasized that he was an uncompromising defender, guider, guardian, enforcer, and otherwise leader of the people. Copying each other, Winckler, Harber and King made an obvious mistake in their translations of a crucial sentence in the above paragraph. While Sommer and Harber left it up to the reader to guess whether the word "*called*" in the sentence "*Anu and Bel called me Hammurabi*" meant "named" or just "called by name", a confused King, without any linguistic or grammatical support, *arbitrarily* made up his interpreting translation "*Anu and Bel called by name me, Hammurabi*". Also without any linguistic or grammatical support, all three scholars *arbitrarily* appended the qualification phrase "*to further the welfare of the people*" following the subject *Anu and Bel*, to the preceding qualifications in the paragraph that were listed before that subject.

The sentence in question is "*ilum u* ^{ilu}*EN-LIL a-na ši-ir ni-ši tu-ub-bi-im šu-mi ib-bu-u*", a rather clear sentence, which can be translated as:
the God (i.e Anu) and god Enlil, for the good of all people, made [wanted] my name Hammurabi
الإلهُ (الإله أنو) والإله إنليل، لِطيبِ (لصالح) سائر الناس، بوّؤ (إختارو) [أرادو] إسمي حَمّورَبي
The word *ši-ir* (سِئر) is related to *šār*, Arabic سأر or سؤر, and means "total" even in the modern Assyriology dictionaries, which claimed it was a "borrowed Sumerian word". Even if that word was from Arabic سير, meaning "proceeding" or "advancing", and the sentence was indeed "to further the good of the people", like the three scholars translated it, it should not be appended to the paragraph parts preceding the subject, "Anu and Bel". I believe the phrase *ši-ir ni-ši* meant "*all people*" to emphasize Hammurabi was a champion of all, weak and strong, rich and poor, which was the key reason for nicknaming Hammurabi, the leader of the masses.
Curiously, Winckler, a "*German orientalist and Bible scholar*"[‡], Harber, a Church of England reverend, and King, a "*most careful, accurate, precise, and suggestive scholar*"[§] according to Robert

[*] Leonard William King. The Code of Hammurabi. 1910.
[†] Mervyn E. J. Richardson (1943-). Hammurabi's Laws, Text, Translation and Glossary. 2000.
[‡] Jewish Virtual Library: A project of AICE. http://www.jewishvirtuallibrary.org/winckler-hugo-x00b0
[§] Robert Williams Rogers. Leonard William King (1869-1919) Assyriologist. *The American Journal of Semitic Languages and Literatures*. January 1920.

Williams Rogers of the Drew Theological Seminary, his close associate who was commissioned to write his obituary, Davies, a professor of Hebrew, and Richardson, a professor of Hebrew and Aramaic languages, have all translatedthe the word *ilum* (literally: The God) as *Anu*. Even though Hummurabi did actually mean *Anu* when he used the word *ilum*, his usage of the word *ilum* alone, instead, is quite significant and should not be arbitrarly replaced by a translator. Hammurabi's usage confirms that the people of Mesopotamia believed in *one* supreme god, *Anu* or "The God of Heaven", long before biblical Abraham! The lower two gods of the Mesopotamian trio gods system, *Enlil* and *Idim*, became the future "downgraded" characters Satan and Adam in the monotheist Abrahamian religions.* Ancient Mesopotamians' belief in one supreme god, like the rest of their kin in the greater Arabian Peninsula and north Africa, indicates they were only "*Mushrikīn*" (in the words of Islam), that is, they associated lower ranking god partners or intermediary gods to their one supreme god.†

Below is the Latin transliteration of paragraph #3, as provided by Harber, followed by my Arabic transliteration, and my modern Arabic and English translations. Numbers were assigned by scholars to record the actual thin columns in a specific "column" (i.e. raw field) on the stele. Words with capital letters are assumed Sumerian words according by scholars. All alternative words transliterations or translations were put between square brackets:

27 i-nu-mi-šu 28 ḫa-am-mu-ra-bi 29 ru-ba-am 30 na-'-dam 31 pa-li-iḫ ili ^{b}ia-ti 32 mi-ša-ra-am 33 i-na ma-tim 34 a-na šu-bi-i-im 35 ra-ga-am u ṣi-nam 36 a-na ḫu-ul-lu-^{b}ki-im 37 dan-nu-um 38 en-ša-am 39 a-na la ḫa-ba-^{b}li-im 40 ki-ma ^{ilu}šamaš 41 a-na SAG.GIG 42 wa-ṣi-e-im-ma 43 ma-tim 44 nu-wu-ri-im 45 ilum 46 u ^{ilu}EN-LIL 47 a-na ši-ir ni-ši 48 tu-ub-bi-im 49 šu-mi ib-bu-u 50
27 حينمْ ذو 28 حمّورأبي [عمّورأبي] [عمّورأفي] [حمّوربي [عموربي]] 29 رؤبمْ [ربأمْ] 30 نأدمْ 31 فلحْ [فلهْ] إلي إياتي [إأتي] 32 ميسرمْ 33 إنَ مأتمْ 34 أنَ سبيمْ 35 رجّمْ و ضغنمْ [صعنمْ] 36 أنَ حلُقمْ 37 دأنمْ 38 عنشمْ 39 أنَ لا حبلمْ 40 كيمَ الشمسْ 41 أنَ سغْ ججْ [سجّجْ] 42 وصيمَ [وصئمْ] 43 مأتمْ 44 نورمْ 45 إلمْ [علمْ] 46 و الإنليل 47 أنَ سئرْ [سيرْ] نئس 48 طوبمْ 49 سُمي إبؤوَ [إبغوْ] 50

حينها (حينذاك)، الإلهُ (الإله أنو) والإله إنليل، لطيب (لصالح) سائر (بقية) (جميع) الناس [للمضي نحو (تحقيق) صلاح الناس]، بوّؤ (إختارو) [بغو (أرادو)] إسمي حمّوربي، داهية (عبقريّ) الإصلاح [مُصلحاً فذّا (عبقريا)] [حارساً (رقيباً) نبهاً (يقظاً)]، مُتّقي الآلهة، لي (بيدي) (فرضْ) العدالة في الارض، لإبعاد الاضطراب (الشغب) [الشرّ] والعنف [والظلم]، لازالة القوي (الظالم) لئلا (لكي لا) يكون الضعيف (المظلوم) مُصطادْ (ضحيّة)، مثل شمس لظلام عقل دامس (لعقل ملتبس) [لظلام دامس]، (انا) خارج (بازغ) (و) مُنوّر الارض.

Then, the God (god Anu) and god Enlil, to (for) the good of the rest of (all) the people [to advance (achieve) the good of the people], assigned (chose) [desired] my name Hammurabi, the reform genius [the genius reformer] [the attentive guardian (overseer)], the gods weary (the gods fearing), to me (in my hand) (the imposition of) the justice in the land, to ward off disturbance [evil] and violence [injustice], to remove the strong (the oppressor) so that the weak (the oppressed) does not become a victim, like a sun to the pitch darkness of mind (i.e. cluelessness of mind) [to a pitch darkness], I am coming out (risen), (and) enlightening the land.

---

* Saad D. Abulhab. The Epic of Gilgamesh: Selected Readings from its Original Early Arabic Language. 2016.

† Dr. Ahmed Mohammedin of Egypt suggested in an Academia.edu session to discuss my preliminary translation of the Hammurabi law code in September 2017 that "changing the wording 'God' into 'Godly creature' or 'Godly' might be more true". He pointed out the following: "In the Ancient Egyptian language, western scholars have labeled all names with the determinative of a 'god' as Gods. This is not true as in many occasions the ancient Egyptians have referred to one name as the only true god."

Referenced Words:

ePSD: bâ'u
dib [PASS] wr. dib; dib$_2$; di-ib "to pass, go along; to go past; to go through; to cross over; to audit; to transfer" Akk. bâ'u; etēqu
ri [IMPOSE] wr. RI; ru "to lay down, cast, place; to set in place, imbue; to lean on; to impose; to throw down; to release, let go; to walk along; to pour out; to lead away" Akk. bâ'u; emēdu; nadû; nasāku; ramû; rehû; tarû; wašaru
ur [DRAG] wr. ur$_3$ "to go along; to wipe clean; to beat, sweep away; to drag; to raise a boat" Akk. bâ'u; kapāru; šabāṭu
AALD: bu'û (v.) يبغي، يختار، يتمنى
AALD: hammu (s.) See ammu العامة، الناس
AALD: ammu (s.) (hammu) عامة الناس
ePSD: rabi sikkati
rabizigatum [OFFICIAL] wr. ra-bi-zi-ga-tum "a military official" Akk. rabi sikkati
ePSD: rabiānu
rabianum [COMMANDER] wr. ra-bi-a-nu-um "commander, a high official" Akk. rabiānu
ePSD: rubû
nun [PRINCE] wr. nun "prince; (as attribute) foremost, best" Akk. rub
ePSD: na'du
nituku [PIOUS] wr. ni$_2$-tuku "pious, attentive" Akk. na'du
ePSD: palāhu
ni teĝ [FEAR] wr. ni$_2$ teĝ$_3$ "to fear, to become afraid" Akk. palāhu; šahātu
šu e [BLESS] wr. šu e$_3$ "to bless; to go out?; to terrify?" Akk. waṣû; palāhu; karābu
ePSD: mīšaru
niĝsisa [JUSTICE] wr. niĝ$_2$-si-sa$_2$ "justice" Akk. mīšaru
ePSD: ešēru
si sa [STRAIGHTEN] wr. si sa$_2$; si si-sa$_2$ "to make straight; to make vertical" Akk. ešēru; šutēšuru
AALD: suppû (s.) (subbû) ينقل بالقوة، يبعد بالقوة، يطرد
ePSD: sapānu
gul [DESTROY] wr. gul; gu-ul "to destroy; to break; to flatten; to carve, cut; to engrave" Akk. abātu; hepû; naqāru; sapānu
sig [FLATTEN] wr. sig$_{10}$ "to flatten, lay flat; to disrespect" Akk. dâṣu; sapānu
tab [FLATTEN] wr. tab "to flatten" Akk. sapānu
ePSD: raggu
NERU [ENEMY] wr. NE.RU "enemy; (to be) wicked, villainous" Akk. ayyābu; raggu
luNERU [EVILDOER] wr. lu$_2$-NE.DU; lu$_2$-NE.RU "evildoer, enemy" Akk. raggu; ayyābu
luniĝNERU [EVILDOER] wr. lu$_2$-niĝ$_2$-NE.RU "evildoer" Akk. raggu
niĝNERU [EVIL] wr. niĝ$_2$-NE.RU; niĝ$_2$-NE.EREN "evil" Akk. raggu
ePSD: ṣenu
azig [VIOLENCE] wr. a$_2$-zig$_3$ "violence" Akk. ṣenu
niĝazig [VIOLENCE] wr. niĝ$_2$-a$_2$-zig$_3$ "malevolent; violent action" Akk. ṣenu
ePSD: halāqu
halam [FORSAKE] wr. ha-lam; gel-le-eĝ$_3$ "(to be) bad, evil; to forsake, forget; to destroy" Akk. halāqu; lapātu; lemnu; mašû
ugu de [DISAPPEAR] wr. u$_2$-gu de$_2$; u$_2$-gu$_3$ de$_2$; ugu de$_2$ "to disappear" Akk. halāqu
uzahal [DISAPPEARANCE] wr. u$_4$-za-hal; u$_4$-za-ha-al "disappearance" Akk. halāqu
zah [DISAPPEAR] wr. zah$_3$; zah$_2$ "to disappear; to move away, withdraw; to stay away; (to be) lost; (to be) fugitive" Akk. duppuru; halāqu; nābutu; šerû

ePSD: enšu
hunu [WEAK] wr. hu-nu; hu-hu-nu "to be weak (of animals); to be crippled; to be helpless" Akk. enšu; hašāru
luGAM [WEAK] wr. lu_2-GAM "weak" Akk. enšu
lusiga [WEAK] wr. lu_2-sig-ga "weak person" Akk. enšu
sig [WEAK] wr. sig "(to be) weak; (to be) low; (to be) thin; (to be) narrow" Akk. enšu; qatnu
ePSD: habālu
heše [OPPRESSED] wr. $heš_5{}^{še}{}_3$; haš "(to be) oppressed; (to be) detained" Akk. habālu; kalû
ePSD: SAG
saĝ [CVVE] wr. $saĝ_5$; saĝ; zag "(compound verb verbal element)"
saĝ [FRONT] wr. saĝ "front side (math.)"
saĝ [HEAD] wr. saĝ "head; person; capital" Akk. qaqqadu; rēšu
ePSD: GIG
gig [SICK] wr. gig "(to be) sick; (to be) troublesome" Akk. marāṣu; marṣu
kib [WHEAT] wr. gig; gib "wheat" Akk. kibtu
ePSD: sag-gig
saĝgig [HEADACHE] wr. saĝ-gig "headache"
ePSD: saĝgiga [HUMANKIND] (4x: Old Babylonian) wr. saĝ-gig_2-ga "humankind". Akk. şalmat qaqqadi "the black-headed ones, mankind"
ePSD: şalmat qaqqadi
saĝgiga [HUMANKIND] wr. saĝ-gig_2-ga "humankind" Akk. şalmat qaqqadi
ePSD: şalmu
alan [STATUE] wr. alan; ^{urud}alan "statue; form" Akk. şalmu
giggi [BLACK] wr. giggi; gi_6-gi_6 "(to be) black" Akk. şalmu
AALD: wāṣû See āṣû
AALD: āṣû (adj.) عاص، خارج، متمرد، يذهب خارج
ePSD: aṣû
e [LEAVE] wr. e_3; i; e "to leave, to go out; to thread, hang on a string; to remove, take away; to bring out; to enter; to bring in; to raise, rear (a child); to sow; to rave; to winnow; to measure (grain) roughly (with a stick); to rent" Akk. aṣû; erēbu; mahû; rubbû; zarû; šakāku
ePSD: nûru
zalag [SHINE] wr. zalag; $zalag_2$; su-lu-ug; sulug "(to be) pure; (fire) light; (to be) bright, to shine" Akk. ebbu; namāru; nûru
AALD: šār (num) المجموع الكلي، 3600
بوأ (لسان العرب) باء إلى الشيء يَبُوءُ بَوْءاً: رجع. ال الأخفش: وباؤوا بغضب من الله: رَجعوا به أي صار عليهم. قال الأصمعي: باءَ بإثْمه، فهو يَبُوءُ به بَوْءاً: إذا أقرّ به. وفي الحديث: أَبُوءُ بنعمتك عليَّ، وأَبُوءُ بذنبي أي أَلتزِمُ وأَرْجِع وأُقِرُّ.
وأصل البَواءِ اللزومُ. وقوله تعالى: والذين تبوّأوا الدار والإيمان، جَعل الإيمان محلاً لهم على المثَل؛ وقد يكون أراد: وتبوّأوا مكان الإيمانِ وبلدَ الإيمان، فحذف. وتبوأ المكان: حلَّه.
بوأ (العباب الزاخر) وتبوَّأتُ منزلاً: أي نزلته، وأباته منزلاً وبوّأته منزلاً وبوَأتُ له منزلاً: بمعنىً، أي هيأْتُه ومكّنتُ له فيه.
حمْوُ (القاموس المحيط) حمْوُ المرأة وحمُوها وحماها وحمْها وحمْؤها: أبو زَوْجِها، ومن كان من قبلِه، والأنْثى: حماةٌ. وحمْوُ الرَّجُلِ: أبو امْرأتِه، أو أخوها، أو عمُّها،
حما (لسان العرب) حمْوُ المرأة وحمْوها وحماها: أبو زوْجها وأخو زوجها، وكذلك من كان من قبله. وفي الحمو أربع لغات: حماً مثل قفاً، وحمْو مثل أبو، وحمٌ مثل أب؛ وحمْوُ الشمس: حرُّها. وحمى أهله في القتال حماية. والحاميةُ: الرجلُ يَحْمي أصحابه في الحرب، وهم أيضاً الجماعة يَحْمون أنفسهم؛ وحَمْةُ الحرِّ: مُعْظَمُه، بالتشديد. وحُميّا كُلِّ شيء: شدَّته وحدَّته. وفعل ذلك في حُميّا شبابه أي في سَوْرته ونشاطه؛ وقال الأصمعي: إنه لحامي الحُمَيّا أي يَحْمي حوْزته وما وليه؛
عمي (لسان العرب) ولقيته صكّة عُميٍّ وصكّة أعمى أي في أشدّ الهاجرة حرّاً، وذلك أن الظَّبي إذا اشتدّ عليه الحرُّ طلب الكِناس وقد برقت عينُه من بياض الشمس ولمعانها، فيسْدرُ بصرُه حتى يصُكّ بنفسه الكناسَ لا يُبْصِرُه، وقيل: هو أشدُّ الهاجرة حرّاً، وقيل: حين كاد الحرُّ يُعْمي من شدَّته، ولا يقال في البرْد، وقيل: حين يقومُ قائمُ الظَّهيرة، وقيل: نصف النهار في شدَّة الحرّ، وقيل: عُميٌّ الحرُّ بعينه،

عمم (الصّحاح في اللغة) العَمّ: أخو الأب، والجمع أعمامٌ وعُمومةٌ. يقال: ما كنتَ عمًّا ولقد عَممْتَ عُمومةً. وبيني وبين فلان عُمومَةٌ، كما يقال أبوّةٌ وخؤولةٌ. والعَمُّ: جماعةٌ من الناس. والعامَّةُ: خلاف الخاصّة. وعمَّ الشيء يَعُمُّ عُموماً: شمل الجماعة.

عمم (لسان العرب) العَمّ: أخو الأب. والعَممُ العامَّةُ اسم للجمع؛ والعَمُّ: الجماعة، وقيل: الجماعة من الحَيّ؛ والأعَمُّ: الجماعة أيضاً؛

رب (مقاييس اللغة) الراء والباء يدلُّ على أصول. فالأول إصلاح الشيء والقيامُ عليه. فالرّبُّ: المالكُ، والخالقُ، والصّاحب. والرّبُّ: المُصْلح للشّيء. يقال رَبّ فلانٌ ضَيعتَه، إذا قام على إصلاحها. والرّبُّ: المُصْلح للشّيء. والله جلّ ثناؤه الرّبُّ؛ لأنه مصلحُ أحوالِ خَلْقه. والرِّبّيُّ العارف بالرّبّ. وربَبْتُ الصّبيَّ أرُبّه، وربّبْته أربّبه.

ربب (الصّحاح في اللغة) ربُّ كلِّ شيءٍ: مالكُهُ. وربَبْتُ القوم: سُسْتُهُمْ، أي كُنْتُ فوقهم. قال أبو نصر: وهو من الرُبوبيَّة. ومنه قول صفوان لأنْ يَرُبّني رجلٌ من قريش أحبُّ إليَّ من أن يرُبّني رجلٌ من هوازن. وربَّ الضَيْعةَ، أي أصلحها وأتمّها.

ربب (لسان العرب) ربُّ كلِّ شيءٍ: مالكُه ومُستحِقُّه؛ وقيل: صاحبُه. والرّبيبُ: الملِكُ؛ قال امرؤُ القيس: فما قاتَلُوا عن ربِّهم وربيبِهم، * ولا آذنوا جاراً، فيظعَنَ سالما أي ملكهُمْ. وربّهُ يَرُبُّهُ رباً: ملكه. وربَبْتُ القومَ: سُسْتُهم أي كنتُ فوقهم.

رأب (الصّحاح في اللغة) رأبْتُ الإناءَ: شعبْتُهُ وأصلحتُه. ومنه قولهم: اللّهم ارْأَبْ بينهم أي أصْلِحْ.

رأب (مقاييس اللغة) الراء والهمزة والباء أصلٌ واحد يدلُّ على ضمٍّ وجمع. تقول: رأبت الأمورَ المتفرّقة؛

رأب (لسان العرب) رأبَ إذا أصْلَح. ورأَبَ الشّيءَ إذا جمعه وشدّه برِفْق. ورأب بين القوم يرْأبُ رأْباً: أصلحَ ما بيْنَهم. وكُلُّ ما أصْلَحْتَه، فقد رأبْته؛

ربأ (لسان العرب) ربَأَ القومَ يرْبَؤهم ربْأً، وربأَ لهم: اطّلَعَ لهم على شرَفٍ. وربأْتُهم وارْتبأْتُهم أي رَقَبْتُهم، وذلك إذا كنت لهم طَليعةً فوق شَرَفٍ. والرَّبيئةُ: الطّليعةُ، وإنما أنّثوه لأن الطّليعة يقال له العين إذ بعَيْنه ينْظُرُ والعين مؤنثة. وإنما قيل له عيْن لأنه يرْعى أمُورهم ويحْرُسُهم. وفي الحديث: مثَلي ومثَلُكم كرجل ذهب يرْبأُ أهله أي يحْفظُهم من عدُوّهم. والاسم: الرّبيئةُ، وهو العين، والطّليعةُ الذي ينظر للقوم لئلا يدْهمَهُم عدُوّ، ولا يكون إلاّ على جبل أو شرَف ينظر منه. ورابأهم: حارسَهم. ورابأْتُ فلاناً إذا حارسْته وحارسَك. ورابأَ الشّيءَ: راقبه. ويقال: ما عرفْتُ فلاناً حتى أرْبأَ لِي أي أشْرفَ لي.

رأف (لسان العرب) الرأْفة: الرحمة، وقيل: أشد الرحمة؛ رأف به يرْأفُ ورئف ورؤُف رأْفة ورآفة. والرّأْفةُ أرقّ من الرحمة ولا تكاد تقع في الكراهة، والرحمةُ قد تقع في الكراهة للمصْلحة.

رفف (العباب الزاخر) أبن دريد: رف الرجل المرأة يرفها رفاً: إذا قبلها بأطراف شفتيه، والرف: مصدر رففت الرجل أرفه رفاً: إذا أحسنت إليه أو أسديت إليه يداً. الرّفَفُ -بالتحريك-: الرّقّةُ، يقال: ثوب رَفيفٌ بيّنُ الرّفَفِ.

رأف (مقاييس اللغة) الراء والهمزة والفاء كلمةٌ واحدة تدلُّ على رِقّة ورحمة، وهي الرّأفة.

رفأ (العباب الزاخر) رفأْتُ الثوب أرْفؤه رفْأً: إذا أصلحت ما وهى منه، وربما لم يُهمز، يقال: من اغتاب خرق ومن استغفر رفأ. وأرفأْتُ السفينة: إذا قرّبتها من الشط، عن هشام أخي ذي الرّمة. وأرْفأَ إليه: لجأ. وأرْفأَ جنح. وأرْفأَ امتَشط. والرّفاءُ -بالكسر والمدّ-: الالْتِئامُ والاتّفاق.

نأد (لسان العرب) النّأْدُ والنّآدى: الداهِيةُ.

نأد (مقاييس اللغة) النون والهمزة والدال كلمةٌ واحدة. يقولون: النّأْدُ والنّآدى: الدّاهية.

الفَلَحُ (القاموس المحيط) والفلاحُ: الفوْزُ، والنّجاةُ، والبقاءُ في الخيْر، والسّحورُ. وأفْلحَ بالشّيءِ: عاشَ به.

فلح (لسان العرب) الفلح والفَلاحُ: الفوز والنجاة والبقاء في النعيم والخير؛ وفلاحُ الدهر: بقاؤه، يقال: لا أفعل ذلك فلاحَ الدهر؛ والفَلاحُ: الفوز بما يُغْتبطُ به وفيه صلاح الحال. وأفْلحَ الرجلُ: ظفِرَ. أبو إسحق في قوله عز وجل: أولئك هم المفلحون؛

فَلّهُ (القاموس المحيط) فلّهُ وفلّلهُ: ثلَمه فتفلّلَ وانفلّ وافْتلّ، و~ القومَ: هزَمهُم، فانْفلّوا وتفلّلوا. وقومٌ فلٌّ: مُنْهزِمون

مسر (لسان العرب) مسَرَ الشّيءَ يمْسُرُه مسْراً: استخرجه من ضيق، والمَسْرُ فعل الماسِر.

اليَسْرُ (القاموس المحيط) اليَسْرُ، بالفتح ويُحرّكُ: اللّينُ، والانْقيادُ، ويسَرَ ييْسِرُ وياسرَه: لاينه. واليَسَرُ، محرّكةً: السّهْلُ، ويسّرهُ: سهّله، يكونُ في الخيْرِ والشّرّ. وياسرَهُ: ساهلَهُ. وتيسّرَ: تسهّل،

يسر (لسان العرب) وياسرَهُ: ساهلَهُ. وتيسّرَ: تسهّل، واليُسْرُ واليسارُ والميسرَةُ والمَيْسُرَةُ، كله: السُهولة والغِنى؛ ويقال: أخذ ما تيسّر وما استَيْسر، وهو ضدّ ما تعسّر والتوى. ويقال: أيسِرْ أخاك أي نفّسْ عليه في الطلب ولا تُعسِرْهُ أي لا تُشدّدْ عليه ولا تُضيّقْ. وقوله تعالى: فما استَيْسرَ من الهدْي؛ قيل: ما تيسّر من الإبل والبقر والشاء، وقيل: من بعير أو بقرة أو شاة. ويسّرَه هو: سهّله، وحكى سيبويه: يسّرَه ووسّعَ عليه وسهّل.

سبي (مقاييس اللغة) السين والباء والياء أصلٌ واحد يدلُّ على أخذِ شي من بلد إلى بلد آخر كرْهاً.

سبي (لسان العرب) السّبْيُ والسِّباءُ: الأسر معروف. وسباه الله يسْبيه سبْياً: لعَنه وغرّبه وأبعده الله كما تقول لعنه الله. ويقال: ما لَه سباهُ الله أي غرّبه، وسَباهُ إذا لعنه؛ والسّبيُّ جِلْد الحيّة الذي تسْلُخُه؛

سبأ (العباب الزاخر) وسبيءُ الحية وسَبِيُّها: سلْخُها. وقال ابن الأعرابي: يقال إنك تريد سُبْأة -بالضم-: أي إنك تريد سفرا بعيدا، سميت سُبْأةَ لأن الإنسان إذا طال سفره سبأَتْه الشمس ولوّحتْه. وأنْسبأ الجلد: انسلخ.

سفا (لسان العرب) وسفت الريحُ التُراب تسْفيه سفْياً: ذرتْه، وقيل: حملتْه فهو سفِيٌّ، وتَسْفي الورَق اليبس سفْياً. وتُرابٌ سافٍ: مسْفِيٌّ، على النسب أو يكون فاعلاً في معنى مفعولٍ. وحكى ابن الأعرابي: سفَتِ الريحُ وأسْفَتْ فلم يُعدّ واحداً منهما. والسافياءُ: الريحُ التي تَحملُ تراباً كثيراً على وجه الأرض تَهْجُمه على الناس؛ قال أبو دُواد: ونُؤْيٍ أضرّ به السافياء، كدرْسٍ من النُونِ حين امّحى قال: والسّفى هو اسمُ كلّ ما سفَتِ الريحُ من كلِّ ما ذكرت. ويقال: السافِياءُ الترابُ يذهبُ مع الريح، وقيل: السافِياءُ الغُبارُ فقط.

رجج (الصّحاح في اللغة) يقال رجّهُ رجّاً، أي حرّكَهُ وزلزله. وارْتجّ البحر وغيره: اضطرب.

رجج (لسان العرب) ورجرجةُ الناس: الذين لا خير فيهم. والرَّجرجةُ: شرارُ الناس. والرَّجرَجةُ: الجماعة الكثيرة في الحرب. ورجَّةُ القوم: اختلاط أصواتهم، ورجَّةُ الرَّعد: صوته. والرَّجُّ: تحريكك شيئًا كحائط إذا حركته، ومنه الرَّجرجة، قال الله تعالى: إذا رُجَّت الأرضُ رجًا؛ معنى رُجّتْ: حُرِّكتْ حركة شديدة وزُلزلتْ. والرَّجرجةُ: الاضطراب. وارْتجَ البحر وغيره: اضطرب؛ وفي ترجمة رخخ: رخَّه شدخه؛ قال ابن مقبل: فلَبْدَه مسُّ القطار، ورخَّه نعاجُ رواف، قبلَ أن يتشددا قال: ويروى ورجَّه، بالجيم؛ ومنه حديث عليٍّ، عليه السلام: وأما شيطان الرَّدهة فقد لقيته بصعقة سمعتُ لها وجْبةَ قلبه ورجَّة صدره؛ وحديث ابن الزبير: جاء فرجَّ البابَ رجًا شديداً أي زعزعه وحركه. والرَّجَجُ الاضطراب. رجارجا الصحاح: والرَّجرجةُ، بالكسر، بقيةُ الماء، في الحوض،الكدرةُ المختلطةُ بالطين. وفي حديث ابن مسعود: لا تقوم الساعة إلا على شرار الناس كرجرجة الماء الخبيث؛ الرِّجرجة، بكسر الراءين: بقية الماء الكدر في الحوض المختلطة بالطين ولا ينتفع بها؛

ضغن (مقاييس اللغة) الضاد والغين والنون أصلٌ صحيحٌ يدلُّ على تغطية شيءٍ في ميل واعوجاج، ولا يدلُّ على خير. من ذلك الضِّغْن والضِّغْن: الحقْد. فأمّا الخليل فقال: يقال للنَّحُوص إذا وحمتْ فاستعصتْ على الجأب: إنَّها لذاتُ شُغْب وضِغْن.

ضغن (لسان العرب) الضِّغْنُ والضَّغَنُ: الحقد، والجمع أضْغانٌ، وكذلك الضَّغينةُ، وجَمْعُها الضَّغائن؛ وفي الحديث: فتكون دماء في عمِّياء في غير ضغينة وحمل سلاح؛ الضِّغْنُ: الحقد والعداوة والبغضاء.

صعن (الصّحاح في اللغة) الصِّعْوَنُّ: الظليمُ، بكسر الصاد وتشديد النون.

ظلم (لسان العرب) الظُّلْمُ: وَضْع الشيء في غير موضعه. والمُتظلِّمُ: الذي يَشْكو رَجُلاً ظلَمه. والمُتظلِّمُ أيضاً: الظالمُ؛ والظِّلِّيمُ، بالتشديد: الكثيرُ الظُّلْم.

حلق (مقاييس اللغة) الحاء واللام والقاف أصول ثلاثة: فالأول تنحية الشعْر عن الرأس، ثم يحمل عليه غيره.

الحَلْقة (القاموس المحيط) وحلق رأسه يَحْلِقُه حلقا وتَحْلاقاً: أزال شعره، كحلّقه واحتلقه.

عنشه (القاموس المحيط) عنشه: عطفه، و~ فلاناً: أزعجه، واستفزّه، وساقه، وطرده. و~ فلاناً: ظلمه.

هبل (مقاييس اللغة) والهَبَّال: الصَّيّاد يهتبل الصَّيد يغترّه، ولذلك سمِّي الذئب هبلاً، لأنه يحتالُ لصيده ويهتبله.وأمّا المَهْبل فمستقرُّ الولد من الرَّحم، وهو عندنا من باب الإبدال، وهو في ذلك أصله مَحْبل.

هبل (الصّحاح في اللغة) الهَبَلُ بالتحريك: مصدر قولك: هبلَتْه أمُّه، أي ثكلته. والإهبالُ: الإثكال. وذئبٌ هبِلٌ: مُحتالٌ.

حبل (مقاييس اللغة) الحاء والباء واللام أصلٌ واحدٌ يدلُّ على امتداد الشيء. ثم يحمل عليه، ومرْجع الفروع مرجعٌ واحد. وزعم ناسٌ أن الأسدَ يقال له حَبيلُ بَراح. والحِبالةُ: حبالة الصائد. ويقال احتبل الصَّيد، إذا صادَهُ بالحبالة. ومن المشتق من هذا الأصل الحِبْل، بكسر الحاء، وهي الداهية. ووجْهُه عندي أنَّ الإنسان إذا دُهِي فكأنه قد حُبل، أي وقع في الحبالة، كالصَّيد الذي يُحبل.

الحَبْلُ (القاموس المحيط) وحبل الصَّيد، واحتبلَه: أخذه بها، أو نصبها له. وإنه لحِبْلٌ من أحبالها: للداهية من الرجال، وللقائم على المال الرَّفيق بسياسته. و"ثار حابلُهم على نابلهم": أوقدوا الشرَّ بينهم.

حبل (لسان العرب) والحَبلان أيضاً: الممتلئ غضباً. وحَبِل الرجلُ إذا امتلأ من شرب اللبن، فهو حَبلانُ، والمرأة حَبْلى. وفلان حَبلان على فلان أي غضبان. وبه حبلٌ أي غضب،

قوق (لسان العرب) القُوقُ والقاقُ، غيرُ مهموز، والقُواق: الطَّويلُ، وقيل: هو القبيحُ الطُّول. والقُوقةُ: الصَّلعةُ. ورجل مُقَوَّق: عظيم الصَّلعة.

قق/اقق (تاج العروس) وقيل: القِقّة. صوتٌ يُصَوِّتُ به الصَّبيُّ أو يُصَوَّتُ له به إذا فزع من شيْءٍ مكْروه، أو فزِعَ إذا وقع في قذر، قاله الزَّمخشريُّ.

قدد (لسان العرب) القَدُّ: القطعُ المستأْصلُ والشَّقُّ طولا. والقَدُّ: قَدْر الشَّيْءِ وتقطيعُه، والْجمعُ أَقُدٌّ وقُدود، وفي حديث جابر:«أُتي بالعبَّاس يوم بدْر أسيرًا ولَمْ يكُنْ عليه ثوْبٌ فنظر لهُ النَّبيُّ» صلّى الله عليه وسلَّم قميصًا فوجدُوا قميص عبد الله بْن أُبيٍّ يُقدَّرُ عليْه فكساهُ إياه أي كان الثوبُ على قَدْره وطوله. والقَيْدُودُ: النّاقةُ الطويلةُ الظهْر.

قدد (تاج العروس) القَدُّ: القطعُ مطلقًا، ومنه قَدّ الطريق يَقُدّه قدًا: قطعه، وهو مجازٌ، والقَدُّ: القدْرُ أي قدْرُ الشيء ومن المجاز: استَقَدّ له: استمرّ. واستَقَدَّ الأمْرُ: استوى. واستقدَّت الإبلُ: استقامتْ على وجْه واحد واستمرّتْ على حالها.

سيغ (لسان العرب) هذا سَيْغُ هذا إذا كان على قدره.

سغغ (العباب الزاخر) سغسغْتُ الشيء في التراب: دسسْته فيه، وقيل: وقيل: دحرجْته فيه. وقال ابن دريد: السَّغسغة: الاضطراب، وقال ابن دريد: السَّغسغة: الاضطراب، والتركيب يدل على دجّ الشيء في الشيء باضطراب وحركة. وصغْصغْت الثَّريدة: مثل سغسغتها.

صغا (لسان العرب) وأصْغى إليه رأسه وسمْعه: أماله. وقال بعضهم: صغوْتُ إليه برأسي أصْغى صَغْواً وصغا وأصْغيْتُ. وأصْغت الناقةُ تُصْغي إذا أمالتْ رأسها إلى الرجل كأنها تستمع شيئا حين يَشُدُّ عليها الرحْل؛

جَأَج (القاموس المحيط) جأج، كمنع: وقف جُبْناً.

جوج (لسان العرب) ابن الأعرابي: الجاجةُ جمع جاج، وهي خرزةٌ وضيعة لا تساوي فلْساً. أبو زيد: الجاجةُ الخرزة التي لا قيمة لها. **غيره:** ما رأيت عليه عاجة ولا جاجة؛ وأنشد لأبي خراش الهذلي يذكر امرأته وأنه عاتبها فاستحيت وجاءت إليه مستحيية: فجاءتْ كخاصي العَيْر، لم تَحْل عاجَة، ولا جاجةً منها تلُوحُ على وشْم يقال: جاء فلان كخاصي العَيْر إذا جاء مستحيياً وخائباً أيضا. وجاج إذا وقف جُبْناً.

أجج (لسان العرب) وقولهم: القومُ في أَجَّة أي في اختلاط؛ وقوله: تكَفَّحَ السَّمائم الأواجج إنما أراد الأَوَاجَّ، فاضطر، ففك الإدغام. أبو عمرو: أَجَج إذا حمل على العدوّ، وجأَج إذا وقف جُبْناً،

كوك (لسان العرب) ابن شميل: الكَيكاء والكَوكَى هما السَّرطانُ أي من لا خير فيه من الرجال.

كيك (لسان العرب) ابن شميل: الكَيكاء والكَوكَى هما السَّرطانُ أي من لا خير فيه من الرجال.

ظلم (مقاييس اللغة) الظاء واللام والميم أصلان صحيحان، أحدهما خلافُ الضِّياء والنور، والآخر وضْع الشَّيء غيرَ موضعه تعدِّياً.فالأول الظُّلْمة، والجمع ظلمات. والظَّلام اسم الظلمة؛ وقد أظلم المكان إظلاماً.

صلم (الصّحَاح في اللغة) ويقال للظليم مُصلَمُ الأذنين، كأنَه مستأصل الأذنين خِلْقَةً. ويسمَى السيفُ صَيْلماً. والاصطِلام: الاستئصالُ.
صنم (لسان العرب) الصَنَمُ: معروفٌ واحدُ الأصْنام، يقال: إنه معرَّب شَمَنْ، وهو الوَثن؛ والصَنمةُ الداهيةُ؛ قال الأزهري: أَصلها صَلَمة._
سجج (لسان العرب) وفي رواية: ظِلٌ الجنة سَجْسج، وقالوا: لا ظلمة فيه ولا شمس؛ وقيل: إِن قدر نوره كالنور الذي بين الفجر وطلوع الشمس. ابن الأعرابي: ما بين طلوع الفجر إلى طلوع الشمس يقال له السَجْسجُ،
سجا (لسان العرب) قال الله تعالى: والضُحى والليل إذا سجا؛ معناه سكن ودام؛ وقال الفراء: إذا أَظلم وركَد في طُوله كما يقال بحرٌ ساجٍ إذا ركد وأظلم، ومعنى رَكَدَ سكن. ابن الأعرابي: سَجا امْتَدَ بظلامه، ومنه البحر الساجي؛ والمتسَجّي: المتغطّي من الليل الساجي لأنه يغطّي بظلامه وسكونه. ابن الأعرابي: السّيجانُ الطيالسة السُودُ، واحدها ساجٌ.
سجو (مقاييس اللغة) السين والجيم والواو أصلٌ يدلُ على سكونٍ وإطباق. يقال* سَجَا اللَيلُ، إذا ادلهمّ وسكن.
وصي (مقاييس اللغة) الواو والصاد والحرف المعتلّ: أصلٌ يدلُّ على وَصلِ شيءٍ بشيء. ووصَيْتُ الشَيءَ: وصَلْتُه. ويقال: وطِئْنا أرضاً واصيةً، أي إنَ نَبتَها متَصلٌ قد امتلأتْ منه. ووصَيْتُ اللَيلَةَ باليوم: وصَلْتُها، وذلك في عملٍ تَعمَلُه. والوصِيَة من هذا القياس، كأنَه كلامٌ يُوصَى أي يُوصَل. يقال: وصَيْتُه توصيةً، وأوصَيْتُه إيصاء.
وَصَى (القاموس المحيط) وَصَى، كوَعَى: خسَ بعدَ رِفْعةٍ، واتَزنَ بعد خِفَةٍ، واتَصلَ، ووَصلَ، و~ الأرضُ وَصْياً ووُصِيًا ووَصاءً ووَصاءَةً: اتَصلَ نَباتُها.
وصي (لسان العرب) ابن الأَعرابي: الوَصِيُّ النبات المُلْتفُ، وأَرض واصِيةٌ: متصلة النبات إذا اتَصل نَبْتها، وربما قالوا تَواصى النبتُ إذا اتصل، وهو نبت واصٍ؛ ووصَى الرجلَ وَصْياً: وصَله. ووصَى الشيءَ بغيره وَصْياً: وصَله. أبو عبيد: وصَيْتُ الشيءَ ووصَلْته سواء؛ ووَصَتِ الأرضُ وَصْياً ووُصِيّاً ووَصاءً ووَصاةً؛ الأخيرة نادرة حكاها أبو حنيفة، كلُّ ذلك: اتصل نباتُها بعضُه ببعض، وهي واصِيةٌ؛ ووصَيْتُ الشيءَ بكذا وكذا إذا وصلته به؛ ويَوصَى: طائر قيل هو الباشَقُ، وقيل: هو الحُرُّ، عراقية ليست من أَبنية العرب.
وأص (لسان العرب) وأَصْتُ به الأَرضَ ووأَص به الأَرضَ وأْصاً: ضربهَا، ومَحص به الأَرض مثله.
وأص (مقاييس اللغة) الواو والهمزة والصاد. يقولون: ما أدري أي الوَئيصةِ هو، أيْ أيِّ الناس هو. والوئيصة: الجماعة.
أصا (القاموس المحيط) أصا النَبْتُ يأْصُو: اتَصلَ، وكثُرَ.
أصا (لسان العرب) وقالوا: ما له حَصاةٌ ولا أَصاةٌ أَي رأْيٌ يرجع إليه. ابن الأَعرابي: أَصى الرجلُ إذا عَقَلَ بعد رُعُونة.
عصو/ي (مقاييس اللغة) العين والصاد والحرف المعتل أصلانِ صحيحان، إلاَ أنَهما متباينان يدلُّ أحدهما على التجمُّع، ويدلُّ الآخر على الفُرْقة.
عصص (لسان العرب) العَصُّ: هو الأَصلُ الكريم وكذلك الأَصُّ. وعَصَ يَعصُ عَصّاً وعَصَصاً: صَلُب واشْتَدَ.
عصا (لسان العرب) ويقال: عَصا إذا صَلُب؛ واعْتَصَت النَواةُ أي اشْتَدَتْ.
العَصُّ (القاموس المحيط) العَصُّ: الأَصْلُ. وعَصَّ، كمَلَّ: صَلُبَ، واشْتَدَ.
سأر (لسان العرب) السُؤْرُ بَقيَة الشيء، وجمعه أَسآرٌ، وسُؤْرُ الفأْرةِ وغيرِها؛ وأَسْأَر منه شيئاً: أَبقى. وفيه سُؤْرَة أي بقية شباب؛ وقد روي بيت الهلالي: إزاء معاشٍ لا يزالُ نِطاقُها شَديداً، وفيها سُؤْرَةٌ، وهي قاعِد (* هذه رواية أخرى للبيت الذي قبله لأن الشاعر واحد وهو حميد ابن ثور الهلالي). التهذيب: وأَما قوله: «وسائرُ الناس هَمج» فإِن أَهل اللغة اتفقوا على أَن معنى سائر في أَمْثال هذا الموضع بمعنى الباقي، من قولك: أَسْأَرْتُ سُؤْراً وسُؤْرَة إذا أَفْضَلْتها وأَبقيتها. والسَّائِرُ الباقي، وكأَنه من سَأَرَ يَسْأَرُ فَهُو سائر. قال ابن الأعرابي فيما رَوى عنه أبو العباس: يقال سَأر وأَسْأَرَ إذا أَفْضَلَ، فهو سائر؛ جعل سَأَرَ وأَسْأَرَ واقعين ثم قال وهو سائر. قال: قال فلا أدري أَراد بالسَّائر المُسْئِر. وفي الحديث: فَضْلُ عائشة على النساء كفَضْلِ الثَّريد على سائر الطعام؛ أَي باقيه؛ والسائر، مهموز: الباقي؛ قال ابن الأَثير: والناس يستعملونه في معنى الجميع وليس بصحيح؛ وتكررت هذه اللفظة في الحديث وكله بمعنى باقي الشيء، والباقي: الفاضِلُ. والسُّؤْرةُ من المال: جَيِّدُهُ، وجمعه سُؤَر.
السُّؤْرُ (القاموس المحيط) السُّؤْرُ، بالضم: البقيةُ، والفضْلَةُ. والسائِرُ: الباقي لا الجميعُ، كما تَوهَم جماعاتٌ، أو قد يُسْتعْمَلُ له.
سير (الصّحَاح في اللغة) وسائرُ الناس: جميعهم. وسارُ الشيءِ: لغةٌ في سائره.
سير (لسان العرب) السَيْرُ: الذهاب؛ سارَ يَسيرُ سَيْراً ومَسيراً وتَسْياراً ومَسِيرةً وسَيْرورَةً؛ سائرُ الناس: جَميعُهم. وسارُ الشيءِ: لغة في سَائِره. وسارُه، يجوز أَن يكون من الباب لسعة باب «س ي ر» وأَن يكون من الواو لأَنها عين، وكلاهما قد قيل؛ قال أَبو ذؤيب يصف ظبية:وسَوَّدَ ماءُ المَرْدِ فاهَا، فلَوْنُهُ كلَوْنِ النَّؤُور، وهي أَدْماءُ سارُها أَي سائرُها؛ التهذيب: وأَما قوله: وسائرُ الناس هَمَجٌ فإِن أَهلَ اللغة اتفقوا على أَن معنى سائر في أَمثال هذا الموضع بمعنى الباقي، من قولك أَسْأَرْتُ سُؤْراً وسُؤْرَةً إذا أَفضلتها. والسِّيرةُ: الطريقة. يقال: سارَ بهم سِيرَةً حسَنَةً.

Part 1

Hammurabi Laws Transliterations and Translations

A Subject Guide to the Law Code of Hammurabi

§ 1 - § 5	Courts and Judiciary Affairs
§ 6 - § 13	Stolen and Missing Property
§ 14	Stealing Children
§ 15 - § 20	Stealing, Hiding, and Finding Slaves
§ 21 - § 24	Home Invasion, Robbery, Deadly Assault, and Liability
§ 25	Stealing by Fire Fighters
§ 26 - § 41	Military Officers and Government Officials Special Laws
§ 42 - § 58	Fields Contracts and Liability
§ 59 - § 66	Orchards Contracts and Liability
§ 67 - § 69	Real Estate and Tenant Affairs
§ 70 - § 76	Merchants Lending and Profits
§ 77 - § ??	Merchants Partnership
§ ?? - § 108	Merchants and Jobbers Relations
§ 109 - § 111	Alewife and Alcohol Sale
§ 112	Cargo Transportation
§ 113 - § 119	Loan Fulfillment and Hostage Taking
§ 120 - § 126	Storage and Lodgment
§ 127 - § 152	Family, Divorce, Wife Adultery, and Dishonor
§ 153 - § 158	Sexual Assault, Daughter Abuse, and Murdering Husband
§ 159 - § 164	Marriage, Dowry and Marriage Endowments
§ 165 - § 174	Inheritance
§ 175 - § 176	Inheritance: Endowed Women Marrying a Slave
§ 177	Inheritance: Orphans and Remarried Widow
§ 178 - § 182	Inheritance: Priestesses, Palace, and Un-endowed Women
§ 183 - § 184	Inheritance: Endowed Concubines
§ 185 - § 194	Adoption and Wet Nurse
§ 195 - § 216	Assault
§ 217 - § 225	Doctors and Veterinarians
§ 226 - § 227	Slave Branding
§ 228 - § 233	Homes, Builders, and Liability
§ 234 - § 240	Boats, Boatmen, and Liability
§ 241 - § 249	Oxen and Donkeys Renting and Liability
§ 250 - § 252	Ox Liability
§ 253 - § 256	Field Laborers, Contractors and Liability
§ 257	Unskilled Workers Hiring
§ 258	Cattle Herdsman Hiring
§ 259 - § 260	Stealing Field Equipment
§ 261 - § 267	Cattle and Sheep Overseer Hiring and Liability
§ 268 - § 273	Working Animals and Carriage Renting
§ 274	Skilled Workers Hiring
§ 275 - § 277	Boats Renting
§ 278 - § 282	Slaves Buying and Ownership

Reading Key

§ # corresponds to a law number

Arabic # corresponds to thin columns within a specific "column" (i.e. band)

Roman # corresponds to "columns" (i.e. band)

All Capital and Light-shaded words are presumed Sumerian words

[ ] Alternative transliterations or translations

( ) Alternative words meanings or clarification notes

... Missing words

| | Assumed words or lines for lost text

§ 1.—V, 26-32

26 šum-ma a-wi-lum ^{b}a-wi-lam 27 u-ub-bi-ir-ma 28 ne-ir-tam e-li-šu 29 id-di-ma 30 la uk-ti-in-šu 31 mu-ub-bi-ir-šu 32 id-da-ak

26 ثَمَّ أويلُم [عويلُم] أَويلَم [عويلَم] 27 يُؤبِرِم 28 نِعرتَم [نحِرتَم] علِي ذو 29 يدِّمَ [يدعِم] 30 لا يُكتِنْ ذو 31 مؤبِرْ ذو 32 يدِكْ

بعد ان (اذا) شخص [رجل] يتهم شخص [رجل]، (و)يدعْ (ويضع) عليه (تهمة) قتل (باراقة الدم)، (و) لا يُثبتها، مُتهمُهُ سوف يُقتَلْ.

If (after) a person [a man] accuses a person [a man], (and) he puts on him a (bloodletting) killing (accusation), (and) he does not prove it, his accuser shall be put to death.

§ 2.—V, 33-56

33 šum-ma a-wi-lum 34 ki-iš-bi 35 e-li a-wi-lim ^{b}id-di-ma 36 la uk-ti-in-šu 37 ša e-li-šu 38 ki-iš-bu na-du-u 39 a-na ^{ilu}Nârim 40 i-il-la-ak 41 ^{ilu}Nâram i-ša-al-^{b}li-a-am-ma 42 šum-ma ^{ilu}Nârum 43 ik-ta-ša-zu 44 mu-ub-bi-ir-šu 45 bîzu i-tab-ba-al 46 šum-ma a-wi-lam ^{b}šu-a-ti 47 ^{ilu}Nârum 48 u-te-ib-bi-^{b}ba-aš-šu-ma 49 iš-ta-al-ma-am 50 ša e-li-šu 51 ki-iš-bi id-du-u 52 id-da-ak 53 ša ^{ilu}Nâram 54 iš-li-a-am 55 bît mu-ub-bi-ri-šu 56 i-tab-ba-al

33 ثَمَّ أويلُم [عويلُم] 34 قِشْبِ [كشْفِ] 35 علِي أويلِم [عويلِم] يدِّمَ [يدعِم] 36 لا يُكتِنْ ذو 37 ذا علِي ذو 38 قشْبُ [كشْفُ] نَدُو 39 أنَ النَهرِم 40 يئِلكْ 41 النَهْرَم يشلِئم [يسلِئم] 42 ثمَّ النَهرُم 43 يكتَسعْ ذوْ [يكتَسعْتَ] [يكتَسأ ذو [يكْتَسأتْ]] 44 مؤبر ذو 45 بيتْ ذو [بيتْ] يتبَل 46 ثمَّ أَويلَم [عويلَم] ذأت 47 النَهْرُم 48 يُطبِعبِذَّم [يُطبِعبا ذُومَ] 49 يستَلمَمْ [إستَلمَمْ] 50 ذا علي ذو 51 قِشْبِ [كشْفِ] إدّوَ 52 يدِكْ 53 ذا النَهْرَم 54 إشلِئم [إسلِئمَ] 55 بيت مؤبِرْ ذو 56 يتبَل

بعد ان (اذا) شخص [رجل] يدَعْ (يضع) (تهمة) شعوذة على شخص [رجل]، (و) لا يثْبتها، الذي عليه (تهمة) الشعوذة واقعة سوف يذهب الى النهر، سوف يغطس النهر (يمتحن محنة النهر)، (و) بعد ان (اذا) يلْفضه النهر، متهمه يأخذ بيته؛ بعد ان (اذا) ذلك الشخص [الرجل] يغْمره (لا يلْفضه) النهر، (و) يُخرجْ سالما، الذي جلبَ (تهمة) الشعوذة عليه سوف يُقتَلْ، الذي غطس (في محنة) النهر سوف يأخذ بيت مُتهمه.

If (after) a person [a man] puts a sorcery (accusation) on a person [a man], (and) he does not prove it, he who on him the sorcery (accusation) fallen shall go to the river, he shall dip (into) the river (shall take the river lying test), (and) if (after) the river expels (rejects) him, his accuser shall take his house; if (after) that person [man], the river submerges him, (and) he emerges unharmed, he who brought the sorcery (accusation) on him shall be put to death, he who dipped into the river shall take the house of his accuser.

§ 3.—V, 57-67

57 šum-ma a-wi-lum 58 i-na di-nim 59 a-na ši-bu-ut 60 ṣa-ar-ra-tim 61 u-zi-a-am-ma 62 a-wa-at iḳ-bu-u 63 la uk-ti-in 64 šum-ma di-nu-um ^{b}šu-u 65 di-in na-bi-iš-tim 66 a-wi-lum šu-u 67 id-da-ak

57 ثُمَّ أويلم [عويلم] 58 إنَ دينمْ 59 أنَ ثبُتْ [شيبتْ] 60 ضرتمْ [صرتمْ] 61 يُزعم 62 أوتْ إقْبو 63 لا يُكتنْ 64 ثُمَّ دينُم ذوو 65 دنْ نبشتم [نفستِمْ] 66 أويلم [عويلم] 67 يدكْ

بعد ان (اذا) شخص [رجل] يزعم (يدّعي) في قضية (جزاء) (وفقا) لشهادة احتيال (لشهادة زور)، (و) لا يثبت مشكوكية (ما) قالَ (بالادلة)، بعد ان (اذا) القضية هذه قضية حياة (أو موت)، الشخصُ [الرجلُ] سوف يُقتَلْ.

If (after) a person [a man], claims in a (court) case (according) to a false testimony, (and) he does not support (prove) the uncertainty of (what) he said, if (after) this case is a life (or death) case, the person [man] shall be put to death.

§ 4.—V, 68-VI, 5

68 šum-ma a-na ši-bu-ut VI, 1 še'im u kaspim 2 u-zi-a-am 3 a-ra-an 4 di-nim šu-a-ti 5 it-ta-na-aš-ši

68 ثُمَّ أنَ ثبُتْ [شيبتْ] 1 سعِمْ [شعِمْ] و كسْفِم 2 يزعم 3 عرنْ [عننْ] 4 دينمْ ذأتِ 5 يتأنتِ [يتعنتِ]

|وفق الفقرة 3| بعد ان (اذا) يدّعي (وفقا) لشهادة حبوب و فضة (شهادة رشوة)، سوف يتحمل (مشقة) تهمة [عقوبة] تلك القضية.

|Referencing §3| If (after) he claims (according) to a grains and silver testimony (on bribe), he shall bear (the hardship) of the charge [the penalty] of that case.

§ 5.—VI, 6-30

6 šum-ma da-a-a-nu-um 7 di-nam i-di-in 8 pu-ru-za-am 9 ip-ru-uš 10 ku-nu-uk-kam 11 u-še-zi-ib 12 wa-ar-ka-^{b}nu-um-ma 13 di-in-šu i-te-ni 14 da-a-a-nam šu-a-ti 15 i-na di-in ^{b}i-di-nu 16 e-ne-im 17 u-ka-an-nu-šu-ma 18 ru-gu-um-ma-am 19 ša i-na di-nim ^{b}šu-a-ti 20 ib-ba-aš-šu-u 21 a-du XII-šu 22 i-na-ad-di-in 23 u i-na pu-uḫ-^{b}ri-im 24 i-na ^{iṣu}kussê 25 da-a-a-nu-ti-šu 26 u-še-it-bu-u-šu-ma 27 u-ul i-ta-ar-ma 28 it-ti da-a-a-ni 29 i-na di-nim 30 u-ul ušta(=ša)-ab

6 ثُمَّ دآنم 7 دينَمْ يدنْ 8 فُرزمْ 9 يفرُسْ 10 كنُكم 11 يُشذبْ 12 ورْكنم 13 دن ذو يتئني [يتنهي] 14 دآنم ذأتِ 15 إنَ دنْ إإدنْ 16 حينئمْ 17 يُكنو ذُوم 18 رُجممْ 19 ذا إنَ دينمْ ذأتِ 20 إبذوَ [إبثوَ] 21 عدو 12–ذو 22 يندنْ 23 و إنَ فهرم 24 إنَ اصوكُسَّي 25 دآنْتي ذو 26 يُشّطْبو ذُوم [يُسّئِتبو ذُومَ] 27 أُل يتأرمَ 28 إتي دآنِ 29 إنَ دينمْ 30 أُل يُثْتَبْ

بعد ان (اذا) حاكم يحكم بقضية (جزاء)، يبتّ (يصدر) قرار، ينجز وثيقة (ملف) قضية مختوم، وراء ذلك يعلّق (يوقف) [ينهي] (سرا) (تنفيذ) حكمه، ذلك الحاكم (الذي) حكم بالحكم، حينئذ سوف يُجلسوه [يستدعوه]، سوف يعطي 12 اضعاف الغرامة التي تواجَدت [ظَهرت] في تلك القضية، وسوف يُبعدوه في (من) كرسي حاكميته في تجمّع (في العلن) (و) سوف لا يعود، (و) لا يجلس مع الحُكّام في قضية.

If (after) a judge judges a (court) case, he decides a verdict, he delivers a sealed court ruling document, afterwards, he slows (suspends) [abandons] (secretly) his judgment (execution), that judge (who) judged in the case, then, they shall seat [call] him in, he shall give 12 fold the fine (amount) that existed [appeared] in that (court) case, and they shall dismiss him in (from) his judging chair in a gathering (publicly), (and) he shall not return, (and) shall not sit in a (court) case with judges.

§ 6.—VI, 31-40

31 šum-ma a-wi-lum 32 ŠA.GA ilim 33 u êkal-lim 34 iš-ri-iḳ 35 a-wi-lum šu-u 36 id-da-ak 37 u ša šu-ur-ga-am 38 i-na ga-ti-šu 39 im-ḫa-ru 40 id-da-ak

31 ثمّ أويلم [عَويلم] 32 شَجا إلمْ [علِم] 33 وهيكلِم 34 يسْرِق 35 أويلم [عَويلم] ذوو 36 يِدكْ 37 وذا سرْجم [سرْقم] 38 إنَ جتي ذو [قتي ذو] 39 إمْخر 40 يِدكْ

بعد ان (اذا) شخص [رجل] يسرق حاجيات إله وقصر، هذا الشخص [الرجل] سوف يُقتلْ، والذي إختار (قبل) بيديه المسروق، سوف يُقتلْ.

If (after) a person [a man] steels the things (belongings) of a god and a palace, this person [man] shall be put to death, and he who chose (accepted) the stolen things in his hands, shall be put to death.

§ 7.—VI, 41-56

41 šum-ma a-wi-lum 42 lu kaspam 43 lu ḫurâṣam 44 lu wardam lu amtam 45 lu alpam lu immeram 46 lu imêram 47 u lu mi-im-ma [b]šum-šu 48 i-na ga-at [b]mâr a-wi-lum 49 u lu warad a-wi-lim 50 ba-lum ši-bi 51 u ri-ik-sa-tim 52 iš-ta-am 53 u lu a-na ma-ṣa-ru-tim 54 im-ḫu-ur 55 a-wi-lum šu-u 56 šar-ra-aḳ id-da-ak

41 ثمّ أويلم [عَويلم] 42 لو كسْفم 43 لو خْراصمْ 44 لو وردمْ لو أمتمْ 45 لو ألفمْ [ألبمْ] [علفمْ [علبمْ]] لو إمْرمْ 46 لو حميرمْ 47 ولو ممّ سمْ ذو 48 إنَ جت [قت] مأرْ أويلم [عَويلم] 49 ولو وردْ أويلِم [عويلِم] 50 بلْمْ ثبي [شيبِ] 51 وركْستِم 52 يستمْ 53 ولو أنَ مصرتِم [نَصرتِم] 54 يمخرْ 55 أويلم [عَويلم] ذوو 56 سارَقْ يدكْ

بعد ان (اذا) شخص [رجل] يشتري بلا (بدون) شهود وعقود لو (ليكن) فضة، لو ذهب [لو حلْي]، لو عبد، لو عبدة، لو ثور، لو خروف، لو حمار، و(حتى) لو أياً إسمه [أي شيء] في (من) يدْ إبن شخص [رجل]، و(حتى) لو عبد شخص [رجل]، و(حتى) لو يختارُ (يقبلُ) للحفظ (للتأمين)، هذا الشخص [الرجل] سوف يُقتلْ كسارق.

If (after) a person [a man] buys without witnesses and contracts, let-it-be silver, let-it-be gold [jewelry], let-it-be male slave, let-it-be female slave, let-it-be ox, let-it-be sheep, let-it-be donkey and (even) let-it-be whatever its name [anything], in (from) the hand of a son of a person [a man], and (even) let-it-be (from) a slave of a person [a man], and (even) let-it-be (that) he chooses (accepts) to (for) safe-keeping, this person [man] shall be put to death as a thieve.

§ 8.—VI, 57-69

57 šum-ma a-wi-lum 58 lu alpam lu immeram [b]lu imêram lu šaḫâm 59 u lu elippam 60 iš-ri-iḳ 61 šum-ma ša i-lim 62 šum-ma ša êkallim 63 a-du XXX-šu 64 i-na-ad-di-in 65 šum-ma ša MAŠ.EN.KAK 66 a-du X-šu i-ri-a-ab 67 šumma šar-ra-[b]ga-nu-um 68 ša na-da-nim [b]la i-šu 69 id-da-ak

57 ثمّ أويلم [عَويلم] 58 لو ألفمْ [ألبمْ] [علفمْ [علبمْ]] لو إمّرمْ لو حميرمْ لو سخمْ 59 ولو علِبمّ 60 يسْرِق 61 ثمّ ذا إلمْ [علِمْ] 62 ثمّ ذا هيكلِمْ 63 عدو 30–ذو 64 يندِنْ 65 ثمّ ذا مَس عَن كأكْ 66 عدو 10–ذو يرأبْ 67 ثمّ سارجنْمْ [سارَقنُمْ] 68 ذا ندانمِْ لا يذو 69 يِدكْ

بعد ان (اذا) شخص [رجل] يسرق، لو (ليكن) ثور، لو خروف، لو حمار، لو خنزير، و(حتى) لو قارب، بعد ان (اذا) لإله، بعد ان (اذا) لقصر، سوف يعطي 30 ضعف؛ بعد ان (اذا) لشخص من العامّة، سوف يُسدِدْ (يعوض) 10 اضعاف؛ بعد ان (اذا) السارق لا يملك ذا الإعطاء (ما للإعطاء) سوف يُقتلْ.

If (after) a person [man] steels, let-it-be an ox, let-it-be a sheep, let-it-be a donkey, and (even) let-it-be a boat, if (after) (it is) of a god, if (after) (it is) of a palace, he shall give 30 fold, if (after) (it is) of an ordinary person, he shall repay (replace) 10 fold, if (after) the thieve does not have that of giving (what to give), he shall be put to death.

§ 9.—VI, 70-VII, 47

70 šum-ma a-wi-lum VII, 1 ša mi-im-mu-šu [b]hal-ḳu 2 mi-im-ma-šu 3 ẖal-ga-am 4 i-na ga-ti [b]a-wi-lim 5 iṣ-ṣa-ba-at 6 a-wi-lum ša ẖu-[b]ul-ḳum 7 i-na ga-ti-šu 8 ṣa-ab-tu 9 na-di-na-nu-um-mi [b]id-di-nam 10 ma-ẖar ši-bi-mi 11 a-ša-am 12 iḳ-ta-bi 13 u be-el ẖu-ul-[b]ḳi-im 14 ši-bi mu-di 15 ẖu-ul-ḳi-ia-mi 16 lu-ub-lam 17 iḳ-ta-bi 18 ša-a-a-ma-nu-um 19 na-di-in 20 id-di-nu-šum 21 u ši-bi 22 ša i-na maẖ-ri-[b]šu-nu 23 i-ša-mu it-ba-lam 24 u be-el ẖu-ul-[b]ḳi-im 25 ši-bi mu-di [b]ẖu-ul-ḳi-šu 26 it-ba-lam 27 da-a-a-nu 28 a-wa-a-ti-šu-nu 29 i-im-ma-ru-ma 30 ši-bu ša maẖ-ri-[b]šu-nu 31 ši-mu-um 32 iš-ša-mu 33 u ši-bu mu-di 34 ẖu-ul-ḳi-im 35 mu-du-zu-nu 36 ma-ẖar i-lim 37 i-ga-ab-bu-ma 38 na-di-na-nu-um 39 šar-ra-aḳ id-da-ak 40 be-el ẖu-ul-ḳi-im 41 ẖu-lu-uḳ-šu 42 i-li-ḳi 43 ša-a-a-ma-nu-um 44 i-na bi-it 45 na-di-na-nim 46 kaspam iš-ḳu-lu 47 i-li-ḳi

70 ثمَ أويلم [عويلم] 1 ذا ممُ ذو حلق 2 مم ذو 3 حلجم [حلقم] 4 إن جتي [قتي] أويلم [عويلم] 5 يضبط 6 أويلم [عويلم] ذا حلقم 7 إن جتي [قتي] 8 ضبط 9 نديننمي إدنم 10 مخر ثبيم [شيبم] 11 أسم 12 يقتبي 13 وبعل حلقم 14 ثبي [شيب] مؤدي [مهدي] 15 حلقيامي 16 لأبلم 17 يقتبي 18 سآمنم 19 ندين 20 إدن ذوم 21 وثبي [شيب] 22 ذا إن مخر ذون 23 إإسم يتبلم 24 وبعل حلقم 25 ثبي [شيب] مؤدي حلق ذو 26 يتبلم 27 دآن 28 أوات ذون 29 يمرم 30 ثب [شيب] ذا مخر ذون 31 سيمم 32 إسأم 33 وثب [شيب] مؤدي [مهدي] 34 حلقم 35 مؤد ذون [مهد ذون] 36 مخر إلم [علم] 37 يجبم [يقبم] 38 نديننم 39 سارق يدك 40 بعل حلقم 41 حلق ذو 42 يلقي 43 سآمنم 44 إن بيت 45 نديننم 46 كسفم إثقل 47 يلقي

بعد ان (اذا) الشخص [الرجل] الذي أي من اشياءه مختفي (مفقود) يضبط (يجد) أي من اشياءه المختفية (المفقودة) في يد شخصٍ [رجلٍ]، الشخص [الرجل] الذي في يديه الشيء المختفي (المفقود) ممسوك يقول "معطيً (بائعً) لي أعطى (باعَ) (هذا)، اشتريت (هذا) امام شهود"، ومالك الشيء المختفي (المفقود) يقول "لأجلب (سأجلب) شهود عارفين بشيئيَ المختفي (المفقود)"؛ المشتري يجلب المعطي (البائع) الذي اعطى (باعَ) والشهود الذين إشترى امامهم، ومالك الشيء المختفي (المفقود) يجلب الشهود العارفين بشيئه المختفي (المفقود)؛ الحكام سوف يتداولون شهاداتهم؛ الشهود الذين أُشتريت الحاجة المُشتراة امامهم، والشهود العارفين بالشيء المختفي (المفقود)، سوف يجيبو (يقولو) امام إله شهاداتهم، (ولذا) المُعطي (البائع) سوف يُقتَلْ كسارق؛ مالك الشيء المختفي (المفقود) سوف يلقي (يأخذ) شيئه المختفي (المفقود)؛ المشتري سوف يلقي (يأخذ) الفضة التي وزنَ (واعطى) في (من) بيت المُعطي (البائع).

If (after) a person [man] who has anything of his things lost, catch (find) any of his lost things in the hands of a person [man]; the person [man] who the lost thing is found in his hands says “an offeror (seller) of mine has offered (sold) (it), I bought (it) in front of witnesses” and the owner of the lost thing says “I shall bring witnesses knowing of (the ownership of) my vanished thing”; the buyer brings the giver (seller) (who) gave (sold) and the witnesses whom he bought in front of them, and the owner of the lost thing brings the witnesses knowing of (the ownership) of his lost thing; the judges shall deliberate (examine) their testimonies; the witnesses whom the bought thing was bought in front of them, and the witnesses knowing (of the ownership) of the lost thing shall answer [say] in front of a god, (and therefore) the giver (seller) shall be put to death as a thieve; the owner of the lost thing shall take (back) his lost thing; the buyer shall find (take back) the silver he measured (and gave) in (from) the house of the giver (seller).

§ 10.—VII, 48-61

48 šum-ma ša-a-a-[b]ma-nu-um 49 na-di-in 50 id-di-nu-šum 51 u ši-bi ša i-na [b]maḫ-ri-šu-nu 52 i-ša-mu 53 la it-ba-lam 54 be-el ḫu-ul-[b]ḳi-im-ma 55 ši-bi mu-di 56 ḫu-ul-ḳi-šu [b]it-ba-lam 57 ša-a-i-ma-nu-um 58 šar-ra-aḳ id-da-ak 59 be-el ḫu-ul-ḳi-im 60 ḫu-lu-uḳ-šu 61 i-li-ḳi

48 ثُمَّ سآمَنَمْ 49 نَدِينْ 50 إدِنُذُومْ 51 وثِبي [شِيب] ذا إنَ مَخرِ ذونُ 52 إِإسَمُ 53 لا يَتْبَلَمْ 54 بَعَلْ حُلْقِمْ 55 ثِبي [شِيب] مؤدي [مُهدي] 56 حُلقِ ذو يِتْبَلَمْ 57 سائمَنُمْ 58 سارَق يدَكْ 59 بَعَلْ حُلْقِمْ 60 حُلُقْ ذو 61 يِلقي

|وفق الفقرة 9| بعد ان (اذا) المشتري لا يجلب المعطي (البائع) الذي اعطاه (باعه) والشهود الذين إشترى امامهم، مالك الشيء المختفي (المفقود) يجلب الشهود العارفين بشيئه المختفي (المفقود)، المشتري سوف يُقتَلْ كسارق؛ مالك الشيء المختفي (المفقود) يلقي (يأخذ) شيئه المختفي (المفقود).

|Referencing §9| If (after) the buyer does not bring the offeror (seller) (who) offered (sold) him and the witnesses whom he bought in front of them, the owner of the vanished thing brings the witnesses knowing of (the ownership) of his vanished thing, the buyer shall be put to death as a thieve; the owner of the vanished thing shall take his vanished thing.

§ 11.—VII, 62-VIII, 3

62 šum-ma be-el [b]ḫu-ul-ḳi-im 63 ši-bi mu-di 64 ḫu-ul-ḳi-šu 65 la it-ba-lam VIII, 1 ṣa-ar 2 tu-uš-ša-am-ma [b]id-ki 3 id-da-ak

62 ثُمَّ بَعَلْ حُلْقِمْ 63 ثِبي [شِيب] مؤدي [مُهدي] 64 حُلقِ ذو 65 لا يَتْبَلَمْ 1 صَرْ [ضَرْ] 2 تَشمَ إدكي [إذكي] 3 يدَكْ

|وفق الفقرة 9| بعد ان (اذا) مالك الشيء المختفي (المفقود) لا يجلب الشهود العارفين بشيئه المختفي (المفقود)، سوف يُقتَل كمحتال [كذاب؛ مخالف] يذكي (يثير) عداوة (فتنة) [إفتراء].

|Referencing §9| If (after) the owner of the lost thing does not bring the witnesses knowing of (the ownership) of his lost thing, he shall be put to death as a cheater [liar; outlaw] stirring up strife [slander].

§ 12.—VIII, 4-13

4 šum-ma na-di-[b]na-nu-um 5 a-na ši-im-tim 6 it-ta-la-ak 7 ša-a-a-ma-nu-um 8 i-na bi-it 9 na-di-na-nim 10 ru-gu-um-me-e 11 di-nim šu-a-ti 12 a-du V-šu 13 i-li-ḳi

4 ثُمَّ نَدِينَنَمْ 5 أنَ سِمتِمْ 6 يتألَكْ 7 سآمَنَمْ 8 إنَ بيتْ 9 نَدِينَنِمْ 10 رُجُمي 11 دينِمْ ذُأتِ 12 عدو 5-ذو 13 يلقي

|وفق الفقرة 9| بعد ان (اذا) المعطي (البائع) يذهب الى المصير (يموت)، المشتري سوف يلقي (يأخذ) 5 اضعاف غرامة تلك القضية في (من) بيت المعطي (البائع).

|Referencing §9| If (after) the giver (seller) goes to destiny (died), the buyer shall take 5 fold the fine (amount) of that (court) case in (from) the house of the giver (seller).

§ 13.—VIII, 14-24

14 šum-ma a-wi-lum [b]šu-u 15 ši-bu-šu [b]la kir-bu 16 da-a-a-nu a-da-nam 17 a-na arḫim VI[kam] 18 i-ša-ak-ka-[b]nu-šum-ma 19 šum-ma i-na arḫim VI[kam] 20 ši-bi-šu [b]la ir-di-a-am 21 a-wi-lum šu-u 22 ṣa-ar 23 a-ra-an di-nim [b]šu-a-ti 24 it-ta-na-aš-ši

14 ثُمَّ أويلُم [عويلُم] ذوو 15 ثِبُ ذو [شيبُ ذو] لا كِربْ 16 دآنُ هدَنَمْ 17 إنَ أرخِمْ 6[كم] 18 يسكَنو ذُومَ 19 ثُمَّ إنَ أرخِمْ 6[كم] 20 ثِبِ ذو [شيبِ ذو] لا يردأمْ 21 أويلُم [عويلُم] ذوو 22 صَرْ [ضَرْ] 23 عَرَنْ [عَنَنْ] دينِمْ ذُأتِ 24 يتأنَت [يتعنت]

|وفق الفقرة 9| بعد ان (اذا) هذا الشخص [الرجل] (مالك الشيء المختفي)، شهوده غير حاضرين، الحكام سوف يضعو له هدنة (مهلة) 6 شهور؛ بعد ان (اذا) لا يصطحب شهوده في ستة شهور، هذا الشخصُ [الرجلُ] مُحتال [كذّاب؛ مُخالف]، سوف يتحمل (مشقة) تهمة [عقوبة] تلك القضية.

|Referencing §9| If (after) this person [man] (the owner of the vanished thing), his witnesses are not present, the judges shall set for him a 6 month respite, if (after) he does not accompany his witnesses in 6 months, this person [this man] is cheater [liar; outlaw], he shall bear (the hardship of) the charge [penalty] to that case.

§ 14.—VIII, 25-29

25 šum-ma a-wi-lum 26 mâr a-wi-lim 27 ṣi-iḫ-ra-am 28 iš-ta-ri-iḳ 29 id-da-ak

25 ثُمَّ أَويلْم [عَويلْم] 26 مأرْ أويلِم [عويلِم] 27 صِهرَمْ [صِغرَمْ] 28 يستَرِقْ 29 يدكْ

بعد ان (اذا) شخص [رجل] يسرق إبن شخص [رجل] صغير، سوف يُقتَلْ.

If (after) a person [a man] steels a young son of a person [a man], he shall be put to death.

§ 15.—VIII, 30-36

30 šum-ma a-wi-lum 31 lu warad êkallim 32 lu amat êkallim 33 lu warad MAŠ.EN.KAK 34 lu amat MAŠ.EN.KAK 35 abullam uš-te-zi 36 id-da-ak

30 ثُمَّ أويلْم [عَويلْم] 31 لو وَرَدْ هيكلِمْ 32 لو وردْ مَس عَن كَأكْ 33 لو أمَتْ هيكلِمْ 34 لو أمَتْ مَس عَن كَأكْ 35 أبُلَّمْ يُستَئزي [يُستَعصي] 36 يدَكْ

بعد ان (اذا) شخص [رجل] يْزيح [يهرّب] من (موقع) حجز (عبيد)، لو (ليكن) عبد قصر، لو عبدُ شخص من العامة، لو عبدة قصر، لو عبدة شخص من العامة، سوف يُقتَلْ.

If (after) a person [man] removes [let escape] from a (slave) confinement (place), let-it-be a palace's slave, let-it-be an ordinary man's slave, let-it-be a palace's female slave, let-it-be an ordinary man's female slave, he shall be put to death.

§ 16.—VIII, 37-48

37 šum-ma a-wi-lum 38 lu wardam lu amtam 39 ḫal-ga-am 40 ša êkallim 41 u lu MAŠ.EN.KAK 42 i-na bi-ti-šu 43 ir-ta-ki-ma 44 a-na ši-si-it 45 na-gi-ri-im 46 la uš-te-zi-a-am 47 be-el bîtim šu-u 48 id-da-ak

37 ثُمَّ أويلْم [عَويلْم] 38 لو وردَمْ لو أمْتَمْ 39 حَلْجَمْ [حلْقَمْ] 40 ذا هيكلِمْ 41 ولو مَس عَن كَأكْ 42 إن بيتِ ذو 43 يرْتَكِمَ 44 أنَ سِستْ 45 نَجِئرِمْ [مَجِئرِمْ] 46 لا يُستَئزيام [يُستَعصيام] 47 بَعلْ بيتِم ذوو 48 يدَكْ

بعد ان (اذا) شخص [رجل] يُلْجِئ في بيته لو (ليكن) عبد، لو عبدة، مختفي(ة) (مفقود(ة))، (ل)قصر و (حتى) لو (ل)شخص من العامة، (و) لا يطرده(ها) [لا يُخرجه(ها)] (بناءا) على أمر الداعي، مالك هذا البيت سوف يُقتَلْ.

If (after) a person [man] harbors in his home a lost, let-it-be a slave, let-it-be a female slave, of a palace, and (even) let-it-be an ordinary man, (and) he does not expel him/her [bring him/her out] to (at) a herold's order, the owner of this house shall be put to death.

§ 17.—VIII, 49-58

49 šum-ma a-wi-lum 50 lu wardam lu amtam 51 ḫal-ga-am 52 i-na ṣi-ri-im 53 iṣ-ba-at-ma 54 a-na be-li-šu 55 ir-te-di-a-aš-šu 56 II šiḳil kaspim 57 be-el wardim 58 i-na-ad-di-iš-šum

49 ثُمَّ أَويلْم [عَويلْم] 50 لو وَرْدَمْ لو أمْتَمْ 51 حَلَجَمْ [حلْقَمْ] 52 إنَ ظِهرِم [ضِهرِم] [صِحرِم] 53 يضْبَطْمَ 54 أنَ بعِلِ ذو 55 يرْتَدأ ذو [يرْتَدأذّو] 56 2 ثِقلْ [شِقِلْ] كَسْفِمْ 57 بَعلْ وَرْدِمْ 58 يندِنْ ذُومْ [ينَدذّومْ]

بعد ان (اذا) شخصً [رجلً] يضبط (يمسك) في البرية لو (ليكن) عبد، لو عبدة، مختفي(ة) (مفقود(ة))، (و) يصطحبه(ها) الى مالكه(ها) ، مالكُ العبد سوف يعطيه 2 مثقال (شقل) فضة.

If (after) a person [man] seizes in the desert (badiyah) a lost, let-it-be a slave, let-it-be a female slave, (and) accompanies him/her (back) to his/her owner, the owner of the slave shall give him 2 Shiqil silver.

§ 18.—VIII, 59-67

59 šum-ma wardum šu-u 60 be-el-šu 61 la iz-za-kar 62 a-na êkallim 63 i-ri-id-di-šu 64 wa-ar-ka-zu 65 ip-pa-ar-ra-aš-ma 66 a-na be-li-šu 67 u-ta-ar-ru-šu

49 ثمَ وَرْدُمْ ذوو 60 بعِلْ ذو 61 لا يذكرْ 62 أنَ هيكلِمْ 63 يردِئي ذو 64 ورْكتْ ذو [وَرْكتْ] 65 يفرسْمْ 66 أنَ بعْلِ ذو 67 يتأرُ ذو

|وفق الفقرة 17| بعد ان (اذا) هذا العبد لا يَذكُر (لا يُسمي) مالكه، (الشخص [الرجل]) سوف يصطحبه الى القصر؛ سوف يتفحصو خلفيته، (و) يعيدوه الى مالكه.

|Referencing §17| If (after) this slave does not say (name) his owner, he shall accompany him to the palace; they shall examine his background, (and) return him to his owner.

§ 19.—VIII, 68-IX, 4

68 šum-ma wardam 69 šu-a-ti 70 i-na bi-ti-šu 71 ik-ta-la-šu 72 wa-ar-ka wardum IX. 1 i-na ga-ti-šu 2 it-ta-aṣ-ba-at 3 a-wi-lum šu-u 4 id-da-ak

68 ثمَ وَرْدَمْ 69 ذأتِ 70 إنَ بيتِ ذو 71 يكْتلَ ذو 72 وَرْكَ وردمْ 1 إنَ جتي ذو [قتي ذو] 2 يتَضْبطْ 3 أويلمْ [عويلمْ] ذوو 4 يدكْ

|وفق الفقرة 17| بعد ان (اذا) ذلك العبد، يحجزه (يحفظه) (الشخص [الرجل]) في بيته، بعدما العبد يُضْبَط (يُمسَك) في يديه (في حوزته)، هذا الشخص [الرجل] سوف يُقتَل.

|Referencing §17| If (after), that slave, he detains (keeps) him in his home, after the slave is caught in his hands (possession), this person [man] shall be put to death.

§ 20.—XI, 5-13

5 šum-ma wardum 6 i-na ga-at 7 ṣa-bi-ta-ni-šu 8 iḫ-ta-li-iḳ 9 a-wi-lum šu-u 10 a-na be-el wardim 11 ni-iš i-lim 12 i-za-kar-ma 13 u-ta-aš-šar

5 ثمَ وردمْ 6 إنَ جتْ [قتْ] 7 ضبطَني ذو 8 يحتلِقْ 9 أويلمْ [عويلمْ] ذوو 10 أنَ بعِلْ وردِمْ 11 نعِشْ إلِمْ [علِمْ] 12 يذَكَرمْ 13 يُتذرْ

|وفق الفقرة 17| بعد ان (اذا) العبد يختفي (يُفقَد) في (من) يد ضابطِه (ماسكِه)، هذا الشخص [الرجل] سوف يقول (يحلف) (ذلك) برفِعَة (بحياة) الإله الى مالك العبد، (و) سوف يُترك (حرا).

|Referencing §17| If (after) this slave vanishes (become lost) in (from) the hand of his holder, this person [man] shall say (declare) (that) in the glory life of god to the slave owner, (and) shall be left (free).

§ 21.—XI, 14-21

14 šum-ma a-wi-lum 15 bi-tam 16 ip-lu-uš 17 i-na pa-ni 18 bi-il-ši-im 19 šu-a-ti 20 i-du-uk-ku-bšu-ma 21 i-ḫa-al-bla-lu-šu

14 ثمْ أوَيلمْ [عَويلمْ] 15 بيتمْ 16 يفلَشْ 17 إنَ فني 18 بلْشِمْ [فلْشِمْ] 19 ذأتِ 20 يدكو ذومَ 21 يخلَلو ذو

بعد ان (اذا) شخص [رجل] يخترق (يسطو على) بيت، سوف يقتلونه في أمام (موقع) ذلك الاختراق، (و) يتركونه ليتعفن.

If (after) person [man] breaches (breaks in) a home, they shall put him to death in front of that breach (place), (and) shall leave him to rot.

§ 22.—XI, 22-27

22 šum-ma a-wi-lum 23 ḫu-ub-tam 24 iḫ-bu-ut-ma 25 it-ta-aṣ-ba-at 26 a-wi-lum šu-u 27 id-da-ak

22 ثمّ أويلم [عويلم] 23 خبْطم 24 يخبْطم 25 يتضْبط 26 أويلم [عويلم] ذوو 27 يدكْ

بعد ان (اذا) شخص [رجل] ينهب (يسلب) نهيبة ، (و) يُضْبَط (يُمسَك)، هذا الشخص [الرجل] سوف يُقتل.

If (after) person [man] robs loot, (and) he is caught, this person [man] shall be put to death.

§ 23.—XI, 28-45

28 šum-ma ḫa-ab-^{b}ba-tum 29 la it-ta-aṣ-ba-at 30 a-wi-lum 31 ḫa-ab-tum 32 mi-im-ma-šu 33 ḫal-ga-am 34 ma-ḫa-ar 35 i-lim 36 u-ba-ar-ma 37 alum 38 u ra-bi-a-nu-um 39 ša i-na ir-ṣi-^{b}ti-šu-nu 40 u pa-di-šu-nu 41 ḫu-ub-tum 42 iḫ-ḫa-ab-tu 43 mi-im-ma-šu 44 ḫal-ga-am 45 i-ri-a-ab-^{b}bu-šum

28 ثمّ خبطمْ 29 لا يتضْبطْ 30 أويلم [عويلم] 31 خبطمْ 32 ممّ ذو 33 حلْجمْ [حلقمْ] 34 مخرْ 35 إلمْ [علِم] 36 يبرمْ 37 أيلمْ 38 وربيانمْ 39 ذا إنَ إرضتِ ذونْ 40 وفدي ذونُ 41 خبطمْ 42 إخبْطو 43 ممّ ذو 44 حلْجمْ [حلقمْ] 45 يرأبو ذومْ

|وفق الفقرة 22| بعد ان (اذا) الناهب (السالب) لا يُضْبَط (لا يُمسَك)، الشخص [الرجل] سوف يُصدّق أمام إله أياً من اشياءه المختفية (المفقودة)، منهوبة؛ العشيرة والزعيم الذين في أرضهم ومحميتهم نُهِبت النهيبة، سوف يسددو له (يعوضوه) أياً من اشياءه المختفية (المفقودة).

|Referencing §22| If (after) the robber is not caught, the person [man] shall confirm in front of god whatever of his vanished (lost), (is) robbed; the tribe and chief in whose land and protectorate the loot was robbed shall repay (replace) anything of his (that is) lost.

§ 24.—XI, 46-50

46 šum-ma na-bi-iš-tum 47 alum u ra-bi-^{b}a-nu-um 48 I ma-na kaspim 49 a-na ni-ši-šu 50 i-ša-ga-lu

46 ثمّ نبستِمْ 47 أيلمْ 38 وربيانمْ 48 1 منَا كسْفمِ 49 أنَ نِيسي ذو 50 يثقلُ

|وفق الفقرة 22| بعد ان (اذا) (المسلوب) حياة (انسان)، العشيرة والزعيم سوف يزنو (ويعطو) الى ناسه (أهله) 1 منَا (رطل) فضة.

|Referencing §22| If (after) (the loot is) a (human) life, the tribe and the chief shall shall measure (and give) to his people (family) 1 Mana (2 lbs.) silver.

§ 25.—XI, 51-65

51 šum-ma i-na bît ^{b}a-wi-lim 52 i-ša-tum 53 in-na-bi-iḫ-ma 54 a-wi-lum 55 ša a-na bu-ul-bli-im 56 il-li-ku 57 a-na nu-ma-at 58 be-el bîtim 59 i-in-šu iš-ši-ma 60 nu-ma-at 61 be-el bîtim 62 il-te-di(=ḳi) 63 a-wi-lum šu-u 64 a-na i-ša-tim ^{b}šu-a-ti 65 in-na-ad-di

51 ثمّ إن بيت أويلم [عويلم] 52 حشاتمْ 53 ينبهمْ [ينفخمْ] 54 أويلم [عويلم] 55 ذا أنَ بُهلمْ 56 إلّكُ 57 أن نُومتْ 58 بعل بيتمْ 59 عينْ ذو يعسيمَ [يئتيمَ] 60 نُومتْ 61 بعل بيتمْ 62 يلْتدي [يتدّي] [يلْتقي] 63 أويلم [عويلم] ذوو 64 أنَ حشاتمْ ذأتِ 65 ينَدي

بعد ان (اذا) نار تهبّ (تشتعل) في بيت شخص [رجل]، (و) الشخص [الرجل] الذي ذهب الى الاطفاء يمنّي [يوجّه (يضع)] عينه على حاجة مالك البيت، (و) يأخذ حاجة مالك البيت، هذا الشخصُ [الرجلُ] سوف يُلقى في تلك النار.

If (after) a fire rages (break out) in a person's [man's] house, (and) the person [the man] who went to the extinguishing allurs [points (puts)] his eye to a house owner's possession, (and) he takes the house owner's possession, that person [man] shall be thrown into that fire.

§ 26.—XI, 66-X, 12

66 šum-ma lu rid ṣâbê 67 u lu bâ'irum 68 ša a-na ḫar-ra-an [b]šar-ri-im 69 a-la-ak-šu X, 1 ga-bu-u 2 la il-li-ik 3 u lu [amêlu]agram 4 i-gur-ma 5 pu-uḫ-šu 6 id-da-ra-ad 7 lu rid ṣâbê 8 u lu bâ'irum šu-u 9 id-da-ak 10 mu-na-ag-gi-[b]ir-šu 11 bî-zu 12 i-tab-ba-al

66 ثمَّ لو رِيدْ صَيبَ 67 و لو بَيئرُمْ [بَيئنُمْ] 68 ذا أنَ حَرَنْ سَرِيمْ [شَرِيمْ] 69 ألَكْ ذو 1 جَبُو [قَبُو] 2 لا يئلِكْ 3 ولو عميل أجْرَمْ 4 يأجْرَم 5 فَه ذو 6 يدرَدْ 7 لو رِيدْ صَيبَ 8 ولو بَيئرُمْ [بَيئنُمْ] ذوو 9 يدَكْ 10 مؤَجِرْ ذو [مُؤنَجِر ذو] 11 بيتْ ذو [بيتْ] 12 يتبَلْ

بعد ان (اذا) لو (ليكن) رائد النُخبة (جنود) و(حتى) لو الموظف (من الأعيان) الذي لرحلة شريف (ملك) مأمور (أَمِرَ) ترسّله (ذهابه)، لا يترسّل (لا يذهب)، و(حتى) لو يستأجر عامل أجر (متعاقد)، (و) يدفع (يرسل) بدله (بدلا عنه)، لو رائد النُخبة و(حتى) لو الموظف، هذا، سوف يُقتل، مُستأجَره (متعاقده) سوف يأخذ بيته.

If (after), let-it-be a leader of an elite (group of soldiers) (an officer) and (even) let-it-be a notable (civil servant) who is ordered his going to (for) a noble's (a royalty's) journey, does not go, and (even) let-it-be he hires a contracted worker to send instead of him, this let-it-be officer and (even) let-it-be notable shall be put to death, his contracted worker shall take his house.

§ 27.—X, 13-X, 29

13 šum-ma lu rid ṣâbê 14 u lu-u bâ'irum 15 ša i-na dan-na-at 16 šar-ri-im 17 tu-ur-ru 18 wa-ar-[ki]-šu 19 eḳil-šu u kirâ-šu 20 a-na ša-ni-im 21 id-di-nu-ma 22 i-li-ik-šu 23 it-ta-la-ak 24 šum-ma it-tu-[b]ra-am-ma 25 ali-šu [b]ik-ta-ašdam 26 eḳil-šu u kirâ-šu 27 u-ta-ar-[b]ru-šum-ma 28 šu-ma i-li-ik-šu 29 i-il-la-ak

13 ثمّ لو رِيدْ صَيبَ 14 و لو بيئرُمْ [بيئنُمْ] 15 ذا إنَ دأنَتْ 16 سرِيمْ [شَرِيمْ] 17 تُرو 18 ورَكْ ذو 19 حقِل ذو وكيرى ذو 20 أنَ ثانِمْ 21 إدنَمْ 22 إلِكْ ذو 23 يتألَكْ 24 ثمّ يتؤرَمَ 25 أيلي ذو يكتَصدَمْ [يقتَصِدَمْ] 26 حقِل ذو وكيرى ذو 27 يتأرُ ذومَ 28 ذُمَا إلِكْ ذو 29 يئلَكْ

بعد ان (اذا) لو (ليكن) رائد النُخبة (الجنود)، و(حتى) لو الموظف (من الأعيان) الذي أصبح منقطِعْ (مفْقودْ) (بينما هو) في خدمة شريف (ملك)، وراءه (بعده)، أعطو حقله وبستانه الى (شخص) ثانٍ (كي) يَترسّل رسالته (يقوم بعمله)، بعد ان (اذا) يعود، (و) يقصد أهله (عشيرته)، سوف يُعيدو له حقله وبستانه، هو (نفسه) سوف يَترسّل رسالته (يقوم بعمله).

If (after) let-it-be the leader of an elite (group of soldiers) (the officer), and (even) let-it-be the notable (the civil servant), who (while) in the service of a noble (royalty) became disconnected (missing), after him, they gave his field and orchard to a second (another) one to run his operation, if (after) he returns, (and) arrives (with) his tribe, they shall return to him his field and his orchard, (and) he (himself) shall run his operation.

§ 28.—X, 30-X, 40

30 šum-ma lu rid ṣâbê 31 u lu-u bâ'irum 32 ša i-na dan-na-at 33 šar-ri-im 34 tu-ur-ru 35 mâr-šu il-kam 36 a-la-kam i-li-i 37 eḳlum u kirûm 38 in-na-ad-di-[b]iš-šum-ma 39 i-li-[ik] a-bi-šu 40 i-il-la-ak

30 ثمّ لو رِيدْ صَيبَ 31 و لو بيئرُمْ [بيئنُمْ] 32 ذا إنَ دأنَتْ 33 سرِيمْ [شَرِيمْ] 34 تُرو 35 مأر ذو إلْكَمْ 36 ألَكَمْ يلعي [يلئي] 37 حقِلَمْ وكيرَمْ 38 ينَّدِنْ ذُومَ [ينَّدِذّومَ] 39 إلِكْ أبي ذو 40 يئلَكْ

بعد ان (اذا)، لو (ليكن) رائد النُخبة (الجنود) و(حتى) لو الموظف (من الأعيان) الذي أصبح منقطِعْ (مفْقودْ) (بينما هو) في خدمة شريف (ملك)، إبنهُ يطيق تَرسُّل الرسالة (القيام بالعمل)، الحقل والبستان سوف تعطى له، (و) سوف يَترسّل رسالة (يقوم بعمل) أبيه.

If (after), let-it-be the leader of an elite (group of soldiers) (the officer) and (even) let-it-be the notable (the civil servant) who (while) in the service of a noble (royalty) became disconnected (missing), his son can handle running the operation, the field and orchard shall be given to him, (and) he shall run his father operation.

§ 29.—X, 41-X, 50

41 šum-ma mâr-šu 42 ṣi-ḫi-ir-ma 43 i-li-ik a-bi-šu 44 a-la-kam 45 la i-li-i 46 ša-lu-uš-ti [b]eḳlim u kirêm 47 a-na um-mi-šu 48 in-na-ad-di-[b]in-ma 49 um-ma-šu 50 u-ra-ab-ba-šu

41 ثُمَّ مأر ذو 42 صِهِرْمَ [صِغِرْمَ] 43 إلِكْ أبي ذو 44 ألَكمْ 45 لا يلِعي [يلِئِي] 46 ثَلْثْتِ حقِلْم وكيرِم 47 أنَ أُمّي ذو 48 ينَدِنْمَ 49 أُمَّا ذو 50 يُرَبّى ذو

|وفق الفقرة 28| بعد ان (اذا) إبنهُ صغير، (و) لا يطيق تَرَسُّل رسالة ابيه (القيام بعمل ابيه)، سوف يعطي (الشخص الثاني المعوّض) ثُلث (عوائد) الحقل والبستان الى أمه، (و) أمُّه سوف تُربّيه.

|Referencing §28| If (after) his son is young, cannot handle running his father operation, (the other man replacing him) shall give one third (the proceeds) of the field and orchard to his mother, (and) his mother shall rear him.

§ 30.—X, 51-XI, 4

51 šum-ma lu rid ṣâbê 52 u lu bâ'irum 53 eḳil-šu kirâ-šu [b]u bî-zu 54 i-na pa-ni [b]il-ki-im 55 id-di-ma 56 ud-da-ab-bi-ir 57 ša-nu-um 58 wa-ar-ki-šu 59 eḳil-šu [b]kirâ-šu 60 u bî-zu 61 iṣ-ba-at-ma 62 šattam III[kam] 63 i-li-ik-šu 64 it-ta-la-ak 65 šum-ma it-tu-[b]ra-am-ma 66 eḳil-šu kirâ-šu u bî-zu 67 i-ir-ri-iš 68 u-ul in-na-ad-[b]di-iš-šum [XI, 1] ša iṣ-ṣa-ab-[b]tu-ma 2 i-li-ik-šu 3 it-ta-al-ku 4 šu-ma [b]i-il-la-ak

51 ثُمَّ لو رِيدْ صيبَ 52 و لو بيئرُمْ [بيئنُمْ] 53 حقِلْ ذو كيرى ذو وبيتْ ذو [بيتْ] 54 إنَ فني إلْكِمْ 55 يدِّمَ [يدعم] 56 يُدَبرْ 57 ثانُمْ 58 ورْكِ ذو 59 حقِلْ ذو كيرى ذو 60 و بيتْ ذو [بيتْ] 61 يضْبطْمَ 62 ستَّمْ [سَنْتَمْ] 3كَم 63 إلِكْ ذو 64 يتألَكْ 65 ثُمّ يترَمَ 66 حقِلْ ذو كيرى ذو وبيتْ ذو [بيتْ] 67 يئرِسْ 68 أُلْ ينَدِنْ ذُومْ [ينَدذّومْ] 1 ذا إضبْطُمَ 2 إلِكْ ذو 3 إتَلْكْ 4 ذُما يئلَكْ

بعد ان (اذا)، لو (ليكن) رائد نُخبة (جنود) و(حتى) لو موظف (من الأعيان) يَدع (يهمل) في (من) البداية رسالة (مهمة عمل) حقله، بستانه، وبيته، (و) يُدّبْر (ويترك)، ورائه (بعده)، (شخص) ثاني (آخر) يضبط (يمسك) حقله بستانه وبيته، (و) يتَرَسَّل رسالته (يقوم بعمله) (ل)ثلاث سنوات؛ بعد ان (اذا) يعود (و) يتحدث عن (يطالب بـ) حقله بستانه وبيته، سوف لن تعطى له؛ الذي ضبطَ (مسك) (الحقل البستان والبيت)، (و) ترسّل رسالته (قام بعمله)، هو (نفسه) سوف يتَرسّل (سيقوم بالعمل).

If (after), let-it-be a leader of an elite (group of soldiers) (an officer) and (even) let-it-be a notable (civil servant) let go (neglects) in (from) the beginning his field, his orchard, and his house, (and) abandons, after him, a second (another) one holds his field, his orchard, and his house, (and) he runs his operation for three years; if (after) he returns (and) request his field, his orchard, and his house, they shall not be given to him; that who held (the field, the orchard, and the house), (and) run his operation, he (himself) shall run (the operation).

§ 31.—XI, 5-12

5 šum-ma ša-at-tam 6 iš-ti-a-at-ma 7 ud-da-ab-[b]bi-ir-ma 8 it-tu-ra-am 9 eḳil-šu kirû-šu [b]u bî-zu 10 in-na-ad-di-[b]iš-šum-ma 11 šu-ma i-li-ik-šu 12 i-il-la-ak

5 ثُمَّ ستَّمْ [سَنْتَمْ] 6 إسْتِياتَمَ [إلْتِياتَمَ] 7 يُدَبرْمَ 8 يترَمْ 9 حقِلْ ذو كيرو ذو وبيتْ ذو [بيتْ] 10 ينَدِنْ ذُومَ [ينَدِّذّومَ] 11 ذُمَا إلِكْ ذو 12 يئلَكْ

|وفق الفقرة 30| بعد ان (اذا) يترُك سنة واحدة، (و) يعود، حقله بستانه وبيته سوف تعطى له، (و) هو (نفسه) سوف يَتَرسّل رسالته (يقوم بعمله).

|Referencing §30| If (after) he leaves (for) one year, (and) returns, his field, his orchard, and his house shall be given to him, (and) he (himself) shall run his operation.

§ 32.—XI, 13-38

13 šum-ma lu rid ṣâbê 14 u lu bâ'iram 15 ša i-na ḫar-ra-an 16 šar-ri-im 17 tu-ur-ru 18 tam-karum ip-tu-^{b}ra-aš-šu-ma 19 ali-šu uš-ta-ak-^{b}ši-da-aš-šu 20 šum-ma i-na bi-ti-šu 21 ša pa-da-ri-im 22 i-ba-aš-ši 23 šu-ma ra-ma-an-šu 24 i-pa-ad-da-ar 25 šum-ma i-na bi-ti-šu 26 ša pa-da-ri-šu 72 la i-ba-aš-ši 28 i-na bît ili ali-šu 29 ip-pa-ad-dar 30 šum-ma i-na bît 31 ili ali-šu 32 ša pa-da-ri-šu 33 la i-ba-aš-ši 34 êkallum i-pa-^{b}ad-da-ri(=ar)-šu 35 eḳil-šu kirû-šu 36 u bî-zu 37 a-na ip-te-ri-šu 38 u-ul in-na-^{b}ad-di-in

13 ثُمَّ لو رِيدْ صيبَ 14 و لو بَيئرُمْ [بيئنم] 15 ذا إنَ حرَنْ 16 سريم [شريمْ] 17 تُرو 18 تمكَارمْ يفطَرذوم [يفطر ذوم] 19 أيل ذو يُستكسِد ذو [يُستقصِد ذو] 20 ثمّ إنَ بيتِ ذو 21 ذا فدرمْ [فطرم] [فدانمْ] 22 يبذي 23 ذُما رأمنْ ذو 24 يفدرْ [يفطرْ] [يفدنْ] 25 ثمَّ إن بيتِ ذو 26 ذا فدرِ ذو [فطرِ ذو] [فدانِ ذو] 27 لا يبذي 28 إنَ بيت إلِ [علِ] أيلِ ذو 29 يفدر [يفطرْ] [يفدنْ] 30 ثمَّ إنَ بيت 31 إلِ [علِ] أيلِ ذو 32 ذا فدرِ ذو [فطرِ ذو] [فدانِ ذو] 33 لا يبذي 34 هيكلُمْ يفدرْ ذو [يفطرْ ذو] [يفدنْ ذو] 35 حقِل ذو كيرُ ذو 36 وبيتْ ذو [بيتْ] 37 أنَ إفطرِ ذو 38 أُلْ ينَدنِ

بعد ان (اذا) لو (ليكن) رائد النُخبة (الجنود) و(حتى) لو الموظف (من الأعيان) الذي أصبح منقطعْ (مفْقودْ) (بينما هو) في رحلة شريف (ملك)، سوف يفتطرِه (سوف يفتديه) متاجر، (و) يجعله يقصد أهله (عشيرته)؛ بعد ان (اذا) يملك في بيته ما للفدية (ما تتطلبه الفدية)، هو (نفسه) سوف يفتدي ذاته؛ بعد ان (اذا) لا يملك في بيته ما للفدية (ما تتطلبه الفدية)، سوف يفتدي (نفسه) في (من) بيت إله عشيرته؛ بعد ان (اذا) لا يملك في بيت إله عشيرته ما للفدية (ما تتطلبه الفدية)، القصر سوف يفتديه؛ سوف لن يعطي حقله، بستانه، وبيته لافتطاره (لافتداءه).

If (after) let-it-be the officer, and (even) let-it-be a the notable (the civil servant), who (while) in a noble (a royalty) journey became disconnected (missing), a merchant shall redeem him, (and) make him arrive (with) his tribe; if (after) he has in his house that of the redemption (the ransom money), he shall redeem himself; if (after) he does not have in his house that of the redemption (the ransom money), he shall redeem (himself) in (from) the house of his tribe's god; if (after) he does not have that of the redemption (the ransom money) in the house of his tribe's god, the palace shall redeem him; he shall not give his field, his orchard, and his house to (for) his redemption.

§ 33.—XI, 39-50

39 šum-ma lu PA.PA 40 u lu-u NU.TUR 41 ṣâb ni-is-ḫa-tim 42 ir-ta-ši 43 u lu a-na ḫarrân 44 šar-ri-im 45 ^{amêlu}agram pu-ḫa-am 46 im-hu-ur-ma 47 ir-te-di 48 lu PA.PA 49 u lu NU.TUR šu-u 50 id-da-ak

39 ثُمَّ لو باباً 40 ولو نوطور 41 صَيبْ نِسْختَمْ 42 يرْتَسي 43 ولو أنَ حرَّنْ 44 سرِيمْ [شَريمْ] 45 عميلأجرمْ فهمْ 46 يمْخرُمْ 47 يرتَدي 48 لو باباً 49 ولو نوطور ذوو 50 يدكْ

بعد ان (اذا) لو (ليكن) قائد عسكري و(حتى) لو حاكم مدني يرتسي (يُوظّف) مجنّد (نخبة) مُستبدَل (مطرود)، و(حتى) لو يختار (يُوظّف) (كـ)عامل أجر (متعاقد) بديل لرحلة شريف (ملك)، (و) يصطحب، لو القائد العسكري و(حتى) لو الحاكم المدني، هذا، سوف يُقتل.

If (after) let-it-be a military commander and (even) let-it-be a civilian administrator settles in (employs) a fired elite (soldier), and (even) let-it-be (that) he selects (hires) (as) a contracted worker to (for) a noble (a royalty) journey, and accompanies, this let-it-be military commander and (even) let-it-be a civilian administrator shall be put to death.

§ 34.—XI, 51-64

51 šum-ma lu PA.PA 52 u lu NU.TUR 53 nu-ma-at rid ṣâbê bil-te-ḳi 54 rid ṣâbê iḫ-ta-[b]ba-al 55 rid ṣâbê a-na ig-ri-im 56 it-ta-di-in 57 rid ṣâbê i-na di-nim 58 a-na dan-nim iš-ta-ra-aḳ 59 ḳi-iš-ti šar-ru-um 60 [a]-na rid ṣâbê id-di-nu 61 il-te-di(=ḳi) 62 lu PA.PA 63 u lu NU.TUR šu-u 64 id-da-ak

51 ثُمَّ لو بابأ 52 ولو نوطور 53 نُومتْ ريدْ صَيب يلْتقي 54 ريدْ صَيبَ يحْتبَل 55 ريدْ صَيب أنَ إجْرمْ 56 يتَدنْ 57 ريدْ صَيب إنَ دينمْ 58 أنَ دأنمْ يسْتَرقْ [يشْتَنَقْ] 59 قِسْطِ [قِشْتِ] سَرُّمْ 60 أنَ ريدْ صَيب إدنْ 61 يلْتدي [يتّدي] [يلْتقي] 62 لو بابأ 63 ولو نوطور ذوو 64 يدكْ

بعد ان (اذا) لو (ليكن) قائد عسكري و(حتى) لو حاكم مدني يأخذ حاجة رائد نُخبة (جنود)، يحتال على رائد نُخبة (جنود)، يعطي رائد نُخبة (جنود) للإيجار (يؤجر)، يسرق [يتصدق بـ] رائد نُخبة (جنود) للقوة (للحماية) [للخدمة] في قضية، يأخذ مُنحة (مكافئة) أعطى شريف (ملك) الى رائد نُخبة (جنود)، لو القائد العسكري و(حتى) لو الحاكم المدني، هذا، سوف يُقتل.

If (after), let-it-be a military commander and (even) let-it-be a civilian administrator takes an officer possession, cheats an officer, gives an officer for rent (hire), steals [grants] an officer to (for) might (protection) [service] in a case, takes an award (a grant) a noble (a royalty) gave to an officer, this let-it-be a military commander and (even) let-it-be a civilian administrator shall be put to death.

§ 35.—XI, 65-XII, 4

65 šum-ma a-wi-lum 66 LID.GUD.ZUN 67 u ṣênê 68 ša šar-ru-um 69 a-na rid ṣâbê 70 id-di-nu XII, 1 i-na ga-ti rid ṣâbê 2 iš-ta-am 3 i-na kaspi-šu 4 i-te-el-li

65 ثُمّ أويلم [عَويلم] 66 لئِدْ جُدْ ظُعُنْ 67 وصِينِ 68 ذا سَرُّمْ 69 أنَ ريدْ صَيبَ 70 إدنْ 1 إنَ جتي [قتي] ريدْ صَيبَ 2 يسْتَمْ 3 إنَ كسْفِ ذو 4 يتَعلّي

بعد ان (اذا) شخص [رجل] يشتري في (من) يَد رائد نُخبة (جنود) غلاظ ابقار العمل والتحميل (الثيران)، والخراف، التي أعطى شريف (ملك) الى رائد النُخبة، (الشخص [الرجل]) سوف يتنازل بفضته (يخسر فضته).

If (after) a person [a man] buys in (from) the hands of an officer the carrying and labor cattle boors (oxen), and sheep that a noble (a royalty) gave to the officer, he shall cede in (give up) (lose) his money.

§ 36.—XII, 5-9

5 eḳlu-um kirûm [b]u bîtum 6 ša rid ṣâbê bâ'irim 7 u na-ši [b]bi-il-tim 8 a-na kaspim 9 u-ul i-na-ad-[b]di-in

5 حِقلْم كيرمْ و بيتمْ 6 ذا ريدْ صَيب بيئرمْ [بيئنمْ] 7 و نأشِ بعلتِمْ 8 أنَ كَسْفِم 9 ألْ ينَدنْ

حقل، بستان، وبيت رائد النُخبة (الجنود)، الموظف (من الأعيان)، ومُستخرِج الإتاوة (الضريبة) سوف لن يُعطى لفضة (لن يُباع).

A field, an orchard, and a house that belong to an officer, a notable (civil servant), and a tax collector shall not be given to (for) silver (shall be sold).

§ 37.—XII, 10-21

10 šum-ma a-wi-lum 11 eḳlam kirâm u bîtam 12 ša rid ṣâbê bâ'irim 13 u na-ši biltim 14 iš-ta-am 15 dup-pa-šu 16 iḫ-ḫi-ib-bi 17 u i-na kaspi-šu 18 i-te-el-li 19 eḳlum kirûm u bîtum 20 a-na be-li-šu 21 i-ta-ar

10 ثُمّ أويلم [عَويلم] 11 حِقلْم كيرمْ و بيتمْ 12 ذا ريدْ صَيب بَيئرمْ [بيئنمْ] 13 و نأشِ بعلتِمْ 14 يستَمْ 15 دُوبا ذو [دُوفا ذو] 16 يهبي 17 وإن كسْفِ ذو 18 يتَعلّي 19 حِقلْم كيرمْ و بيتمْ 20 أنَ بعْلِ ذو 21 يتأرْ

بعد ان (اذا) شخص [رجل] يشتري حقل، بستان، وبيت عائد الى رائد نُخبة (جنود)، موظف (من الأعيان)، ومُستخْرِج إتاوة (ضريبة)، سوف يحطّم لوحه (لوح ملكيته) ويتنازل بفضته (يخسر فضته)، سوف يُعيد الحقل، البستان، والبيت الى صاحبه.

If (after) a person [a man] buys a field, an orchard, and a house that belong to an officer, a notable (civil servant), and a tax collector, he shall smash (to fine pieces) his tablet (deed tablet) and cede in (give up) (lose) his money, he shall return the field, the orchard, and the house to its owner.

§ 38.—XII, 22-30

22 rid ṣâbê bâ'irum 23 u na-ši biltim 24 i-na eḳlim kirêm [b]u bîtim 25 ša il-ki-šu 26 a-na aš-ša-ti-šu 27 u mârti-šu 28 u-ul i-ša-bad-da-ar 29 u a-na i-il-[b]ti-šu 30 u-ul i-na-[b]ad-di-in

22 رِيدْ صَيب بَيئرمْ [بيئنمْ] 23 و نأش بعلتمْ 24 إنَ حقلمْ كيريمْ و بيتمْ 25 ذا إلك ذو 26 أنَ أستِ ذو 27 ومأرت ذو 28 أُلْ يسدرْ [يسدنْ] 29 وأن إلتِ ذو [إهلت ذو] 30 أُلْ يندنْ

رائد النُخبة (الجنود)، الموظف (من الأعيان)، ومُستخْرِج الإتاوة (الضريبة) سوف لا يُخصّص (يُملّك حصة) الى أمرأته (زوجته) وبنته في (من) حقل، بستان، وبيت رسالته (مهمة عمله) ولا يعطي الى (مقابل) التزاماته (القانونية).

An officer, a notable (civil servant), and a tax collector shall not allocate (deed) to his woman (wife) and his daughter in (from) the field, the orchard, and the house of his operation, and not give to (for) his (legal) obligation.

§ 39.—XII, 31-38

31 i-na eḳlim kirêm bu bîtim 32 ša i-ša-am-mu-ma 33 i-ra-aš-šu-u 34 a-na aš-ša-ti-šu 35 u mârti-šu 36 i-ša-ad-dar 37 u a-na e-ḫi-bil-ti-šu 38 i-na-ad-di-in

31 إنَ حقلمْ كيريمْ و بيتمْ 32 ذا إسمَمْ 33 إرسو 34 أن أساتِ ذو 35 ومأرت ذو 36 يسدرْ [يسدنْ] 37 وأن إهلتِ ذو 38 يندنْ

|وفق الفقرة 38| في (من) الحقل، البستان، والبيت الذي إشترى، (و) رسى (استقر به)، سوف يُخصّص (يُملّك حصة) الى أمرأته (زوجته) وبنته، ويعطي الى (مقابل) التزاماته (القانونية).

|Referencing §38| He shall allocate to his woman (wife) and his daughter, and give to (for) his (legal) obligation, in (from) the field, the orchard, and the house that he bought, (and) settled in.

§ 40.—XII, 39-48

39 aššatum tamkarum 40 u il-kum a-ḫu-u-um 41 eḳil-šu kirâ-šu 42 u bî-zu ana kaspim 43 i-na-ad-di-in 44 ša-a-a-ma-nu-um 45 i-li-ik eḳlim 46 kirêm u bîtim 47 ša i-ša-am-mu 48 i-il-la-ak

39 أستَم تمكَارمْ 40 وإلكُم أخومْ 41 حقلِ ذو كيري ذو 42 و بيتْ ذو [بيت] أن كسفمْ 43 يندنْ 44 سآمَنمْ 45 إلكْ حقلمْ 46 كيريمْ و بيتمْ 47 ذا إسمو 48 يئلكْ

الإمرأة (الزوجة)، المتاجر، و المترسّل (القائم على العمل، المُستعمِل) القاصد قصدهم (المشابه لهم) سوف يعطي حقله، بستانه، وبيته لفضة (يمكن ان يبيع)؛ المشتري سوف يترسل رسالة (سوف يستخدم) الحقل، البستان، والبيت الذي اشترى.

A woman (wife), a (land) merchant, and a runner (an operator) with similar objective shall give his/her field, his/her orchard, and his/her house to (for) silver; the buyer shall run the operation of the field, the orchard, and the house that he bought.

§ 41.—XII, 49-62

49 šum-ma a-wi-lum 50 eḳlam kirâm u bîtam 51 ša rid ṣâbê bâ'irim 52 u na-ši bi-il-tim 53 u-bi-iḫ 54 u ni-ip-la-tim 55 id-di-in 56 rid ṣâbê bâ'irum 57 u na-ši bi-il-tim 58 a-na eḳli-šu kirê-šu [b]u bîti-šu 59 i-ta-ar 60 u ni-ip-la-tim 61 ša in-na-ad-[b]nu-šum 62 i-tab-ba-al

49 ثمَّ أويلُم [عويلُم] 50 حقْلَم كيرَمْ و بيتَمْ 51 ذا ريدْ صيبْ بيئرِمْ [بيئنِمْ] 52 و نأش بعلْتمْ 53 يُبخْ 54 و نفلْتمْ 55 يدنْ 56 ريدْ صيبِ بيئرمْ [بيئنُمْ] 57 و نأش بعلتمْ 58 أنَ حقلِ ذو كيري ذو و بيتِ ذو 59 يتأرْ 60 و نفلْتمْ 61 ذا إندنْ ذُومْ 62 يتبلْ

بعد ان (اذا) شخص [رجل] يضعَف (يكسر قيمة) حقل، بستان، وبيت رائد النُخبة (الجنود)، الموظف (من الأعيان)، ومُستخرِج الإتاوة (الضريبة)، ويعطي (رسميا) عربون، رائد النُخبة (الجنود)، الموظف (من الأعيان)، ومُستخرِج الإتاوة (الضريبة) سوف يُرجع (يسترجع) حقله، بستانه، وبيته، ويأخذ (يُصادر) العَربون الذي أعطوه.

If (after) a person [a man] bargains down (the value of) a field, an orchard, and a house of an officer, a notable (civil servant), and a tax collector, and gives a sworn-in payment (deposit), the officer, the notable (civil servant), and the tax collector shall return (take back) his field, his orchard, and his house, and take the sworn-in payment (the deposit) that they gave him.

§ 42.—XII, 63- XIII, 5

63 šum-ma a-wi-lum 64 eḳlam a-na ir-ri-ᵇšu-tim 65 u-še-ṣi-ma 66 i-na eḳlim še'am ᵇla uš-tab-ši 67 i-na eḳlim ši-ip-ᵇri-im XIII, 1 la e-bi-ši-im 2 u-ka-an-nu-šu-ma 3 še'am ki-ma i-te-šu 4 a-na be-el eḳlim 5 i-na-ad-di-in

63 ثمَّ أويلُم [عويلُم] 64 حقْلَمْ أن إريستِمْ 65 يُسئصِمَ 66 إنَ حقلِمْ سعَمْ [شعَمْ] لا يُستبذي [يُستبثي] 67 إنَ حقلِمْ سبرِمْ [سفرِمْ] 1 لا يعبشِمْ [يعفشِمْ] [يعفسِمْ] 2 يُكنو ذومَ 3 سعَمْ [شعَمْ] كيمَ يتئ ذو 4 أنَ بعَلْ حقلِمْ 5 يندنْ

بعد ان (اذا) شخص [رجل] يُوثّق (يرتبط بـ) (يتعهد) حقل للفلاحة (حسب المحصول)، (و) لا يوجدْ [يُظهِر (ينشر)] (ينمّي) حبوب في الحقل، (لانه) لايضع مهارة العمل (اللازمة) في الحقل، سوف يُجلسوه [يستدعوه]، (و) سوف يعطي الى مالك الحقل حبوب كما (بكمية حبوب) جيرانه.

If (after) a person [a man] takes on a field to (for) farming (based on crop), (and) he does not make exist [make appear] (grow) grains in the field, (because) he does not put the (required) work skill in the field, they shall seat [call] him in, (and) he shall give to the owner of the field as much grains as (harvested by) his neighbor.

§ 43.—XIII, 6-16

6 šum-ma eḳla-am ᵇla i-ri-iš-ma 7 it-ta-di 8 še'am ki-ma i-te-šu 9 a-na be-el eḳlim 10 i-na-ad-di-in 11 u eḳlam ša id-ᵇdu-u 12 ma-a-a-ri 13 i-ma-aḫ-ḫa-aṣ 14 i-ša-ak-ka-ᵇak-ma 15 a-na be-el eḳlim 16 u-ta-ar

6 ثمَّ حقْلَمْ لا يئرِسمَ 7 يتدي 8 سعَمْ [شعَمْ] كيمَ يتئ ذو 9 أنَ بعَلْ حقلِمْ 10 يندنْ 11 وحقْلَمْ ذا إدّو 12 معرِ 13 يمحَصْ 14 يشككَمْ [يشققَمْ] 15 أنَ بعَلْ حقلِمْ 16 يُتأرْ

|وفق الفقرة 42| بعد ان (اذا) (الشخص [الرجل]) لا يفلح (و) يَدعْ (يترك) الحقل، سوف يعطي الى مالك الحقل حبوب كما (بكمية حبوب) جيرانه، والحقل الذي أدَعَ (ترَكَ) جدب (غير خصب)، سوف يضرب (يكسّر)، يُشقق (يهوّي)، (و) يُعيد الى مالك الحقل.

|Referencing §42| If (after) he does not farm, (and) let go (leaves), the field, he shall give to the owner of the field as much grains as (harvested by) his neighbor, and the field that he had let go (had left) unfit for cultivation, he shall strike (breakup), harrow (aerate), (and) return to the owner of the field.

§ 44.—XIII, 17-34

17 šum-ma a-wi-lum 18 eḳlam KI.KAL 19 a-na šattim IIIᵏᵃᵐ 20 a-na te-ip-ti-tim 21 u-še-ṣi-ma 22 a-aḫ-šu id-di-ma 23 eḳlam la ip-te-te 24 i-na ri-bu-tim 25 ša-at-tim 26 eḳlam ma-a-a-ri 27 i-ma-aḫ-ḫa-aṣ 28 i-mar-ra-ar 29 u i-ša-ak-ᵇka-ak-ma 30 a-na be-el eḳlim 31 u-ta-ar 32 u X GAN.E 33 X ŠE.GUR 34 i-ma-ad-da-ad

17 ثمَّ أويلم [عويلم] 18 حقِلمْ كيع [قيع] كهل 19 أنَ ستّمْ [سنتِم] 3 كأم 20 أنَ تفتحتم [تفتيتِمْ] 21 يسئصم 22 أخ ذو [أهْ ذو] يدِّم [يدعم] 23 حقِلمْ لا يفتتح [يفتتي] 24 إن ربعتِم 25 ستّمْ [سنتِم] 26 حقِلمْ معر 27 يمحص 28 يمعْرِر 29 ويشككم [يشققم] 30 أنَ بعل حقِلمْ 31 يتأرْ 32 و 10 قنْع 33 10 سع [شع] جرْ [كرْ] 34 يمددْ

بعد ان (اذا) شخص [رجل] يُوثّق (يرتبط بـ) (يتعهد) حقل أرض بور (مُهملة) للتفتيحة (للتأهيل) لثلاث سنوات، (و) يدَعْ جانبه (يضع جانبا) (يترك)، (و) لا يهيئ الحقل في السنة الرابعة، (الشخص [الرجل]) سوف يضرب (يكسّر)، يجرّد (من الادغال) ويْشقق (يهوّي) الحقل الجدِب (الغير خصب)، (و) يُعيد الى مالك الحقل، و سوف يُمد (يجهّز) 10 كُر حبوب (لكل) 10 قنع (قاطع حقل).

If (after) a person [a man] takes on a fallow (neglected) land field for habilitation (development) for three years, (and) he let go (to) his side (put aside), (and) he does not habilitate (develop) the field in the fourth year, he shall strike (breakup), cleanup (weed) and harrow (aerate) the unfit for cultivation field, (and) return to the owner of the field, and he shall supply 10 Kur of grains (for every) 10 Qan'i (field sectors).

§ 45.—XIII, 35-46

35 šum-ma a-wi-lum 36 eḳil-šu a-na biltim 37 a-na ir-ri-ši-im 38 id-di-in-ma 39 u bilat eḳli-šu 40 im-ta-ḫa-ar 41 wa-ar-ka eḳlam 42 ilu Adad ir-ta-ḫi-iṣ 43 u lu bi-ib-bu-lum 44 it-ba-al 45 bi-ti-iḳ-tum 46 ša ir-ri-ši-im-ma

35 ثمَّ أويلم [عويلم] 36 حقِلْ ذو أنَ بعِلتِمْ 37 أنَ إريسمْ 38 يدنمَ 39 وبعِلتْ حقِلْ ذو 40 يمتخرْ 41 وركَ حقلمْ 42 إل هداد يرتحِص 43 ولو ببلمْ 44 يتبلْ 45 بتِقتمْ 46 ذا إريسمَ

بعد ان (اذا) شخص [رجل] يعطي حقله للإتاوة (حسب الإيجار) الى فلاح، ويختار (يستلم كاملا) إتاوة حقله، بعدما الإله هدّاد (إله الرعد والعوصف) يعصر (يعصُفْ) الحقل، و(حتى) لو يحمل (يأخذ) المحصول، الخسارة للفلاح (على الفلاح).

If (after) a person [a man] gives his field to (for) a rent-fee (basis) to a farmer, and he chooses (receives in full) his field rent-fee (amount), after the god Haddad (god of thunder and storm) squashes (ruins) the field, and (even) let-it-be that he carries away the crop, the loss of (on) the farmer (the renter).

§ 46.—XIII, 47-57

47 šum-ma bilat eḳli-šu 48 la im-ta-ḫar 49 u lu a-na mi-iš-bla-ni 50 u lu a-na ša-lu-uš 51 eḳlam id-di-in 52 še'am ša i-na eḳlim 53 ib-ba-aš-šu-u 54 ir-ri-šum 55 u be-el eḳlim 56 a-na ap-ši-te-im 57 i-zu-uz-zu

47 ثمَّ بعِلتْ حقِلْ ذو 48 لا يمتخرْ 49 ولو أنَ مثلنِ 50 ولو أنَ ثلثْ 51 حقِلمْ يدنْ 52 سعَم [شعَمْ] ذا إنَ حقِلمْ 53 إبذوَ [إبثوَ] 54 إريسمْ 55 وبعَلْ حقِلمْ 56 أنَ عفشيتيم [عفسيتيمْ] 57 يززّ

|وفق الفقرة 45| بعد ان (اذا) لا يختار (لا يستلم كاملا) إتاوة حقله، و(حتى) لو يعطي الحقل على المثل (النصف)، و(حتى) لو على الثلث (من الاتاوة)، الفلاح ومالك الحقل سوف يفرقو (سوف يتقاسمو) الحبوب التي تواجَدت [ظهرَت] (بعد العاصفة) في الحقل الى (حسب) العمل (المُنجز من قبل الفلاح) [الى (حسب) المقايضة].

|Referencing §45| If (after) he does not choose (receive in full) his field rent-fee, and (even) let-it-be he gives the field (based) on half, and (even) let-it-be (based) on third, (of the rent-fee), the farmer and the owner of the field shall divide (share) the grains that existed [appeared] (after the storm) in the field (according) to labor (done by the farmer) [to (based on) barter].

§ 47.—XIII, 57-70

58 šum-ma ir-ri-šum 59 aš-šum i-na ša-[b]at-tim 60 maḫ-ri-tim 61 ma-na-ḫa-ti-šu 62 la il-lu(=ḳu)-u 63 eḳlam e-ri-ša-am [b]iḳ-ta-bi 64 be-el eḳlim 65 u-ul u-up-pa-as 66 ir-ri-su-ma 67 eḳil-šu i-ni-ri-[b]iš-ma 68 i-na ebûrim 69 ki-ma ri-ik-[b]sa-ti-šu 70 še'am i-li-ḳi

58 ثُمَّ إريسُمْ 59 هذُمْ إنَ ستّمْ [سنْتِم] 60 مخْرتِمْ 61 مناحتِ ذي 62 لا إلّؤو [إلعوَ] 63 حقْلمْ أرسَمْ يقْتَبي 64 بَعَلْ حقلِمْ 65 أُلْ يُعفَس [يئْبَس] 66 إريسُمْ 67 حقِلْ ذو ينئرِسمْ 68 إنَ حبرِمْ 69 كيمَ ركْستِ ذو 70 سعمْ [شعمْ] يلقي

بعد ان (اذا) فلاح يسأل (يطلب) فلاحة الحقل (من فلاح آخر)، هذا لأنه ما أطاقَ كدْحها (مشقّتها) في السنة الماضية، مالك الحقل سوف لن يلوم [يجادل]؛ فلاحا سيفْلحُ حقله، (و) في (موسم) الثمار (الحصاد) سيأخذ الحبوب كما (حسب) عقْده.

If (after) a farmer asks (requests) field farming (by another farmer), that is because he could not handle its hard work in the past year, the owner of the filed shall not blame [argue]; a farmer shall farm his field, (and) in (at) harvest (time), he shall take grains as (according to) his contract.

§ 48.—XIII, 71-XIV, 17

71 šum-ma a-wi-lum 72 ḫu-bu-ul-lum 73 e-li-šu XIV, 1 i-ba-aš-ši-ma 2 eḳil-šu 3 [ilu]Adad 4 ir-ta-ḫi-iṣ 5 u lu-u [b]bi-ib-bu-lum 6 it-ba-al 7 u lu-u [b]i-na la me-e 8 še'um i-na eḳlim 9 la it-tab-ši 10 i-na ša-at-tim šu-a-ti 11 še'am a-na be-el [b]ḫu-bu-ul-[li] 12 u-ul u-ta-ar 13 dup-pa-šu 14 u-ra-ad-da-ab 15 u ṣi-ib-tam 16 ša ša-at-tim [b]šu-a-ti 17 u-ul i-na-[b]ad-di-in

71 ثُمَّ أويلُم [عويلُم] 72 حبلُمْ 73 علي ذو 1 يبذِمَ 2 حقِلْ ذو 3 إلْهَداد 4 يرتَهصْ 5 و لوو ببلُمْ 6 يتبَلْ 7 و لوو إنَ لا مئي 8 سعَمْ إنَ حقلِمْ 9 لا يتبْذي [يتبْثي] 10 إنَ ستّمْ [سنْتِم] ذأتِ 11 سعَمْ [شعمْ] أنَ بعَلْ حبُلِ 12 أُلْ يُتأرْ 13 دوبا ذو [دُوفا ذو] 14 يُردَبْ 15 و ضِبطمْ 16 ذا ستّمْ [سنْتِم] ذأتِ 17 أُلْ ينْدنْ

بعد ان (اذا) شخص [رجل] يملك سنَدْ (حبوب) عليه، (و) الإله هداد (إله الرعد والعوصف) يعصر (يعصُفْ) الحقل، ولو (وليكن) له أن يحمل (يأخذ) (هداد) المحصول، ولو (وليكن) له أن لا تتواجد [تظهر (تنتشر)] (تنمو) حبوب في الحقل بلا ماء (بسبب قلة الماء)، (الشخص [الرجل]) سوف لن يعيد حبوب الى مالك السنَدْ في تلك السنة، سوف يَلغي لوح (السند)، وسوف لن يعطي قَبضْ (أرباح) تلك السنة.

If (after) a person [a man] has a (grain) bond on (owed by) him, (and) the god Haddad (god of thunder and storm) squashes (ruins) the field, and let-it-be for him (that) he (Haddad) carries away the crop, and let-it-be for him that grains do not exist [appear] (grow) in the field in no (without) water, he shall not return grains to the owner of the (grains) bond in that year, he shall void the bond-tablet, and he shall not give the profits of that year.

§ 49.—XIV, 18-44

18 šum-ma a-wi-lum 19 kaspam it-ti [b]tamkarim 20 il-ḳi-ma 21 eḳil ip-še-tim 22 ša še'im u lu [b]šamaššammim 23 a-na tamkarim id-di-in 24 eḳlam e-ri-iš-ma 25 še'am u lu-u [b]šamaššammam 26 ša ib-ba-aš-šu-u 27 e-si-ip ta-ba-al 28 iḳ-bi-šum 29 šum-ma ir-ri-šum 30 i-na eḳlim še'am 31 u lu šamaššammam 32 uš-tab-ši 33 i-na ebûrim še'am [b]u šamaššammam 34 ša i-na eḳlim [b]ib-ba-aš-šu-u 35 be-el eḳli-ma 36 i-li-ḳi-ma 37 še'am ša kaspi-šu 38 u ṣi-ba-zu 39 ša it-ti tamkarim 40 il-ḳu-u 41 u ma-na-ḫa-at 42 e-ri-ši-im 43 a-na tamkarim 44 i-na-ad-di-in

18 ثُمَّ أويلُم [عويلُم] 19 كسفَمْ إتي تَمكارِمْ 20 يلْقيمَ 21 حقلْ عفشتِمْ [عفستِمْ] 22 ذا سعِمْ [شعِمْ] ولو سمسمِمْ 23 أنَ تمْكارِمْ يدنْ 24 حقلَمْ أرسمَ 25 سعَمْ [شعَمْ] ولو سمَسمَمْ 26 ذا إبذو [إبثو] 27 أسفْ [عسفْ] تبلْ 28 يقْبي ذوم 29 ثُمَّ إريسُمْ 30 إنَ حقلِم سعَم [شعَمْ] 31 ولو سمسمَمْ 32 يُستبذي [يُستبثي] 33 إنَ حبرِمْ سعَمْ [شعَمْ] و سمسمَمْ 34 ذا إنَ حقلِمْ إبذو [إبثوَ] 35 بَعلْ حقلِمْ 36 يلقيمَ 37 سعَمْ [شعَمْ] ذا كَسفِ ذو 38 و ضبطْ ذو [ضِبتُ] 39 ذا إتي تمْكارِمْ 40 إلْقو 41 ومناحتْ 42 أرسِمْ 43 أنَ تمْكارِمْ 44 ينْدنْ

بعد ان (اذا) شخص [رجل] يلقي (يأخذ) فضة مع (من) متاجر، (و) يعطي الى المتاجر (كضمان) حقلْ عَملْ حبوب و (حتى) لو سمسم، يقول له "إفلحْ (إزرعْ) الحقل، إجْني (و)خذْ الحبوب و (حتى) لو السمسم التي تواجدَت [ظهرت] (نمت) (به)"؛ بعد ان (اذا) الفلاح (المُستأجر) يوجدْ [يُظهر (يُنشر)] (يُنمّي) حبوب و(حتى) لو سمسم في الحقل، مالك الحقل (الشخص [الرجل]) سوف يأخذ الحبوب و(حتى) لو السمسم التي تواجدَت [ظهرت] (نمت) في الحقل في (موسم) الثمار (الحصاد)، (و) سوف يُعطي للمتاجر حبوب (بقيمة) فضته التي أخذ مع (من) المتاجر وقبضها (ربحها)، ومشقة (كدح) الفلاحة.

If (after) a person [a man] takes silver with (from) a merchant, (and) he gives to the merchant (for security) a working field of grains and (even) let-it-be sesame, he says to him "farm the field, the grains and (even) let-it-be the sesame that existed [appeared] (grown) (in it), harvest and take"; if (after) the farmer (the renter) make exist [make appear] (grows) grains and (even) let-it-be sesame in the field, the owner of the field (the person [the man]) shall take the grains and (even) let-it-be sesame that existed [appeared] (grown) in the field in (at) harvest (time), (and) he shall give to the merchant the (equivalent) grains of his silver that he took with (from) the merchant and its profit, and the farming hard work (cost).

§ 50.—XIV, 45-55

45 šum-ma eḳlam ir-ša-am 46 u lu-u 47 eḳil šamaššammim 48 ir-ša-am id-di-in 49 še'am u šamaššammam 50 ša i-na eḳlim 51 ib-ba-aš-šu-u 52 be-el eḳli-ma 53 i-li-ḳi-ma 54 kaspam u ṣi-ba-zu 55 a-na tamkarim ^{b}u-ta-ar

45 ثمّ حِقلمْ إرسَمْ 46 ولوو 47 حِقلْ سَمَسمَمْ 48 إرسَمْ يدِنْ 49 سَعَمْ [شعَمْ] و سَمَسمَمْ 50 ذا إنَ حِقلِمْ 51 إبذوَ [إبثوَ] 52 بَعلْ حِقلِمْ 53 يلقِيمَ 54 كَسفَمْ و ضبطْ ذو [ضِبتْ] 55 أنَ تمكارِمْ يتأرْ

|وفق الفقرة 49| بعد ان (اذا) (الشخص [الرجل]) يعطي (كضمان) حقل فالح (مزروع (بالحبوب))، ولو (وليكن) له حقل سمسم، مالك الحقل سوف يأخذ الحبوب والسمسم التي تواجدَت [ظهرت] (به)، (و) سوف يُعيد الى المتاجر الفضة وقبضها (ربحها).

|Referencing §49| If (after) he gives (for security) a farmed (planted (with grains)) field, and let-it-be for him a sesame field, the owner of the field shall take the grains and sesame that existed [appeared] (grown) in the field, (and) shall return to the merchant the silver and its profit.

§ 51.—XIV, 56-66

56 šum-ma kaspam 57 a-na tu-ur-ri-im 58 la i-šu 59 šamaššammam 60 a-na ma-ḫi-ra-^{b}ti-šu-nu 61 ša kaspi-šu 62 u ṣi-ib-ti-šu 63 ša it-ti tamkarim ^{b}il-ku-u 64 a-na pî ṣi-im-^{b}da-at 65 šar-ri-im 66 a-na tamkarim ^{b}i-na-ad-di-in

56 ثمّ كَسفَمْ 57 أنَ تؤرِمْ 58 لا إإذو [إإتو] 59 سمسمَمْ 60 أنَ مخراتِ ذُونْ 61 ذا كَسفِ ذو 62 و ضِبطِ ذو 63 ذا إتي تمكارِمْ إلكو [إلقو] 64 أنَ فِيي صِمدَتْ [ضِمدَتْ] 65 سرِيمْ [شرِيمْ] 66 أنَ تمكارِمْ ينَدنْ

|وفق الفقرة 50| بعد ان (اذا) ما له [ما أوتي] (ليس عنده) الفضة للإعادة، (الشخص [الرجل]) سوف يعطي الى المتاجر سمسم (بقدر) فضته التي أخذ مع (من) المتاجر وقبضها (ربحها)، لمُقابلهم، الى (حسب) تصريح الشريف (الملك).

|Referencing §50| If (after) he does not the silver to (for) the return, he shall give to the merchant the (equivalent) sesame of his silver that he took with (from) the merchant and its profit, to (as) their (the money and profits) substitute, (according) to the declaration (words) of the noble (the royalty).

§ 52.—XV, 1-6

XV, 1 šum-ma ir-ri-šum 2 i-na eḳlim še-am 3 u lu šamaššammam 4 la uš-tab-ši 5 ri-ik-sa-ti-šu 6 u-ul in-ni

1 ثمّ إرِيسمْ 2 إنَ حِقلِمْ سَعَمْ [شعَمْ] 3 ولو سَمَسمَمْ 4 لا يُستَبذي [يُستَبثي] 5 رِكستِ ذو 6 أُلْ ينئِي [ينهِي]

|وفق الفقرة 49| بعد ان (اذا) الفلاح (المستأجِر) لا يوجدْ [لا يُظْهِر (يُنشِر)] (لا يُنمّي) حبوب و(حتى) لو سمسم في الحقل، (الفلاح (المُستأجِر)) سوف لن (يستطع ان) ينقض [يُنهي] (يترك) عقده.

|Referencing §49| If (after) the farmer does not make exist [make appear] (grows) grains and (even) let-it-be sesame in the field, he shall not (be able to) nullify [end] his contract.

§ 53.—XV, 7-20

[7] šum-ma a-wi-lum [8] a-na |kâri|-šu [9] du-|un-nu|-nim [10] a-aḫ-šu |id-di-ma| [11] kâri-|šu| [12] la u-dan-|ni-in-ma| [13] i-na kâri-|šu| [14] bi-tum it-te-|ip-ti| [15] u ugaram ᵇme-e uš-ta-bil [16] a-wi-lum [17] ša i-na kâri-šu [18] bi-tum ib-bi-tu-u [19] še'am ša u-ḫal-li-ḳu [20] i-ri-a-ab

[7] ثمَّ أَويلُم [عَويلْم] [8] أنَ |كَيْرِ| ذو [9] |دُؤنُنِمْ| [10] أخْ ذو [أهْ ذو] يدِّمَ [يدعمَ] [11] كَيْرِ ذو [12] لا |يُدأنِنْمْ| [13] إنَ كَيرِ ذو [14] بِتُّمْ |يتَفْتِح يتَفْتِي|] [15] و عُقرَمْ [أُقرَمْ] مَئي يُستَبِل [16] أويلُم [عَويلْم] [17] ذا إنَ كَيرِ ذو [18] بِتّمْ إبتو [19] سعمْ [شعَمْ] ذا أُحلِق [20] يرأَبْ

بعد ان (اذا) شخص [رجل] يدَع جانبه (يضع جانبا) (يترك) القوة (قوة إندفاع الماء) الى حوضه، (و) لا يقوّي (جدران) حوضه، (ثم) ينفَتحَ شق في حوضه وتحَمل (تأخذ) المياه (المندفعة) حقل مثمر (بحبوب)، الشخص [الرجل] الذي إنشَقّ شق في حوضه سوف يسدّد (يعوض) الحبوب التي أزالَ.

If (after) a person [a man] let go (to) his side (put aside) (abandons) the (water flow) strength to his reservoir, (and) does not strengthen (the walls of) his reservoir, (then) a breach gets open in his reservoir and the waters carry (take) away a (grains) yielding field, the person [the man] whom a breach was breached in his reservoir shall repay (replace) the grains he swept away.

§ 54.—XV, 21-30

[21] šum-ma še'am ri-a-ba-am [22] la i-li-i [23] šu-a-ti [24] u bi-ša-šu [25] a-na kaspim [26] i-na-ad-di-nu-ma [27] mâr+ugarê [28] ša še'i-šu-nu [29] mu-u ub-lu [30] i-zu-uz-zu

[21] ثُمَّ سعمْ [شعَمْ] رِأبَمْ [22] لا يلعِي [يلِئي] [23] ذأتِ [24] و بيذا ذو [25] أنَ كسْفِمْ [26] ينَدنُمَ [27] مأر+عجَري [مأر+أُجَري] [28] ذا سَعِي ذُونْ [شَعِي ذُون] [29] مؤ أُبْلو [30] يُزُّز

|وفق الفقرة 53| بعد ان (اذا) لا يطيق تسديد تلك الحبوب، ذلك (الشخص [الرجل]) وممتلكاته سوف يعطو للفضة (يبيعو)، ابناء (اصحاب) الحقول المثمرة (بحبوب) الذين حَمل (أخذ) الماء حبوبهم سوف يفرقو (سوف يتقاسمو) (الفضة).

|Referencing §53| If (after) he cannot handle repaying (replacing) that grains, that (person [man]) and and his goods [possessions] they shall give for silver (sell), the owners of the (grains) yielding fields whom the water had carried (took) away their grains shall divide (share) (the silver).

§ 55.—XV, 31-38

[31] šum-ma a-wi-lum [32] a-tap-pa-šu [33] a-na ši-ki-tim ip-te [34] a-aḫ-šu id-di-ma [35] eḳil i-te-šu [36] me-e uš-ta-bil [37] še'am ki-ma i-te-šu [38] i-ma-ad-da-ad

[31] ثُمَّ أَويلُم [عَويلْم] [32] عتفَ ذو [33] أنَ سكِتِمْ يفتَحِ [يفْتَي] [34] أخْ ذو [أهْ ذو] يدِّمَ [يدعِمَ] [35] حقِلْ يتئ ذو [36] مئي يُستَبِل [37] سَعَم [شَعَمْ] كيمَ يتئ ذو [38] يمَدَدْ

بعد ان (اذا) (الشخص [الرجل]) يفتح قناته (المائية) الى سكّة (زرع)، يدَعْ جانبه (يضع جانبا) (يترك)، (و) تحْمل (تخرّب) المياه حقل جيرانه (المزروع)، سوف يُمِد (يجهّز) حبوب كما (بمقدار حبوب) جيرانه.

If (after) a person [a man] opens his (water) channel to a (planted) track (and) let go (to) his side (put aside) (abandons), (and) the waters carry (take) away (destroy) his neighbor (planted) field, he shall supply grains as much as his neighbor (grains).

§ 56.—XV, 39-45

39 šum-ma a-wi-lum 40 me-e ip-te-ma 41 ip-še-tim [b]ša eḳil i-te-šu 42 me-e uš-ta-bil 43 X GAN.E 44 X ŠE.GUR 45 i-ma-ad-da-ad

39 ثمَّ أويلم [عويلم] 40 مي ذو يفتحم [يفتيم] 41 عِفشَتِم [عفستِم] ذا حقلْ يتئ ذو 42 مئي يُستبِل 43 10 قنْع 44 10 سع [شع] جرْ [كُرْ] 45 يمدَدْ

|وفق الفقرة 55| بعد ان (اذا) الشخص [الرجل] يفتح مياهه (مياه قناته) (و) المياه تحْمل (تخرّب) عمل حقل جيرانه (الغير مزروع)، (الشخص [الرجل]) سوف يُمد (يجهّز) 10 كُر حبوب (لكل) 10 قنع (قاطع حقل).

|Referencing §55| If (after) the person [the man] opens his waters (water channels), (and) the waters carry (take) away (destroy) the work of his (unplanted) neighbor field, he shall supply 10 Kur of grains (for every) 10 Qan'i (field sectors).

§ 57.—XV, 46-64

46 šum-ma rê'um 47 a-na ša-am-mi 48 ṣênê šu-ku-lim 49 it-ti be-el eḳlim 50 la im-ta-gar-ma 51 ba-lum be-el eḳlim 52 eḳlam ṣênê 53 uš-ta-ki-il 54 be-el eḳlim eḳil-šu 55 i-iṣ-ṣi-id 56 rê'um ša i-na ba-lum 57 be-el eḳlim 58 eḳlam ṣênê 59 u-ša-ki-lu 60 e-li-nu-um-ma 61 X GAN.E 62 XX ŠE.GUR 63 a-na be-el eḳlim 64 i-na-ad-di-in

46 ثمَّ رعومْ 47 أن ثمي 48 ضين تؤكلم 49 إتي بعَل حقلِم 50 لا يمتجرم 51 بلم بعَل حقلِم 52 حقلَم ضين 53 يُستأكل 54 بعَل حقلم حقلْ ذو 55 يحصِد 56 رعومْ ذا إن بلُم 57 بعَل حقلِم 58 حقلَم ضين 59 أُتأكلو 60 علينُم 61 10 قنْع 62 20 سع [شع] جرْ [كُرْ] 63 أن بعَل حقلِم 64 يندِن

بعد ان (اذا) راعي لا يتحاقل (يشتري حق زرع في الارض) مع مالك حقل لتأكيل خراف حشيش، (و) يؤكِل الخراف الحقل بلا (بدون) (علم) مالك الحقل، مالك الحقل سوف يحصد (حشيش) حقله، الراعي الذي أكّلَ الخراف الحقل في (من) بدون (موافقة) مالك الحقل، علاوة (على ذلك)، سوف يعطي الى مالك الحقل 20 كُر حبوب (لكل) 10 قنع (قاطع حقل).

If (after) a shepherd does not buy (in-ground plantation right) with (from) a field owner to (for) grass feeding sheep, (and) he feeds the sheep (on) the field without (the knowledge of) the owner of the field, the owner of the field shall reap his filed (grass), on top (of that) (in addition), the shepherd, who without (the agreement of) the owner of the field fed the sheep (on) the field, shall give to the owner of the field 20 Kur of grains (for every) 10 Qan'i (field sectors).

§ 58.—XV, 65- XVI, 3

65 šum-ma iš-tu [b]ṣênê 66 i-na ugarim 67 i-te-li-a-nim 68 ka-an-nu [b]ga-ma-ar-tim 69 i-na abullim 70 it-ta-aẖ-la-lu 71 rê'um ṣênê 72 a-na eḳlim id-di-ma 73 eḳlam ṣênê 74 uš-ta-ki-il 75 rê'um eḳlum u-ša-ki-lu 76 i-na-ṣa-ar-ma 77 i-na ebûrim 78 X GAN.E XVI, 1 LX ŠE.GUR 2 a-na be-el eḳlim 3 i-ma-ad-da-ad

65 ثمَّ إستْ ضين 66 إن عقرم [أقرم] 67 إتعليانم 68 كنو جمرتم 69 إن أبلّم 70 إتخلّل 71 رعومْ ضين 72 أن حقلم يدم [يدعم] 73 حقلَم ضين 74 يُستأكل 75 رعومْ حقلُمْ أُتأكلو 76 ينظرَم 77 إن حبرم 78 10 قنْع 1 60 سع [شع] جرْ [كُرْ] 2 أن بعَل حقلِم 3 يمدَدْ

|وفق الفقرة 57| بعد ان (اذا) أولما (حالما) صعدت (رعت) الخراف في الحقل المثمر (بحبوب)، (و) تخللت (نفذت من) كُنّ الحبَس (المأوى) في [من] (موقع) الحجز، الراعي يدعْ الخراف للحقل (الغير مزروع) (و) يؤكِل الخراف الحقل، الراعي سوف يراقب الحقل (الذي) أكّلَ، (و) سوف يُمد (يجهّز) الى مالك الحقل 60 كُر حبوب (لكل) 10 قنع (قاطع حقل)، في (موسم) الثمار (الحصاد).

|Referencing §57| If (after) once the sheep went up the (grains) yielding field, (and) broke through (escaped) the imprisonment shelter (the sheepfold) in [from] the confinement (place), the shepherd let go the sheep to the (unplanted, grass) field, (and) feed the sheep (on) the field, the shepherd shall

watch the field he fed (on), (and) he shall supply to the owner of the field 60 Kur of grains (for every) 10 Qan'i (field sectors), in (at) harvest (time).

§ 59.—XVI, 4-9

4 šum-ma a-wi-lum 5 ba-lum be-el kirêm 6 i-na kirê a-wi-lim 7 i-ṣa-am ik-ki-is 8 ½ ma-na kaspim 9 i-ša-ḳal

4 ثُمَّ أويلُم [عَويلُم] 5 بَلُمْ بَعَلْ كيريمْ 6 إنَ كيري أويلم [عَويلم] 7 عِصَمْ يكِسْ [يقِصْ] 8 1\2 مَنَا كَسْفِمْ 9 يثْقَلْ

بعد ان (اذا) شخص [رجل] يكسر [يقص] عود شجر صلب في بستان شخص [رجل]، بلا (بدون) (علم) مالك البستان، (الشخص [الرجل]) سوف يَزن (ويعطي) 1\2 رطل فضة.

If (after) a person [a man] breaks a solid tree branch in (another) person [man] orchard without (the knowledge of) the owner of the orchard, he shall measure (and give) ½ Mana (1 lb.) silver.

§ 60.—XVI, 10-26

10 šum-ma a-wi-lum 11 eḳlam a-na kirêm ^{b}za-ga-bi-im 12 a-na NU.kirêm ^{b}id-di-in 13 NU.kirûm 14 kirâm iz-ḳu-up 15 šattam IV^{kam} 16 kirâm u-ra-ab-ba 17 i-na ḫa-mu-uš-tim 18 ša-at-tim 19 be-el kirêm 20 u NU.kirûm 21 mi-it-ḫa-ri-iš 22 i-zu-zu 23 be-el kirêm 24 zitti-šu 25 i-na-za-ak-ma 26 i-li-ḳi

10 ثُمَّ أويلُم [عَويلُم] 11 حِقْلَمْ أنَ كيريمْ زَجَبِمْ [سَقَبِمْ] [سَقَفِمْ] 12 أنَ نُؤ كيريمْ يدِنْ 13 نُؤ كيريمْ 14 كيريمْ يزْقُفْ [يسْقُفْ] 15 سَتَّمْ [سَنْتَمْ] 4كَمْ 16 كيريمْ يُربَا 17 إنَ خَمُسْتِمْ 18 سَتِّمْ [سَنْتِمْ] 19 بَعَلْ كيريمْ 20 و نُؤ كيريمْ 21 مِتْحَرِتْ [مِتْخَرِتْ] 22 يُزُّزْ 23 بَعَلْ كيريمْ 24 زِتّي ذو 25 ينَزَكْمَ [ينَسَقْمَ] 26 يلِقي

بعد ان (اذا) شخص [رجل] يعطي حقل الى بستاني (متعهد بساتين) لنَصب (لزراعة) بستان، (و) البستاني ينْصِبْ (يزرع) بستان، يربي البستان أربعة سنوات، في السنة الخامسة مالك البستان والبستاني سوف يفرقو (سيقسمو) (ارض البستان) بالتساوي، مالك البستان سوف يحدّدْ حصته (و) يأخذ.

If (after) a person [a man] gives a field to a gardener (to) for erecting (planting) an orchard, (and) the gardener erects (plants) an orchard, raises (rears) the orchard for 4 years, in the fifth year, the owner of the orchard and the gardener shall divide (share) (the orchard), equally, the owner of the orchard shall sort out his portion and take (it).

§ 61.—XVI, 27-33

27 šum-ma NU.kirûm 28 eḳlam i-na za-ga-bi-im 29 la ig-mur-ma 30 ni-di-tam i-zi-ib 31 ni-di-tam 32 a-na li-ib-bi ^{b}zitti-šu 33 i-ša-ka-nu-šum

27 ثُمَّ نُؤ كيريمْ 28 حِقْلَمْ إنَ زَجَبِمْ [سَقَبِمْ] [سَقَفِمْ] 29 لا يجْمُرْمْ 30 نِدِئْتِمْ يعْزِبْ 31 نِدِئْتِمْ 32 أنَ لِبّ زِتّي ذو 33 يسكَنو ذُومْ

|وفق الفقرة 60| بعد ان (اذا) البستاني (متعهد بساتين) لا يشمل كل الحقل في نَصْبْ (زراعة) (البستان)، (و) يترك منطقة غير مروية (غير مزروعة)، سوف يضعو المنطقة الغير مروية (الغير مزروعة) في داخل حصته.

|Referencing §60| If (after) the gardener does not include the entire field in the erecting (the planting), he leaves unwatered (unplanted) area, they shall place the unwatered (unplanted) area inside his portion.

§ 62.—XVI, 34-47

34 šum-ma eḳlam 35 ša in-na-ad-nu-šum 36 a-na kirêm ^{b}la iz-ḳu-up 37 šum-ma abšênum 38 bilat eḳlim 39 ša ša-na-tim 40 ša in-na-du-u 41 NU.kirûm 42 a-na be-el eḳlim 43 ki-ma i-te-šu 44 i-ma-ad-da-ad 45 u eḳlam ši-ip-ra-am 46 i-ib-bi-eš-ma 47 a-na be-el eḳlim ^{b}u-ta-a-ar

34 ثُمَّ حِقْلَمْ 35 ذا إِنْدَنْ ذُومْ 36 أَنَ كيريمْ لا يزْقُفْ [يسقُفْ] 37 ثمّ أبشينَمْ [هبشينَمْ] 38 بِعلَتْ حقْلِمْ 39 ذا سناتِمْ 40 ذا إِنْدُوَ 41 نَؤْ كيريمْ
42 أَنَ بَعلْ حقْلِمْ 43 كيمَ يتئْ ذو 44 يمدَدْ 45 و حقْلَمْ سبْرِمْ [سِفرِمْ] 46 يثبيشَمْ [يعفيشَمْ] [يعفيسَمْ] 47 أَنَ بعَلْ حقْلِمْ يُتأرْ

|وفق الفقرة 60| بعد ان (اذا) لا ينْصِبْ (يزرع) الى بستان الحقل الذي أعطوه، بعد ان (اذا) أتاوة (محصول) الحقل للسنوات التي رميَ (أُهمِلَ) (كانت) حَرِش (شعير للعلف)، البستاني سوف يُمِد (يجهّز) حبوب كما (بكمية حبوب) جيرانه الى مالك الحقل، و سوف يضع البستاني مهارة عمل الحقل (اللازمة)، (و) يعيد الى مالك الحقل.

|Referencing §60| If (after) he does not erect (plant) to an orchard the field they gave him, if (after) the produce of the field during the years it was thrown away (neglected) (was) wild barley (for animal feed), the gardener shall supply as much grains as (harvested by) his neighbor to the owner of the field, and he shall put the (required) field work skill, to return to the owner of the field.

§ 63.—XVI, 48-57

48 šum-ma eḳlam KI.KAL 49 eḳlam ši-ip-ra-am 50 i-ib-bi-eš-ma 51 eḳlu(=a-na) be-el eḳlim 52 u-ta-a-ar 53 u X GAN.E 54 X ŠE.GUR 55 ša ša-at-tim 56 iš-ti-a-at 57 i-ma-ad-da-ad

48 ثُمَّ حِقْلَمْ كيعْ [قيعْ] كهلْ 49 حِقْلَمْ سبْرَمْ [سِفْرَمْ] 50 يثبيشَمْ [يعفيشَمْ] [يعفيسَمْ] 51 حِقْلَنَ بعَلْ حقْلِمْ 52 يُتأرْ 53 و 10 قنْعِ 54 10
سِعْ [شعْ] جُرْ [كُرْ] 55 ذا سَتِّمْ [سَنْتِمْ] 56 إسْتياتَمْ [إلْتياتَمْ] 57 يمَدَدْ

|وفق الفقرة 60| بعد ان (اذا) (أصبح الحقل) حقل أرض بور (مُهملة)، سوف يهيء (يضع) مهارة عمل الحقل (اللازمة)، (و) يعيد حقل مالك الحقل، وسوف يُمد (يجهّز) 10 كُر حبوب (لكل) 10 قنع (قاطع حقل)، للسنة الواحدة (لكل سنة).

|Referencing §60| If (after) (the field becomes) a fallow (neglected) land field, he shall put the (required) field work skill (and) return the field of the field owner, and he shall supply 10 Kur of grains (for every) 10 Qan'i (field sectors) of one (for each) year.

§ 64.—XVI, 58-70

58 šum-ma a-wi-lum 59 kirâ-šu 60 a-na NU.kirêm 61 a-na ru-ku-bi-im 62 id-di-in 63 NU.kirûm 64 a-di kirûm ṣa-ab-tu 65 i-na bi-la-at kirêm 66 ši-it-ti-in 67 a-na be-el kirêm 68 i-na-ad-di-in 69 ša-lu-uš-tam 70 šu-u i-li-ḳi

58 ثُمَّ أويلم [عويلَمْ] 59 كيريَ ذو 60 أَنَ نَؤْ كيريمْ 61 أَنَ رُكُبِمْ 62 يدِنْ 63 نَؤْ كيريُمْ 64 عدي [حدي] كيريُمْ ضَبْطُ 65 إِنَ بِعلَتْ كيريمْ 66 ثِتِّنْ
67 أَنَ بَعلْ كيريمْ 68 ينَدِنْ 69 ثَلُثْتَمْ 70 ذوو يلقي

بعد ان (اذا) شخص [رجل] يعطي بستانه الى بستاني (متعهد بساتين) للإتيان (للجَني) [للاقامة (عليها)]، البستاني سوف يعطي الى مالك البستان ثلثين في (من) محصول البستان حتى (مادامت) البستان ممسوكة، هو يأخذ الثُلث.

If (after) a person [a man] gives his orchard to a gardener to (for) mounting (reaping) [to (for) handling], the gardener shall give to the owner of the orchard two thirds in (from) orchard's produce as long as the orchard is in (his) possession, he shall take one third.

§ 65.—XVI, 71-77

71 šum-ma NU.kirûm 72 kirâm la u-ra-ᵇak-ki-ib-ma 73 bi-il-tam um-ta-di 74 NU.kirûm 75 bi-la-at kirêm 76 a-na i-te-šu 77 |i-ma-ad-da-ad|

71 ثُمَّ نَؤْ كيريُمْ 72 كيريَمْ لا يُركِبْمَ 73 بِعلِتَمْ يمْتَدي [يبْتَدي] [يمْتَطي] [يمْتَعطي] 74 نَؤْ كيريُمْ 75 بِعلَتْ كيريَمْ 76 أَنَ يتئْ ذو 77 |يمدَدْ|

|وفق الفقرة 64| بعد ان (اذا) البستاني (متعهد بساتين) لا يأتي (لا يجني) [لا يُقيم (على)] البستان، يُبَدّد (يُشَتّت) [يُقلّلْ] المحصول، البستاني سوف يُمِدّ (يجهّز) محصول بستان الى (حسب) جيرانه.

|Referencing §64| If (after) the gardener does not mount (does not reap) [does not handle] the orchard, scatters [reduces] the produce; the gardener shall supply orchard produce to (based on) his neighbor.

§§ 66-99, which were presumably contained in the erased five bands (row fields) of the Louvre museum stele were partially replaced from other tablet fragments found

§ 66
L66 (BL §A; MSS P, Q, I; Roth gap a)

šumma awīlum kaspam itti tamkārum ilqēma tamkāršu īsiršuma, mimma ša nadānim la ibaššīšum, kirāšu ištu tarkibtim ana tamkārim iddinma suluppī mala ina kirîm ibbaššû ana kaspika tabal iqbīšum tamkārum šû ul immaggar suluppī ša ina kirîm ibbaššû bēl kirîmma ileqqēma kaspam u ṣibassu ša pī ṭuppišu tamkāram ippalma suluppī watrūtim ša ina kirîm ibbaššû bēl kirîmma ileqqe

ثُمَّ أويلُم [عَويلُم] كَسْفَمْ إتي تمكارِمْ يلْقيمَ تمْكارِ ذو يسِرْ ذُومْ ممَّ ذا نَدانمْ لا يبْذِي ذُومْ [يبثّي ذُومْ] كِيرا ذو إسْتُ تركبْتِمْ أنَ تمكارِمْ يدنَمَ سلُفَّ ملَئ إن كيريمْ إبَّذو [إبثّوَ] أنَ كَسفك تبَلْ يقْبي ذُومْ تمكارُمْ ذوو أُلْ يمَّجرْ سلُفَّ ذا إنَ كيريمْ إبَّذوَ [إبثّوَ] بَعَلْ كيريمَّ يلْقيمْ كَسْفَمْ و ضِبطْ ذو [ضِبَتْ] ذا فيي دُوبِّ ذو [دُوفِّ ذو] تمكارَمْ يئفَلْمَ سلُفِّ وَتْرُتِمْ ذا إنَ كيريمْ إبَذو بَعَلْ كيريمَّ يلْقي

بعد ان (اذا) شخص [رجل] يلقي (يأخذ) فضة مع (من) متاجر، (و) (ل)متاجره، يسرُّه (يخفي عنه)، (و) لا يُوجِد له [لا يُظهِر له] أيّ ذا إعطاء (أي فضة)، (ثم) يعطي بستانه الى المتاجر أوّلما (حالما (موسم) الإتيان (الجَني) [(موسم) الاقامة (عليها)]، (و) يقول له "خُذْ كامل التمر (الذي) تواجدَ [ظهرَ] في البستان الى (مقابل) فضتكَ"، هذا المتاجر سوف لن (بامكانه ان لا) يوافق؛ مالك البستان سوف يلقي (يأخذ) التمر الذي تواجدَ [ظهرَ] في البستان، (و) سوف يتحمّل (دين) الفضة وربحها ذا (حسب) تصريح (كلمات) لوحه (لوح سنده) للمتاجر، (و) مالك البستان سوف يلقي (يأخذ) تمرِ الوترِ (التنقيص) (التمر بعد تنقيص قيمة الدَين) الذي تواجدَ [ظهرَ] في البستان.

If (after) a person [a man] takes silver with (from) a merchant, (and) (to) his merchant, he conceals to him (cheats on) him, (and) he does let him get [see] anything of (for) giving (any silver), (then) he gives his orchard to the merchant once (it is) mounting (reaping) (season) [handling (season)], (and) he says "take the full dates that existed [appeared] in the orchard to (for) your silver", this merchant shall (may) not approve; the owner of the orchard shall take the dates that existed [appeared] in the orchard, (and) he shall take upon (the debt of) the silver and its profit of (according to) the declaration (words) of his (bond) tablet (to) the merchant, (and) the owner of the orchard shall take the dates of the reduction (dates after reducing the debt value) that existed [appeared] in the orchard.

§ 67
67+a (BL §C, MSSP, Q, Frag. Noug. JA 245; Roth gap c)

|šumma ....| ana šimim |.......| ul inaddiššum šumma še'am kaspam u bīšam ana bīt ilkim ša bīt itēšu ša išāmu inaddin ina mimma ša iddinu ītelli bītum ana |bēlišu| itâr šumma bītum šû ilkam la išu išâm ana bītim šuāti še'am kaspam u bīšam inaddin

ثُمَّ |......| أنَ سمِمْ |.....| أُلْ ينَدِنْ ذُومْ [ينَدِذّومْ] ثُمَّ سعَمْ [شعَمْ] كسْفَمْ و بيذَمْ أنَ بيت إلكِمْ ذا بيت يتئ ذو ذا إسَأمُ ينَدِنْ إن ممَّ ذا إدِّنْ يتَعلّي بيتُمْ أنَ بَعَلْ ذو يتأرْ ثُمَّ بيتُمْ ذوو إلكَمْ لا يذو يسَمْ أنَ بيتِمْ ذأُتِ سعَمْ [شعَمْ] كسْفَمْ و بيذَمْ ينَدِّنْ

بعد ان (اذا) |............| للشراء (للبيع) |............| سوف لن يعطيه؛ بعد ان (اذا) يعطي حبوب، فضة، وممتلكات الى (لشراء) بيت الرسالة (بيت العمل) العائد لبيت جيرانه (جيران البيت) الذي أُشْتُرِيَ، سوف يتنازل بأي الذي أعطاه، سوف يُعيد البيت الى مالكه؛ بعد ان (اذا) هذا البيت لا يملك رسالة (ليس بيت عمل)، سوف يشتري، سوف يعطي حبوب، فضة، وممتلكات الى (لشراء) ذلك البيت.

If (after) |.................| to (for) buying (for sell) |..............|, he shall not buy; if (after) he gives grains, silver, and goods [possessions] to (for buying) the work house of its neighboring house that was bought, he shall cede in (give up) (lose) whatever he gave, he shall return the house to its owner; if (after) this house does not have work (purpose), he shall buy, he shall give grains, silver, and goods [possessions] to (for buying) that house.

§ 68

68+b (BL §H, §G; MSSP, R, Roth gap e)

|šumma .....| nabalkattaka dunnin ištu bītika ibbalakkatunim ana bēl nidītim nidītka epuš |ištu| nidītika |bītī| ipallašūnim iqbi šibī iškun |.......| ina nabalkattim |.........| nabalkattim |........| bēl |.....| šumma |.......| bēl |.......| mimma |.......| iriab.

|ثُمَّ ....| نَبَلْكَتُكَ دؤنُنْ إسْتُ بيتِكَ إبْلَكَّتُنِمْ أنَ بَعَلْ نديتِمْ نديْتَكَ عفْش [عفْس] |هذُمْ| نديْتِكَ |بيتي| إفَلَّسْنِمْ يقبي ثِبي [شيبِ] إسكُنْ |....| إنَ نَبَلْكَتِّمْ |...........| نَبَلْكَتِّمْ |.....| بَعلْ |.......| ثُمَّ |.......| بَعَلْ |.......| مِمَّ |.......| يرأبْ

|بعد ان (اذا) ....| يقول الى مالك الارض الندية "قوّي حجارتك (التي) أخلَطت أساس بيتك، إبني أرضك الندية"، "هذا لان أرضك الندية (النزيزة) أخفضت بيتي"، يضع شهود، |...|

|If (after)...............|, he says to the owner of the wetland "strengthen your stone mixed (in) your house's foundation, build your wetland", "that is because your wetland has lowered (down) my house", he sets (brings in) witnesses, |..|

§ 69

69+c (BL §J, §E; MSS P, R, s; Roth gap g)

"|šumma awīlum ..... ina ....| awīlum ašbumma kasap kiṣrišu gamram ša šanat ana bēl |bītim| iddinma bēl bītim ana waššābim ina ūmīšu la malûtim waṣâm iqtabi bēl bītim aššum waššabim ina ūmīšu la malûtim ina bītišu |ušēṣû| ina kaspim ša waššābum |iddinušum ītelli|

|ثُمَّ أَويلْم [عَويلْم] ..... إنَ ....|، أويلْم [عَويلْم] أثْبُمَّ كَسَفْ كِصْرِ ذو [قِصْرِ ذو] جمْرَمْ ذا سَنَتْ أنَ بَعلْ |بيتِمْ| يدِّنْم بعَلْ بيتِمْ أنَ وَثّابِمْ إنَ أُومِ ذو لا مَلؤتِم وَصئَمْ يقْتَبي بعَلْ بيتِمْ هذُمْ وثّابِمْ إنَ أُومِ ذو لا مَلؤتِم إنَ بيتِ ذو |إسئصوَ| إنَ كَسْفِمْ ذا وَثّابُمْ إدِّنْ ذُومْ يتَعلّي

|بعد ان (اذا) شخص [رجل] ...... في ....| الشخص [الرجل] المقيم يعطي فضة إلتزامه (إيجاره)، مجموع (ايجار) السنة، الى مالك البيت، (ثم) مالك البيت يقول للمقيم الغير مكمتل في يومه (في مُدته) "أخْرُجْ"، هذا لأنه أخرجَ المقيم الغير مكمتل في يومه (في مُدته) في (من) بيته، سوف يتنازل بالفضة التي أعطاه المُقيم.

If (after) a person [a man] |...................................|, the settled person [man] (the tenant) gives the silver of his obligation (his rent), the total (amount) of the year, to the owner of the house (the landlord), (then) the owner of the house (the landlord) says to the settler (who is) not complete in his day (term) "leave", that is because he forced the settler (who is) not complete in his day (term) to leave, he shall cede in (give up) (lose) the silver that the settler gave him.

§ 70
§5.9 (BAL L70+d; $_{\text{MS}}$ S; BL §L; Roth §5.9 gap t)

šumma tamkārum še'am u kaspam ana ẖubullim iddin ana 1 kurrum 1 pān 4 sūt še'am ṣibtam ileqqe šumma kaspam ana ẖubullim iddin ana 1 šiqil kaspim 1/6 u 6 uṭṭit ṣibtam ileqqe

ثُمَّ تَمْكَارُمْ سَعَمْ [شَعَمْ] و كَسْفَمْ أنَ حُبُلِّمْ يدِنْ أنَ 1 كُرِّمْ 1 فانْ [فارْ] 4 سوت سَعَمْ [شَعَمْ] ضِبطَمْ يلقّي ثُمَّ كَسْفَمْ أنَ حُبُلِّمْ يدِنْ أنَ 1 ثِقِلْ [شِقِلْ] كَسْفِمْ 1\6 و 6 عُطِّتْ [حُطِّتْ] ضِبطَمْ يلقّي

بعد ان (اذا) متاجر يعطي حبوب وفضة للدين (بسند)، سوف يأخذ 1 ققار (سلّة) (و) 4 سوت حبوب للكُرْ الواحد، بعد ان (اذا) يعطي فضة للدين، سوف يأخذ 1\6 (مثقال (شقل)) و 6 حبات (فضة) ربح لمثقال (لشقل) الفضة الواحد.

If (after) a merchant gives grains and silver to (for) loan (bond), he shall take 1 Far (basket) (and) 1 Sut (of) grains to one (for each) Kur, if (after) (it is) silver, he shall take 1/6 Shiqil and 6 grains (of silver) to one (for each) Shiqil silver (as) profit.

§ 71
§5.9 (BAL L71+d; $_{\text{MS}}$ S; BL §M; Roth §5.9 gap u)

šumma awīlum ša ẖubullam iršu kaspam ana turrim la išu še'am u kaspam kīma ṣimdat šarrim u ṣibassu 1 kurrum še'am 1 pān ana šattim ileqqe šumma tamkārum ṣibat ẖubulli |...| ana 1 kur |...| 1/6 u 6 uṭṭit |...| uwatterma ilqe ina |mimma| ša iddinu ītelli

ثُمَّ أويلُم [عَويلُم] ذا حُبُلَّمْ إرْسو كَسْفَمْ أنَ تؤرِّم لا يذو سَعَمْ [شَعَمْ] كيمَ صِمْدَتْ [ضِمْدَتْ] سرِّمْ و ضِبطْ ذو [ضِبَتْ] 1 كُرِّمْ سَعَمْ [شَعَمْ] 1 فانْ [فارْ] أنَ ستّمْ [سَنْتِمْ] يلقّي ثُمَّ تَمْكَارُمْ ضِبَطْ حُبُلِّ |....| أنَ 1 كُرْ |أنَ 1 ثِقِلْ [شِقِلْ] كَسْفِمْ| 1\6 و 6 عُطِّتْ [حُطِّتْ] |ضِبطَمْ| يُوتَرِّمَ يلقي إنَ مِمَّ ذا إدِّنْ يتَعلّي

|وفق الفقرة 70| بعد ان (اذا) الشخص [الرجل] الذي أرسى (وضعَ على عاتقه) الدين (بسند) لا يملك الفضة للإعادة، (المتاجر) سوف يأخذ حبوب كما (حسب) تصريح الشريف (الملك) و ربحه، 1 ققار (سلّة) (لكل) 1 كُرُّمْ حبوب، للسنة، بعد ان (اذا) المتاجر |يُغير| ربح الدين، ينْقِص (كمية) 1\6 (مثقال (شقل)) و 6 حبات (فضة) |ربح لمثقال (لشقل) الفضة الواحد| لكُرْ (الحبوب) الواحد (يُنقص قيمة كُرْ الحبوب مقابل فضة الربح)، (و) يأخذْ (حبوب)، سوف يتنازل في (عن) أيّ ما أعطى (الدين).

|Referencing §70| If (after) the person [the man] who settled in (put upon himself) the loan (bond) does not have silver for returning, (the merchant) shall take grains as (according to) the declaration (words) of the noble (the royalty) and its profit, 1 Far (basket) (for each) one Kur of grains, to (for each) year; if (after) the merchant |changes| the profit of the loan, he reduces (the amount of) the 1/6 Shiqil and 6 grains (of silver) |to one (for each) Shiqil silver profit| to (for) a Kur of grains (he reduces the value of a Kur of grains against the profit of silver), (and) he takes (grains), he shall cede in (give up) (lose) whatever he gave.

§ 72
§5.13 (BAL L72+e; $_{\text{MS}}$ S; BL §0; Roth gap w)

šumma tamkārum |....| ana |....| ṣibtam |....| ilteqēma |....| u lu še'am |u lu kaspam| mala |imẖur u lu| la uštaẖriṣma ṭuppam eššam la išṭur u lu ṣibātim ana qaqqadim uṭṭeẖẖi tamkārum šû še'am mala ilqû uštašannāma utâr.

ثُمَّ تمْكارِمْ |....| أنَ |....| ضِبطَمْ |....| يلْتقيمَ |....| و لو سَعَمْ [شَعَمْ] |ولو كَسْفَمْ| ملَئ |يمخُرْ و لو| لا يستخْرِصمَ دُوبَمْ [دُوفَمْ] عشّمْ [عسّمْ] لا يسْطُرْ و لو ضِباطِمْ أنَ قَقْدِمْ يطّحي تمكارُمْ ذوو سَعَمْ [شَعَمْ] ملَئ إلقو يُستَثْنَم يتأر

بعد ان (اذا) تاجر |..........................|، و (حتى) لو يختار (يستلم) كامل الحبوب، و (حتى) لو الفضة، و(حتى) لو لا يخصِم (و) لا يسطّر (لا يدوّن) اللوح المطلوب، و(حتى) لو يَضع (يُضيف) أرباح الى المقدار، هذا المتاجر سوف يثنّي (يُضاعف) كامل الحبوب (التي) أخذ، (و) يُعيد.

If (after) a merchant |.....................|, and (even) let-it-be he chooses (receives) the full (amount of) grains, and (even) the silver, and (even) let-it-be he does not deduct, (and) does not write the required tablet, and (even) let-it-be he lays (adds) profits to the amount , this merchant shall double the full (amount of) grains, (and) return.

§ 73

§5.13 (BAL L75+e; $_{MS}$ S; BL §P; Roth gap x)

šumma tamkārum še'am u kaspam ana ẖubullim iddinma inūma ana ẖubullim iddinu kaspam ina abnim maṭītim u še'am ina šūtim maṭītim iddin u inūma imẖuru kaspam ina abnim |rabītim u| še'am ina šūtim rabītim imẖur |tamkārum sû| ina |mimma ša iddinu ītelli|

ثمَّ تمكارُمْ سعَمْ [شعَمْ] و كسفَمْ أنَ حبُلِّمْ يدنمَ حينُم أنَ حبُلِمْ إدنُ كسفَمْ إنَ أبنِمْ معطيتِمْ [مَطيتِمْ] و سعَمْ [شعَمْ] إنَ ذؤتِمْ معطيتِمْ [مَطيتِمْ] يدنْ و حينُمَ إمخُرُ كسفَمَ إنَ أبنِمْ |ربيتِمْ و| سعَمْ [شعَمْ] إنَ ذؤتِمْ ربيتِمْ يمخُرْ |تمكارُمْ ذووا| إنَ ممَّ ذا إدِّنُ يتعلّي

بعد ان (اذا) متاجر يعطي حبوب وفضة للدين (بسند)، (و) حينما (عندما) أعطى للدين، يعطي الفضة في الذروة الواطئة (سوق الطلب الواطئ) والحبوب في ذات (الذروة) الواطئة، وحينما (عندما) إختارَ (استلمَ)، يختار (يستلم) الفضة في الذروة العالية (سوق الطلب العالي) والحبوب في ذات (الذروة) العالية، هذا المتاجر سوف يتنازل في (عن) أيّ ما أعطى (الدين).

If (after) a merchant gives grains and silver to (for) loan (bond), (and) when he gave (for) loan (bond), he gives the silver in the low peak (low demand market) and the grains in that (same) low, (and) when he chose (received), he choose (receives) the silver in the high peak (high demand market) and the grains in that (same) high, this merchant shall cede in (give up) (lose) whatever he gave.

§ 75

§5.15 (BAL L75+e; $_{MSS}$ P, S; BL §R; Roth gap z)

šumma awīlum še'am u kaspam itti tamkārim ilqēma še'am u kaspam ana turrim la išu bīšamma išu mimma ša ina qātišu ibaššû maẖar šībī kima ubbalu ana tamkārišu inaddin tamkārum ul uppas imaẖẖar.

ثمَّ أويلُم [عَويلُم] سعَمْ [شعَمْ] و كَسفَمْ إتي تَمْكارِمْ يلْقيمَ سعَمْ [شعَمْ] و كَسفَمْ أنَ تؤرِّمْ لا يذو بيذَمَّ يذو مِمَّ ذا إنَ جتي ذو [قتي ذو] إبذّوَ مَخَرْ ثبي [شيبِ] كيمَ أُبّلو أنَ تمكارِ ذو ينَدِنَ تَمْكارُمْ أُلْ يُعْفَس [يُئْبَس] يمخّر

بعد ان (اذا) شخص [رجل] يأخذ حبوب وفضة مع (من) متاجر، (و) لا يملك الحبوب والفضة للإعادة، سوف يعطي لمتاجره، كما (بقدر ما) حُمِّلَ (أُعطيَ)، الحاجيات (التي) يملك، أيّ التي تواجدَت [ظَهرت] في يديه (في حوزته) أمام شهود؛ المتاجر سوف لن يلوم [يجادل]، سوف يختار.

If (after) a person [a man] takes grains and silver with (from) a merchant, (and) he does not have the grains and silver to (for) returning, he shall give to his merchant, as (as much as) he was loaded (was givin), the things (the belongings) that he has, whatever that existed [apeared] in his hands (his possession), in front of witnesses; the merchant shall not blame [argue], he shall choose.

§ 77
L77+f (fragment cc; BL §U; $_{MS}$ S)

{šumma awīlum ana awīlim kaspam ana tappûtim iddin nēmelam u butuqqâm ša ibbašû maḫar ilim mitḫāriš izuzzū

ثُمَّ أويلُم [عَويلُم] أنَ أويلِم [عويلِم] كَسْفَمْ أنَ تبعُتِمْ يدِنْ نَملَمْ و بُتُقَّمْ ذا يبّذُو [يبّثُو] مَخرْ إلِمْ [علِم] متحَرت يزُزُّو

بعد ان (اذا) شخص [رجل] يعطي الى شخص [رجل] فضة للولاء (للشراكة)، سوف يفرقو (يتقاسمو) الفائض (العوائد) والخسارة التي سوف يوجدو [يظهرو] (يحققو) أمام إله بالتساوي.

If (after) a person [a man] gives to a person [a man] silver to (for) loyalty (partnership), they shall divide the abundance (the dividends) that they shall make exist [appear] (have) in front of a god, equally.

.

.

.

.

§ 100.—XVII, 1-7
L100 (BL §V; $_{MS}$ S)

|..........................| [XVII, 1] ṣi-ba-a-at kaspim [2] ma-la il-ḳu-u [3] i-sa-ad-dar-ma [4] ûmi-šu [5] i-ma-an-nu-[b]u-ma [6] tamkari-šu [7] i-ip-pa-al

{šumma tamkārum ana šamallém kaspam ana |nadānim u maḫārim| iddinma ana ḫarrānim iṭrussu šamallûm ina ḫarrānim |...| šumma ašar illiku |nēmelam| itamar ṣibāt kaspim mala ilqû isaddarma ūmīšu imannūma tamkāršu ippal}

ثمَّ تمكارُمْ أنَ سملَّمْ كسْفَمْ أنَ |نَدنِم و مَخرِم| يدنَم أنَ حَرّانِم يطرُس [يترِصُّ] سمَلَّمْ إنَ حَرّانِمْ |...| ثمَّ أشَرْ إلِّكْ |نملَمْ| يتأمرْ [1] ضِبَطْ كَسْفَمْ [2] ملئ إلقوَ [3] يسَدَرْمَ [يسَدَنمَ] [4] أومِ ذو [5] يمَنّومَ [6] تمْكارِ ذو [7] يئفَلْ

بعد ان (اذا) متاجر يعطي الى مُتَعهّد فضة للإعطاء والإستلام (للبيع والشراء)، (و) يجهّز للرحلة، (و) المُتَعهّد |يذهب| في الرحلة، بعد ان (اذا) (المُتَعهّد) يرى فائض (عوائد) حيث تَرسّلَ (ذَهبَ)، سوف يُخصّص كامل قباض (أرباح) الفضة (التي) لقي (أخذ)، (و) يعِدّ (يسجل) أيامها، (و) يتحمل (تكاليف) متاجره.

If (after) a merchant gives to a jobber silver to (for) giving and receiving (selling and buying (trading)), (and) he arranges to (for) the journey, (and) the jobber |goes| in the journey, if (after) he sees abundance (dividends) where he went, he shall allocate the full profits of the silver he took, (and) count (mark) its days, (and) shall take upon (the expenses of) the merchant.

§ 101.—XVII, 8-14

[8] šum-ma a-šar [b]il-li-ku [9] ne-me-lam [10] la i-ta-mar [11] kaspam il-ḳu-u [12] uš-ta-ša-na-ma [13] šamallûm a-na tamkarim [14] i-na-ad-di-in

[8] ثمَّ أشَرْ إلِّكْ [9] نَملَمْ [10] لا يتأمرْ [11] كَسْفَمْ إلْقوَ [12] يُستَثنَمَ [يتّثنَم] [13] سمَلَّمْ أنَ تمْكارِم [14] ينَدنْ

|وفق الفقرة 100| بعد ان (اذا) لا يرى فائض (عوائد) حيث تَرسّلَ (ذَهبَ)، سوف يضاعف الفضة (التي) أخذ، (و) المُتَعهّد سوف يعطي الى المتاجر.

|Referencing §100| If (after) he does not see abundance (dividends) where he went, the jobber shall double the silver he took, (and) shall give to the merchant.

§ 102.—XVII, 15-23

[15] šum-ma tamkarum [16] a-na šamallîm [17] kaspam a-na ta-ad-[b]mi-iḳ-tim [18] it-ta-di-[b]in-ma [19] a-šar il-li-ku [20] bi-ti-iḳ-tam [21] i-ta-mar [22] ga-ga-ad kaspim [23] a-na tamkarim [b]u-ta-ar

[15] ثمّ تمكارمْ [16] أنَ سملّمْ [17] كسفمْ أن تدمقتمْ [تدمجتمْ] [18] يتدنمْ [19] أشرْ إلّكْ [20] بتقتمْ [21] يتأمرْ [22] ججدْ كسفمْ [23] أن تمكارمْ يتأرْ

|وفق الفقرة 100| بعد ان (اذا) متاجر يعطى الى مُتعهّد فضة للإنضمام (معه)، (والمُتعهّد) يرى (يعاني) خسارة حيث ترسّل (ذهب)، (المُتعهّد) سوف يعيد الى المتاجر عطية الفضة (بدون ارباح).

|Referencing §100| If (after) a merchant gives silver to (for) affiliation to a jobber, (and) he (the jobber) sees loss where he went, he shall return to the merchant the given silver (without profits).

§ 103.—XVII, 24-31

[24] šum-ma ḫar-ra-nam [25] i-na a-la-ki-šu [26] na-ak-ru-um [27] mi-im-ma [b]ša na-šu-u [28] uš-ta-ad-di-šu [29] šamallûm [b]ni-iš i-lim [30] i-za-kar-ma [31] u-ta-aš-šar

[24] ثمّ حرانمْ [25] إنَ ألكِ ذو [26] نكرمْ [27] ممّ ذا نسو [28] يُستأدي ذو [يُتأدي ذو] [29] سملّمْ نعشْ إلمْ [علِم] [30] يذكرمْ [31] يُتذرْ

|وفق الفقرة 100| بعد ان (اذا) (المُتعهّد) في (عند) ترسّله (ذهابه) الرحلة، أيّ ما (كان) ماضيا به (حامل)، محتال [غريب] يدعه (يُذهبْه) (يسرقه)، المُتعهّد سوف يقول (يحلف) (ذلك) برفعَة (بحياة) الإله، (و) سوف يُترك (حرا).

|Referencing §100| If (after) (the jobber) in his going the journey, a swindler (a con artist) let it go (robs it), whatever that he was carrying, confiscated it, the jobber shall say (declare) (that) in the glory life of god, (and) shall be left (free).

§ 104.—XVII, 32-45

[32] šum-ma tamkarum [33] a-na šamallîm [34] še'am šipâtam šamnam [35] u mi-im-ma [b]bi-ša-am [36] a-na pa-ša-ri-im [37] id-di-in [38] šamallûm kaspam [39] i-sa-ad-dar-ma [40] a-na tamkarim [41] u-ta-ar [42] ša-mallûm [b]ka-ni-ik kaspim [43] ša a-na tamkarim [44] i-na-ad-di-nu [45] i-li-ḳi

[32] ثمّ تمكارمْ [33] أنَ سملّمْ [34] سعمْ [شعمْ] شعفيتمْ سمنمْ [35] و ممّ بيذمْ [36] أن فشارمْ [فشأنمْ] [37] يدنْ [38] سملّمْ كسفمْ [39] يسدرمْ [يسدنْمْ] [40] أنَ تمكارمْ [41] يتأرْ [42] سملّمْ كانكْ [كينكْ] كسفمْ [43] ذا أنَ تمكارمْ [44] إندنْ [45] يلقي

بعد ان (اذا) متاجر يعطي الى مُتعهّد حبوب، خصال صوف، سمن و أي ممتلكات (اخرى) للتجارة، المُتعهّد سوف يُخصّص الفضة (المكتسبة)، (و) يعيد للمتاجر؛ المُتعهّد سوف يأخذ (بالمقابل) (وصل) ضمانة الفضة التي أعطى للمتاجر.

If (after) a merchant gives to a jobber grains, wool bundles, oil, and whatever goods [possessions] to (for) trading, the jobber shall allocate the silver (made), (and) return to the merchant; the jobber shall take the guarantee (receipt) of the silver that he gave to the merchant.

§ 105.—XVII, 46-54

[46] šum-ma šamallûm [47] i-te-gi-ma [48] ka-ni-ik kaspim [49] ša a-na tamkarim [50] id-di-nu [51] la il-te-ḳi [52] kaspi la ka-ni-[b]ki-im [53] a-na ni-ik-ka-[b]az-zi-im [54] u-ul iš-ša-ak-ka-an

[46] ثمْ سملّمْ [47] يتعجّيم [يتعجّهمِ] [48] كانكْ [كينكْ] كسفمْ [49] ذا أنَ تمكارمْ [50] إدنْ [51] لا يلْتقي [52] كسفِ لا كانكمْ [كينكمْ] [53] أنَ نكسمِ [نقصمِ] [54] ألْ يسكنْ

|وفق الفقرة 104| بعد ان (اذا) المُتعهّد يتهاون (يهمل) [يتعنْجَه (يتجاهل)]، (و) لا يأخذ (وصل) ضمانة الفضة التي أعطى للمتاجر، سوف لن يضع (يضيف) الى (حساب) النقصان (الدائن) الفضة عديمة (وصل) الضمانة.

|Referencing §104| If (after) the jobber ignores [be self-conceit], (and) he does not take the guarantee (receipt) of the silver he gave to the merchant, he shall not put (add) in the (credit) account the silver of (with) no guarantee (receipt).

§ 106.—XVII, 55-67

55 šum-ma šamallûm 56 kaspam it-ti ᵇtamkarim 57 il-ḳi-ma 58 tamkari-šu 59 it-ta-ki-ir 60 tamkarum šu-u 61 i-na ma-ḫar i-lim ᵇu ši-bi 62 i-na kaspim li-ḳi-im 63 šamallâm u-ka-an-ma 64 šamallûm kaspam 65 ma-la il-ḳu-u 66 a-du III-šu a-na tamkarim 67 i-na-ad-di-in

55 ثُمَّ سَمَلْمْ 56 كَسْفَمْ إتي تَمْكَارِمْ 57 يلْقِيمَ 58 تَمْكَارِ ذو 59 يتّكِرْ 60 تَمْكَارُمْ ذوو 61 إنَ مَخَرْ إلِمْ [علِمْ] و ثِبي [شَيبِ] 62 إنَ كَسْفِمْ لِقِيمْ 63 سَمَلَّمْ يُكَنْمَ 64 سَملُمْ كَسْفَمْ 65 مَلاْ إلْقُوَ 66 عدو 3–ذو أنَ تَمْكَارِمْ 67 يندِنْ

بعد ان (اذا) مُتَعَهّد يلقي (يأخذ) فضة مع (من) متاجر، (و) يتنكّر (الى) متاجره، هذا المتاجر سوف يُجْلِس (يستدعي) المُتَعَهّد في امام إله وشهود في أخذ الفضة، المُتَعَهّد سوف يعطي الى المتاجر 3 أضعاف كامل (بقدر) (ما) أخذ (من) الفضة.

If (after) a jobber takes silver with (from) a merchant, (and) denies (to) his merchant, this merchant shall seat [call] in the jobber in front of a god and the witnesses in the money taking, the jobber shall give to the merchant 3 fold the full (amount) silver he took.

§ 107.—XVII, 68-XVIII, 14

68 šum-ma tamkarum 69 šamallâm i-ḳi-ip-ma 70 šamallûm mi-im-ma 71 ša tamkarum id-di-nu-šum 72 a-na tamkari-šu XVIII, 1 ut-te-ir 2 tamkarum mi-im-ma 3 ša šamallûm 4 id-di-nu-šum 5 it-ta-ki-ir-šu 6 šamallûm šu-u 7 i-na ma-ḫar i-lim ᵇu ši-bi 8 tamkaram u-ka-an-ma 9 tamkarum ᵇaš-šum šamallî-šu 10 ik-ki-ru 11 mi-im-ma ᵇša il-ḳu-u 12 a-du VI-šu 13 a-na šamallîm 14 i-na-ad-di-in

68 ثُمَّ تَمْكَارُمْ 69 سَمَلَّمْ يقِفْمَ 70 سَملُمْ مِمَّ 71 ذا تَمْكَارُمْ إدِنْ ذُومْ 72 أنَ تَمْكَارِ ذو 1 يُتِئرْ 2 تَمْكَارُمْ مِمَّ 3 ذا سَملَّمْ 4 إدِنْ ذُومْ 5 يتّكِرْ ذو 6 سَملُّمْ ذوو 7 إنَ مَخَرْ إلِمْ [علِم] و ثِبي [شَيبِ] 8 تَمْكَارَمْ يكَنْمَ 9 تَمْكَارُمْ هَذُمْ سَملِّ ذو 10 إكِرْ 11 مِمَّ ذا إلْقُوَ 12 عدو 6–ذو 13 أنَ سَملَّمْ 14 يندِنْ

بعد ان (اذا) متاجر يصطفي (ينتقي) مُتَعَهّد، (و) المُتَعَهّد يعيد الى متاجره ايّ ما أعطاه المتاجر، (ثم) المتاجر، أيّ ما أعطاه المُتَعَهّد، يتنكره (ينكره)، هذا المُتَعَهّد سوف يُجْلِس (يستدعي) المتاجر أمام إله وشهود، والمتاجر سوف يعطي 6 أضعاف أيّ ما أخذ الى المُتَعَهّد، هذا لانه تنكر (نكر الى) مُتَعَهّده.

If (after) a merchant selects a jobber, (and) the jobber returns to the merchant whatever that the jobber gave him, (then) the merchant, whatever the jobber gave him, he retreats on it (denies it), that jobber shall seat [call] in the merchant in front of the a god and witnesses, and the merchant shall give 6 fold whatever he took to the jobber, that is because he denied (to) his jobber.

§ 108.—XVIII, 15-25

15 šum-ma ŠAL.GEŠ.TIN.NA 16 a-na šîm šikarim 17 še'am la im-ta-ḫar 18 i-na abnim ᵇra-bi-tim 19 kaspam im-ta-ḫar 20 u KI.LAM šikarim 21 a-na KI.LAM še'im ᵇum-ta-di 22 ŠAL.GEŠ.TIN.NA ᵇšu-a-ti 23 u-ka-an-nu-ši-ma 24 a-na me-e 25 i-na-[ad]-du-u-ši

15 ثُمَّ سَعَلْ [شَهلْ] جَعَتّنَ [جَسْتِنَ] 16 أنَ سيمْ سِكَارِمْ 17 سَعَمْ [شَعَمْ] لا يمتَخرْ 18 إنَ أبْنِمْ ربيتِمْ 19 كَسفَمْ يمتَخرْ 20 و كيلَمْ سِكَارِمْ 21 أنَ كيلَمْ سَعِمْ [شَعِمْ] يُمْتَدي [يَبْتَدي] [يُمْتَطي] [يُمْتَعطي] 22 سَعَلْ [شَهلْ] جَعَتِّنَ [جَسْتِنَ] ذَأتِ 23 يُكَنو ذِيمَ 24 أنَ مئي 25 يندُو ذي

بعد ان (اذا) إمرأة [عجوزة] نبيذ (خمّارة) لا تختار (لا تقبل) حبوب لشراء (مقابل شراء) مشروب (كحولي)، تختار (تقبل) فضة في الذروة العالية (سوق الطلب العالي)، وتُبَدّدْ (تْشَتت) [تُقَلّلْ] معيار (قيمة) المشروب (الكحولي) الى (وفق) معيار (قيمة) الحبوب، تلك الخمّارة سوف يُجلسوها [يستدعوها]، (و) سوف يرموها [يَدعونها] في الماء.

If (after) an alewife does not accept grains for alcohol drink purchase, she accepts silver in the high peak (high demand market), and she scatters [reduces] the scale (the value) of alcohol drink to the scale (the value) of grains, that alewife, they shall seat [call] her in, (and) shall throw [let go] her in the water.

§ 109.—XVIII, 26-35

26 šum-ma ŠAL.GEŠ.TIN.NA 27 ṣa-ar-ru-tum 28 i-na bîti-ša 29 it-tar-ka-zu-ma 30 ṣa-ar-ru-tim [b]šu-nu-ti 31 la iṣ-ṣa-ab-[b]tam-ma 32 a-na êkallim 33 la ir-di-a-am 34 ŠAL.GEŠ.TIN.NA [b]ši-i 35 id-da-ak

26 ثُمَّ سَعَلْ [شَهلْ] جَعَتَّن [جَسْتِنَ] 27 صَروتُمْ [ضَروتُمْ] 28 إنَ بيت ذا 29 يترَكَزَم [يتَرْكَسَمَ] 30 صَروتَمْ [ضَروتَمْ] ذونوتِ 31 لا يضَبْطَم
32 أنَ هيكَلِمْ 33 لا يرْدِيَمْ 34 سَعَلْ [شَهلْ] جَعَتَّن [جَسْتِنَ] ذيي 35 يدَكْ

بعد ان (اذا) إمرأة [عجوزة] نبيذ (خمّارة) يتَجمعو في بيتها مجرمين، (و) لا تضبط (تحجز) هؤلاء المجرمين، (و) لا تُعيد الى القصر، هذه الخمّارة سوف تُقْتَلْ.

If (after) an alewife, outlaws gather in her home, (and) she does not hold these outlaws, (and) does not bring back to the palace, this alewife shall be put to death.

§ 110.—XVIII, 36-44

36 šum-ma aššatum NIN.AN 37 ša i-na MAL.GE.A 38 la wa-aš-ba-at 39 bît GEŠ.TIN.NA [b]ip-te-te 40 u lu a-na šikarim 41 a-na bît GEŠ.TIN.NA 42 i-te-ru-ub 43 a-wi-il-tam [b]šu-a-ti 44 i-ḳal-lu-u-ši

36 ثُمَّ أسْتَمْ نِن عَنْ 37 ذا إنَ مَلْجِئا 38 لا وَثْبَتْ 39 بيت سَعَلْ [شَهلْ] جَعَتَّن [جَسْتِنَ] يفْتَتِح [يفْتَتِي] 40 ولو أنَ سِكارِمْ 41 أنَ بيت سَعَلْ
[شَهلْ] جَعَتَّن [جَسْتِنَ] 42 يتأرَبْ 43 أولِتَم [عولِتَم] ذأتِ 42 يقلُو ذي

بعد ان (اذا) الإمرأة (المتزوجة) الكاهنة التي في ملجأها لا (غير) مقيمة تفتح بيت خمّارة، و(حتى) لو تدخل (طلبا للمساعدة) الى بيت خمّارة لمشروب (كحولي) (لعمل مشروب كحولي)، تلك الشخصة [الإمرأة]، سوف يقلوها (يحرقوها).

If (after) a priestess (married) woman, who is not residing in her sanctuary, opens an alewife house and (even) let-it-be she enters (seeking help) to an alewife house to (for) alcohol drink (to make alcohol drink), that (female) person [woman], they shall burn her.

§ 111.—XVIII, 45-49

45 šum-ma ŠAL.GEŠ.TIN.NA 46 LX ḲA šikarim U.SA.KA.NI 47 a-na di-ib-tim id-di-in 48 i-na ebûrim 49 L ḲA še'im i-li-ḳi

45 ثُمَّ سَعَلْ [شَهلْ] جَعَتَّن [جَسْتِنَ] 46 60 قا سِكارِمْ يُسكَن 47 أنَ دِبْتِم [دِفتِمْ] يدِنْ 48 إنَ حبْرِمْ 49 50 قا سعِمْ [شعِمْ] يلِقي

بعد ان (اذا) إمرأة [عجوزة] نبيذ (خمّارة) تضع 60 قا (دلو) مشروب (كحولي)، تعطي للجانب (للخزن)، سوف تلقي (تأخذ) 50 قا (دلو) حبوب في (موسم) الثمار (الحصاد).

If (after) an alewife sets (puts) 60 Qa (buckets) of alcohol, gives (them) to (for) the side (for reserve), she shall take 50 Qa (buckets) of grains in (at) harvest (time).

§ 112.—XVIII, 50-74

50 šum-ma a-wi-lum 51 i-na ḫar-ra-nim 52 wa-ši-ib-ma 53 kaspam ḫurâṣam abnam 54 u bi-iš ga-ti-šu 55 a-na a-wi-lim 56 id-di-in-ma 57 a-na ši-bu-ul-tim 58 u-ša-bil-šu 59 a-wi-lum šu-u 60 mi-im-ma ša šu-bu-lu 61 a-šar šu-bu-lu 62 la id-[di-]in-ma 63 it-ba-al 64 be-el ši-bu-ul-tim 65 a-wi-lam šu-a-ti 66 i-na mi-im-ma 67 ša šu-bu-lu-ma 68 la id-di-nu 69 u-ka-an-nu-šu-ma 70 a-wi-lum šu-u 71 a-du V-šu mi-im-ma 72 ša in-na-ad-nu-šum 73 a-na be-el [b]ši-bu-ul-tim 74 i-na-ad-di-in

50 ثُمّ أويلُم [عَويلُم] 51 إنَ حرانِمْ 52 وثبَم 53 كسْفَمْ خُراصَمْ أبْنَمْ 54 وبيذْ جتي ذو [قتي ذو] 55 أنَ أويلِم [عَويلِم] 56 يدنَمْ 57 أنَ سبْلْتِمْ 58 يُسبِلْ ذو 59 أويلُم [عَويلُم] ذوو 60 مِمّ ذا سُبُلْ 61 أشرْ سُبُلْ 62 لا يدنَمْ 63 يتْبلْ 64 بعَلْ سبْلْتِمْ 65 أويلَم [عَويلَم] ذأتَ 66 إنَ مِمّ 67 ذا سُبُلَمْ 68 لا إدِنُ 69 يُكَنْ ذُومَ 70 أويلُم [عَويلُم] ذوو 71 عدو 5-ذو مِمّ 72 إندْنو ذُومْ 73 أن بَعَلْ سبْلْتِمْ 74 ينَدِنْ

بعد ان (اذا) شخص [رجل] جالس (قائم) برحلة، (و)يعطي فضة، ذهب [حُلي]، احجار كريمة وممتلكات يده (ممتلكاته اليدوية) الى شخص [رجل]، (و)ينقلها لنقلية (كنقلية)؛ هذا الشخص [الرجل] لا يعطي (و) يأخذ أياً ما نُقِلْ حيث نُقِلْ؛ مالك النقلية، (لـ)ذلك الشخص [الرجل]، سوف يُجلسه (يستدعيه) في (بخصوص) أي ما نُقِلْ (و) لا أعطى، (و) هذا الشخص [الرجل] سوف يعطي 5 اضعاف أيّ شيء أعطاه الى مالك النقلية.

If (after) a person [a man] sitting (involved) in a trip, (and) gives to a person [a man] silver, gold [jewelry], and his hand (portable) goods [possessions], (and) he transports them to (as) transported goods (cargo); that person [man] does not give (back) (and) take whatever (was) transported wherever (was) transported; the owner of the cargo, (to) that person [man], he shall seat [call] in (regard to) whatever (was) transported (and) he did not give (back), (and) that person [man] shall give (back) 5 fold whatever he gave him to the owner of the transported goods.

§ 113.—XVIII, 75-XIX, 16

75 šum-ma a-wi-lum 76 e-li a-wi-lim XIX, 1 še'am u kaspam ^{b}i-šu-ma 2 i-na ba-lum ^{b}be-el še'im 3 i-na na-aš-pa-^{b}ki-im 4 u lu i-na ma-^{b}aš-ka-nim 5 še'am il-te-ḳi 6 a-wi-lam šu-a-ti 7 i-na ba-lum ^{b}be-el šê'im 8 i-na na-aš-pa-ki-im 9 u lu i-na maškanim 10 i-na še'im li-ḳi-im 11 u-ka-an-nu-šu-ma 12 še'am ma-la il-ḳu-u 13 u-ta-ar 14 u i-na mi-im-^{b}ma šum-šu 15 ma-la id-di-nu 16 i-te-el-li

75 ثُمّ أويلُم [عَويلُم] 76 علي أويلِم [عَويلِم] 1 سعَمْ [شعَمْ] و كسفَمْ يذوم 2 إنَ بلُمْ بعَلْ سعِمْ [شعِمْ] 3 إنَ نسْفكِمْ [مَسْفكِمْ] 4 ولو إن مَسْكنِمْ 5 سعَمْ [شعَمْ] يلتقي 6 أويلَم [عَويلَم] ذأت 7 إنَ بلَمْ بعَلْ سعِمْ [شعِمْ] 8 إنَ نسْفكِمْ [مَسْفكِمْ] 9 ولو إن مَسْكنِمْ 10 إنَ سعِمْ [شعِمْ] لِقيم 11 يُكنو ذُومَ 12 سعَمْ [شعَمْ] ملأ إلْقوُ 13 يُتأرْ 14 و إنَ مِمّ سُمْ ذو 15 ملأ إدِنُ 16 يتعلّي

بعد ان (اذا) شخص [رجل] يملك على شخصٍ [رجلٍ] (طلَبْ) حبوب وفضة، (و) يلقي (يأخذ) حبوب بلا (بدون) (علم) مالك الحبوب في (من) مسفك (مكدس) و(حتى) لو في (من) مخزن، ذلك الشخص سوف يُجلسوه (يستدعوه) في (بخصوص) أخذَ الحبوب بلا (بدون) (علم) مالك الحبوب في (من) مسفك (مكدس) و(حتى) لو في (من) مخزن، سوف يعيد كامل (بقدر) (ما) أخذ (من) حبوب، وسوف يتنازل بكامل (بقدر) (ما) أعطى (من) أيِّ إسمه [من أي شيء].

If (after) a person [a man] have grains and money (hold) over (another) person [man], (and) he takes grains from a shed and (even) let-it-be from storehouse (silo), without (the knowledge of) the owner of the grains, that person [man], they shall seat [call] in (regard to) grains taking from the shed and (even) let-it-be from the storehouse (the silo) without (the knowledge of) the owner of the grains, he shall return the full (amount) he took grains, (and) he shall cede in (give up) (lose) the full (amount) he gave in (of) whatever its name [anything].

§ 114.—XIX, 17-25

17 šum-ma a-wi-lum 18 e-li a-wi-lim 19 še'am u kaspam 20 la i-šu-ma 21 ni-bu-zu ^{b}it-te-bi 22 a-na ni-bu-tim 23 iš-ti-a-at 24 ⅓ ma-na kaspim 25 i-ša-ḳal

17 ثُمّ أويلُم [عَويلُم] 18 علي أويلِم [عَويلِم] 19 سعَمْ [شعَمْ] و كَسفَمْ 20 لا يذوم 21 نبؤ ذو [نبؤتْ] يتبئي 22 أنَ نبؤتِم 23 إسْتيات 24 1\3 منا كَسفِمْ 25 يثقَلْ

بعد ان (اذا) شخص [رجل] لا يملك على شخصٍ [رجلٍ] (طلَبْ) حبوب وفضة، (و) يتباوئ (يعوّض يأخذ) رهينتها، (المباوئ) سوف يَزن (ويعطي) 1\3 رطل فضة للرهينة (عن الرهينة) الواحدة.

If (after) a person [a man] does not have grains and silver (hold) over a (another) person [man], (and) he substitutes (by seizing) its hostage, he (the holder) shall measure (and give) 1/3 Mana (<1 lb.) silver to one (for each) hostage.

§ 115.—XIX, 26-37

26 šum-ma a-wi-lum 27 e-li a-wi-lim 28 še’am u kaspam 29 i-šu-ma 30 ni-bu-zu ib-bi-ma 31 ni-bu-tum 32 i-na bît ne-bi-ša 33 i-na ši-ma-ti-ša 34 im-tu-ut 35 di-nu-um šu-u 36 ru-gu-um-ma-am 37 u-ul i-šu

26 ثمَّ أويلم [عَويلم] 27 علي أويلم [عويلم] 28 سعمْ [شعَمْ] و كسفمْ 29 يذومْ 30 نبؤ ذو [نبؤتْ] يبئيم 31 نبؤتمْ 32 إنَ بيت نبئي ذا 33 إنَ سمتَ ذا 34 يمتُتْ 35 دينمْ ذوو 36 رُجمم 37 ألْ يذو

بعد ان (اذا) شخص [رجل] يملك على شخصٍ [رجلٍ] (طَلَبْ) حبوب وفضة، (و) يباوئ (يعوّض بأخذ) رهينتها، (و) الرهينة يموت في (وفق) مصيره (يموت طبيعيا) في بيت مرتهنه، قضية (الجزاء) هذه لا تملك (لا تتضمن) غرامة.

If (after) a person [a man] does have grains and silver (hold) over a (another) person [man], (and) he substitutes (by seizing) its hostage, (and) the hostage dies in (according to) his destiny (dies naturally) in his holder’s house, this (court) case does not have fine (penalty).

§ 116.—XIX, 38-53

38 šum-ma ni-bu-tum 39 i-na bît ne-bi-ša 40 i-na ma-ḫa-zi-im 41 u lu i-na uš-bšu-ši-im 42 im-tu-ut 43 be-el ni-bu-tim 44 tamkari-šu 45 u-ka-an-ma 46 šum-ma mâr a-wi-lim 47 mâr-šu i-du-uk-ku 48 šum-ma warad a-wi-lim 49 ⅓ ma-na kaspim 50 i-ša-ḳal 51 u i-na mi-im-ma bšum-šu 52 ma-la id-di-nu 53 i-te-el-li

38 ثمَّ نبؤتمْ 39 إنَ بيت نبئي ذا 40 إنَ محزمْ 41 ولو إنَ أشْشمْ 42 يمتُتْ 43 بعَلَ نبؤتمْ 44 تمكار ذو 45 يكنمْ 46 ثمَّ مأرْ أويلم [عويلم] 47 مأرْ ذو يدكو 48 ثمَّ وردْ أويلم [عويلم] 49 1\3 منا كسفم 50 يثقلْ 51 و إنَ مم سمْ ذو 52 ملأ إدنْ 53 يتعلّي

|وفق الفقرة 115| بعد ان (اذا) الرهينة يموت في بيت مُرتهنه في (من) الشدّة (شدة الأخذ)، و(حتى) لو في (من) التهيج (الإنفعال)، مالك الرهينة سوف يُجلس (يستدعي) متاجره (مُقرضه المُرتهن)؛ بعد ان (اذا) (الرهينة) ابن شخص [رجل]، سوف يُقتل إبنه (ابن المُقرِض المُرتهن)؛ بعد ان (اذا) (الرهينة) عبد شخص [رجل]، (المُقرِض المُرتهن) سوف يَزن (ويعطي) (الى المالك) 1\3 رطل فضة (للرهينة الواحدة)، (و) سوف يتنازل بكامل (بقدر) (ما) أعطى (من) أيٍ إسمه [من أي شيء] .

|Referencing §115| If (after) the hostage dies in the house of his holder in (from) the harshness (of seizing), or (even) let-it-be (from) the overexcitement (the worry), the owner of the hostage shall seat [call in] his merchant (the lender/holder); if (after) (the hostage is) a son of a person [a man], his son (the son of the merchant) shall be put to death; if (after) (the hostage is) a slave of a person [a man], he (the merchant) shall measure (and give) (to the owner) 1/3 Mana (<1 lb.) silver, and he shall cede in (give up) (lose) the full (amount) he gave (of) whatever its name [anything].

§ 117.—XIX, 54-67

54 šum-ma a-wi-lam 55 e-ḫi-il-tum 56 iṣ-ba-zu-ma 57 aššа-zu mâr-šu bu mâra-zu 58 a-na kaspim bid-di-in 59 u lu a-na ki-iš-bša-a-tim 60 it-ta-an-di-in 61 šattam IIIkam 62 bît ša-a-a-ma-bni-šu-nu 63 u ka-ši-ši-šu-nu 64 i-ib-bi-šu i-na ri-bbu-tim 65 ša-at-tim 66 an-du-ra-ar-šu-nu 67 iš-ša-ak-ka-an

54 ثمَّ أويلَم [عويلم] 55 إهلتمْ 56 يضبطْ ذومَ [يضبطمَ] 57 أسّتْ ذو [أسّتوَ] مأرْ ذو ومأرتوَ 58 أنَ كسفمِ يدنْ 59 ولو أنَ كسأتمْ 60 يتندنْ 61 ستّمْ [سنتمْ] 3كمْ 62 بيت سآمني ذونْ 63 وكسئسِ ذونْ 64 50 يئبشو [يعفشو] [يعفسو] يبئي ذو إنَ ربعتمْ 65 ستّمْ [سنتمِ] 66 أندرر ذونْ [أدُّررْ ذونْ] 67 يسكنْ

بعد ان (اذا) شخص [رجل] يضْبَطْه (يمسكه) التزام (قانوني) (دَيْن)، (و) يعطي لفضة (يبيع) إمرأته (زوجته)، إبنه، وبنته، و(حتى) لو يعطي للخدمة، سوف يؤدو عمل بيت مُشتَريهم ومُطالبِهِمْ (مُستَخدِمِهم) ثلاث سنوات، في السنة الرابعة سوف يُقَرْ (يتم) تحررهم.

If (after) a person [a man], a (legal) obligation (debt) holds him (he is in debt), (and) he gives to (for) silver (sells) his woman (wife), his son, and his daughter, and (even) let-it-be he gives for service; they shall conduct the work of (shall service) the house of their buyer and their demander (holder) three years, in the fourth year their freedom shall be set.

§ 118.—XIX, 68-73

68 šum-ma wardam u lu amtam 69 a-na ki-iš-ša-tim 70 it-ta-an-di-in 71 tamkarum u-še-ti-iḳ 72 a-na kaspim i-na-ad-din 73 u-ul ib-ba-gar

68 ثُمَّ وردُمْ ولو أمْتَمْ 69 أنَ كِسأتِمْ 70 يتَنْدِنْ 71 تَمكارُمْ يُسأتِقْ [يَتأتِقْ] 72 أنَ كَسفِمْ يندِنْ 73 أُل يبجَر [يفجَرْ] [يبقَرْ]

|وفق الفقرة 117| بعد ان (اذا) يعطي عبد و(حتى) لو عبدة للخدمة، (ثم) المتاجر يتّقي (يستبدل)، يعطي للفضة (يبيع العبد او العبدة)، سوف لن يُنازَعْ (يُقاضى) (عليه).

|Referencing §117| If (after) he gives to (for) silver a male slave, and (even) let-it-be a female slave, (if) the merchant exchanges, gives (the slaves) for money (sells them), he shall not be contended (legally challenged) (for).

§ 119.—XIX, 74- XX, 3

74 šum-ma a-wi-lam 75 e-ḫi-il-tum 76 iṣ-ba-zu-ma 77 ama-zu ša mârê ul-du-šum 78 a-na kaspim it-ta-din XX, 1 kaspam tamkarum [b]iš-ḳu-lu 2 be-el amtim [b]i-ša-ḳal-ma 3 ama-zu [b]i-pa-dar

74 ثُمَّ أويلَم [عَويلَم] 75 إهِلتُمْ 76 يضبَطْ ذُومَ [يضبَطمَ] 77 أما ذو [أمتُ] مأري أُلدو ذُومْ 78 أنَ كَسفِمْ يتَدِنْ 1 كَسفَمْ تَمكارُمْ إثْقُلو 2 بَعَل أمتِمْ يثَقلَمَ 3 أما ذو [أمتُ] يفدَرْ [يفدَنْ]

بعد ان (اذا) شخص [رجل] يضْبَطْه (يمسكه) التزام (قانوني) (عليه دَيْن)، (و) يعطي للفضة (يبيع) عبدَته (التي) ولدت له أولاد، مالك العبدة سوف يَزِن (ويعطي) الفضة (التي) وَزَنَ (واعطى) (له) المتاجر، (كي) يفتدي عبدته.

If (after) a person [a man], a (legal) obligation (debt) holds him (he is in debt), (and) he gives to (for) silver (sells) his female slave (who) has borne him children, the owner of the female slave shall measure (and give) the silver (that) the merchant measured (and gave) (him), to rdeem his female slave.

§ 120.—XX, 4-23

4 šum-ma a-wi-lum 5 še'i-šu a-na na-aš-[b]pa-ku-tim 6 i-na bît a-wi-lum 7 iš-pu-uk-ma 8 i-na ga-ri-tim 9 i-ib-bu-u-um [b]it-tab-ši 10 u lu be-el bîtim 11 na-aš-pa-kam [b]ip-te-ma 12 še'am il-ḳi 13 u lu še'am [b]ša i-na bîti-šu 14 iš-ša-ap-ku 15 a-na ga-am-ri-im 16 it-ta-ki-ir 17 be-el še'im [b]ma-ḫar i-lim 18 še'i-šu u-ba-ar-ma 19 be-el bîtim 20 še'am ša il-ḳu-u 21 uš-ta-ša-na-ma 22 a-na be-el še'im 23 i-na-ad-di-in

4 ثُمَّ أويلُم [عَويلُم] 5 سَعي ذو [شَعي ذو] أنَ نَسفَكتِمْ [مَسفَكتِمْ] 6 إنَ بيت أويلُم [عويلُم] 7 يسفُكَمْ 8 إنَ جريّتِمْ [قَريّتِمْ] 9 إبؤمْ يتَبْذي [يتَبْثي] 10 ولو بَعَلْ بيتِمْ 11 نَسفَكمَ يفتَحمَ [يفتَيمَ] 12 سَعَمْ [شَعَمْ] يلقي 13 ولو سعَمْ [شعَمْ] ذا إنَ بيت ذو 14 إسفَكو 15 أنَ جمرِمْ 16 يتّكرْ 17 بَعَلْ سعِمْ [شعِمْ] مخَرْ إلِمْ [علِمْ] 18 سعي ذو [شعي ذو] يُبَرَّمَ 19 بَعَلْ بيتِمْ 20 سعَمْ [شعَمْ] ذا إلقُوَ 21 يُستَثنَمَ [يُتَثَّنَمَ] 22 أنَ بَعَلْ سعِمْ [شعِمْ] 23 ينَدِنْ

بعد ان (اذا) شخص [رجل] يكدّس حبوبه للتكديس (للخزن) في بيت شخص [رجل]، (و) يتواجَد [يظهر] في المَجْمع (المخزن) تعويض (إستبدال حبوب)، ولو (وليكن) أن يفتح مالك البيت المَسفك (المكدس)، (و) يلقي (يأخذ) حبوب، ولو (وليكن) أن يتنكر لمجموع (كمية) الحبوب التي كدّسَ في بيته، مالك الحبوب سوف يُصدّق أمام إله (كمية) حبوبه، (و) مالك البيت سوف يضاعف (كمية) الحبوب التي أخذَ، (و) يعطي الى مالك الحبوب.

If (after) a person [a man] piles his grains for piling (storage) in the house of (another) person [man], (and) a (grains) substitution exists [appears] in the storehouse, and (even) let-it-be that the owner of the house opens the shed, (and) takes grains, and (even) let-it-be that he denies to (about) the total amount of the grains that he piled in his house, the owner of the grains shall confirm in front of a god (the amount of) his grains, the owner of the grains shall double (the amount of) the grains that he took, (and) give to the owner of the grains.

§ 121.—XX, 24-30

24 šum-ma a-wi-lum 25 i-na bît a-wi-lim 26 še'am iš-pu-uk 27 i-na ša-na-at 28 a-na I ŠE.GUR.E bV ḲA še'im 29 ID na-aš-pa-ki-im 30 i-na-ad-di-in

24 ثُمَّ أويلُم [عَويلُم] 25 إنَ بيت أويلِم [عويلِم] 26 سعَمْ [شعَمْ] يسْفُكْ 27 إنَ سنَتْ 28 أنَ 1 سعِ [شعِ] جُرِ [كُرِ] 5 قا سعَمْ [شعَمْ] 29 عِدْ نَسْفكِمْ 30 يندِنْ

بعد ان (اذا) شخص [رجل] يكدّس حبوب في بيت شخص [رجل]، سوف يعطي 5 قا (دلو) حبوب لكُرِّ الحبوب الواحد في السنة (ل)حساب (ايجار) مَسفك (مَكدس).

If (after) a person [a man] piles grains in the house of (another) person [man], he shall give 5 Qa (buckets) of grains per one Kur of grains (stored) in a year (for) shed (rent) rate,.

§ 122.—XX, 31-43

31 šum-ma a-wi-lum 32 a-na a-wi-lim 33 kaspam ḫurâṣam 34 u mi-im-ma šum-šu 35 a-na ma-ṣa-ru-tim 36 i-na-ad-di-in 37 mi-im-ma ma-la 38 i-na-ad-di-nu 39 ši-bi u-kal-lam 40 ri-ik-sa-tim 41 i-ša-ak-ka-an-ma 42 a-na ma-ṣa-ru-tim 43 i-na-ad-di-in

31 ثُمْ أويلُم [عَويلُم] 32 أنَ أويلِم [عَويلِم] 33 كسفُمْ خُراصَمْ 34 ومِمّ سمْ ذو 35 أنَ مصرتِم [نصرَتِمْ] 36 يندِنْ 37 مِمّ ملأْ 38 إندِنْ 39 ثِبي [شيبِ] يُكلِّمْ 40 رِكستِمْ 41 يسكنمْ 42 أنَ مصرتِم [نصرَتِمْ] 43 يندِنْ

بعد ان (اذا) شخص [رجل] يعطي الى شخص [رجل] فضة، ذهب [حُلي] وأيا (كان) إسمه [أي شيء كان] للحفظ (للإتمان)، كامل (بقدر) (ما) أعطى (من) أيٍ (من اي شيء)، سوف يُريهُنْ (الى) شهود، يضع عقد، (و) يعطي للحفظ (للإتمان).

If (after) a person [a man] gives to a person [a man] silver, gold [jewelry], and whatever its name (and anything else), for safe-keeping , the full (amount) he gave (of) anything, he shall show to witnesses, establish a contract, (and) give for safe-keeping.

§ 123.—XX, 44-52

44 šum-ma ba-lum ši-bi 45 u ri-ik-sa-tim 46 a-na ma-ṣa-ru-tim 47 id-di-in-ma 48 a-šar id-di-nu 49 it-ta-ak-ru-šu 50 di-nu-um šu-u 51 ru-gu-um-ma-am 52 u-ul i-šu

44 ثُمّ بَلُمْ ثِبي [شيبِ] 45 و رِكْستِمْ 46 أنَ مصرتِم [نصرتِمْ] 47 يدِنمْ 48 أشرَ إدِنْ 49 يتكرْ ذو 50 دينُمْ ذوو 51 رُجْمَمْ 52 أُلْ يذو

|وفق الفقرة 122| بعد ان (اذا) يعطي بلا (بدون) شهود وعقد للحفظ (للإتمان)، (و) حيثُ أعطى يتنكروه (ينكروه)، قضية (الجزاء) هذه لا تملك (لا تتضمن) غرامة.

|Referencing §122| If (after) he gives without witnesses and contract for safe-keeping, (and) where he gave, they they deny it (on him), this (court) case does not have fine (penalty).

§ 124.—XX, 53-65

53 šum-ma a-wi-lum 54 a-na a-wi-lim 55 kaspam ḫurâṣam 56 u mi-im-ma šum-šu 57 ma-ḫar ši-bi 58 a-na ma-ṣa-ru-tim 59 id-di-in-ma 60 it-ta-ki-ir-šu 61 a-wi-lam šu-a-ti 62 u-ka-an-nu-šu-ma 63 mi-im-ma [b]ša ik-ki-ru 64 uš-ta-ša-na-ma 65 i-na-ad-di-in

53 ثمّ أويلم [عويلم] 54 أنَ أويلم [عويلم] 55 كسفم خراصم 56 وممّ سمْ ذو 57 مخرْ ثبي [شيبِ] 58 أنَ مصرتمْ [نصرتِم] 59 يدنمْ 60 يتكّرْ ذو 61 أويلم [عويلم] ذأتِ 62 يكنو ذومَ 63 ممّ ذا إكرْ 64 يستثنمَ [يتّثنم] 65 يندنْ

بعد ان (اذا) شخص [رجل] يعطي الى شخص [رجل] فضة، ذهب [حُلي]، وأيا (كان) إسمه [أي شيء كان] أمام شهود للحفظ (للإتمان)، (و) (الشخص [الرجل]) يتنكّره (ينكر له)، ذلك الشخص [الرجل] سوف يُجلسوه [يستدعوه]، (و) أيّ ما أنكرَ سوف يثنّي (يُضاعف)، (و) يعطي.

If (after) a person [a man] gives to (another) person [man] silver, gold [jewelry], and whatever its name (anything it was), in front of witnesses, for safe-keeping, (and) he denies (to) him, that same person [man], they shall seat [call] him, (and) whatever he retreated on (denied) he shall double, (and) give.

§ 125.—XX, 66-XXI, 7

66 šum-ma a-wi-lum 67 mi-im-ma-šu 68 a-na ma-ṣa-ru-tim id-[b]di-in-ma 69 a-šar id-di-nu 70 u lu i-na bi-[b]il-ši-im 71 u lu i-na na-ba- 72 al-ka-at-tim 73 mi-im-mu-šu 74 it-ti mi-im-me-e 75 be-el bîtim iḫ-ta-li-iḳ [b]be-el bîtim ša i-gu-ma 76 mi-im-ma ša a-na 77 ma-ṣa-ru-tim [b]id-di-nu-šum-ma 78 u-ḫal-li-ḳu 79 u-ša-lam-ma XXI. 1 a-na be-el ŠA-GA 2 i-ri-a-ab 3 be-el bîtim 4 mi-im-ma-šu [b]ḫal-ga-am 5 iš-te-ne-i-ma 6 it-ti šar-ra-[b]ga-ni-šu 7 i-li-ḳi

66 ثمّ أويلم [عويلم] 67 ممّ ذو 68 أن مصرتمْ [نصرتمْ] يدنمْ 69 أشرْ إدنْ 70 ولو إن بلشمْ [فلشمْ] 71–72 ولو إن نبلكتمْ 73 ممّ ذو 74 إتي ممّي 75 بعلْ بيتمْ يحتلقْ بعلْ بيتمْ ذا إجوْم [إهجعْم] 76 ممّ ذا أن 77 مصرتمْ [نصرتمْ] إدنْ ذومَ 78 أُحلقْ 79 يُسلمَ 1 أنَ بعلْ شجا 2 يرأبْ 3 بعلْ بيتمْ 4 ممّ ذو حلجمْ [حلقمْ] 5 يستنأيمَ [يتنأيمَ] 6 إتي سرجنِ ذو [سرقنِ ذو] 7 يلقي

بعد ان (اذا) شخص [رجل] يعطي أيا من أشياءه للحفظ (للإتمان) (الى مالك بيت)، (و) حيث أعطى، و(حتى) لو في اختراق (سطو)، و(حتى) لو في احداث نهب، يفْقدْ أي من اشياءه مع أيّ من أشياء مالك البيت، مالك البيت الذي تقاعس (اهمل) سوف يُأمن اي ما أعطوه للحفظ (للإتمان) (و) فَقَد، (و) سوف يُسدد (يعوض) الى مالك الحاجيات؛ مالك البيت سوف يتعقّب ايا من أشياءه المفقودة، (و) يلقي مع (يأخذ من) سارقه.

If (after) a person [a man] gives anything of his for safe-keeping (to a house owner), (and) where he gave, and (even) let-it-be in a breach (break in), and (even) let-it-be in a riot, he loses anything of his with anything of the house owner, the house owner who neglected shall secure (guarantee) anything he was given for safe-keeping, (and anything) he lost, (and) shall repay (replace) to the owners of the things (belongings); the house owner shall pursue anything of his lost, to find with (take from) his thieve.

§ 126.—XXI, 8-24

8 šum-ma a-wi-lum 9 mi-im-mu-šu 10 la ḫa-li-iḳ-ma 11 mi-im-[me]-šu 12 ḫa-li-[iḳ] [b]iḳ-ta-bi 13 ba-ab-ta-šu 14 u-te-ib-bi-ir 15 ki-ma mi-im-mu-šu 16 la ḫal-ḳu 17 ba-ab-ta-šu 18 i-na ma-ḫar i-lim 19 u-ba-ar-šu-ma 20 mi-im-ma 21 ša ir-gu-mu 22 uš-ta-ša-na-ma 23 a-na ba-ab-ti-šu 24 i-na-ad-di-in

8 ثمْ أويلمْ [عويلمْ] 9 ممّ ذو 10 لا حلقمْ 11 ممّي ذو 12 حلقْ يقتبي 13 ببْتَ ذو 14 يُتعبرْ 15 كيمَ ممّ ذو 16 لا حلقْ 17 ببْتَ ذو 18 إنَ مخرْ إلمْ [علِم] 19 يُبرْ ذومَ 20 ممّ 21 ذا إرْجمَ 22 يُستثنمَ [يتّثنمَ] 23 أنَ ببْتِ ذو 24 يندنْ

|وفق الفقرة 125| بعد ان (اذا) الشخص [الرجل] أيّه (أي من أشياءه) غير مفقود، يقول (يدّعي) أي من أشياءه مفقود، يستخرج من (يبْتز) مغفلّه (ضحيته)، كما (بمقدار) أي من أشياءه الغير مفقودة سوف يصدّق له، ضحيته (لضحيته)، أمام إله، (و) سوف يضاعف (قيمة) أي من اشياءه التي غرّم، (و) يعطي الى ضحيته.

|Referencing §125| If (after) a person [a man], anything of his is not lost, says (claims) anything of his is lost, he obtains from (he swindles) his fool (his victim), as much as the non-lost of anything of his, he shall confirm to him, his victim, in front of a god, (and) he shall double whatever he fined (penalized), (and) give to his victim.

§ 127.—XXI, 25-34

25 šum-ma a-wi-lum 26 e-li NIN.AN 27 u aš-ša-at a-wi-lim 28 u-ba-nam ᵇu-ša-at-ri-iṣ-ma 29 la uk-ti-in 30 a-wi-lam šu-a-ti 31 ma-ḫar da-a-a-ni 32 i-na-ad-du-u-šu 33 u mu-ut-ta-zu 34 u-gal-la-bu

25 ثمّ أويلم [عويلم] 26 علي نِنْ عَنْ 27 و أسّتْ عويلمْ 28 أبنَمْ يسترْصَمْ [يتترصّمْ] 29 لا يكتِنْ 30 أويلم [عويلم] ذأتِ 31 مخر دآن 32 يندو ذو 33 و مُتّتْ ذو [مُتتْ] [مطّتْ ذو [مطّتْ]] 34 يجلبو [يُجلفو]

بعد ان (اذا) شخص [رجل] يلصق (تهمة) عار على كاهنة وإمرأة (زوجة) شخص [رجل]، (و) لا يثبت (بالادلة)، ذلك الشخص [الرجل] سوف يرموه [يدعونه] أمام الحكام، و سوف يدمغو (يُعلّمو على) جبينه [يجلفو (يستأصلو)] حاجبه].

If (after) a person [a man] sticks (lays) a (charge of) disgrace on a priestess and a person's [a man's] woman (wife), (and) he does not prove (with evidence), they shall throw [let go] in front of the judges that person [man], and they shall brand (mark) his forehead [scrap off (remove) his eye brow].

§ 128.—XXI, 35-41

35 šum-ma a-wi-lum 36 aš-ša-tam 37 i-ḫu-uz-ma 38 ri-ik-sa-ti-ša 39 la iš-ku-un 40 zinništum ši-i 41 u-ul aš-ša-at

35 ثمّ أويلم [عويلم] 36 أستَمْ 37 يحزمْ 38 ركْستِ ذا 39 لا يسْكنْ 40 ذنِثْتمْ ذي 41 ألْ أستْ

بعد أن (اذا) شخص [رجل] يحوز على (يأخذ) إمرأة (كزوجة)، (و) لا يضع (لها) عقدها، هذه الأنثى ليست زوجة.

If (after) a person [a man] takes a woman (wife), (and) he does not set (her) a contract, that female is not a wife.

§ 129.—XXI, 42-53

42 šum-ma aš-ša-at ᵇa-wi-lim 43 it-ti zi-ka-ri-im 44 ša-ni-im 45 i-na i-tu-lim 46 it-ta-aṣ-bat 47 i-ka-zu-šu-nu-ti-ma 48 a-na me-e 49 i-na-ad-du-u-ᵇšu-nu-ti 50 šum-ma be-el ᵇaš-ša-tim 51 aš-ša-zu u-ba-la-aṭ 52 u šar-ru-um 53 wara-zu u-ba-la-aṭ

42 ثمّ أستْ أويلم [عويلم] 43 إتي ذكرِمْ 44 ثانمْ 45 إنَ إتلمْ 46 إتّضبَطْ 47 يكسعو ذونُتيَم [يكسؤ ذونُتيَم] 48 أنَ مئي 49 يندو ذونُتي 50 ثمّ بَعَل أستِمْ 51 أسّتْ ذو [أسّتْ] يبلطْ 52 و سرّمْ 53 وردْ ذو [ورتْ] يُبلط

بعد ان (اذا) إمرأة (زوجة) شخص [رجل] ضُبطَتْ (مُسكَتْ) في (حالة) تضاجع مع ذكَرْ (رجل) ثاني، سوف يسوقوهما (مُقيدين)، (و) يرموهما [يدعونها] في الماء (النهر)؛ بعد ان (اذا) مالك إمرأة (زوجة)، سوف (يستطع ان) يحْي (ينقذ) إمرأته (زوجته)، و (بعد ان (اذا)) شريف (ملك)، سوف (يستطع ان) يحْي (ينقذ) عبده.

If (after) a woman (a wife) of a person [a man] was caught with another male (man) in a laying down position (having sex), they shall chase them (tied), (and) shall throw [let go] them in the water (the river); if (after) (he is) the owner of the woman (wife) (the husband), he can keep alive (save) his woman (wife), and (if (after)) (he is) a nobel (a royalty), he can keep alive (save) his male slave.

§ 130.—XXI, 54-67

54 šum-ma a-wi-lum 55 aš-ša-at a-wi-lim 56 ša zi-ka-ra-am 57 la i-du-u-ma 58 i-na bît a-bi-ša 59 wa-aš-ba-at 60 u-kab-bil-ši-ma 61 i-na zu-ni-ša 62 it-ta-ti-bil-ma 63 iṣ-ṣa-ab-tu-šu 64 a-wi-lum šu-u 65 id-da-ak 66 zinništum ši-i 67 u-ta-aš-šar

54 ثمَّ أويلم [عويلم] 55 أستْ أويلم [عويلِم] 56 ذا ذكرَمْ 57 لا إدُومَ [إهدُومَ] 58 إنَ بيت أبي ذا 59 وَثْبتْ 60 يُكبلْ ذيمَ 61 إنَ زونِ ذا [ذون ذا] 62 يتتلمَ 63 إضبْطُ ذو 64 أويلم [عويلم] ذوو 65 يدكْ 66 ذنثتْمْ ذيي 67 يُتذَرْ

|وفق الفقرة 129| بعد ان (اذا) شخص [رجل]، (ل)إمرأة (لزوجة) الشخص [الرجل] (الآخر) التي ما عرفت الذكَر (مسبقا) (و)مقيمة في بيت أبيها [زوجها]، يكبلّها (و) يتضاجع بجماعها (بمَعيتها) [في عَيْبِها]، (و) ضبطوه (مسكوه)، هذا الشخص [الرجل] هذا سوف يُقتل، هذه الانثى سوف تُترك (حرة).

|Referencing §129| If (after) a person [a man], (to) the woman (wife) of (another) person [man] who did not know (beforehand) the male (and) was residing in her father's [husband's] house, he holds her (by force) (and) lay down (have sex) in her company [in her private part], (and) they caught him, that person [man] shall be put to death, that female shall be left (free).

§ 131.—XXI, 68-76

68 šum-ma aš-sa-at 69 a-wi-lim 70 mu-za u-ub-bi-bir-ši-ma 71 it-ti zi-ka-ri-im bša-ni-im 72 i-na u-tu-lim 73 la iṣ-ṣa-bi-it 74 ni-iš i-lim 75 i-za-kar-ma 76 a-na bîti-ša i-ta-ar

68 ثمَّ أستْ 69 أويلِم [عويلم] 70 مؤتْ ذا [مؤتا] يؤبرْ ذيمَ 71 إتي ذكرِمْ ثانمْ 72 إنَ أُتْلمْ 73 لا يضبطْ 74 نعشْ إلمْ [علم] 75 يذكَرمَ 76 أنَ بيت ذا يتأرْ

بعد ان (اذا) إمرأة (زوجة) شخص [رجل] يتهمها زوجها، (و) لا يضبط(ها) (يمسك(ها)) في (حالة) تضاجع مع ذكَر (رجل) ثاني، سوف تقول (تحلف) (ببراءتها) برفعة (بحياة) الإله، (و) تعود الى بيتها.

If (after) a woman (a wife) of a person [a man], her husband accuses her, (and) he does not catch (her) in a laying down position (having sex) with another male (man), she shall say (declare) (her innocence) in the glory life of god, (and) she return to her house.

§ 132.—XXI, 77-XXII, 6

77 šum-ma aš-ša-at 78 a-wi-lim 79 aš-šum zi-ka-bri-im ša-ni-im 80 u-ba-nu-um 81 e-li-ša 82 it-ta-ri-iṣ-ma 83 it-ti zi-ka-bri-im XXII, 1 ša-ni-im 2 i-na u-tu-lim 3 la it-ta-aṣ-bba-at 4 a-na mu-ti-ša 5 iluNâram 6 i-ša-al-li

77 ثمَّ أستْ 78 أويلِم [عويلِم] 79 هذمْ ذكرِمْ ثانمْ 80 أبنمْ 81 علي ذا 82 يترصَمْ 83 إتي ذكرِمْ 1 ثانمْ 2 إنَ أُتلمْ 3 لايتَضبْطْ 4 أنَ مؤتي ذا 5 إلنَهرَم 6 يشلئ [يسلِئ]

بعد ان (اذا) إمرأة (زوجة) شخص [رجل]، تَلتصق عليها تهمة عار، هذا لأن (بسبب) ذكَرْ ثاني (آخر)، (و) لا تُضبط (تُمسك) في (حالة) تضاجع مع الذكَر الثاني (الآخر)، سوف تغطس النهر (تمتحن محنة النهر) لزوجها (لسمعة زوجها).

If (after) a woman (a wife) of a person [a man], a charge of disgrace sticks (lays) over her, that is because of a second (another) male (man), (and) she is not caught in a laying down position (having sex) with the second (other) male, she shall dip (into) the river (shall take the river lying test) to (for) her husband (reputation).

§ 133.—XXII, 7-17

7 šum-ma a-wi-lum 8 iš-ša-li-bil-ma 9 i-na bîti-šu 10 ša a-ka-lim 11 i-ba-aš-ši 12 |aš-ša|-zu 13 |i-na bî|-za b|wa-az-za-a|t 14 |pa-gar-š|a 15 |i-na-ṣa-a|r 16 |a-na bîtim ša-ni|-im 17 |u-ul i-ir|-ru-ub

7 ثمَّ أويلم [عَويلم] 8 يسلِلمْ 9 إنَ بيتِ ذو 10 ذا أكلمْ 11 يبذي 12 أستْ ذو [أسْتْ] |13 .... 14 فقرْ ذا 15 ينصرْ 16 أن بيتِم ثانمْ 17 أُلْ| يأرْبْ

بعد ان (اذا) شخص [رجل] يختفي، (و) يملك ما للأكل (متطلبات المعيشة) في بيته، إمرأته (زوجته) |.........|، سوف تحفظ جسدها، سوف لن| تدخل (طلبا للمساعدة) |في بيت ثاني|.

If (after) a person [a man] disappears, (and) he has that of feeding (living necessities) in his house, his wife |..........|, she shall keep (secure) her body, she shall not seek help [she shall not enters (seeking help) in a second (another) home.

§ 133A.—XXII, 18-26

18 š|um-ma| zinništum ši-i 19 |pa|-gar-ša 20 la iṣ-ṣur-ma 21 a-na bîtim ša-ni-im 22 i-te-ru-ub 23 zinništam šu-a-ti 24 u-ka-an-nu-ši-ma 25 a-na me-e 26 i-na-ad-du-u-ši

18 ثمَّ دنِثْتمْ ذيي 19 فقرْ ذا 20 لا يصرمْ 21 أن بيتِم ثانمْ 22 يتأرْبْ 23 دنِثْتمْ ذأتْ 24 يكَنو ذيمَ 25 أنَ مَئي 26 ينَدُو ذي

|وفق الفقرة 133A| بعد ان (اذا) هذه الانثى (الزوجة) لا تحفظ جسدها، تدخل (طلبا للمساعدة) في بيت ثاني، تلك الأنثى (الزوجة) سوف يُجلسوها (يستدعوها)، (و) يرموها [يَدعونها] في الماء (النهر).

|Referencing §133A| If (after) this female did not secure her body, (and) she enters (seeking help) in a second (another) home, that female (wife) they shall seat [call] her in, (and) shall throw [let go] her in the water (river).

§ 134.—XXII, 27-36

27 šum-ma a-wi-lum 28 iš-ša-ᵇli-il-ma 29 i-na bîti-šu 30 ša a-ka-li-im 31 la i-ba-aš-ši 32 aš-ša-zu 33 a-na bîtim ša-ni-im 34 i-ir-ru-ub 35 zinništum ši-i 36 ar-nam ᵇu-ul i-šu

27 ثمَّ أويلم [عَويلم] 28 يسَلِلمْ 29 إنَ بيت ذو 30 ذا أكلِمْ 31 لا يبذي 32 أستْ ذو [أسْتْ] 33 أنَ بيتمْ ثانمْ 34 يأرْبْ 35 دنِثْتمْ ذيي 36 عرْنَمْ [عنَمْ] أُلْ يذو

بعد ان (اذا) شخص [رجل] يختفي، (و) لا يملك ما للأكل (متطلبات المعيشة) في بيته، (ثم) إمرأته (زوجته) تدخل (طلبا للمساعدة) في بيت ثاني، هذه الانثى لا تملك (ليس عليها) تهمة [عقوبة].

If (after) a person [a man] disappears, (and) he does not have that of feeding (living necessities) in his house, (then) his woman (wife) entered (seeking help) in a second (another) home, this female (the wife) does not have (owe) charge [penalty].

§ 135.—XXII, 37-56

37 šum-ma a-wi-lum 38 iš-ša-ᵇli-il-ma 39 i-na bîti-šu 40 ša a-ka-li-im 41 la i-ba-aš-ši 42 a-na pa-ni-šu 43 aš-ša-zu 44 a-na bîtim ša-ni-im 45 i-te-ru-ub-ma 46 mârê ᵇit-ta-la-ad 47 i-na wa-ar-ka 48 mu-za it-tu-ra-ᵇam-ma 49 ali-šu 50 ik-ta-aš-dam 51 zinništum ši-i 52 a-na ḫa-wi-ri-ša 53 i-ta-ar 54 mârê wa-ar-ki 55 a-bi-šu-nu 56 i-il-la-ku

37 ثمَّ أويلم [عَويلم] 38 يسلِلمْ 39 إنَ بيت ذو 40 ذا أكلِمْ 41 لا يبذي 42 أنَ فني ذو 43 أستْ ذو [أسْتْ] 44 أنَ بيتمْ ثانمْ 45 يتأرْبْ 46 مَأري يتلَدْ 47 إنَ وركْ 48 مُؤتْ ذا [مُؤتا] يتؤرَمْ 49 أيلي ذو 50 يقتصْدمْ 51 دنِثْتمْ ذيي 52 أنَ خوري ذا 53 يتأرْ 54 مأري وركْ 55 أبي ذُونْ 56 يئلكو

بعد ان (اذا) شخص [رجل] يختفي، (و) لا يملك في بيته ما للأكل (متطلبات المعيشة)، (ثم) إمرأته (زوجته) تدخل (طلبا للمساعدة) في بيت ثاني، تَلِدْ أبناء، لوجهه (علنا)، فيما بعد زوجها يعود، (و) يقصد أهله (عشيرته)، هذه الانثى سوف تعود الى صفيّها (زوجها)، الأبناء سوف يترسلو (يذهبو) وراء (الى) أبيهم.

If (after) a person [a man] disappears, (and) he does not have in his house that of feeding (living necessities), (then) his woman (wife) enters (seeking help) in a second (another) home, gives birth to (new) children, to his face (openly), hereinafter, her husband returns, (and) arrives (with) his tribe, this female (wife) shall return to her chosen (her first husband), the children go after (to) their father.

§ 136.—XXII, 57-72

57 šum-ma a-wi-lum 58 ali-šu ^{b}id-di-ma 59 it-ta-bi-it 60 wa-ar-ki-šu 61 aš-ša-zu 62 a-na bîtim ša-ni-im 63 i-te-ru-ub 64 šum-ma a-wi-lum ^{b}šu-u 65 it-tu-ra-am-ma 66 aš-ša-zu 67 iṣ-ṣa-ba-at 68 aš-šum ali-šu 69 i-zi-ru-ma 70 in-na-bi-tu ^{b}aš-ša-at mu-na-ab-tim 71 a-na mu-ti-ša 72 u-ul i-ta-ar

57 ثُمَّ أَويلُم [عَويلُم] 58 أيلي ذو يدِّمَ [يدعِم] 59 يتَبِتْ 60 وَرْكِ ذو 61 أستَ 62 أن بيتِم ثانِمْ 63 يتأرُبْ 64 ثُمَّ أويلُم [عويلُم] ذوو 65 يتؤرَم 66 أسَّتْ ذو [أسَّتُ] 67 يضبَطْ 68 هَذوم أيلي ذو 69 إزرُمَ [إزعِرُمَ] 70 إنبتْ أسّتْ منَبتِمْ 71 أنَ مُؤتي ذا 72 أُلْ يتأر

بعد ان (اذا) شخص [رجل] يَدَعْ (يهمل) أهله، (و) ينقطع (يهجر)، وراءه (بعده) إمرأته (زوجته) تدخل (طلبا للمساعدة) في بيت ثاني؛ بعد ان (اذا) هذا الشخص [الرجل] يعود، (كي) يضبط (يمسك) إمرأته (زوجته)، إمرأة (زوجة) المنقطع (الهاجر) سوف لن تعود الى زوجها، هذا لأن (الشخص [الرجل]) إزدرى [أساء معاملة] أهله (و) قاطَعَ (هَجرَ).

If (after) a person [a man] let go (neglects) (and) abandons his family, after him, his woman (wife) enters (seeking help) in a second (another) home, if (after) this person [the man] returns, to catch (hold) his woman (wife), the woman (wife) of the abandoner shall not return to her husband, that is because he scorned [mistreated] his family (and) abandoned,

§ 137.—XXII, 73-XXIII, 13

73 šum-ma a-wi-lum 74 a-na ^{sal}šu-ge-tim 75 ša mârê ul-du-šum ^{b}u lu aššatim ša mârê 76 u-šar-šu-šu 77 e-ṣi-bi-im 78 pa-ni-šu 79 iš-ta-ka-an 80 a-na zinništim šu-a-ti 81 še-ri-iḳ-ta-ša 82 u-ta-ar-ru-ši-im 83 u mu-ut-ta-at 84 eḳlim kirêm u bi-ši-im XXIII, 1 i-na-ad-di-nu-^{b}ši-im-ma 2 mârê-ša 3 u-ra-ab-ba 4 iš-tu mârê-ša 5 ur-ta-ab-bu-u 6 i-na mi-im-ma 7 ša a-na mârê-ša 8 in-na-ad-nu 9 ṣi-it-tam 10 ki-ma ab-lim ^{b}iš-te-en 11 i-na-ad-di-nu-^{b}ši-im-ma 12 mu-tu ^{b}li-ib-bi-ša 13 i-iḫ-ḫa-az-zi

73 ثُمَّ أويلُم [عَويلُم] 74 أنَ سَعَلْ [شَهلْ]شوقتِمْ [سَعَلْ [شَهلْ]شوجَتِمْ] 75 ذا مَأري أُلدو ذُومْ ولو أستِمْ ذا مَأري 76 أُشرَتو ذو [أُشرَثو ذو] 77 عضِبِمْ [حصِبِمْ] 78 فَني ذو 79 يستَكَنْ 80 أنَ ذِنِشْتِمْ ذُأَت 81 شَنِقْتَ ذا [شَرِقْتَ ذا] 82 يتأَرُ ذيمْ 83 و مُؤتَتْ [مُعطَتْ] 84 حقْلِمْ كيريمْ و بيذِمْ 1 ينَدِنُ ذيمَ 2 مَأري ذا 3 يُربَى 4 إستُ مَأري ذا 5 أُرْتَبُوَ 6 إنَ مِمَّ 7 ذا أنَ مَأري ذا 8 إندَنو 9 ضِحتَمْ 10 كيمَ أبلِمْ [أبنِمْ] إستَنْ 11 ينَدِنو ذيمَ 12 مُؤتو لِبِّ ذا 13 يحزي [يأخذي]

بعد ان (اذا) شخص [رجل] يضع وجهته الى (يتوجه نحو) القطيعة [الإدبار] عن الجارية التي ولدت له أولاد، و(حتى) لو الإمرأة (الزوجة) التي أنجبتهُ [بَلَتْهُ] أولاد؛ الى تلك الانثى، سوف يعيدو لها صدقتها، ويعطون لها معطيات (عوائد) الحقل والبستان والممتلكات، (كي) تربي أبناءها؛ أَولَما (حالما) تَرَبّو أبناءها، سوف يعطونها نَفَقة بقدر (نفقة) حَملْ مسؤولية (ابن) [ابن] واحد في (من) أي ما أعطو الى أبناءها، (و) سوف تحيز (تأخذ) زوج قلبها (اختيارها).

If (after) a person [a man] set his face (eye) on the estrangement [leaving] of the concubine who borne (from) him children, and (even) the woman (the wife) who begot him children, to that female, they shall return to her her endowment, and they shall give to her (from) the earnings of the field, orchard, and goods [possessions], to raise up her children; once her children are grown up, they shall give her a disbursement (an allocation) (alimony) as much as one (child) responsibility [child] in (from) whatever they gave to (for) her children, (and) she shall take (marry) the husband of her heart (her choice).

§ 138.—XXIII, 14-24

[14] šum-ma a-wi-lum [15] ḫi-ir-ta-šu [16] ša mârê [b]la ul-du-šum [17] i-iz-zi-ib [18] kaspam ma-la [19] tir-ḫa-ti-ša [20] i-na-ad-di-iš-[b]ši-im [21] u še-ri-iḳ-tam [22] ša iš-tu [b]bît a-bi-ša ub-lam [23] u-ša-lam-[b]ši-im-ma [24] i-iz-zi-ib-ši

[14] ثمَّ أويلم [عَويلم] [15] خيرتَ ذو [16] ذا مأري لا أُلدو ذومْ [17] يعزِبْ [18] كسفَمْ ملأ [19] ترحَتِ ذا [طرْحَتِ ذا] [20] ينَدِذّيم [يندِنْ ذيمْ] [21] و شنِقْتَمْ [شرِقْتَمْ] [22] ذا إسْتُ بيت أبي ذا يُبْلَمْ [23] يُسلَمْ ذِيم [24] يعزِبْ ذي

بعد ان (اذا) شخص [رجل] يترك (يطلق) زوجته التي ما ولدت له أولاد، سوف يعطيها كامل (بقدر) طرحتها (مهرها) فضة، و سوف يُأمّن الصدقة التي أولّما (في البداية) يجلب بيت ابيها، (كي) يتركها.

If (after) a person [a man] leaves (divorces) his wife who have not borne him children, he shall give her the full (amount) of her dowry silver, and secure (guarantee) the endowment that once (first) her father's house brings, to leave (divorce) her.

§ 139.—XXIII, 25-29

[25] šum-ma tir-ḫa-tum [26] la i-ba-aš-ši [27] I ma-na kaspim [28] a-na u-zu-ub-[b]bi-im [29] i-na-ad-di-iš-[b]ši-im

[25] ثمَّ ترِحتُمْ [طِرْحتُمْ] [26] لا يبذي [27] 1 منَا كَسفِمْ [28] أنَ عزُبِمْ [29] ينَدِذّيم [يندِنْ ذيمْ]

|وفق الفقرة 138| بعد ان (اذا) (الشخص [الرجل]) لا يملك (قدر فضة) الطرحة (المهر)، سوف يعطيها للطلاق 1 منا (رطلان) فضة.

|Referencing §138| If (after) (the person [the man]) does not have the dowry (amount of silver), he shall give her for divorce 1 Mana (2 lbs.) silver.

§ 140.—XXIII, 30-32

[30] šum-ma MAŠ.EN.KAK [31] ⅓ ma-na kaspim [32] i-na-ad-di-iš-[b]ši-im

[30] ثمّ مَس عَن كَأكْ [31] 1\3 منَا كَسفِمْ [32] ينَدِذّيم [يندِنْ ذيمْ]

|وفق الفقرة 138| بعد ان (اذا) (الشخص [الرجل]) شخص من العامة، سوف يعطيها 1\2 منا (رطل) فضة.

|Referencing §138| If (after) (the person [the man]) is an ordinary man, he shall give her 1/2 Mana (1 lb.) silver.

§ 141.—XXIII, 33-59

[33] šum-ma aš-ša-at [b]a-wi-lim [34] ša i-na bît [b]a-wi-lim [35] wa-aš-ba-at [36] a-na wa-ṣi-im [37] pa-ni-ša [38] iš-ta-ka-an-ma [39] zi-ki-il-tam [40] i-za-ak-ki-il [41] bî-za [b]u-za-ap-pa-aḫ [42] mu-za u-ša-[b]am-da [43] u-ka-an-nu-[b]ši-ma [44] šum-mamu-za [45] e-ṣi-ib-ša 46 iḳ-ta-bi [47] i-iz-zi-ib-ši [48] ḫa-ra-an-ša [49] u-zu-ub-bu-ša [50] mi-im-ma [51] u-ul in-na-ad-[b]di-iš-ši-im [52] šum-ma mu-za [53] la e-ṣi-ib-ša [b]iḳ-ta-bi [54] mu-za zinništam ša-ni-tam [55] i-iḫ-ḫa-az [56] zinništum ši-i [57] ki-ma amtim [58] i-na bît mu-ti-ša [59] uš-ša-ab

[33] ثمّ أستْ أويلم [عَويلم] [34] إنَ بيت أويلم [عَويلم] [35] وثبتْ [36] أنَ [وصئِمْ] [وأصِمْ] [وهصِمْ] [وصِمْ] [37] فني ذا [38] يستَكَنمْ [39] زِكلتَمْ [سكِلتَمْ] [شكِلتَمْ] [زقِلتَمْ] [دكِلتَمْ] [40] يزكِلْ [يسكِلْ] [يشكِلْ] [يزقِلْ] [يدكِلْ] [41] بيتْ ذا [بيتْ] يُزفِح [يُسفِحْ] [42] مؤتْ ذا [مؤتا] يُسمِدْ [43] يُكنو ذيم [44] ثمَّ مؤتْ ذا [مؤتا] [45] إعضبْ ذا [إحصبْ ذا] [46] يقتبي [47] يعزِبْ ذي [48] حرَنْ ذا [49] عزُبُ ذا [50] مِمَّ [51] ألْ ينَدِّذيم [يندِنْ ذيمْ] [52] ثمَّ مؤتْ ذا [مؤتا] [53] لا إعضبْ ذا [إحصبْ ذا] يقتبي [54] مؤتْ ذا [مؤتا] ذنِثتَمْ ثانتمْ [55] يحزْ [يأخذْ] [56] ذنِثتُمْ ذيي [57] كيمَ أمتِمْ [58] إنَ بيت مؤتي ذا [59] يُثب

بعد ان (اذا) إمرأة (زوجة) شخص [رجل] مقيمة في بيت الشخص [الرجل] تضع وجهها (تتوجه) للخروج (للانفصال)، (و) تقصّر تقصير (تتراخى رخاء) [تستَقرد استقرادا (تتصرّف بحمق)]، تبَدّدْ (تهمل) بيتها، تتكبر على (تستَقِلْ) زوجها، سوف يُجلسوها

(يستدعوها)؛ بعد ان (اذا) زوجها يقول "سوف اقاطعها [أدبر عنها]"، (زوجها) سوف يتركها (يطلقها)، (عند) رحيلها، (عند) تركها (طلاقها)، سوف لا تُعطى أي شيء؛ بعد ان (اذا) زوجها يقول "سوف لا اقاطعها [لا أدبر عنها]"، زوجها سوف يحيز (يأخذ) أنثى (زوجة) ثانية (اخرى)؛ هذه الأنثى (الزوجة الاولى) سوف تقيم في بيت زوجها كعبدة.

If (after) a person's [a man's] woman (wife) residing in the person's [the man's] set her face (eye) on leaving (divorce), (and) commits negligence [behaves like monkey (fool)] [flirts flirtation], wastes (neglect) her house, belittles her husband, they shall seat [call] her in; if (after) her husband says "I shall estrange [leave] her", her husband shall leave her, (at) her departure, her leaving (divorce), she shall not be given anything; if (after) her husband says "I shall not estrange [leave] her", her husband shall take a second (another) female (wife); this female (the first wife) shall reside in her husband's house as a female slave.

§ 142.—XXIII, 60-XXIV, 5

60 šum-ma zinništum ^{b}mu-za i-zi-ir-ma 61 u-ul ta-aḫ-ḫa-^{b}za-an-ni 62 iḳ-ta-bi 63 wa-ar-ka-za 64 i-na ba-ab-ti-ša 65 ip-pa-ar-ra-^{b}aš-ma 66 šum-ma na-aṣ-^{b}ra-at-ma 67 ḫi-di-tam 68 la i-šu 69 u mu-za(g) 70 wa-zi-ma 71 ma-ga-al 72 u-ša-am-^{b}da-ši 73 zinništum ši-i XXIV, 1 ar-nam ^{b}u-ul i-šu 2 še-ri-iḳ-ta-ša 3 i-li-ḳi-ma 4 a-na bît a-bi-ša 5 it-ta-al-la-ak

60 ثمَّ ذنثْتمْ مؤتْ ذا [مؤتا] يزرِم [يزعِرم] 61 ألْ تحزني [تأخذني] 62 يقتبي 63 وركَتْ ذا [وركَت] 64 إنَ ببْتِ ذا 65 يفرَسْم 66 ثمْ نصرتم 67 حدتم 68 لا يذو 69 و مؤتْ ذا [مؤتا] 70 وأزمَ [وهسِم] [وهزم] [وزيم] [وأصِم] [وهصِم] [وصئم] 71 مجل 72 يسمْدَ ذي 73 ذنثتمْ ذيي 1 عرنمْ [عنمْ] ألْ يذوَ 2 شنقْتَ ذا [شرقتَ ذا] 3 يلقيم 4 أن بيت أبي ذا 5 يتألكْ

بعد ان (اذا) أنثى تزدري [تسيء التصرف مع] زوجها، تقول (له) "سوف لن تحيزني (تأخذني)"، سوف يتفحصو خلفيتها (سوابقها) في (خصوص) ضحيتها (زوجها)؛ بعد ان (اذا) (كانت) حافظة (أمينة)، (و) لا تملك حديّة (شدة)، وزوجها متطاول (معتدي) [مستبد (متعنت)] [متسكّع]، (و) يتكبر عليها (يستقلّها) بشكل كبير، هذه الانثى لا تملك (ليس عليها) تهمة [عقوبة]، سوف تأخذ صدقتها، (و) تذهب الى بيت ابيها.

If (after) a female (a woman) scorns [mistreats] her husband, (and) says (to him) "you shall not take (have) me", they shall examine her background in (in regard to) her victim (the husband); if (after) she was protective, (and) does not have stubbornness [rudeness], and her husband was greatly confrontational (abusive) [oppressive (arrogant)] [gadabout], this female (wife) does not have charge [penalty], she shall take her endowment, (and) go to her father's house.

§ 143.—XXIV, 6-12

6 šum-ma la na-^{b}aṣ-ra-at-ma 7 wa-zi-a-at 8 bi-za ^{b}u-za-ap-pa-aḫ 9 mu-za u-ša-am-da 10 zinništam šu-a-ti 11 a-na me-e 12 i-na-ad-du-u-ši

6 ثمّ لا نصرتم 7 وأزِئتْ [وهسِئتْ] [وهزِئتْ] [وزيئتْ] [وأصِئتْ] [وهصِئتْ] [وصِئتْ] 8 بيتْ ذا [بيتْ] يزفح [يُسفح] 9 مؤتْ ذا [مؤتا] يسمْدَ 10 ذنثتمْ ذآتي 11 أنَ مئي 12 يندو ذي

|وفق الفقرة 142| بعد ان (اذا) (كانت) لا حافظة (لا أمينة)، متطاولة [متعنتة] [متسكّعة]، تبدّدْ (تهمل) بيتها، تتكبر على (تستقلْ) زوجها، ذات الانثى، سوف يرمونوها [يدعونها] في الماء (النهر).

|Referencing §142| If (after) she was not protective, (and) was confrontational [arrogant] [gadded], wastes (neglects) her house, belittles (does not take seriously) her husband, that female (wife), they shall throw [le go] her in the water (river).

§ 144.—XXIV, 13-27

13 šum-ma a-wi-lum 14 aššatam i-ḫu-^{b}uz-ma 15 aššatum ši-i 16 amtam a-na mu-ti-ša 17 id-di-in-ma 18 mârê uš-tab-ši 19 a-wi-lum šu-u 20 a-na ^{šal}šu-ge-tim 21 a-ḫa-zi-im 22 pa-ni-šu 23 iš-ta-ka-an 24 a-wi-lam ^{b}šu-a-ti 25 u-ul i-ma-ag-^{b}ga-ru-šu 26 ^{šal}šu-ge-tam 27 u-ul i-iḫ-ḫa-az

13 ثمّ أويلُم [عويلُم] 14 أسّتَمْ يحزُم [يأخُذَم] 15 أسّتُمْ ذيي 16 أمتَمْ أنَ مؤتي ذا 17 يدنَمْ 18 مأري يُستبذي [يُستَبثي] 19 أويلُم [عَويلُم] ذوو 20 أنَ سعل [شهل]شوقتِمْ [سعل [شهل]شوجتِمْ] 21 أحزِمْ [أخذِمْ] 22 فني ذو 23 يستَكن 24 أويلَم [عويلَم] ذأتِ 25 ألْ يمجرْ ذو 26 سعل [شهل]شوقتَمْ [سعل [شهل]شوجتَمْ] 27 ألْ يحزْ

بعد ان (اذا) شخص [رجل] يحيز (يأخذ) إمرأة (زوجة)، (و) هذه الإمرأة (الزوجة) تعطي الى زوجها عبدة، (كي) تنمّي الاولاد، (ثم) هذا الشخص [الرجل] يضع وجهته (يتوجّه) لحيازة (لأخذْ) جارية، ذلك الشخص [الرجل] سوف لن يوافقونه، سوف لن يحيز (يأخذ) جارية.

If (after) a person [a man] takes a woman (wife), (and) this woman (wife) gives a female slave to her husband, to raise up children, (then) this person [man] set his face (eye) on taking a concubine, that person [man], they shall not approve him, he shall not take a concubine.

§ 145.—XXIV, 28-42

28 šum-ma a-wi-lum 29 aššatam i-ḫu-uz-ma 30 mârê la u-šar-^{b}ši-šu-ma 31 a-na ^{šal}šu-ge-tim 32 a-ḫa-zi-im 33 pa-ni-šu 34 iš-ta-ka-an 35 a-wi-lum šu-u 36 ^{šal}šu-ge-tam 37 i-iḫ-ḫa-az 38 a-na bîti-šu 39 u-še-ir-ri-^{b}ib-ši 40 ^{šal}šu-ge-tum ^{b}ši-i 41 it-ti aššatim 42 u-ul uš-ta-^{b}ma-aḫ-ḫa-ar

28 ثمّ أويلُم [عويلُم] 29 أسّتَم يحزَم [يأخُذَمَ] 30 مأري لا يُشرت ذُوم [يُشرْث ذُومَ] 31 أنَ سعل [شهل]شوقتِم [سعل [شهل]شوجتِمْ] 32 أحزِمْ [أخذِمْ] 33 فني ذو 34 يستَكن 35 أويلُم [عويلُم] ذوو 36 سعل [شهل]شوقتَمْ [سعل [شهل]شوجتَمْ] 37 يحزْ [يأخذْ] 38 أنَ بيت ذو 39 يُسئِرِبْ ذي [يتئِرِبْ ذي] 40 سعل [شهل]شوقتُمْ [سعل [شهل]شوجتُمْ] ذيي 41 إتي أسّتِمْ 42 ألْ يستَمْخِرْ

بعد ان (اذا) شخص [رجل] يحيز (يأخذ) إمرأة (زوجة)، لاتنجبهُ [تبليه] أولاد، (ثم) يضع وجهته (يتوجّه) لحيازة (لأخذْ) جارية، هذا الشخص [الرجل] سوف يحيز (يأخذ) جارية، سوف يُدخِلها في بيته (للمُساعدة في انجاب اطفال)، هذه الجارية سوف لن تعادل (مرتبة) الزوجة.

If (after) a person [a man] takes a woman (wife), (and) she does not beget him children, (and) he set his face (eye) on taking a concubine, this person [man] shall not take a concubine, he shall let her enter his house (to help getting him children), this concubine shall not equal (in status) with his woman (wife).

§ 146.—XXIV, 43-59

43 šum-ma a-wi-lum 44 aššatam i-ḫu-uz-ma 45 amtam a-na mu-ti-ša 46 id-di-in-ma 47 mârê it-ta-^{b}la-ad 48 wa-ar-ka-nu-um 49 amtum ši-i 50 it-ti ^{b}be-el-ti-ša 51 uš-ta-tam-ḫi-ir 52 aš-šum mârê ^{b}ul-du 53 be-li-za 54 a-na kaspim 55 u-ul i-na-ad-^{b}di-iš-ši 56 ab-bu-ut-tam 57 i-ša-ak-ka-^{b}an-ši-ma 58 it-ti amâti 59 i-ma-an-nu-ši

43 ثمّ أويلُم [عويلُم] 44 أسّتَمْ يحزُم [يأخُذَم] 45 أمتَمْ أنَ مؤتي ذا 46 يدنَمَ 47 مأري يتألَد 48 وركَنُمْ 49 أمتُمْ ذيي 50 إتي بَعلَت ذا 51 يُستتَمخِرْ 52 هذَمْ مأري ألْدو 53 بعلت ذا [بعلتا] 54 أن كسفِمْ 55 ألْ ينَدذي [ينَدنْ ذي] 56 أبُتَمْ 57 يسكنْ ذيمَ 58 إتي أماتي 59 يمنّو ذي

بعد ان (اذا) شخص [رجل] يحيز (يأخذ) إمرأة (زوجة)، (و) تعطي الى زوجها عبدة، (والعبدة) تَولد أبناء، وراء ذلك هذه العبدة تحاول ان تتعادل (بالمرتبة) مع مالكتها؛ هذا لانها ولدت أولاد، مالكتها سوف لن تعطيها للفضة (تبيعها)، سوف تضعها (تجعلها) مُقيمة (ليست للبيع)، (ولكن) سوف تعدّها مع (بحساب) العبيد.

If (after) a person [a man] takes a woman (wife), (and) she gives to her husband a female slave, (and) she gives birth to children, afterwards this female slave attempts to be equal with her owner (the wife); that is because she gave birth to children, her owner shall not give her to (for) silver (sell her), she shall set (treat) her as a resident (not for sale), (but) she shall count her with the slaves.

§ 147.—XXIV, 60-64

60 šum-ma mârê 61 la u-li-id 62 be-li-za 63 a-na kaspim 64 i-na-ad-di-[b]iš-ši

60 ثمَّ مَاري 61 لا أُلدْ 62 بَعلِتْ ذا [بَعلتا] 63 أن كَسفِمْ 64 ينددِّي [ينَدنْ ذي]

|وفق الفقرة 146| بعد ان (اذا) (العبدة) ما ولَدتْ أبناء، مالكتها سوف تعطيها للفضة (تبيعها).

|Referencing §146| If (after) (the female slave) have not borne children, her owner shall give her to (for) silver (sell her).

§ 148.—XXIV, 65-81

65 šuma a-wi-lum 66 aš-ša-tam 67 i-ḫu-uz-ma 68 la-'a-bu-um 69 iṣ-ṣa-ba-az-zi 70 a-na ša-ni-tim 71 a-ḫa-zi-im 72 pa-ni-šu 73 iš-ta-ka-an 74 i-iḫ-ḫa-az 75 aš-ša-zu 76 ša la-'a-bu-um 77 iṣ-ba-tu 78 u-ul i-iz-[b]zi-ib-ši 79 i-na bîtim i-pu-šu 80 uš-ša-am-ma 81 a-di ba-al-ṭa-at [b]it-ta-na-aš-ši-ši

65 ثمَّ أويلم [عويلم] 66 أستَمْ 67 يحزَمْ [يأخذَمْ] 68 لأبم [لَعبُمْ] 69 يضبَطْ ذي [يضبَطي] 70 أنَ ثانتمْ 71 أحزمْ [أخذمْ] 72 فني ذو 73 يستكَنْ 74 يحزْ [يأخذْ] 75 أستّ ذو [أستّ] 76 ذا لأبم [لَعبُمْ] 77 إضبَطْ 78 أُلْ يعزِبْ ذي 79 إنَ بيتِمْ إعفشو [إعفُسو] 80 يُسم [يُشمَ] 81 عَدي [حَدي] بلْطَتْ 82 يتأنَت ذي [يتعنَت ذي]

بعد ان (اذا) شخص [رجل] يحيز (يأخذ) إمرأة (زوجة)، (و) يلزمها (يعتريها) المرض، (ثم) يضع وجهته (يتوجّه) لحيازة (لأخذْ) ثانية (اخرى)، سوف يحيز (يأخذ) (امرأة ثانية)؛ زوجته التي لَزَمَ (إعْترى) المرض، سوف لن يتركها، سوف تستقر [تأمن] في بيت هيّئ (هو)، (و) سوف يتحمل مشقتها حتى (مادامت) (هي) حيّة (على قيد الحياة).

If (after) a person [a man] takes a woman (wife), a terminal illness seizes her, (then) set his face (eye) on taking a second (another) (woman), he shall take (the second woman); his woman (wife) who was seized by terminal illness, he shall not leave her, she shall settle in a house he prepared (equipped), (and) he shall bear her hardship (her responsibility) until (as long as) she is alive.

§ 149.—XXV, 1-9

1 šum-ma zinništum ši-i 2 i-na bît mu-ti-ša 3 wa-ša-ba-am 4 la im-ta-gar 5 še-ri-iḳ-ta-ša 6 ša iš-tu [b]bît a-bi-ša 7 ub-lam 8 u-ša-lam-šim-ma 9 it-ta-al-la-ak

1 ثمَّ ذنِثْتمْ ذيي 2 إنَ بيت مُؤتي ذا 3 وَثبَمْ 4 لا يمتجرَ 5 شنِقْتَ ذا [شَرِقْتَ ذا] 6 ذا إستُ بيت أبي ذا 7 يُبْلَمْ 8 يُسلَمْ ذِيمَ 9 يتألّكْ

|وفق الفقرة 148| بعد ان (اذا) هذه الانثى (الزوجة المريضة) لا تقبل الاقامة في بيت زوجها، سوف يُأمّن صدقتها التي أوّلما (في البداية) يجلب بيت ابيها، (و) سوف تذهب.

|Referencing §148| If (after) this female (the sick wife) does not accept residing in her husband's house, he shall secure (guarantee) her endowment that once (first) her father's house brings, (and) she shall go.

§ 150.—XXV, 10-25

10 šum-ma a-wi-lum 11 a-na aš-ša-ti-šu 12 eḳlam kirâm bîtam 13 u bi-ša-am 14 iš-ru-uḳ-šim 15 ku-nu-uk-kam 16 i-zi-ib-ši-im 17 wa-ar-ki [b]mu-ti-ša 18 mârê-ša u-ul [b]i-ba-ga-ru-ši 19 um-mu-um 20 wa-ar-ka-za 21 a-na mâri-ša 22 ša i-ra-am-mu 23 i-na-ad-di-in 24 a-na a-ḫi-im 25 u-ul i-na-ad-di-in

10 ثمَّ أويلم [عويلم] 11 أنَ أستَ ذو 12 حقلَم كيرَم بيتَم 13 و بيذَم 14 يشنُق ذيم [يشرُق ذيم] 15 كُنكَم 16 يعزب ذيم 17 ورك مؤتي ذا 18 مأري ذا ألْ يبجرو ذي [يفجرو ذي] [يبقرو ذي] 19 أمم 20 ورك ذا [وركت] 21 أنَ مأري ذا 22 ذا يرأمو 23 يندنَ 24 أنَ أخم 25 ألْ يندنَ

بعد ان (اذا) شخص [رجل]، الى إمرأته (زوجته)، يتصدّق (يوصي) لها حقل، بستان، بيت، وممتلكات، يترك لها وثيقة (وصية) مختومة، وراء (موت) زوجها، أبناءها سوف لن ينازِعوها (يُقاضوها)؛ الأم، بعدها (بعد موتها)، سوف (ربما) تعطي الى ابنها الذي تَحبّ، سوف (ربما) لن تعطي الى شقيق (له).

If (after) a person [a man], to his woman (wife), he endows her a field, an orchard, a house, and possessions, leaves her a sealed document (will), after her husband (death), her children shall not contend her (legally challenge) her; the mother, after her (death), shall (may) give to the child whom she loves, shall (may) not give to (his) sibling.

§ 151.—XXV, 26-51

26 šum-ma zinništum 27 ša i-na bît a-wi-lim 28 wa-aš-ba-at 29 aš-šum be-el ^{b}ḫu-bu-ul-lim 30 ša mu-ti-ša 31 la ṣa-ba-ti-ša 32 mu-za ^{b}ur-ta-ak-ki-is 33 dup-pa-am 34 uš-te-zi-ib 35 šum-ma ^{b}a-wi-lum šu-u 36 la-ma zinništam šu-a-ti 37 i-iḫ-ḫa-zu 38 ḫu-bu-ul-lum 39 e-li-šu 40 i-ba-aš-ši 41 be-el ḫu-bu-ul-^{b}li-šu 42 aš-ša-zu 43 u-ul i-ṣa-^{b}ba-tu 44 u šum-ma ^{b}zinništum ši-i 45 la-ma a-na bît ba-wi-lim 46 i-ir-ru-bu 47 ḫu-bu-ul-lum 48 e-li-ša 49 i-ba-aš-ši 50 be-el ḫu-bu-ul-^{b}li-ša 51 mu-za u-ul ^{b}i-ṣa-ba-tu

26 ثمَّ ذنِثتَم 27 ذا إنَ بيت أويلم [عويلم] 28 وثبَت 29 هذَم بَعلَ حبلَم 30 ذا مؤتي ذا 31 لا ضَبط ذا 32 مؤتَ ذا [مؤتَ] يرتَكس 33 دُوبَم [دُوفَم] 34 يُستعزِب 35 ثمَّ أويلم [عويلم] ذوو 36 لما ذنثتَم ذأتِ 37 يحز 38 حبلَم 39 علي ذو 40 يبذي 41 بَعلَ حبلِ ذو 42 أستَ ذو [أستَ] 43 ألْ يضبط 44 ثمَّ ذنِثتَم ذيي 45 لما أنَ بيت أويلِم [عويلِم] 46 يئرب 47 حبلَم 48 علي ذا 49 يبذي 50 بَعلَ حبلِ ذا 51 مؤتَ ذا [مؤتَ] ألْ يضبَطُ

بعد ان (اذا) انثى (امرأة) مقيمة في بيت شخص [رجل] (زوج) تُعاقد زوجها ليترك لوح مختوم، هذا لأن مالك سند (دَين) زوجها لا (غير) ملْزِم (قضائيا) لها؛ بعد ان (اذا) الشخص [الرجل] (الزوج) يملك عليه سند (دَين) قبل ان يحيز (يأخذ) المرأة، (المالك) سوف لن يمسكْ (قضائيا) زوجته؛ بعد ان (اذا) الانثى (الزوجة) تملك عليها سند (دَين) قبل ان تدخل الى بيت الشخص [الرجل] (الزوج)، مالك سندها سوف لن يمسك (يلْزِم قضائيا) زوجها.

If (after) a female (wife) residing in a person's [man's] (husband's) house contracts her husband to leave a sealed tablet, that is because the owner of her husband bond (debt) is not holding (obliging) on her; if (after) this person [this man] (the husband) has on him a bond (debt) before he takes the woman (the wife), he (the owner) shall not hold his wife (responsible); if (after) this woman (this wife) has on her a bond (debt) before she enters to the person's [the man's] (the husband's) house, the owner of her bond shall not hold her husband (responsible).

§ 152.—XXV, 52-60

52 šum-ma iš-tu 53 zinništum ši-i 54 a-na bît a-wi-lim 55 i-ru-bu 56 e-li-šu-nu 57 ḫu-bu-ul-lum 58 it-tab-ši 59 ki-la-la-šu-nu 60 tamkaram i-ip-pa-lu

52 ثمَّ إستُ 53 ذنِثتَم ذيي 54 أنَ بيت أويلِم [عويلم] 55 إرُبْ 56 علي ذُون 57 حبلَم 58 يتبذي [يتبثي] 59 كلالَ ذُون 60 تمكارَم يئفلو

|وفق الفقرة 151| بعد ان (اذا) أولما (حالما) هذه الانثى (الزوجة) دخلت في بيت الزوج، السند (الدَين) يتواجد [يظهر] (ينمو) عليهم، كلاهم سوف يتحملو (دين) المتاجر.

|Referencing §151| If (after) once this female (the wife) entered in the house of the person [the man] (the husband), the bond (the debt) exists [occurs] (grows) on them, both shall take upon (the debt of) the merchant.

§ 153.—XXV, 61-66

61 šum-ma aš-ša-at [b]a-wi-lim 62 aš-šum zi-ka-[b]ri-im 63 ša-ni-im 64 mu-za uš-di-ik 65 zinništam šu-a-ti [b]i-na ga-ši-ši-im 66 i-ša-ak-ka-nu-ši

61 ثُمَّ أَسْتْ أَويلِم [عَويلِم] 62 هَذْمْ ذِكَرِمْ 63 ثانِمْ 64 مؤتْ ذا [مؤتَ] يُسْدِكْ 65 ذنِثْتَمْ ذأتِ إنَ جَسِسِمْ [قَسِسِمْ] 66 يسكنو ذي

بعد ان (اذا) إمرأة (زوجة) شخص [رجل] تطعنْ زوجها، هذا بسبب رجل ثاني (آخَر)، تلك الانثى، سوف يقرّوها (يخرقوها للموت) بعصا (بخازوق).

If (after) a person's [man's] woman (a wife) stabs her husband, that is because of a second (another) male (man), that female (wife), they shall set her (penerate (impale) her to death) in (with) a stick.

§ 154.—XXV, 67-71

67 šum-ma a-wi-lum 68 mâra-zu 69 il-ta-ma-ad 70 a-wi-lam šu-a-ti 71 alam u-še-iz-[b]zu-u-šu

67 ثُمَّ أَويلُم [عَويلُم] 68 مأرتْ ذو [مأرتَ] 69 يلْتَمَدْ 70 أويلم [عَويلَم] ذأتِ 71 أيلَمْ يُشْئزو ذو [يُشْئِتو ذو]

بعد ان (اذا) شخص [رجل] يبلي بضرب بنته، سوف يفرقونه (يبعدونه عن) الاهل.

If (after) a person [a man] batters his daughter, that person [man], they shall seperate him of (set him aside from) the family.

§ 155.—XXV, 72- XXVI, 1

72 šum-ma a-wi-lum 73 a-na mâri-šu 74 kallâtam [b]i-ḫi-ir-ma 75 mâr-šu il-ma-zi 76 šu-u wa-ar-[b]ka-nu-um-ma 77 i-na zu-ni-ša 78 it-ta-ti-il-ma 79 iṣ-ṣa-ab-tu-šu 80 a-wi-lam šu-a-ti 81 i-ka-zu-šu-ma 82 a-na me-e XXVI, 1 i-na-ad-du-u-ši

72 ثُمَّ أويلُم [عَويلُم] 73 أنَ مأرِ ذو 74 كلّتَمْ [كنّتَمْ] يخرِمَ 75 مأرْ ذو يلْمَدْ ذي [يلْمَدي] [يلْمَسْ ذي [يلْمَسي]] 76 ذوو ورْكَنُمَ 77 إنَ زونِ ذا [ذونِ ذا] 78 يتتِلْمَ 79 إصَبْطْ ذو 80 أَويلَم [عَويلَم] ذأتِ 81 يكَسعو ذُومَ [يكسؤ ذُومَ] 82 أنَ مئي 1 ينَدو ذي

بعد ان (اذا) شخص [رجل] يختار كَنّة (عروس (زوجة)) الى إبنه، (و) إبنه يلتصق (يقترن) بها [يلمسها]، (و) وراء ذلك، هو (الأب) يتضاجع بجماعها (بمَعيتها) [في عَيْبِها]، (و) يمسكوه، ذلك الشخص [الرجل]، سوف يسوقونه (مقيدا)، (و) يرمونه في الماء (النهر).

If (after) a person [a man] selects a pride (wife) to his son, (and) his son weds [touches] her, (and) afterwards, he (the father) lays down (have sex) in her company [in her private part], (and) they catch (hold) him, they shall chase him (tied), (and) shall throw him in the water (the river).

§ 156.—XXVI, 2-17

2 šum-ma a-wi-lum 3 a-na mâri-šu 4 kallâtam 5 i-ḫi-ir-ma 6 mâr-šu la il-[b]ma-zi-ma 7 šu-u i-na zu-ni-ša 8 it-ta-ti-il 9 ½ ma-na kaspim 10 i-ša-ḳal-[b]ši-im-ma 11 u mi-im-ma 12 ša iš-tu 13 bît a-bi-ša 14 ub-lam 15 u-ša-lam-[b]ši-im-ma 16 mu-tu [b]li-ib-bi-ša 17 i-iḫ-ḫa-az-zi

2 ثُمَّ أويلُم [عَويلُم] 3 أنَ مأرِ ذو 4 كلّتَمْ 5 يخرِمَ 6 مأرْ ذو لا يلْمَدْ ذي [يلْمَدي] [يلْمَسْ ذي [يلْمَسي]] 7 ذوو إنَ زونِ ذا [ذونِ ذا] 8 يتتِلْ 9 2\1 مَنا كسفِمْ 10 يثْقَلْ ذيمَ 11 و ممَّ 12 ذا إسْتْ 13 بيت أبي ذا 14 يُبلَمْ 15 يسلَمْ ذيمَ 16 مؤتو لبِّ 17 يحزّي

بعد ان (اذا) شخص [رجل] يختار كَنّة (عروس (زوجة)) الى إبنه، (و) إبنه لا يلتصق (يقترن) بها [لا يلمسها]، (اذا) هو (الأب) يتضاجع بجماعها (بمَعيتها) [في عَيْبِها]، سوف يَزن (ويعطي) لها نصف رطل فضة، وسوف يأمّن أيّ الذي أولّما (في البداية) يجلب بيت ابيها، (و) سوف تحيز (تأخذ) زوج قلبها (اختيارها).

If (after) a person [a man] selects a bride (wife) to his son, (and) his son does not wed [touch] her, (if) he (the father) lay down (have sex) in her company, he shall measure (and give) her ½ Mana (1 lb.) silver, and shall secure (guarantee) anything that once (first) her father's house brings, (and) she shall take (marry) the husband of her heart (her choice).

§ 157.—XXVI, 18-23

18 šum-ma a-wi-lum 19 wa-ar-ki ᵇa-bi-šu 20 i-na zu-un ᵇum-mi-šu 21 it-ta-ti-il 22 ki-la-li-šu-nu 23 i-ḳal-lu-u-ᵇšu-nu-ti

18 ثُمَّ أويلُم [عَويلُم] 19 ورْكِ أبي ذو 20 إنَ زونْ [ذونْ] أمي ذو 21 يتَتِلْ 22 كِلالِ ذُونو 23 يقلُو ذُنوتي

بعد ان (اذا) شخص [رجل]، وراء (موت) أبيه، يتضاجع بجماع (بمَعية) [في عَيْبْ] أمّه، كلاهما، سوف يحرقونهما.

If (after) a person [a man], following (the death of) his father, lay down (have sex) in the company [in the private part] of his mother, both of them, they shall burn them.

§ 158.—XXVI, 24-32

24 šum-ma a-wi-lum 25 wa-ar-ki ᵇa-bi-šu 26 i-na zu-un 27 ra-bi-ti-šu 28 ša mârê ᵇwa-al-da-at 29 it-ta-aṣ-ba-at 30 a-wi-lum šu-u 31 i-na bît a-ba 32 in-na-az-za-aḫ

24 ثُمَّ أويلُم [عَويلَم] 25 ورْكِ أبي ذو 26 إنَ زونْ [ذونْ] 27 رَبيتي ذو 28 ذا مأريي ولَدَتْ 29 إتْضَبَطْ 30 أويلَم [عَويلَم] ذوو 31 إنَ بيت أبا 32 ينَزَحْ [ينَسَحْ] [ينَسَخْ]

|وفق الفقرة 157| بعد ان (اذا) شخص [رجل]، وراء (موت) أبيه، مُسِكَ (يتضاجع) بجماع (بمَعية) [في عَيْبْ] زوجة أبيه التي ولَدت أبناء (من ابيه)، هذا الشخص [الرجل] سوف يُزاح [يُنحّى] في (من) بيت الأب.

|Referencing §157| If (after) a person [a man], following (the death of) his father, was caught (laying down (having sex)) in the company [in the private part] of his step mother, this person [this man] has removed himself in (from) the father's house.

§ 159.—XXVI, 33-46

33 šum-ma a-wi-lum 34 ša a-na bît ᵇe-mi-šu 35 bi-ib-lam 36 u-ša-bi-lu 37 tir-ḫa-tam id-di-nu 38 a-na zinništim ša-ni-tim 39 up-ta-al-li-ᵇis-ma 40 a-na e-mi-šu 41 mârat-ka 42 u-ul a-ḫa-az ᵇiḳ-ta-bi 43 a-bi mârtim 44 mi-im-ma 45 ša ib-ba-ab-ᵇlu-šum 46 i-tab-ba-al

33 ثُمَّ أويلَم [عَويلَم] 34 ذا أنَ بيت عمِّ ذو 35 ببْلَمْ 36 أُسَبِلْ 37 ترْحَتَمْ [طرْحَتَمْ] إدِنْ 38 أنَ ذنِثْتِمْ ثانِتِمْ 39 يُفْتَلِسْمَ [يبْتَلِسْمَ] 40 أنَ عمي ذو 41 مأرَتْك 42 ألْ أحز يقْتَبي 43 أبي مأرْتِم 44 ممَّ 45 ذا إبَبْلُ ذُوم 46 يتَبَلْ

بعد ان (اذا) الشخص [الرجل] الذي نَقلَ محصول الى بيت عمّه (ابو خطيبته)، أعطى (ك)طرحة (كمهر)، يتأمَلْ الى أنثى ثانية (أخرى)، (و) يقول الى عمّه "سوف لن أحزَ (أأخْذ) بنتك"، أبو البنت (العَم) سوف يأخذ أي ما محصول أعطاه.

If (after) the person [the man] who has transported crop to his uncle (future father-in-law), gave as dowry, longs to another female, (and) tells his uncle "I shall not take your girl (daughter)", the father of the girl shall take whatever he transported (gave) to him.

§ 160.—XXVI, 47-59

47 šum-ma a-wi-lum 48 a-na bît e-mi-im 49 bi-ib-lam 50 u-ša-bi-il 51 tir-ḫa-tam 52 id-di-in-ma 53 a-bi mârtim 54 mârti-i u-ul a-na-ᵇad-di-ik-kum 55 iḳ-ta-bi 56 mi-im-ma ma-la 57 ib-ba-ab-lu-šum 58 uš-ta-ša-an-na-ma 59 u-ta-ar

47 ثُمَّ أويلَم [عَويلَم] 48 أنَ بيت عمِنْ 49 ببْلَمْ 50 يُسَبِلْ 51 ترْحَتَمْ [طرْحَتَمْ] 52 يدِنَمْ 53 أبي مأرْتِمْ 54 مأرْتِيي ألْ أندِكُمْ 55 يقْتَبي 56 ممَّ ملَئْ 57 إبَبْلُ ذُومْ 58 يُستَثْنَمَ [يُثَنَّمَ] 59 يتأرْ

|وفق الفقرة 159| بعد ان (اذا) شخص [رجل] ينقل محصول الى بيت العم (ابو الخطيبة)، يعطي (ك)طرحة (كمهر)، (و) ابو البنت يقول "سوف لن أعطيك بنتي"، (ابو البنت) سوف يضاعف كامل (بقدر) (ما) أعطاه (من) أيٍ (من أي شيء)، (و) يُعيد.

|Referencing §159| If (after) the person [the man] transports crop to the uncle (the future father-in-law), gives as dowry, (and) the father of the girl says "I shall not give you my girl", he (the father of the girl) shall double the full (amount) he transported (gave) to him (of) anything, (and) return.

§ 161.—XXVI, 60-77

60 šum-ma a-wi-lum 61 a-na bît e-mi-šu 62 bi-ib-lam u-ša-bil 63 tir-ḫa-tam 64 id-di-in-ma 65 i-bi-ir-šu 66 ug-dar-ri-zu 67 e-mu-šu 68 a-na be-el aš-ša-tim 69 mârti-i u-ul ᵇta-aḫ-ḫa-az 70 iḳ-ta-bi 71 mi-im-ma ma-la 72 ib-ba-ab-lu-šum 73 uš-ta-ša-an-na-ma 74 u-ta-ar 75 u aš-ša-zu 76 i-bi-ir-šu 77 u-ul i-iḫ-ḫa-az

60 ثُمَّ أويلم [عويلم] 61 أنَ بيت عمٍّ ذو 62 ببلَمْ يُسبلْ 63 ترْحَتَمْ [طرْحتَمْ] 64 يدنَمْ 65 إبرْ ذو 66 يُجْدَرئِ ذو [يُجدرئِت] [يُجتَرئ ذو [يُجتَرئِت]] 67 عمُّ ذو 68 أنَ بَعلْ أستِمْ 69 مأرَتيي ألْ تحزْ 70 يقتَبي 71 مِمَّ ملئ 72 إببَلُ ذوم 73 يُستَثنَم [يتَثّنَم] 74 يُتأرْ 75 و أسّتْ ذو [أسّتْ] 76 إبِرْ ذو 77 ألْ يحزْ

بعد ان (اذا) شخص [رجل] يَنقل محصول الى بيت عمِّه (ابو خطيبته)، يعطي كطرحة (كمهر)، (و) صاحب له يتحدّاه (على البنت)، (ثم) عمُّه (ابو خطيبته) يقول الى مالك (سيد) الإمرأة (الخطيب) "سوف لن تحيز (تأخذ) بنتي"، (عمُّه) سوف يضاعف كامل (بقدر) ما أعطاه، (و) يعيد، وصاحبه سوف لن يحيز (يأخذ) إمرأته (خطيبته).

If (after) a person [a man] transports crop to the uncle (future father-in-law), gives (it) as dowry, (and) a fellow of his challenges him (for the girl), (then) his uncle (father-in-law) says to the owner (master) of the woman (the future husband) "you shall not take my girl", he (the father-in-law) shall double the full (amount) he transported (given) to him (of) anything, (and) return, and his fellow shall not take his woman (fiancé).

§ 162.—XXVI, 78-XXVII, 6

78 šum-ma a-wi-lum 79 aš-ša-tam 80 i-ḫu-uz 81 mârê u-li-zum-ma 82 zinništum ši-i 83 a-na ši-im-tim XXVII, 1 it-ta-la-ak 2 a-na še-ri-iḳ-ᵇti-ša 3 a-bu-ša 4 u-ul i-ra-ᵇag-gu-um 5 še-ri-iḳ-ta-ša 6 ša mârê-ša-ma

78 ثُمَّ أويلم [عويلم] 79 أستَمْ 80 يحزْ 81 ماريي يألدْ ذومَ [يألتمَ] 82 ذنِثتُمْ 83 أن سمتِمْ 1 يتألكْ 2 أنَ شنقتِ ذا [شرقتِ ذا] 3 أبو ذا 4 ألْ يرَجمْ 5 شنقتَ ذا [شرقتَ ذا] 6 ذا مأري ذامَ

بعد ان (اذا) شخص [رجل] يحز (يأخذ) إمراة (زوجة)، تولد له ابناء، (و) الانثى (الزوجة) تذهب الى المصير (تموت)، أبوها سوف لن يُغرِّم عن (يُطالب بـ) صَدَقتها، صَدَقتها لأبناءها.

If (after) a person [a man] takes a woman (wife), she bears him children, (and) the female (the wife) goes to destiny (dies), her father shall not fine (penalize) (for) her endowment, her endowment of (for) her children.

§ 163.—XXVII, 7-23

7 šum-ma a-wi-lum 8 aš-ša-tam 9 i-ḫu-uz-ma 10 mârê la u-ᵇšar-ši-šu 11 zinništum ši-i 12 a-na ši-im-tim 13 it-ta-la-ak 14 šum-ma tir-ḫa-tam 15 ša a-wi-lum šu-u 16 a-na bît e-mi-šu ᵇub-lu 17 e-mu-šu 18 ut-te-ir-šum 19 a-na še-ri-iḳ-ti 20 zinništim šu-a-ti 21 mu-za u-ul ᵇi-ra-ag-gu-um 22 še-ri-iḳ-ta-ša 23 ša bît a-bi-ša-ma

7 ثُمَّ أويلم [عَويلم] 8 أستَمْ 9 يحزمْ 10 مأري لا يُشرتِ ذو [يُشرْثِ ذو] 11 ذنِثتُمْ ذيي 12 أن سمِتمْ 13 يتألكْ 14 ثُمّ ترحتم [طرْحتَمْ] 15 ذا أويلْم [عويلْم] ذوو 16 أنَ بيت عمِّ ذو أبْلو 17 عمُّ ذو 18 يُتئِر ذومْ 19 أنَ شنقتِ [شرقتِ] 20 ذنِثتمْ ذأت 21 مؤتْ ذا [مؤت] ألْ يرجمْ 22 شَنقتَ ذا [شرقتَ ذا] 23 ذا بيت أبي ذامَ

بعد ان (اذا) شخص [رجل] يحز (يأخذ) إمراة (زوجة)، (و) لا تنجبهُ [تُبليه] أولاد، (ثم) هذه الانثى (الزوجة) تذهب الى المصير (تموت)؛ بعد ان (اذا) عمّه يعيدهُ (يعيدُ له) الطرحة (المهر) التي جلَبَ هذا الشخص [الرجل] الى بيت عمّه (ابو زوجته)، زوجها سوف لن يغْرّم (يُطالب بـ) صدَقة تلك الانثى (الزوجة)، صدَقتها لبيت أبيها.

If (after) a person [a man] takes a woman (wife), (and) she does not beget him children, (then) this female (wife) goes to destiny (dies); if (after) his uncle (father-in-law) returns (to) him the dowry which this person [man] brought to his uncle (father-in-law), her husband shall not fine (penalize) for that female (wife) endowment, her endowment of (for) her father's house (her family).

§ 164.—XXVII, 24-32

24 šum-ma e-mu-šu 25 tir-ḫa-tam 26 la ut-te-ir-šum 27 i-na še-ri-iḳ-[b]ti-ša 28 ma-la [b]tir-ḫa-ti-ša 29 i-ḫar-ra-aṣ-ma 30 še-ri-iḳ-ta-ša 31 a-na bît a-ta(=bi)-ša 32 u-ta-ar

24 ثمّ عمّ ذو 25 ترحتمْ [طرحتمْ] 26 لا يتئر ذومْ 27 إنَ شنقتِ ذا [شرقتِ ذا] 28 ملئ ترحتِ ذا [طرحتِ ذا] 29 يخرصمْ [يحرصمْ] 30 شنقتَ ذا [شرقتَ ذا] 31 أنَ آتا ذا 32 يتأرْ

|وفق الفقرة 163| بعد ان (اذا) عمّه (ابو زوجته) لا يعيدهُ (لا يعيدُ له) الطرحة (المهر)، (الزوج) سوف يفرزْ [يقتطع] كامل (بقدر) طرحتها (مهرها) في (من) صدَقتها، (و) يُعيد (بقية) صدَقتها الى آتيها (معطيها) (بيت ابوها).

|Referencing §164| If (after) his uncle (father-in-law) does not return (to) him the dowry, he shall set aside (deduct) as much as the full (amount) of her dowry in (from) her endowment, (and) shall return (the rest of) her endowment to its bringer (its giver) (her family).

§ 165.—XXVII, 33-50

33 šum-ma a-wi-lum 34 a-na mâri-šu 35 ša i-in-šu [b]maḫ-ru 36 eḳlam kirâm u bîtam 37 iš-ru-uḳ 38 ku-nu-kam iš-tur-šum 39 wa-ar-ka a-bu-um 40 a-na ši-im-tim 41 it-ta-al-ku 42 i-nu-ma aḫ-ḫu 43 i-zu-uz-zu 44 ḳi-iš-ti a-bu-um 45 id-di-nu-šum 46 i-li-ḳi-ma 47 e-li-nu-um-ma 48 i-na ŠA-GA bît a-ba 49 mi-it-ḫa-ri-iš 50 i-zu-uz-zu

33 ثمّ أويلم [عويلم] 34 أنَ مأري ذو 35 ذا عينْ ذو مخرْ 36 حقلمْ كيرمْ و بيتمْ 37 يشنقْ [يشرقْ] 38 كنكمْ يسترْ ذومْ [يسطرْ ذومْ] 39 وركَ أبومْ 40 أنَ سمتمْ 41 إتلكْ 42 حينمَ أخو 43 يززو 44 قسطِ [قشتِ] أبومْ 45 إدنْ ذومْ 46 يلقمْ 47 علينمْ 48 إنَ شجا بيت أبا 49 متحرتْ [متخرتْ] 50 يززو

بعد ان (اذا) شخص [رجل] يتصدّق (يوصي) حقل، بستان، وبيت، الى إبنه الذي عيْنه مُختارة (الى ابنه المفضّل)، يُسطّر (يُدوّن) له وثيقة (وصية) مختومة، بعدما الأب (قد) ذهب الى المصير (مات)، حينما (عندما) الاخوة يفرقو (يقسمو)، (الابن) سوف يلقي (يأخذ) مِنحة (ما) أعطاه الاب، (و) علاوة (على ذلك)، (الاخوة) سوف يفرقو (سوف يتقاسمو) في حاجيات بيت الاب بالتساوي.

If (after) a person [a man] endows a field, an orchard, and a house to his son who is his eye's chosen (his favorite son), writes for him a sealed document (will), after the father has gone to destiny (died), when the brothers divide, he (the favorate son) shall take the grant his father gave him, (and) additionally, they shall divide in (share) the things (the belongings) of the father's house, equally.

§ 166.—XXVII, 51-73

51 šum-ma a-wi-lum 52 a-na mârê ša ir-šu-u 53 aš-ša-tim i-ḫu-uz 54 a-na mâri-šu 55 ṣi-iḫ-ri-im 56 aš-ša-tam 57 la i-ḫu-uz 58 wa-ar-ka a-bu-um 59 a-na ši-im-tim 60 it-ta-al-ku 61 i-nu-ma aḫ-ḫu 62 i-zu-uz-zu 63 i-na ŠA.GA bît a-ba 64 a-na a-ḫi-šu-nu 65 ṣi-iḫ-ri-im 66 ša aš-ša-tam 67 la iḫ-zu 68 e-li-a-at 69 zi-it-ti-šu 70 kaspi tir-ḫa-tim 71 i-ša-ak-ka-[b]nu-šum-ma 72 aš-ša-tam 73 u-ša-aḫ-[b]ḫa-zu-šu

51 ثُمَّ أَويلم [عَويلُم] 52 أنَ مأريي ذا إرْسو 53 أسّتيم يحزْ 54 أنَ مأري ذو 55 صِهرم [صِغرَمْ] 56 أسّتمْ 57 لا يحزْ 58 وَرك أبوُمْ 59 أنَ سمتِمْ 60 إتَلْكُ 61 حينُم أخوُ 43 يُززوُ 63 إنَ شجا بيت أبا 64 أنَ أخي ذُونوُ 65 صِهرَمْ [صِغرَمْ] 66 ذا أسّتمْ 67 لا إحزْ 68 عِليات 69 زِتّي ذو 70 كسْفِ ترْحتِم [طِرحتِمْ] 71 يسكنو ذُومَ 72 أسّتمْ 73 يُتحزو ذو

بعد ان (اذا) شخص [رجل] يُحيز (يأخذ) نساء (زوجات) الى الابناء الذين إستقرو (بلغو)، لا يحز (يأخذ) إمراة (زوجة) الى إبنه الصغير، بعدما الأب (قد) ذهب الى المصير (مات)، حينما (عندما) الاخوة يفرقو (يقسمو)، علاوة على حصته في (من) حاجيات بيت الاب، لأخيهم الصغير الذي ما حاز (أخذ) إمراة (زوجة)، (الاخوة) سوف يضعو له مال طرحة (مهر)، (كي) يجعلونه يحيز (يأخذ) إمراة (زوجة).

If (after) a person [a man] takes women (wives) for the sons who settled (matured), does not take a woman (a wife) to his young son, after the father has gone to destiny (died), when the brothers divide (share), in addition to his portion in (from) his father's things (belongings), to their young brother who did not take a woman (a wife), they shall set (put) for him dowry money, to enable him to take a woman (a wife).

§ 167.—XXVII, 74-XXVIII, 8

74 šum-ma a-wi-lum 75 aš-ša-tam 76 i-ḫu-uz-ma 77 mârê u-li-zum 78 zinništum ši-i 79 a-na ši-im-tim 80 it-ta-la-ak 81 wa-ar-ki-ša 82 zinništam ša-ni-tam 83 i-ta-ḫa-^{b}az-ma 84 mârê it-ta-^{b}la-ad 85 wa-ar-ka-nu-um 86 a-bu-um ^{b}a-na ši-im-tim 87 it-ta-al-ku XXVIII, 1 mârê a-na um-^{b}ma-tim 2 u-ul i-zu-^{b}uz-zu 3 še-ri-iḳ-ti 4 um-ma-ti-šu-nu 5 i-li-ḳu-ma 6 ŠA.GA bît a-ba 7 mi-it-ḫa-ri-iš 8 i-zu-uz-zu

74 ثُمَّ أَويلم [عَويلم] 75 أسّتمْ 76 يحزْمَ 77 مأريي يُألِدْ ذُومَ [يألِتُمْ] 78 ذنِشْتُمْ ذيي 79 أنَ سمتِمْ 80 يتألكْ 81 وَرك ذا 82 ذنِشْتُمْ ثانتمَ 83 يتحَزْمَ 84 مأريي يتألِدْ 85 وركنُمْ 86 أبوُمْ أنَ سمتِمْ 87 إتَلكُ 1 مأريي أنَ أُماتِمْ 2 أُلْ يُززوُ 3 شَنِقْتِ [شَرِقْتِ] 4 أُماتِ ذُونو 5 يلِقوُمَ 6 شجا بيت أبا 7 مِتْحرِتْ [مِتْخرِتْ] 8 يُززوُ

بعد ان (اذا) شخص [رجل] يحيز (يأخذ) إمراة (زوجة)، (و) تولد له أبناء، (و) الانثى (الزوجة) تذهب الى المصير (تموت)، وراءها (بعدها) يحيز (يأخذ) انثى (زوجة) ثانية (اخرى) (و) تولد له ابناء، وراء ذلك، الأب (قد) ذهب الى المصير (مات)؛ الابناء للامهات سوف لن يفرقو (لن يقسمو) (كل شيء)، سوف يلقو (يأخذو) صدقات (مُهر) أمهاتهم، سوف يفرقو (يقسمو) حاجيات بيت الاب بالتساوي.

If (after) a person [a man] takes a woman (a wife), (and) she bears him children, (and) that woman (wife) goes to destiny (dies), after her, he takes a second (another) woman (wife), (and) she bears children, afterwards, the father has gone to destiny (died); the children to (of) the mothers shall not divide (share) (all), they shall take their (respective) mothers' family dowries, (and) they shall divide (share) the things (the belongings) of the father's house, equally.

§ 168.—XXVIII, 9-24

9 šum-ma a-wi-lum 10 a-na mâri-šu 11 na-sa-ḫi-im 12 pa-nam iš-ta-ka-an 13 a-na da-a-a-ni 14 mâri-i a-na-za-aḫ ^{b}iḳ-ta-bi 15 da-a-a-nu 16 wa-ar-ka-zu 17 i-par-ra-su-ma 18 šum-ma mârum ^{b}ar-nam kab-tam 19 ša i-na ab-lu-tim 20 na-sa-ḫi-im 21 la ub-lam 22 a-bu-um mâri-šu 23 i-na ab-lu-tim 24 u-ul i-na-za-aḫ

9 ثُمَّ أَويلم [عَويلم] 10 أنَ مأري ذو 11 نَسحِمْ [نَسخِمْ] 12 فَنَمْ يستَكَنْ 13 أنَ دآنِ 14 مأري أنزَحْ [أنَسحْ] [أنَسخْ] يقْتَبي 15 دآنْ 16 ورك ذو 17 يفَرَسمَ 18 ثُمَّ مأرمْ عرْنَمْ [عنّمْ] كَبْتَمْ 19 ذا إنَ أبلتِمْ [أبنتِمْ] 20 نَسَحِمْ [نَسَخِمْ] 21 لايُبلَمْ 22 أبوُمْ مأري ذو 23 إنَ أبلتِمْ [أبنتِمْ] 24 أُلْ يَنزَحْ [يَنَسحْ] [يَنَسخْ]

بعد ان (اذا) شخص [رجل] يضع الوجه الى (يتوجه نحو) ازاحة (تنحية) إبنه (من مسؤوليته) [التبرأ (من) إبنه]، يقول للحكام "سوف أزيح (أنحّي) إبني (من مسؤوليتي) [أتبرأ من ابني]"، الحكام سوف يتفحصو خلفيته (سوابقه)؛ بعد ان (اذا) الإبن لا يحملْ (مسؤولية) التهمة [العقوبة] الضخمة التي في (المبررة ل) تنحية (ازاحة) حملْ المسؤولية [التبرأ (من) مسؤولية البنوّة]، الأب سوف لن يزيح (ينحّي) في (من) حَملْ المسؤولية [مسؤولية البنوّة] إبنه.

If (after) a person [a man] set the face to (toward) the removal of his son (from responsibility) [to disown his son], he says to the judges "I shall remove my son (from responsibility) [disown my son]", the judges shall examine his background; if (after) the son does not bear (the responsibility for) the huge charge [penalty] that is in (that justifies) the removal of the bearing of (son) responsibility [the disowning of sonship], the father shall not remove in (from) the bearing of (son) responsibility [from sonship] his son.

§ 169.—XXVIII, 25-37

25 šum-ma ar-nam kab-tam 26 ša i-na ab-lu-tim 27 na-sa-ḫi-im 28 a-na a-bi-šu 29 it-ba-lam 30 a-na iš-ti-iš-šu 31 pa-ni-šu ub-ba-lu 32 šum-ma ar-nam ᵇkab-tam 33 a-di ši-ni-šu 34 it-ba-lam 35 a-bu-um mâri-šu 36 i-na ab-lu-tim 37 i-na-za-aḫ

25 ثمّ عرنَمْ [عنَمْ] كبْتمْ 26 ذا إنَ أبلتِمْ [أبنتِمْ] 27 نسحِمْ [نسخِمْ] 28 أنَ أبي ذو 29 يتبلَمْ 30 أنَ إستِتْ ذو 31 فني ذو يُبلو 32 ثمّ عرنَمْ [عنَمْ] كبتَمْ 33 عدي [حَدي] ثيني ذو 34 يتبلَمْ 35 أبومْ مأري ذو 36 إنَ أبلتِمْ [أبنتِمْ] 37 ينزَحْ [ينسَحْ] [ينسَخْ]

|وفق الفقرة 168| بعد ان (اذا) (الإبن) يتحمل لأبيه (مقابل ابيه) (مسؤولية) التهمة [العقوبة] الضخمة التي في (المبررة ل) تنحية (ازاحة) حَملْ المسؤولية [التبرأ (من) مسؤولية البنوّة]، لأوّلته (لمرّته الاولى) سوف يتحملو (يطيقو) (الحكام) وجهه (يغفرو له)؛ بعد ان (اذا) (الإبن) يتحمل (مسؤولية) التهمة [العقوبة] الضخمة، حتى (مادامت) ثانيته (مرّته الثانية)، الأب سوف يزيح (ينحّي) في (من) حَملْ المسؤولية [مسؤولية البنوّة] إبنه.

|Referencing §168| If (after) he (the son) bears to (in front of) his father (the responsibility for) the huge charge [penalty] that is in (that justifies) the removal of the bearing of (son) responsibility [the disowning of sonship], to (for) his first (time), they (the judges) shall bear (tolerate seeing) his face (shall forgive him); if (after) he (the son) bears (the responsibility for) the huge charge [penalty], until (as long as) (it is) his second (time), the father shall remove in (from) the bearing of (son) responsibility [from sonship] his son.

§ 170.—XXVIII, 38-61

38 šum-ma a-wi-lum 39 ḫi-ir-ta-šu 40 mârê u-li-zum 41 u ama-zu 42 mârê u-li-zum 43 a-bu-um 44 i-na bu-ul-ti-šu 45 a-na mârê ša amtum 46 ul-du-šum 47 mârû-u-a ᵇiḳ-ta-bi 48 it-ti mârê ᵇḫi-ir-tim 49 im-ta-nu-šu-nu-ti 50 wa-ar-ka ᵇa-bu-um 51 a-na ši-im-tim 52 it-ta-al-ku 53 i-na ŠA.GA ᵇbît a-ba 54 mârê ḫi-ir-tim 55 u mârê amtim 56 mi-it-ḫa-ri-iš 57 i-zu-uz-zu 58 TUR.UŠ TUR ḫi-ir-tim 59 i-na zi-it-tim 60 i-na-za-ak-ma 61 i-li-ḳi

38 ثمّ أويلم [عويلم] 39 خيرتَ ذو 40 مأريي يألدْ ذومْ [يألتمَ] 41 و أما ذو [وأمات] 42 مأريي يألدْ ذومْ [يألتم] 43 أبومْ 44 إنَ بلْتِ ذو [بلْطِ ذو] 45 أنَ مأريي ذا أمتمْ 46 ألْدو ذومْ 47 مأروا يقْتبي 48 إتي مأريي خيرتمْ 49 يمتنو ذونْ 50 ورك أبومْ 51 أنَ سمتمْ 52 إتلّكْ 53 إنَ شَجا بيت أبا 54 مأريي خيرتمْ 55 و مأريي أمتمْ 56 متحرتْ [متخرتْ] 57 يزّزوْ 58 طرسْ تَرْ [طرْ] خيرتمْ 59 إنَ زتّيمْ 60 ينزكمَ [ينسقمَ] 61 يلقي

بعد ان (اذا) شخص [رجل]، زوجته تولد له ابناء، وعبدته تولد له ابناء، (و) ألاب (الشخص [الرجل])، في عنفوانه [في حياته]، يقول للابناء الذين ولدَت له العبدة "أبنائي"، يعدّهم مع (بحساب) ابناء الزوجة؛ بعدما الأب (قد) ذهب الى المصير (مات)، ابناء

الزوجة وابناء العبدة سوف يفرقو (سوف يتقاسمو) في حاجيات بيت الاب، بالتساوي؛ فتى [ابن] الزوجة المُختار [البِكر]، سوف يحدّدْ في الحصّة (و) يأخذ (سوف يكون له الخيار الاول).

If (after) a person [a man], his wife bears him children, and his female slave bears him children, (and) the father (the person [the man]), in his bloom [in his life], says to the children that the female slave bore him "my children", count them with the children of the wife; after the father has gone to destiny (died), the children of the wife and the children of the female slave shall divide in (share) the things (the belongings) of the father's house, equally; the chosen [the first] son of the wife shall determine in the portion (and) take (he shall have first choice).

§ 171.—XXVIII, 62-XXIX, 5

[62] u šum-ma a-bu-um [63] i-na bu-ul-ti-šu [64] a-na mârê ša amtum [b]ul-du-šum [65] mârû-u-a [b]la iḳ-ta-bi [66] wa-ar-ka [b]a-bu-um [67] a-na ši-im-tim [68] it-ta-al-ku [69] i-na ŠA.GA bît a-ba [70] mârê amtim [71] it-ti mârê [b]ḫi-ir-tim [72] u-ul i-zu-uz-zu [73] an-du-ra-ar [74] amtim u mârê-ša [75] iš-ta-ak-ka-an [76] mârê ḫi-ir-tim [77] a-na mârê amtim [78] a-na wa-ar-du-tim [79] u-ul i-ra-ag-gu-mu [80] ḫi-ir-tum [81] še-ri-iḳ-ta-ša [82] u nu-du-na-am [83] ša mu-za [84] id-di-nu-ši-im [85] i-na dub-bi-im [86] iš-tu-ru-ši-im [87] i-li-ḳi-ma [88] i-na šu-ba-at [89] mu-ti-ša uš-ša-ab [XXIX, 1] a-di ba-al-ṭa-at [b]i-ik-ka-al [2] a-na kaspim [3] u-ul i-na-ad-[b]di-in [4] wa-ar-ka-za [5] ša mârê-ša-ma

[62] و ثمَّ أبومْ [63] إنَ بلْتِ ذو [بلْطِ ذو] [64] أنَ مأريي ذا أمتمْ ألْدو ذومْ [65] مأروا لا يقتبي [66] ورك أبومْ [67] أنَ سمتمْ [68] إتلكْ [69] إنَ شجا بيت أبا [70] مأريي أمتمْ [71] إتي مأريي خيرتمْ [72] ألْ يززوْ [73] أندرر [أدّرْ] [74] أمتمْ ومأريي ذا [75] يستكنْ [76] مأريي خيرتمْ [77] أنَ مأريي أمتمْ [78] أنَ وردتمْ [79] ألْ يرجمو [80] خيرتمْ [81] شنقتِ ذا [شرقت ذا] [82] و نُدنمْ [83] ذا موْت ذا [موْتَ] [84] إدنَ ذيمْ [85] إنَ دوبمْ [دوفمْ] [86] إستؤرْ ذيمْ [إسطؤرْ ذيمْ] [87] يلقيمَ [88] إنَ ثبتَ [89] مؤتي ذا يثبْ [1] عدي [حدي] بلطتْ يئكلْ [2] أنَ كسفمْ [3] ألْ يندنِ [4] وركتْ ذا [وركتَ] [5] ذا مأريي ذامَ

|وفق الفقرة 170| وبعد ان (و اذا) الأب لا يقول "أبنائي" للابناء الذين ولدَلت له العبدة، في عنفوانه [في حياته]، بعدما الأب (قد) ذهب الى المصير (مات)، ابناء العبدة مع ابناء الزوجة سوف لا يفرقو (لا يتقاسمو) في حاجيات بيت الاب، سوف يُقرّ (يتم) تحرر العبدة وابناءها، ابناء الزوجة، لابناء العبدة، سوف لن يُغرّمو (يُطالبو) للعبودية؛ الزوجة سوف تلقي (تأخذ) صدقتها و عَطاياها التي اعطاها زوجها، سطّرَ لها (دوّنَ لها) في لوح (سند)، (و) سوف تقيم في مقام (بيت) زوجها، سوف تأكل (تَنْعَمْ) حتى (مادامت) حيّة (على قيد الحياة)، (المقام) سوف لن يُعطى للفضة (لن يباع)، وراءها (بعد موتها سيكون) لأبناءها.

|Referencing §168| And after (and if) the father does not say "my children" to the children that the female slave bore him, in his bloom [in his life], after the father has gone to destiny (died), the children of the female slave with the children of the wife shall not divide (share) in the things (the belongings) of the father's house, the freedom of the female slave and her children shall be set, the children of the wife, to the children of the female slave, shall not fine (demand) to slavery; the wife shall take her endowment and her givings (presents) that her husband gave her, wrote her in a tablet, she shall settle in her husband's dwelling (house), she shall enjoy (the house) until (as long as) she is alive, it (the dwelling) shall not be given for silver (shall not be sold), after her (death) (it is) of (for) her children.

§ 172.—XXIX, 6-40

[6] šum-ma mu-za [7] nu-du-un-na-am [8] la id-di-iš-ši-im [9] še-ri-iḳ-ta-ša [10] u-ša-la-mu-[b]ši-im-ma [11] i-na ŠA.GA [12] bît mu-ti-ša [13] ṣi-it-tam [14] ki-ma ablim [b]iš-te-en [15] i-li-ḳi [16] šum-ma mârê-ša [17] aš-šum i-na bîtim [b]šu-zi-im [18] u-za-aḫ-ḫa-mu-ši [19] da-a-a-nu [20] wa-ar-ka-za [21] i-par-ra-su-ma [22] mârê ar-nam [23] i-im-mi-du [24] zinništum ši-i [25] i-na bît mu-ti-ša [26] u-ul uz-zi [27] šum-ma zinništum ši-i [28] a-na wa-ṣi-im [29] pa-ni-ša [30] iš-ta-ka-an [31] nu-du-un-na-am [32] ša mu-za [33] id-

di-nu-ši-im 34 a-na mârê-ša 35 i-iz-zi-ib 36 še-ri-iḳ-tam 37 ša bît a-bi-ša 38 i-li-ḳi-ma 39 mu-ut li-ib-^{b}bi-ša 40 i-iḫ-ḫa-az-zi

6 ثُمّ مؤتْ ذا [مؤتْ] 7 نْدُنَم 8 لا يدذْ ذيمْ [يدنْ ذيمْ] 9 شنقتْ ذا [شرقْتْ ذا] 10 يسلَمْ ذيمَ 11 إنَ شَجا 12 بيت مؤتي ذا 13 ضِحْتمْ 14 كيم أبْلمْ [أبْنمْ] إسْتَنْ 15 يلقي 16 ثمّ مأريي ذا 17 هذمْ إن بيتمْ ذو ذيم [ذوتمْ] 19 يزحمو ذي [يزهمو ذي] 19 دآنُ 20 وركَتْ ذا [وركَتْ] 21 يفرسومَ 22 مأريي عرْنَمْ [عنّمْ] 23 يمدو 24 ذنِثْتمْ ذيي 25 إنَ بيت مؤتي ذا 26 ألْ يؤزي [يُعْصي] 27 ثُمّ ذنثْتمْ ذيي 28 أنَ [وصئمْ] [وأصمْ] [وهصمْ] [وصمْ] 29 فني ذا 30 يسْتكنْ 31 نْدُنَمْ 32 ذا مؤتْ ذا [مؤتْ] 33 إدنُ ذيمْ 34 أنَ مأريي ذا 35 يعزبْ 36 شنقْتمْ [شرقْتمْ] 37 ذا بيت أبي ذا 38 يلقيمَ 39 مؤتْ لبّ ذا 40 يحزي

|وفق الفقرة 171| بعد ان (اذا) زوجها لا يعطي لها عَطايا، سوف يُأمّنو لها (يعطوها) صدقتها، سوف تلقي (تأخذ) نَفَقة بقدر (نفقة) حَملْ مسؤولية (ابن) [(نفقة) ابن] واحد في (من) حاجيات بيت زوجها؛ بعد ان (اذا) الحكام يتفحصو بعدها (بعد ذاك) أبناءه، هذا لأنهم يزاحموها (يضايقوها) في البيت العائد لها، (و) يجهّزو (ويضعو على) الابناء التهمة [العقوبة]، (الابناء) سوف لن يُخْرجو [لن يَطردو] هذه الانثى (الزوجة) في (من) بيت زوجها؛ بعد ان (اذا) هذه الانثى (الزوجة) تضع وجهها (تتوجه) للخروج (للانفصال)، سوف تترك عَطيتها التي أعطاها زوجها الى ابناءها، سوف تأخذ الصدقة التي لبيت أبيها، (و) سوف تحيز (تأخذ) زوج قلبها (اختيارها).

|Referencing §171| If (after) her husband does not give her givings (presents), they shall secure her (family) endowment for her, she shall take a disbursement (an allocation) as much as one (son) responsibility bearing [son] in (from) the things (the belongings) of the father's house; if (after) the judges examine (investigate) after that his children, that is because they harass her in her own home, (and) furnish (put on) the children the charge [penalty], the children shall not force out that female (wife) in (from) her husband's house, if (after) this female (the wife) set her face (eye) on leaving (her house), she shall leave to her children the givings (presents) that her husband gave her, she shall take the endowment of her father's house, (and) shall take the husband of her heart (her choice).

§ 173.—XXIX, 41-50

41 šum-ma zinništum ši-i 42 a-šar i-ru-bu 43 a-na mu-ti-ša 44 wa-ar-ki-im 45 mârê it-ta-la-ad 46 wa-ar-ka zinništum ši-i ^{b}im-tu-ut 47 še-ri-iḳ-ta-ša 48 mârê maḫ-ru-tum 49 u wa-ar-ku-tum 50 i-zu-uz-zu

41 ثُمَّ ذنثْتمْ ذيي 42 أشَرْ إرْبُ 43 أنَ مؤتي ذا 44 وركِمْ 45 مأريي يتَلَدْ 46 وركَ ذنِثْتمْ ذيي يمْتُتْ 47 شنَقتَ ذا [شَرقْتَ ذا] 48 مأريي مَخْرُتَم 49 و ورَكْتُمْ 50 يزّزوْ

|وفق الفقرة 172| بعد ان (اذا) هذه الانثى (الزوجة)، حيث دخلت، تولد ابناء الى زوجها الاخير (اللاحق)، بعدما هذه الانثى (الام) تموت، ابناء (الزوج) المتقدم (السابق) و (الزوج) المتأخر (اللاحق) سوف يفرقو (سوف يتقاسمو) صدقتها.

|Referencing §172A| If (after) this female (wife), where (in the house) she entered (later), she bears (new) children to her later husband, after this female (wife) dies, the children of the advanced (former husband) and the latter (later husband) shall divide (share) her endowment.

§ 174.—XXIX, 51-56

51 šum-ma a-na mu-ti-ša 52 wa-ar-ki-im 53 mârê la it-^{b}ta-la-ad 54 še-ri-iḳ-ta-ša 55 mârê ḫa-wi-ri-^{b}ša-ma 56 i-li-ḳu-u

51 ثمّ أنَ مؤتي ذا 52 وَرْكِمْ 53 مأريي لا يتلَدْ 54 شنَقْتَ ذا [شَرقْتَ ذا] 55 مأريي خوري ذامَ 56 يلقَوَ

|وفق الفقرة 172| بعد ان (اذا) هذه الانثى (الزوجة)، لا تولد ابناء الى زوجها الاخير (اللاحق)، أبناء صفيّها (زوجها الاول) يلقو (يأخذو) صدقتها.

|Referencing §172A| If (after) she does not bear (new) children to her later husband, the children of her chosen (her first husband) shall take her endowment.

§ 175.—XXIX, 57-68

57 šum-ma lu warad [b]êkallim 58 u lu warad 59 MAŠ.EN.KAK 60 mârat a-wi-lim 61 i-ḫu-uz-ma 62 mârê 63 it-ta-la-ad 64 be-el wardim 65 a-na mârê 66 mârat a-wi-lim 67 a-na wa-ar-[b]du-tim 68 u-ul i-ra-ag-gu-um

57 ثُمّ لو وَرَدْ هيكلِمْ 58 ولو وردْ 59 مَس عَن كَاكْ 60 مأرتْ أويلِم [عَويلِم] 61 يحزُمْ 62 مأريي 63 يتلَدْ 64 بعَلْ وردِمْ 65 أنَ مأريي 66 مأرتْ أويلِم [عَويلِم] 67 أنَ وَردُتِمْ 68 أُلْ يرجُمْ

بعد ان (اذا)، لو (ليكن) عبد قصر، و(حتى) لو عبد شخص من العامة، يحيز (يأخذ) بنت شخص [رجل]، (والبنت) تولد أبناء، مالك العبد، لأبناء بنت الشخص [الرجل]، سوف لن يُغرّم (يُطالب) للعبودية.

If (after), let-it-be a palace's slave, and (even) let-it-be an ordinary man's slave takes (marries) a daughter of a person [a man], (and) she gives birth to children, the owner of the slave, to the children of the daughter of the person [the man], shall not fine (demand) to slavery.

§ 176.—XXVIII, 69-XXX, 21

69 u šum-ma [b]warad êkallim 70 u lu warad MAŠ.EN.KAK 71 mârat a-wi-lim 72 i-ḫu-uz-ma 73 i-nu-ma i-ḫu-zu-ši 74 ga-du-um 75 še-ri-iḳ-tim 76 ša bît a-bi-ša 77 a-na bît warad êkallim 78 u lu warad MAŠ.EN.KAK 79 i-ru-ub-ma 80 iš-tu in-ne-im-du 81 bîtam i-pu-šu 82 bi-ša-am ir-šu-u 83 wa-ar-ka-nu-um-ma 84 lu warad êkallim 85 u lu warad MAŠ.EN.KAK 86 a-na ši-im-tim 87 it-ta-la-ak 88 mârat a-wi-lim 89 še-ri-iḳ-ta-ša 90 i-li-ḳi 91 u mi-im-ma 92 ša mu-za u ši-i XXX. 1 iš-tu [b]in-ne-im-du 2 ir-šu-u 3 a-na ši-ni-šu 4 i-zu-uz-zu-ma 5 mi-iš-lam [b]be-el wardim 6 i-li-ḳi 7 mi-iš-lam 8 mârat a-wi-lim 9 a-na mârê-ša [b]i-li-ḳi 10 šum-ma [b]mârat a-wi-lim 11 še-ri-iḳ-tam [b]la i-šu 12 mi-im-ma [b]ša mu-za u ši-i 13 iš-tu [b]in-ne-im-du 14 ir-šu-u 15 a-na ši-ni-šu 16 i-zu-uz-zu-ma 17 mi-iš-lam [b]be-el wardim 18 i-li-ḳi 19 mi-iš-lam 20 mârat a-wi-lim 21 a-na mârê-ša [b]i-li-ḳi

69 و ثمّ وردْ هيكلِمْ 70 ولو وردْ مَس عَن كَاكْ 71 مأرتْ أويلِم [عَويلِم] 72 يحزُمْ 73 حينمَ إحزُ ذي 74 جدُمْ [قدُمْ] 75 شنقتَمْ [شرقتَمْ] 76 ذا بيت أبي ذا 77 أنَ بيت وَردْ هيكلِمْ 78 ولو وَردْ مَس عَن كَاكْ 79 يأرُبمْ 80 إستُ إنئمْدو [إنعمْدو] 81 بيتمْ إعفُشو [إعفُسو] 82 بيذمْ إرْسُو 83 وركَنُمْ 84 لو وَردْ هيكلِمْ 85 ولو وَردْ مَس عَن كَاكْ 86 أنَ سمْتمْ 87 يتألكْ 88 مأرتْ أويلِم [عَويلِم] 89 شنقتْ ذا [شرقتْ ذا] 90 يلقِي 91 و ممَّ 92 ذا مؤتْ ذا [مؤتْ] و ذيي 1 إستُ إنئمْدو [إنعمْدو] 2 إرْسُو 3 أنَ ثِيني ذو 4 يزُّزمْ 5 مثلَمْ بعَلْ وردِمْ 6 يلقِي 7 مثلَمْ 8 مأرتْ أويلِم [عَويلِم] 9 أنَ مأريي ذا يلقِي 10 ثُمّ مأرتْ أويلِم [عَويلِم] 11 شنقتَمْ [شرقتَمْ] لا يذو 12 ممَّ ذا مؤتْ ذا [مؤتْ] و ذيي 13 إستُ إنئمْدو [إنعمْدو] 14 إرْسُو 15 أنَ ثِيني ذو 16 يزُّزمْ 17 مثلَمْ بعَلْ وردِمْ 18 يلقِي 19 مثلَمْ 20 مأرتْ أويلِم [عَويلِم] 21 أنَ مأريي ذا يلقِي

وبعد ان (اذا)، عبد قصر، و(حتى) لو عبد شخص من العامة، يحيز (يأخذ) بنت شخص [رجل]، (و) حينما (عندما) حازها (أخذها)، تدخُلْ الى بيت عبد القصر، ولو عبد الشخص من العامة، أُسوة (أُسوة مع) الصدقة التي لبيت أبيها، (و) أوّلما (حالما) إلتصقو (إقترنو)، بنو (هيئو) بيت، أرسو (وضعو) ممتلكات (اثاث)، (ثم) وراء ذلك، لو عبد القصر، ولو عبد الشخص من العامة، يذهب الى المصير (يموت)؛ بنت الشخص [الرجل] سوف تلقي (تأخذ) صدقتها، وسوف يفرقو (يقسمو) لإثنينه (لنصْفيه) أيّ الذي زوجها وهي أوّلما (حالما) إلتصقو (إقترنو) أرسو (وضعو)، مالك العبد سوف يلقي (يأخذ) نصف، بنت الشخص [الرجل] سوف تلقي (تأخذ) لأبناءها نصف؛ بعد ان (اذا) البنت شخص [رجل] لا تملك صدقة، أيّما الذي زوجها وهي أوّلما (حالما) إلتصقو (إقترنو) أرسو

(وضعو)، سوف يفرقو (يقسمو) لإثنينه (لنصّفيه)، مالك العبد يلقي (يأخذ) نصف، بنت الشخص [الرجل] تلقي (تأخذ) لأبناءها نصف.

If (after), let-it-be a palace's slave, and (even) let-it-be an ordinary man's slave takes (marries) a daughter of a person [a man], (and) when he took her, she enters to the house of the palace's slave, and (even) let-it-be the ordinary man's slave along with the endowment of her father's house, (and) once they coupled, they established a house, settled in (put in) goods [possessions], afterwards, let-it-be the palace's slave, and (even) let-it-be the ordinary man's slave goes to destiny (dies); the daughter of the person [the man] shall take her endowment, and whatever that her husband and she settled in (put in) once they coupled, they shall divide (share) to its twos (its halfs), the owner of the slave shall take (one) half, the daughter of the person [the man] shall take (one) half to (for) her children; if (after) the daughter of the person [the man] does not have an endowment, whatever that her husband and she settled in (put in), once they coupled, they shall divide (share) to its twos (its halfs), the owner of the slave shall take (one) half, the daughter of the person [the man] shall take (one) half to (for) her children.

§ 177.—XXX, 22-60

22 šum-ma NU.MU.SU 23 ša mârê-ša 24 ṣi-iḫ-ḫi-ru 25 a-na bîtim ša-ni-im 26 e-ri-bi-im 27 pa-ni-ša 28 iš-ta-ka-an 29 ba-lum da-a-a-ni 30 u-ul i-ir-ru-ub 31 i-nu-ma 32 a-na bîtim ša-ni-im 33 i-ir-ru-bu 34 da-a-a-nu 35 wa-ar-ka-at 36 bît mu-ti-ša 37 pa-ni-im 38 i-par-ra-su-ma 39 bîtam ša mu-ti-ša 40 pa-ni-im 41 a-na mu-ti-ša 42 wa-ar-ki-im 43 u zinništim šu-a-ti 44 i-pa-ak-ki-du-ma 45 dup-pa-am 46 u-še-iz-zi-bu-[b]šu-nu-ti 47 bîtam i-na-ṣa-ru 48 u ṣi-iḫ-ḫi-ru-tim 49 u-ra-ab-bu-u 50 u-ni-a-tim 51 a-na kaspim 52 u-ul i-na-ad-di-nu 53 ša-a-a-ma-nu-um 54 ša u-nu-ut 55 mârê NU.MU.SU 56 i-ša-am-mu 57 i-na kaspi-šu 58 i-te-el-li 59 ŠA.GA a-na be-li-šu 60 i-ta-ar

22 ثمْ نمس [نُقّسْ] [نُكّسْ] 23 ذا ماريي ذا 24 صهيرْ [صغيرْ] 25 أنَ بيتمْ ثانمْ 26 إربمْ 27 فني ذا 28 يستكنْ 29 بلمْ دآنِ 30 أُلْ يئرِب 31 حينمْ 32 أن بيتمْ ثانمْ 33 يئرِبْ 34 دآنْ 35 وركتْ 36 بيت مؤتي ذا 37 فنيمْ 38 يفرسمْ 39 بيتمْ ذا مؤتي ذا 40 فنيمْ 41 أن مؤتي ذا 42 وركمْ 43 و ذنثتمْ ذأتِ 44 يفكدوم [يفقدوم] 45 دوبمْ [دوفمْ] 46 يشزبو ذنوتي [يشذبو ذنوتي] 47 بيتمْ ينصرو 48 و صهيرتمْ [صغيرتمْ] 49 يربوَ 50 عنياتمْ 51 أن كسفمْ 52 أُلْ يندنو 53 سآمنمْ 54 ذا عنْتْ 55 مأريي نُمُسْ [نُقّسْ] [نُكّسْ] 56 إإسمْ 57 إنَ كسْف ذو 58 يتعلّي 59 شَجا أنَ بعْلِ ذو 60 يتأرْ

بعد ان (اذا) الأرملة التي أبناءها صغار تضع وجهها (عينها) (تتوجه) الى دخول بيت ثاني (آخرْ)، سوف لا تدخل بلا (بدون) (علم) الحكام؛ حينما (عندما) تدخل الى بيت ثاني (آخرْ)، الحكام سوف يتفحصو خلفية (حالة) بيت زوجها المتقدم (السابق)، (و) سوف يُعلّقو (يُعهدو) الى زوجها الاخير (اللاحق) وتلك الانثى (الزوجة) البيت الذي لزوجها المتقدم (السابق)، سوف يُعلّمونَهما (يُبيّنونَهما) (يكتبون لهما) لوح (سند)، (هُما) سوف يحفظو البيت و يربّو الصغار (الأبناء)، سوف لن يعطو للفضة (يبيعو) العُدّيات (الحاجيات)، المشتري الذي إشترى عُدّة (حاجيات) أبناء أرملة سوف يتنازل بفضته (يخسر فضته)، سوف يُعيد الحاجيات الى مالكها.

If (after) the widow whose children are young set her face (eye) on entering a second (another) house, she shall not enter without (the knowledge of) the judges; when she enters to a second (another) house, the judges shall examine the background (status) of her former husband, (and) they shall entrust the house of her former husband to her later husband and that female (widow), they shall mark them [clarify them] (write for them) a tablet; they (the widow and new husband) shall protect the house and rear the young (children), they shall not give for silver (sell) the things [belongings], a buyer who bought widow's children things [belongings] shall cede in (give up) his silver, shall return the things [belongings].

§ 178.—XXX, 61-XXXI, 19

61 šum-ma NIN.AN ᵇŠAL(?) 62 u lu zinništum zi-ik-ᵇru-um 63 ša a-bu-ša 64 še-ri-iḳ-tam 65 iš-ru-ḳu-ši-im 66 dup-pa-am 67 iš-tu-ru-ši-im 68 i-na dup-pi-im 69 ša iš-tu-ru-ši-im 70 wa-ar-ka-za 71 e-ma e-li-ša 72 ṭa-bu na-da-nam 73 la iš-tur-ši-im-ma 74 ma-la li-ib-bi-ša 75 la u-ša-am-zi-ši 76 wa-ar-ka a-bu-um 77 a-na ši-im-tim 78 it-ta-al-ku 79 eḳil-ša u kirâ-ša 80 aḫ-ḫu-ša 81 i-li-ḳu-ma 82 ki-ma e-mu-uḳ 83 zi-it-ti-ša 84 ŠE.BA NI.BA ᵇu ŠIG.BA 85 i-na-ad-di-nu-šim-ma 86 li-ib-ba-ša 87 u-ṭa-ab-bu 88 šum-ma aḫ-ḫu-ša 89 ki-ma e-mu-uḳ 90 zi-it-ti-ša 91 ŠE.BA NI.BA u ŠIG.BA 92 la it-ta-ad-ᵇnu-ši-im-ma XXXI,1 li-ib-ba-ša 2 la uṭ-ṭi-ib-bu 3 eḳil-ša u kirâ-ša 4 a-na ir-ri-ši-im 5 ša e-li-ša ᵇṭa-bu 6 i-na-ad-di-in-ma 7 ir-ri-za 8 it-ta-na-aš-ši-ši 9 eḳlam kirâm 10 u mi-im-ma 11 ša a-bu-ša 12 id-di-nu-ši-im 13 a-di ba-al-ṭa-at ᵇi-kal 14 a-na kaspim 15 u-ul i-na-ad-di-in 16 ša-ni-a-am 17 u-ul u-up-pa-al 18 ab-lu-za 19 ša aḫ-ḫi-ᵇša-ma

61 ثمَّ نِنْ عَنْ سَعَلْ [شَهَلْ] 62 ولو ذنِثْتمْ ذِكْرمْ 63 ذا أبو ذا 64 شنِقْتمْ [شرِقْتمْ] 65 إشْنُقْ ذيمْ [إشْرُقْ ذيمْ] 66 دُوبمْ [دُوفمْ] 67 إسْطُرْ ذيمْ 68 إنَ دُوبِمْ [دُوفِمْ] 69 ذا إسْطُرُ ذيمْ 70 ورْكَتْ ذا [ورْكَت] 71 إيما علي ذا 72 طبُ ندنَمْ 73 لا إسْطُرُ ذيمْ 74 ملئ لبِّ ذا 75 لا يُسمْدُ ذي ذي [يُسمْتِ ذي] 76 ورك أبُومْ 77 أنَ سمْتِمْ 78 إتلكُ 79 حقلْ ذا وكيرَ ذا 80 أخوُ ذا 81 يلقومْ 82 كيمَ عمُقْ 83 زتّي ذا 84 سعبَ [شعبَ] نحيبَ و سجْبَ 85 يندنُ ذيمَ 86 لبَّ ذا 87 يُطبو 88 ثمَّ أخوُ ذا 89 كيمَ عمُقْ 90 زتّي ذا 91 سعبَ [شعبَ] نيبَ و سجْبَ 92 لا يتدْنُ ذيمَ 1 لبَّ ذا 2 لا أُطبو 3 حقلْ ذا وكيرَ ذا 4 أنَ إريسمْ 5 ذا علي ذا طبُ 6 يندنمْ 7 إرسْ ذا [إرتَ] 8 يتأنتِ ذي [يتَعنتِ ذي] 9 حقلَمْ كيرمْ 10 و ممَّ 11 ذا أبو ذا 12 إدنُ ذيمْ 13 عدي [حدي] بلْطتْ يكلْ 14 أنَ كسفِمْ 15 أُلْ يندنُ 16 ثانيامْ 17 أُلْ يؤفلْ 18 أبلُ ذا [أبلُتَ] 19 ذا أخيي ذامَ

بعد ان (اذا) الإمرأة [العجوز] الكاهنة، و(حتى) لو أنثى الطاعة (المُطيعة او الخادمة في قصر)، التي تصدّقها (تصدّق عليها) ابوها صدقة، سطّرَ لها (دوّن لها) لوح (سند)، (الأب) لا (ما) سطّرَ لها (دوّنَ لها) "وراءها (بعدها)، أينما (حيثما) عليها مُسرْ (مُسر لقلبها) مُعطى" في اللوح (السند) الذي سطّرَ لها (دوّن لها)، كامل (مسرّة) قلبها، لم يقصده لها، بعدما الأب (قد) ذهب الى المصير (مات)، اخوانها يلقو (يأخذو) حقلها وبستانها، (و) يعطونها حبوب، زيت، وصوف، مثل حق (بمقدار) حصتها، (و) يطيبو (يسرّو) قلبها؛ بعد ان (اذا) اخوانها لا يعطوها حبوب، زيت، وصوف، كما حق (بمقدار) حصتها، (و) لا يطيبو (لا يسرّو) قلبها، سوف تعطي حقلها وبستانها الى الفلاح (المُستأجر) الذي عليها مُسرْ (مُسر لقلبها)، (و) فلاحها (مستأجرها) سوف يتحمَل مشقتها، سوف تأكل (تَنْعَمْ من) الحقل، البستان، وأيّ ما اعطاها ابوها حتى (مادامت) حيّة (على قيد الحياة)، سوف لن تعطي للفضة (تبيع)، سوف لن تُحمّل (تودع الى) (تتعَهد الى) ثانيا (آخرا)، حمَلْها (أملاكها) لإخوانها.

If (after) the priestess woman [the old priestess], and (even) let-it-be an obedience female (a palace's disciple or servant) whose father endowed her an endowment, wrote her a tablet, he has not written her "after her, wherever on her pleasing (whoever pleases her heart) shall be given" in the table he wrote her, her full heart (choice), he does not intend it for her, after the father has gone to destiny (died), her brothers shall take her field and her orchard, (and) shall give her grains, oil, and wool, as worthy as her portion, (and) shall please her heart; if (after) her brothers do not give her grains, oil, and wool, as worthy as her portion, (and) do not please her heart, she shall give her field and her orchard to the farmer (renter) who is over her pleasing (who pleases her heart), (and) her farmer (renter) shall bear their hardship (their responsibility), she shall enjoy (the fruit of) the field, the orchard, and whatever her father gave her until (as long as) she is alive, she shall not give for silver (sell), she shall not load (pledge) to a second (to another), her load (her property) (will be) of (for) her brothers.

§ 179.—XXXI, 20-42

20 šum-ma NIN.AN ŠAL(?) 21 u lu zinništi zi-ᵇik-ru-um 22 ša a-bu-ša 23 še-ri-iḳ-tam 24 iš-ru-ḳu-ši-im 25 ku-nu-kam 26 iš-tu-ru-ši-im 27 i-na dup-pi-im 28 ša iš-tu-ru-ši-im 29 wa-ar-ka-za 30 e-

ma e-li-ša ᵇṭa-bu 31 na-da-nam 32 iš-tur-ši-im-ma 33 ma-la li-ib-bi-ša 34 uš-tam-zi-ši 35 wa-ar-ka a-bu-um 36 a-na ši-im-tim 37 it-ta-al-ku 38 wa-ar-ka-za 39 e-ma e-li-ša ṭa-bu 40 i-na-ad-di-in 41 aḫ-hu-ša 42 u-ul i-ba-ᵇag-ga-ru-ši

20 ثُمّ نِن عَنْ سَعَلْ [شَهَلْ] 21 ولو ذنثتي ذِكْرُم 22 ذا أبو ذا 23 شَنقتَمْ [شرقتَمْ] 24 إشْنُقْ ذيمْ [إشْرُقْ ذيمْ] 25 كُنكُمْ 26 إسْطُرْ ذيمْ 27 إن دُوبِمْ [دُوفِمْ] 28 ذا إسْطُرْ ذيمْ 29 ورْكَتْ ذا [ورْكَت] 30 أيما علي ذا 31 طَبْ نَدنَمْ 32 إسْطُرْ ذيمْ 33 ملئ لبّ ذا 34 يُستَمْدْ ذي ذي [أُسْتَمْتي ذي] 35 ورك أبوْمْ 36 أنَ سِمتِمْ 37 إتلْكُ 38 ورْكَتْ ذا [ورْكَت] 39 إيما علي ذا طبْ 40 ينَدِنَمْ 41 أخوو ذا 42 ألْ يبَجَرو ذي [يفجرو ذي] [يبقَرو ذي]

بعد ان (اذا) الإمرأة الكاهنة [العجوز الكاهنة]، و(حتى) لو أنثى الطاعة (المُطيعة او الخادمة في قصر) التي تصدّقها (تصدّق عليها) أبوها صدقة، سطّرَ لها (دوّن لها) وثيقة (وصية) مختومة، (الأب) سطّرَ لها (دوّنَ لها) "وراءها (بعدها)، أيّما عليها مُسرْ (مُسر لقلبها) مُعطى" في اللوح (السند) الذي سطّرَ لها (دوّنَ لها)، كامل (مسرّة) قلبها يتقصّده لها، بعدما ذهب الأب الى المصير (مات)، وراءها (بعد موتها)، سوف تعطي أينما (حيثما) عليها مُسرْ (مُسر لقلبها)، إخوانها سوف لن ينُازعوها (يُقاضوها).

If (after) the priestess woman [the old priestess], and (even) let-it-be the obedience female (the palace's disciple or servant) whose father has endowed her an endowment, wrote her a tablet, he has written her "after her, wherever on her pleasing (whoever pleases her heart) shall be given" in the table he wrote her, her full heart (choice), he intends it to her, after the father has gone to destiny (died), after her (passing), she shall give wherever on her pleasing (whoever pleases her heart), her brothers shall not contend (legally challenge) her.

§ 180.—XXXI, 43-59

43 šum-ma a-bu-um 44 a-na mârti-šu 45 ˢᵃˡkallâtim 46 u lu zinništi zi-ᵇik-ru-um 47 še-ri-iḳ-tam 48 la iš-[ru]-uḳ-ši-im 49 wa-ar-ka a-bu-um 50 a-na ši-im-tim 51 it-ta-al-ku 52 i-na ŠA.GA bît a-ba 53 ṣi-it-tam ki-ma 54 ab-lim iš-te-en 55 i-za-az-ma 56 a-di ba-al-ṭa-at 57 i-ik-ka-al 58 wa-ar-ka-za 59 ša aḫ-ḫi-ša-ma

43 ثُمّ أبوْمْ 44 أنَ مأرتي ذو 45 سعل [شهل] كلتِمْ 46 ولو ذنثتي ذِكرُمْ 47 شَنقتَمْ [شرِقتَمْ] 48 لا يشنُق ذيمْ [يشرُق ذيمْ] 49 ورك أبوْمْ 50 أنَ سِمتِمْ 51 إتلْكُ 52 إنَ شَجا بيت أبا 53 ضِحتَمْ كيمَ 54 أبلِمْ [أبنِمْ] إستَنْ 55 يززمْ 56 عدي [حدي] بلْطَتْ 57 يئكَلْ 58 وركَتْ ذا [ورْكَتْ] 59 ذا أخيي ذامَ

بعد ان (اذا) الأب، لإبنته الكُنّة (العروس (الزوجة))، و(حتى) لو أنثى الطاعة (المُطيعة او خادمة القصر)، لا يتصدّقها (يتصدّق عليها) صدقة، بعدما الأب (قد) ذهب الى المصير (مات)، سوف تقتسمْ (تأخذ جزء) نَفَقة بقدر (نفقة) حَملْ مسؤولية (ابن) [(نفقة) ابن] واحد في (من) حاجيات بيت الاب، (و) سوف تأكل (تنْعَم) حتى (مادامت) حيّة (على قيد الحياة)، وراءها (بعد موتها) (جزءها) لإخوانها.

If (after) the father, to his daughter the bride, and (even) let-it-be an obedience female (a palace's disciple or servant), does not endow her an endowment, after the father has gone to destiny (died), she shall share a disbursement (an allocation) as much as one (son) responsibility bearing [son] in (from) the things (the belongings) of the father's house, (and) she shall enjoy (the house) until (as long as) she is alive, after her (passing) (her share) of (for) her brothers.

§ 181.—XXXI, 60-75

60 šum-ma a-bu-um 61 ˢᵃˡ?ḳadištam 62 u lu NU.PAR 63 a-na ilim iš-ši-ma 64 še-ri-iḳ-tam 65 la iš-ru-uḳ-ši-im 66 wa-ar-ka a-bu-um 67 a-na ši-im-tim 68 it-ta-al-ku 69 i-na ŠA.GA bît a-ba 70 IGI.III.GAL ablûti-ša 71 i-za-az-ma 72 a-di ba-al-ṭa-at 73 i-ik-ka-al 74 wa-ar-ka-za 75 ša aḫ-ḫi-ša-ma

60 ثُمَّ أبوُمْ 61 سعل [شهل] قَدِسْتَمْ 62 ولو نوبَرْ 63 أنَ إلمْ يعسِيمَ [يئتِيم] 64 شنَقتَمْ [شَرِقتَمْ] 65 لا يشْنَقْ ذيم [يشْرُقْ ذيمْ] 66 وَرْكَ أبوُمْ
67 أنَ سِمتِمْ 68 إتَلْكُ 69 إنَ شَجا بيت أبا 70 إجي 3 جَلْ أبلْتي ذا [أبْنْتي ذا] 71 يزَّزَمْ 73 عدي [حدي] بَلْطَتْ 74 يئكَلْ 75 وَرْكَتْ ذا [وَرْكَتَ]
59 ذا أخيي ذامَ

بعد ان (اذا) أبْ يُمَنّي [يوجّه] (يَنْذُر) (بنت) قدّيسة (ورعة)، و(حتى) لو (بنت) متجافية (غير ورعة) للإله، (و) لا يتصدّقها (لا يتصدّق عليها) صدقة، بعدما الأب (قد) ذهب الى المصير (مات)، (هي) سوف تقتسمْ (تأخذ جزء) 1\3 حَمِلْ مسؤوليته (لابن) [(مسؤولية) بنْوّته] في (من) حاجيات بيت الاب، (و) سوف تأكل (تَنْعَمْ) حتى (مادامت) (هي) حيّة (على قيد الحياة)، وراءها (بعدها)، (الجزء) لإخوانها.

If (after) a father dedicates [directs] to the god a devotee [pure] (daughter), and (even) let-it-be a withdrawn (non-devoted) (daughter), (and) he does not endow her an endowment, after the father has gone to destiny (died), she shall share 1/3 his bearing of (son) responsibility [his sonship] in (from) the things (the belongings) of the father's house, (and) she shall enjoy (the house) until (as long as) she is alive, after her (the share is) of (for) her brothers.

§ 182.—XXXI, 76-XXXII, 1

76 šum-ma a-bu-um 77 a-na mârti-šu 78 aššat ^{ilu}Marduk 79 ša Bâbili.KI 80 še-ri-iḳ-tam 81 la iš-ru-uḳ-ši-im 82 ku-nu-kam 83 la iš-tur-ši-im 84 wa-ar-ka ^{b}a-bu-um 85 a-na ši-im-tim 86 it-ta-al-ku 87 i-na ŠA.GA ^{b}bît a-ba 88 IGI.III.GAL ablûti-ša 89 it-ti aẖ-ẖi-ša 90 i-za-az-ma 91 il-kam 92 u-ul i-il-la ak 93 aššat ^{ilu}Marduk 94 wa-ar-ka-za 95 e-ma e-li-ša 96 ṭa-bu $^{XXXII, 1}$ i-na-ad-di-in

76 ثُمَّ أبوُمْ 77 أنَ مأرتي ذو 78 أسّتْ الْمَرْدوكْ [الْمأرْ دوكْ] 79 ذا بابلِ كيعِ [قيع] 80 شنَقِتَمْ [شَرِقتَمْ] 81 لا يشْنُقْ ذيم [يشْرُقْ ذيمْ] 82
كُنُكَمْ 83 لا يسْطُرْ ذيمْ 84 وَرَكَ أبوُمْ 85 أنَ سِمتِمْ 86 إتَلْكْ 87 إنَ شَجا بيت أبا 88 إجي 3 جَلْ أبلْتي ذا [أبْنْتي ذا] 89 إتي أخيي ذا 90 يزّزَمْ 91
إلْكَمْ 92 إلْ يئِلَكْ 93 أسّتْ الْمَرْدوكْ [الْمأرْ دوكْ] 94 وَرْكَتْ ذا [وَرْكَتَ] 95 71 إيما علِي ذا 96 طَبُ 1 ينَدِمْ

بعد ان (اذا) الأبْ، لإبنته، إمرأة (كاهنة) الإله مَرْدوكْ (إبن العاصِفْ (إبن إنليل)) ذا أرض بابل، لا يتصدّقها (لا يتصدّق عليها) صدقة، لا يسطّرْ لها (يدوّنْ لها) وثيقة (وصية) مختومة، بعدما الأب (قد) ذهب الى المصير (مات)، سوف تقتسمْ (تأخذ جزء) مع إخوانها 1\3 حَمِلْ مسؤوليته (لابن) [(مسؤولية) بنْوّته] في (من) حاجيات بيت الاب، (و) سوف لن تَتَرسّل الرسالة (لن تقوم بالعمل)؛ إمرأة (كاهنة) الإله مَرْدوكْ سوف تعطي (جزءها) أينما (حيثما) عليها مُسِرْ (يسرّ قلبها)، وراءها (بعد موتها).

If (after) the father, to his daughter, (who is) a woman (a priestess) of the god Marduk (Ma'arduk: son of the storm maker (son of Enlil)) of the land of Babylon, he does not endow her an endowment, he does not write her a sealed document (will), after the father has gone to destiny (died), she shall share with her brothers 1/3 his bearing of (son) responsibility [his sonship] in (from) the things (the belongings) of the father's house, (and) she shall not run the operation (shall not do the work); a woman (a priestess) of the god Marduk shall give wherever on her pleasing (whoever pleases her heart), after her (passing),

§ 183.—XXXII, 2-14

2 šum-ma a-bu-um 3 a-na mârti-šu ^{b}šu-ge-tim 4 še-ri-iḳ-tam 5 iš-ru-uḳ-ši-im 6 a-na mu-tim 7 id-di-iš-ši 8 ku-nu-uk-kam 9 iš-tur-ši-im 10 wa-ar-ka ^{b}a-bu-um 11 a-na ši-im-tim 12 it-ta-al-ku 13 i-na ŠA.GA ^{b}bît a-ba 14 u-ul i-za-az

2 ثُمَّ أبوُمْ 3 أنَ مأرَتي ذو شوقتِمْ [شوجَتِمْ] 4 شنَقتَمْ [شَرِقتَمْ] 5 يشْنَقْ ذيمْ [يشْرُقْ ذيمْ] 6 أنَ مؤتِمْ 7 يدِذْ ذِي [يدِنْ ذِي] 8 كُنُكَمْ 9
يسطُرْ ذيمْ 10 وَرَكَ أبوُمْ 11 أنَ سِمتِمْ 12 إتَلْكُ 13 إنَ شَجا بيت أبا 14 أُلْ يزّزْ

بعد ان (اذا) الأبْ، لإبنته الجارية، يتصدّقها (يتصدّق عليها) صدقة، يعطيها الى زوج (يزوجها)، يسطّرْ لها (يدوّنْ لها) وثيقة (وصية) مختومة، بعدما الأب (قد) ذهب الى المصير (مات)، سوف لن تقتسِمْ (تأخذ جزء) في (من) حاجيات بيت الاب.

If (after) a father, to his daughter, the concubine, endows her an endowment, gives her to a husband, writes her a sealed document (will), after the father has gone to destiny (died), she shall not share (does not have a share) in (from) the things (the belongings) of the father's house.

§ 184.—XXXII, 15-30

15 šum-ma a-wi-lum 16 a-na mârti-šu 17 šu-ge-tim 18 še-ri-iḳ-tam 19 la iš-ru-uḳ-šim 20 a-na mu-tim 21 la id-di-iš-ši 22 wa-ar-ka [b]a-bu-um 23 a-na ši-im-tim 24 it-ta-al-ku 25 aḫ-ḫu-ša 26 ki-ma e-mu-uḳ [b]bît a-ba 27 še-ri-iḳ-tam 28 i-šar-ra-ḳu-[b]ši-ma 29 a-na mu-tim 30 i-na-ad-di-nu-ši

15 ثمّ أويلم [عويلم] 16 أنَ مأرتي ذو 17 شوقتِمْ [شوجتِمْ] 18 شنِقتَمْ [شرِقتَمْ] 19 لا يشنُق ذيم [يشرُق ذيم] 20 أنَ مؤتِمْ 21 لا يدِذْ ذي [يدِنْ ذي] 22 ورك أبومْ 23 أنَ سمِتمْ 24 إتلَكْ 25 أخو ذا 26 كيم عمُقْ بيت أبا 27 شنِقتَمْ [شرِقتَمْ] 28 يشنَقو ذيم [يشرَقو ذيم] 29 أنَ مؤتِمْ 30 يندِنو ذي

بعد ان (اذا) شخص [رجل]، لإبنته الجارية، لا يتصدّقها (لا يتصدّق عليها) صدقة، لا يعطيها الى زوج، بعدما الأب (قد) ذهب الى المصير (مات)، إخوانها، سوف يتصدّقونها (يتصدّقو عليها) صدقة كما حق (حسب قيمة) بيت الاب، (و) سوف يعطونها الى زوج (يزوجونها).

If (after) a person [a man], to his daughter, the concubine, does not endow her an endowment, does not give her to a husband, after the father has gone to destiny (died), her brothers shall endow her an endowment as worthy as the father 's house, (and) they shall give her to a husband.

§ 185.—XXXII, 31-38

31 šum-ma a-wi-lum 32 ṣi-iḫ-ra-am 33 i-na me-e-šu 34 a-na ma-ru-tim 35 il-ḳi-ma 36 ur-ta-ab-bi-šu 37 tar-bi-tum ši-i 38 u-ul ib-ba-ag-gar

31 ثمّ أويلم [عويلم] 32 صِهْرَمْ [صِغْرَمْ] 33 إنَ مئي ذو 34 أنَ مأرُتِمْ 35 يلْقِيمْ 36 يُرْتَبي ذا 37 تربيتمْ ذيي 38 أُلْ يبجَرْ [يفجَرْ] [يبقَرْ]

بعد ان (اذا) شخص [رجل] يلقي (يأخذ) (طفل) صغير في حُسنه وصفاءه (في يفاعته) للبنوّة (للتبنّي)، (و) يربّيه، هذه التربْيةْ (ذات التربية هذا) (هذا الطفل المُتربّى أو المُتبنّى) سوف لن يُنازَعْ (يُقاضى) (عليه).

If (after) a person [a man] takes a youngster in his youth (purity) to (for) sonship (adoption), (and) rears him, that reared one (that foster child) shall not be contended (legally challenged) (for).

§ 186.—XXXII, 39-49

39 šum-ma a-wi-lum 40 ṣi-iḫ-ra-am 41 a-na ma-ru-tim [b]il-ḳi 42 i-nu-ma 43 il-ḳu-u-šu 44 a-ba-šu 45 u um-ma-šu 46 i-ḫi-a-aṭ 47 tar-bi-tum ši-i 48 a-na bît a-bi-šu 49 i-ta-ar

39 ثمّ أويلم [عويلم] 40 صِهْرَم [صِغْرَمْ] 41 أنَ مأرُتِمْ يلْقِي 42 حينَمْ 43 إلْقُو ذو 44 أبا ذو 45 و أما ذو 46 يخِئَطْ [يخطَئْ] 47 تَرْبيتُمْ ذيي 48 أنَ بيت أبي ذو 49 يتأرْ

بعد ان (اذا) شخص [رجل] يلقي (يأخذ) (طفل) صغير للبنوّة (للتبنّي)، (و) حينما (بعدما) لَقاه (أخذه)، (الصغير) يخطئ بحق (يأذى) أبيه وأمه (المتبنيان)، هذه التربْيةْ (ذات التربية هذا) (هذا الطفل المُتربّى أو المُتبنّى) سوف يعود الى بيت أبيه.

If (after) a person [a man] takes a youngster to (for) sonship (adoption), when (after) he took him, (the youngster) mistreats his (adopted) father and mother, that reared one (that foster child) shall return to his father's house.

§ 187.—XXXII, 50-53

[50] mâr NER.SE.GA [51] mu-za-az êkallim [52] u mâr zinništi zi-ik-[b]ru-um [53] u-ul ib-ba-ag-gar

[50] مأر نَعَرْسَجا [نَعَرْصَجا] [نَحَرْسَجا] [نَحَرْصَجا] [51] مُعزَزْ [مُؤزَزْ] هيكلِمْ [52] ومأر ذنِثْتي ذِكْرُمْ [53] أُلْ يبجرْ [يفجرْ] [يبقَرْ]

إبن المُلازم (المُرابط)، مُثقَلْ (حارس) القصر، و إبن أنثى الطاعة (المُطيعة او الخادمة في قصر) سوف لن يُنازَعْ (يُقاضى) (عليه).

The son of the attendant, the encumbered (guard) of the palace, and the son of the obedience female (the disciple or servant of the palace) shall not be contended (legally challenged) (for).

§ 188.—XXXII, 54-59

[54] šum-ma mâr ummânim [55] mâram a-na tar-bi-tim [56] il-ḳi-ma [57] ši-bi-ir ga-ti-šu [58] uš-ta-ḫi-zu [59] u-ul ib-ba-gar

[54] ثُمَّ مأرْ أُمّانِمْ [55] مأرَمْ أنَ تَرْبيتِمْ [56] يلْقِيمَ [56] سِبِرْ [سِفِرْ] جَتي ذو [قَتي ذو] [56] يُسْتَحِزْ ذو [يُسْتَحِزوَ] [57] أُلْ يبجَرْ [يفَجَرْ] [يبقَرْ]

بعد ان (اذا) ابن أمانة (مهنة) يلقي (يأخذ) إبن للتربية (للتبنّي)، (و) يُحيزُه (يعلّمه) مهارة عمل يده، سوف لن يُنازَعْ (يُقاضى) (عليه).

If (after) a son of profession (a professional) takes a son to (for) rearing (for adoption), (and) makes him gain (teaches him) the skill of his hand, he shall not be contended (legally challenged) (for).

§ 189.—XXXII, 60-64

[60] šum-ma ši-bi-ir [b]ga-ti-šu [61] la uš-ta-ḫi-zu [62] tar-bi-tum ši-i [63] a-na bît a-bi-šu [64] i-ta-ar

[60] ثُمَّ سِبِرْ [سِفِرْ] جَتي ذو [قَتي ذو] [61] لا يُسْتَحِزْ ذو [يُسْتَحِزوَ] [62] تَرْبيتُمْ ذيي [63] أنَ بيت أبي ذو [64] يتأرْ

|وفق الفقرة 188| بعد ان (اذا) لا يُحيزُوَ (لا يعلّمه) مهارة عمل يده، هذه التَرْبيةُ (ذات التربية هذا) (هذا الطفل المُتربّى أو المُتبنّى) سوف يعود الى بيت أبيه.

|Referencing §188| If (after) he does not make him gain (does not teach him) the skill of his hand, that reared one (that foster child) shall return to his father's house.

§ 190.—XXXII, 65-74

[65] šum-ma a-wi-lum [66] ṣi-iḫ-ra-am [67] ša a-na ma-ru-ti-šu [68] il-ḳu-šu-ma [69] u-ra-ab-bu-šu [70] it-ti mârê-šu [71] la im-ta-nu-šu [72] tar-bi-tum ši-i [73] a-na bît a-bi-šu [74] i-ta-ar

[65] ثُمَّ أويلُم [عَويلُم] [66] صِهْرَمْ [صِغْرَمْ] [67] ذا أنَ مأرُتِ ذو [68] إلْقُو ذُومْ [69] أُربوَ ذو [70] أتي مأريي ذو [71] لا يمْتَنو ذو [72] تَرْبيتُمْ ذيي [73] أنَ بيت أبي ذو [74] يتأرْ

بعد ان (اذا) شخص [رجل]، (الطفل) الصغيرَ الذي لقاه (أخذه) لبنوّته (لتبنّيه) (و) ربّاه، لا يعدّه مع (بحساب) أبناءه، هذه التَرْبيةُ (ذات التربية هذا) (هذا الطفل المُتربّى أو المُتبنّى) سوف يعود الى بيت أبيه.

If (after) a person [a man], the youngster whom he took to (for) his sonship (his adoption), (and) reared him, he does not count him with his children, that reared one (that foster child) shall return to his father's house.

§ 191.—XXXII, 75-95

[75] šum-ma a-wi-lum [76] ṣi-iḫ-ra-am [77] ša a-na ma-ru-ti-šu [78] il-ḳu-šu-ma [79] u-ra-ab-bu-u-šu [80] bî-zu i-bu-uš [81] wa-ar-ka mârê [82] ir-ta-ši-ma [83] a-na tar-bi-tim na-sa-ḫi-im [84] pa-nam iš-ta-ka-an [85] mârum šu-u tal-ku-zu [86] u-ul it-ta-al-la-ak [87] a-bu-um mu-ra-bi-šu [88] i-na ŠA.GA-šu [89] IGI.III.GAL ablûti-šu [90] i-na-ad-di-iš-šum-ma [91] it-ta-la-ak [92] i-na eḳlim kirêm [93] u bîtim [94] u-ul i-na-ad-di- [95] iš-šum

75 ثُمَّ أويلم [عويلم] 76 صهرمْ [صغرمْ] 77 ذا أنَ مأرْت ذو 78 إلْقو ذُومَ 79 أُربو ذو 80 بيتْ ذو [بيتْ] يئبُش [يعفُش] [يعفُس] 81 ورْك مأريي 82 يرتسيم 83 أن تربيتِم نسحِم [نسخِم] 84 فنمْ يستكنْ 85 مأرمْ ذوو تألكْ ذو [تألكْتْ] 86 ألْ يتألكْ 87 أبوم مربي ذو 88 إن شَجا ذو 89 إجي 3 جلْ أبلْتي ذو [أبنْتي ذو] 90 يندنْ ذُومْ [ينْدذّومْ] 91 يتألكْ 92 إنَ حقلِمْ كيريم 93 و بيتِمْ 94–95 ألْ يندنْ ذُومْ [ينْدذّومْ]

بعد ان (اذا) شخص [رجل]، (الطفل) الصغيرَ الذي لقاه (أخذه) لبنوته (لتبنّيه) (و) ربّاه يعمل (يبني) (للاب) بيته، بعدما (الشخص [الرجل]) يرتسي (يكتسب) أبناء، (و) يضع الوجه (يتوجّه) لازاحة التربْيةُ (ذات التربية) (الابن المُتربّى أو المُتبنّى)، هذا الابن (المُتبنّى) سوف لن يترسّلْ ترسّلهُ (لن يذهب مذهبهُ) (لن يذهب خالي اليدين)؛ الأب، مُربّيه، سوف يعطيه 1\3 حمْل مسؤوليته (لإبن) [(مسؤولية) بنُوّته] (و) يترسّل (يذهب)، سوف لن يعطيه (حصة) في (من) الحقل، البستان، والبيت.

If (after) a person [a man], the youngster whom he took to (for) his sonship (his adoption) (and) reared him builds (for the father) his house, after he (the person [the man]) settles in (acquires) (his own) children, (and) set the face to (toward) the removal of the reared one (the foster child), that (adopted) son shall not go his way (empty handed); the father, the one who reared him, shall give him 1/3 his bearing of (son) responsibility [his sonship], (and) he goes, he shall not give him (a share) in (from) the field, the orchard, and the house.

§ 192.—XXXII, 96-XXXIII, 9

96 šum-ma mâr NER.SE.GA XXXIII, 1 u lu mâr zinništi zi-^{b}ik-ru-um 2 a-na a-bi-im 3 mu-ra-bi-šu 4 u um-mi-im 5 mu-ra-bi-ti-šu 6 u-ul a-bi ^{b}at-ta 7 u-ul um-mi ^{b}at-ti iḳ-ta-bi 8 lišâni-šu 9 i-na-ak-ki-su

96 ثُمّ مأر نَعرْسَجا [نَعرْصَجا] [نَحرْسَجا] [نَحرْصَجا] 1 ولو مأر ذنِثْتي ذِكرْمْ 2 أنَ أبيمْ 3 مُربّي ذو 2 و أُميمْ 3 مُربّيةِ ذو 2 ألْ أبي 3 أتَّ 2 ألْ أُمي أتِّ 3 يقْتبي 2 لِسانِ ذو 3 ينّكِسو [ينّقصو]

بعد ان (اذا) إبن ملازم (مُرابط) (حارس أو مسؤول في قصر)، و(حتى) لو إبن أنثى الطاعة (مُطيعة او خادمة في قصر)، يقول الى الأب، مربّيه، و الأم، مربّيته، "أنتَ لستَ أبي، أنتِ لستِ أمي"، سوف يقطعو لسانه.

If (after) the son of an attendant (palace's guard), and (even) let-it-be the son of an obedience female (a palace's disciple or servant), says to the father, the one who reared him, and the mother, the one who reared him, "you are not my father, you are not my mother", they shall shorten (cut) his tongue.

§ 193.—XXXIII, 10-22

10 šum-ma mâr NER.SE.GA 11 u lu mâr zinništi zi-^{b}ik-ru-um 12 bît a-bi-šu 13 u-wi-id-di-ma 14 a-ba-am 15 mu-ra-bi-šu 16 u um-ma-am 17 mu-ra-bi-zu 18 i-ṣi-ir-ma 19 a-na bît a-bi-šu 20 it-ta-la-ak 21 i-in-šu 22 i-na-za-ḫu

10 ثُمّ مأر نَعرْسَجا [نَعرْصَجا] [نَحرْسَجا] [نَحرْصَجا] 11 ولو مأر ذنِثْتي ذِكرْمْ 12 بيت أبي ذو 13 يؤدِمَ [يودِمَ] 14 أبمْ 15 مُربّي ذو 16 وأُممْ 17 مُربّيتْ ذو [مُربّيةْ] 18 يصرِمَ [يزرِمْ] [يزعرِمْ] 19 أنَ بيت أبي ذو 20 يتألكْ 21 عينْ ذو 22 ينزَحو [ينسَحو] [ينسَخو]

بعد ان (اذا) إبن المُلازم (المُرابط) (الحارس أو المسؤول في قصر)، و(حتى) لو إبن أنثى الطاعة (المُطيعة او الخادمة في قصر)، يَصِلْ (يهتدي الى) [يودّ] بيت أبيه، (و) يقاطع [يزدري] الأب، مربّيه، والأم، مربّيته، (و) يترسّل (يعود) الى بيت أبيه، سوف يزيحو (يزيلو) عينه.

If (after) the son of an attendant (a palace's guard), and (even) let-it-be the son of an obedience female (a palace's disciple or servant), reaches [desires] his father's house, (and) boycott [scorns] the father, the one who reared him, and the mother, the one who reared him, (and) he goes (returns) to his father's house, they shall remove his eyes.

§ 194.—XXXIII, 23-40

23 šum-ma a-wi-lum 24 mâra-šu a-na mu-še-^{b}ni-iḳ-tim 25 id-di-in-ma 26 mârum šu-u 27 i-na ga-at ^{b}mu-še-ni-iḳ-tim 28 im-tu-ut 29 mu-še-ni-iḳ-tum 30 ba-lum a-bi-šu 31 u um-mi-šu 32 mâram ša-ni-a-am-ma 33 ir-ta-ka-aš 34 u-ka-an-nu-ši-ma 35 aš-šum ba-lum a-bi-šu 36 u um-mi-šu 37 mâram ša-ni-a-am 38 ir-ku-šu 39 tulê-ša 40 i-na-ak-ki-su

23 ثمَّ أَويلم [عَويلم] 24 مأرَ ذو أنَ مُسنِقتِم [مُتأنِقتِم] 25 يدنِمَ 26 مأرمْ ذوو 27 إنَ جتْ [قتْ] مُسنِقتِم [مُتأنِقتِم] 28 يمتُتْ 29 مُسنِقتُمْ [مُتأنِقتُمْ] 30 بَلمْ أبي ذو 31 وأُمي ذو 32 مأرَمْ ثانيامَ 33 يرتَكَسْ 34 يُكنو ذيمَ 35 هذَمْ بَلمْ أبي ذو 36 وأُمي ذو 37 مأرَمْ ثانيامْ 38 إرْكُسو 39 تُلِيي ذا [تُلعِي ذا] 40 ينَكِسو [ينقِصو]

بعد ان (اذا) شخص [رجل] يعطي إبنه الى المُرضعة، (و) هذا الابن يموت في يدْ المُرضعة، المُرضعةُ تُعيد [تستبدل] ابناً ثانيا (آخرا) بلا (بدون) (علم) أبيه وأمه، سوف يُجلسوها [يستدعوها]، (و) سوف يقطعو ثدييها، هذا لأنها أعادت [استبدلت] إبناً ثانيا (آخرا) بلا (بدون) (علم) أبيه وأمه.

If (after) a person [a man] gives his child to the wet nurse, (and) this child dies in the hands of the wet nurse, the wet nurse gives back [substitutes] a second (another) child without (the knowledge of) his father and mother, they shall seat [call] her in, (and) they shall cut her breasts, that is because she gave back [substituted] a second (another) child without (the knowledge of) his father and mother.

§ 195.—XXXIII, 41-44

41 šum-ma mârum a-ba-šu 42 im-ta-ḫ̮a-aṣ 43 rittê-šu 44 i-na-ak-ki-su

41 ثمَّ مأرمْ أبا ذو 42 يمْتَحصْ 43 رتّيي ذو 44 ينَكِسو [ينَقِصو]

بعد ان (اذا) إبن يضرب أبيه، سوف يقطعو كفّيه [أصابيعه].

If (after) a son strikes his father, they shall cut his hand fists [his fingers].

§ 196.—XXXIII, 45-49

45 šum-ma a-wi-lum 46 i-in mâr a-wi-lim 47 uḫ̮-tab-bi-it 48 i-in-šu 49 u-ḫ̮a-ap-pa-du

45 ثمَّ أويلُم [عويلُم] 46 عينْ مأرْ أويلِم [عويلِم] 47 يُختَبِطْ 48 عينْ ذو 49 يُهَبدو [يُخبَطو]

بعد ان (اذا) شخص [رجل] يسلِب عَين إبن شخص [رجل]، سوف يستخرجو (يقتلعو) [يسلبو عينه].

If (after) a person [a man] robs the eye of a son of a person [a man], they shall pluck out his eye [rob his eye].

§ 197.—XXXIII, 50-53

50 šum-ma NER.PAD.DU ^{b}a-wi-lim 51 iš-te-bi-ir 52 NER.PAD.DU-šu 53 i-še-ib-bi-ru

50 ثمَّ نَرْفَدُ [مَرْفَدُ] أويلِم [عَويلِم] 51 يسْتَبِرْ [يتَّبِرْ] 52 نَرْفَدُ ذو [مَرْفَدُ ذو] 53 يسَئِبرو [يتَئِبْرو]

|وفق الفقرة 196| بعد ان (اذا) (الشخص [الرجل]) يكسر (يهشم) عَظْمْ شخص [رجل]، سوف يكسرو (يهشّمو) عظمه.

|Referencing §196| If (after) (a person [a man]) breaks a bone of a person [a man], they shall break his bone.

§ 198.—XXXIII, 54-59

54 šum-ma i-in ^{b}MAŠ.EN.KAK 55 uḫ̮-tab-bi-it 56 u lu NER.PAD.DU ^{b}MAŠ.EN.KAK 57 iš-te-bi-ir 58 I ma-na kaspim 59 i-ša-ḳal

54 ثمَّ عِينْ مَس عَن كَأكْ 55 يُخْتَبِطْ 56 ولو نَرْفَدُ [مَرْفَدُ] مَس عَن كَأكْ 57 يسْتَبِرْ [يتَّبِرْ] 58 1 منَا كَسْفِمْ 59 يثَقلْ

|وفق الفقرة 196| بعد ان (اذا) (الشخص [الرجل]) يسْلب عَين شخص من العامة، و(حتى) لو يكسر (يهشم) عَظْمْ شخص من العامة، سوف يَزن (ويعطي) 1 رطل فضة.

|Referencing §196| If (after) (a person [a man]) robs the eye of an ordinary person, and (even) let-it-be he breaks a bone of an ordinary person, he shall measure (and give) 1 Mana (2 lbs.) silver.

§ 199.—XXXIII, 60-65

60 šum-ma i-in ᵇwarad a-wi-lim 61 uḫ-tab-bi-it 62 u lu NER.PAD.DU ᵇwarad a-wi-lim 63 iš-te-bi-ir 64 mi-ši-il ᵇšîmi-šu 65 i-ša-ḳal

60 ثمَّ عينْ وَردْ أويلم [عويلم] 61 يُختَبطْ 62 ولو نَرفَدْ [مَرفَدْ] وَردْ أويلم [عويلم] 63 يستَبرْ [يتبّرْ] 64 مثِلْ سيم ذو 65 يثقلْ

|وفق الفقرة 196| بعد ان (اذا) (الشخص [الرجل]) يسْلب عَين (بصر) عبد شخص [رجل]، و(حتى) لو يكسر (يهشم) عَظْمْ عبد شخص [رجل]، سوف يَزن (ويعطي) نصف (قيمة) شراءه (فضّة).

|Referencing §196| If (after) (a person [a man]) robs the eye of a slave, and (even) let-it-be he breaks a bone of a slave, he shall measure (and give) half his purchase value (in silver).

§ 200.—XXXIII, 66-70

66 šum-ma a-wi-lum 67 ši-in-ni ᵇa-wi-lim 68 me-iḫ-ri-šu 69 it-ta-di 70 ši-in-na-šu ᵇi-na-ad-du-u

66 ثمَّ أويلُم [عويلُم] 67 سنّ أويلم [عويلم] 68 مئخْري ذو 69 يتدي 70 سنّ ذو ينَدْو

بعد ان (اذا) شخص [رجل] يدَعْ (يُسقِطْ) سنْ شخص [رجل] مقابيله [معادل له]، سوف يَدعون (يُسقِطون) سنّه.

If (after) a person [a man] let go (cause to fall) a tooth of a person [a man] in front of him [equal to him], they shall throw (cause to fall) his tooth.

§ 201.—XXXIII, 71-74

71 šum-ma ši-in-ni 72 MAŠ.EN.KAK it-ta-di 73 ⅓ ma-na kaspim 74 i-ša-ḳal

71 ثُمَّ سنّ 72 مَس عَن كَأكْ يتدي 73 1\3 مَنا كَسْفِمْ 59 يثقلْ

|وفق الفقرة 200| بعد ان (اذا) (الشخص [الرجل]) يدَعْ (يُسقِطْ) سنْ شخص من العامة، سوف يَزن (ويعطي) 1\3 رطل فضة.

|Referencing §200| If (after) (the person [the man]) let go (cause to fall) a tooth of an ordinary person, he shall measure (and give) 1/3 Mana (<1 lbs.) silver.

§ 202.—XXXIII, 75-81

75 šum-ma a-wi-lum 76 li-e-it a-wi-lim 77 ša e-li-šu ra-bu-u 78 im-ta-ḫa-aṣ 79 i-na pu-uḫ-ri-im 80 i-na ᵐᵃšᵃᵏḳinazi alpim 81 I ŠU.ŠI im-maḫ-ḫa-aṣ

75 ثمَّ أويلُمْ [عَويلُمْ] 76 لِئتْ [لِيتْ] أويلِم [عويلِم] 77 ذا علي ذو ربُو 78 يمْتَحَصْ 79 إنَ فُهرِمْ 80 إنَ مسكقِناز ألفِمْ [ألبِمْ] [علفِمْ [علبِمْ]] 81 1 سُتّ يمَحَصْ

بعد ان (اذا) شخص [رجل] يَضرب صفحة عنق [خدّ] الشخص [الرجل] الذي عليه قائم (عليه آمر)، (الشخص [الرجل]) سوف يُضربْ 60 (جَلْدة) بسوطْ جلد ثور في تجمع (امام الملئ).

If (after) a person [a man] strikes (slaps) the neck side [cheek] of a person [a man], who is superior (presiding) over him, he shall be stricken (belted) 60 (whips) in (with) an ox skin whip in an (open) gathering.

§ 203.—XXXIII, 82-87

82 šum-ma mâr a-wi-lim 83 li-e-it mâr a-wi-lim 84 ša ki-ma šu-a-ti 85 im-ta-ḫa-aṣ 86 I ma-na kaspim 87 i-ša-ḳal

82 ثمَّ مأرْ أويلم [عَويلم] 83 لِئتْ [لِيتْ] مأرْ أويلم [عَويلم] 84 ذا كيمَ ذأتْ 85 يمْتَحَصْ 86 1 منا كَسْفِمْ 87 يثقَلْ

بعد ان (اذا) إبن شخص [رجل] يَضرب صفحة عُنق [خد] إبن الشخص [الرجل] الذي مثل ذلك (ذاك)، (الشخص [الرجل]) سوف يَزن (ويعطي) 1\3 رطل فضة.

If (after) a son of a person [a man] strikes (slaps) the neck side [cheek] of a son of a person [a man], who is the same as that, he shall measure (and give) 1/3 Mana (<1 lbs.) silver.

§ 204.—XXXIII, 88-91

88 šum-ma MAŠ.EN.KAK 89 li-e-it MAŠ.EN.KAK 90 im-ta-ḫa-aṣ 91 X šiḳil kaspim i-ša-ḳal

88 ثمَّ مَس عَن كَاكْ 89 لِئتْ [لِيتْ] مَس عَن كَاكْ 90 يمْتَحَصْ 91 10 ثقلْ [شقلْ] كَسْفَمْ يثقَلْ

بعد ان (اذا) شخص من العامة يَضرب صفحة عُنق [خد] شخص من العامة، سوف يَزن (ويعطي) 10 مثقال (شقل) فضة.

If (after) an ordinary person strikes (slaps) the neck side [cheek] of an ordinary person, he shall measure (and give) 10 Shiqil silver.

§ 205.—XXXIII, 92-XXXIV, 3

92 šum-ma warad a-wi-lim 93 li-e-it mâr a-wi-lim XXXIV, 1 im-ta-ḫa-aṣ 2 u-zu-un-šu 3 i-na-ak-ki-su

92 ثمَّ وَرَدْ أويلِم [عَويلِم] 93 لِئتْ [لِيتْ] مأرْ أويلِم [عَويلِم] 1 يمْتَحَصْ 2 أُذنْ ذو 3 ينَكِسو [ينَقصو]

بعد ان (اذا) عبد شخص [رجل] يَضرب صفحة عُنق [خد] إبن شخص [رجل]، سوف يقطعو أذنه.

If (after) a slave of a person [a man] strikes (slaps) the neck side [cheek] of a son of a person [a man], they shall cut his ear.

§ 206.—XXXIV, 4-13

4 šum-ma a-wi-lum [b]a-wi-lam 5 i-na ri-is-[b]ba-tim 6 im-ta-ḫa-aṣ-ma 7 zi-im-ma-am 8 iš-ta-ka-an-šu 9 a-wi-lum šu-u 10 i-na i-du-u 11 la am-ḫa-zu 12 i-tam-ma 13 u A.ZU [b]i-ip-pa-al

4 ثمَّ أويلُم [عَويلُم] أويلَم [عَويلَم] 5 إنَ رِسْبَتِم 6 يمْتَحَصْمَ 7 زِممْ [سِممْ] 8 يستَكَنْ ذو 9 أويلُم [عَويلُم] ذوو 10 إنَ إدْوَ [إهدُوَ] 11 لا أمْحَصْ ذو [أمْحَتْ] 12 يتأمَ 13 و أزو [أسو] يئفَلْ

بعد ان (اذا) شخص [رجل] يضرب شخص [رجل] في سَقْطة (بالخطئ) [في شِجار]، (و) يضع له (يسبب له) شَقْ (جرح)، هذا الشخص [الرجل] سوف يَفْضي "ما ضَرَبته" فيما (بينما) عَرِفَ (مسبقا)، وسوف يتحمل (تكاليف) الطبيب.

If (after) a person [a man] strikes a person (a man) in a stumble (in an error) [in quarrel], set on him (cause him) injury, this person [this man] shall notify (inform) “I did not strike him” in (while) he knew (beforehand), (and) he shall take upon (the expenses of) the doctor.

§ 207.—XXXIV, 14-19

14 šum-ma i-na ma-[b]ḫa-zi-šu 15 im-tu-ut 16 i-tam-ma-ma 17 šum-ma mâr a-wi-lim 18 ½ ma-na kaspim 19 i-ša-ḳal

14 ثمَّ إنَ مَحزي ذو 15 يمتُتْ 16 يتأمَ 17 ثمَّ مأرْ أويلِم [عَويلِم] 18 1\2 منا كَسْفَمْ 19 يثقَلْ

|وفق الفقرة 206| بعد ان (اذا) (المضروب) يموت في (من) الشدة (شدة الضرب)، (الشخص [الرجل]) سوف يَفْضي (كما اعلاه)، (و) بعد ان (اذا) (المضروب) إبن شخص [رجل]، سوف يَزن (ويعطي) 1\2 رطل فضة.

|Referencing §206| If (after) (the beaten) dies in (from) the harshness (of strike), he shall notify (inform) (as above), (and) if (after) (the beaten) is a son of a person, he shall measure (and give) 1/2 Mana (1 lb.) silver.

§ 208.—XXXIV, 20-22

[20] šum-ma mâr MAŠ.EN.KAK [21] ⅓ ma-na kaspim [22] i-ša-ḳal

[20] ثُمَّ مَس عَن كَأكْ [18] 1\3 مَنا كَسْفِم [19] يثقلْ

|وفق الفقرة 207| بعد ان (اذا) (المضروب) شخص من العامة، سوف يَزن (ويعطي) 1\3 رطل فضة.

|Referencing §207| If (after) (the beaten is a son of) ordinary person, he shall measure (and give) 1/3 Mana (<1 lb.) silver.

§ 209.—XXXIV, 23-30

[23] šum-ma a-wi-lum [24] mârat a-wi-lim [25] im-ḫa-aṣ-ma [26] ša li-ib-bi-ša [27] uš-ta-di-ši [28] X šiḳil kaspim [29] a-na ša li-ib-[b]bi-ša [30] i-ša-ḳal

[23] ثُمَّ أويلم [عَويلْم] [24] مأرتْ أويلِم [عَويلِم] [25] يمْحَصْمَ [26] ذا لِبَّ ذا [27] يُسْتَدي [يُتَّدي] [28] 10 ثِقِلْ [شِقِلْ] كَسْفِمْ [30] أنَ ذا لِبَّ ذا [19] يثقَلْ

بعد ان (اذا) شخص [رجل] يضرب بنت شخص [رجل]، يدَعْ (يُسْقِطْ) الذي في داخلها (جنينها)، (الشخص [الرجل]) سوف يَزن (ويعطي) 10 مثقال (شقل) فضة الى (عن) الذي في داخلها (عن جنينها).

If (after) a person [a man] strikes the daughter of a person [a man], (and) lets go (drops) that of her inside (her fetus), he shall measure (and give) 10 Shiqil silver to (for) that of her inside (her fetus).

§ 210.—XXXIV, 31-34

[31] šum-ma zinništum ši-i [32] im-tu-ut [33] mâra-zu [34] i-du-uk-ku

[31] ثُمَّ ذنِثْتُمْ ذيي [32] يمْتُتْ [33] مأرَتْ ذو [مأرَتْ] [34] يدكُو

|وفق الفقرة 209| بعد ان (اذا) هذه الانثى (البنت) تموت، سوف يقتلو بنته.

|Referencing §209| If (after) that female (daughter) dies, they shall kill his daughter.

§ 211.—XXXIV, 35-40

[35] šum-ma mârat [b]MAŠ.EN.KAK [36] i-na ma-ḫa-zi-im [37] ša li-ib-bi-ša [38] uš-ta-ad-di-ši [39] V šiḳil kaspim [40] i-ša-ḳal

[35] ثُمَّ مأرتْ مَس عَن كَأكْ [36] إنَ مَحزِمْ [37] ذا لِبَّ ذا [38] يُسْتَدي ذي [يُتَّدي ذي] [39] 5 ثِقِلْ [شِقِلْ] كَسْفِمْ [40] يثقَلْ

|وفق الفقرة 209| بعد ان (اذا) بنت شخص من العامة (التي) يدَعُها (يُسْقِطُها) (جنينها) في (من) الشدّة (شدة الضرب)، سوف يَزن (ويعطي) 5 مثقال (شقل) فضة (عن جنينها).

|Referencing §209| If (after) a daughter of an ordinary person, (whom) he makes her let go (makes her drop) that of her inside (her fetus) in (from) the harshness (of strike), he shall measure (and give) 5 Shiqil silver.

§ 212.—XXXIV, 41-44

[41] šum-ma zinništum ši [42] im-tu-ut [43] ½ ma-na kaspim [44] i-ša-ḳal

[41] ثُمَّ ذنِثْتُمْ ذي [42] يمْتُتْ [43] 1\2 مَنا كَسْفِمْ [40] يثقَلْ

|وفق الفقرة 211| بعد ان (اذا) هذه الانثى (البنت) تموت، سوف يَزن (ويعطي) 1\2 رطل فضة.

|Referencing §211| If (after) that female (daughter) dies, he shall measure (and give) 1/2 Mana (1 lb.) silver.

§ 213.—XXXIV, 45-50

45 šum-ma amat a-wi-lim 46 im-ḫa-aṣ-ma 47 ša li-ib-bi-ša 48 uš-ta-ad-di-ši 49 II šiḳil kaspim 50 i-ša-ḳal

45 ثُمَّ أمَتْ أويلِم [عَويلِم] 46 يمْحَصْمَ 47 ذا لبِّ ذا 48 يُستأدي ذي [يَتأدي ذي] 49 2 ثِقِلْ [شِقِلْ] كَسْفِمْ 50 يثقَلْ

|وفق الفقرة 209| بعد ان (اذا) (الشخص [الرجل]) يضرب عبدة شخص [رجل]، (و) يدعُها (يُسقِطُها) الذي في داخلها (جنينها)، سوف يزن (ويعطي) 2 مثقال (شقل) فضة (عن جنينها).

|Referencing §209| If (after) the female slave of a person (a man), he makes her let go (makes her drop) that of her inside (her fetus), he shall measure (and give) 2 Shiqil silver.

§ 214.—XXXIV, 51-54

51 šum-ma amtum ši-i 52 im-tu-ut 53 ⅓ ma-na kaspim 54 i-ša-ḳal

51 ثُمَّ أمتُمْ ذيي 42 يمْتُتْ 43 1\3 مَنَا كَسفِمْ 40 يثقَلْ

|وفق الفقرة 213| بعد ان (اذا) هذه العبدة تموت، سوف يَزن (ويعطي) (الشخص [الرجل]) 1\3 رطل فضة.

|Referencing §211| If (after) that female slave dies, he shall measure (and give) 1/3 Mana (<1 lb.) silver.

§ 215.—XXXIV, 55-66

55 šum-ma A.ZU 56 a-wi-lam ^{b}zi-im-ma-am kab-tam 57 i-na GIR.NI siparrim 58 i-bu-uš-ma 59 a-wi-lam ^{b}ub-ta-al-li-iṭ 60 u lu na-gab-ti ^{b}a-wi-lim 61 i-na GIR.NI siparrim 62 ip-te-ma 63 i-in a-wi-lim 64 ub-ta-al-li-iṭ 65 X šiḳil kaspim 66 i-li-ḳi

55 ثُمَّ أزو [أسو] 56 أويلَم [عَويلَم] زمَمْ [سمَمْ] كَبْتَمْ 57 إنَ جِرْنِ [جرز] سفرِّمْ [صفرِّمْ] 58 يئبُشْمَ [يعفُشْمَ] [يعفُسْمَ] 59 أويلَم [عَويلَم] يُبْتَلِطْ 60 ولو نَجَبْتِ [نجفْتِ] أويلِم [عويلِم] 61 إنَ جِرْنِ [جرز] سفرِّمْ [صفرِّمْ] 62 يفْتَحْمَ [يفْتيمَ] 63 عينْ أويلِم [عَويلِم] 64 يُبْتَلِطْ 65 10 ثِقِلْ [شِقِلْ] كَسفِمْ 19 يلِقي

بعد ان (اذا) طبيب يعمل (لـ)شخص [(لـ)رجل] شق (جرح) كبير بمِشْرَط نحاس، (و) يحي (يشفي) الشخص [الرجل]، و(حتى) لو يفتح دُمّلْ (عين) شخص [رجل] بمِشْرَط نحاس، (و) يحي (يشفي) عين الشخص [الرجل]، (الطبيب) سوف يلقي (يأخذ) 10 مثقال (شقل) فضة.

If (after) a doctor makes (to) a person [a man] in a large cut (with) a bronze lancet, (and) he keeps alive (heals) the person (the man), and (even) let-it-be that he opens a (swelled eye) abscess of a person [a man] in (with) a bronze lancet, (and) he keeps alive (heals) the eye of the person (the man), he shall take 10 Shiqil silver.

§ 216.—XXXIV, 67-69

67 šum-ma mâr MAŠ.EN.KAK 68 V šiḳil kaspim 69 i-li-ḳi

67 ثُمَّ مأرْ مَس عَن كَاكْ 68 5 ثِقِلْ [شِقِلْ] كَسفِمْ 69 يلِقي

|وفق الفقرة 215| بعد ان (اذا) (المريض) إبن شخص من العامّة، (الطبيب) سوف يلقي (يأخذ) 5 مثقال (شقل) فضة.

|Referencing §215| If (after) (the patient is) a son of an ordinary person, he (the doctor) shall take 5 Shiqil silver.

§ 217.—XXXIV, 70-73

70 šum-ma warad a-wi-lim 71 be-el wardim ba-na A.ZU 72 II šiḳil kaspim 73 i-na-ad-di-in

70 ثُمَّ ورَدْ أويلِم [عويلِم] 71 بَعَلْ ورِدِمْ أنَ أزو [أسو] 72 2 ثِقِلْ [شِقِلْ] كَسْفِمْ 73 ينَدِنْ

|وفق الفقرة 215| بعد ان (اذا) (المريض) عبد شخص [رجل]، مالك العبد سوف يعطي الى الطبيب 2 مثقال (شقل) فضة.

|Referencing §215| If (after) (the patient is) a slave of a person (a man), the owner of the slave shall give (to the doctor) 2 Shiqil silver.

§ 218.—XXXIV, 74-83

74 šum-ma A.ZU a-wi-lam 75 zi-im-ma-am kab-tam 76 i-na GIR.NI siparrim 77 i-bu-uš-ma 78 a-wi-lam uš-ta-mi-it 79 u lu na-gab-ti a-wi-lim 80 i-na GIR.NI siparrim 81 ip-te-ma i-in a-wi-lim 82 uḫ-tab-bi-it 83 rittê-šu i-na-kisu

74 ثُمَّ أزو [أسو] أويلَم [عويلَم] 75 زِمَمْ [سِمَمْ] كَبْتَمْ 76 إن جِرْنِ [جِرْزْ] سِفَرِمْ [صِفَرِّمْ] 77 يئِبُشْمَ [يعفُشْمَ] [يعفُسْمَ] 78 أويلَم [عويلَم] يُسْتَمِتْ 79 ولو نَجبْتِ [نَجفْتِ] أويلِم [عويلِم] 80 إن جِرْنِ [جِرْزْ] سِفَرِّمْ [صِفَرِّمْ] 81 يفْتَحْمَ [يفْتيم] عينْ أويلِم [عويلِم] 82 يُخْتَبِطْ 83 رِتّيي ذو ينَكِسو [ينَقِّصو]

بعد ان (اذا) طبيب يعمل (ل)شخص [(ل)رجل] شق (جرح) كبير بمِشْرَط نحاس، (و) يُميت (يسبب موت) الشخص [الرجل]، و(حتى) لو يفتح بمِشْرَط نحاس دُمّلْ (عين) شخص [رجل]، (و) يسلب عين الشخص [الرجل]، سوف يقطعو كفّيه [أصابيعه].

If (after) a doctor makes (to) a person [a man] a large cut in (with) a bronze lancet, (and) he causes the death of the person (the man), and (even) let-it-be that he opens in (with) a bronze lancet a (swelled eye) abscess of a person [a man], (and) he robs the eye of the person (the man), they shall cut his hand fists [his fingers].

§ 219.—XXXIV, 84-88

84 šum-ma A.ZU zi-ma-am kab-tam 85 warad MAŠ.EN.KAK 86 i-na GIR.NI siparrim 87 i-bu-uš-ma uš-ta-mi-it 88 wardam ki-ma wardim i-ri-ab

84 ثُمَّ أزو [أسو] زِمَمْ [سِمَمْ] كَبْتَمْ 85 ورَدْ مَس عَن كَاكْ 86 إن جِرْنِ [جِرْزْ] سِفَرِمْ [صِفَرِّمْ] 87 يئِبُشْمَ [يعفِشْمَ] [يعفُسْمَ] يُسْتَمِتْ 88 وَرْدَمْ كيم وردِمْ يرأِبْ

بعد ان (اذا) طبيب يعمل بمِشْرَط نحاس شق (جرح) كبير (ل)عبد شخص من العامة، (و) يُميت (ويسبب موت)، (الطبيب) سوف يُسدّد (يعوض) (للمالك) عبد (آخر) مثل (بقيمة) العبد (الميت).

If (after) a doctor makes in (with) a bronze lancet (to) a slave of an ordinary person, a large cut, (and) he causes death, he shall repay (replace) (to the owner) a slave like (with the same value of) the (dead) slave.

§ 220.—XXXIV, 89-94

89 šum-ma na-gab-ta-šu 90 i-na GIR.NI siparrim 91 ip-te-ma 92 i-in-šu uḫ-tab-da (=it) 93 kaspam mi-ši-il 94 šîmi-šu i-ša-ḳal

89 ثُمَّ نَجبْتَ ذو [نَجفْتَ ذو] 90 إنَ جِرْنِ [جِرْزْ] سِفَرِّمْ [صِفَرْمْ] 91 يفْتَحْمَ [يفْتيمَ] 92 عينْ ذو يُهْتَبْدَ [يُخْتَبْطَ] 93 كَسْفَمْ 94 مِثِلْ سِيمِ ذو يثْقَلْ

|وفق الفقرة 219| بعد ان (اذا) (الطبيب) يفتح دُمّلْه (دُمّلْ عينه) بمِشْرَط نحاس، (و) يقتَلِعَ [يسلبَ] عينه، (الطبيب) سوف يَزن (ويعطي) (المالك) نصف (قيمة) شِراءه، فضّة.

|Referencing §219| If (after) (the doctor) opens his (swelled eye) abscess in (with) a bronze lancet, (and) he plucks out his eye [robs his eye], he shall measure (and give) half his purchase value, (in) silver.

§ 221.—XXXIV, 95-XXXV, 9

95 šum-ma A.ZU 96 NER.PAD.DU a-wi-lim XXXV, 1 še-bi-ir-tam 2 uš-ta-li-im 3 u lu še-ir ḫa-nam 4 mar-ṣa-am 5 ub-ta-al-li-iṭ 6 be-el ṣi-im-mi-im 7 a-na A.ZU 8 V šiḳil kaspim 9 i-na-ad-di-in

95 ثُمَّ أزو [أسو] 96 نَرْفَدْ [مَرْفَدْ] أويلِم [عويلِم] 1 سبِرتَمْ [تبرْتَمْ] 2 يُستَلِمْ 3 ولو سأرْ حانَمْ [حآنَمْ] 4 مرضَمْ 5 يُبتَلِطْ 6 بَعَلْ صمِمِ [ضِمِمْ] 7 أنَ أزو [أسو] 8 5 ثِقِلْ [شقِلْ] كسفِمْ 9 ينَدِنْ

بعد ان (اذا) طبيب يُأمن (يجبّر) عظم شخص [رجل] مكسور، و(حتى) لو يحي (يشفي) سائرِ (عظام) الحواني (زوجي الاضلاع الكبار على الجانبين) المريضة (المُبْتلية)، صاحب التضميد (المُضمَّد) سوف يعطي للطبيب 5 مثقال (شقل) فضة.

If (after) a doctor secures (bandages) the broken bone of a person (a man), and (even) let-it-be he keeps alive (heals) all his afflicted super-ribs (two on each side), the possessor of the bandage (the bandaged) shall give to the doctor 5 Shiqil silver.

§ 222.—XXXV, 10-12

10 šum-ma ᵇmâr MAŠ.EN.KAK 11 III šiḳil kaspim 12 i-na-ad-di-in

ثُمَّ مأرْ مَس عَن كَأكْ 68 3 ثِقِلْ [شِقِلْ] كَسْفِمْ 69 ينَدِنْ

|وفق الفقرة 221| بعد ان (اذا) (المُجَبّر) إبن شخص من العامّة، سوف يعطي (الطبيب) 3 مثقال (شقل) فضة.

|Referencing §221| If (after) (the patient is) a son of an ordinary person, he shall give (to the doctor) 3 Shiqil silver.

§ 223.—XXXV, 13-17

13 šum-ma ᵇwarad a-wi-lim 14 be-el wardim 15 a-na A.ZU 16 II šiḳil kaspim 17 i-na-ad-di-in

70 ثُمَّ ورَدْ أويلِم [عَويلِم] 71 بَعَلْ ورْدِمْ أنَ أزو [أسو] 72 2 ثِقِلْ [شِقِلْ] كسْفِمْ 73 ينَدِنْ

|وفق الفقرة 221| بعد ان (اذا) (المُجَبّر) عبد شخص [رجل]، مالك العبد سوف يعطي الى الطبيب 2 مثقال (شقل) فضة.

|Referencing §221| If (after) (the patient is) a slave of a person (a man), the owner of the slave shall give (to the doctor) 2 Shiqil silver.

§ 224.—XXXV, 18-28

18 šum-ma A.ZU alpim 19 u lu imêrim 20 lu alpam u lu imêram 21 ṣi-im-ma-am kab-tam 22 i-bu-uš-ma 23 ub-ta-al-li-iṭ 24 be-el alpim ᵇu lu imêrim 25 IGI.VI.GAL kaspim 26 a-na A.ZU 27 ID-šu 28 i-na-ad-di-in

18 ثُمَّ أزو [أسو] ألفِمْ [ألبِمْ] [علفِمْ [علبِمْ]] 19 ولو حمِيرِمْ 20 ألفَمْ [ألبَمْ] [علفَمْ [علبَمْ]] ولو حميرَمْ 21 زِمَمْ [سِمَمْ] كَبْتَمْ 22 يئبُشْمَ [يعفُشْمَ] [يعفِسْمَ] 23 يُبْتَلِطْ 24 بعَلْ علَفِمْ ولو حمِيرِمْ 25 إجي 6 جَلْ كسفِمْ 26 أنَ أزو [أسو] 27 عِدْ ذو 28 ينَدِنْ

بعد ان (اذا) طبيب الثور وحتى لو طبيب الحمار يعمل (لـ)ثور وحتى لو (لـ)حمار، شق (جرح) كبير، (و) يحي (يشفي)، مالك الثور، و(حتى) لو الحمار، سوف يعطي 1\6 مثقال (شقل) فضة للطبيب (لـ)حسابه (لحساب اجره).

If (after) a doctor of ox, and (even) let-it-be a donkey, makes (to) an ox, and (even) let-it-be a donkey, a large cut, (and) he keeps alive (heals), the owner of the ox, and (even) let-it-be the donkey, shall give 1/6 Shiqil silver to the doctor (for) his (fee) rate.

§ 225.—XXXV, 29-35

29 šum-ma alpam u lu imêram 30 zi-im-ma-am [b]kab-tam 31 i-bu-uš-ma 32 uš-ta-mi-it 33 IGI.IV.GAL šîmi-šu 34 a-na be-el alpim bu lu imêrim 35 i-na-ad-di-in

29 ثُمَّ ألفَمْ [ألبِمْ] [علفَمْ [علبِمْ]] ولو حِميرَمْ 30 زِمَمْ [سِمَمْ] كبْتَمْ 31 يئبُشْمَ [يعفُشْمَ] [يعفُسْمَ] 32 يُستَمتْ 33 إجي 4 جَل سيمِ ذو
34 أنَ بَعَلْ ألفِمْ [ألبِمْ] [علفِمْ [علبِمْ]] ولو حِميرِمْ 35 ينْدنْ

|وفق الفقرة 224| بعد ان (اذا) (الطبيب) يعمل (ل)ثور وحتى لو (ل)حمار، شق (جرح) كبير، (و) يُميت (يسبب الموت)، (الطبيب) سوف يعطي 1\4 (قيمة) شراءه (من الفضة) الى مالك الثور، و(حتى) لو الحمار.

|Referencing §224| If (after) (the doctor) makes (to) an ox, and (even) let-it-be a donkey, a large cut, (and) he causes death, the owner of the ox, and let-it-be the donkey, he shall give 1/4 its purchase value (in silver) to the owner of the ox, and (even) let-it-be the donkey.

§ 226.—XXXV, 36-42

36 šum-ma gallabum 37 ba-lum be-el wardim 38 ab-bu-ti 39 wardi la še-e-im 40 u-gal-li-ib 41 rittê [b]gallabim šu-a-ti 42 i-na-ak-ki-su

36 ثُمَّ جلَّبُمْ 37 بلَمْ بعَلْ ورْدِمْ 38 أبْتِ 39 ورْدِ لا سئِمْ 40 يُجلِّبْ 41 رتِّيي جلَّبِمْ ذأتِ 42 ينَكِسو [ينَقِّصو]

بعد ان (اذا) دامغ (مُعَلّمْ) يدمغ (يُعلّمْ) بلا (بدون) (علم) مالك العبد "مقيم، لا شراء (ليس للبيع)"، سوف يقطعو كفّي [أصابيع] ذلك الدامغ (المُعَلّمْ).

If (after) a brander brands (marks) without (the knowledge of) the owner of the slave “resident, no purchase (not for sale)”, they shall cut the hand fists [fingers] of that brander.

§ 227.—XXXV, 43-55

43 šum-ma a-wi-lum 44 gallabam i-da-aṣ-ma 45 ab-bu-ti 46 wardi la še-e-im 47 ug-da-al-li-ib 48 a-wi-lam šu-a-ti 49 i-du-uk-ku-šu-ma 50 i-na bâbi-šu 51 i-ḫa-al-la-[b]lu-šu 52 gallabum i-na i-du-u 53 la u-gal-li-bu 54 i-tam-ma-ma 55 u-ta-aš-šar

43 ثُمَّ أويلُم [عويلُم] 44 جلَّبَمْ يدصَمْ 45 أبْتِ 46 ورْدِ لا سئِمْ 47 يُجدَلِبْ [يُجتَلِبْ] 48 أويلَم [عويلَم] ذأتِ 49 يدكو ذُوم 50 إنَ بابِ ذو 51 يخلَلو ذو 52 جلَّبُمْ إنَ إإدُوَ [إهدُوَ] 53 لا أُجلِبُ 54 يتأمم 55 يتَذَرْ

|وفق الفقرة 226| بعد ان (اذا) شخص [رجل] يخدع (يوقعْ ب) دامغ (مُعَلّمْ)، (كي) يدمغ (يُعلّمْ) "مقيم، لا شراء (ليس للبيع)"، ذلك الشخص [الرجل] سوف يقتلونه، (و) يتركونه ليتعفن في (عند) بابه (باب بيته)، الدامغ (المُعَلّمْ)، سوف يَفْضي (بأنه) ما دمَغَ (ما علّمَ) فيما (بينما) عَرفَ (مسبقا)، (و) سوف يُترك (حرا).

|Referencing §226| If (after) a person (a man) misleads a brander to brand (marks) “resident, no purchase (not for sale)”, they shall put him to death, (and) leave him to rot in (front of) his door, the brander shall notify (inform) “I did not brand” in (as) he knew (beforehand), to be left (free).

§ 228.—XXXV, 56-63

56 šum-ma bânûm 57 bîtam a-na a-wi-lim 58 i-bu-uš-ma 59 u-ša-ak-li-[b]ilšum 60 a-na I SAR bîtim 61 II šiḳil kaspim 62 a-na ḳi-iš-ti-šu 63 i-na-ad-di-iš-šum

56 ثُمَّ بانُمْ 57 بيتَمْ أنَ أويلِم [عويلِم] 58 يئبُشْمَ [يعفُشْمَ] [يعفُسْمَ] 59 يُشكْلِل ذُوم 60 أنَ 1 سَرْ بيتِمْ 61 2 ثِقِلْ [شِقِلْ] كَسْفِمْ 62 أنَ قِسْطِ ذو [قِشْتِ ذو] 63 ينَدِنْ ذُوم [ينَدِذّوم]

بعد ان (اذا) بنّاء يعمل (يبني) [رجل] بيت الى شخص، (و) يُكْمِله (حسب الاتفاق)، (الشخص [الرجل]) سوف يعطيه لمكافئته 2 مثقال (شقل) فضة لسرْ (صف طابوق) البيت الواحد.

If (after) a builder makes (builds) a house to (for) a person [a man], (and) complete (as agreed), he shall give him to (for) his award 2 Shiqil silver to one (for each) house sar (row of bricks).

§ 229.—XXXV, 64-72

64 šum-ma bânûm 65 a-na a-wi-lim 66 bîtam i-bu-uš-ma 67 ši-bi-ir-šu 68 la u-dan-ni-in-ma 69 bîtum i-bu-šu 70 im-ku-ut-ma 71 be-el bîtim ᵇuš-ta-mi-it 72 bânûm šu-u id-da-ak

64 ثمّ بانمْ 65 أنَ أويلم [عويلِم] 66 بيتمْ يئبُشمَ [يعفشْمَ] [يعفِسمْ] 67 سبِرْ ذو 68 لا يُدأننِم 69 بيتمْ إإبُشُ [إعفَشُ] [إعِفسُ] 70 يمكْتمَ [يمقطمَ] 71 بَعلَ بيتِمْ يُستمتِ 72 بانمْ ذوو يدكَ

بعد ان (اذا) بنّاء يعمل (يبني) بيت الى شخص [رجل]، (و) لا يقوّي كُنهه (بناءه)، (و) البيت (الذي) بني يتهاوى، (و) يقتل مالك البيت، هذا البنّاء سوف يُقتل.

If (after) a builder makes (builds) a house for a person [a man], (and) he does not strengthen its core, (and) the house crumbles down, (and) it causes the death of the owner of the house, this builder shall be put to death.

§ 230.—XXXV, 73-76

73 šum-ma mâr be-el bîtim 74 uš-ta-mi-it 75 mâr bânîm šu-a-ti 76 i-du-uk-ku

73 ثمّ مأر بَعلْ بيتِمْ 74 يُستَمتِ 75 مأر بانمْ ذأتِ يدكو

|وفق الفقرة 230| بعد ان (اذا) (البيت المتهاوي) يقتل إبن مالك البيت، سوف يقتلو إبن ذلك البنّاء.

|Referencing §230| If (after) it causes the death of a son of the owner of the house, they shall put to death the son of the builder.

§ 231.—XXXV, 77-81

77 šum-ma warad be-el bîtim 78 uš-ta-mi-it 79 wardam ki-ma wardim 80 ana be-el bîtim 81 i-na-ad-di-in

77 ثمّ ورد بعَلْ بيتِمْ 78 يُستمِتْ 79 وردمْ كيم وردِمْ 80 أنَ بعلْ بيتِمْ 81 ينَدنْ

|وفق الفقرة 230| بعد ان (اذا) (البيت المتهاوي) يقتل عبد مالك البيت، (البناء) سوف يعطي عبدا مثل (بقيمة) العبد (المقتول).

|Referencing §230| If (after) it causes the death of a slave of the owner of the house, he shall give a slave like (with the same value of) the (dead) slave.

§ 232.—XXXV, 82-92

82 šum-ma ŠA.GA 83 uḫ-ta-al-li-iḳ 84 mi-im-ma 85 ša u-ḫal-li-ḳu 86 i-ri-ab 87 u aš-šum bîtam i-bu-šu 98 la u-dan-ni-nu-ma 89 im-ku-tu 90 i-na ŠA.GA 91 ra-ma-ni-šu 92 bîtam im-ku-tu i-ib-bi-eš

82 ثمَّ شَجا 83 يُحْتَلِقْ 84 مِمَّ 85 ذا أُحلِقُ 86 يرِأبْ 87 و هَذَمْ بيتَم إإبُشُ [إعفَشُ] [إعِفسُ] 88 لا إدأننِمْ 89 إمكُتُ [إمقْطُ] 90 إنَ شَجا 91 رأمَني ذو 92 بيتَم إمكُتْ [إمقْطُ] يئبيَشْ [يعفِيَشْ] [يعفِيَسْ]

|وفق الفقرة 230| بعد ان (اذا) (البيت المتهاوي) يضيّعْ (يحطّمْ) حاجيات، (البنّاء) سوف يُسدد (يعوض) أيّما (حاجيات) أزال (حطّمَ)، (و) هذا لأن البيت (الذي) بنى ما قوّى (تكوينه)، (ف)هوى، (البناء) سوف يعمل (يبني) في (من) حاجيات ذاته (على حسابه) البيت (الذي) هوى.

|Referencing §230| If (after) it causes the loss (it destroys) things (belongings), he shall repay (replace) whatever that it made lost (it destroyed), and that is because he did not strengthen the house he made (built), (and) it crumbled down, in (from) his own things (belongings) (on his own expense), he shall make (rebuild) the house (that) crumbled down.

§ 233.—XXXV, 93-XXXVI, 3

93 šum-ma bânûm bîtam 94 a-na a-wi-lim i-bu-uš-ma 95 ši-bi-ir-šu 96 la uš-te-iṣ-bi-ma 97 igarum iḳ-tu-up 98 bânûm šu-u XXXVI, 1 i-na kaspim [b]ra-ma-ni-šu 2 igaram šu-a-ti 3 u-dan-na-an

93 ثمَّ بانمْ بيتمْ 94 أنَ أويلم [عَويلِم] يئبُشمَ [يعفْشمَ] [يعفْسمَ] 95 سبرْ ذو 96 لا يستعصبِمَ [يستعظبِمَ [يستئصبِمَ]] 97 إجرمْ [حجَرمْ] يقْتبْ [يقْطفْ] 98 بانمْ ذوو 1 إنَ كسفمْ رأمني ذو 2 إجرمْ [حجَرمْ] ذأتِ 3 يُدأننْ

بعد ان (اذا) بنّاء يعمل (يبني) بيت الى شخص [رجل]، (و) لا يشدّ (يربط) [لا يُحسن عمل] كُنهه (بناءه)، (و) السطح (السقف) [الحائط] يقتب (يحدّب لضغط الوزن) [يرتخى]، هذا البنّاء سوف يقوّي ذلك السطح (السقف) [الحائط] في (من) فضته ذاته (على حسابه).

If (after) a builder makes (builds) for a person [a man] a house, (and) he does not tighten [does not do well] its core, (and) the roof [the wall] bends (sags) [loses vigor (declines)], this builder shall strengthen that roof [wall] in (from) his own silver (on his own expense).

§ 234.—XXXVI, 4-9

4 šum-ma malaḫum 5 elippi LX GUR 6 a-na a-wi-lim ip-ḫi 7 II šiḳil kaspim 8 a-na ḳi-iš-ti-šu 9 i-na-ad-di-[b]iš-šum

4 ثمَّ ملاحُمْ 5 علِفّ [علِبّ] 60 جرْ [كرْ] 6 أنَ أويلِم [عَويلِم] يفحي 7 2 ثقِلْ [شقِلْ] كسْفِمْ 8 أنَ قسْطِ ذو [قشْتِ ذو] 9 ينْدِنْ ذوْمْ [ينْدِذّومْ]

بعد ان (اذا) بلّام يكسو (يقيّر) قُفّة (عبّارة نهر) (بسعة) 60 كُر لشخص (الرجل) ، سوف يعطيه لمكافئته 2 مثقال (شقل) فضة.

If (after) a boatman seals (with tar) a boat of 60 Kur (capacity) to (for) a person [a man], he shall give him to (for) his award 2 Shiqil silver.

§ 235.—XXXVI, 10-26

10 šum-ma malaḫum 11 elippam [b]a-na a-wi-lim 12 ip-ḫi-ma 13 ši-bi-ir-šu 14 la u-tak-[b]ki-il-ma 15 i-na ša-at-tim-ma [b]šu-a-ti 16 elippum ši-i 17 iz-za-par 18 ḫi-di-tam ir-ta-ši 19 malaḫum 20 elippam šu-a-ti 21 i-na-ḳar-ma 22 i-na ŠA.GA [b]ra-ma-ni-šu 23 u-dan-na-an-ma 24 elippam dan-na-tam 25 a-na be-el elippim 26 i-na-ad-di-in

10 ثمَّ ملاحُمْ 11 علِفّمْ [علِبّمْ] 12 أنَ أويلِم [عَويلِم] يفحيمَ 13 سبرْ ذو 14 لا يُتكلْمَ [يتأكلْمَ] 15 إنَ ستّمَ [سنْتمَ] ذأتِ 16 علِفّمْ [علِبّمْ] ذيي 17 يزفرْ [يزبرْ] 18 حدِتمْ يرتسي 19 ملاحُمْ 20 علِفّمْ [علِبّمْ] ذأتِ 21 ينقرْمَ 22 إنَ شجا رأمني ذو 23 يُدأننْمَ 24 علِفّمْ [علِبّمْ] دأنتمْ 25 أنَ بعَلْ علِفّمْ [علِبّمْ] 26 ينْدِنْ

بعد ان (اذا) بلّام يكسو (يقيّر) قُفّة (عبّارة نهر) لشخص (لرجل)، (و) لا يغذّي (يُشبع) كُنهها (صلبها)، (و) هذه القُفة تُنَفّس (تنثقب) في تلك السنة، تَرتسي (تواجه) حدّة (شدة)، البلّام سوف يتحرّى (و) يقوي (يُصلّح) تلك القُفّة في (من) حاجيات ذاته (على حسابه)، (و) سوف يعطي قُفّة قوية (صالحة) الى مالك القُفّة.

If (after) a boatman seals (with tar) a boat to (for) a person [a man], (and) he does not feed (fill well) its core, (and) this boat punctures (allows water in) in that year, (and) settles in (faces) hardship (difficulty), the boatman shall troubleshoots, (and) strengthens (fixes) that boat in (from) his own things (belongings) (on his own expense), (and) he shall give to the owner of the boat a strong (a fixed) boat.

§ 236.—XXXVI, 27-37

27 šum-ma a-wi-lum 28 elippi-šu 29 a-na malaḫim 30 a-na ig-ri-im 31 id-di-in-ma 32 malaḫum [b]i-gi-ma 33 elippam ut-te-bi 34 u lu uḫ-ta-[b]al-li-iḳ 35 malaḫum elippam 36 a-na be-el elippim 37 i-ri-a-ab

27 ثمَّ أويلم [عَويلُم] 28 علفَّ ذو [علبَّ ذو] 29 أنَ ملاحمْ 30 أنَ إجرمْ 31 يدنمَ 32 ملاحمْ يعجّيمَ [يعجهمَ] 33 علفّمْ [علبّمْ] يُطبع 34 ولو يُحتَلق 35 ملاحمْ علفمّ [علبمّ] 36 أنَ بعَلْ علفّمْ [علبمّ] 37 يرأبْ

بعد ان (اذا) شخص (رجل) يُعطي قُفّته (عبّارته) الى بلّام للإيجار (يؤجر)، (و) البلّام يهمل [يتجاهل] (و) يُغرق القُفّة (العبّارة)، و (حتى) لو يُضيّع، البلّام سوف يُسَدّدْ (يعوض) الى مالك القُفّة (العبّارة) القُفّة (عبّارة).

If (after) a person [a man] gives his boat to a boatman to (for) rent, (and) the boatman neglects (and) sinks the boat, and (even) let-it-be he loses (it), the boatman shall repay (replace) to the owner of the boat the (lost) boat.

§ 237.—XXXVI, 38-55

38 šum-ma a-wi-lum 39 malaḫam ᵇu elippam 40 i-gur-ma 41 še'am šipâtam šamnam suluppam 42 u mi-im-ma ᵇšum-šu 43 ša ṣi-nim 44 i-ṣi-en-ši 45 malaḫum šu-u 46 i-gi-ma 47 elippam ut-te-ib-bi 48 u ša li-ib-ᵇbi-ša 49 uḫ-ta-al-li-ḳ 50 malaḫum 51 elippam ša u-te-ᵇib-bu-u 52 u mi-im-ma 53 ša i-na li-ib-bi-ša 54 u-ḫal-li-ḳu 55 i-ri-a-ab

38 ثمَّ أويلم [عَويلُم] 39 ملاحمْ و علفّم [علبّم] 40 يئجُرمَ 41 سعَمْ [شعَمْ] شعفيتَم سمْنَم سُلُفّمْ 42 و ممَّ سمْ ذو 43 ذا ظعنمْ 44 يظعَنْ 45 ملاحمْ ذوو 46 يعجيّمَ [يعجّهمَ] 47 علفّمْ [علبّمْ] يُطبع 48 و ذا لبَّ ذا 49 يحتَلقْ 50 ملاحمْ 51 علفّمْ [علبّمْ] ذا أُطبعُ 52 و ممَّ 53 ذا إنَ لبَّ ذا 54 أحلقْ 55 يرأبْ

بعد ان (اذا) شخص (رجل) يستأجر بلّام و قُفّة (عبّارة)، (و) يحمّل حبوب، خصال صوف، سمن، تمر، و أيا (كان) إسمه [أي شيء كان] من الحمولة، (ثم) هذا البلّام يهمل [يتجاهل] (عمله)، (و) يُغرق القُفّة (العبّارة)، و يُضّيع الذي في داخلها (حمولتها)، البلّام سوف يُسَدّدْ (يعوض) القُفّة (العبّارة) التي أغرقَ، و أيّ الذي أضاع في (من) داخلها (حمولتها).

If (after) a person [a man] rents (hires) a boatman and (with) a boat, he loads (it) grains, wool bundles, oil, dates, and whatever its name (anything) of the load (the cargo), (then) this boatman neglects, (and) he sinks the boat, and loses that of its inside (the cargo), the boatman shall repay (replace) the boat he sunk, and whatever he lost in (from) its inside (the cargo).

§ 238.—XXXVI, 56-61

56 šum-ma malaḫum 57 elippi a-wi-lim 58 u-te-ib-bi-ma 59 uš-te-li-a-aš-ši 60 kaspi mi-ši-il ᵇšî-mi-ša 61 i-na-ad-di-|in|

56 ثمَّ ملاحمْ 57 علفّمْ [علبّمْ] أويلم [عَويلم] 58 يُطبعمَ [يتَعبمَ] 59 يُستَلياذّي [يُستَلياً ذي] 60 كَسْفَ مِثلْ سيمِ ذا 61 يندنْ

بعد ان (اذا) البلّام يُغرِق قُفّة (عبّارة) شخص (رجل)، (و) يستّلها (يُخرجُها)، سوف يعطي (المالك) فضّة نصف (قيمة) شراءها.

If (after) a boatman sinks a person's [a man's] boat, (and then) plucks (pulls) it out, he shall give (the owner) half its purchase value, (in) silver.

§ 239.—XXXVI, 62-66

62 šum-ma a-wi-|lum| 63 malaḫam |i-gur| 64 VI |ŠE.GUR| 65 i-na ša-na|-at| 66 i-na-ad-|di|-ᵇiš-|šum|

62 ثمَّ أويلم [عَويلُم] 63 ملاحمْ |يئجرْ| 64 6 |سعِ [شع] جرْ [كرْ]| 65 إنَ سنَتْ 66 يندنْ ذومْ [يندذّومْ]

بعد ان (اذا) شخص (رجل) يستأجر بلّام، سوف يعطيه في السنة، 6 كُر حبوب.

If (after) a person [a man] rents (hires) a boatman, he shall give him in a year, 6 Kur grains.

§ 240.—XXXVI, 67-80

67 šum-ma |elippum| 68 ša ma-ḫi-ir-|tim| 69 elippam ša mu-|uk|-ᵇki-el-bi-|tim| 70 im-ḫa-aṣ-ma 71 ut-te-ib-bi 72 be-el elippim ša elippu-šu ᵇte-bi-a-at 73 mi-im-ma ša i-na ᵇelippi-šu ḫal-ḳu 74

i-na ma-ḫar i-lim 75 u-ba-ar-ma 76 ša ma-ḫi-ir-tim 77 ša elippam ša mu-uk-[b]ki-el-bi-tim 78 u-te-ib-bu-u 79 elippi-šu u mi-im-[b]ma-šu ḫal-ga-am 80 i-ri-a-ab-šum

67 ثمّ إعلفمْ [علبمْ]| 68 ذا مَخرِتمْ 69 علفمَ [علبمَ] ذا مُقئلبتمْ [مُقئلفتمْ] 70 يمحصَمْ 71 يُطبع 72 بَعلَ علِفمْ [علِبمْ] ذا علفٌ ذو [علِبٌ ذو] طَبعتْ 73 ممّ ذا إنَ علِفٌ ذو [علِبٌ ذو] حلَقْ 74 إنَ مخرَ إلمْ [علِمْ] 75 يُبرمْ 76 ذا مَخرِتمْ 77 ذا علِفمْ [علِبمْ] ذا مكألبتمْ 78 أطبعُ 79 علِفٌ ذو [علِبٌ ذو] و ممّ ذو حلَجمْ [حلقمْ] 80 يرأبْ ذومْ

بعد ان (اذا) قُفّة (عبّارة) ماخرة (شاقة لتيار النهر) تضرب (و) تُغرق قُفّة (عبّارة) جارفة (سائرة مع تيار النهر)، مالك القُفّة (العبّارة) التي قُفّتُه (عبّارتُه) غرقَتْ سوف يصّدَق امام إله أيّما مفقود في قُفّته (عبّارته)، صاحب (القُفّة (العبّارة) الماخرة الذي أغرقَ القُفّة (العبّارة) الجارفة سوف يُسدّدْ (يعوض) له قُفّتَه (عبّارتَه) وايا من أشياءه المفقودة.

If (after) a (water current) facing boat strikes (and) sinks a (water current) drifting boat, the owner of the boat whose boat is sunk (submerged) shall confirm in front of a god whatever that is in his boat vanished (lost), that of (the owner of) the (water current) facing (boat) who sank (caused the sinking of) the (water current) drifting boat shall repay (replace) (to) him his boat and whatever (things) of his vanished (lost).

§ 241.—XXXVI, 81-84

81 šum-ma a-wi-lum 82 alpam a-na ni-bu-tim 83 it-te-bi 84 ⅓ ma-na kaspim i-ša-ḳal

81 ثمّ أويلم [عويلم] 82 ألفمْ [ألبمْ] [علفمْ [علبمْ]] أنَ نبؤتمْ 83 يتبئي 84 1\3 منا كسفم يثقلْ

بعد ان (اذا) شخص (رجل) يتباوئ (يعوض بأخذ) ثور للرهينة (كرهينة)، سوف يزن (ويعطي) (لمالكه) 1\3 رطل فضة.

If (after) a person [a man] substitutes (by seizing) for (as) a hostage an ox, he shall give (to its owner) 1/3 Mana (<1 lb.) silver.

§ 242-243.—XXXVI, 85-91

85 šum-ma a-wi-lum 86 a-na šattim I i-gur 87 ID GUD.DA.UR.RA 88 IV ŠE.GUR 89 ID GUD.UD.LID.SAG 90 III ŠE.GUR a-na be-li-šu 91 i-na-ad-di-in

85 ثمّ أويلم [عويلم] 86 أنَ 1 ستّمْ [سنَتمْ] يئجرْ 87 عِدْ جدا عُرا 88 4 سعِ [شعِ] جرْ [كُرْ] 89 عِدْ جُدْؤدْ لئِدْ سَجْ 90 3 سعِ [شعِ] جرْ [كُرْ] أنَ بَعلِ ذو 91 يندِنْ

|مقارنتا بالفقرة 241| بعد ان (اذا) شخص (رجل) يستأجر لسنة، سوف يعطي 4 كُر حبوب (ل)حساب (ايجار) بقر جرْ (حراثة)، 3 جرار حبوب (ل)حساب (ايجار) واحد أبقار غلاظ النقل، لمالكه.

|In comparison to §241| If (after) a person (a man) rents for a year, he will give 4 Kur grains (for) a plowing cattle boor (rent) rate, 3 Kur grains (for) a transportation cattle boor (rent) rate, to its owner.

§ 244.—XXXVII, 1-5

XXXVII, 1 šum-ma a-wi-lum 2 alpam imêram i-gur-ma 3 i-na ṣi-ri-im 4 UR.MAH id-du-uk-šu 5 a-na be-li-šu-ma

1 ثمّ أويلم [عويلم] 2 ألفمْ [ألبمْ] [علفمْ [علبمْ]] حميرمْ يئجرْمَ 3 إنَ ظهرِم [ضهرِم] [صحرم] 4 عرمخ يدكْ ذو 4 أن بَعلِ ذومَ

بعد ان (اذا) شخص (رجل) يستأجر ثور، (أو) حمار، (و) حيوان مفترس [أسد] يقتله (يأكله) في البرية، (الخسارة) لمالكه.

If (after) a person [a man] rent an ox, (or) donkey, (and) a ferocious creature [a lion] kills (eats) it in the desert (badiyah), (the loss is) to its owner.

§ 245.—XXXVII, 6-13

6 šum-ma a-wi-lum 7 alpam i-gur-ma 8 i-na me-gu-tim 9 u lu i-na ma-ḫa-ᵇzi-im 10 uš-ta-mi-it 11 alpam ki-ma alpim 12 a-na be-el alpim 13 i-ri-a-ab

6 ثمَّ أويلم [عويلم] 7 ألفمْ [ألبمْ] [علفمْ [علبمْ]] يئجرْمَ 8 إنَ معجتم [معجهتمْ] 9 ولو إن محزمْ 10 يُستمِتْ 11 ألفمْ [ألبمْ] [علفمْ [علبمْ]] كيمَ ألفمْ [ألبمْ] [علفمْ [علبمْ]] 12 أنَ بعلَ ألفمْ [ألبمْ] [علفمْ [علبمْ]] 12 يرأبْ

بعد ان (اذا) شخص (رجل) يستأجر ثور، (و) (الثور) يموت في (من) الإهمال [التجاهُلْ] و (حتى) لو في (من) الشدّة (شدة السوق)، (الشخص (الرجل) سوف يسدّدْ (يعوض) ثورا الى مالك الثور كالثورِ (الميت).

If (after) a person [a man] rent an ox, (and) it dies in (from) neglect, and (even) let-it-be the harshness (of labor), he shall repay (replace) to the owner of the ox an ox like (with the same value of) the (dead) ox.

§ 246.—XXXVII, 14-21

14 šum-ma a-wi-lum 15 alpam i-gur-ma 16 šêpi-šu iš-te-bi-ir 17 u lu la-bi-a-an-šu 18 it-ta-ki-is 19 alpam ki-ma alpim 20 a-na be-el alpim 21 i-ri-a-ab

14 ثمَّ أويلم [عويلم] 15 ألفمْ [ألبمْ] [علفمْ [علبمْ]] يئجرْمَ 16 ظيفِ ذو [سيفِ ذو] يستبرْ [يتبّرْ] 17 ولو لبأن ذو 18 يتكسْ [يتقصْ] 19 ألفمْ [ألبمْ] [علفمْ [علبمْ]] كيمَ ألفمْ [ألبمْ] [علفمْ [علبمْ]] 20 أنَ بعلَ ألفمْ [ألبمْ] [علفمْ [علبمْ]] 21 يرأبْ

بعد ان (اذا) شخص (رجل) يستأجر ثور، (و) يكسر (يهشّم) وظيفه (مستدق اطرافه)، و(حتى) لو يقطع (يحزّ) لَبانه (نحره)، (الشخص (الرجل) سوف يسدّدْ (يعوض) الى مالك الثورِ ثور كالثورِ (المجروح).

If (after) a person [a man] rent an ox, (and) he breaks its lower leg, and (even) let-it-be he cut its throat, he shall repay (replace) to the owner of the ox an ox like (with the same value of) the (injured) ox.

§ 247.—XXXVII, 22-27

22 šum-ma a-wi-lum 23 alpam i-gur-ma 24 în-šu uḫ-tab-da(=it) 25 kaspi mi-ši-il šîmi-šu 26 a-na be-el alpim 27 i-na-ad-di-in

22 ثمَّ أويلم [عويلم] 23 ألفمْ [ألبمْ] [علفمْ [علبمْ]] يئجرْمَ 24 عينْ ذو يُختبط [يهتبدَ] 25 كسفِ مثِلْ سيمِ ذو 26 أنَ بعلَ ألفمْ [ألبمْ] [علفمْ [علبمْ]] 66 يندنْ

بعد ان (اذا) شخص (رجل) يستأجر ثور، (و) يسلب [يقتلع] عينه، (الشخص (الرجل)) سوف يعطي الى مالك الثورِ فضةِ نصف (قيمة) شراءه.

If (after) a person [a man] rent an ox, (and) he robs his eye [plucks out his eye], he shall give to the owner of the ox half its purchase value, (in) silver.

§ 248.—XXXVII, 28-35

28 šum-ma a-wi-lum 29 alpam i-gur-ma 30 ḳar-ni-šu iš-bi-ir 31 zibba-zu it-ta-ki-is 32 u lu šêr pasutti-šu 33 it-ta-sa-ak 34 kaspi IGI.IV.GAL šîmi-šu 35 i-na-ad-di-in

28 ثمَّ أويلم [عويلم] 29 ألفمْ [ألبمْ] [علفمْ [علبمْ]] يئجرْمَ 30 قرْنِ ذو يسبرْ [يتبرْ] 31 زبَّ ذو [زبّتْ] [ذبَّ ذو [ذبّتْ]] يتكسْ [يتقصْ] 32 ولو شعَرْ فستِّ ذو [فسطِّ ذو] 33 يتسكْ [يتصكْ] 34 كسفِ إجي 4 جلْ سيمِ ذو 35 يندنْ

بعد ان (اذا) شخص (رجل) يستأجر ثور، (و) يكسر قرنه، يقطع ذيله [شعر ذيله]، و(حتى) لو يُجرْد (يُذهب عبر الحك والضرب) شعَرْ بيت شعْره (الشعر المنبسط الطويل فوق رأسه ورقبته الذي يشبه الخيمة أو الشبكة)، سوف يعطي (الى المالك) فضّة 1\4 (سعِرْ) شراءه (قيمته).

If (after) a person [a man] rent an ox, (and) he breaks its horn, cut its tail [cut its tail hair], and (even) let-it-be he scraps off its hair-tent (the tent-like long straight hair on its head and neck), he shall give (to the owner) 1/4 its purchase value, in silver.

§ 249.—XXXVII, 36-43

36 šum-ma a-wi-lum 37 alpam i-gur-ma 38 i-lum im-ḫa-zu-ma 39 im-tu-ut 40 a-wi-lum ša alpam ^{b}i-gu-ru 41 ni-iš i-lim 42 i-za-kar-ma 43 u-ta-aš-šar

36 ثمْ أويلمْ [عويلمْ] 37 ألفمْ [ألبمْ] [علفمْ [علبمْ]] يئجرمْ 38 إلمْ [علمْ] يمحص ذوم [يمحتمْ] 39 يمتُتْ 40 أويلمْ [عويلمْ] ذا ألفمْ [ألبمْ] [علفمْ [علبمْ]] إجرُ 41 نِعش إلمْ [علِم] 42 يذّكرمْ 43 يُتذرْ

بعد ان (اذا) شخص (رجل) يستأجر ثور، (و) الإله يضربه (بشدّة (مرض)) (و) يموت، الشخص (الرجل) الذي أجّرَ الثور سوف يقول (يحلف) (بذلك) برِفعَة (بحياة) الإله، (و) سوف يُترك حرا.

If (after) a person [a man] rent an ox, (and) god strikes it (with hardship (sickness)), (and) it dies, the person [the man] who rented the ox shall say (declare) (that) in the glory life of god, (and) shall be left (free).

§ 250.—XXXVII, 44-51

44 šum-ma alpum zu-ga-am 45 i-na a-la-ki-šu 46 a-wi-lam 47 ik-ki-ib-ma 48 uš-ta-mi-it 49 di-nu-um šu-u 50 ru-gu-um-ma-am 51 u-ul i-šu

44 ثمّ ألفمْ [ألبمْ] [علفمْ [علبمْ]] زجّمْ [سوقمْ] 45 إنَ ألكِ ذو 46 أويلم [عويلمَ] 47 يكّبمَ [يقّبمْ] 48 يُستمِتْ 49 دينُمْ ذوو 50 رُجمم 51 أُلْ يذو

بعد ان (اذا) ثور ينطح شخص [رجل] في (عند) ترسّله (ذهابه) مُزدحَما [سوقا]، (و) يُميت، قضية (الجزاء) هذه لا تملك (لا تتضمن) غرامة.

If (after) an ox gores a person [a man] in (during) his going to a crowded place [a market], (and) causes death, this (court) case does not have fine (penalty).

§ 251.—XXXVII, 52-65

52 šum-ma alap a-wi-lim 53 na-ak-ka-a|m-ma| 54 ki-ma na-ak-ka-^{b}pu-u 55 ba-ab-ta-šu 56 u-še-di-šum-ma 57 ḳar-ni-šu 58 la u-šar-ri-im 59 alpi-šu la u-sa-^{b}an-ni-iḳ-ma 60 alpum šu-u 61 mâr a-wi-lim 62 ik-ki-ib-ma 63 uš-ta-mi-it 64 ½ |ma|-na kaspim 65 i-|na|-ad-di-in

52 ثمّ ألفْ [ألبْ] [علفْ [علبْ]] أويلِم [عويلِم] 53 إنكبْ [نقبْ]| 54 كيم نكبو [نقبو] 55 ببَت ذو 56 يُسئِد ذوم [يُسهِد ذومَ] [يتئِد ذومَ [يتْهِد ذومَ]] 57 قرْن ذو 58 لا يَشرِمْ 59 ألفَ ذو [ألبَ ذو] [علفَ ذو [علبَ ذو]] لا يُزنِقمَ [يُصنِقمَ] 60 ألفمْ [ألبمْ] [علفمْ [علبمْ]] ذوو 61 مأرْ أويلُم [عويلُم] 62 يكّبمَ [يقّبمَ] 63 يُستَمِتْ 64 1\2 منَا كسفمَ 65 يندِنْ

بعد ان (اذا) ثور شخص [رجل]، نطحْ كنطحْوَ، يخبروه (يعْلموه) (مصير) ضحيته، لا يقطع (اعلى) قرنه، لا يربط (أرجُل) ثوره، (و) هذا الثور ينطح ابن شخص [رجل]، (و) يُميت، سوف يعطي 1\2 رطل فضة.

If (after) an ox of a person [a man], a gore like its gore, they inform (alert) him about (the fate of) its victim (fate), (and) he does not cut (the top of) his horn, does not shacke his ox (legs), (and) this ox gores a son of a person [a man], (and) causes death, he shall give ½ Mana silver.

§ 252.—XXXV, 66-68

66 |šum-ma| warad a-wi-lim 67 ⅓ ma-na kaspim 68 i-na-ad-di-in

66 ثم وردْ أويلِم [عويلِم] 67 1\3 منَا كسفمَ 68 يندِنْ

|وفق الفقرة 251| بعد ان (اذا) (الميت) عَبد شخص [رجل]، سوف يعطي 1\3 رطل فضة.
|Referencing §251| If (after) (the dead is) a slave of a person [a man], he shall give 1/3 Mana silver.

§ 253.—XXXVII, 69-82

69 šum-ma a-wi-lum ᵇa-wi-lam 70 a-na pa-ni eḳli-šu 71 u-zu-uz-zi-im 72 i-gur-ma 73 al-dá-a-am 74 [i]-ḳi-ip-šu 75 [LID].GUD.ZUN ᵇip-ki-zum 76 [a-na] eḳlim e-ri-ši-im ᵇu-ra-ak-ki-su 77 šum-ma a-wi-lum šu-u 78 ŠE.ZIR u lu ŠÀ.GAL 79 iš-ri-iḳ-ma 80 i-na ga-ti-šu 81 it-ta-aṣ-ba-at 82 rittê-šu i-na-ak-ki-su

69 ثُمَّ أويلم [عَويلَم] أويلم [عَويلَم] 70 أنَ فَني حقلِ ذو 71 أُززِمْ 72 يئجُرمْ 73 ألْداءَم [هَلْداءَم] 74 يقفْ ذو 75 لئدْ جُدْ ظُعُنْ يفْكِدْ ذُوم [يفْكِتَم] [يفْقدْ ذُوم [يفْقِتَم]] 76 أنَ حقلِمْ أرسِمْ يُركِسُ ذو 77 ثُمَّ أويلم [عَويلَم] ذوو 78 سعِ [شعِ] ذرْ [زغِرْ] ولو سعا [شعا] جَلْ 79 يسْرقَم 80 إنَ جَتي ذو [قَتي ذو] 81 يتَضْبَطْ 82 رِتّيي ذو ينَكّسو [ينَقّصو]

بعد ان (اذا) شخص [رجل] يستأجر شخص [رجل] لتقسيم (لمناصفة) واجهة حقلِ، ينتقيه (ينتقي له) بذوره، يعْهده غلاظ أبقار العمل والتحميل (الثيران)، (و) يعاقده لفلاحة الحقل، بعد ان (اذا) هذا الشخص [الرجل] يسرق ذئر [زغر] الحبوب (حبات الحبوب)، و(حتى) لو عظيم الحبوب (سنابل الحبوب)، (و) تُضْبَط (تُمسَك) في يديه (في حوزته)، سوف يقطعو كفّيه [أصابيعه].
If (after) a person [a man] rents (hires) a person [a man] to (for) dividing (fifty-fifty) his field's front, he selects his seeds, entrusts him (with) the carrying and labor cattle boors (oxen), (and) contracts him (for) the field farming, if (after) this person [man] steals the small ones of the grains (the seeds), and (even) let-it-be the great ones of the grains (the spikes), (and) they are caught in his hands (possession), they shall cut his (hand) fists [fingers].

§ 254.—XXXVII, 83-87

83 šum-ma al-dá-a-am 84 il-ḳi-ma LID.GUD.ZUN 85 u-te-en-ni-iš 86 ta-a-na še'im ša im-ri-ru 87 i-ri-ab

83 ثُمَّ ألْداءَم [هَلْداءَم] 84 يلْقِيمَ لئدْ جُدْ ظُعُنْ 85 يتَئنِتْ [يتَعنِتْ] 86 تأنَ [تأمْ] سعِمْ [شعِمْ] ذا إمْرِرْ 87 يرأبْ

|وفق الفقرة 253| بعد ان (اذا) (المُستأجَر) يلقي (يأخذ) بذور، (و) يُحمِّل غلاظ أبقار العمل والتحميل (الثيران) مشقّة (يستخدمهم)، (المُستأجَر) سوف يسدد (يعوض) (المالك) مثل (كمية) الحبوب التي نَكش (أخذ لنفسه).
|Referencing §253| If (after) he (the hired one) takes the seeds, (and) exhausts (put to work) the carrying and labor cattle boors (oxen), he shall repay (replace) (the owner) the same (amount of) grains he has hoed (took for himself).

§ 255.—XXXVII, 88-96

88 šum-ma LID.GUD.ZUN 89 a-wi-lim a-na ig-ri-im 90 it-ta-di-in 91 u lu ŠE.ZIR iš-ri-iḳ-ma 92 i-na eḳlim la uš-tab-ši 93 a-wi-lam šu-a-ti 94 u-ka-an-nu-šu-ma 95 i-na ebûrim X GAN.E 96 LX ŠE.GUR i-ma-ad-da-ad

88 ثُمَّ لئدْ جُدْ ظُعُنْ 89 أويلِم [عَويلِم] أنَ إجْرِمْ 90 يتَدِنْ 91 ولو سعِ [شعِ] ذرْ [زغِرْ] يسْرِقَمْ 92 إنَ حقلِمْ لا يُستَبذي [يُستَبثي] 93 أويلَم [عَويلَم] ذأتِ 94 يُكَنو ذُومَ 95 إنَ حبَرمْ 10 قَنَع 96 60 سعِ [شعِ] جرْ [كَرْ] يمَدَدْ

|وفق الفقرة 253| بعد ان (اذا) الشخص [الرجل] (المُستأجَر) يعطي غلاظ أبقار عمل وتحميل (ثيران) الشخص [الرجل] للايجار، و (حتى) لو يسرق ذئر [زغر] الحبوب (حبات الحبوب) (و) لا يوجدْ [يُظْهِر (ينشر)] (لا ينمّي) في الحقل، ذلك الشخص [الرجل] ((المُستأجَر) سوف يُجلسوه [يستدعوه]، (و) سوف يمُدُّ (يجهّز) (المالك) 60 كُر حبوب (لكل) 10 قنع (قاطع حقل)، في موسم الحصاد.

|Referencing §253| If (after) he (the hired one) gives to (for) rent the carrying and labor cattle boors (oxen) of the person [the man], and (even) let-it-be he steals the small ones of the grains (the seeds) (and) does not make exist [make appear] (grow) in the field, they shall seat [call] in that person [man] (the hired one), (and) he shall supply 60 Kur of grains (for every) 10 Qan'i (field sectors), in (at) harvest (time).

§ 256.—XXXVII, 97-100

97 šum-ma bi-ḫa-zu 98 a-pa-lam la i-li-i 99 i-na eḳlim šu-a-ti [b]i-na GUD.LID.ZUN 100 im-ta-na-aš-ša-ru-šu

97 ثمَّ بِحزْ [بحزْ ذو] 98 أفلَمْ لا يلِعي [يلئِي] 99 إنَ حقِلِمْ ذأت إن جَدْ لئِدْ طَعَنْ 100 يمْتَنسرو ذو [يمْتَنصرو ذو]

|وفق الفقرة 255| بعد ان (اذا) (المُستأجَر) لا يطيق تحمّلَ (حمل) شدته (عقوبته)، سوف يحرروه (يضعوه) [يحددوه (يحبسوه)] في ذلك الحقل، في (مع) (قطيع) أبقار غِلاظ العمل والتحميل (الثيران).

|Referencing §255| If (after) he (the hired one) cannot handle bearing his hardship (his punishment), they shall free (put) him [confine him] in that field, in (with) the cattle of the carrying and labor boors (the oxen).

§ 257.—XXXVII, 101-XXXVIII, 4

101 šum-ma a-wi-lum XXXVIII, 1 AK.ŠU i-gur 2 VIII ŠE.GUR 3 i-na šattim I[kam] 4 i-na-ad-di-iš-šum

101 ثُمَّ أويلم [عويلم] 1 عَكَشُ [علَكْ شو] يئِجرْ 68 8 سعِ [شعِ] جرْ [كُرْ] 68 إنَ ستِّمْ [سَنْتِمْ] 1كم 68 ينَدِنْ ذُومْ [ينَدِذّومْ]

بعد ان (اذا) شخص [رجل] يستأجر عامل يد، سوف يعطيه 8 كُر حبوب في السنة الواحدة.

If (after) a person [a man] rent (hires) a hand-laborer, he shall give him 8 Kur of grains in one (per) year.

§ 258.—XXXVIII, 5-9

5 šum-ma a-wi-lum 6 ŠÀ.GUD i-gur 7 VI ŠE.GUR 8 i-na šattim I[kam] 9 i-na-ad-di-iš-šum

5 ثُمَّ أويلم [عَويلم] 6 شعا جَدْ يئِجرْ 7 6 سعِ [شعِ] جرْ [كُرْ] 8 إنَ ستِّمْ [سَنْتِمْ] 1كم 9 ينَدِنْ ذُومْ [ينَدِذّومْ]

بعد ان (اذا) شخص [رجل] يستأجر ناشر ماشية (راعي ماشية)، سوف يعطيه 6 كُر حبوب في السنة الواحدة.

If (after) a person [a man] rent (hires) a cattle herdsman, he shall give him 6 Kur of grains in one (per) year.

§ 259.—XXXVIII, 10-15

10 šum-ma a-wi-lum 11 GIŠ.APIN i-na ugarim 12 iš-ri-iḳ 13 V šiḳil kaspim 14 a-na be-el GIŠ.APIN 15 i-na-ad-di-in

10 ثُمَّ أَويلم [عَويلْم] 11 جِشْ أفِنْ [أبِنْ] إنَ عُقَرِمْ [أُقَرِمْ] 12 يسْرِقْ 13 5 ثِقِلْ [شِقِلْ] كسْفِمْ 14 أنَ بَعَلْ جِشْ أفِنْ [أبِنْ] 15 ينَدِنْ

بعد ان (اذا) شخص [رجل] يسرق خشبة محراث في (من) حقل، سوف يعطي 5 مثقال (شقل) فضة الى مالك خشبة المحراث.

If (after) a person [a man] steals a plow (wood) in (from) a field, he shall measure (and give) 5 Shiqil silver to the owner of the plow (wood).

§ 260.—XXXVIII, 16-20

16 šum-ma GIŠ.APIN.TUK.KIN 17 u lu GIŠ.GAN.UR 18 iš-ta-ri-iḳ 19 III šiḳil kaspim 20 i-na-ad-di-in

16 ثُمَّ جِشْ أفِنْ [أبِنْ] تُكِّنْ 18 ولو جِشْ جَنُرْ 12 يسْتَرِقْ 19 3 ثِقِلْ [شِقِلْ] كَسْفِمْ 15 ينَدِنْ

|وفق الفقرة 259| بعد ان (اذا) شخص [رجل] يسرق شفرة (نصل) خشبة محراث، و(حتى) لو خشبة مَدَق (هاون)، سوف يعطي 3 مثقال (شقل) فضة.

|Referencing §259| If (after) he steals a blade of a plow (wood), and (even) let-it-be a pestle (wood), he shall measure (and give) 3 Shiqil silver.

§ 261.—XXXVIII, 21-27

21 šum-ma a-wi-lum 22 nâḳidam ^{b}a-na LID.GUD.ZUN 23 u ṣênê 24 ri-im i-gur 25 VIII ŠE.GUR 26 i-na šattim I^{kam} 27 i-na-ad-di-iš-šum

21 ثُمَّ أويلُم [عَويلُم] 22 نِقدَمْ أنَ لئِدْ جُدْ ظُعُنْ 23 و ضِينِ 24 رِعيِمْ يئجُرْ 25 8 سِعِ [شِعِ] جُرْ [كُرْ] 26 إنَ سَتِّمْ [سَنْتِمْ] 1كَم 27 ينَدِنْ ذُوم [ينَدِذُّومْ]

بعد ان (اذا) شخص [رجل] يستأجر ناظر لرعي (للعناية بـ) غِلاظ أبقار العمل والتحميل (ثيران) والخراف، سوف يعطيه 8 كُر حبوب في السنة الواحدة.

If (after) a person [a man] rents (hires) an overseer to (for) tending the carrying and labor cattle boors (oxen) and sheep, he shall give him 8 Kur of grains in one (per) year.

§ 262.—XXXVIII, 28-36

28 šum-ma a-wi-lum 29 alpam u lu immeram 30 a-na . . . .

28 ثُمَّ أويلُم [عَويلُم] 29 ألفَمْ [ألبَمْ] [عَلفَمْ [عَلبَمْ]] ولو حِميرَمْ 30 أنَ ....

بعد ان (اذا) شخص [رجل] .... ثور، و(حتى) لو حمار، ....

If (after) a person [a man] .... an ox, and (even) let-it-be a donkey ....

§ 263.—XXXVIII, 37-43

37 šum-ma |alpam| ^{b}u lu immeram 38 ša in-na-ad-nu-šum 39 uḫ-ta-al-li-iḳ 40 alpam ki-ma [alpim] 41 immeram ki-ma |immerim| 42 a-na be-li-|šu-nu| 43 i-ri-a-|ab|

37 ثُمَّ ألفَمْ [ألبَمْ] [عَلفَمْ [عَلبَمْ]] ولو حِميرَمْ 38 ذا إندَنْ ذُوم 39 يُحتلِقْ 40 ألفَمْ [ألبَمْ] [عَلفَمْ [عَلبَمْ]] كيمَ ألفِمْ [ألبِمْ] [عَلفِمْ [عَلبِمْ]] 41 حِميرَمْ كيمَ حِميرِمْ 42 أنَ بَعلِ ذُونُ 27 يرأبْ

|وفق الفقرة 262| بعد ان (اذا) (الشخص [رجل]) يُضيعْ الثور، و(حتى) لو الحمار الذي أعطوه، سوف يسدّدْ (يعوض) ثورا كالثورِ، حمارا كالحمارِ الى مالكهم.

|Referencing §262| If (after) a person [a man] loses the ox, and (even) let-it-be the donkey, that they gave him, this person [man] shall repay (replace) an ox like (with the same value of) the (lost) ox, a donkey like (with the same value of) the (lost) donkey to their owner.

§ 264.—XXXVIII, 44-60

44 šum-ma |rê'um| 45 ša LID.GUD.|ZUN| 46 u lu ṣênê 47 a-na ri-im 48 in-na-ad-nu-šum 49 ID-šu mimma(?) ḫar(?)-ra-tim 50 ma-ḫi-ir 51 li-ib-ba-šu ṭa-ab 52 LID.GUN.ZUN 53 |uz|-za-aḫ-ḫi-ir 54 ṣênê 55 uz-za-aḫ-ḫi-ir 56 ta-li-id-tam ^{b}um-ta-di 57 a-na pî ri-ik-^{b}sa-ti-šu 58 ta-li-id-tam 59 u bi-il-tam 60 i-na-ad-di-in

45 ثُمَّ رِعُمْ 45 ذا لئِدْ جُدْ ظُعُنْ 46 ولو ضِينِ 47 أنَ رِعيِمْ 48 إندَنْ ذُومْ 49 عِدْ ذو مِمَّ؟ خرتِمْ؟ 50 مَخِرْ 51 لبَّ ذو طبْ 52 لئِدْ جُدْ ظُعُنْ 53 يصَهِرْ [يصَغِرْ] 54 ضِينِ 55 يصَهِرْ [يصَغِرْ] 56 تَلِدتَمْ يُمتَدي [يُبْتَدي] [يُمْتَطي] [يُمْتَعطي] 57 أنَ فيي رِكْستِ ذو 58 تَلِدتَمْ 58 و بِعلِتَمْ 58 ينَدِنْ

بعد ان (اذا) الراعي الذي أعطوه غلاظ أبقار عمل وتحميل (ثيران)، و(حتى) لو خراف، للرعي (للعناية)، أيّما (كان) إختيار (طلب) حساب (أجره) (كان) مُختارْ (مقبول)، قلبه (كان) مسرور، (ثم) يُقلّلْ غلاظ أبقار العمل والتحميل (الثيران)، يُقلّلْ الخراف، يُبدّدْ (يُشتّت) [يُقلّلْ] الأولاد المنتجة، سوف يعطي (الى المالك) الأولاد المنتجة والمنتجات (منتجات الماشية والخراف) الى (حسب) تصريح (كلمات) عقده.

If (after) the shepherd whom they gave the carrying and labor cattle boors (oxen), and (even) let-it-be the sheep, to (for) tending, whatever his (pay) rate choice (request) (was) chosen, his heart (was) pleased, (then) he reduces (the number of) the carrying and labor cattle boors (oxen), reduces (the number of) the sheep, scatters [reduces (the number of)] the newly born, he shall give (to the owner) the newly born (according) and the produce (of the oxen and sheep) (according) to the declaration (words) of his contract.

§ 265.—XXXVIII, 61-75

61 šum-ma rê'um 62 ša LID.GUD.ZUN 63 u ṣênê 64 a-na ri-im 65 in-na-ad-nu-šum 66 u-sa-ar-[b]ri-ir-ma 67 ši-im-tam [b]ut-ta-ak-ki-ir 68 u a-na kaspim 69 it-ta-di-in 70 u-ka-an-nu-šu-ma 71 a-du X-šu [b]ša iš-ri-ḳu 72 LID.GUD.ZUN 73 u ṣênê 74 a-na be-li-šu-nu 75 i-ri-a-ab

61 ثمَّ رعِمْ 62 ذا لئِدْ جدْ ظعْنْ 63 وضينِ 64 أنَ رعِيمْ 65 إندنْ ذومْ 66 يُسررِمْ 67 سمِتمْ يتكرْ 68 و أنَ كسفِمْ 69 يتدِنْ 70 يُكنو ذومْ 71 عدو 10–ذو ذا إسرِقْ 72 لئِدْ جدْ ظعْنْ 73 و ضينِ 74 أنَ بعلِ ذونْ 75 يرأبْ

بعد ان (اذا) الراعي الذي أعطوه غلاظ أبقار العمل والتحميل (الثيران) والخراف للرعي (للعناية) يَسْرُرْ (يخفي ويغش) (و) يتنكّر (الى) الأمانة (الوديعة) ويعطي لفضة (ويبيع)، سوف يُجلسوه (يستدعوه)، (و) سوف يُسَدِدْ (يعوض) 10 أضعاف الذي سرق، (بـ)غلاظ ماشية عمل وتحميل و(بـ)خراف، الى مالكهم.

If (after) the shepherd whom they gave to (for) tending carrying and labor cattle boors (oxen) and sheep, conceals (cheats), (and) denies (about) the consignment and gives for silver (sells), they shall seat (call) him in, (and) he shall repay (replace) 10 fold what he stole, (in) carrying and labor cattle boors (oxen) and sheep, to their owner.

§ 266.—XXXVIII, 76-81

76 šum-ma i-na tarbaṣim 77 li-bi-it i-lim [b]it-tab-ši 78 u lu UR.MAH id-du-uk [b]rê'um ma-ḫar ilim 79 u-ub-ba-am-ma 80 mi-ki-it-ti tarbaṣim 81 be-el tarbaṣim i-maḫ-ḫar-šu

76 ثمَّ إنَ تربضِمْ [تربصِمْ] 77 لبتْ إلِمْ [علِمْ] يتبْذي [يتبّثي] 78 ولو عرْمخْ يدكْ رعِمْ مخرْ إلِمْ [علِمْ] 79 يُبأمَ 80 مكتِ [مقط] تربضِمْ [تربصِمْ] 81 بعلْ تربضِمْ [تربصِمْ] يمخرْ ذو

|وفق الفقرة 265| بعد ان (اذا) غضب إله (حادث قاتل) يتواجد [يظهر] (يحلّ) في المأوى، و(حتى) لو حيوان مفترس [أسد] يَقتُل، الراعي سوف يبوء (يجيب) امام إله، (و) متهاوي (صريع) المأوى، مالك المأوى سوف يواجهه (يتحمل خسارته).

|Referencing §265| If (after) a rage of god (an act of god) exists [occurs] in the sheepfold, and (even) let-it-be a ferocious creature [a lion] kills (eats), the shepherd shall answer in front of a god, (and) the fallen (the casualty) of the sheepfold, the owner of the sheepfold shall face it (bear its loss).

§ 267.—XXXVIII, 82-89

82 šum-ma rê'um i-gu-ma 83 i-na tarbaṣim kaz-za-tam uš-tab-ši 84 rê'um ḫi-di-it kaz-za-tim 85 ša i-na tarbaṣim u-ša-ab-šu-u 86 LID.GUN.ZUN u ṣênê 87 u-ša-lam-ma 88 a-na be-li-šu-nu 89 i-na-ad-di-in

82 ثمَّ رعِمْ يعجُومَ [يعجُهُمْ] 83 إنَ ترْبضِمْ [ترْبصِمْ] كزتمْ يُستبذي [يُستبثي] 84 رعِمْ حدتْ كزتمْ 85 ذا إنَ ترْبضِمْ [ترْبصِمْ] أُسبْذوَ [أُسبْثوَ] [أُتبْذوَ [أُتبْثو]] 86 لئدْ جدْ ظعَنْ و ضِينَ 87 يُسلمْ 88 أنَ بعلِ ذونْ 89 يندنْ

|وفق الفقرة 265| بعد ان (اذا) الراعي يهمل (يتجاهل)، (و) يوجدْ [يُظهر (ينشر)] (يُحلّ) الكزاز (التشنج من شدة البرد) في المأوى، الراعي سوف يأمّن غلاظ أبقار عمل وتحميل (ثيران) وخراف شدة الكزاز الذي أوجدَ [أظهرَ (نشرَ)] (أحلّ) في المأوى، (و) سوف يعطي الى مالكهم.

|Referencing §265| If (after) the shepherd neglects, (and) makes exist [makes appear] (causes) paralysis from hypothermia in the sheepfold, the shepherd shall secure (guarantee) the carrying and labor cattle boors (oxen) and sheep (of) the severe hypothermia that he made existed [caused to occur] in the sheepfold (in), (and) he shall give to their owner.

§ 268.—XXXVIII, 90-92

90 šum-ma a-wi-lum alpam 91 a-na di-a-ši-im i-gur 92 20 ḲA še'im ID-šu

90 ثمَّ أويلم [عَويلم] ألفمْ [ألبمْ] [علفمْ [علبمْ]] 91 أنَ دياسِمْ يئجُرْ 92 20 قا سعِمْ [شعِمْ] عدْ ذو

بعد ان (اذا) شخص (رجل) يستأجر ثور للدياسة (للجَش)، 20 قا (دلو) حبوب حسابه (ايجاره)

If (after) a person [a man] rents (hires) an ox for threshing its (rent) rate is 20 Qa (buckets) grains.

§ 269.—XXXVIII, 93-95

93 šum-ma imêram 94 a-na di-a-ši-im i-gur 95 10 ḲA še'im ID-šu

90 ثمَّ حميرَنْ 91 أنَ دياسِمْ يئجُرْ 92 10 قا سعِمْ [شعِمْ] عدْ ذو

|وفق الفقرة 268| بعد ان (اذا) يستأجر حمار للدياسة (للجَش)، 10 قا (دلو) حبوب حسابه (ايجاره)

|Referencing §268| If (after) he rents (hires) a donkey for threshing its (rent) rate is 10 Qa (buckets) grains.

§ 270.—XXXVIII, 96-98

96 šum-ma lalâm 97 a-na di-a-ši-im i-gur 98 I ḲA še'im ID-šu

90 ثمَّ لعلمْ 91 أنَ دياسِمْ يئجُرْ 92 1 قا سعِمْ [شعِمْ] عدْ ذو

|وفق الفقرة 268| بعد ان (اذا) يستأجر تيس للدياسة (لجَش الحبوب)، 1 قا (دلو) حبوب حسابه (ايجاره)

|Referencing §268| If (after) he rents (hires) a male goat for threshing its (rent) rate is 1 Qa (bucket) grains.

§ 271.—XXXVIII, 99-XXXIX, 2

99 šum-ma a-wi-lum 100 LID.GUD.ZUN ṣumbam 101 u mu-ur-te-ᵇdi-ša i-gur XXXIX, 1 i-na ûmi Iᵏᵃᵐ CLXXX ḲA še'im 2 i-na-ad-di-in

99 ثمَّ أويلم [عَويلم] 100 لئدْ جدْ ظعَنْ صُمبَمْ [صُفَمْ] 101 و مُرْتَدئي ذا يئجُرْ 1 إنَ أوم 1كم 180 قا سعِمْ [شعِمْ] 2 يندنْ

بعد ان (اذا) شخص (رجل) يستأجر غلاظ أبقار عمل وتحميل (ثيران)، عربة نقل، ومصطَحبُها (قائدها)، سوف يعطي 180 قا (دلو) حبوب في اليوم الواحد.

If (after) a person [a man] rents (hires) carrying and labor cattle boors (oxen), transportation carriage, and its accompanier (its driver), he shall give 180 Qa (buckets) grains in one (per) day.

§ 272.—XXXIX, 3-7

3 šum-ma a-wi-lum 4 ṣumba-ma 5 a-na ra-ma-ni-ša ^{b}i-gur 6 i-na ûmi I^{kam} XL ḲA še'im 7 i-na-ad-di-in

3 ثُمَّ أويلم [عَويلْم] 4 صُمْبَم [صُفَّم] 5 أنَ رَأمَني ذا يِئجرْ 6 إنَ أُومِ 1 كمْ 40 قا سَعِم [شَعِمْ] 7 يندِنْ

|وفق الفقرة 271| بعد ان (اذا) الشخص (الرجل) يستأجر عربة نقل لذاتها (فقط)، سوف يعطي 40 قا (دلو) حبوب في اليوم الواحد.

|Referencing §271| If (after) a person [a man] rents a transportation carriage in (by) itself (only) he shall give 40 Qa (buckets) grains in one (per) day.

§ 273.—XXXIX, 8-19

8 šum-ma a-wi-lum 9 ^{amêlu}agram i-gur 10 iš-tu ri-eš ^{b}ša-at-tim 11 a-di ḫa-am-ši-im ^{b}arḫi-im 12 VI ŠE kaspim 13 i-na ûmi I^{kam} 14 i-na-ad-di-in 15 iš-tu ši-^{b}ši-im arḫi-im 16 a-di ta-ak-ti-da ^{b}ša-at-tim 17 V ŠE kaspim 18 i-na ûmi I^{kam} 19 i-na-ad-di-in

8 ثُمَّ أويلم [عَويلْم] 9 عميلأجرَمْ يِئجر 10 إسْتَ رأس سَتّمْ [سَنْتَمْ] 11 عدي [حدي] خَمْسِمْ أرحِمْ 12 6 سع [شع] كسْفِمْ 13 إنَ أُومِ 1 كمْ 14 يندِنْ 15 إسْتُ سِسِمْ [سِتِمْ] أرحِمْ 16 عدي [حَدي] تكْتِدَ [تكْتِتَ] [تقْتِتَ] سَتّمْ [سَنْتَمْ] 17 5 سع [شع] كسفِمْ 18 إنَ أُومِ 1 كمْ 19 يندِنْ

بعد ان (اذا) شخص (رجل) يستأجر عامل أجر (متعاقد)، سوف يعطي (الأجير) 6 حبّات فضة في اليوم الواحد أوّلما (من) رأس السنة حتى (ما دام) الشهر الخامس، 5 حبّات فضة في اليوم الواحد أوّلما (من) الشهر السادس حتى (ما دامت) نهاية السنة.

If (after) a person [a man] hires a contracted worker, he shall give 6 grains of silver in one (per) day once (from) the head of the year until (as long as) the fifth month, 5 grains of silver in one (per) day once (from) the sixth month until (as long as) the end of the year.

§ 274.—XXXIX, 20-44

20 šum-ma a-wi-lum 21 mâr ummânim 22 i-ig-ga-ar 23 ID ^{amêlu} . . . . . 24 V ŠE kaspim 25 ID ^{amêlu}GAB.A 26 V ŠE kaspim 27 [ID] ^{amêlu}KAD 28 [VŠE] kaspim 29 [ID] ^{amêlu}GUL 30 . . . . [ŠE] kaspim 31 [ID] ^{amêlu}GA(?) 32 . . . [ŠE] kaspim 33 ID . . . . tu(?) 34 . . . [ŠE] kaspim 35 [ID] . . . nangarim 36 IV ŠE kaspim 37 ID SA 38 IV ŠE kaspim 39 ID AT.KIT 40 . . . ŠE kaspim 41 ID ^{amêlu}bânîm 42 . . . [ŠE] kaspim 43 i-na [ûmi] I^{kam} 44 [i-na-ad-di]-in

20 ثُمَّ أويلم [عويلْم] 21 مأرْ أُمانِمْ 22 يِئجرَ 23 عِدْ عميل|...| 24 5 سع [شع] كسْفِمْ 25 عِدْ عميلجبا [عميلجابا] 26 5 سع [شع] كسْفِمْ 27 عِدْ عميلكعد [عميلقعد] 28 5 سع [شع] كسْفِمْ 29 عِدْ عميلجول 30 |...| سع [شع] كسْفِمْ 31 عِدْ عميل|...| 32 |...| سع [شع] كسْفِمْ 33 عِدْ عميل... 34 ... سع [شع] كسْفِمْ 35 عِدْ |...| نَنْجَرِمْ 36 4 سع [شع] كسْفِمْ 37 عِدْ |عميلسها| 38 4 سع [شع] كسْفِمْ 39 عِدْ أتْ قتْ [أتْ قِطْ] 40 ... سع [شع] كسْفِمْ 41 عِدْ عميلبَنيم 42 |...| سع [شع] كسْفِمْ 43 إنَ أُومِ 1 كمْ 44 |إيندِنْ|

بعد ان (اذا) شخص (رجل) يستأجر ابن أمانة (مهنة)، سوف يعطي 5 حبّات فضة (لـ)حساب (أجر) ......، 5 حبّات فضة (لـ)حساب (أجر) عامل حفر (حفّار)، 5 حبّات فضة (لـ)حساب (أجر) عامل حصير وقتب (حائك)، 5 حبّات فضة (لـ)حساب (أجر) عامل صخر (قاطع صخر)، ... حبّات فضة (لـ)حساب (أجر) ......، ... حبّات فضة (لـ)حساب (أجر) ......، ... حبّات فضة (لـ)حساب (أجر) عامل نجارة (نجّار)، 4 حبّات فضة (لـ)حساب (أجر) عامل سياج [عامل حَزم قصب] (سيّاج)، 4 حبّات فضة (لـ)حساب (أجر) آتي حطب (حطّاب)، ... حبّات فضة (لـ)حساب (أجر) عامل بناء (بنّاء)، في اليوم الواحد.

If (after) a person [a man] hires a son of profession (a professional), he shall give 5 grains of silver (for) the (pay) rate of ..... worker, 5 grains of silver (for) the (pay) rate of a (well) digger, 5 grains of silver (for) the (pay) rate of a (saddle and mat) knitting worker, 5 grains of silver (for) the (pay) rate of a stone cutting worker, ... grains of silver (for) the (pay) rate of ....., ... grains of silver (for) the (pay) rate of ....., ... grains of silver (for) the (pay) rate of a carpentry worker, 4 grains of silver (for) the (pay) rate of a (reed bunch) fence maker, 4 grains of silver (for) the (pay) rate of a bush collector (a bushman), ... grains of silver (for) the (pay) rate of a construction worker, in one (per) day.

§ 275.—XXXIX, 45-48

[45] |šum-ma| a-wi-lum [46] |elippam| i-gur [47] i-na ûmi I[kam] [48] III ŠE kaspim ID-ša

[45] ثمَّ أويلم [عويلم] [46] |عِلفَّمْ [علبَّمْ]| يئجرْ [47] إنَ أومِ 1[كم] [48] 3 سعِ [شعِ] كسفمْ عدْ ذا

بعد ان (اذا) شخص (رجل) يستأجر قُفّة (عبّارة)، 3 حبّات فضة في اليوم الواحد حسابها (حساب ايجارها).

If (after) a person (a man) rents a boat, its (rent) rate is 3 grains of silver in one (per) day.

§ 276.—XXXIX, 49-52

[49] šum-ma ma-ḫi-ir-tam i-gur [50] II½ ŠE kaspim [b]ID-ša [51] i-na ûmi I[kam] [52] i-na-ad-di-in

[49] ثمَّ مَخرْتمْ يئِجرْ [50] 2.5 سعِ [شعِ] كسفمْ عدْ ذا [51] إنَ أومِ 1[كم] [52] ينَدنْ

|وفق الفقرة 275| بعد ان (اذا) يستأجر (قُفّة (عبّارة)) ماخرة (شاقّة لتيار النهر)، سوف يعطي 2.5 حبّات فضة في اليوم الواحد (ل)حسابها (لحساب ايجارها).

|Referencing §275| If (after) (he rents) a boat, he shall give 2.5 grains of silver in one (per) day (for) its (rent) rate.

§ 277.—XXXIX, 53-57

[53] šum-ma a-wi-lum [54] elippi LX GUR i-gur [55] i-na ûmi I[kam] [56] IGI.VI.GAL kaspim [b]ID-ša [57] i-na-ad-di-in

[53] ثمَّ أويلم [عَويلم] [54] عِلفِّ [عِلبِّ] 60 جُرْ [كُرْ] يئِجرْ [55] إنَ أومِ 1[كم] [56] إجي 6 جَلْ كَسفمْ عدْ ذا [57] ينَدنْ

بعد ان (اذا) شخص (رجل) يستأجر قُفّة (عبّارة) (بسعة) 60 كُر، سوف يعطي في اليوم الواحد 1\6 (مثقال (شقل)) فضة (ل)حسابها (لحساب ايجارها).

If (after) aperson (a man) rents a boat of 60 Kur (capacity), he shall give, in one (per) day, 1/6 (Shiqil) silver (for) its (rent) rate is.

§ 278.—XXXIX, 58-66

[58] šum-ma a-wi-lum [59] wardam amtam i-ša-am-ma [60] arḫi-šu la im-la-ma [61] bi-en-ni e-li-šu [62-63] im-ta-ku-ut a-na na-di-na-ni-šu u-ta-ar-ma [64] ša-a-a-ma-nu-um [65] kaspam iš-ḳu-lu [66] i-li-ḳi

[58] ثمَّ أويلم [عويلم] [59] وردَمْ أمْتمْ يسمَّ [60] أرْخِ ذو لا يملَئمْ [61] بيِنَ [بئِنِّ] علِي ذو [63-62] يمتَكُتْ [يمتَقُطْ] أنَ ندنَنِ ذو يُتأرمَ [64] سآمَنمْ [65] كسفَمْ إثْقلِو [65] يلِقي

بعد ان (اذا) شخص (رجل) يشتري عبد، عبدة، (و) يقع (يأتي) عليه (مرض) الصّرَعْ (و) لا (ولم) يُكمل شهره، سوف يُعيد الى معطيه (بائعه)، (و) المشتري سوف يلقي (يأخذ) الفضة (التي) وزنَ (واعطى).

If (after) a person [a man] buys a male slave, a female slave, (and) epilepsy falls upon him/her, (while) he/she does not complete his/her month, he shall return (him/her) to his/her giver (seller), (and) the buyer shall take (back) the silver he measured (and gave).

§ 279.—XXXIX, 67-71

67 šum-ma a-wi-lum 68 wardam amtam i-ša-am-ma 69 ba-ag-ri [b]ir-ta-ši 70 na-di-na-an-šu 71 ba-ag-ri i-ip-pa-al

58 ثمّ أويلم [عويلم] 59 وردمْ أمتمْ يسمّ 60 بجرِ يرتسي 70 ندنَنْ ذو 57 بجرِ يئفلْ

بعد ان (اذا) شخص (رجل) يشتري عبد، عبدة، (و) يرتسي (يجتلب) نزاع (مقاضاة)، مُعطيه (بائعه) سوف يتحمل (كلفة) النزاع (المقاضاة).

If (after) a person [a man] buys a male slave, a female slave, (and) he/she settles in (brings in) challenge (legal claim), his/her giver (seller) shall take upon (the cost of) the challenge (the legal claim).

§ 280.—XXXIX, 72-87

72 šum-ma a-wi-lum 73 i-na ma-at 74 nu-ku-ur-tim 75 wardam amtam ša [b]a-wi-lim 76 iš-ta-am 77 i-nu-ma 78 i-na li-ib-bu mâtim 79 it-ta-al-kam-ma 80 be-el wardim u lu amtim 81 lu wara-zu u lu ama-zu 82 u-te-id-di 83 šum-ma wardum u amtum šu-nu 84 mârê ma-tim 85 ba-lum kaspima 86 an-du-ra-ar-šu-nu 87 iš-ša-ak-ka-an

72 ثمّ أويلم [عويلم] 73 إنَ مأتْ 74 نكرتمْ 75 وردمْ أمتمْ ذا أويلم [عويلم] 76 يستمْ 77 حينمْ 78 إنَ لبُّ مأتمْ 79 يتلكمْ 80 بعلْ وردمْ ولو أمتمْ 81 لو وردْ ذو [ورتْ] ولو أمتْ ذو [أمتْ] 82 يتئدي [يتهدي] 83 ثمّ وردمْ ولو أمتمْ ذوو 84 مأريي مأتمْ 85 بلمْ كسفمِ 86 أندررْ ذون [أدّررْ ذونْ] 87 يسكَنْ

بعد ان (اذا) شخص (رجل) يشتري عبد، عبدة شخص (رجل) (آخرْ) في ارض (بلاد) غريبة، حينما (عندما) يترسّلْ (يرجع) لأرضِ (لبلد) القلب (لبلاده)، (و) مالك العبد، و (حتى) لو العبدة، يعرف عن [يهتدي الى] (يجد) عبده، و(حتى) لو عبدته، بعد ان (اذا) العبد، و(حتى) لو العبدة إبناء الارض (ابناء بلاده)، سوف يُقرّ (يتم) تحررهم بلا (بدون) (أخذ) فضة.

If (after) a person [a man] buys a male slave, a female slave, of a person [a man] in an alien land (region), when he comes (back) to the land (region) of his heart (his region), (and) the owner of the male slave, and (even) let-it-be the female slave, knows about (finds out) [reaches to] his male slave, and (even) let-it-be his female slave, if (after) the male slave, and (even) let-it-be the female slave, are descendants of the land (buyer's region), their freedom shall be set without (giving) silver.

§ 281.—XXXIX, 88-96

88 šum-ma mârê ma-tim [b]ša-ni-tim 89 ša-a-a-ma-nu-ma 90 i-na ma-ẖar i-lim 91 kaspam iš-ḳu-lu 92 i-ga-ab-bi-ma 93 be-el wardim u lu amtim 94 kaspam iš-ḳu-lu a-na tamkarim 95 i-na-ad-di-in-ma 96 lu wara-zu lu ama-zu i-pa-aḳ

88 ثمّ مأريي مأتمْ ثانتِمْ 89 سآمنمْ 90 إنَ مخرْ إلمْ [علمْ] 91 كسفمْ إثقلو 92 يجبمْ [يقبمْ] 93 بعلْ وردمْ ولو أمتمْ 94 كسفمْ إثقلو أن تمكارمِ 95 يندنمْ 96 لو وردْ ذو [ورتْ] ولو أمتْ ذو [أمتْ] يئبقْ [يعفقْ]

|وفق الفقرة 279| بعد ان (اذا) (العبد او العبدة) إبناء ارض (بلاد) ثانية (أخرى)، المشتري سوف يجيب [يقول] أمام إله (كمية الفضة (التي) وزنَ (واعطى)، (و) مالك العبد، و (حتى) لو العبدة، سوف يعطي الفضة (التي) وزنَ (واعطى)، الى المتاجر (المشتري)، (و) سوف يُذهب بدون إثم او خوف (سوف يعتق) عبده، و(حتى) لو عبدته [سوف يُرجِع عبده، و(حتى) لو عبدته].

|Referencing §279| If (after) they are descendants of a second (another) land (region), the buyer shall answer [say] in front of a god the (amount of) silver he measured (and gave), (and) the owner of the male slave, and (even) let-it-be the female slave shall give the silver he measured (and gave), to the merchant (the buyer), (and) he shall make go without fear or guilt (shall release) [shall bring back] his male slave, and (even) let-it-be his female slave.

§ 282.—XXXIX, 97-102

97 šum-ma wardum a-na be-li-šu 98 u-ul be-li at-ta 99 iḳ-ta-bi 100 ki-ma wara-zu 101 u-ka-an-šu-ma 102 be-el-šu u-zu-un-šu [b]i-na-ak-ki-is

97 ثُمَّ وَرْدُمْ أَنَ بَعْلِ ذو 98 أُلْ بَعْلي أتَّ 99 يقْتبي 100 كيمَ وَرَدْ ذو [وَرَتُ] 101 يُكَنْ ذُومَ 102 بَعَلْ ذو أُذْنْ ذو 3 ينَّكِسْ [ينَّقِصْ]

بعد ان (اذا) عبد يقول لمالكه "أنت لست مالكي"، (مالكه) سوف يُجلسه (يستدعيه) كعبده، (و) مالكه سوف يقطع اذنه (بنفسه).

If (after) a slave says to his owner “you are not my owner”, he (the owner) shall seat [call] him in as his slave, (and) his owner (himself) shall cut his ear.

Part 2

Appendixes and Reference Indexes

1

Letters Substitutions Guides

al-Jibūrī Letters Substitutions Rules

From: *Qamūs al-Lughah al-Akkadiyyah al-ʿArabiyyah*

Akkadian Arabic throat letters (أ، ح، هـ، ع، غ، ض، ظ، ث، ذ) **=> Hamzah** (’) **=> ē, ī, ū, û , ā, â**

e.g. ba’lum = bēlum بعل | ẖaqlum = ēqlum حقل | ĝrub = ērub غرب

Nūn (n) **with sukūn** (stop) **+ Arabic lip letter** (b, p, m) **=> Arabic lip letter repeated** (bb, pp, mm)

e.g. kanpum => kappum | anpum => appum

Letter with sukūn (stop) **+ Arabic teeth letter** (t, d, ṭ, s, š) **=> Lām + Arabic teeth letter** (t, d, ṭ, s, š)

e.g. išdu => ildu | išṭur => ilṭur | iššī => ilšī | ištakan => iltakan | ušubtu => ušultu

Mīm (m) **+ Arabic teeth letter** (t, d, ṭ, s, š) **=> Nūn** (n) **+ Arabic teeth letter** (t, d, ṭ, s, š)

e.g. imdud => indud | imtu => intu | amiš => aniš | imtanum => intanum

Rā’(r) **+ Nūn** (n) **=> Nūn** (n) **+ Nūn** (n) **=> NūnNūn** (nn)

e.g. arnu => annu | ibqurnisu => ibqunnisu

Two assimilated letters => Nūn (n) **with sukūn** (stop) **+ One assimilated letter**

e.g. inazziq => inanziq | inaddi => inandi | immagar => imangar | nammuri => nanmuri

Two words joind by two assimilated letters L1-L2 => One word, repeated assimilated letter L2

e.g. şit-šamaši => şissamiši | sinm-yattum => sinyyatum | umam-kal => umakkal

Strong Sumerian letter sounds => Akkadian letter sounds

ث => ش   ذ => ط   ذ => ئ   ذ => ز   ظ => ص   ض => ص   ق <=> ك

Arabic Letters Substitutions

From: *Lisān al-ʿArab*

ت <=> ظ	س (+ ق،ط،غ،خ،غ) => ص	ز <=> س	أ <=> ع
ت <=> ض	س <=> ش	ز <=> ص	أ <=> هـ
ذ <=> ث	س <=> ت	ك <=> ق	ب <=> م
ذ <=> ض	ف <=> ب	م <=> ن	د <=> ط
	ت <=> ط	ن => ر	د <=> ذ

Latin Arabic Letters Substitutions

Compiled by the Author through his Research

Latin Letter	Possible Arabic Letter(s)	Latin Letter	Possible Arabic Letter(s)
A (àáāâ)	ا أ آ ع هـ	S	س ش ص ظ
B	ب	Š	ش س ذ ض ث ظ
D	د ذ ض ط	Ṣ	ص ض ظ
E (èē)	أ إ ي ح ع غ هـ	T	ت ط ث ذ
G	ج ق غ	Ṭ	ط ت
H (ẖ)	خ ح هـ	U (úū)	ؤ و ع
I (íī)	إ ي ع ح هـ	W	و
K	ك ق خ	Y	ي
L	ل	Z	ز ذ ص ظ
M	م	ʾ Hamzah	أ ع غ ح هـ ض ظ ث ذ
N	ن	a	◌َ
P	ف ب	e	◌َ ◌ِ
Q (ḵ)	ق ك	i	◌ِ
R	ر	u	◌ُ

2

List of Linguistic Tools

Modern Assyrian Akkadian Etymological Tools:

The Electronic Pennsylvania Sumerian Dictionary (ePSD)
http://psd.museum.upenn.edu/epsd/index.html

The Akkadian-Arabic Language Dictionary (AALD)
A concise Arabic translation of CAD by Ali Y. al-Jubouri, professor of Akkadian and Cuneiform studies in the University of Mosul.

Historical Arabic Etymological Tools (995 CE - 1791 CE)

al-Baheth al-Arabi الباحث العربي
http://www.baheth.info/

Lisān al-ʿArab لسان العرب
Magāyīs al-Lughah مقاييس اللغة
al-Ṣaḥḥāh fī al-Lughah الصحاح في اللغة
al-Qāmūs al-Muḥīṭ القاموس المحيط
al-ʿUbāb al-Zākhir العباب الزاخر

al-Muʿjam المعجم
http://www.almougem.com/Home/index

Tāj al-ʿArūs تاج العروس
Maqālīd al-ʿUlūm مقاليد العلوم
al-Taʿrifāt التعريفات
al-Muṣbāḥ al-Munīr المصباح المنير
Lisān al-ʿArab لسان العرب
Mukhtār al-Ṣaḥḥāḥ مختار الصحاح
Shams al-ʿUlūm شمس العلوم
Asās al-Balāghah أساس البلاغة
Ṭalabat al-Ṭalabah طلبة الطلبة
Mujmal al-Lughah مجمل اللغة
Maqāyīs al-Lughah مقاييس اللغة
Ṣaḥḥāḥ al-ʿArabīyah صحاح العربية
Muntakhab al-Ṣaḥḥāḥ منتخب الصحاح
al-Muḥīṭ fī al-Lughah المحيط في اللغة
Tahdhīb al-Lughah تهذيب اللغة
al-Mudhakkar wa-al-Muʾannath المُذكر والمؤنث
al-ʿAyn العين

3

Referenced Words Index

§ 1.—V, 26-32

AALD: awīlu See amīlu
ePSD: amēlu
<u>ili</u> [<u>MAN</u>] wr. i_3-li_2 "man" Akk. amēlu
<u>lu</u> [<u>PERSON</u>] wr. lu_2; mu-lu; mu-lu_2; lu_{10}; lu_6 "who(m), which; man; (s)he who, that which; of; ruler; person" Akk. amēlu; ša
AALD: ubburu (v.) يتهم بجريمة؛ يربط، يُحيط
AALD: mubbiru (s.) المتهم
ePSD: nêru
<u>sag</u> [<u>SCATTER</u>] wr. sag_2; sag_3; sag_7 "to throw (down); to scatter, disperse; to kill, to beat" Akk. dâku; nasāku; nêru; sapāhu
<u>saĝ ĝeš ra</u> [<u>KILL</u>] wr. saĝ ĝeš ra "to kill" Akk. nêru
ePSD: kânu
<u>gin</u> [<u>ESTABLISH</u>] wr. gin_6; gi-na; gi-in; ge-en; gin "(to be) permanent; to confirm, establish (in legal contexts), verify; (to be) true; a quality designation; medium quality" Akk. kânu; kīnu
ePSD: dâku
<u>gaz</u> [<u>KILL</u>] wr. gaz; gaz_2; kaz_8 "to kill, slaughter; to grind, grate; to beat; to thresh (grain); to execute, impose a death sentence; to break" Akk. dâku; habātu; hašālu; kaşāşu; pa'āşu; šagāšu
<u>gi</u> [<u>KILL</u>] wr. gi_4 "kill" Akk. dâku
<u>rah</u> [<u>BEAT</u>] wr. rah_2; ra-ah "to beat, kill; to break, crush; to flood; to thresh (grain with a flail)" Akk. dâku;

ثمم (لسان العرب) وثَمَّ، بفتح الثاء: إشارة إلى المكان؛ وثُمَّ وثُمَّت وثُمَّتْ، كلها: حرف نسَق والفاء في كل ذلك بدل من الثاء لكثرة الاستعمال.
الليث: ثُمَّ حرف من حروف النَسق لا يُشْرَك ما بعدها بما قبلها إلا أنها تبيِّن الآخر من الأوَّل،
ثم (مقاييس اللغة) الثاء والميم أصلٌ واحد، هو اجتماعٌ في لين. يقال ثممْتُ الشيء ثمّاً، إذا جمعته. وأكثرُ ما يُستعمل في الحشيش.
وثم (لسان العرب) وقال المزني: وجدْتُ كلأً كثيفاً وَثيمةً؛ قال: الوَثيمةُ جماعةٌ من الحشيش أو الطعام. يقال: ثم لها أي اجْمعْ لها.
أبر (لسان العرب) وإبرة العقرب: التي تلدغُ بها، وفي المحكم: طرف ذنبها. وأَبرته تأْبُره وتأْبِره أبْراً: لسعته أي ضربته بإبرتها. وفي حديث أسماء بنت عُميس: قيل لعلي: ألا تتزوَج ابنة رسول الله صلى الله عليه وسلم؟ فقال: مالي صفْراء ولا بيضاءُ، ولست بمأْبور في ديني فيُوَرِّي بها رسولُ الله صلى الله عليه وسلم، عني، إني لأوّلُ من أَسلم،؛ المأْبور: من أَبرته العقربُ أي لَسعَتْه بإبرتها، يعني لست غير الصحيح الدين ولا المُتهمَ في الإسلام فيتألَّفني عليه بتزويجها إياي، ويروى بالثاء المثلثة وسنذكره. والإبرَة والمِئبرَة، الأَخيرة عن اللحياني: النميمة. والمآبرُ النمائم وإفساد ذاتِ البين؛ قال النابغة: وذلك منْ قوْلٍ أتاك أقْوله، ومنْ دسّ أعدائي إليك المآبرا
نحر (مقاييس اللغة) والعالم بالشَيء المجرَّب نحْرير، وهو إن كان من القياس الذي ذكرناه، بمعنى أنه ينحر العلمَ نحراً، كقولك: قتلتُ هذا الشَيء عِلْماً.
نَحْرُ (القاموس المحيط) وانْتحر: قتَلَ نفْسه،
نعر (لسان العرب) قال شمر: النَاعِرُ على وجهين: النَاعِرُ المُصوّتُ والنَاعِرُ العِرْقُ الذي يسيل دماً. ونعَر عِرْقُه ينْعرُ نُعوراً ونَعيراً، فهو نَعّارٌ ونعُورٌ: صوَت لخروج الدم؛ قال العجاج: وبَجّ كلَّ عاندٍ نعُورِ، قضْبَ الطَبيبِ نائطَ المصْفُورِ وهذا الرجز نسبه الجوهري لرؤبة؛ قال ابن بري: وهو لأبيه العجاج، ومعنى بجّ شقّ، يعني أن الثور طعن الكلبَ فشق جلده. والعَاندُ: العرق الذي لا يرْقأُ دمُه. قال شمر: النَاعِرُ على وجهين: النَاعِرُ المُصوّتُ والنَاعِرُ العِرْقُ الذي يسيل دماً. ونعَر عِرْقُه ينْعِرُ نُعوراً ونعيراً، فهو نَعّارٌ ونعُورٌ: صوَت لخروج الدم؛ قال الأزهري: قرأت في كتاب

أبي عمر الزاهد منسوباً إلى ابن الأعرابي أنه قال: جرح تَعَارٌ، بالعين والتاء، وتَغَارٌ، بالغين والتاء، ونَعَارٌ، بالعين والنون، بمعنى واحد، وهو الذي لا يَرْقَأُ، فجعلها كلها لغات وصححها. ونَعَرَ القومُ: هاجوا واجتمعوا في الحرب. وقال الأصمعي في حديث ذكره: ما كانت فتنةٌ إلاَّ نَعَرَ فيها فلانٌ أي نَهَضَ فيها. وفي حديث الحَسَن: كلما نَعَرَ بهم ناعِرٌ اتَّبَعُوه أي ناهِضٌ يدعوهم إلى الفتنة ويصيح بهم إليها.

دعع (لسان العرب) دَعَّه يَدُعُّه دَعًّا: دفَعَه في جَفْوة، وقال ابن دريد: دَعَّه دَفَعَه دَفْعاً عنيفاً.

يدع (لسان العرب) وأَيْدَعَ الحجَّ على نفسه: أَوْجَبه، وذلك إذا تطيَّبَ لإِحْرامه؛ وقول جرير أَيْدَعُوا أي أَوْجَبُوا على أنفسهم؛ ابن الأعرابي: أَوْذَمْتُ يميناً وأَيْدَعْتُها أي أَوْجَبتُها.

دع (مقاييس اللغة) الدال والعين أصلٌ واحد مُنقاسٌ مطَّرِد، وهو يدلُّ على حركة ودَفْع واضطراب. فالدَّعُّ: الدفع؛ يقال دَعَعْتُه أَدُعُّه دَعّاً.

دعو (مقاييس اللغة) وتداعَت الحِيطان، وذلك إذا سقط واحدٌ وآخَرُ بعده، فكأنَّ الأوّل دعا الثاني. وربَّما قالوا: داعَيْناها عليهم، إذا هدَمْناها، واحداً بعد آخر. ودَواعِي الدَّهر: صُروفه، كأنّها تُميل الحوادث. ويُحمَل على الباب مجازاً أنْ يقال :دعا فُلاناً مَكانُ كذا، إذا قصَد ذلك المكان، كأنَّ المكان دعاه.

دعا (لسان العرب) ودَعا الرجلَ دَعْواً ودُعاءً: ناداه، والاسم الدعْوة. وتَداعى القومُ: دعا بعضُهم بعضاً حتى يجتمعوا؛ ودعاه إلى الأَمير: ساقَه. ويقال: ما الذي دعاك إلى هذا الأَمْرِ أي ما الذي جرَّكَ إليه واضْطَرَّك. وقوله عز وجل: أَنْ دَعَوْا للرحمن وَلداً؛ أَي جعلوا، وأَنشد بيت ابن أَحمر أَيضاً وقال أَي كنت أَجعل وأُسَمِّي؛

المَدْعَةُ (القاموس المحيط) والمَدْعِيُّ: المُتَهَمُ في نَسَبِه، قِيلَ: مَنْسوبٌ إلى المَدْعَةِ، أو من الدَّعْوَةِ في النَّسَبِ على لُغَةِ مَنْ يقولُ: دَعَيْتُ في دَعَوْتُ.

دأى (الصَّحاح في اللغة) وجمع الدأْيِ دَئِيٌّ. أبو زيد: دَأَيْتُ للشيء أَدْأَى له دأْياً، إذا خَتَلْتَهُ، مثل أدوْتُ له. ودَأَوْتُ له: لغةٌ في دَأَيْتُ. يقال: الذئب يَدْأَى للغزال ليأخذه، أي يَخْتِلُهُ، مثل يأدو.

الدَّأْيُ (القاموس المحيط) ودَأَيْتُ للشيءِ، كَسَعَيْتُ: خَتَلْتُه.

دأي (لسان العرب) ودَأَوْتُ له: لغة في دأَيْت. ودأَوْتُ له: مثل أَدَيْتُ له؛

أدي (مقاييس اللغة) الهمزة والدّال والياء أصلٌ واحد، وهو إيصال الشيء إلى الشيء أو وصوله إليه من تلقاء نفسه. قال الخليل: أدّى فلان يؤدِّي ما عليه أداءً وتأْدِيَةً.

أَدَاهُ (القاموس المحيط) أَدَاهُ تأْدِيَةً: أَوْصَلَهُ، وقَضاهُ، والاسمُ: الأداءُ.

عول (لسان العرب) والعَوْل: المُستعان به، وقد عَوَّل به وعليه. وأَعْوَل عليه وعَوَّل، كلاهما: أَدلَّ وحمَل. ويقال: عَوِّلْ عليه أَي اسْتَعِنْ به. وعَوَّل عليه: اتَّكَلَ واعْتَمد؛

عالَ (القاموس المحيط) والعَوْلُ: كُلُّ ما عالَكَ، والمُسْتَعانُ به، وقوتُ العِيال. وعَوَّلَ عليه مُعَوَّلاً: اتَّكَلَ واعْتَمَدَ، والاسمُ، كعِنَبٍ. وعِيَلُكَ، ككَيِّسٍ وكِتابٍ: من تَتَكَفَّلُ بِهِم.

أول (لسان العرب) والآل: السراب، وقيل: الآل هو الذي يكون ضُحى كالماء بين السماء والأَرض يرفع الشُّخوص ويَزْهاها، فأَما السَّراب فهو الذي يكون نصف النهار لاطِئاً بالأَرْض كأَنه ماء جار، وقال ثعلب: الآل في أَول النهار؛ وأَنشد: إِذ يَرْفَعُ الآلُ رأْس الكلب فارتفعا وقال اللحياني: السَّراب يذكر ويؤنث؛ وفي حديث قُسّ بن ساعدَة: قَطَعتُ مَهْمَهاً وآلاً فآلا الآل: السَّراب، والمَهْمَهُ: القَفْر. الأَصمعي: الآل والسراب واحد، وخالفه غيره فقال: الآل من الضحى إِلى زوال الشمس، والسراب بعد الزوال إِلى صلاة العصر، واحتجوا بأَن الآل يرفع كل شيء حتى يصير آلاً أَي شَخْصاً، وآلُ كل شيء: شَخْصه، وأَن السراب يخفض كل شيء فيه حتى يصير لاصقاً بالأَرض لا شخص له؛ والآل: الخَشَبُ المُجَرَّد؛ ومنه قوله: آلٌ على آلٍ تَحمَّلَ آلا فالآل الأَول: الرجل، والثاني السراب، والثالث الخشب؛ وقول أَبي دُواد: عَرَفْت لها مَنزلاً دارساً، وآلاً على الماء يَحْمِلْن آلا فالآل الأَولِ عيدانُ الخَيْمة، والثاني الشخص؛ قال: وقد يكون الآل بمعنى السراب؛

كنو (مقاييس اللغة) الكاف والنون والحرف المعتل يدلُّ على توريةٍ عن اسم بغيره. يقال: كنيت عن كذا. إذا تكلَّمت بغيره مما يُستَدلُّ به عليه. وكُنَى الرُّؤيا هي الأَمثالُ التي يَضرِبُها مَلَكُ الرُّؤيا، يَكْني بها عن أَعيان الأُمور.

الدَكُّ (القاموس المحيط) الدَكُّ: الدَّقُّ والهَدْمُ،

دكك (لسان العرب) والدَّك: الدقَ، وقد دَكَكْتُ الشيء أَدُكُّه دَكّاً إِذا ضربته وكسرته حتى سَوَّيته بالأَرض؛

§ 2.—V, 33-56

ePSD: kaššaptu
sibsib [SORCERESS] wr. sibsib "sorceress" Akk. kaššaptu
ePSD: kišpu
niĝak [MAGIC] wr. niĝ$_2$-ak; niĝ$_2$-ak-ak "magic" Akk. kišpu
AALD: kišpū (pl. only) (See kašāpu) كشف، سحر، شعوذة
AALD: kašāpu (v.) يسحر؛ يرمي سحرا، شرا

kašāšu
u [RIDE] wr. u_5 "to ride; attatchment to a plow; upper pivot of a door; ship's cabin; to gain control" Akk. hinnu; kašāšu; rakābu; rikbu; šagammu
ePSD: bašû
ĝal [BE] wr. $ĝal_2$; ma-al; $^{ga}{}_2gal_2$ "to be (there, at hand, available); to exist; to put, place, lay down; to have" Akk. bašû; šakānu
ePSD: bušu
niĝ [THING] wr. $niĝ_2$; $aĝ_2$ "thing, possesion; something" Akk. bušu; mimma
ePSD: alāku
dirig [FLOAT] wr. dirig "to drift (clouds); to float, glide (along/down); to go; to soak, steep, dissolve in liquid" Akk. alāku; mahāhu; mahāru; neqelpû
ĝen [GO] wr. ĝen; ma "to go; to flow" Akk. alāku
AALD: šalû (v.) šalû يغمر نفسه؛ يخضع للمحنة
AALD: tēbibtu (s.) التطهير، التظيف
ePSD: ţebû
su [SINK] wr. su; su_3 "to submerge; to sink" Akk. ţebû
ePSD: ţebû (v.) يغمر، يُغرق، يُهبَط، يلغي وثيقة
ePSD: ţebû (v.) see tebû
ePSD: tebû
šu zig [RAISE THE HAND] wr. šu zig_3 "'to raise the hand'; to rise; to plunder" Akk. nanduru; qātu našû; tebû
zig [RISE] wr. zig_3 "to issue; to levy, raise, muster; to swell; to expend; to rise" Akk. dekû; gapāšu; tebû; şītu
ePSD: šalû ša mê
luĝa [SUBMERGE] wr. $luĝ_2$ "to submerge oneself in water" Akk. šalû ša mê

القَشْبُ (القاموس المحيط) القَشْبُ: الخَلْطُ، وسقْيُ السَمِّ والإصابةُ بالمكْروه، والمُسْتَقْذَرُ ،المُسْتَقْذَرُ، والافْتِراءُ، واكْتِسابُ الحَمْدِ أو الذَمِّ، كالاقْتِشاب، والإفْسادُ، واللَّطْخُ بالشيءِ، والتَعْييرُ. وإزالَةُ العَقْلِ،

قشب (لسان العرب) وقِشْبُ الطعام: ما يُلْقى منه مما لا خير فيه. وكلُّ قذر قَشْبٌ وقِشْبٌ. وقَشَب الشيءَ: دنَسه. وقشبه بشَرٍّ إذا رماه بعلامة من الشَرِّ، يُعْرفُ بها. وفي حديث عمر، رضي الله عنه، قال لبعض بنيه: قَشَبكَ المالُ أي أفْسدَك وذهب بعَقْلك. والقِشْبةُ الخسيسُ من الناس، يمانية.

كشف (لسان العرب) الكَشْفُ: رفعُك الشيء عما يُواريه ويغطّيه، كشَفه يكشِفه كشْفاً وكشّفه فانكشف وتكشّف. وكَشَفه عن الأمر: أكرهه على إظهاره.

سبسب (لسان العرب) وسَبْسَب إذا شتم شتْماً قبيحاً.

ألك (لسان العرب) ويقال: ألَك بين القوم إذا ترسَل ألْكاً وأُلوكاً والاسم منه الألُوك، وهي الرسالة، وكذلك الألُوكة والمَأْلُكة والمَألُك، فإن نقلته بالهمزة قلت ألَكْتُه إليه رسالةً، والأصل أألَكْتُه فأخرت الهمزة بعد اللام وخففت بنقل حركتها على ما قبلها وحذفِها، فإن أمرتَ من هذا الفعل المنقول بالهمزة قلت ألِكْني إليها برسالة، وكان مقتضى هذا اللفظ أن يكون معناه أرْسِلْني إليها برسالة، إلا أنه جاء على القلب إذ المعنى كُنْ رسولي إليها بهذه الرسالة فهذا على حد قولهم: ولا تَهَيّبَني المَوْماةُ أركبها أي ولا أتهيَّبُها، وكذلك ألِكْني لفظه يقضي بأن المخاطب مُرْسَلٌ والمتكلم مُرْسِل، وهو في المعنى بعكس ذلك، وهو أن المخاطب مُرْسِل والمتكلم مرْسَل؛

بيي (لسان العرب) حَيّاك الله وبيّاك، قيل: حيّاك ملَّكك، وقيل: أبقاك، ويقال: اعتَمدك بالمُلْك، وقيل: أصْلحك، وقيل: قرّبك؛ الأخيرة حكاها الأصمعي عن الأحمر. ويقال: بَيَّنْتُ الشيء وبَيَّيْتُه إذا أوضحته. والتَّبيِّي التبيين من قرب.

بيض (لسان العرب) وبيْضةُ كل شيء حوْزَتُه. ويقال: بَيَّضْت الإناءَ إذا فرّغْتَه، وبيَّضْته إذا ملأْته، وهو من الأضداد.

السَلَى (القاموس المحيط) ووقَعُوا في سَلَى جَملٍ: أمْرٍ صَعْبٍ، لأنَّ الجَمَلَ لا سَلى له.

سلا (لسان العرب) وفي المثَل: وقع القومُ في سَلى جمَلٍ، ووقع في سَلى جمَلٍ أي في أمرٍ لا مَخْرج له لأن الجمل لا سلى له، وإنما يكون للناقةِ، وقيل: يحتمل أن يكون أصله ما سلأْتَم، بالهمز، من السّلاءِ وهو السَمْنُ، فترك الهمز فصارت ألِفاً ثم قُلبت الألفُ ياءً. ويقال للأمْرِ إذا فات: قدِ انقطع السَلى؛ يُضْرب مثلاً للأمْر يفوت وينقطِع. الجوهري: يقال انقطع السَلى في البطن إذا ذهبت الحيلة، كما يقال: بلغ السِكّينُ العظمَ.

شلا (لسان العرب) وقوله: اشْتَلَيْت واستشْليت سواءٌ في المعنى، وكلُّ منْ دعَوْته فقد أشْلَيْته، وكلُّ من دعوْته حتى تُخْرجه وتُنجِيَه من الضَيق أو من الهلكة أو من موضِع أو مكانٍ فقد استَشْليته واشْتليته، وأنشد بيت القُطامي.

تعب (لسان العرب) وأتْعب إناءَه وقدحه: ملأه،

طبع (الصَحاح في اللغة) وطَبِع أيضاً بمعنى كَسِل. وطبِعَ السيفُ، أي علاه الصدأُ. وطَبَعْتُ السقاءَ وغيره تَطْبيعاً: ملأته، فتطَبع، أي امتلأَ.

الطَبْعُ (القاموس المحيط) وطَبَع عليه، كمنع: ختم، و~ السيف، و~ الدَرْهم، و~ الجرّة من الطِّين: عملها، و~ الدَلْو: ملأها، و~ الإناءُ: امْتلأ.
طبع (مقاييس اللغة) الطاء والباء والعين أصلٌ صحيح، وهو مثَلٌ على نهايةٍ ينتهي إليها الشيء حتى يختم عندها يقال طبَعت على الشيء طابعاً. ثم يقال على هذا طَبْعُ الإنسان وسجيّتُه. ومن ذلك طبَعَ اللهُ على قَلْب الكافر، كأنَّه ختم عليه حتى لا يصل إليه هُدىً ولا نُور، فلا يوفَّق لخير.
طبع (لسان العرب) وقال أبو إسحق النحوي: معنى طبع في اللغة وختم واحد، وهو التغْطِيةُ على الشيء والاستيثاقُ من أن يدخله شيء كما قال تعالى: أم على قلوب أَقفالُها، وقال عز وجل: كلاَّ بلْ ران على قلوبهم؛ معناه غطّى على قلوبهم، وكذلك طبع الله على قلوبهم؛ وطِبْعُه مِلْؤُه. وتطبّعَ النهرُ بالماء. فاض به من جوانبه وتدفّق. والطِّبْعُ، بالكسر: النهر، وجمعه أطباع، قال لبيد: فتولّوا فاتراً مَشْيُهُمْ، كرَوايا الطِّبْع هَمَّتْ بالوَحَلْ وقيل: الطِّبْعُ هنا المِلْءُ، وقيل: الطِّبْعُ هنا الماء الذي طُبِعتْ به الرَاوِيةُ أي مُلِئَتْ. قال الأزهري: ولم يعرف الليث الطِّبْعَ في بيت لبيد فتحيّر فيه، فمرّة جعله المِلْءَ، وهو ما أخذ الإناءُ من الماءِ، ومرة جعله الماء، قال: وهو في المعنيين غير مصيب. والطِّبْعُ في بيت لبيد النهر، وهو ما قاله الأصمعي، وسمي النهر طِبْعاً لأن الناس ابتدَؤُوا حفره، وهو بمعنى المفعول كالقِطْف بمعنى المقْطوف، والنِّكْث بمعنى المنْكوث من الصوف، وأما الأنهار التي شقَّها الله تعالى في الأرض شقًا مثل دَجْلة والفُرات والنيل وما أشبهها فإنها لا تسمى طُبوعاً، إنما الطُّبُوعُ الأنهار التي أَحْدثها بنو آدم واحتفروها لمَرافقهم؛ وناقة مُطَبَّعةٌ ومُطَبَعةٌ: مُثْقلةٌ بحمْلِها على المثل كالماء؛
كسأ (لسان العرب) وكَسَأَ القومَ يَكْسَؤُهم كسْأً: غلَبهم في خُصُومة ونحوها. ويقال للرجل إذا هَزم القومَ فمَرَّ وهو يطْرُدُهم: مرَّ فلان يكْسَؤُهم ويكْسَعُهم أي يَتْبَعُهم.
كسع (لسان العرب) الكَسْعُ: أَنْ تَضْرِبَ بيدك أو برجلك بصدر قدمك على دبر إنسان أو شيء. كَسَعه بكذا وكذا إذا جعله تابعاً له ومَذْهباً به؛ وفي نوادر الأعراب: كَسَعَ فلان فلاناً وكسَحه وثَفَنه ولَظَه ولاظَه يَلُظُّه ويَلُوظُه ويَلأَظُه إذا طرَده.
كسع (الصَحاح في اللغة) الكَسْعُ: أن تضرِب دُبر الإنسان بيدك أو بصدر قدمك. يقال: اتَّبع فلانٌ أدبارهم يكْسَعُهُمْ بالسيف، مثل يكْسَؤُهم، أي يطردهم.

§ 3.—V, 57-67

ePSD: dīnu
did [LAWSUIT] wr. di "lawsuit, trial; legal decision" Akk. dīnu
AALD: dīnu (s.) قضية
AALD: šību (s.) شاهد، الرجل الاشيب
AALD: šībūtu (s.) الشهادة، الدليل؛ الشيب، الكبر
AALD: iqbû (s.) See qabû امر، توجيه
ePSD: qabû
di [SPEAK] wr. di "non-finite imperfect stem of dug[to speak]" Akk. atwû; dabābu; qabû
dug [SPEAK] wr. dug_4 "to speak, talk, say; to order; to do, perform; to negotiate" Akk. atwû; dabābu; epēšu; qabû
e [SPEAK] wr. e; na-be_2-a; be_2; ne; da-me; na-be_2; e_7 "perfect plural and imperfect stem of dug[to speak]" Akk. atwû; dabābu; qabû
AALD: qabû (v.) يقول، يخبر، يؤدي شهادة
AALD: qabû (v.) (qabā'û) يتعهَد، يُجير، يُعد، يُعطي امرا، يجعل شخص يعطي امرا
AALD: awatu See amatu
AALD: amatu (awatu) (s.) قضية رسمية في المحكمة، الشأن، الشيء، المحتوى، القرار، النطق
ePSD: sarru
hulu [BAD] wr. hul; hul_3 "to destroy; (to be) bad-smelling, maloderous; (to be) bad, evil; (to be) slight, lightweight; (to be) false; (to be) criminal, dishonest; enemy; to raid; to strike the eyes; blinker, winker, one with vision problems" Akk. abātu ša īni; bēšu; lapātu ša īni; ṣabru; lemnu; masku; qallu; sarru; zāmânû
lu'IM [CRIMINAL] wr. lu_2-IM "criminal; false, fraudulent" Akk. sarru
lul [FALSE] wr. lul "(to be) false; (to be) criminal" Akk. sarru
lulul [LIAR] wr. lu_2-lul "liar" Akk. sarru
AALD: ṣarru See sarru
AALD: sarru (adj.) جريمة، غش، مجرم، سارق
AALD: ṣarru See ṣerru
AALD: ṣerru (s.) الزوجة الثانية، الضرَة

دين (الصّحاح في اللغة) وفي الحديث: "الكَيِّسُ من دان نفسه وعمل لما بعد الموت. الجزاءُ والمكافأةُ. يقال: دانهُ ديناً، أي جازاه. يقال: كما تدينُ تُدانُ، أي كما تُجازي تُجازى، أي تُجازى بفعلك وبحسب ما عملت. وقوله تعالى: "أإنا لمدينون" أي مجزيُّون محاسَبون. والدينُ الطاعةُ. ودان له، أي أطاعه.

دين (مقاييس اللغة) الدال والياء والنون أصلٌ واحد إليه يرجع فروعُه كلُّها. ومنه: مَالِكِ يَوْمِ الدِّينِ [الفاتحة 4]،أي يوم الحكم. وقال قومٌ: الحساب والجزاء.

ثبت (لسان العرب) وتثبّت في الأَمر والرَّأْي، واستثْبت: تأَنّى فيه ولم يَعْجَل. واسْتَثْبت في أَمره إِذا شاور وفحَص عنه. وتقول أيضاً: لا أَحْكُم بكذا، إِلا بثَبْت أَي بحُجَّة. وفي حديث صوم يوم الشك: ثم جاء الثَّبتُ أَنه من رمضان؛ الثَّبتُ، بالتحريك: الحجة والبينة. وفي حديث قتادة بن النُّعمان: بغير بَيِّنة ولا ثَبت. وثابته وأَثْبته: عرَفه حَق المَعْرفة. وطعَنه فأَثْبت فيه الرُّمْح أَي أَنفذه. وأَثْبت حجته: أَقامها وأَوْضحها.

زعم (مقاييس اللغة) الزاء والعين والميم أصلان: أحدهما القولُ من غير صحّةٍ ولا يقين، والآخر التكفُّل بالشيء.فالأول الزَّعم والزُّعم.

زعم (لسان العرب) والتَّزَعُّمُ التَّكَذُّبُ؛

ضرط (لسان العرب) وتكلم فلان فأضرط به فلان أي أنكر قوله. يقال: أضرط فلان بفلان إذا استخفّ به وسخر منه، وكذلك ضَرّط به أي هَزِئ به وحكى له بفيه فِعْل الضارِط.

صرط (لسان العرب) الأزهري: قرأ ابن كثير ونافع وأبو عمرو وابن عامر وعاصم والكسائي: اهْدنا الصِّراط المستقيم، بالصاد، وقرأ يعقوب بالسين، قال: وأَصل صاده سين قلبت مع الطاء صاداً لقُرب مخارجها. الجوهري: الصراطُ والسراطُ والزِّراطُ الطريق؛

زور (لسان العرب) والزُّور: الكذب والباطل، وقيل: شهادة الباطل.

زور (الصّحاح في اللغة) الزور: الكذب. ويقال للقوس: زَوْراءُ لميلها، وللجيش: أَزْوَرُ. والازْوِرارُ عن الشيء: العدولُ عنه. وقد ازْوَرَّ عنه ازوراراً، وازوارَّ ازْويراراً، وتزاور عنه تزاوُراً، كلُّه بمعنى عدلَ عنه وانحرف. وزُرْتُهُ أَزُورُهُ زَوْراً وزيارةً وزوارةً أيضاً.

سرر (لسان العرب) والسريرةُ: عمل السر من خير أو شر.

سرر (الصّحاح في اللغة) وأَسْرَرْتُ الشيءَ: كتمْتُهُ، وأعْلَنْتُهُ أيضاً، فهو من الأضداد.

الضَرُّ (القاموس المحيط) أو من ضارَهُ ضِراراً ومُضارَةً: إذا خالفه.

ضرر (لسان العرب) الضَّرّ والضُّرُّ لغتان: ضد النفع. والضَّرُّ المصدر، والضُّرّ الاسم، وقيل: هما لغتان كالشَّهْد والشُّهْد، فإِذا جمعت بين الضَّرّ والنفع فتحت الضاد، وإِذا أَفردت الضُّرّ ضَمَمْت الضاد إِذا لم تجعله مصدراً، كقولك: ضَرَرْتُ ضَرّاً؛ هكذا تستعمله العرب. أَبو الدُّقَيْش: الضَّرّ ضد النفع، والضُّر، بالضم، الهزالُ وسوء الحال. والضَّرَرُ: سوء الحال، وجمعه أَضْرٌّ؛ والضررُ الضِّيقُ، وقيل: لا تُضارُّون في رُؤْيته أَي لا يُخالِفُ بعضُكم بعضاً فيُكَذِّبه.

ضرأ (القاموس المحيط) ضَرأ، كجمعَ: خفيَ.

ضرأ (العباب الزاخر) أبو عمرو: ضَرأ يضْرَأُ: إذا خفي.

ضرا (الصّحاح في اللغة) وفلانٌ يمشي الضراء، إذا مشى مستخفياً فيما يوارى من الشجر. ويقال للرجل إذا خَتَلَ صاحبه: هو يمشي له الضَراء ويدبُّ له الخمر. واسْتَضْرَيْتُ للصيد، إذا ختلته من حيث لا يعلم.

صري (لسان العرب) وقد تكررت هذه اللفظة في أَحاديث منها قوله، صلى الله عليه وسلم: لا تَصُرُّوا الإِبل والغنم، فإِن كان من الصَّرّ فهو بفتح التاء وضم الصاد، وإِن كان من الصَّرْي فيكون بضم التاء وفتح الصاد، وإِنما نَهى عنه لأَنه خِداعٌ وغِشٌّ.

أوا (لسان العرب) أَوَيْتُ مَنْزِلي وإلى منزلي أُوِيّاً وإِوِيّاً وأَوَيْتُ وتأَوَّيْتُ وأْتَوَيْتُ، كله: عُدْتُ؛ وقالوا: أَوتا عليك، بالتاء، وهو التهلف على الشيء، عزيزاً كان أَو هيناً. قال النحويون: إِذا جعلت أَوْ اسماً ثقلت واوها فقلت أَوٌّ حَسنةٌ، وتقول دع الأَوَّ جانباً، تقول ذلك لمن يستعمل في كلامه افْعلْ كذا أَو كذا، وكذلك تثقل لَوْ إِذا جعلته اسماً؛ وقال أَبو زُبَيْد: إِنَّ لَيْتاً وإِنَّ لَوّاً عَناءُ وقول العرب: أَوِّ من كذا، بواو ثقيلة، هو بمعنى تَشَكّي مشقة أَو همّ أَو حزن. وأَوْ: حرف عطف. وأَو: تكون للشك والتخيير، وتكون اختياراً.

أمت (لسان العرب) أَمَتَ الشيءَ يأْمِتُه أَمْتاً، وأَمَّتَه: قَدَرَهُ وحَزَره. والأَمْتُ الانْخفاضُ، والارْتفاعُ، والاختلافُ في الشيء. وأَصله من الأَمْتِ بمعنى الحَزْر، والتقدير، لأَنّ الشك يدخلهما؛

قباهُ (القاموس المحيط) قباهُ: جَمَعَهُ بأَصابعه، و~ البناء: رفعهُ،

قَبَّ (القاموس المحيط) قَبَّ القَوْمُ يَقِبُّون قُبوباً: صَخِبوا في الخُصومة، و~ الأَسَدُ، و~ الفَحْلُ قَبّاً وقَبيباً: سُمع قَعْقَعَةُ أَنْيابِه، و~ نابُهُ: صَوَّتَتْ، وقَعْقَعتْ،

قبب (لسان العرب) قَبَّ القومُ يَقِبُّون قَبّاً: صخِبُوا في خُصومة أَو تَمار. وقال بعضهم: القَبِيبُ الصوتُ، فعَمّ به. والقَبْقَبةُ والقَبِيبُ: صوتُ جَوْف الفرس. والقَبْقبةُ والقَبْقابُ: صوتُ أَنياب الفحل، وهديرُه؛ وقيل: هو تَرْجيع الـهَدير. وقَبْقَب الأَسدُ والفحل قَبْقبة إِذا هدر. والقَبْقابُ: الجمل الـهَدَّار. ورجلٌ قَبْقابٌ وقُباقِبٌ: كثير الكلام، أَخطأَ أَو أَصاب؛ وقيل: كثير الكلام مُخَلِّطُه؛

قبب (تاج العروس) وقال بعضهم: القَبِيب: الصوتُ، فعَمّ به. والقابَةُ في قولهم؛ ما سمِعْنا العام قابَةً؛ أَي صَوْت الرَّعْدِ يَذْهَبُ بِهِ إِلى القبيب، وهو الصوتُ، على ما تقدّم.

قبء (المحيط في اللغة) وقبوته: إذا علوته. وقبيت على الرجل: عدوت عليه في أمره. وقبأت الشيء: إذا أخفيته. ويقال للرفعة في النحو: قبوة لانضمام الشفتين بها.
قبب (اساس البلاغة) ومن المجاز: هو قب قومه، وهو القب الأكبر وهو الشيخ الذي عليه مدار أمرهم.
قب (مجمل اللغة) والقابة: صوت الرعد، من قولهم: ما سمعنا العام قابة.
قبب (العين) ويقال لشيخ القوم هو قبهم.

§ 4.—V, 68-VI, 5

ePSD: kaspu
<u>kugbabbar</u> <u>[SILVER]</u> wr. kug-babbar; kug-babbar$_2$ "silver" Akk. Kaspu
AALD: kaspu (s.) الفضة كوسيلة تعامل، النقود
ePSD: išīnu
<u>isin</u> <u>[STALK]</u> wr. išin; i$_3$-si-na; e-si-na; isin$_x$(|ŠE.IGI.TUR|); isim$_2$; isim$_3$ "culm, grain stalk, stem" Akk. išīnu
AALD: še'u (s.) شعير، حنطة، حبة الصنوبر
AALD: še'û (v.) يسعى، يناضل من اجل
AALD: arnu (s.) (annu) الذنب، الاثم، الجريمة؛ العقوبة، الغرامة
ePSD: enēšu
<u>šer</u> <u>[WEAKEN]</u> wr. še-er "to weaken" Akk. enēšu
AALD: enēšu (v.) يضعف، يفقر، يرتجف، يهتز، يتداعى See also anšu

قسب (مقاييس اللغة) القاف والسين والباء يدلّ على مِثْل ما دلّ عليه الذي قبله. يقولون: [القَسْب]: التّمر اليابس. والقَسْب: الصُّلب من كلّ شيء.
قسب (الصّحاح في اللغة) القَسْبُ: الصلبُ.
قزب (مقاييس اللغة) القاف والزاء والباء، فيه من طرائف ابن دريد: القَزب الصَّلابة والشِّدّة. قزب الشيءُ: صلُب.
القَزْبُ (القاموس المحيط) القَزْبُ: النِّكاحُ الكثيرُ، وبالكسر: اللَّقَبُ، وبالتَّحريك: الصَّلابةُ، والشِّدَّةُ. قَزِبَ، كفَرِح. والقازِبُ: التاجرُ الحريصُ، مرَّةً في البحْرِ ومرَّةً في البرّ.
قصب (مقاييس اللغة) القاف والصاد والباء أصلان صحيحان، يدلُّ أحدهما على قطْع الشَّيء، ويدلُّ الآخر على امتدادٍ في أشياء مجوَّفة.
قصف (مقاييس اللغة) القاف والصاد والفاء أصلٌ صحيحٌ يدلُّ على كسرٍ لشيء.
الكِسْفةُ (القاموس المحيط) الكِسْفةُ، بالكسر: القِطْعةُ من الشيء،
كسف (الصّحاح في اللغة) الكِسْفَةُ: القطعة من الشيء. يقال: أعطني كِسْفة من ثوبك؛ والجمع كِسْفٌ وكِسَفٌ.
كسف (تهذيب اللغة) فقال: كلُّ شيءٍ قطعته فقد كسفته. قال، ويقال: كسفت الشمسُ إذا ذهب ضوءُها، وكسَف القمر إذا ذهب ضوءُه، وكسَف الرَّجلُ إذا نكس طرْفه، وكسفت حالُه إذا تغيرتْ. قال: وكسفت الشمسُ وخسفت بمعنىً واحد. وقال شمرٌ: قال أبو زيد: كسفت الشمسُ تكسِفُ كسوفا إذا اسْودّت بالنهار، وكسفت الشمسُ النّجومَ إذا غلب ضوءُها النجومَ فلم يَبْدُ منها شيءٌ، والشمسُ حينئذ كاسفةٌ للنجوم.
كسب (مقاييس اللغة) الكاف والسين والباء أصلٌ صحيحٌ، وهو يدلُّ على ابتغاء وطلبٍ وإصابة.
كسب (لسان العرب) والكَسْبُ: الطَّلَبُ والسَّعْيُ في طلَب الرزق والـمَعيشةِ؛ ابن الأَثير: يقال: كَسَبْتُ زيداً مالاً، وأَكْسَبْتُ زيداً مالاً أَي أَعنْتُه على كَسْبه، أَو جعلْتُه يكْسِبُه،
ثم (مقاييس اللغة) الثاء والميم أصلٌ واحد، هو اجتماعٌ في لين. يقال ثَمَمْتُ الشيءَ ثَمّاً، إذا جمعته. وأكثرُ ما يُستعمل في الحشيش.
وثم (لسان العرب) وقال المزني: وَجَدْتُ كلأً كثيفاً وثِيمةً؛ قال: الوثيمةُ جماعةٌ من الحشيش أو الطعام. يقال: ثِمْ لها أي اجْمَعْ لها.
سعم (لسان العرب) وسَعَمَه وسَعَّمَه: غذاه. وسَعَمَ إبلَه: أرعاها. والمُسَعَّمُ الحسَنُ الغِذاء، والغين المعجمة لغة.
سعا (لسان العرب) والسَّعْيُ: الكَسْبُ، وكلُّ عملٍ من خير أو شرّ سَعْي، والفعلُ كالفعْل. وفي التنزيل: لِتُجْزَى كلُّ نفْس بما تَسْعَى. وسَعَى لهم وعليهم: عَمِلَ لهم وكَسَبَ. وأَسْعَى غيره: جعَله يَسْعَى؛ وقد روي بيتُ أَبي خِراش: أَبْلِغْ عَلِيّاً، أَطال اللهُ ذُلَّهُمُ أَنَّ البُكَيْرَ الذي أَسْعَوْا به هَمَلُ أَسْعَوْا وأَشْعَوْا.
سعع (لسان العرب) السَّعِيعُ: الزُّؤانُ أَو نحوه مما يخرج من الطعام فيرمى به، واحدته سَعِيعةٌ. والسَّعِيعُ: الشَّيْلَمُ.
الشَّغوشُ (القاموس المحيط) الشَّغوشُ، كصَبورٍ: بُرٌّ ذُو شَيْلَمٍ رديءٌ،
شعع (لسان العرب) وشَعُّ السُّنبل وشَعاعُه وشُعاعُه: سَفاه إِذا يبِس ما دام على السُّنْبُل. وقد أَشَعَّ الزرْعُ: أَخرج شَعاعه.
شعا (لسان العرب) أَشْعَى القومُ الغارةَ إِشْعاءً: أَشْعَلُوها. وغارةٌ شَعْواءُ: فاشِيةٌ متفرِّقةٌ؛ والشَّعْوانةُ: الجُمَّةُ من الشَّعَر المُشعانّ. وشجرة شَعْواءُ: مُنْتَشِرةُ الأَغصان. الغارةُ تَشْعَى شَعاً إِذا انتشرت، فهي شَعْواءُ،
شعي (مقاييس اللغة) الشين والعين والحرف المعتل، أُصلٌ يَدُلُّ على مثل ما دلَ عليه الذي قَبْلَه. يقال أَشْعَى القومُ الغارةَ إِشعاء، إذا أَشْعَلُوها.

عنا (لسان العرب) عنن (لسان العرب) قال الأزهري: قولهم أخذتُ الشيءَ عَنْوة يكون غلبَة، ويكون عن تسليم وطاعة ممن يؤخذُ منه الشيء؛
وقال أبو الهيثم: العناء الحبْس في شدة وذلّ. وفي حديث آخر: أطْعِموا الجائعَ وفكُّوا العاني، قال: ولا أراه مأخوذاً إلا من الذّل والخُضوع.
والتَّعْنية: الحبس؛ وعانى الشيءَ: قاساه. والمُعاناةُ: المُقاساة. يقال: عاناه وتَعنّاه وتَعنّى هو؛
عرن (مقاييس اللغة) العين والراء والنون أصلٌ صحيحٌ واحد يدلّ على ثباتٍ وإثباتِ شيء، كالشّيء المركب. من ذلك العِرنين، وهو الأنف،
والجمع عرانين سمّي بذلك كأنّه عُرن على الأنف، أي رُكِّب. وكذلك اللّحم عرينٌ، لأنه مُثْبتٌ مركّبٌ على الجسم.
عنت (مقاييس اللغة) العين والنون والتاء أصلٌ صحيح يدلّ على مشقّة وما أشبه ذلك، ولا يدلّ على صحّة ولا سهولة. قال الزّجاج: العنت في اللغة: المشقّة الشديدة.
عنت (الصّحاح في اللغة) العَنَتُ: الإثمْ. وقد عَنِتَ الرجل. وقال تعالى: "عزيزٌ عليه ما عَنِتُّمْ. "ذلك لمن خَشيَ العنتَ منكم" يعني الفجور والزنا.
والعَنَتُ أيضاً: الوقوع في أمر شاقّ. وقد عنِتَ وأعْنتَهُ غيره.
العَنَتُ (القاموس المحيط) العَنَتُ، محركةً: الفسادُ، والإثْمُ، والهلاكُ، ودُخولُ المَشقّةِ على الإنسانِ، وأعْنَتَهُ غيرُهُ، ولِقاءُ الشّدّة، والزّنى، والوَهْيُ،
والانْكسارُ، واكتِسابُ المأثَمِ. وعَنّته تعْنيتاً: شدّدَ عليه، وألْزمه ما يَصْعُبُ عليه أداؤه. والعُنْتوتُ: يبيسُ الخلى، وجبلٌ مُستَدِق في الصّحراءِ، وأوّلُ
كلّ شيءٍ، والشّاقّةُ المصعدِ من الآكام، كالعنوت. والعانِتُ: المرأة العانسُ.
عنس (مقاييس اللغة) العين والنون والسين أصلٌ صحيح واحدٌ يدلّ على شدّةٍ في شيء وقوّة.
أنت (القاموس المحيط) أنتَ يأنِتُ أنيتاً: أنّ، و~ فُلاناً: حَسَدَهُ، فهو مأنوتٌ وأنيتٌ، و~ الشّيءَ: قَدَرَه.
أنت (مقاييس اللغة) الهمزة والنون والتاء، شذّ عن كتاب الخليل في هذا النَسق،وكذلك عن ابن دريد. وقال غيرهما: وهو يأنِت أي يزْحر.

§ 5.—VI, 6-30

ePSD: parāsu
tar [CUT] wr. tar; tar^{ar} "to cut down; to untie, loosen; to cut; to scatter, disperse; to decide" Akk. harāşu; parāsu; paţāru; sapāhu
ePSD: parāsu; harāşu
kud [CUT] wr. kud; gur$_5$ "to break off, deduct; to separate, cut off; to cut; to incise; to decide; to make clear" Akk. harāşu; napādu; parāsu; harāşu; parāsu; harāşu
AALD: purussû (s.) (pursû (القرار القانوني، الحل، القرار
ePSD: kanāku
gug [SEAL] wr. gug$_6$ "to seal" Akk. kanāku
kišib rah [SEAL] wr. kišib rah$_2$ "to seal" Akk. kanāku
AALD: warkû See arkû
ePSD: arkatu
aga [REAR] wr. a-ga; a-ba "rear; a building or a part of a building" Akk. arkatu
eĝir [BACK] wr. eĝir; eĝir$_5$(LUM); egir$_4$; eĝir$_6$(MURGU$_2$) "back, rear; after; estate, inheritence" Akk. arkatu
ePSD: warkatu
murgu [SHOULDER] wr. murgu$_2$; murgu "shoulder; back" Akk. pūdu; warkatu
ePSD: ragāmu
inim ĝar [SUE] wr. inim ĝar; inim ga$_2$-ga$_2$ "to sue, to make a legal claim" Akk. baqāru; ragāmu
AALD: tēnû (s.) تبديل؛ بديل، تعويض
AALD: enû (v.) يزيل، ينقل، يغير، يلغي، يقلب، يبطل، يتبادل، يحل محل
AALD: ēnû (s.) البديل، الاستبدال
ePSD: šebû
lum [FRUIT] wr. lum "(to be) full, replete, satisfied (with); (to be) grown (tall); to fruit; (to be) fructified; to shine" Akk. enēbu; unnubu; namāru; šebû; šihu
ePSD: bašû
ĝal [BE] wr. ĝal$_2$; ma-al; $^{ga}{}_2$gal$_2$ "to be (there, at hand, available); to exist; to put, place, lay down; to have" Akk. bašû; šakānu
ePSD: bušu
niĝ [THING] wr. niĝ$_2$; aĝ$_2$ "thing, possesion; something" Akk. bušu; mimma
ePSD: işu
ĝeš [TREE] wr. ĝeš; mu; u$_5$ "tree; wood; a description of animals" Akk. işu
ePSD: kussû
ašte [CHAIR] wr. ašte$_2$; ^{ĝeš}aš-te; ^{ĝeš}iš-de$_3$ "chair, throne; seat, dwelling; shrine, chapel; a unit of area"

Akk. kussû; sukku; šubtu

durĝar [CHAIR] wr. ^{ĝeš}dur$_2$-ĝar; dur$_2$-gar; dur$_2$-gar^{urudu} "chair" Akk. kussû

guza [CHAIR] wr. ^{ĝeš}gu-za; gu-za; gu$_2$-za; ^{ĝeš}guza; ^{ĝeš}aš-te "chair, stool, throne" Akk. kussû

ePSD: nadānu

šum [GIVE] wr. šum$_2$; ze$_2$-eĝ$_3$ "to give" Akk. nadānu

AALD: *adi (prep.) (hadi, hadu, qadi, qadu) حتى، طالما، مع الاعداد والوقت ومضاعفاتهما

فرز (لسان العرب) والفِرْزَةُ كالفِرْزِ. وأَفْرز له نصيبَه: عَزَلَ. والفِرْزُ في الحديث: النصيبُ المفْرُوزُ. وقد فَرَزْتُ الشيء وأَفْرَزْتُه إِذا قسمته.

والفِرزُ النصيب المفْرُوزُ لصاحبه، واحداً كان أَو اثنين: وفرزَهُ يفْرِزُه فرْزاً وأَفْرزه: مازَهُ. الجوهري: الفَرْزُ مصدر قولك فَرَزْتُ الشيء أَفْرِزُه إِذا عزلته عن غيره ومزْتَه، والقِطعةُ منه فِرْزَةٌ، بالكسر. وفارَز فلانٌ شريكه أَي فاصله وقاطعه. قال بعض أَهل اللغة: الفَرْزُ قريب من الفَزْرِ، تقول: فرَزْتُ الشيء من الشيء أَي فصلته.

فرس (لسان العرب) ويقال: هو يتفرَّس إِذا كان يتَثَبَّتُ وينظرُ. قال: أَنا أَفرسُ بالرجال؛ يريد أَبْصرُ وأَعرفُ. ورجل فارس بالأَمر أَي عالم به بصير. والفِراسة، بكسر الفاء: في النَّظر والتَّثَبت والتأَمل للشيء وابصر به، يقال إِنه لفارس بهذا الأَمر إِذا كان عالماً به. والفَرْصَة ريح الحَدَب، والفَرْس: ريح الحَدَب. والفِرْناس، مثل الفِرْصاد: من أَسماء الأَسد مأْخوذة من الفَرْسِ، وهو دقّ العُنُق، نونه زائدة عند سيبويه.

فرص (لسان العرب) والفَرْسُ، بالسين: الكسرُ. والفَرْصُ الشَقُّ. والفَرْصُ القطعُ. وفَرَصَ الجِلْدَ فَرْصاً: قطعَه. والمِفْرَصُ والمِفْراصُ: الحديدةُ العريضةُ التي يقطع بها، وقيل: التي يُقعطع بها الفضةُ؛

فرض (لسان العرب) فَرَضْت الشيء أَفْرِضه فَرْضاً وفَرَّضْتُه للتكثير: أَوْجبْته. وفرض الله علينا كذا وكذا وافْتَرضَ أَي أَوْجب.

ركا (لسان العرب) وأَرْكَيْت في الأَمْر: تأَخَّرْت. ابن الأَعرابي: ركاه إِذا أَخَّره.

ورك (لسان العرب) قال: وقال أَبو زياد التَوَرُّك التَبَطُّؤُ عن الحاجة. وقال أَبو حنيفة: وَرِكُ الشجرة عَجُزها. قال الأَصمعي: ورَكْتُ الجبل تَوْريكاً، أَي جاوزته.

شسب (لسان العرب) الشَاسبُ: لغة في الشَازِبِ، وهو النَحِيف اليابسُ من الضُمْر، الذي قد يَبِس جلده عليه؛

شذب (مقاييس اللغة) الشين والذال والباء أَصلٌ يدلُّ على تجريدِ شيءٍ من قِشره، ثم يُحمَل عليه. فالشَّذْب: قَشْر اللَّحم. وكلُّ شيءٍ نحَّيتَه عن شيءٍ فقد شَذَبته. ومن الباب: التَّشذيب: التقطيع. فأَمَا الشوْذب فمن هذا الباب أَيضاً، وهو الطَوِيلُ من كلّ شيء، كأَنّه في طوله مشذَّب، أَي مجرَّد؛

شذب (لسان العرب) قال: ولا يقال للبائنِ الطُّول إِذا كان كثير اللحم مُشذَّبٌ حتى يكون في لحمه بعضُ النُّقصان؛ يقال: فرسٌ مُشَذَّبٌ إِذا كان طويلاً، ليس بكثير اللحم. وفي حديث علي، كرَم الله وجهه، شذَّبهم عنا تَخرُّم الآجال. وشَذَب عنه شَذْباً أَي ذبَّ.

كنن (لسان العرب) الكِنُّ والكِنَّةُ والكِنانُ: وقاء كل شيءٍ وسِتْرُه. وكَنَّ الشيءَ يَكُنُّه كَنَّاً وكُنوناً وأَكَنَّه وكَنَّنَه: ستره؛ وأَكننْتُه في نفسي: أَسْرَرْتُه. وفي التنزيل العزيز: أَو أَكنَنْتُم في أَنفسكم؛ أَي أَخفيْتم.

كنن (الصَحّاح في اللغة) الكِنُّ: السُترة؛

وكن (لسان العرب) قال أَبو عبيدة: هي الأُكْنة والوُكْنَة والوُقْنة والأُقْنةُ. الأَصمعي: الوَكْرُ والوَكْنُ جميعاً المكان الذي يدخل فيه الطائر والوُكْنة اسم لكل وَكْر وعُشّ، والتَوكُّنُ: حُسْنُ الاتّكاء في المجلس؛ قال الشاعر: قلتُ لها: إِيَاكِ أَن توكَني، في جِلْسةٍ عندي، أَو تلْبَني أَي تَرَبَعي في جِلْسَتِك. وتوكَّن أَي تمكَّن. والواكِنُ الجالس؛

الوَنَى (القاموس المحيط) ووَناهُ القَومُ: تركُوهُ، و~ الكُمَّ: شمَرَهُ. ووَنَّى توْنيةً: إِذا لم يَجِدَّ في العمَلِ.

وني (لسان العرب) الوَنا: الفَتْرةُ في الأَعمال والأُمور. وامرأَةٌ وناةٌ وأَناةٌ وأَنِيَةٌ: حليمةٌ بطيئةُ القِيام، الهمزة فيه بدل من الواو؛

أني (لسان العرب) وأَنَى أُنِيَاً فهو أَنِيٌّ: تأَخر وأَبطأَ. ويقال: لا تُؤنِ فُرْصَتَك أَي لا تؤخرها إِذا أَمْكَنَتْك. وكل شيء أَخَّرته فقد آنيْتَه. الجوهري: آناه يُؤنيه إِيناء أَي أَخَّره وحَبَسه وأَبطأَه؛

أنا (الصَحّاح في اللغة) وتأَنَّى في الأَمر، أَي تَرفق وتَنظَر. وآناهُ يُؤنيه إِيناءً، أَي أَخَّرَهُ وحبسَهُ وأَبطأَه.

نأت (لسان العرب) ونأَتَ إِذا أَنَّ، مثل نَهت.

نِيهٌ (القاموس المحيط) ونَفْسٌ ناهةٌ: مُنْتَهِيَةٌ عن الشيء.

ناهَ (القاموس المحيط) والنَّوْهُ، ويُضَمُّ: الانْتهاءُ عن الشيء.

نوه (لسان العرب) وناهَتْ نفسي عن الشيء تَنْوهُ وتَناهُ نَوْهاً: انتهت، وقيل: نُهْتُ عن الشيء أَبَيْتُه وتركته.

عَنَ (القاموس المحيط) ورأَيْتُه عَيْن عُنَة، أَي: الساعة. وأَعْننْتُ بعُنَةٍ لا أَدْري ما هي: تَعرَّضْتُ لشيءٍ لا أَعْرِفُهُ. وهْوَ عَنانٌ عن الخَيْرِ، كشَدَّادٍ: بطيءٌ.

عنن (لسان العرب) عَنَ الشيءُ يَعِنُ ويَعُنُ عنناً وعُنوناً: ظَهَر أَمامك؛ وعَنَ يعِنُ ويَعُنُ عنَاً وعُنوناً واعْتَنَ: اعترَضَ وعَرَض؛ وعن: معناها ما عدا الشيء، تقول: رميت عن القوسْ لأَنه بها قَذَفَ سهمه عنها وعدَّاها، والاعْتِنانُ: الاعتراض. وامرأَة معَنَّة: تَعْتنُ وتعْترض في كل شيء؛ ويقال: هو لك بين الأَوْبِ والعنَن إِمَا أَن يؤُوبَ إِليك، وإِما أَن يعْرِضَ عليك؛ قال ابن مقبل: تُبْدي صُدوداً، وتُخْفي بيننا لطَفاً يأْتي محارِمَ بين الأَوْبِ والعَنَن. وقيل معناه بين الطاعة والعصيان.

الرَجْمُ (القاموس المحيط) الرَجْمَ: القتْلُ، والقذْفُ، والغيبُ، والظنُّ، والخليلُ، والنديمُ، واللَعْنُ، والشَتْمُ، والهجرانُ، والطَرْدُ ورَمْيٌ بالحجارة، واسْمُ ما يُرجَمُ به

رجم (مقاييس اللغة) الراء والجيم والميم أصلٌ واحدٌ يرجع إلى وجهٍ واحد، وهي [الرَمْي بـ] الحجارة، ثم يستعار ذلك. من ذلك الرِّجام، وهي الحجارة. يقال رُجم فلانٌ، إذا ضُرب بالحجارة. وقال بعضهم: الرَجام حجرٌ يشدُّ بطرف عَرْقُوة الدَلو، ليكون أسرعَ لانحدارها.والذي يستعار من هذا قولُهم: رَجَمْتُ فلاناً بالكلام ، إذا شتَمْته. وذُكر في تفسير ما حكاه عز وجلّ في قصة إبراهيم عليه السلام: لَئِنْ لَمْ تَنْتَهِ لأَرْجُمَنَّكَ [مريم 46] أي لأشْتُمَنَّك؛ وكأنه إذا شتمه فقد رجَمه بالكلام، أي ضربه به، كما يُرجَم الإنسان بالحجارة. وقال قوم: لأرجُمنك: لأقتُلنك.

سحت (مقاييس اللغة) السين والحاء والتاء أصلٌ صحيح منقاس. يقال سُحِت الشيء، إذا استؤصل، وأسْحت.

شيع (لسان العرب) وأشاع ببوله إشاعةً: حذف به وفرّقه. وأشاعت الناقة ببولها واشتاعت وأوْزغت وأزْغلت، كل هذا: أرسلته متفرّقاً ورمَته رَمْياً وقطّعته ولا يكون ذلك إلا إذا ضرَبها الفحل.

شع (مقاييس اللغة) الشين والعين في المضاعف أصلٌ واحد يدلّ على التفرُّق والانتشار.

شعب (مقاييس اللغة) الشين والعين والباء أصلان مختلفان، أحدهما يدلّ على الافتراق، والآخر على الاجتماع.

السَّبُ (القاموس المحيط) السَّبُ: سيْرٌ فوقَ العنق.

الشَطْبُ (القاموس المحيط) وشطب: قطعَ، ومالَ، و~ عنهُ: عدلَ وبَعُد. والشَطائبُ: الفرقُ المُختلفةُ.

شطب (لسان العرب) وشطَب عن الشيء: عَدل عنه. الأصمعي: شطف وشطَب إذا ذهب وتباعد.

البذُّ (القاموس المحيط) البذُّ: الغلبةُ، و~ من التمرِ: المُنتثِرُ، والبذيذةُ: النصيبُ. وابْتذذْتُ حقّي: أخذْتُه.

بذذ (لسان العرب) والعرب تقول: بذّ فلان فلاناً يَبُذّه بذّاً إذا ما علاه وفاقه في حسن أو عمل كائناً ما كان. وتمربذٌّ: مُتفرّق لا يلْزَق بعضه ببعض كفذٍّ؛

بث (مقاييس اللغة) الباء والثاء أصلٌ واحد، وهو تفريق الشيء وإظهاره؛ والله تعالى خلق الخلْق وبثّهم في الأرض لمعاشهم. وبثَثْتُ الطَعامَ والتمرَ إذا قلبْته* وألقيتَ بعضه على بعض، وبثَثْتُ الحديث أي نشرْته.

بثَّ (القاموس المحيط) وأبثَثْتُك: أظهرْتُه لك. وتمرٌ بثٌّ: مُتفرِّقٌ، منْثورٌ.

بثث (الصَحاح في اللغة) بَثَّ الخبرَ وأبثَّه بمعنىً، أي نشره. يقال: أبْثَثْتُك سرّي، أي أظهرته لك. وبثّث الخبرَ، شُدّد للمبالغة، فانْبثَّ أي انتشر.

بثث (لسان العرب) بثَّ الشيءَ والخَبرَ يَبُثّه ويبِثّه بثّاً، وأبثَّه، بمعنى، فانبثَّ: فرّقه فتفرّق، ونشره؛ قال: أبْثَثْتُك أي أظْهرْتُ لك بثّي. وفي حديث أم زرع: لا تبُثُّ حديثنا تبْثيثاً؛ وبُثَّت البُسُطُ إذا بُسطت. قال الله عز وجل: وزرابيُّ مَبْثُوثةٌ؛ قال الفراءُ: مبْثوثة كثيرة. وقوله عز وجل: فكانتْ هباءً مُنبثّاً؛ أي غُباراً مُنتشراً. وتمْرٌ بثٌّ إذا لم يُجوّد كنْزُه فتفرَّق؛ ويروى تنُثُّ، بالنون، بمعناه. واستبثّه إياه: طلب إليه أن يبُثّه إياه. ويقال: أبثَثْتُ فلاناً سرّي، بالألف، إبثاثاً أي أطلعْتُه عليه وأظهرْته له. وبثَّثْتُ الخبر، شُدّد للمبالغة، فانبثَّ أي انتشر. وبثْبثْتُ الأمرَ إذا فتّشت عنه وتخبرْته. وبثْبثْتُ الخبر بثْبثةً: نشرْتُه، والغُبار: هيّجته.

بسس (الصَحاح في اللغة) وبسستُ المال في البلاد فانبسّ، إذا أرسلته فتفرّق فيها، مثل بثثْتُه فانبثّ.

البيُّ (القاموس المحيط) وبيّيتُ الشيءَ تَبييًا: بيّنْتُه، وأوْضحْتُه.

بيي (لسان العرب) حَيّاك الله وبيّاك، قيل: حَيّاك ملّكك، وقيل: أبقاك، ويقال: اعتمدك بالمُلْك، وقيل: أصلحك، وقيل: قرّبك؛ الأخيرة حكاها الأصمعي عن الأحمر. ويقال: بَيّنْتُ الشيء وبيّيْتُه إذا أوضحته. والتّبيِيُّ التبيين من قرب.

بيض (لسان العرب) وبيْضةُ كل شيء حوْزتُه. ويقال: بيَضْت الإناء إذا فرّغته، وبيّضته إذا ملأته، وهو من الأضداد.

بدا (لسان العرب) بدا الشيءُ يَبْدو بَدْواً وبُدُوّاً وبداءً وبداً؛ الأخيرة عن سيبويه: ظهر. وكل شيء أظهرته فقد أبديته وبدّيته؛ وأبديْته أنا: أظهرته.

كسا (لسان العرب) والكُسْيُ: مؤخر العجز، وقيل: مؤخر كل شيء، والجمع أكساء؛

كرس (لسان العرب) وتكرّس أُسُّ البناء: صَلُب واشتدّ. والكُرْسيّ معروف واحد والكراسي، وربما قالوا كِرْسيّ؛ بكسر الكاف. قال الزجاج: وهذا القول بَيّنٌ لأن الذي نعرفه من الكُرْسي في اللغة الشيء الذي يُعتَمد عليه ويُجْلس.

صيا (لسان العرب) الصَيَةُ: ما يَخْرُجُ من رحمِ الشاة بعد الولادة. والصَيَةُ: أُنثى الطائر الذي يقال له الهامّ. وصيصيَةُ الثَّور: قَرْنه لاحتصانه به من عَدُوّه؛ وصيصيَةُ الديك: مِخْلبان في ساقيه، وقيل: صيصيَةُ الديك وغيره من الطَّيْر الإصْبع الزائدةُ التي في مُؤخرِ رجله، وقيل: صيصيَةُ الدّيك شوكته لأنه يَتحصّنُ بها.

أصا (القاموس المحيط) أصا النبْتُ يأصُو: اتصل، وكثُر.

عصا (لسان العرب) العصا: العُودُ، أُنثى.

سبع (لسان العرب) وسبَعَ القومَ يسبَعُهم، بالفتح، سبْعاً: صار سابعهم. وسبَعه يس○بَعُه (يستبِعُه) سبْعا: طعن عليه وعابه وشتمه ووقع فيه بالقول القبيح.

سبي (لسان العرب) ويقال: ما له سباهُ الله أي غرّبه، وسباه. إذا لعنه؛ ومنه قول امرئ القيس: فقالت: سَباك الله إنك فاضحي أي أبْعدك وغرّبك؛ ومنه قول الآخر: يفُضّ الطّلْح والشّرْيان هضْباً، وعُود النّبْع مُجتلباً سَبيًا ومنه السَبْيُ لأنه يُغرب عن وطنه، والمعنى متقارب لأن اللّعْن إبْعاد.

يندا (القاموس المحيط) وتندّى: تسخّى، وأفضَل، كأندى، فهو نديُّ الكفّ. وأندى: كثُر عطاياه، أو حسُن صوْتُه.

ندا (الصَحَاح في اللغة) والندى: الجود. ورجلٌ ندٍ، أي جواد. وفلان أَندى من فلان، إذا كان أكثر خيراً منه. وفلان يَتَندَى على أصحابه، أي يتسخَّى. ولا تقل يُنَدّي على أصحابه.

ندي (لسان العرب) النَدَى: البلَلُ. والنَدى: السَخاء والكرم. وتندَّى عليهم ونَدِيَ : تسخَّى ، وأَنْدى ندَى كثيراً كذلك. وأَنْدى عليه: أَفضل. وأَنْدى الرَّجلُ: كثر نداه أي عَطاؤه، وأَنْدى إذا تَسخَّى، وأَنْدى الرجلُ إذا كثر نداه على إخوانه، وكذلك انْتدى وتندَّى. وفلان يَتَندَى على أَصحابه: كما تقول هو يَتسخَّى على أَصحابه، ولا تقل يُنَدّي على أَصحابه.

ودن (لسان العرب) ودَنَ الشيءَ يدِنُه وَدْناً ووِداناً، فهو مَوْدون ووَدينٌ أي منقوع، فاتَّدَن: بَلَّهُ فابْتَلَّ؛ وَدِين أي مَوْدُونٍ مبلول من وَدَنْتُه أَدِنُه وَدْناً إذا بللته.

عَدا (القاموس المحيط) عَدا عَدْواً وعُدُوّا وعدواناً، محرّكَةً، وتَعْداءً و~ عنه: جاوزَهُ، وتركَهُ، كتَعدَّاهُ. وأعْدى الأمْرَ: جاوزَ غيْرَهُ إليه، وعَدا: فِعْلٌ يُسْتَثْنى به، مَعَ ما وبدُونه.

عد (مقاييس اللغة) العين والدال أصلٌ صحيح واحد لا يخلو من العَدّ الذي هو الإحصاء. ومن الإعداد الذي هو تهيئة الشَيء. والعَدد مقدار ما يُعدُّ، ويقال: ما أكثَرَ عديدَ بني فلان وعَددهم. وإنّهم ليتعادُّون ويتعدَّدُون على عشرة آلاف، أي يزيدون عليها.

العَدُّ (القاموس المحيط) العَدُّ: الإِحْصاءُ، والاسمُ: العَدَدُ والعَديدُ، كالعِدِّ والعِدادِ، بكسرهما، و~ من القَوْم: مَنْ يُعَدُّ فيهم. والعَديدةُ: الحِصَّةُ.

§ 6.—VI, 31-40

ePSD: mahāru

BU'I [FACE] wr. BU-I "to face" Akk. mahāru

šu gid [ACCEPT] wr. šu gid$_2$ "to accept" Akk. mahāru

šu teĝ [ACCEPT] wr. šu teĝ$_4$; šu teĝ$_3$ "to accept" Akk. leqû; mahāru

ePSD: šarrāqu

luniĝzuha [THIEF] wr. lu$_2$-niĝ$_2$-zuh-a "thief" Akk. šarrāqu

ePSD: šarāqu

zuh [STEAL] wr. zuh "to steal" Akk. šarāqu

ePSD: šurqu

niĝzuha [STOLEN GOODS] wr. niĝ$_2$-zuh-a "stolen goods" Akk. šurqu

ePSD: šaĝan

šaĝan [FLASK] wr. šaĝan; ^{dug}šaĝan "a flask" Akk. šikkatu

šaĝan [MERCHANT] wr. šaĝan-la$_2$; šaĝan "an apprentice merchant" Akk. šamallû

ePSD: ŠA.GA$_2$

šaĝar [OPPRESSED] wr. šaĝa; ša-ĝa$_2$; šaĝa$_x$(LU$_2$) "a wronged person; (to be) slain; (to be) afflicted, oppressed" Akk. hablu; šagšu

ePSD: šagāšu

gaz [KILL] wr. gaz; gaz$_2$; kaz$_8$ "to kill, slaughter; to grind, grate; to beat; to thresh (grain); to execute, impose a death sentence; to break" Akk. dâku; habātu; hašālu; kaşāşu; pa'āşu; šagāšu

ePSD: ekallu

egal [PALACE] wr. e$_2$-gal "palace; temple" Akk. ekallu

AALD: êkallu (s.) الهيكل، القصر الملكي، الغرفة الرئيسية للقصر

مخر (مقاييس اللغة) الميم والخاء والراء أصلٌ يدل على شَقّ وفتح. يقال مَخرت السَفينةُ الماءَ مخراً: شقَّته.

مخر (الصَحَاح في اللغة) وامْتَخَرْتُ القومَ: انتقيت خيارهم ونُخْبَتَهُم. والمِخْرةُ والمُخْرَةُ: الشيء الذي تختاره. والماخورُ: مجلسُ الفُسَّاقِ.

مخر (لسان العرب) وامْتَخَرَ الشيءَ: اخْتاره. والماخُورُ: بَيْتُ الريبة، وهو أيضاً الرجل الذي يَلي ذلك البيتَ ويقود إليه.

خرت (مقاييس اللغة) الخاء والراء والتاء أصلٌ يدلُّ على تثَقُّبٍ وشِبْهه. فالخُرْت: ثَقْب الإبرة والأخرات: الحَلَق في رؤوس النُّسوع. والخِرّيتُ: الرجلُ الدَليلُ الماهر بالدَّلالة. وسُمّي بذلك لشقّه المَفازة، كأنه يدخُل في أخْرَاتِها. ويقال خرَتْنا الأرض، إذا عَرفْناها فلم تَخْفَ علينا طرقُها.

هكل (مفاييس اللغة) الْهاءُ وَالْكافُ وَاللَّامُ يَدُلُّ عَلَى إِشْرافٍ وَعُلُوٍّ.

هكل (تهذيب اللغة) أما هكل فقد استعمل منه الهَيْكل وهو البناء المرتفع تُشبَهُ به الفرسُ الطويل، ومنه قول امرىء القيس: بمُنْجرِدٍ قَيْدِ الأوابد هَيْكلِ

هكل (العين) والهيْكلُ: بيتٌ للنَصارى فيه صنمٌ على خِلْقَةِ مريم عليها السَلام فيما يُذْكَرُ، قال: مَشْيَ النَصارى حول بيت الهَيكَلِ

هكل (لسان العرب) والهيْكلُ الضخمُ من كل شيء. الهيْكل النبت الذي طال وعظُم وبلغ وكذلك الشجر، واحدته هيْكله. وهَيْكل الزرع: نما وطال. الهَيْكلُ: البناء المُشرف. والهَيْكلُ بيت الأصنام.

هكل (تاج العروس) والهيْكلُ: البناءُ المُشْرِفُ قيلَ هذا هو الأَصْلُ ثم سُمّي به بُيوتُ الأَصْنام مجازاً.

سجا (لسان العرب) سَجى الميتَ: غطّاه. وسَجَّيْت الميت تسجيةً إذا مددْت عليه ثوباً. التَسْجِيَةُ: أن يُسجَّى الميتُ بثوب أي يُغطَّى به؛

شجج (الصَحاح في اللغة) وشَجّت السفينةُ البحر، أي شقّته.
شجج (لسان العرب) الشَّجَة: واحدةُ شِجاج الرَّاس، وهي عشر: الحارصةُ وهي التي تَقشرُ الجلد ولا تُدميه، والدَامية وهي التي تُدميه، والباضِعةُ وهي التي تشق اللحم شقّاً كبيراً، والسّمْحاقُ وهي التي يبقى بينها وبين العظم جلدة رقيقة،
شجا (لسان العرب) وأشْجَيْتُ فلاناً عنّي: إمّا غريمٌ، وإما رجُلٌ سألك فأعْطيته شيئاً أرْضيْته به فذهب فقد أشْجيْته. ويقال للغريم: شَجيَ عنّي يَشْجى أي ذهب. وأشْجاه الشيءُ: أغصَه. وفي مثلِ للعرب: ويلٌ للشَجي من الخلي، وقد تُشدد ياءُ الشَجي فيما حكاه صاحب العين، قال ابن سيده: والأول أعرف. قال ابن بري: قال أبو جعفر أحمد بن عبيد المعروف بأبي عَصيدة الصواب ويلٌ الشَّجيّ من الخَليّ، بتشديد الياء، وأما الشَّجي، بالتخفيف، فهو الذي أصابه الشّجا وهو الغصَصُ، وأما الحزينُ فهو الشَّجيُّ، بتشديد الياء، قال: ووجهه أن يكون المفعولَ من شجوْته أشْجوه، فهو مشْجُوٌّ وشَجيٌّ، كما تقول جرحْته فهو مجْروحٌ وجريحٌ، وأما شَج، بالتخفيف، فهو اسمُ الفاعل من شَجي يَشْجى، فهو شَجٍ؛ قال أبو زيد: الشَجي المشغول والخلي الفارغُ. وقيل: معنى قولهم ويلٌ للشَجيّ من الخَليّ ويل للمهموم من الفارغ، قال: وشَجي إذا غصّ. أبو العباس في الفصيح عن الأصمعي: ويلٌ للشَجيّ من الخَليّ، بتثقيل الياء فيهما؛ وأنشد: ويلُ الشَجيّ من الخَليّ، فإنه نصِبُ الفؤاد، بحُزْنه مهمومُ والشَجْوُ: الحاجة.
سرق (مقاييس اللغة) السين والراء والقاف أصلٌ يدلّ على أخْذ شيء في خفاء وستر.

§ 7.—VI, 41-56

ePSD: lu [PERSON] wr. lu$_2$; mu-lu; mu-lu$_2$; lu$_{10}$; lu$_6$ "who(m), which; man; (s)he who, that which; of; ruler; person" Akk. amēlu; ša
ePSD: wardu
ama'atud [SLAVE] wr. ama-a-tud; ama-tu "house-born slave" Akk. dušmû; wardu
ePSD: alpu
gud [OX] wr. gud; gu$_3$-ra "bull, ox; cattle; calf; lion" Akk. alpu; lī'um
ePSD: immeru
udu [SHEEP] wr. udu; e-ze$_2$ "sheep" Akk. Immeru
ePSD: imēru
anše [EQUID] wr. anše "donkey; equid" Akk. imēru
ePSD: hurāşu
KU'UDKI [GOLD] wr. KU$_3$.UD.KI "gold" Akk. hurāşu
kugsig [GOLD] wr. kug-sig$_{17}$ "gold" Akk. hurāşu
ePSD: šâmu
sa [PAY FOR] wr. sa$_{10}$ "to pay for, buy; to be paid for, sell" Akk. šâmu
ePSD: māru
dumu [CHILD] wr. dumu; du$_5$-mu "child, son, daughter" Akk. māru
dumunita [SON] wr. dumu-nita "son" Akk. māru
hibira [SON] wr. hibira "son" Akk. māru
AALD: balu (conj. prep.) (balum) بلا، بدون
ePSD: riksu
dagan [TOTALITY] wr. da-gan "totality; assembly; band" Akk. kullatu; puhru; riksu
dim [POST] wr. dim; dim$_3$; ^{geš}dim "post, pillar, pole; binding, knot, bond" Akk. mahrašu; makūtu; riksu; timmu
ePSD: rakāsu
kešed [BIND] wr. keš$_2$ "to bind" Akk. rakāsu
sir [BIND] wr. sir$_3$; sir$_2$ "to bind" Akk. rakāsu
tag [TOUCH] wr. tag "to touch, take hold of; to bind; to attack" Akk. lapātu; rakāsu
zu kešed [GATHER] wr. zu$_2$ keš$_2$ "to gather, to assemble; to organize; to bind" Akk. kaşāru; rakāsu
AALD: rikištu See rikistu
AALD: maşru (see naşāru)
AALD: naşāru (v.) ينصر، يحافظ، يراقب، ينتظر، يحمي
AALD: maşşartu (s.) (see manşārtu) يراقب، يحرس
ePSD: maşşartum
ennuĝ [IMPRISONMENT] wr. en-nu-ĝa$_2$; en-nuĝ$_x$(NUN); en-nu-uĝ$_3$; en-nu-uĝ$_5$; en-uĝ$_3$-ĝa$_2$ "watch, guard; watch (as a division of night time); imprisonment; prison" Akk. maşşartum

لو (مقاييس اللغة) اللام والواو كلمةٌ أداة، وهي لو، يُتمنَّى بها. وأهل العربية يقولون: لو يدلُّ على امتناع الشيء لامتناع غيره، ووقوعه لوقوع غيره. نحو قولهم لو خرج زيد لخرجت.

لو (الصَحاح في اللغة) لَوْ: حرفُ تمنٍ، وهو لامتناع الثاني من أجل امتناع الأوَّل، تقول: لَوْ جئتني لأكرمتك. وهو خلافُ إنْ التي للجزاء، لأنَّها توقع الثانية من أجل وجود الأول.

خرص (مقاييس اللغة) وأصلٌ آخر، يقال للحلْقة من الذهب خُرْصٌ

الخِرْصُ (القاموس المحيط) والخُرْصُ، بالضم ويُكسرُ: حَلْقةُ الذهب والفضة، أو حَلْقةُ القُرْط، أو الحَلْقةُ الصغيرةُ من الحُلِيّ

ورد (مقاييس اللغة) الواو والراء والدال: أصلان، أحدهما الموافاة إلى الشيء،

ورد (لسان العرب) وفي اللغة: ورد بلد كذا وماء كذا إذا أَشرف عليه، دخله أو لم يدخله، قال: فالوُرودُ، بالإجماع، ليس بدخول. الجوهري: ورد فلان وُرُوداً حضر، وأورده غيره واسْتَوْرده أي أَحْضَره. ابن سيده: تورَّده واستَوْرَده كوَرَده كما قالوا: علا قِرْنَه واستعلاه. والوِرْدُ القَطيعُ من الطَّيْر. والوِرْدُ الجَيْشُ على التشبيه به؛ والورْدُ الإبل بعينها.

أما (لسان العرب) الأَمَةُ: المَمْلوكةُ خلاف الحُرَّة.وفي التهذيب: الأَمة المرأَة ذات العُبودة، وقد أَقرَت بالأُمُوَة.

حمر (لسان العرب) والحمارُ: النَّهّاق من ذوات الأَربع، أَهلِياً كان أَو وَحْشِياً. وقال الأَزهري: الحمارُ العَيْرُ الأَهْليُّ والوحشي، وجمعه أَحْمِرَة وحُمُرٌ وحميرٌ وحُمْرٌ وحُمُورٌ، وحُمُراتٌ جمع الجمع، كَجُزُراتٍ وطُرُقاتٍ، والأُنثى حِمارة. واليحمور أَيضاً: دابة تشبه العنْزَ؛ وقيل: اليحمور حمار الوحش.

أمر (لسان العرب) والإِمَّرُ الخروف. والإِمَّرَةُ الرِّخْلُ، والخروف ذكر، والرِّخْلُ أُنثى.

علب (مقاييس اللغة) العين واللام والباء أصلانِ صحيحان، يدلُّ أحدهما على غِلَظٍ في الشيء وجُسْأة، والآخر على أثَر.جانبي عنقه.

حدل (لسان العرب) من الثور أَي من علب الثَّور من عقب الثَّور.

ألب (لسان العرب) والتَّأْلَبُ الشَّدِيدُ الغَلِيظُ الـمُجْتَمِعُ من حُمُرِ الوَحْش. والتَّأْلَبُ الوعِلُ، والأُنثى تأْلَبةٌ، تاؤه زائدة لقولهم أَلَبَ الحِمارُ أُتُنَه.

علف (لسان العرب) ورجل عُلْفُوف: جافٍ كثير اللحم والشعر. والعلِّف الكثير الأَكل.

ألف (مقاييس اللغة) الهمزة واللام والفاء أصل واحد، يدلُّ على انضمام الشيء إلى الشيء، والأشياء الكثيرة أيضاً.

لفف (لسان العرب) اللَّفَف: كثرةُ لحم الفخذين، وهو في النساء نعت، وفي الرجال عيب. لَفَّ لَفّاً ولَفَفاً، وهو أَلَفُّ. ورجل أَلفُّ: ثقيل. الأَلفُّ الرجل الثقيل البطيء.

مرا (لسان العرب) ابن الأَعرابي: المَرِيءُ الطعام (قوله« المرئ الطعام» كذا بالأصل مهموزاً وليس هومن هذا الباب. وقوله« المري الرجل» كذا في الأصل بلا ضبط ولعله بوزن ما قبله.) الخفيف، والمري الرجل المقبول في خلقه وخُلُقه.

مَرُؤ (القاموس المحيط) والمَرْءُ، مُثَلَّثة الميم: الإِنسانُ، أو الرَّجُلُ، ولا يُجْمَعُ من لَفْظِه، أو سُمِعَ: مَرْؤُون، والذِّئْبُ، وهي بهاءٍ، ويقالُ: مَرَةٌ والامرأة.

مرأ (لسان العرب) الـمُرُوءة: كَمالُ الرُّجُولِيَّة. مَرُؤَ الرجلُ يَمْرُؤُ مُرُوءة، فهو مَرِيءٌ، على فعيل، وتَمَرَّأَ، على تَفَعَّلَ: صار ذا مُروءة. والمَرْءُ: الإِنسان. تقول: هذا مَرْءٌ، وكذلك في النصب والخفض تفتح الميم، هذا هو القياس. وقد ورد في حديث الحسن: أَحْسِنُوا مَلأَكُمْ أَيها الـمَرْؤُون. قال ابن الأَثير: هو جَمْعُ المَرْءِ، وهو الرَّجل. وأَلحقوا أَلف الوصل في المؤَنث أَيضاً، فقالوا: امْرأَةٌ، فإِذا عرَّفوها قالوا: الـمَرأَة. وقد حكى أَبو علي: الامْرأَة. الليث: امْرأَةٌ تأْنيث امْرِئٍ.

مرأ (العباب الزاخر) وتقول: هذا امرؤ ورأيت امرأً ومررت بأمرئٍ معرباً من مكانين، وهذه امرأةٌ؛ مفتوحة الراء على كل حال، فإن صغَّرت أسقطت ألف الوصل فقلت: مُرَيءٌ ومُرَيْئَةٌ، وفي حديث النبي -صلى الله عليه وسلم-: إني لأكْرَه أن أرى الرجل ثائراً فرِيْصُ رقبته قائماً على مُرَيْئَته يضربُها. تصغيرُه المرأة استضعاف لها واستصغار لُيري أن الباطش بمثلها في ضعفها لئيم،

سوم (لسان العرب) السَّوْمُ: عَرْضُ السِّلْعَة على البيع. وسامني الرجلُ بسِلْعته سَوْماً: وذلك حين يذكر لك هو ثمنها، والاسم من جميع ذلك السُّومَةُ والسِّيمَةُ. وإِنه لغالي السِّيمة والسُّومة إِذا كان يُغْلي السَّوْم.

بل (مقاييس اللغة) الباء واللام في المضاعف له أصولٌ خمسة هي معظم الباب. ومن ذلك التي هي العطيّة. قال الخليل: يقال للإنسان إذا حسُنَتْ حالُه بعد الهزال: قد ابتلَّ وتبلَّل. ويقولون: "لا أفعلُ كذا ما بَلَّ بَحْرٌ صُوفَةً" ويقال للبخيل: ما تَبُلُّ إحدى يديْه الأُخْرَى. ومنه "بُلُّوا أرحامكم ولو بالسَّلام". ويقال لا تبلُك عندي بالَّةٌ ولا بلالٌ ولا بَلالِ على وزن حَذامِ. والأصل الثالث: أخذ الشَّيء والذَّهابُ به. يقال بَلَّ فلانٌ بكذا، إذا وقَعَ في يده. قال ذو الرُّمَّة: ويقولون: "لَئن بَلَّ به لَيبلَّن بما يودّه. ويقال: إنه لَبِلٌّ بالقرينة. ويقولون: إنه لَيبِلُّ بهِ الخَيْرُ، أي يوافقُه.

بلو/ي (مقاييس اللغة) الباء واللام والواو والياء، أصلان: أحدهما إخلاق الشيء، *والثاني نوعٌ من الاختبار، ويحمل عليه الإخبار أيضاً.فأمّا الأول فقال الخليل: بلِيَ يَبْلَى فهو بالٍ. قال ابنُ الأعرابيّ: يقال ابتليْتُه فأبلاني، أي استخبرْتُه فأخبَرَني. ذكر ما شذَّ عن هذين الأصلين: قال الخليل: تقول: الناس بذي بِلِيّ وذي بَلِيّ، أي هم متفرِّقون. قال أبو زيد: هم بذي بليانٍ أيضاً، وذلك إذا بَعُدَ بعضُهم [عن بعض] وكانوا طوائفَ مع غير إمامٍ يجمعُهم.

بلا (لسان العرب) بَلَوْتُ الرجل بَلْواً وبَلاءً وابْتَلَيْتُه: اخْتَبَرْتُه، وبَلاهُ يَبْلُوه بَلْواً إِذا جَرَّبَه واخْتَبَره. وأَبْلَيْت الرجل: أَحلفته. وابتلى هو: استحْلَف واستَعْرَف؛ وأَبلَيت فلاناً يميناً إِبْلاءً إِذا حلفت له فطَيَّبت بها نفسه، ويقال: ابتليْت أَي استحْلَفتُ؛ يقال: ما باليته وما باليت به أَي لم أَكترث به. وفي الحديث: هؤلاء في الجنة ولا أُبالي وهؤلاء في النار ولا أُبالي؛ وحكى الأَزهري عن جماعة من العلماء: أَن معناه لا أَكره. وحديث الرجل مع عَمَله وأَهلِه وماله قال: هو أَقلُّهم به بالَةً أَي مبالاةً.

ثبي (مقاييس اللغة) الثاء والباء والياء أصلٌ واحد، وهو الدوام على الشيء. قاله الخليل.والتصغير فيهما ثُبَيَّة، وقياسُه ما بدأنا به الباب في ذكر التثبية، وهو من ثَبَى على الشيء إذا دام.

ثبت (الصَحاح في اللغة) ثَبتَ الشيءُ ثَباتاً وثُبوتاً؛ وأَثْبَتَهُ غيره وثَبَّتَهُ، بمعنىً.

رَكزَ (القاموس المحيط) وارْتكزَ: ثَبتَ، والمَركَزُ: وسَطُ الدائرة، ومَوْضعُ الرّجُلِ، ومَحلُّه، وحيثُ أُمِرَ الجُنْدُ أن يلْزَموهُ. والرِّكْزُ الصوتُ الخفيُّ، وقيل: هو الصوت ليس بالشديد. وفي حديث ابن عباس في قوله تعالى: فرّتْ من قسْورة، قال: هو رِكْز الناس، قال: الرِّكْزُ الحِسّ والصوت الخفي فجعل القَسْورَةَ نفسها رِكْزاً لأن القسورة جماعة الرجال،

رَكزَ (القاموس المحيط) وارْتكزَ: ثَبتَ،

ركس (لسان العرب) الرِّكْسُ: الجماعة من الناس، وقيل: الكثير من الناس، والرِّكْسُ شبيه بالرَّجيع. يقال: رَكسْتُ الشيء وأرْكَسْتُه إذا رَدَدْته ورَجعْته، وفي رواية: إنه رِكِيس، فعيل بمعنى مفعول؛ ومنه الحديث: اللهم أركِسْهما في الفتنة رَكْساً؛ والرَّكْسُ: قلبُ الشيء على رأسه أو رَدُّ أوله على آخره؛ وقال شمر: بلغني عن ابن الأعرابي أنه قال المَنْكوس والمَرْكوس المُدبر عن حاله. والرَّكْسُ رَدُّ الشيء مقلوباً. والرَّاكِسُ: الهادي، وهو الثور الذي يكون في وَسطِ البَيْدر عند الدِّياس والبقر حوله تدور ويرْتكسُ هو مكانه، والأُنثى راكسة.

نصَرَ (القاموس المحيط) نصَرَ المَظْلومَ نصْراً ونُصوراً: أعانَهُ، ونصَرَهُ منه: نَجّاهُ وخلَّصَهُ، وهو ناصِرٌ ونُصَرٌ، كصُرَدٍ، من نُصّارٍ وأنْصارٍ ونَصْرٍ، كصَحْبٍ. والنَّصيرُ: الناصرُ.

نظر (مقاييس اللغة) النون والظاء والراء أصلٌ صحيح يرجع فروعُه إلى معنىً واحد وهو تأمُّلُ الشَّيء ومعاينته، ثم يُستعار ويُتَّسع فيه. ويقولون: نظرْتُه، أي انتظرته.

نظر (لسان العرب) النَّظَر: حِسُّ العين، نظَره يَنْظُره نظَراً ومَنْظَراً ومَنْظرة ونظَر إليه. وناظُورُ الزرع والنخل وغيرهما: حَافِظُه؛ والطاء نبطيَّة.

مصر (لسان العرب) والمِصْرُ الحاجِزُ والحدُّ بين الشيئين؛ وأهلُ مصْرَ يكتبون في شروطهم: اشترى فلان الدار بمُصُورِها أي بحدودها، وكذلك يكْتُبُ أهلُ هجَر. والمِصْرُ الحدّ في كل شيء، وقيل: المصر الحَدُّ في الأَرض خاصة.الجوهري: مِصْر هي المدينة المعروفة، تذكر وتؤنث؛ عن ابن السراج. والمِصْران الكوفةُ والبصْرةُ؛ والمصر الحاجز بين الشيئين.

نصر (مقاييس اللغة) النون والصاد والراء أصلٌ صحيح يدلُّ على إتيان خير وإيتائه. والنَّصْر العطاء.

نصَرَ (القاموس المحيط) نصَرَ المَظْلومَ نصْراً ونُصوراً: أعانَهُ، ونصَرَهُ منه: نَجّاهُ وخلَّصَهُ، وهو ناصِرٌ ونُصَرٌ، كصُرَدٍ، من نُصّارٍ وأنْصارٍ ونَصْرٍ، كصَحْبٍ. والنَّصيرُ: الناصرُ. ورجلٌ نصْرٌ، وقومٌ نصْرٌ، أو النُّصْرَةُ: حُسْنُ المعونةِ.

§ 8.—VI, 57-69

ePSD: riābu

<u>sug</u> <u>[REPLACE]</u> wr. sug_6 "to repay a loan; to replace" Akk. apālu; riābu

ePSD: MAŠ.EN.KAK

<u>mašga'en</u> <u>[STATUS]</u> wr. MAŠ.EN.KAK; MAŠ.KAK "a social status or profession" Akk. muškēnu

AALD: muškēnu (maškēnu) المسكين؛ العامي، الفقير، المحروم، نعت شخص يعتمد على الملك

رأب (لسان العرب) رَأَبَ إذا أَصْلَح. ورَأَبَ الصَّدْعَ والإِناءَ يرْأَبه رَأْباً ورأْبةً: شعبه، وأصْلحه؛ وكلُّ ما أصْلحْته، فقد رأَبْته؛ ومنه قولهم: اللهم ارْأَبْ بينهم أي أصلِحْ؛ والرُّؤْبةُ، مهموزةٌ: ما تُسَدُّ به الثُّلْمة؛

رعب (مقاييس اللغة) الراء والعين والباء أصولٌ ثلاثة: أحدها الخوف، والثاني المَلْء، والآخر القطْع.

كيك (لسان العرب) ابن شميل: الكَيْكاء والكَوْكى هما السَّرطانُ أي من لا خير فيه من الرجال.

كوك (لسان العرب) ابن شميل: الكَيْكاء والكَوْكى هما السَّرطانُ أي من لا خير فيه من الرجال.

الكَيْكَةُ (القاموس المحيط) والكَيْكاءُ: مَنْ لا خَيْرَ فيه.

مأس (لسان العرب) المأس: الذي لا يلتفت إلى موعظة أحد ولا يقبل قوله. ويقال: رجل ماسٌ بوزن مال أي خفيف طياش، وسنذكره أيضاً في موس، وقد مسأَ ومَأَس بينهم يَمْأَسُ مأْساً ومأَساً: أفسد؛

موس (لسان العرب) رجل ماسٌ مثل مالٍ: خفيف طيَّاش لا يلتفت إلى موعظة أحد ولا يقبل قوله؛

§ 9.—VI, 70-VII, 47

ePSD: halāqu

<u>zah</u> <u>[DISAPPEAR]</u> wr. zah_3; zah_2 "to disappear; to move away, withdraw; to stay away; (to be) lost; (to be) fugitive" Akk. duppuru; halāqu; nābutu; šerû

ePSD: šiqlu

<u>giĝ</u> <u>[UNIT]</u> wr. $gi\hat{g}_4$ "a unit of weight, shekel; a unit of area; a unit of volume" Akk. šiqlu

ePSD: šaqālu

<u>la</u> <u>[HANG]</u> wr. la_2; la; lal_2 "to supervise, check; to weigh, weigh (out), pay; to hang, balance, suspend, be suspended; to show, display; to bind; binding, (yoke-)team; to press, throttle; to winnow (grain); to carry" Akk. alālu; hanāqu; hiāţu; kamû; kasû; şimittu; kullumu; šaqālu; šuqalulu; zarû

حلق (لسان العرب) قال ابن سيده: حلَق اللبن ذهب، والحالق التي ذهب لبنها؛ كلاهما عن كراع. والحالق: الضامر. وحلَق الشيءَ يَحْلِقه حلْقاً: قشره،

الحلْقةُ (القاموس المحيط) وحلق رأسه يَحلِقُه حلْقا وتَحْلاقاً: أزالَ شَعرَه، كحلَّقه واحْتلقه. لأنَّهُ يَحلِقُ النبات كما يَحلِقُ الشَّعرَ.

ضبا (لسان العرب) وأضْبَى الرجلُ على ما في يدَيْه: أَمْسك، لغةٌ في أضْبأَ؛

ضبْته (القاموس المحيط) و~ عليه: أشْرفَ ليظفرَ به،

ضبط (لسان العرب) الضَبْطُ: لزوم الشيء وحَبْسه، ضَبط عليه وضَبطه يضبُط (* قوله «يضبط» شكل في الأصل في غير موضع بضم الباء، وهو مقتضى اطلاق المجد وضبط هامش نسخة من النهاية يوثق بها، لكن الذي في المصباح والمختار أنه من باب ضرب.) ضَبْطاً وضَباطة، وقال الليث: الضَبْطُ لزومُ شيء لا يفارقه في كل شيء، وضَبْطُ الشيء حفظُه بالحزم، والرجل ضابطٌ أي حازِمٌ.

ضَبَطَهُ (القاموس المحيط) ضَبَطَهُ ضَبْطاً وضَباطةً: حفظَهُ بالحزْمِ. ورجُلٌ وجملٌ ضابِطٌ وضَبَنْطى، كحبَنْطى: قويٌّ شديدٌ. وأضْبَطُ: يَعمَلُ بيدَيْهِ جميعاً وهي ضبطاء. وتضَبَّطَهُ: أخَذَهُ على حَبْسٍ وقَهْرٍ،

رمم (لسان العرب) وفي الحديث: فأَرَمَّ القومُ. قال أبو عبيد: أرَمَّ الرجل إرْماماً إذا سكت فهو مُرِمٌّ. والإرْمام السكوت. وأرَمَّ القومُ أي سكتوا؛ وقال حُميد الأرقط: يرِدْن، والليلُ مُرِمٌّ طائره، مُرْخَى رِواقاه هُجُودٌ سامره وكلّمه فما ترَمْرَم أي ما ردَّ جواباً. وترَمْرَم القومُ: تحركوا للكلام ولم يتكلّموا. التهذيب: أما التَرَمْرُمُ فهو أن يحرِّك الرجل شفتيه بالكلام. يقال: ما ترَمْرَم فلان بحرف أي ما نطق؛ الجوهري: وترَمْرَم إذاحَرَّك فاه للكلام؛

مرا (لسان العرب) ابن الأنباري: في قولهم مارى فلان فلاناً معناه قد استخرج ما عنده من الكلام والحُجَة، مأخوذ من قولهم مَرَيْت الناقة إذا مسحتَ ضَرْعها لِتدرّ. أبو زيد: المَرِيُّ الناقة تُحلب على غير ولد ولا تكون مَرِياً ومعها ولدها، وهو غير مهموز، وجمعها مَرايا.

ثقل (لسان العرب) وقوله تعالى: وأخرجت الأرض أثقالها؛ أثقالُها: كنوزُها ومَوْتاها؛ قال الفراء: لَفظَتْ ما فيها من ذهب أو فضة أو ميت، وقيل: معناه ما فيها من كنوز الذهب والفضة، ويقال: أعطه ثِقْله أي وَزْنه. المِثْقال في الأصل: مقدار من الوزن أيَّ شيءٍ كان من قليل أو كثير، فمعنى مِثْقال ذرَّة وزن ذرَّة، والناس يطلقونه في العرف على الدينار خاصة وليس كذلك؛ والمِثْقال: واحد مثاقيل الذهب. قال الأصمعي: دينار ثاقل إذا كان لا ينقص، ودنانير ثَواقِل؛ ومِثْقال الشيء: ميزانُه من مثله.

ثقل (الصّحاح في اللغة) والمِثْقالُ: واحد مثاقيلِ الذهب. قال الأصمعي: دينارٌ ثاقِلٌ، إذا كان لا ينقص. ودنانيرُ ثَواقِلُ. ومِثْقالُ الشيء: ميزانُهُ من مثله. وقولهم: ألقى عليه مَثاقيلَهُ، أي مؤونَتَهُ.

§ 11.—VII, 62-VIII, 3

AALD: tuššu (s.) كذب، افتراء، كلام خبيث
AALD: tušama See tuša
AALD: tuša (adv.) في ما اذا، في الواقع

تسس (العباب الزاخر) ابن الأعرابي: التُسُس -بضمّتين-: الأُصول الرديئة.
التُسُسُ (القاموس المحيط) التُسُسُ، بضمتين: الأُصُولُ الرَدِيَّةُ.
تسا (لسان العرب) ابن الأعرابي: ساتاهُ إذا لعب معه الشَفَلَّقة، وتاساهُ إذا آذاهُ واستَخَفَّ به، والله أعلم.
توس (لسان العرب) وتاساه إذا آذاه واستخف به.
وشم (لسان العرب) ويقال: بيننا وشِيمةٌ أي كلام شرّ أو عداوة.
الوَشْمُ (القاموس المحيط) والوَشِيمَةُ: الشَرُّ، والعداوةُ.
وشم (مقاييس اللغة) الواو والشين والميم: كلمةٌ واحدةٌ تدلُّ على تأثيرٍ في شيءٍ تزييناً له. ويتّسعون في هذا فيقولون: ما أصابتنا العام وشْمة، أي قطْرةٌ من مطر، وذلك لأنّ بالقطر تُوشَم الأرض. وربَما قالوا: كانت: بيني وبينه وشِيمةٌ، أي كلام. ولا يكون ذلك إلا في كلام عداوة. وهذا تمثيلٌ.
وشي (مقاييس اللغة) الواو والشين والحرف المعتل: أصلان، أحدُهما يدلُّ على تحسين شيءٍ وتزيينه، والآخر على نماءٍ وزيادة.
وشي (لسان العرب) ووَشّاه: نمْنَمه ونقشه وحَسَنه، ووشى الكذِبَ والحديثَ: رقمه وصَوَّره. والنَمّامُ يَشِي الكذبَ: يُؤَلِّفُه ويُلَوِّنه ويُزَيِّنه. الجوهري: يقال وَشى كلامَه: أي كذب. وأَوْشى الشيءَ: علمه؛ عن ابن الأعرابي؛ وأنشد: غَرَّاء بلْهاء لا يَشْقَى الضَجِيعُ بها، ولا تُنادي بما تُوشِي وتَستمِعُ لا تُنادِي به أي لا تُظْهِره.
دك (مقاييس اللغة) والأصل الآخر يقرب من باب الإبدال، فكأنّ الكاف فيه قائمةٌ مقام القاف. يقال دكَكْت الشيء، مثل دققته، وكذلك دكّكته.
دقق (لسان العرب) الدَقُّ: مصدر قولك دَقَقْت الدَواء أَدُقُّه دقاً، وهو الرَضُّ. والدَقُّ: الكسر والرَضُّ في كلِ وجه، ودَقَّ الشيءِ يدُقُّه إذا أظهره؛ ومنه قول زهير:ودَقّوا بينهم عِطْرَ مَنْشِمِ أي أظهروا العُيوب والعداوات. ويقال في التهدد: لأدُقَّنَّ شُقورَك أي لأُظهِرنَّ أُمورَك. والمُداقَّةُ في الأمر: التَداقُّ. والمُداقَّة: فعل بين اثنين، يقال: إنه لَيُداقُّه الحساب.
ذكا (مقاييس اللغة) الذال والكاف والحرف المعتلّ أصلٌ واحد مطَّرِدٌ منقاس يدلُّ على حدَّةٍ [في] الشيء ونفاذ.
ذَكَتِ (القاموس المحيط) واسْتَذْكَتْ: اشْتَدَّ لَهَبُها، وهي ذَكِيَّةٌ. وذَكَّاها وأذْكاها: أوْقدها.

§ 12.—VIII, 3-13

AALD: šīmtu
nam [FATE] wr. nam; na-ağ$_2$ "determined order; will, testament; fate, destiny" Akk. šīmtu
namtar [FATE] wr. nam-tar "sickness; fate, destiny; a demon" Akk. murşu; namtaru; šīmtu
AALD: šimtu (s.) عاقد العزم، الوصية، الميثاق

ذمم (لسان العرب) والذِّمّة العهد والكفالة، وجمعها ذِمامٌ. وفلان له ذِمّة أي حق والذَمامةُ والذَمامة: الحق كالذِمّة؛ قال ذو الرمة: تَكُنْ عَوْجة يَجزيكما الله عندها بها الأجرَ، أو تُقضى ذِمامةُ صاحب ذِمامة: حُرْمةٌ وحق. وفي الحديث ذكر الذِمَّة والذِمام، وهما بمعنى العَهْد والأمان والضَمان والحُرْمة والحق، وسُمِّيَ أهل الذِمّة ذِمّة لدخولهم في عهد المسلمين وأمانهم.

سمت (مقاييس اللغة) السين والميم والتاء أصلٌ يدل على نهج وقصدِ وطريقة. يقال سَمتَ، إذا أخذ النَهج. وكان بعضُهم يقول: السَمْت: السَير بالظنّ والحدْس. وهو قول القائل:ويقال إنّ فلاناً َحسنُ السَمْتِ، إذا كان مستقيمَ الطريقةِ متحرّياً لفعل الخير. والفعل منه سَمت.
ويقال سمت سَمْته، إذا قصد قصده.

سمت (لسان العرب) السَمْتُ: حُسْنُ النَحْو في مذْهب الدِّينِ، والفعلُ سَمت يَسْمُتُ سمْتا، وإنه لحَسَنُ السَمْت أي حسن القَصْدِ والمذْهب في دينه ودنْياه. والسَمْتُ الطريقُ؛ يقال: الْزَمْ هذا السَمْتَ؛ وسمْتُ الطريقِ: قصْدُه. والسَمْتُ السَيْرُ على الطَريق بالظنّ؛ سمت يسْمُتُ، بالضم، أي قصد؛ وقال الأصمعي: يقال تعمَده تعمُداً، وتسمّته تسمُتاً إذا قصد نحْوه. وقال شمر: السَمْتُ تنسُمُ القصْد. وفي حديث عوف بن مالك: فانطلقت لا أدري أين أذهبُ، إلاَ أنني أُسمّتُ أي ألْزمُ سمْت الطريق؛ يعني قصْدَه؛ ال أبو العباس: يقال سَمت العاطس تَسميتاً، وشمّته تشْميتاً إذا دعا له بالهُدي وقصْد السَمْتِ المستقيم؛ والأصل فيه السين، فقُلبتْ شيناً. قال ثعلب: والاختيار بالسين، لأنه مأْخوذ من السَمْت، وهو القَسْدُ والمَحجَة. وقال أبو عبيد: الشين أعلة في كلامهم، وأكثر. والسَمْتُ هيئة أهل الخير. يقال: ما أَحسَن سَمْته أي هدْيه.

§ 13.—VIII, 14-24

ePSD: arhu
<u>ab</u> [<u>COW</u>] wr. ab$_2$ "cow" Akk. arhu; littu
<u>immal</u> [<u>COW</u>] wr. immal$_2$; im-ma-al; immal; immal$_x$(|NUN.LAGAR|) "wild cow; cow" Akk. arhu; littu
<u>itud</u> [<u>MOON</u>] wr. itud; itud$_x$(|UD.AN.ŠEŠ.KI|); i$_3$-ti; iti$_7$; i-ti; itud$_x$(|UD@s|); itud$_x$(|UD×BAD|) "month; moon" Akk. arhu
<u>šilam</u> [<u>COW</u>] wr. šilam; $^{ab}{}_2$šilam; $^{ab}{}_2$šilam$_2$; ša$_3$-lam; šallam$_2$; $^{ab}{}_2$NUN.LAGAR "cow; bovine" Akk. arhu; littû
ePSD: karābu
<u>siškur</u> [<u>PRAYER</u>] wr. siškur$_2$; siškur "prayer; blessing; offering, sacrifice, rites; to pour (a libation), sacrifice; to intercede" Akk. karābu; naqû; nīqu
<u>šu e</u> [<u>BLESS</u>] wr. šu e$_3$ "to bless; to go out?; to terrify?" Akk. waşû; palāhu; karābu
<u>šu mu</u> [<u>PRAY</u>] wr. šu mu$_2$ "to pray" Akk. karābu
ePSD: redû
<u>us</u> [<u>FOLLOW</u>] wr. us$_2$ "(to be) of a lesser quality; to drag; to stretch; to accompany, follow; a qualification of grain; to thresh (grain) by treading; to coagulate?" Akk. diāšu; redû; šadādu

كرب (لسان العرب) وكُلُّ شيءٍ دنا: فقد كَرَبَ. وكلُّ دانٍ قريبٍ، فهو كارِبٌ. أبو زيد: أكْرَب الرجلُ إكْراباً إذا أحْضَر وعدا.

ردد (الصَحاح في اللغة) وتقول: رَدَّه إلى منزله. وردَّ إليه جواباً: أي رجع. واستردَّهُ الشيءَ: سأله أن يَرُدَّهُ عليه. والرِدّيدي: الردَ. وفي الحديث: "لا رِدّيدي في الصدقة". ورادَّهُ الشيءَ: أي رَدّه عليه. وشيءٌ رَدٌّ، أي رديء.

ردد (لسان العرب) الرد: صرف الشيء ورَجْعُه. وتَرَدّد وتراد: تراجع.

ردأ (لسان العرب) رَدأ الشيءَ بالشيءِ: جعله له رِدْءاً. وأَرْدَأَهُ أعانه. وترادأ القومُ: تعاونوا. وأرْدَأْته بنفسي إذا كنت له رِدْءاً، وهو العَوْنُ. وفلان رِدْءٌ لفلان أي يَنصُرُه ويشُدُّ ظهره. وقال الليث: تقول ردأْتُ فلاناً بكذا وكذا أي جعلْته قُوّةً له وعماداً كالحائط ترْدؤه من بناءٍ تُلزقُه به. وتقول: أَرْدأْت فلاناً أي رَدأْته وصرْتُ له رِدْءاً أي مُعيناً. وترادؤوا أي تعاونُوا. والرِّدْءُ: المُعينُ.

ردي (مقاييس اللغة) والكلمة الأخرى أردأت، إذا أعنْت. وفلان رِدْءُ فلانٍ، أي مُعينه. قال الله جلَ جلالُه* في قصة موسى: فأَرْسِلْهُ معِيَ رِدْءاً يُصدِّقني [القصص 34].

روح (لسان العرب) والرَّواحُ: نقيضُ الصَباح، وهو اسم للوقت، وقيل: الرَّواحُ العشيُّ، وقيل: الرَواحُ من لَدُن زوال الشمس إلى الليل. يقال: راحوا يفعلون كذا وكذا ورُحْنا رَواحاً؛ يعني السَيْرَ بالعَشيِّ؛ وسار القوم رَواحاً وراحَ القومُ، كذلك. وخرجوا برِياحٍ من العشيِّ، بكسر الراء، ورَواحٍ وأَرْواحٍ أي بأَوَلٍ. وعشيّةٌ: راحةٌ؛ وإذا قالت العرب: راحت الإبل ترُوحُ وتَراحُ رائحةً، فرواحُها ههنا أَن تأْوي بعد غروب الشمس إلى مُراحِها الذي تبيت فيه. ابن سيده: والإراحةُ ردُّ الإبل والغنم من العشيّ إلى مُراحها حيث تأْوي إليه ليلاً، وقد أَراحها راعيها يُريحُها. قال في قوله:
مُعاوِيَ، من ذا تجْعلُون مكاننا، إذا دلَكتْ شمسُ النهار براحِ يقول: إذا أظلم النهار واسْتُريح من حرِّها، يعني الشمس، لما غشيها من غبرة الحرب فكأنها غاربة؛ كقوله: تَبْدُو كواكبُه، والشمسُ طالعةٌ، لا النُورُ نُورٌ، ولا الإظْلامُ إظْلامُ وقيل: دَلَكَتْ براحٍ أي غربَتْ، والناظرُ إليها قد توقّى شُعاعها براحته.

روح (مقاييس اللغة) الراء والواو والحاء أصلٌ كبير مطّرد، يدلُّ على سَعةٍ وفُسْحةٍ واطّراد. والرَّواح: العشيُّ؛ وسمِّي بذلك لرَوح الرِّيح، فإنَّها في الأغلب تهُبّ بعد الزَّوال. وراحوا في ذلك الوقت، وذلك من لَدُنْ زوالِ الشّمس إلى الليل. وأرحْنا إبلَنا: ردَدْناها ذلك الوقتَ.

رحي (مقاييس اللغة) الراء والحاء والحرف المعتلُّ أصلٌ واحد، وهي الرَّحى الدائرة. ثم يتفرّع منها ما يقاربُها في المعنى. من ذلك رحَى الحرب، وهي حوْمتُها.

أرخ (الصَحاح في اللغة) التأْريخُ: تعريف الوقت. والإراخُ: بقَرُ الوحش، الواحدةُ إرْخٌ. الليث: والأَرْخُ والإِرْخُ والأُرْخيُّ البقر، وخص بعضهم به الفتيّ منها، والجمع آراخ وإراخ، والأنثى أَرْخة وإِرْخة، والجمع إراخٌ لا غير. والأَرْخُ الأنثى من البقر البِكْرُ التي لم يَنْزُ عليها الثيران؛ قال أبو حنيفة: الأَرْخُ والإِرْخُ الفتية من بقر الوحش، وقال ابن السكيت: الأَرْخ بقر الوحش.

أرخ (مقاييس اللغة) الْهمْزةُ والرّاءُ والْخاءُ كلمةٌ واحدةٌ عربيّةٌ، وهي الإراخُ لبقرِ الْوحْش. وأمّا تأْريخُ الْكتاب فقدْ سمع، وليس عربيًا ولا سمع منْ فصيح.
رخا (لسان العرب) والرَّخاء: سعة العيْش، وقد رخُو ورخا يرْخُو ويرْخى رخاً، فهو راخ ورخيٌّ أي ناعم، وزاد في التهذيب: ورخي يرْخى وهو رخيُّ البال إذا كان في نَعْمة واسع الحال بيْنَ الرَّخاء، ممدودٌ. ويقال: إنه في عيْش رخيٍّ.
أرخ (تاج العروس) أرخَ الكتاب، بالتخفيف، وقضيّته أنّه كنصر وأرّخه بالتشديد، وآرخه بمدّ الهمزة: وقّته، أرْخًا وتأْريخًا ومؤارخة. ومثله التّوريخُ، وزعم يعقوبُ أنّ الواو بدلٌ من الهمزة. وقيل: إنّ التّأريخ الذي يؤرّخه الناسُ ليس بعربيّ محْض، وإنّ المسلمين، أخذوه من أهْل الكتاب. قال شيخنا: وقد أنكرَ جماعةٌ استعمالَه مخففًا، والصّوابُ ورودُه واستعماله، كما أورده ابن القطّاع وغيره. والخِلاف في كونه عربياً أو ليس بعربيّ مشهور، وقيل هو مقلوب من التأْخير. والأرْخ، بفتح فسكون، وهو الصحيح، قاله أبو منصور، ويُكسر، نُقل عن الصّيداويّ: الذّكرُ من البقر، ويقال: الأنثى من البقر البكْرُ التي لم ينزُ عليها الثيران. والأرْخيُّ، بالضّم: الفتيّ منه أي من البقر، ومنهم من عمّ به البقرَ كالأرْخ والإرْخ، قاله أبو حنيفة، والجمع آراخٌ وإراخٌ، والأنثى أرخه، محركة، وإرْخة، والجمع إراخٌ لا غير. أو الإراخ ككتاب: بقرُ الوحْش، الواحد إرْخة. ويُطلق على المذكّر والمؤنّث، وهو ظاهرُ كلام الجوهريّ. والأرْخيّة ولدُ الثّيتل، وقال ابن السّكّيت: الأرْخ بقرُ الوحْش. فجعله جنْسًا، فيكون الواحد على هذا القول أرْخة، مثْل بطّ وبطّة، وتكون الأرْخة تقع على الذّكر والأنثى، يقال: أرْخة ذكرٌ وأرْخة أنثى، كما يقال بطّة ذكرٌ وبطّة أنثى. الأرْخ ولدُ البقرة الصّغيرُ. وقيل: إنّ التاريخ مأْخوذ منه، كأنّه شيءٌ حدث كما يحدُث الولدُ .وقال ابنُ الأعرابيّ وأبو منصور: الصحيحُ الأرْخ بالفتح، والذي حكاه الصّيداويّ فيه نظرٌ، والّذي قاله اللّيث أنّه يقال له الأرْخيّ لا أعرفه، كذا في التهذيب. وقالوا من الأرْخ ولد البقرة أرخْتُ أرْخًا.
ءرخ (المصباح المنير) أرّخْت الْكتاب بالتّثْقيل في الْأشْهر والتّخْفيفُ لُغةٌ حكاها ابنُ الْقطّاع إذا جعلْت لهُ تاريخًا وهُو مُعرّبٌ وقيل عربيٌّ وهُو بيانُ انْتهاء وقْته ويُقالُ ورّخْتُ على الْبدلِ والتّوْريخُ قليلُ الاسْتعْمال وأرّخْت الْبيّنة ذكرْت تاريخًا وأطْلقْت أيْ لمْ تذْكُرْهُ. الْهلال وإنّما يظْهرُ باللّيْل فجعلُوهُ ابْتداءَ التّاريخ والْأحْسنُ ذكْرُ الْأقلّ ماضيًا كان أوْ باقيًا.

§ 14.—VIII, 24-29

ePSD: şehru
banda [JUNIOR] wr. $banda_3^{da}$ "(to be) junior; small; (to be) wild, fierce" Akk. ekdu; şehru
genna [CHILD] wr. genna "(to be) small; (young) child" Akk. şehru; šerru
زغر (مقاييس اللغة) الزاء والغين والراء أُصَيْلٌ. يقال زَغر الماءُ وزخر. وليس هذا عندي من جهةِ الإبدال؛ لأن قياس زَغر قياسٌ صحيح، وسيجيء *في الرباعيّ مايصحّحه. وذكر ابن دُريد أنّ الزّغر الاغتصاب؛ يقال زَغرْت الشيء زَغْراً. قال: والزغْر فعلٌ مُماتٌ.
زغد (لسان العرب) ونهر زَغّاد: كثير الماءِ، وقد زَغَدَ وزخر وزغر بمعنى واحد؛
صهر (مقاييس اللغة) الصاد * والهاء والراء أصلان: أحدهما يدلّ على قُربَى، والآخر على إذابة شيء.
صغر (مقاييس اللغة) الصاد والغين والراء أصلٌ صحيح يدلّ على قِلّة وحقارة. من ذلك الصّغَر: ضدّ الكِبَر. والصّغير: خلاف الكبير.
صغر (لسان العرب) الصّغرْ: ضد الكبر. وصَغّره وأصْغَره: جعله صَغيراً.

§ 15.—VIII, 30-36

ePSD: abullu
abula [GATE] wr. abul; abul-la; a-bul_5-la "gate" Akk. abullu
murub [MIDDLE] wr. $murub_6$; $murub_4$; $murub_2$; murub; $murub_3$ "middle; female genitals, vulva; buttocks, rump; knob; mouth; gate (of city or large building); space between, distance; link; hips" Akk. abullu; birītu; bişşūru; pinku; pû; qablu; qinnatu; ûru
ePSD: aşû
e [LEAVE] wr. e_3; i; e "to leave, to go out; to thread, hang on a string; to remove, take away; to bring out; to enter; to bring in; to raise, rear (a child); to sow; to rave; to winnow; to measure (grain) roughly (with a stick); to rent" Akk. aşû; erēbu; mahû; rubbû; zarû; šakāku
AALD: tezû (v.) (tēşû) يطرح، يُفرغ، يُبرّز، يُفرزْ
افل (لسان العرب) قال الليث: إذا استقر اللّقاح في قرار الرَّحم قيل قد أفل، ثم يقال للحامل آفل.
العَبْلُ (القاموس المحيط) والعُنْبَلُ والعُنْبُلَةُ، بضمّهما: البظْرُ.
عبل (مقاييس اللغة) العين والباء واللام أصلٌ صحيحٌ يدلّ على ضخَم وامتداد وشدّة. من ذلك العبْلُ من الأجسام، وهو الضّخم. تقول: عبُل يعْبُل عبالة.
أبل (مقاييس اللغة) الهمزة والباء واللام بناء على أصول ثلاثة: [على] الإبل، وعلى الاجتزاء، وعلى الثّقل، و[على] الغلبة. وقال بعضهم: تأبّل على الميت حزن عليه. وأبلت الميت مثل أبّنْت. ويقال أبل الرجل يَأبل أبلاً إذا غلب وامتنع. والأبلة الثّقل.
أبل (لسان العرب) ويقال: إن فعلت ذلك فقد خرجت من أبلته أي من تبعته ومذمته. وأبلت الإبل بالمكان أبولاً: أقامت؛ وإبل أوابلُ وأُبّلٌ وأُبّالٌ ومؤبّلة: كثيرة، وقيل: هي التي جُعلتْ قطيعاً قطيعاً، وأبلت أبلاً وأبولاً: كثُرت. وأبلت تأبلُ: تأبّدت. قال: الأبلةُ، بفتح الهمزة والباء، الثّقل والطّلبة، وقيل هو من الوبال، وأبّل الرجلَ: كأبّنه؛ عن ابن جني؛ اللحياني: أبّنْت الميت تأبيناً وأبّلته تأبيلاً إذا أثنيت عليه بعد وفاته.
بلل (لسان العرب) وبلِلْت به بَللاً وبلالة وبُلولاً وبلِلْت: مُنيت به وعُلّقته. وبللْته: لزمته؛ قال: دَلْو تمأى دُبغتْ بالحُلّب، بُلّتْ بكفّي عزب مُشذّب، فلا تُقعسرْها ولكن صوّب تقعسرها أي تعازّها. أبو عمرو: بلّ يبِلّ إذا لزم إنساناً ودام على صحبته، وبلّ يَبلّ مثلها؛
عصا (لسان العرب) والعِصيانُ خلافُ الطّاعة. واستعْصى عليه الشيءُ: اشْتدّ كأنه من العِصيان؛ وعصى الطائرُ يَعْصي: طار؛

عصو/ي (مقاييس اللغة) العين والصاد والحرف المعتل أصلانِ صحيحان، إلاّ أنّهما متباينان يدلّ أحدهما على التجمّع، ويدلّ الآخر على الفُرْقة. والأصل الآخَر: العِصيانُ والمَعصية. يقال: عَصَى، وهو عاصٍ، والجمع عُصاة وعاصون. والعاصي: الفَصيل إذا عَصَى أمّه في اتِّباعها.
صت (مقاييس اللغة) الصاد والتاء أصلٌ يدلّ على نزاعٍ وخصومةٍ وافتراق، يقال للجلَبة الصَّتيت. وما زلتُ أُصاتُّ فلاناً، أي أخاصمُه. والصَّتُّ، فيما يقال: الصَّدْم. والصَّتيت: الفِرْقة.
عزو/ي (مقاييس اللغة) ولأنَّ معنى التعزّي هو أن يتأسّى بغيره فيقول: "حالي مثلُ حالِ فلان. ولذلك قيل: تأسَّى، أي جعل أمره أُسوة أمرِ غيره. فكذلك التعزّي.
أزا (لسان العرب) قال رؤبة: تَغْرِفُ من ذي غَيِّثٍ وتُوزي وأزى يأْزِي أَزْياً وأُزِيّاً: انقبض واجتمع.
زوي (لسان العرب) الزَّيُّ: مصدر زوى الشيءَ يَزْويه زَيّاً وزَوْياً فانْزوى، نَحّاه فتنحَّى. وزواهُ: قبضه. وزوَيْت الشيءَ: جمعته وقبضته. زواهُم الدَّهرُ أي ذهب بهم؛ قال بشر: فقد كانت لنا، ولهُنّ حتى زوتها الحربُ، أيامٌ قِصارُ قال: زوتها ردّتها. وقد زوَوْهم أي ردُّوهم. وزوى اللهُ عني الشرَّ أي صرَفه. وزوَيْت الشيء عن فلان أي نحّيته. وأزْوى الرجلُ إذا جاء ومعه آخرُ. وزوْزَيْته وزوْزَيت به إذا طردْته. وزوْزى: نصب ظَهْره وقارب خَطْوه في سُرْعة. واسْتوْزى كزوْزى؛

§ 16.—VIII, 37-47

ePSD: nagiru
niĝir [HERALD] wr. niĝir; li-bi-ir "herald" Akk. Nagiru
ePSD: šasû
gu de [SAY] wr. gu_3 de_2 "to say (addressing someone); to call; to read out" Akk. ?; nabû; šasû
gu rah [SHOUT] wr. gu_3 ra-ah; gu_3 ra "to shout" Akk. šasû

ركا (لسان العرب) وأرْكَيْت إليه: لجأْت.
سوس (لسان العرب) والسَّوْسُ: الرِّياسةُ، يقال ساسوهم سَوْساً، وإذا رأَسُوه قيل: سَوّسُوه وأَساسوه. وساس الأمرَ سياسةً: قام به، ورجل ساسٌ من قوم ساسة وسُوّاس؛ وسَوَّسه القومُ: جعلوه يَسُوسُهم. ويقال: سُوِّس فلانٌ أمرَ بني فلان أي كُلِّف سياستهم. الجوهري: سُسْتُ الرعية سياسة. وسُوِّس الرجلُ أُمور الناس، على ما لم يُسَمَّ فاعله، إذا مُلِّكَ أمرَهم؛ وفلان مُجَرَّبٌ قد ساسَ وسِيسَ عليه أي أَمَرَ وأُمِرَ عليه.
نجر (لسان العرب) النَّجْر والنِّجارُ والنُّجارُ: الأَصْلُ والحسَبُ.
جأر (الصِّحاح في اللغة) الجُؤارُ مثل الخوار. يقال: جأر الثور يَجأرُ أي صاح.
جأر (القاموس المحيط) جأر، كمَنَع، جأْراً وجُؤاراً: رفع صوْتَهُ بالدُّعاء، وتضرَّع، واسْتغاث، و~ البقرةُ والثَّورُ: صاحا،
جأر (لسان العرب) جأَر يَجْأَرُ جأْراً وجُؤاراً: رفع صوته مع تضرع واستغاثة. وفي التنزيل: إذا هُمْ يجأَرُون؛ وقال ثعلب: هو رفع الصوت إليه بالدعاء. وجأَر الرجلُ إلى الله عز وجل إذا تضرَّع بالدعاء. وفي الحديث: كأني أنظر إلى موسى له جُؤارٌ إلى ربه بالتلبية؛
نقر (لسانِ العرب) وفلانٌ كريمُ النَّقير أي الأَصل. وبيني وبينه مُناقَرةٌ ونِقارٌ وناقِرةٌ ونقْرةٌ أي كلام؛ عن اللحياني؛ والمُناقَرةُ مراجعةُ الكلام بين اثنين وبثُّهما أحاديثَهما وأُمورَهما. والتَّنْقيرُ عن الأمر: البحث عنه. ورجل نَقّارٌ: مُنقِّرٌ عن الأُمور والأَخبار. الجوهري: دعوتهم النَّقَرى أي دعْوةً خاصة، وهو الانْتِقار أيضاً، وقد انْتقَرَهُم؛ والرجل يُنَقِّرُ باسم رجل من جماعة يخصه فيدعوه، يقال: نَقَر باسمه إذا سماه من بينهم. والنَّقْرُ صوت اللسان، وهو إلزاق طرفه بمخرج النون ثم يُصوِّتُ به فيَنْقُر بالدابة لتسير؛ والنَّقْرُ أن يضع لسانه فوق ثناياه مما يلي الحنكَ ثم ينْقُر. ابن سيده: والنَّقْرُ أن تُلْزِق طرف لسانك بحنكك وتفْتح ثم تُصوّت، وقيل: هو اضطراب اللسان في الفم إلى فوق وإلى أسفل؛ وقد نقَر بالدابة نقْراً وهو صُوَيْتٌ يزعجه.

§ 17.—VIII, 49-58

ePSD: şēru
aneden [STEPPE] wr. an-eden "the high steppe" Akk. şēru
eden [BACK] wr. eden "back, upper side" Akk. şēru
muš [SNAKE] wr. muš "snake" Akk. şēru
sanimmara [BACK] wr. sa-nim-ma-ra "back" Akk. şēru
sug [BACK] wr. sug "steppe, open country; back, upperside, upper part" Akk. elītu; şēru
ePSD: šiqlu
giĝ [UNIT] wr. $gi\hat{g}_4$ "a unit of weight, shekel; a unit of area; a unit of volume" Akk. šiqlu

بدا (لسان العرب) بَدا الشيءُ يَبْدُو بَدْواً وبُدُوّاً وبَداءً وبَداً؛ الأَخيرة عن سيبويه: ظهر.وكل شيء أظهرته فقد أَبْدَيْتَه. ويقال: بَدا لي شيءٌ أي ظهر. وقال الليث: البادية اسم للأرض التي لا حضَر فيها، وإذا خرج الناسُ من الحضَر إلى المراعي في الصَّحاري قيل: قد بَدَوا، والإسم البَدْوُ.
صحر (مقاييس اللغة) الصاد والحاء والراء أصلان: أحدهما البَراز من الأرض، والآخر لونٌ من الألوان.فالأوّل الصحراء: الفضاء من الأرض. ويقال أصحر القومُ، إذا برَزُوا.
الضَّهْرُ (القاموس المحيط) الضَّهْرُ: السُّلَحْفاةُ، وأعْلى الجبل، كالضَّاهِر، وخِلْقَةٌ فيه من صَخْرةٍ تُخالفُ جِبِلَّته، وجبلٌ باليمن. والضَّاهِرُ: الوادي.
ظهر (مقاييس اللغة) الظاء والهاء والراء أصلٌ صحيحٌ واحدٌ يدلُّ على قوّة وبروز. من ذلك ظهَرَ الشيءُ يظهرُ ظهوراً فهو ظاهر، إذا انكشف وبرز. ويقولون: سلكْنا الظَّهر: يريدون طريق البرّ، وذلك لظهوره وبروزه.
صراهُ (القاموس المحيط) صراهُ يصْريه: قطعهُ، ودفعهُ، ومنعهُ، وحفظهُ، وكفاهُ، ووقاهُ، و~ ماءهُ: حبسهُ في ظَهْرِه بامتناعه عن النِّكاح، وتقدَّم، وتأخَّر، وعلاَ، وسَفل، ضِدٌّ، وعَطف، وأنْجى إنسانا من هَلَكة، و~ فلاً في يد فُلان: بَقِيَ مَحْبوساً، و~ بينهم: فصَل.
سقل (مقاييس اللغة) السين والقاف واللام ليس بأصل، لأنَّ السين فيه مبدلة عن صاد.

صقل (لسان العرب) الصَقْلُ: الجلاءِ. صقل الشيء يصْقُله صَقْلاً وصِقالاً، فهو مَصْقُولٌ وصَقيلٌ: جَلاهُ، والاسم الصِقالُ، وهو صاقِلٌ والجمع صَقلةٌ؛
مثقال (شمس العلوم) المثْقال: وزن مَعْلومُ القَدْرِ.
ثقل (المصباح المنير) ثَقُلَ الشَّيْءُ بِالضَّمِّ ثِقَلاً وِزَانُ عِنَبٍ وَيُسَكَّنُ لِلتَّخْفِيفِ فَهُوَ ثَقِيلٌ وَالثِّقْلُ الْمَتَاعُ وَالْجَمْعُ أَثْقَالٌ مِثْلُ: سَبَبٍ وَأَسْبَابٍ قَالَ الْفَارَابِيُّ الثِّقْلُ مَتَاعُ الْمُسَافِرِ وَحَشَمُهُ وَالثَّقَلَانِ الْجِنُّ وَالْإِنْسُ وَأَثْقَلَهُ الشَّيْءُ بِالْأَلِفِ أَجْهَدَهُ. وَالْمِثْقَالُ وَزْنُهُ دِرْهَمٌ وَثَلَاثَةُ أَسْبَاعِ دِرْهَمٍ وَكُلُّ سَبْعَةِ مَثَاقِيلَ عَشَرَةُ دَرَاهِمَ قَالَ الْفَارَابِيُّ وَمِثْقَالُ الشَّيْءِ مِيزَانُهُ مِنْ مِثْلِهِ وَيُقَالُ أَعْطِهِ ثِقْلَهُ وِزَانُ حِمْلٍ أَيْ وَزْنَهُ.
ثقل (لسان العرب) والمِثْقال: واحِدُ مثاقِيلِ الذَّهَبِ. قال الأَصمعي: دينارٌ ثاقل إِذا كان لا يَنْقُصُ، ودنانيرُ ثواقل؛ ومِثْقال الشَّيْءِ: ميزانُه من مِثْلِه.
ومِثْقال الشيء: ما آذَنَ وزنَه فثَقُل ثِقْلَه.
ثقل (مختار الصحاح) الثِّقْلُ وَاحِدُ (الْأَثْقَالِ) كَحِمْلٍ وَأَحْمَالٍ وَمِنْهُ قَوْلُهُمْ أَعْطَاهُ ثِقْلَهُ أَيْ وَزْنَهُ. وَ(الْمِثْقَالُ) وَاحِدُ (مَثَاقِيلِ) الذَّهَبِ وَ(مِثْقَالُ) الشَّيْءِ مِيزَانُهُ مِنْ مِثْلِهِ.
ثقل (صحاح العربية) الثِقْلُ: واحد الأثْقال، مثل حِمْلٍ وأحمالٍ. ومنه قولهم: أعطه ثِقْلَهُ، أي وزنه. وثقل الشئ الشئ في الوزن يَثْقُلُهُ ثَقْلاً.
ثقل (منتخب الصحاح) قال الأصمعي: دينارٌ ثاقلٌ، إذا كان لا ينقص. ودنانيرُ ثواقلُ. ومثقالَ الشيءِ: ميزانُهُ من مثله.
ثقا (المحيط في اللغة) والمِثْقالُ: وَزْنٌ مَعْلومٌ قَدْرُه. ومِثْقالُ الشَّيْءِ: ميزانُه، وثِقْلُ الشَّيْءُ: وزن.
ثقل (تهذيب اللغة) وأصل الثَقَل أنّ العرَب تقول لكلّ شيء نفيس مَصُون: ثَقَل، وأصلُه في بيض النعام المصُون. قال: والمثقال: وَزْنٌ معلومٌ قدرُه، ومثقال الشيء: ميزانُه من مثله.
ثقل (العين) والمِثقال وزن معلوم قدره. ومثقال الشيء: ميزانه من مثله.
شقل (تاج العروس) وقال ابنُ الأَعْرابِيّ: شَقَلَ الدِّينارَ: وَزَنَهُ. وشَوْقَلَ الرَّجُلُ: تَرَزَّنَ حِلْمًا ووَقارًا. وشَوْقَلَ الدِّينارَ: عايَرَهُ وصَحَّحَه. ويقالُ: عنْده دَراهِمُ شَقْلة. وشَقْلَة من دَراهم، لكَثِيرَة منها مُصَحَّحة معايِرَة: عامِّيَّة.
شقل (لسان العرب) ابْنُ الأَعرابي: الشَّقْل الوَزْنُ، يُقَالُ: اشْقُل لِي هَذا الدِّينارَ أَي زِنْه، قَالَ: وقَدْ شَقَلْته
شقل (مجمل اللغة) الشاقول: شيء يمسكه الذارع. والشقل: الوزن، وفيها نظر.
شقل (مقاييس اللغة) الشِّينُ وَالْقَافُ وَاللَّامُ لَيْسَ بِشَيْءٍ، وَقَدْ حُكِيَ فِيهِ مَا لَا يُعَرَّجُ عَلَيْهِ.
شقل (المحيط في اللغة) الشّاقُوْلُ: خَشَبَةٌ قَدْرُ ذِراعَيْنِ في رَأْسِها زُجٌّ. واشْتُقَّ منه اسْم للذكر. والشَّشْقَلَةُ: كلمةٌ حِمْيَرِيَّةٌ للصَيارِفَة وهي المُعايَرَةُ، يقولون: شَشْقَلْنا الدَّراهِمَ والدَّنانيرَ: أي عيرْناها.
شقل (تهذيب اللغة) قال: الشَّقْلُ: الوزن، يقال: اشْقُلْ لي هذا الدينار أي زِنْه، قال :وشَوْقَلَ الرَجل إذا تَرَزَّن حِلمًا ووقارًا، وشَوْقَل إذا عَيَّر ديناره تعييرًا مُصححًا.
شقل (العين) وشقلْتُ الدنانير: عيرتها، وهي كلمة عبادية حيرية ليست بعربية محضة.

§ 18.—VIII, 59-67

ePSD: parāsu

<u>tar</u> <u>[CUT]</u> wr. tar; tar^{ar} "to cut down; to untie, loosen; to cut; to scatter, disperse; to decide" Akk. harāṣu; parāsu; paṭāru; sapāhu

ePSD: târu

<u>gi</u> <u>[TURN]</u> wr. gi$_4$; gi "to turn, return; to go around; to change status; to return (with claims in a legal case); to go back (on an agreement)" Akk. lamû; târu

<u>gur</u> <u>[TURN]</u> wr. gur "to reject (legal evidence), to turn away; to turn, return" Akk. sahāru; târu

فرس (لسان العرب) ويقال: إن فلاناً لفارس بذلك الأمر إذا كان عالماً به. ويقال: هو يتفرَّس إذا كان يتثبَّتُ وينظرُ. ورجل فارس بالأمر أي عالم به بصير. والفِراسة، بكسر الفاء: في النَّظر والتَّثبت والتأمل للشيء وابصر به، يقال إنه لفارس بهذا الأمر إذا كان عالماً به. والأصل في الفَرْس دَقُّ العُنُق، ثم كثُر حتى جُعل كل قتل فَرْساً؛ وفرَس الشيءَ فرْساً: دَقه وكسَرَهُ؛ وفرَس السَّبُعُ الشيءَ يفرسُه فَرْساً.
تور (لسان العرب) وأَترْتُ الشيءَ: جئت به تارةً أخرى أي مرَّةً بعد مرة؛ قال: ومنه يقال أَتأَرْتُ النَّظرَ إليه أي أدمته تارةً بعْد تارةٍ. وأَتأَرْته بصري: أَتبعْته إياه. والتَّارةُ: الحين والمرَّة، ألفها واو، جمْعُها تاراتٌ وتِيَرٌ؛ والتَّورُ الرسول بين القوم، عربي صحيح؛ ابن الأعرابي: التَّورةُ الجارية التي تُرسلُ بين العُشاق. أبو عمرو: فلان يُتارُ على أن يُؤْخذ أي يُدار على أن يؤْخذ؛
عود (الصّحاح في اللغة) عادَ إليه يعودُ عَوْدةً وعَوْداً: رجع. العَوْدُ: الرُّجوعُ. و العَوْدُ: ثاني البَدْءِ. والمَعادُ: المصيرُ والمرجعُ. والمُعاودَةُ: الرجوع إلى الأمر الأوَّل. وعاوَدهُ بالمسألة، أي سأله مرة بعد أخرى. والمُعاوِدُ: المُواظِبُ، والبطلُ. واسْتعاده: سأله أن يفْعله ثانياً، وأن يعودَ. وأعاده إلى مكانِه: رَجَعه، وأعاد الكلامَ: كرَّرَه.

§ 19.—VIII, 68-IX, 4

ePSD: kalû

<u>aga kar</u> <u>[DEFEAT]</u> wr. aga kar$_2$; aga$_3$ kar$_2$ "to defeat; to conquer; to surround; to besiege" Akk. kalû; kaşāru

<u>ešela</u> <u>[BOUND]</u> wr. ešela "(to be) bound" Akk. hanāqu; kalû; kamû

<u>gala</u> <u>[SINGER]</u> wr. gala; gala$_{10}$ "lamentation singer" Akk. kalû

<u>heše</u> <u>[OPPRESSED]</u> wr. heš$_5^{še}_3$; haš "(to be) oppressed; (to be) detained" Akk. habālu; kalû

كلأ (لسان العرب) وقد كلأه يَكْلَؤه كلأ وكِلاءَ وكِلاءة، بالكسر: حرسه وحفظه. واكْتلأ منه اكْتِلاءً: احْترس منه. وكالأه مُكالأةً وكِلاءً: راقبه. واكْتلأ كُلأةً وتكلأها: تسلّمها. والكلأ، مهموز مقصور: ما يُرْعى.

§ 20.—XI, 5-13

ePSD: pašāru
<u>bur</u> <u>[SPREAD]</u> wr. bur_2; bur "to release, free; to reveal; to spread out, cover" Akk. pašāru; šuparruru
<u>u'en</u> <u>[RELEASE]</u> wr. u_3-en; u_3-en_3 "to release" Akk. pašāru
ePSD: ašāru
<u>na deg</u> <u>[CLEAR]</u> wr. na deg_x(RI); ša di; ša di-di; ša di-di_5; ša di_5 "to make clear, explain; to consecrate, purify; to separate; to clear out, cut out" Akk. ašāru; elēlu; hasāsu
<u>šuš</u> <u>[COVER]</u> wr. $šuš_2$; šuš; $šuš_5$ "to sink down; to cloud over; to cover, to spread over; to envelop, overwhelm; covering; surface; to raise (clothes)" Akk. ašāru; erēpu; katāmu; sahāpu; sehpu; šaqû ša lubši
ePSD: nīš šarrim tamû
<u>mu lugalak pad</u> <u>[SWEAR]</u> wr. mu lugal pad_3 "to swear by the king's name" Akk. nīš šarrim tamû
AALD: nīšu (s.) (nēšu) nīšu ilim قسم الحياة، بحياة الاله
AALD: nīšu (s.) الارتفاع، الزيادة، الترقية، التشريف
AALD: nêšu (s.) (na'āšu) يعيش، يجلب الحياة، يستمر في الحياة

مسر (الصَحاح في اللغة) ومسر الشيء، أخرجه من ضيق.
مشر (مقاييس اللغة) ومَشَرْتُ الشَيء. فرَقتهُ.
بشر (لسان العرب) وأبْشرَت الأرضُ إبْشاراً: بَذرتْ
بذر (مقاييس اللغة)الباء والذال والراء أصلٌ واحد، وهو نَثْرُ الشيء وتفريقُه.
مذر (لسان العرب) قال: ويتمذَّرُ يتفرق، قال: ومنه قوله: تفرّق القومُ شذر مذر
ذرر (لسان العرب) ذَرَّ الشيءَ يذُرُّه: أخذه بأطراف أصابعه ثم نثره على الشيء. وذرَرْتُ الحبَّ والملح والدواء أذُرُّه ذرّاً: فرَقته؛
ذرا (لسان العرب) ذَرت الريح الترابَ وغيره تذْرُوه وتذْريه ذرْواً وذرْياً وأذْرَتْهُ وذرَتْه: أطارته وسفته وأذهبَتْه، وقيل: حملته فأثارته وأذْرته إذا ذرَت التُراب وقد ذرا هو نفسُه. وذرَوْتُه أنا أي طيَّرته وأذهبْته؛
وذر (لسان العرب) ابن السكيت: يقال ذرْ ذا، ودعْ ذا، ولا يقال وَذرْته ولا ودعْته، وأما في الغابر فيقال يذرُه ويدعُه وأصله وَذرهُ يذرُه مثال وَسِعه يسعُه، ولا يقال واذِرٌ لا وادِعٌ، ولكن تركته فأنا تارك. وقال الليث: العرب قد أماتت المصدر من يذرُ والفعلَ الماضي، فلا يقال وَذرهُ ولا واذِرٌ، ولكن تركه وهو تارك، قال: واستعمله في الغابر والأمر فإذا أرادوا المصدر قالوا ذرْهُ تركاً، ويقال هو يذرُه تركاً. وحكي عن بعضهم: لم أذرْ ورائي شيئاً، وهو شاذ، والله أعلم.
نشش (لسان العرب) ونشَّ الشيءَ: نِصفُه. والنَشُّ: السَوْقُ الرَفيق، ويروى بالسين، وهو السَوْق الشديد؛ وقال شمر: نَشْنشَ الرجلُ الرجلَ إذا دفعه وحرَكه. ونَشْنشَ ونشَّ: ساق وطرَد.
نشأ (مقاييس اللغة) النون والشين والهمزة أصلٌ صحيح يدلُّ على ارتفاع في شيءوسمو. ونَشأ السَحابُ: ارتفع. وأنْشأه الله: رفعه.
نشأ (القاموس المحيط) نشأ، كمنع وكرُم، نشْئاً ونُشوءاً ونشاءً ونشْأةً ونشاءةً: حيي، وربا وشبَّ، و~ السَحابةُ: ارْتفعتْ.
نعش (لسان العرب) نعشَه اللهُ ينْعشُه نعْشاً وأنْعشَه: رفعه. وانْتعشَ: ارتفع. والانْتعاشُ: رَفْعُ الرأس. وقال ابن السكيت: نعشَه اللهُ أي رَفعَه، ولا يقال أنْعشَه وهو من كلام العامَة، ونعَشْتُ له: قلت: له نعشَك اللهُ؛ قال رؤبة: وإنْ هوى العاثرُ قُلنا: دَعْدعا له، وعالَيْنا بتَنْعيش لعا وقال شمر: النَعْشُ البقاءُ والارتفاع. يقال: نعشَه الله أي رَفعَه اللهُ وجبره. قال: والنَعْشُ منْ هذا لأنه مرتفع على السرير. وفي حديث عمر، رضي الله عنه: انْتعشْ نعشَك اللهُ؛ معناه ارْتفِعْ رفعَك اللهُ؛ وفي حديث جابر: فانْطلَقنا به ننْعشُه أي نُنْهضه ونقَوّي جأْشَه. ونعشْت الشجرةَ إذا كانت مائلةً فأقمْتها. والرَبيعُ ينْعَشُ الناسَ: يُعيشُهم ويُخْصِبهم؛

§ 21.—XI, 14-21

AALD: pilšu (s.) الكسر، الصدع، الفتحة، الحفرة، النفق، الخرم، الثقب
AALD: palāšu (v.) يطعن، يثقب، يخترق، يقتحم
AALD: palāşu See balāşu
AALD: balāşu (v.) يحدق، يتمعن
AALD: palāsu (v.) (palāšu) يحدق، يتمعن
AALD: halālu (v.) يتخلَل، يعلق، يتسلّل، ينسلَ، يدُبَ، يحتجز، ينتظر، يربط، زمجرة، خرخرة (الصدر)، زئزئة

بلس (لسان العرب) أبْلسَ الرجلُ: قُطع به؛ والبلاسُ: المِسْحُ، والجمع بُلُسٌ. وأهل المدينة يسمون المِسْحَ بلاساً، وهو فارسي معرب، ومن دعائهم: أرانيك اللهُ على البلس، وهي غرائرُ كبارٌ من مُسُوح يجعل فيها التين ويُشهَرُ عليها من يُنكَلُ به وينادى عليه، والإبْلاسُ: الحَيْرة؛ ومنه الحديث: ألم تر الجنَ وإبلاسَها أي تحيُّرَها ودهشَها.
فشش (لسان العرب) تتبُّع السَرَقِ الدون، فشَه يفُشّه فشّاً؛ وفشَّ القُفْل فشّاً: فتحه بغير مفتاح. والانْفشاش: الانكسار عن الشيء والفشَلُ.

الخَلُّ (القاموس المحيط) وتَخَلَّلَهُ: ثَقَبهُ ونفذهُ. واخْتَلَّه بالرُّمْحِ: نَفَذَهُ وانْتَظَمه. وتَخَلَّلَهُ به: طَعَنه طَعْنَةً إثْرَ أُخْرى. و~ بالمَكانِ وغيرِه: غابَ عنه وتركَهُ،
خلل (الصَحَاح في اللغة) وأَخَلَّ الرجل بمركزه، أي تركه.
خلل (لسان العرب) واخْتَلَّه بسهم: انْتَظمه. واخْتَلَّه بالرمح: نفذه، يقال: طَعَنته فاخْتَلَّلت فؤداه بالرُّمح أي انتظمته؛ وفي رأيه خَلَل أي انتشار وتفرُّق.
وأخَلَّ بالمكان وبمَرْكَزه وغيره: غاب عنه وتركه.

§ 22.—XI, 22-27

AALD: habātu (v.) يقترض
AALD: habātu (v.) يخبط، يسرق، يغتصب اموال، يرتكب جريمة سرقة، يخطف
AALD: hubtu (s.) السَرقة، الغنائم، الأسلاب، الاسير، سجين حرب

خَبطَه (القاموس المحيط) خَبطَه يَخْبطُه: ضَرَبه شديداً، وكذا البعيرُ بيدِه الأرضَ،
خبط (لسان العرب) خَبطَه يَخْبطُه خَبْطاً: ضربه ضرْباً شديداً. ويقال: خبطَه إذا سأله؛ ومنه قول زهير: يوْماً ولا خابطاً من مالِه وَرِقا والخَبْطُ: طَلَبُ المعروف، خَبطَه يَخْبطُه خبْطاً واخْتَبطَه. والمُخْتَبِطُ: الذي يَسْألُك بلا وسِيلة ولا قَرابةٍ ولا معرفة. وخَبطَه بخير: أَعطاه من غير معرفة بينهما؛ وخبطَه الشيطانُ وتَخَبَّطَه: مسَّه بأذىً وأفسَده.
هبط (العباب الزاخر) الهابط: المنحطُ. وهَبطَه يهبطه هبطاً: أي أنزلَه،
هبط (لسان العرب) والهَبْطُ أن يقع الرجل في شرَ. والهَبْطُ الذُّلُّ.
حبط (لسان العرب) ويقال: حَبِطَ دم القتيل يَحْبَطُ حبْطاً إذا هُدِرَ.
هبت (مقاييس اللغة) الهاء والباء والتاء كلمةٌ تدلُّ على ضربٍ متتابع. وهُبِتَ الرَّجُل يُهْبَتُ.
هبت (لسان العرب) الهَبْتُ: الضَرْبُ. وهبَتَ الرجل يهْبِتُه هبْتاً: ذَلَّلَهُ.
حفت (لسان العرب) الحفْتُ: الاهْلاكُ. حَفتَه اللهُ حفْتاً: أَهْلكه، ودقَّ عُنُقه؛ قال الأزهري: لم أسمع حَفتَه بمعنى دقَّ عُنُقَه لغير الليث؛
خمط (العباب الزاخر) وقال الأصمعي :التَخمُّطُ: القهر والأخذُ بالغلبة،
همط (لسان العرب) الهَمْطُ: الظلم. هَمطَ يَهْمِطُ هَمْطاً: خلط بالأباطِيلِ. وهَمطَ الرجلَ واهْتَمطَه: ظلمه وأخذ منه ماله على سبيل الغَلَبة والجَوْر؛

§ 23.—XI, 28-45

AALD: ālu (s.) الاهل، المدينة (كهيئة اجتماعية)، القرية، العزبة، الملكية
ePSD: rabû
<u>kingal</u> [OFFICIAL] wr. kingal; kin-gal "grandee; crown authority over land, labor recruiter"
Akk. mu'erru; rabû
buluĝ [GROW] wr. buluĝ$_3$; buluĝ$_5$; bu-lu-ug; buluĝ "to grow up, rear, make grow; novice; foster child"
Akk. rabû; tarbûtu
ePSD: erşetu
<u>arali</u> [EARTH] wr. a-ra-li; arali; arali$_x$(|URU×GAL|) "earth, land; underworld" Akk. erşetu
ePSD: pâdu
<u>ur</u> [COLLECT] wr. ur$_5$ "to confine, imprison" Akk. pâdu
AALD: pâdû (adj.) عديم الرحمة، قاسي الفؤاد، قاس

برو/ي (مقاييس اللغة) الباء والراء والحرف المعتلّ بعدهما وهو الواو والياء أصلان: أحدهما تسويةُ الشَيءِ نحتاً، والثَاني التعرُّض والمحاكاة.
بَرى (القاموس المحيط) وانْبَرى له: اعْتَرضَ. وتبرَّيْتُ لِمَعْرُوفِه: تعرَّضْتُ. وباراهُ: عارضَهُ، و~ امرأتَهُ: صالَحها على الفِراقِ. وتَبارَيا: تعارضا.
برر (الصَحّاح في اللغة) وبرَّ فلانٌ في يمينه، أي صدَقَ.
برر (لسان العرب) البِرُّ: الصِّدْقُ والطاعةُ. وبرِرْتُ والدي، بالكسر، أَبَرُّهُ برّاً وقد برَّ والده يَبَرُّه ويَبِرُّه برّاً، فيَبرُّ على بَرِرْتُ ويبِرُّ على بَرَرْتُ على حَدِّ ما تقدّم في اليمين؛ وهو برٌّ به وبارٌّ؛ عن كراع، وأَنكر بعضهم بارٌّ. والبُرُّ: نقيض الكِنّ؛ وقد بَرْبَر في كلامه بَرْبَرةً إذا أكثر. والبَرْبَرةُ: الصوتُ وكلامٌ من غضَب؛
أَهْلُ (القاموس المحيط) أَهْلُ الرجُلِ: عشيرتُه، وذَوُو قُرْباهُ، ج: أَهْلون وأهالٍ وآهالٌ وأَهْلاتٌ، ويُحرَكُ. وأَهَل يأْهُلُ ويأْهِلُ أهولاً، وتأَهَل واتَّهَل: اتَّخذَ أَهْلاً. وأَهْلُ الأمرِ: وُلاتُه، و~ للبيتِ: سُكَّانُه،
وأل (لسان العرب) وقال بعضهم: مَن أَطاف بالرجل وحلّ معه من قرابته وعشيرته فهو إيلَتُه. وقال العكلي: هو من إيلَتِنا أي من عشيرتنا.
لتهذيب: وأيْلة قرية عربيّة كأنها سميت أيلة لأن أهلها يؤولون إليها، وأمَا إلْيَةُ الرجل فقراباته، وكذلك لِيَتُه.
ربب (الصَحَاح في اللغة) رَبُّ كلِّ شيءٍ: مالكُهُ.
ربا (لسان العرب) رَبا الشَيءُ يَرْبُو رُبُوّاً ورِباءً: زاد ونما.
عرص (الصَحَاح في اللغة) العَرْصَةُ: كلُّ بُقعةٍ بين الدُور واسعةٍ ليس فيها بناءٌ، والجمع العِراصُ والعَرَصاتُ.
عرض (مقاييس اللغة) وكان ابنُ الأعرابي يقول: الأعراض: الجبال والأودَية والسحاب، الواحد عِرْض. كذا قال بكسر العين، ورُوي عنه أيضاً بالفتح. وقال أبو عبيدة :العَرض: سَنَد الجبل. فأمَا عَرُوض الشِّعر فقال قوم: مشتقٌ من العَرُوض، وهي النَاحية، كأنَه ناحيةٌ من العِلْم. والمعارض: جمع مَعْرَض وهي بلاد تُعْرَضُ فيها الماشيةُ للرَعْي.

أرض (لسان العرب) الأَرْض: التي عليها الناس، وكل ما سفل، فهو أَرض؛
فيد (لسان العرب) والتَّفَيُّدُ: التبَخْتُرُ. والفَيّادُ: المتبَخْتِر؛ وهو رجل فَيّادٌ ومُتَفَيِّدٌ. أنشد ابن الأعرابي لأَبي النجم: ليس بِمُلْتاثٍ ولا عَمَيْثَلِ، وليس بالفَيّادة المُقَصْمِلِ أي هذا الراعي ليس بالمُتَجَبِّر الشديد العصا.
فدي (مقاييس اللغة) الفاء والدال والحرف المعتل كلمتان متباينتان جداً. فالأولى: أنْ يُجعل شيءٌ مكان شيءٍ حِمىً له، والأُخرى شيءٌ من الطَّعام.فالأولى قولك: فديتُه أفديه، كأنّك تحميه بنفسك أو بشيءٍ يعوِّض عنه.

§ 24.—XI, 46-50

ePSD: manû
mana [UNIT] wr. ma-na "a unit of weight" Akk. manû
AALD: manû (v.) يعتبر، يعد، يعد ويسجل، يعين او يسلم
ePSD: nišū
umia [PEOPLE] wr. u_2-mi-a "people" Akk. nišū

منا (الصِّحاح في اللغة) المنا مقصور: الذي يوزن به، والتثنية منوان، والجمع أَمْناءٌ، وهو أفصح من المَنِّ. ويقال: مُنِيَ له، أي قُدِّر. ويقال: مُنِيَ له، أي قُدِّر.
منن (الصِّحاح في اللغة) والمَنُّ: المَنا، وهو رطلان، والجمع أَمْنانٌ، وجمع المَنا أَمْناءٌ.
أنس (لسان العرب) الإنسان: معروف؛ وذلك أَن المعهود في الكلام إذا قيل للناس من أَنتم قالوا: ناس من بني فلان، والأَنَسُ: أَهل المَحَلِّ، والجمع آناسٌ؛ وقالوا: كيف ابنُ إنْسِك أي كيف نفْسُك. أبو زيد: تقول العرب للرجل كيف ترى ابن إنْسِك إذا خاطبت الرجل عن نفسك. الأَحمر: فلان ابن إنْس فلان أي صَفِيُّه وأَنيسُه وخاصته. قال الأَزهري: وأَصل الإنس والأَنس والإنسان من الإيناس، وهو الإبْصار. والنَّاتُ: لغة في الناس على البدل الشاذ؛ ويقال للمرأَة أَيضاً إنسانٌ ولا يقال إنسانة، والعامة تقوله.
نوس (لسان العرب) النَّاسُ: قد يكون من الإنس ومن الجن،

§ 25.—XI, 51-65

ePSD: išātu
izi [FIRE] wr. izi; izi_2 "fire; brazier" Akk. išātu; pendû
ePSD: napāhu
bar [BURN] wr. bar_7 "to burn; to fire (pottery)" Akk. napāhu
bur [GLOW] wr. bur_2; bu_7 "light; to glow, shine" Akk. napāhu; nūru
kar [BLOW] wr. kar_2-kar_2; kar_2 "to blow; to light up, shine; to rise" Akk. napāhu
kur [BURN] wr. kur "to burn, light up" Akk. napāhu
lu [FLARE] wr. lu_9 "to flare up" Akk. napāhu
AALD: napāhu (v.) ينفخ، يشعل النار
ePSD: belû
ten [EXTINGUISH] wr. te-en; ten "to extinguish" Akk. belû
AALD: balû (v.) (belû) يصبح خامدا، ينتهي، يبيد، يطفئ
AALD: īnu (s.f.) (ēnu) عين
AALD: numātu (s.f.) (nuwātu) اثاث، ادوات منزلية
ePSD: nadû
gurud [THROW] wr. gurud; $gurud_2$ "to throw, place" Akk. nadû
ku [PLACE] wr. ku "to place, lay (down), lay eggs; to spread, discharge" Akk. nadû; uşşu
ri [IMPOSE] wr. RI; ru "to lay down, cast, place; to set in place, imbue; to lean on; to impose; to throw down; to release, let go; to walk along; to pour out; to lead away" Akk. bâ'u; emēdu; nadû; nasāku; ramû; rehû; tarû; wašaru
šub [FALL] wr. šub "to fall; to drop, lay (down); to thresh (grain)" Akk. habātu; maqātu; nadû

حش (مقاييس اللغة) ويقال حشَشْتُ النار، إذا أثقبتها، وهو من الأصل الذي ذكرناه، كأنّك جعلت ثقوبها كالحشيش لها تأكلُه.
حوش (لسان العرب) وقال أَبو عُبَيْدة فيما روى عنه أبو عبيد وابن الأَعرابي: إنما هو جمْعُ محاشك، بكسر الميم، جعلوه من مَحَشْته أي أَحْرقته لا من الحَوْش، وقد فسر في الثلاثي الصحيح أنهم يتحالفون عند النار؛ وأما المَحاشُ، بفتح الميم، فهو أَثاث البيت، وأَصله من الحَوْش وهو جمع الشيء وضمه.
حشش (لسان العرب) وحَشَّ النارَ يَحُشُّها حَشّاً: جمع إليها ما تفرق من الحطب، وقيل: أَوقدها، وقال الأَزهري: حَشَشْتُ النارَ بالحطب، فزاد بالحطب؛ وفي حديث الرؤيا: وإذا عنده نار يَحُشُّها أَي يُوقدها؛ ومنه حديث أَبي بصير: وَيْلُ أُمِّه محشُّ حَرْبٍ لو كان معه رجال ومنه حديث عائشة تصف أَباها، رضي الله عنهما: وأَطفأَ ما حَشَّتْ يهود أَي ما أَوقدت من نيران الفتنة والحرب. وحَشْحَشْتُه النَّارُ: أَحْرقَتْه.
نبه (لسان العرب) النُّبْه: القِيامُ والانْتباهُ من النوم، وقد نَبَهَ وأَنبهه من النوم فتنَبَّه وانْتبه، وانْتبه من نومه: استيقظ، والتنبية مثله؛ ونَبَّهْتُه أَنا: رفعته من الخمول.
هبب (لسان العرب) وأَهَبَّه: نَبَّهه، وأَهْبَبْتُه أَنا.

نبه (مقاييس اللغة) النون والباء والهاء أصلٌ صحيح يدلُّ على ارتفاع وسمُوّ.
نفخ (مقاييس اللغة) النون والفاء والخاء: أصلٌ صحيح يدلُّ على انتفاخ وعلوّ. منه انتفخ الشَيءُ انتفاخاً.
نفخ (لسان العرب) النَفْخ: معروف، نَفخ فيه فانْتَفخ. ابن سيده: نَفخ بفمه يَنْفُخ نفْخاً إذا أخرج منه الريح يكون ذلك في الاستراحة والمعالجة ونحوهما؛ وفي الخبر: فإذا هو مُغْتاظٌ يَنْفُخ؛ ونفخ النارَ وغيرها ينفخها نفْخاً ونفيخاً. والنَّفيخ: الموكل بنفْخ النار؛ والمِنْفاخ: الذي يُنْفخ به في النار وغيرها.
المَنفوهُ (القاموس المحيط) واسْتَنْفه: اسْتراح.
بلِيَ (القاموس المحيط) والبَلاءُ يكونُ مِنْحة، ويكونُ مِحْنةً.
بلا (لسان العرب) وبَلاه كأَبْلاهُ؛ وبَلِيَ الثوبُ يَبْلى بلًى وبلاء وأَبلاه هو؛ يقال: ما باليته وما باليت به أي لم أكترث به. وفي الحديث: هؤلاء في الجنة ولا أبالي وهؤلاء في النار ولا أُبالي؛ وحكى الأزهري عن جماعة من العلماء: أن معناه لا أكره. وفي حديث ابن عباس: ما أُباليه بالةً.
البَهْلُ (القاموس المحيط) والإبْهالُ: إرْسالُك الماءَ فيما بَذرْتَه. وبَهْلاً، أي: مَهْلاً.
مهل (لسان العرب) وفلان ذو مَهَل، بالتحريك، أي ذو تقدُّم في الخير، ولا يقال في الشر. يقال: مَهَّلته وأَمْهلته أي سكَّنته وأَخَّرته.
نوي (لسان العرب) ويروى: ولما تَنْتَوي بنواتي أي لم تقض حاجتي؛ ويقال: لي في بني فلان نَواةٌ ونِيَّةٌ أي حاجة. والنَّوى: الحاجة.
نوم (لسان العرب) ورجلٌ نائمٌ ونَؤُومٌ ونُومةٌ ونَومٌ؛ الأخيرة عن سيبويه، من قوم نيامٍ ونُوَّم، على الأصل، ونُيَّم، على اللفظ، قلبوا الواو ياءً لقربها من الطرف، ونِيَّم، عن سيبويه، كسروا لمكان الياء، ونُوَّام ونُيَّام، الأخيرة نادرة لبعدها من الطرف؛ والنِّيمُ: الفَرْوُ، وفي الصحاح: النِّيم الفَرْوُ الخَلَق. والنِّيم: كلُّ لَيِّن من ثوبٍ أو عَيْشٍ. والنِّيمُ: النَّعْمةُ التامَّةُ.
أتي (لسان العرب) الإتْيان: المَجيء. وأَتَّى للماء: وجَّه له مَجْرى. ويقال: أَتِّ لهذا الماء فتُهَيِّئَ له طريقه.
عسو/ي (مقاييس اللغة) وأهلُ العلم يقولون: عَسَى من الله تعالى واجبٌ، في مثل قوله تعالى: عَسَى اللهُ أَنْ يَجعَلَ بَيْنَكُمْ وَبَيْنَ الَّذِينَ عَادَيْتُمْ مِنْهُمْ مَوَدَّةً [الممتحنة 7].
عسا (لسان العرب) عَسا الشيخُ يَعْسو عَسْواً وعُسُوّاً وعُسِيّاً مثلُ عُتِيّاً وعساءً وعَسْوَةً وعَسِيَ عَسًى، كلُّه: كَبِرَ مثلُ عَتِيَ. وأما الأصمعي فقال: ظَنِّي بهم كعَسى أي ليس بثبت كعَسى، يريد أن الظَّن هنا وإن كان بمعنى اليقين فهو كعَسى في كونها بمعنى الطمع والرجاء، وجوائزُ الأمثال ما جاز من الشعر وسار. وهو عَسِيٌّ أن يَفْعل كذا وعَسٍ أي خَليقٌ؛ قال ابن الأعرابي: ولا يقال عَسى.
أدا (الصَحاح في اللغة) وأَدَوْتُ له، أي خَتَلْته. وتأدَّى إليه الخبر، أي انتهى. ويقال: استَأداهُ مالاً، إذا صادره واستخرجه منه.
أَدَاهُ (القاموس المحيط) و~ فلاناً مالاً: صادرَهُ، وأخذه منه.
ندأ (لسان العرب) نَدأَ اللحمَ يَنْدَؤه نَدْءاً: أَلقاهُ في النار،
نَدأَهُ (القاموس المحيط) و~ اللَّحْمَ: أَلْقاهُ في النار، أو دَفنه فيها، و= خَوَّفَهُ وذَعرَه، وضَرب به الأرضَ، و~ عليهم: طَلَع،
نَدَّ (القاموس المحيط) نَدَّ البَعيرُ يَنِدُّ نَدّاً ونَديداً ونُدوداً ونِداداً: شَرَد ونَفَر. وإبِلٌ نُدُدٌ، محركة: مُتفرِّقةٌ، وأَنَدَّها ونَدَّدها.وذَهبُوا أناديد وتَناديدَ: تفرَّقُوا في كُلِّ وجْهٍ. والتَّنادُّ: التَّفرُّقُ، والتَّنافُرُ،
لتد (لسان العرب) لَتَده بيده: كوكَزه.
لَتَدهُ (القاموس المحيط) لَتَدهُ بيده يَلْتِدُهُ: لكَزهُ.

§ 26.—XI, 66-X, 12

ePSD: rēdû
aga'us [SOLDIER] wr. aga-us$_2$; aga$_3$-us$_2$ "a soldier" Akk. rēdû
AALD: rēdû (s.) (rādiu) رئيس العمال، المرشد، الدليل، الجندي، رسول او جاجب المحكمة، مساعد المأمور، سائق او تاجر الماشية
AALD: redû (v.) (radā'u, redu) ... يسوق: حيوانات، عربات؛ يُرسل، ينقل بضائع، يقود، يتولى
ePSD: Akk. gallû "demon; constable".
ePSD: ṣābu
erin [PEOPLE] wr. erin$_2$; eri-na; erin$_9$ "people; troops" Akk. ṣābu
AALD: ṣēbû (s.) المهنة، الحرفة
ePSD: bā'eru
šukud [FISHERMAN] wr. šu-ku$_6$; šu-|HA@g|; $^{lu}{}_2$šu-ku$_6$ "fisherman; hunter, catcher" Akk. bā'eru
ePSD: harrānu
kaskal [WAY] wr. kaskal "way, road; journey, caravan" Akk. harrānu
šušer [ROAD] wr. šu-še-er "far away lands; road" Akk. harrānu; nasīkātu
ePSD: šarru
HUŠma [KING] wr. HUŠ-ma "king" Akk. šarru
ePSD: gepû
rig [UNMNG] wr. rig$_7$ "?" Akk. gepû
ePSD: igru
addir [HIRE] wr. addir "hire, wage" Akk. igru
ePSD: puhtu
šuzigu [SUBSTITUTE] wr. šu-zi$_3$-gu "substitute" Akk. puhtu

ePSD: amēlu
ili [MAN] wr. i$_3$-li$_2$ "man" Akk. amēlu
lu [PERSON] wr. lu$_2$; mu-lu; mu-lu$_2$; lu$_{10}$; lu$_6$ "who(m), which; man; (s)he who, that which; of; ruler; person" Akk. amēlu; ša
lulu [MAN] wr. lu$_2$-lu$_7$; lu$_2$-lu$_7$^{lu} "man; humanity" Akk. amēlu; lullû
na [MAN] wr. na "man" Akk. amēlu
ur [MAN] wr. ur "man" Akk. amēlu
za [MAN] wr. za "man" Akk. amēlu

رود (لسان العرب) الرَّوْدُ: مصدر فعل الرائد، والرائد: الذي يُرْسل في التماس النُّجْعة وطلب الكلإِ، والجمع رُوّاد مثل زائر وزُوّار. وأَصل الرائد الذي يتقدَّم القوم يُبْصر لهم الكلأَ ومساقط الغيث؛ ورجل رادٌ: بمعنى رائد،

الرَّوْدُ (القاموس المحيط) الرَّوْدُ: الطَّلَبُ، كالرِّيادِ والارْتِيادِ والذَّهابِ والمَجيءِ، والمُراوِدةُ والرِّوادُ والرِّيدُ، بكسرهما. والإِرادةُ: المَشيئَةُ. والرَّائِدُ: يَدُ الرَّحى، والمُرْسَلُ في طَلَبِ الكَلأ. ورِيادُ الإِبِلِ: اخْتِلافُها في المَرْعى مُقْبِلَةً ومُدْبِرَةً،

ردأ (لسان العرب) وأَرْدَأَه أَعانَه. وتقول: أَرْدَأْت فلاناً أَي رَدَأْته وصرْتُ له رِدْءاً أَي مُعيناً. وترادَؤُوا أَي تعاوَنُوا. والرِّدْءُ: الـمُعِينُ. ورَدَأْته أَي أَعَنْتُه.

صيب (لسان العرب) الصُّيَّابُ والصُّيَّابة: أَصلُ القوم. وفلان من صُيَّابةِ قومه وصُوَّابةِ قومه أَي من مُصاصِهم وأَخْلَصِهم نَسَباً. وصُيَّابةُ القوم: جماعتهم؛ عن كراع. وقوم صُيَّابٌ أَي خِيار؛ والصُّيَّابةُ: السَّيِّدُ.

بأر (لسان العرب) وقيل: هو الأَجير الذي ينزل البئر فينقيها أَو يخرج منها شيئاً وقع فيها فيموت.

البَئْرُ (القاموس المحيط) وابْتَأَرَ: حفر، و~ الشيءَ: خَبأَهُ، أو ادَّخَرَهُ، و~ الخَيْرَ: قَدَّمَهُ، أو عَمِلَهُ مَسْتوراً. ويقال للذَّخيرة يَدَّخِرها الإِنسان: بَئِيرَةٌ.

قال أَبو عبيد: في الابْتِئار لغتان: يقال ابْتَأَرْتُ وائْتَبَرْتُ ابْتِئاراً وائتباراً؛ وقال القطامي: فإِن لم تَأْتَبِرْ رَشَداً قُرَيْشٌ، فليس لسائر لناس ائْتِبارُ يعني اصطناع الخير والمعروف وتقديمه.

البَيْنُ (القاموس المحيط) والبَيانُ: الإِفْصاحُ مع ذَكاءٍ.

بين (لسان العرب) والبَيِّن من الرجال: الفصيح. ابن شميل: البَيِّن من الرجال السَّمْح اللسان الفصيح الظريف العالي الكلام القليل الرتج.

بين (الصّحاح في اللغة) والبيانُ الفصاحةُ واللَسَنُ.

حرن (مقاييس اللغة) الحاء والراء والنون أصلٌ واحد، وهو لزوم الشي للشيء لا يكادُ يفارقه.

ثرا (لسان العرب) الثَّرْوَة: كثْرة العَدَد من الناس والمال. يقال: ثَرْوة رجالٍ وثَرْوة مالٍ، والفَرْوة كالثَّرْوة فاؤه بدل من الثاء. ورجل ثَرِيَ وأَثْرى: كثير المال.

شري (لسان العرب) واستشْرتْ بينهم الأُمورُ: عظُمت وتفاقمَتْ. وإِبلٌ شَراةٌ كسَراةٍ أَي خِيارٌ؛

سرا (لسان العرب) السَّرْوُ: المُروءةُ والشَّرَفُ. وسَراةُ المال: خِيارُه، الواحد سَرِيٌّ. فقال: ومن اقْتَدَحَ المَرْخَ والعفارَ فقد اخْتارَ واسْتارَ. وأَخَذْت سَراته أَي خِيارَه. وتَسَرَّيْته: أَخَذْت أَسراه؛ والسَّرِيُّ: المُخْتار. ومنه حديث الأَنصار: افترَقَ ملَؤُهم وقُتِلَت سَرَواتُهم أَي أَشْرافُهم.

أجر (مقاييس اللغة) الهمزة والجيم والراء أصلان يمكن الجمعُ بينهما بالمعنى، فالأول الكِراء على العمل، والثاني جَبْر العظم الكسير. فأمّا الكِراء فالأجر والأُجْرة. وكان الخليل يقول: الأجر جزاء العمل، والفعل أجَرَ يأجُرُ أجْرا، والمفعول مأجور.

سرر (الصّحاح في اللغة) وقد يعبر بالسرير عن المُلْكِ والنَعمةِ؛ وسرُّ الوادي: أفضلُ مَوضعٍ فيه والجمع أسِرَّةٌ.

السَّرُّ (القاموس المحيط) والسَّريرُ، كأميرٍ: ع بدِيارِ بني دارِمٍ أو بني كِنانة، ومَمْلَكَةٌ بين بلادِ اللاَّنِ، وبابِ الأبوابِ، لها سلطانٌ برأسِهِ ومِلَّةٌ ودينٌ مُفْرَدٌ، ووادٍ.

عمل (لسان العرب) املُ: هو الذي يتولى أُمور الرجل في ماله ومِلْكه وعمله، ومنه قيل للذي يَسْتَخْرج الزكاة: عامل. والعمَل: المِهْنة والفِعْل، والجمع أَعمال، عَمِلَ عَمَلاً، وأَعْمَله غيرُه واسْتَعْمله، واعْتَمل الرجلُ: عَمِلَ بنفسه؛ ورجل عَمِلٌ: ذو عَمَلٍ؛

أمل (لسان العرب) الأَمَل والأَمْل والإِمْل: الرَّجاء؛ ابن الأَعرابي: الأَمَلة أَعوان الرجل، واحدهم آمل.

فهه (لسان العرب) فَهَّ عن الشيء يَفَهُّ فَهّاً: نسيَه. وأَفَهَّهُ غيرُهُ: أَنْساه. ويقال: خرجت لحاجةٍ فأَفَهَّني عنها فلانٌ حتى فَهِهْتُ أَي أَنسانيها.

بدل (مقاييس اللغة) ويقولون بدَّلْتُ الشيءَ إذا غيَّرته وإنْ لم تأتِ له ببَدَل.

جبأ (مقاييس اللغة) الجيم والباء والهمزة أصلان: أحدهما التنحِّي عن الشيء. يقال جبأت عن الشيء، إذا كععت.

جبأ (لسان العرب) جبأَ عنه يَجْبأُ: ارْتَدع. وجبأْتُ عن الأَمر: إِذا هِبْتَه وارْتَدَعْت عنه. ابن الأَعرابي: الإِجْباء: ان يُغَيِّبَ الرجلُ إِبلَه، عن الـمُصَدِّق. يُقالُ: جبأَ عن الشيءِ: توارى عنه، وأَجْبَيْتُه إِذا وارَيْتَه. وجَبأَ الضَّبُّ في جُحْره إِذا اسْتَخْفى.

كعع (لسان العرب) وتَكَعْكَعَ: هابَ القومَ وتركهم بعدما أَرادهم وجَبُن عنهم، لغة في تَكَأْكَأَ وتكَعْكَعَ الرجلُ وتكَأْكأَ إِذا ارْتدع. وفي حديث الكسوف: قالوا له ثم رأَيناك تكَعْكَعْت أَي أَحْجَمْتَ وتأَخَّرْت إِلى وراءٍ.

كيع (الصّحاح في اللغة) الكسائي: كِعْتُ عن الشيء أكيعُ وأَكاعُ، لغة في كعَعْتُ عن الأمر أكِعُّ، إذا هِبْتَهُ وجبُنتَ.

درأ (لسان العرب) الدَّرْءُ: الدَّفْع. دَرأَهُ يَدْرَؤُهُ دَرْءاً ودَرْأَةً: دفَعَه. في الحديث: اللهم إِني أَدْرأُ بك في نُحورهم أَي أَدْفع بك لتَكْفِيني أَمرَهم، ودرأ الشيءِ بالشيءِ (قوله «ودرأ الشيء بالشيء إلخ» سهو من وجهين الأول: أن قوله وأرداه اعانه ليس من هذه المادة. الثاني: ان قوله ودرأ الشيء إلخ صوابه وردأ كما هو نص المحكم وسيأتي في ردأ ولمجاورة ردأ لدرأ.)

دَرَأَهُ (القاموس المحيط) دَرَأَهُ، كجَعَلَهُ، دَرْءاً ودَرْأَةً: دفَعَهُ،

§ 27.—X, 13-X, 29

ePSD: dannu
<u>kalag</u> <u>[STRONG]</u> wr. kal-ga; kalag; kal-la "(to be) strong, powerful, mighty; to reinforce; to provide for" Akk. dannu; kubbû
<u>lirum</u> <u>[STRENGTH]</u> wr. lirum; $lirum_3$; $lirum_2$; $lirum_6$; $lirum_7$; $lirum_8$ "strength; force; (to be) strong, powerful, mighty, great; (to be) resistant, obstinate, combative, quarrelsome; a noble; (crook of the) arm; wrestler" Akk. abaru; dannu; emûqu; gāmiru; kamiru; kirimmu; umašu; šapṣu; šitnunu; šitpuṣu
<u>urun</u> <u>[EXALTED]</u> wr. $urun_x$(EN); u_{18}-ru; uru; uru_{15} "(to be) exalted; (to be) strong" Akk. dannu; šapsu; ṣīru
ePSD: tarû
<u>ri</u> <u>[IMPOSE]</u> wr. RI; ru "to lay down, cast, place; to set in place, imbue; to lean on; to impose; to throw down; to release, let go; to walk along; to pour out; to lead away" Akk. bâ'u; emēdu; nadû; nasāku; ramû; rehû; tarû; wašaru
ePSD: kirû
<u>kiri</u> <u>[ORCHARD]</u> wr. $^{ĝeš}kiri_6$; $kiri_6$ "(fruit) plantation, orchard" Akk. kirû
ePSD: kašādu
<u>sa dug</u> <u>[ARRIVE]</u> wr. sa_2 dug_4 "to arrive; to cause to arrive (regularly)" Akk. kašādu
<u>sa</u> <u>[EQUAL]</u> wr. sa_2; sa_x(ZAG); se_3 "to equal, compare, compete, be equal to, rival" Akk. kašādu; mašālu; šanānu

دين (مقاييس اللغة) الدال والياء والنون أصلٌ واحد إليه يرجع فروعُه كلُّها. وهو جنسٌ من الانقياد والذُّل. فالدِّين: الطاعة، يقال دان لـه يَدِين دِيناً، إذا أصْحَبَ وانقاد وطَاعَ.
الدَّيْنُ (القاموس المحيط) ودِنْتُه أدِينُه: خَدَمْتُهُ، وأحْسَنْتُ إليه، ومَلَكْتُه،
دعن (لسان العرب) وقال أبو عمرو في تفسير شعر ابن مُقبل: أُدْعِنت الناقةُ وأُدعن الجمل إذا أُطيل ركوبه حتى يَهْلِك، رواه بالدال والنون.
ذعن (مجمل اللغة) ذعن: أذعن الرجل: انقاد، يذعن إذعانًا، وبناؤه ذعن، إلا أن استعمالهُ أذعن. وناقة مذعان: سلسة الرأس منقادةٌ.
الذَّانُ (القاموس المحيط) الذَّانُ: العَيْبُ.
ذين (لسان العرب) الذَّيْنُ والذَّانُ: العيب. وذَامه وذَانه وذابه إذا عابه. وقال أبو عمرو: هو الذَّيْمُ والذَّامُ والذانُ والذابُ بمعنى واحد؛
ضن (المحيط في اللغة) والضَنَنُ: الرَّجُلُ الشُّجَاعُ.
دن (تهذيب اللغة) وقال الليثُ: الدَّنَ ما عَظُم من الرَّواقيد، ثعلب عن ابن الأعرابي: الأدنَ الَّذي كأنَ صُلْبه دَنَ،
ذأن (لسان العرب) غيره: الذُّؤْنون نبت ينبت في أُصول الأَرْطى والرِّمْثِ والألاء، تنشقُّ عنه الأَرض فيخرج مثل سواعد الرجال لا ورق له،
تري (لسان العرب) التهذيب خاصة: ابن الأعرابي تَرى يَتْري إذا تَراخى في العَمِلِ فعمل شيئاً بعد شيء.
ترر (لسان العرب) وتَرَّ الرجلُ عن بلاده تُروراً: بَعُدَ. وأَتَرَّه القضاءُ إتْراراً: أبعده. وتَرَّ بسلْحه وهَذَّ به وهَرَّ به رمى به. وتَرَّ بسَلْحِه يَتِرُّ: قذف به. وتُرَّ في يده: دفع. والتُّرُّ: الأصل. يقال: لأَضْطرَّنَك إلى تُرِّكَ وقُحاحِك. انفرد وقد أَتَرُّوه إتْراراً. ابن الأعرابي: تَرْتَرَ إذا استرخى في بدنه وكلامه. وقال أبو العباس: التارَ المسترخي من جوع أو غيره؛ وأنشد: ونُصْبِحُ بالغداةِ أترَّ شَيْءٍ قوله: أتَرّ شيء أي أرخى شيء من امتلاء الجوف، ونمسي بالعشي جياعاً قد خلت أجوافنا؛ قال: ويجوز أن يكون أترَّ شيء أمْلأ شيء من الغلام التَّارِ، وقد تقدم. قال أبو العباس: أَترَّ شيء أرخى شيء من التعب.
تَرَّ (القاموس المحيط) تَرَّ العَظْمُ يَتُرُّ ويتِرُّ تَرّاً وتُروراً: بان، وانْقَطَعَ، وقطعَ،
طرر (لسان العرب) وطَرَّتْ يداه تَطِرّ وتَطُرُّ: سقطتْ، وتَرَّت تَتُرّ وأَطَرَّها هو وأتَرَّها.
طرأ (لسان العرب) طَرَأَ على القوم يطْرَأُ طَرْءاً وطُرُوءاً: أَتاهم من مكانٍ، أو طَلَعَ عليهم من بلدٍ آخَر، أو خرج عليهم من مكانٍ بعيدٍ فُجاءة، أو أتاهم من غير أن يَعْلَمُوا، أو خَرج عليهم من فَجْوةٍ.
كَرا (القاموس المحيط) كرا الأرضَ يَكْرُوها: حفرَها،
قرا (الصَّحَاح في اللغة) والقَرِيُّ: مجرى الماء في الروض، والجمع أَقرِيَةٌ وقُرْيانٌ. وتقول: تَقَرَّيْتُ المياه، أي تتبَّعتها. وقَرَيْتُ الماء في الحوض، أي جمعت. واسم ذلك الماء قِرًى.
مكر (لسان العرب) والمَكْرُ سَقْيُ الأَرض؛ يقال: امْكُروا الأرض فإِنها صُلْبَةٌ ثم احرثوها، يريد اسقوها.والمَكْرةُ السَّقْية للزرع. يقال: مررت بزرع مَمْكُورٍ أي مَسْقِيّ. ومكَرَ أَرضه يَمْكُرُها مكْراً: سقاها.

§ 28.—X, 30-X, 40

ePSD: lē'û
<u>a ĝal</u> <u>[STRONG]</u> wr. a_2 $ĝal_2$ "to be strong" Akk. lē'û
<u>atuku</u> <u>[POWERFUL]</u> wr. a_2-tuku "powerful, able-bodied" Akk. igigallu; lē'û
<u>da</u> <u>[WRITING BOARD]</u> wr. ^{ĝeš}da "writing board" Akk. lē'û

ePSD: lû
piriĝ [LION] wr. piriĝ; piriĝ$_3$; bi$_2$-ri-iĝ$_3$; ^{ĝeš}piriĝ; piriĝ$_2$ "lion; bull, wild bull" Akk. lû; lābu; nēšu; rīmu
ePSD: lullû
lulu [MAN] wr. lu$_2$-lu$_7$; lu$_2$-lu$_7$^{lu} "man; humanity" Akk. amēlu; lullû
لعا (لسان العرب) قال الليث: يقال كلبة لَعْوةٌ وذئبة لَعْوةٌ وامرأة لَعْوة يعني بكل ذلك الحريصة التي تقاتل على ما يؤكل، والجمع اللَّعواتُ. واللَّعْوُ واللَّعا الشَّره الحَريص، رجل لَعْوٌ ولَعاً، منقوص، وهو الشره الحريص، واللاعي: الذي يُفزعه أدنى شيء؛ عن ابن الأعرابي؛ واللاعي: الخاشي؛
لأي (لسان العرب) اللَّأى: الإبطاء والاحْتباس، بوزن اللَّعا، واللأى: الجهْد والشدَّة والحاجة إلى الناس؛ قال: واللأيُ المشقة والجهد. واللأى، بوزن اللَّعا: الثَّور الوحشيّ؛ قال اللحياني: وتثنيته لأيان، والجمع ألآء مثل ألْعاع مثل جبَل وأجبال، والأنثى لآة مثل لَعاةٍ ولأى، بغير هاء، هذه عن اللحياني، وقال: إنها البقرة من الوحش خاصة. ابن الأعرابي: لآةٌ وألاة بوزن لَعاة وعَلاة.
لأو (مقاييس اللغة) اللام والهمزة والحرف المعتلّ كلمتان: إحداهما الشِّدَّة، والأخرى حيوان. فالأولى اللأْواء: الشّدة.

§ 29.—X, 41-X, 50

ePSD: šalāš
eš [THREE] wr. eš$_5$; eš-a-bi; eš$_{10}$; am$_3$-mu-uš "three; triplets" Akk. takšû; šalāš
ePSD: šalšu
šušana [FRACTION] wr. šušana "one third" Akk. šalšu
ePSD: rabû
buluĝ [GROW] wr. buluĝ$_3$; buluĝ$_5$; bu-lu-ug; buluĝ "to grow up, rear, make grow; novice; foster child" Akk. rabû; tarbûtu
ثلث (لسان العرب) الثَّلاثة: مِن العدد، في عدد المذكر، معروف، والمؤنث ثلاث. وثَلَثَ الاثنين يَثْلِثهما ثَلْثاً: صار لهما ثالثاً.
با (القاموس المحيط) رَبا رُبُوّاً، كعُلُوّ، ورِباءً: زاد، ونما، وارْتَبَيْتُه، ورَبَيْتُ رباءً ورُبِيّاً: نشأْتُ. ورَبَيْتُه تَرْبِيةً: غَذَوْتُه،

§ 30.—X, 51-XI, 4

AALD: pānû
igi [FACE] wr. igi; i-bi$_2$; igi$_3$; i-gi "first, earlier; front; face" Akk. mahrum; pānû
AALD: depāru (v.) (debāru) يُشبع، يُتخم، يُقنع
AALD: debāru معنى غير معروف
ePSD: erištu
niĝaldi [REQUEST] wr. niĝ$_2$-al-di "request" Akk. erištu
ePSD: rašû
lidim [GET] wr. lidim "to get" Akk. rašû
tuku [ACQUIRE] wr. tuku "to acquire, get; to marry" Akk. rašû
فني (لسان العرب) الفَناء: نقيض البقاء، والفعل فَنِي يفْنَى نادر؛ والفِناء سَعةٌ أمامَ الدار، يعني بالسعة الاسم لا المصدر، والأفْنِية السَّاحات على أبواب الدور؛
دبر (مقاييس اللغة) الدال والباء والراء. أصل هذا الباب أنّ جُلَّه في قياسٍ واحد، وهو آخر الشَّيء وخَلْفُه خلافُ قُبُله. وعلى ذلك يفسَّر قوله جلَّ ثناؤه: واللّيلِ إذا دبرَ [المدثر 33]، يقول: تبع النَّهارَ. ودبرَ بالقِمار، إذا ذَهب به.
الدُّبُرُ (القاموس المحيط) الدُّبُرُ، بالضم وبضمتين: نقيضُ القُبُلِ، و~ من كُلّ شيءٍ: عَقِبُه ومؤخَرُه. ودبرَ: وَلَّى، كأدْبَرَ، وتدابروا: تقاطعوا. واسْتَدْبَرَ: ضدُّ اسْتَقْبَلَ،
سنت (لسان العرب) ابن الأعرابي: أَسْتَنَ الرَّجُلُ وأَسْنَتَ إذا دَخَلَ في السنة.
رسا (لسان العرب) رَسَا الشَّيءُ يَرْسُو رُسُوّاً وأَرْسَى: ثَبَتَ، وأَرْساه هو. ورَسَوْتُ عنه حديثاً أَرْسُوهُ رَسْواً، ورَسَا عنه حديثاً رَسْواً: رَفعه وحَدَّث به عنه؛ ورَسَسْتُ الحديث أَرُسُّه في نفسي أي حَدَّثْتُ به نفْسي؛ ولفظ النهاية: إني لأسمع الحديث أرسه في نفسي واحدث به الخادم، أرسه في نفسي أي اثبته إلخ). فأُحدِّثُ به أَرُسُّه في نفسي؛ قال أبو عبيد: أبتدئ بذكر الحديث ودرْسه في نفسي وأُحدِّثُ به خادمي أَسْتَذْكِرُ الحديث؛ وقال الفراء: معناه أُرَدِّدُه وأُعاوِدُ ذِكْره.

§ 31.—XI, 5-12

ePSD: išten
aš [ONE] wr. aš "one" Akk. išten
ePSD: ištēn
diš [ONE] wr. diš; de-eš-šu$_2$; di-id; di-t- "one" Akk. ištēn
ešda [ONE] wr. eš$_3$-da "one" Akk. ištēn
ur [HE] wr. ur$_5$; ur "he; that, this same; maid, female slave; one; corresponding (to one another); like (one another)" Akk. amtu; ištēn; mithāru; šû
أَسْتُ (القاموس المحيط) أَسْتُ الدَّهْر: قِدَمُه.

أست (لسان العرب) ترجمها الجوهري: قال أبو زيد: ما زال على اسْتِ الدَّهْرِ مَجْنُوناً أي لم يَزلْ يُعْرفُ بالجُنون، وهو مثْلُ أَسِّ الدَّهْرِ، وهو القِدمُ، فأَبدلوا من إِحدى السينين تاء، كما قالوا للطَّسِّ طَسْتٌ؛

سته (لسان العرب) واسْتُ الدهر: أَوَّلُ الدهر. أبو عبيدة: يقال كان ذلك على اسْتِ الدَّهْرِ وعلى أُسِّ الدهر أي على قِدَم الدهر؛

§ 32.—XI, 13-38

AALD: tamkāru (s.) See makāru (v.) التاجر، المُقرض

ePSD: tamkāru

damgar [MERCHANT] wr. dam-gar$_3$ "merchant, trader" Akk. tamkāru

ibira [MERCHANT] wr. ibira; ibira$_2$ "merchant, businessman" Akk. tamkāru

AALD: iptu (s.f.) الإتاوة

AALD: ipţirū (s.) See paţāru (v.) السعر الذي يدفع لتحرير سبيل، فدية

AALD: paţāru (v.) يفطر، يفك

ePSD: paţāru

duh [LOOSEN] wr. duh; ze$_2$-eb "to loosen, release; to open" Akk. paţāru

tar [CUT] wr. tar; tar^{ar} "to cut down; to untie, loosen; to cut; to scatter, disperse; to decide" Akk. harāşu; parāsu; paţāru; sapāhu

ePSD: padû

uš gu [SPARE] wr. uš gu$_7$; uš$_2$ gu$_7$ "to spare; to release" Akk. padû

ePSD: ramānu

mete [ONE'S OWN] wr. me-te; ni$_2$-te "one's own" Akk. ramānu

ni [SELF] wr. ni$_2$ "self" Akk. ramānu

مكر (مقاييس اللغة) الميم والكاف والراء كلمتانِ متباينتان: إحداهما المَكْر: الاحتيال والخداع.

المَكْرُ (القاموس المحيط) المَكْرُ: الخَديعَةُ، وهو ماكِرٌ ومَكَّارٌ ومَكُورٌ، والمَغْرَةُ. والتَّمْكيرُ: احْتِكارُ الحُبوبِ في البُيوت.

فطر (لسان العرب) فطَرَ الشيءَ يَفْطُرُه فطْراً فانْفطر وفطَّره: شقه.

بطر (مقاييس اللغة) الباء والطاء والراء أصلٌ واحد وهو الشَقّ.

بتر (لسان العرب) البَتْرُ: اسْتِئْصالُ الشيء قطعاً.

فتر (لسان العرب) الفَتْرَةُ: الانكسار والضعف.

فطر (مقاييس اللغة) الفاء والطاء والراء أصلٌ صحيحٌ يدلُّ على فَتْح شيءٍ وإبرازِه. من ذلك الفِطْرُ من الصَوم. يقال: أَفْطَرَ إفطاراً.

الفَطْرُ (القاموس المحيط) الفَطْرُ: الشَقُّ. والفِطرَةُ: صَدَقةُ الفِطْرِ، والخِلْقَةُ التي خُلِقَ عليها المَوْلودُ في رَحِمِ أُمِّه، والدِّين. وذَبَحْنا فطيرَةً وفَطُورَةً: شاةً يومَ الفِطْر.

صدق (مقاييس اللغة) و[من] الباب الصَّدَقة: ما يتصدَّق به المرءُ عن نفسه وماله.

فدى (الصِّحاح في اللغة) ويقال: فَداهُ وفاداهُ إذا أعطى فداءه فأنقذه وفداه بنفسه. وفَدَاهُ تَفْدِيَةً، إذا قال له جُعِلت فِداءك. والفِديَةُ والفَدى والفِداءُ، كله بمعنى.

فدي (لسان العرب) فَدَيْتُه فَدًى وفِداء وافْتَدَيْتُه؛ والفداء أن تشتريه، فَدَيْته بمالي فداء وفَدَيْتُه بنَفْسي.

رأم (مقاييس اللغة) الراء والهمزة والميم أصلٌ يدل على مُضامَّةٍ وقُرْبٍ وعَطْف.

رَئِمَ (القاموس المحيط) رَئِمَ الشيءَ، كسَمِعَ: أحَبَّه، وألِفَهُ، و~ الجُرْحُ رَأْماً ورِئْماناً: انْضَمَّ للبُرْءِ، و~ النَّاقَةُ ولَدَها: عَطَفَتْ عليه، ولَزِمَتْه، فهي رَؤُومٌ ورائِمَةٌ ورائِمٌ.

روم (لسان العرب) رام الشيءَ يَرومُهُ رَوْماً ومَراماً: طلبه، ومنه رَوْمُ الحركة في الوقف على المرفوع والمجرور؛ قال ابن سيده: والمرامُ المطلَبُ.

§ 33.—XI, 39-50

ePSD: PA.PA

sisig [BREEZE] wr. sig-sig; ^{tumu}si-si-ig; si-si-ga; sig$_3$-sig$_3$ "ghost?; storm; breeze, wind" Akk. mehû; zīqīqu?; šāru

ePSD: PA

ugula [OVERSEER] wr. ugula "instructor; overseer, foreman" Akk. aklu; šāpiru

ePSD: NU.TUR

nubanda [OVERSEER] wr. nu-banda$_3$; nu-banda$_3$^{da} "overseer, captain" Akk. laputtû

ePSD: nasāhu

bur [TEAR] wr. bur$_{12}$; bu$_7$ "to tear out" Akk. nasāhu

deg [COLLECT] wr. deg$_x$(RI) "to take; to gather up, glean; to tear out; to collect, pick up" Akk. ahāzu; laqātu; leqû; nasāhu

dirig [TEAR] wr. dirig "to tear out" Akk. nasāhu

<u>suh</u> [EXTRACT] wr. suh_5; suh "to tear out; to extract; to choose" Akk. nasāhu
<u>zi</u> [CUT] wr. zi_2; zi; zi_x(|IGI@g|) "to cut, remove; to erase" Akk. baqāmu; barāšu; naţāpu; nasāhu
نطر (لسان العرب) النَّاطِر والنَّاطور من كلام أهل السَّواد: حافظ الزرع والتَّمر والكَرْم، ابن الأعرابي: النَّطرة الحفظ بالعينين، بالطاء، قال: ومنه أخذ النَّاطور.
بأبأ (لسان العرب) وبَأْبأَ الرَّجُلُ: أسْرَعَ. وبأْبأْنا أي أسْرَعْنا. وتبأْبأْتُ تبأْبُؤاً إذا عدوْتُ. وقال أبو عمرو: البُؤْبُؤ: العالِمُ المُعلِّمُ. ويقال: البُؤْبُؤ إنسانُ العيْنِ. وفي التهذيب: البُؤْبُؤ: عَيْرُ العيْنِ. ابن السكيت: يُبأْبئه: يُفدِّيه، بُؤْبُؤ: سيدٌ كريمٌ، بِئْباؤُه: تفديتُه،
بوب (لسان العرب) وبَوَّبَ الرَّجلُ إذا حمل على العدُوِّ. وقال الليث: البابيَّةُ هديرُ الفحْلِ في ترْجيعه. وقال رؤبة: بغَبْغَةٍ مرّاً ومرّاً بابيا وقال أيضاً: يَسُوقُها أعْيَسُ، هدّارٌ، بَبِبٌ، إذا دعاها أقبلتْ، لا تَتَئِبْ (وقوله «يسوقها أعيس إلخ» أورده الصاغاني أيضاً في ب ب ب.) وهذا بابةُ هذا أي شَرْطه.
شرط (لسان العرب) وأشْرَط فلان نفسه لكذا وكذا: أعْلَمها له وأعدَّها؛ ومنه سمي الشُّرَطُ لأنهم جعلوا لأنفسهم علامة يُعْرَفُون بها، الواحد شُرْطةٌ وشُرَطِيٌّ؛ قال ابن أحمر:فأشْرَط نفسه حرصاً عليها، وكان بنفْسِه حَجِئاً ضَنِينا والشُّرْطةُ في السُّلْطان: من العلامة والإعْداد. ورجل شُرْطِيٌّ وشُرَطِيٌّ: منسوب إلى الشُّرطة، والجمع شُرَطٌ، سموا بذلك لأنهم أعَدُّوا لذلك وأعْلَمُوا أنفسهم بعلامات، وقيل: هم أوَل كتيبة تشهد الحرب وتتهيأ للموت. وشُرَطُ السلطان: نُخْبةُ أصحابه الذين يقدِّمهم على غيرهم من جنده؛
نسح (لسان العرب) والمنساحُ: شيءٌ يُدْفعُ به الترابُ ويُذْرى به. قال الأزهري: ما ذكره الليث في النَّسْح لم أسمعه لغيره، قال: وأرجو أن يكون محفوظاً. الجوهري: نسحَ الترابَ نَسْحاً أذراه، ونسح نسحاً: طمع.
نسخ (الصِّحاح في اللغة) نَسَخَتِ الشمسُ الظلَّ وانْتَسَخَتْهُ: أزالته. ونَسَخَتِ الريحُ آثار الدار: غَيَّرتها.
نسخ (لسان العرب) والنَّسْخ إبطال الشيء وإقامة آخر مقامه؛ والنسخ نقل الشيء من مكان إلى مكان وهو هو؛ ونسخ الشيء بالشيء ينسخه وانتسخه: أزاله به وأداله؛ والشيء ينسخ الشيء نَسْخاً أي يزيله ويكون مكانه.

§ 34.—XI, 51-64

ePSD: qiāšu
<u>ba</u> [ALLOT] wr. ba "to divide into shares, share, halve; to allot" Akk. qiāšu; zâzu
<u>šubarzi</u> [PRESENT] wr. šu-bar-zi "present" Akk. qiāšu
AALD: qīāšu (s.) qīltu See qâšu منحة، مكافئة، بخشيش
ePSD: habālu
<u>heše</u> [OPPRESSED] wr. $heš_5{}^{še}{}_3$; haš "(to be) oppressed; (to be) detained" Akk. habālu; kalû
ePSD: hablu
<u>šaĝar</u> [OPPRESSED] wr. šaĝa; šа-ĝa$_2$; šaĝa$_x$(LU$_2$) "a wronged person; (to be) slain; (to be) afflicted, oppressed" Akk. hablu; šagšu
AALD: hābilu (s.) See habālu فاعل الشر، السارق
ePSD: šarāqu
<u>zuh</u> [STEAL] wr. zuh "to steal" Akk. šarāqu
ePSD: šarāku
<u>a ru</u> [DEDICATE] wr. a ru "to dedicate" Akk. šarāku
<u>sag rig</u> [BESTOW] wr. sag rig_7 "to bestow" Akk. šarāku
هبل (مقاييس اللغة) والهَبَّال: الصَّيَّاد يهتبل الصَّيد يغترُّه، ولذلك سمِّي الذِّئب هبلاً، لأنه يَحتالُ لصيده ويهتبله.وأمَّا المَهْبِل فمستقرُّ الولد من الرَّحِم، وهو عندنا من باب الإبدال، وهو في ذلك أصله محْبل.
هبل (الصِّحاح في اللغة) الهبَلُ بالتحريك: مصدر قولك: هَبِلَتْهُ أُمُّه، أي ثكلتْهُ. والإهبالُ: الإثْكال. وذِئْبٌ هَبِلٌ: مُحتالٌ.
حبل (مقاييس اللغة) الحاء والباء واللام أصلٌ واحدٌ يدلُّ على امتداد الشيء. ثمّ يحمل عليه، ومَرْجع الفروع مرجعٌ واحد. وزعم ناسٌ أنَّ الأسد يقال له حَبيلُ بَراحٍ. والحِبالة: حِبالة الصائد. ويقال احتبلَ الصيدَ، إذا صادهُ بالحبالة. ومن المشتق من هذا الأصلِ الحِبْل، بكسر الحاء، وهي الداهية. ووجْهُهُ عنديَ أنَّ الإنسان إذا دُهي فكأنَه قد حُبل، أي وقع في الحِبالة، كالصَّيد الذي يُحبَل.
الحَبْلُ (القاموس المحيط) وحبلَ الصَّيْد، واحْتَبلَهُ: أخذَهُ بها، أو نصَبَها له. وإنه لحِبْلٌ من أحْبالِها: للداهية من الرجالِ، وللقائم على المالِ الرَّفيق بسياسته. و"ثارَ حابِلُهم على نابِلِهم": أوقدوا الشَّرَّ بينهم.
حبل (لسان العرب) والحَبْلان أيضاً: الممتلئ غضباً. وحَبِل الرجلُ إذا امتلأ من شرب اللبن، فهو حَبْلانُ، والمرأة حَبْلى. وفلان حَبْلان على فلان أي غضبان. وبه حَبَلٌ أي غضب،
سَرَق (القاموس المحيط) واسْترقَهُ: جاءَ مُسْتتِراً إلى حِرْزٍ، فأخَذ مالاً لِغَيْرِه، والاسْمُ: السَّرِقَةُ، بالفتح، وكفَرِحةٍ وكتِفٍ. والتَّسْريقُ: النِّسْبةُ إلى السَرِقةِ. والمُسْترقُ: الناقصُ الضَّعيفُ الخلْقِ، والمُستمِعُ مُخْتفِياً. والاسْتراق: الخَتْل سِراً كالذي يستمع، والكَتَبةُ يَسْترِقُون من بعض الحسابات. والمُسارقة والاسْتراق والتَّسرُّق: اختلاس النظر والسمع؛
شرك (لسان العرب) وشاركت فلاناً: صرت شريكه. واشْتركنا وتَشاركنا في كذا وشَرِكْتُه في البيع والميراث أشْرَكُه شَرِكةً، والإسم الشِّرْك؛
سرق (مقاييس اللغة) السين والراء والقاف أصلٌ يدلُّ على أخْذ شيء في خفاء وستر. واسترَقَ السَّمعَ، إذا تسمَّع مختفياً.
وقش (لسان العرب) ووَقَشَ منه وَقْشاً: أصاب منه عطاء. الجوهري: بنو أُقَيش قومٌ من العرب، وأصل الألف فيه واو مثل أُقِّتَتْ ووُقِّتَت،

شنق (الصَحاح في اللغة) الشَنَقُ في الصدقة: ما بين الفريضتين. وفي الحديث: "لا شناق" أي لا يؤخذ من الشنق حتى يتم. والشَنَقُ أيضاً: ما دون الدية، وذلك أن يسوقَ ذو الحمالةِ الدية كاملة، فإذا كانت معها دِياتُ جراحاتٍ فتلك هي الأَشْناقُ. كأنها متعلِّقة بالدية العُظمى.قسط (الصَحاح في اللغة) والقِسْطُ الحِصَّةُ والنصيب.

القِسْطُ (القاموس المحيط) والاقْتِساطُ: الاقْتِسامُ. والحِصَّةُ من الشيء، والمِقْدارُ، والرِّزْقُ، والمِيزانُ، والكُوزُ. وتَقَسَّطُوا الشيءَ بينَهُم: اقْتَسَمُوهُ بالسَّوِيَّة.

قسط (لسان العرب) وفي الحديث: أَنَّ اللهَ لا ينامُ ولا ينبغي له أَن ينام، يَخْفِضُ القِسْطَ ويرفعُه؛ القِسْطُ: الميزانُ، سمي به من القِسْطِ العَدْلِ، والقِسْطُ الحِصَّةُ والنَّصيبُ. يقال: أَخذ كل واحد من الشركاء قِسْطَه أَي حِصَّتَه.

§ 35.—XI, 65-XII, 4

AALD: elû (alû) (v.) يعلو، يصعد، يفقد، يخسرغرامة، يفقد، يتحمل مسؤلية
ePSD: luʾtu
me [STIFFNESS] wr. me "stiffness" Akk. luʾtu
ePSD: gud [OX] (17947x: ED IIIa, ED IIIb, Old Akkadian, Lagash II, Ur III, Early Old Babylonian, Old Babylonian, 1st millennium, unknown) wr. gud; gu_3-ra "bull, ox; cattle; calf; lion" Akk. alpu; lī'um
ePSD: GUD.GIŠ
gudĝeš [OX] wr. gud-ĝeš "a draught ox"
AALD: ṣênu (v.) See ṣēnu يحمل الحمولة
AALD: ṣēnu (adj.) مُحمَل
AALD: ṣēnu (s.f.) الضأن (الاغنام والماعز)، اغنام وماعز

لود (لسان العرب) عنُقٌ أَلوَدُ: غليظ. ورجل أَلوَدُ: لا يكادُ يميلُ إِلى عَدْلٍ ولا إِلى حقٍّ ولا يَنْقادُ لأَمر؛ وقد لود يَلْوَدُ لَوداً وقَومٌ أُلوادٌ. قال الأَزهري: هذه كلمة نادرة؛ وقال رؤبة: أَسْكَتَ أَجْراسَ القُرومِ الأُلواد وقال أَبو عمرو: الأَلْوَدُ الشديد الذي لا يُعْطي طاعة، وجمعه أُلواد؛ وأَنشد: أَغلبَ غلاَّباً أَلدَّ أَلودا

ولد (لسان العرب) ووَلَدُه: رهطه في معنى. وتوالَدُوا أَي كثروا، ووَلَد بعضهم بعضاً. ويقال في تفسير قوله تعالى: مالُه وولدُه إِلا خساراً؛ أَي رهْطُه.

جدد (لسان العرب) وشاةٌ جَدَّاءُ: قليلةُ اللبن يابسة الضَّرْع، وكذلك الناقة والأَتان؛ وقيل: الجَدّاءُ من كل حَلوبة الذاهبةُ اللبن عن عيب، والجَدودةُ: القليلةُ اللبن من غير عيب، والجمع جَدائدُ وجِدادٌ. ابن السكيت: الجَدودُ النعجة التي قلّ لبَنُها من غير بأْس، وناقة جَدَّاءُ: يابسة الضَّرْ والجَدَّاءُ من الغنم والإِبل: المقطوعة الأُذن. وفي التهذيب: والجَدَّاء الشاةُ المقطوعة الأُذُن. والأَصمعي: يقال للناقة إِنها لَمِجَدَّةٌ بالرَّحْل إِذا كانت جادَّة في السير.

جدا (لسان العرب) والجادي الجراد لأَنه يَجْدي كل شيء أَي يأْكله؛ والجَدْيُ: الذكر من أَولاد المَعز، والجمع أَجْدٍ وجِداءٌ، ولا تقل الجَدايا، ولا الجِدى، بكسر الجيم، والجَدايةُ والجِداية جميعاً: الذكر والأُنثى من أَولاد الظباء إِذا بلغ ستة أَشهر أَو سبعة وعدا وتَشدَّد، وخص بعضهم به الذكر منها. غيره: الجداية بمنزلة العَناق من الغنم،

ظبي (تاج العروس) والظَّبْيَةُ: الشَّاةُ. وأَيْضاً: البَقَرَةُ.

الظَّبْيُ (القاموس المحيط) والظَّبْيَةُ: الأُنْثَى، والشاةُ، والبقرةُ، وفَرْجُ المرأةِ، والجِرابُ، أو الصغيرُ، ومُنْعَرَجُ الوادي، ورَجُلٌ (بليدٌ)، وثلاثةُ أفراسٍ، وماآن، ومَوْضِعان.

ظبي (تهذيب اللغة) ظبي: الأُنثى من الظِّباء ظَبْية، والذكر ظَبْيٌ، أبو عبيد عن الأصمعيّ :يقال لكلِ ذاتِ خُفٍ أو ظِلْفٍ: الحياء، ولكل ذاتِ حافرٍ: الظَّبْيَةُ، قال: وللسباعِ كلها: الثَّفْرُ، قال: وقال الفرّاء: يقال لِلكلبة ظَبْية، وشَقْحةٌ، ولذوات الحافر ظَبْيَةٌ، وفي الحديث أنه أُهْدِيَ للنبي صلى الله عليه وسلم ظَبيةٌ فيها خَرَزٌ فأعطى الأهل منها والعزب، وقال الليث: الظَّبْيَةُ جهاز المرأة والنَاقة، يعني حياءها، والظَبْيَةُ شبهُ العِجْلة والمَزادة، قال: وإذا خرج، تَخْرُجُ امرأة قُدامه تُسمى ظَبْيَة، وهي تُنْذِرُ المسلمين.

جعد (لسان العرب) وبعير جعد: كثير الوبر جَعْده.

ظعن (لسان العرب) ظَعَنَ يَظْعَنُ ظَعْناً وظَعَناً، بالتحريك، وظُعوناً: ذهب وسار. والظَّعُون من الإِبل: الذي تركبه المرأَة خاصة، وقيل: هو الذي يُعْتَملُ ويُحْتَمل عليه. وفرس مِظْعانٌ: سَهْلة السَّير، وكذلك الناقة.

ظعن (الصَحاح في اللغة) ظَعَن، أي سار، ظَعْناً وظَعَناً بالتحريك. أراد: يا ظعينةُ. الكسائي: الظعونُ: البعير الذي يُعتمل ويُحمَل عليه.

ظعن (مقاييس اللغة) الظاء والعين والنون أصلٌ واحدٌ صحيحٌ يدلُّ على الشُّخوص من مكانٍ إلى مكان. والظَّعُون: البعير الذي يُعَدُّ للظَّعَن.

جرر (لسان العرب) وبعير جَرُورٌ: يُسْنَى به، وجمعه جُرُرٌ. الجوهري: الجَرِيرُ حَبْلٌ يجعل للبعير بمنزلة العِذار للدابة غَيْرُ الزِّمام، وبه سمي الرجل جَريراً. ابن سيده: والجِرَّةُ ما يُفِيضُ به البعيرُ من كرشه فيأْكله ثانية. والجَرْجَرَةُ: تَرَدُّدُ هدير الفحل، وهو صوت يردده البعير في حَنْجَرته، وقد جَرْجَرَ؛

صعن (لسان العرب) الصَّعَوْنُّ، بكسر الصاد وتشديد النون: الدَّقيقُ العُنق الصغير الرأْس من أَيّ شيء كان، وقد غلب على النَّعام، والأُنثى صَعَوْنَّةٌ.

ضين (لسان العرب) الضِّينُ والضَّيْنُ: لغتان في الضأْن، فإِما أَن يكون شاذاً، وإِما أَن يكون من لفظ آخر؛ قال ابن سيده: وهو الصحيح عندي.

ضأن (لسان العرب) الضَّائنُ من الغنم: ذو الصوف، ويُوصَفُ به فيقال: كَبْش ضائنٌ، والأُنثى ضائنة. والضائنُ: خلافُ الماعز، والجمع الضَّأْنُ والضَّأَنُ مثل المَعْز والمَعَز. والضَّئِينُ والضِّئِينُ: تميمية. والضَّيْن والضِّين، غير مهموزين؛

ضأن (مقاييس اللغة) الضاد والهمزة والنون أُصَيلٌ صحيح، وهو بعض الأنعام.
علا (لسان العرب) وعالِ عنّي وأعْلِ عنّي: تنحَّ. وعال عليَّ أي احمِلْ؛ وعلى: حرف جرّ، ومعناه استعْلاء الشيء، وعلينا أميرٌ: كقولك عليه مالٌ لأنه شيء اعْتلاهُ، وهذا كالمثَل كما يَثْبت الشيءُ على المكان كذلك يَثْبت هذا عليه، فقد يتَّسع هذا في الكلام، ولا يريد سيبويه بقوله عليه مال لأنه شيء اعْتلاه أنّ اعْتلاه من لفظ على، إنما أراد أنها في معناها وليست من لفظها، وكيف يظن بسيبويه ذلك وعلى من ع ل ي واعتلاه من ع ل و؟وقد تأْتي على بمعنى في؛ وقالوا: ثبتَ عليه مالٌ أي كثر، وكذلك يقال: علَيْه مالٌ، يريدون ذلك المعنى، ولا يقال له مالٌ إلا من العين كما لا يقال عليه مالٌ إلاّ من غير العين؛ وفي الحديث: عليكم بكذا أي افْعلوه، وهو اسمٌ للفعل بمعنى خذ، يقال: علَيْك زيداً وعليك بزيدٍ أي خذه. ويقولون: علَيْه دَيْن، وعلا الفرسَ: ركِبه. وأعْلى عنه: نزل.

§ 36.—XII, 5-9

ePSD: biltu

gun [LOAD] wr. gun$_2$; gu$_2$-un "load; yield; rent, tax, tribute; a unit of weight" Akk. biltu

niĝguna [TRIBUTE] wr. niĝ$_2$-gu$_2$-na "tribute, rent, tax" Akk. biltu

u [LOAD] wr. u$_2$ "load" Akk. biltu

AALD: nāši biltu (nāš biltu) See nāšû المستأجر لحقل مُلك للدولة

ePSD: našû

gaĝ [CARRY] wr. gaĝ$_x$(IL$_2$); ga-aĝ$_3$ "to carry" Akk. našû

gur [LIFT] wr. gur$_3$-ru; guru$_3$; gur; gur$_{17}$; guru$_6$ "bearer; to lift, carry" Akk. našû; nāšû

il [RAISE] wr. il$_2$; il$_5$; $il_2{}^{ll}{}_2$ "to raise, carry" Akk. našû

ePSD: nāšû

gur [LIFT] wr. gur$_3$-ru; guru$_3$; gur; gur$_{17}$; guru$_6$ "bearer; to lift, carry" Akk. našû; nāšû

نأش (مقاييس اللغة) النون والهمزة والشين كلمةٌ تدلّ على أخْذ وبطش.
النَّأْشُ (القاموس المحيط) النَّأْشُ، كالمنْع: التَناوُلُ، كالتَناوُش، والأخْذُ،
نأش (لسان العرب) التناؤشُ، بالهمز: التأخُّرُ والتباعدُ. ابن سيده: نَأَشَ الشيءَ أخَّره وانْتأَش هو تأخَّر وتباعدَ. قال: وقد يجوز أن يكون من النَأْشِ، وهو الطلبُ، ونأَشه اللهُ نأْشاً كنَعشه أي أحْياه ورفعه؛ وانْتأَشه الله أي انْتزعه.
نوش (لسان العرب) ناشَه بيده ينُوشُه نوْشاً: تناوله؛ وقال ثعلب: التناوُش. بلا همز، الأخْذُ من قُرْب، والتناؤشُ، بالهمز، من بُعد، وقد تقدم ذكره أولَ الفصل. ونُشْتُ الرجلَ نوْشاً: أنلْته خيراً أو شرّاً. وقد ناشَه ينُوشُه نوْشاً إذا تناوله وأخذه؛ ونُشْتُ الشيء نوْشاً: طلبْتُه. وانْتَشْتُ الشيءَ: استخرجْته؛
بعل (لسان العرب) والبعْل ما أُعطي من الإتاوة على سقْي النخل؛ وبعْلُ الشيء: ربُّه ومالكُه. وباعله: جالسه. وهو بَعْلٌ على أهله أي ثِقْلٌ عليهم. وفي الحديث: أن رجلاً قال للنبي،صلى الله عليه وسلم: أبايعك على الجهاد، فقال: هل لك من بَعْلٍ؟ البعْل: الكلُّ؛

§ 37.—XII, 10-21

ePSD: ţuppu

dub [TABLET] wr. dub "tablet" Akk. ţuppu

ePSD: dibbu

dib [BOARD] wr. dib "board" Akk. dibbu

AALD: dibbu (s.) (dippu) لوح (خشبي)

ePSD: hepû

gul [DESTROY] wr. gul; gu-ul "to destroy; to break; to flatten; to carve, cut; to engrave" Akk. abātu; hepû; naqāru; sapānu

rah [BEAT] wr. rah$_2$; ra-ah "to beat, kill; to break, crush; to flood; to thresh (grain with a flail)" Akk. dâku; diāšu; hepû; rahāşu; rapāsu

AALD: hepû (v.) (hebû, hapû, habû) يحطم، يدمر، يكسر نصا (لوحا)

دوف (العباب الزاخر) الدوف الخلط والبل، يقال: دفت الدواء وغيره: أي بللته بماء أو بغيره، فهو مدوف ومدووف: أي مبلول؛
ديف (لسان العرب) وداف الشيء يديفه: لغة في دافه يَدُوفُه إذا خلطه.
دبب (لسان العرب) دبَّ النَمْلُ وغيره من الحيوان على الأرض، يدبُّ دبّاً ودبيباً: مشى على هِينته.
دفف (لسان العرب) والدَّفيفُ: العدْوُ. الصحاح: الدَفيفُ الدَّبيبُ وهو السَيرُ اللَّيِنُ؛ وفي حديث لُحوم الأضاحي: إنما نهيْتُكم عنها من أجلِ الدَّافَة؛ هم قوم يسيرون جماعة سَيْراً ليس بالشَّديد. يقال: هم قوم يدفُّونَ دفيفاً. الدَفُّ والدَّفَّةُ: الجنْبُ من كل شيء، بالفتح لا غير؛ وأنشد الليث في الدفَّة: ووانية زجَرْتُ، عل وَجاها، قريح الدَفتيْنِ من البطانِ وقيل: الدَفُّ صفْحةُ الجنب؛ ودفَّ الأمْرُ يدِفُّ واسْتَدفَّ: تهيّأ وأمكن. يقال: خذ ما دفَّ لك واسْتَدفَّ أي خذ ما تهيّأ وأمكن وتسهّلَ مثل اسْتطفّ، والدال مبدلة من الطاء. واسْتدفَّ أمْرُهم أي اسْتتبَّ واستقام؛
الدَّفُّ (القاموس المحيط) الدَّفُّ، بالفتح: الجَنْبُ من كُلِّ شيءٍ، أو صَفْحَتُهُ، ودَفّتا المُصْحَفِ: ضِمامَتاهُ،
دفف (العباب الزاخر) الدَّفُّ -بالفتح-: الجنب، ودفا البعير: جنباه،
طوب (لسان العرب) يقال للداخل: طوْبَـة وأوْبَـة، يُريدونَ الطَّيِّبَ في المعنى دون اللَّفظ، لأن تلك ياءٌ وهذه واو. والطُّوبَةُ: الآجُرَة، شامية أو رومية. قال: الآجر الطين.

طوب (الصَحَاح في اللغة) الطُوب: الآجُرّ بلغة أهل مصر.
هبا (لسان العرب) والهباء دُقاق التُرب ساطعُه ومَنثُوره على وجه الأرض. ويقال: أَهبى التراب إهباء، وهي الأهابيّ؛ والهابي من التراب: ما ارْتفع ودَقَ؛
هبب (لسان العرب) وهبَّ السيفُ يَهُبّ هباً وهبَّة وهبَة إذا قطع.
هب (مقاييس اللغة) الهاء والباء مُعظمُ بابه الانتباه والاهتزاز والحركة، وربما دلّ على رِقّة شيء. وهزَزْتُ السَيف فهبّ هبّة. وهبّته: هزّته ومَضاؤه في ضريبته. ويقال لقطع الثّوب: هبَبٌ.

§ 38.—XII, 22-30

ePSD: aššatu
dam [SPOUSE] wr. dam "spouse" Akk. aššatu; mutu
ePSD: elâtu
sibta [SHARE] wr. sib$_2$-ta "additional share" Akk. elâtu
AALD: sidru (s.) (sadru) See sadāru السَطر، الصَف، خط المعركة، قرابين
AALD: illatu (s.f.) (illitu) القافلة، الحزمة، العائلة، الجماعة، الحشد
AALD: e'iltu (s.) (i'iltu) (OB: ehiltu, ihiltu, iheltu) See e'ēlu الزام مسؤلية قانونية
AALD: e'ēlu (v.) (a'alu) يعلق، يربط، يلزم
AALD: adāru (v.) (See: adirtu, adiru) يقلق، يسبب الازعاج او الخوف

السَتَه (القاموس المحيط) السَتَه، ويُحرَكُ: الاسْتُ. والسَه، ويُضمّ مُخففة: العجُزُ، أو حَلْقةُ الدُبُر.
سته (لسان العرب) الجوهري: والاسْتُ العجُزُ، وقد يُرادُ بها حلْقة الدبر، وأصله ستَهٌ على فعَل، بالتحريك، يدل على ذلك أن جمعه أسْتاه مثل جَمل وأجمال، ولا يجوز أن يكون مثل جِزْع وقفْل اللذين يجمعان أيضاً على أفعال، لأنك إذا رَددْت الهاء التي هي لام الفعل وحذفت العين قلت سَهٌ، بالفتح؛ قال ابن خالويه: فيها ثلاث لغات: سَهٌ وستٌ واسْتٌ. والسَتَهُ عِظمُ الاسْت. والسَتَه مصدر الأسْتَه، وهو الضَخْمُ الاست. قال النحويون: أصل الاسْت ستَهٌ، فاستثقلوا الهاء لسكون التاء، فلما حذفوا الهاء سكنت السين فاحتيج إلى ألف الوصل، كما فعل بالاسْم والابْن فقيل الاسْتُ، قال: ومن العرب من يقول السَه، بالهاء، عند الوقف يجعل التاء هي الساقطة، ومنهم من يجعلها هاء عند الوقف وتاء عند الإدراج،
سطر (مقاييس اللغة) السين والطاء والراء أصلٌ مطَرد يدلُ على اصطفاف الشيء، كالكتاب والشجر، وكلّ شيء اصطفّ.
سطر (لسان العرب) السَطْرُ والسَطَرُ: الصَفُ من الكتاب والشجر والنخل ونحوها؛ والسَطْرُ الخَطُ والكتابة، وهو في الأصل مصدر. وسطر يَسْطُر إذا كتب؛ قال أبو سعيد الضرير: سمعت أعرابيّاً فصيحاً يقول: أسْطرَ فلانٌ اسمي أي تجاوز السَطْرَ الذي فيه اسمي، فإذا كتبه قيل: سَطرَهُ
سدر (مقاييس اللغة) السين والدال والراء أصلٌ واحدٌ يدلُ على شبه الحَيْرة واضطراب الرأي. يقولون: السادر المتحيّر. ويقولون سدِر بصرُهُ يَسْدَر، وذلك إذا اسمدَ وتحيّر. ويقولون: السّادر هو الذي لا يبالي ما صَنَع، ولا يهتمّ بشيء.
سدر (لسان العرب) وقال ابن السكيت: جاء ينفض أزْدرَيه، بالزاي وذلك إذا جاء فارغاً ليس بيده شيء ولم يقْض طَلبته. أبو عمرو: سمعت بعض قيس يقول سَدَلَ الرجُل في البلاد وسدَر إذا ذهب فيها فلم يثْنِه شيء.
سدل (مقاييس اللغة) السين والدال واللام أصلٌ واحدٌ يدلُ على نزول الشيء من عُلْوٍ إلى سُفْلٍ ساتراً لـه. يقال منه أرخى اللّيل سُدوله، وهي سُتُرُه.
سدن (مقاييس اللغة) السين والدال والنون أصلٌ واحد لشيء مخصوص. يقال إنّ السِدانة الحجابة. وسدنة البيت: حجبتُه. ويقولون: السَدن السِتر. فإنْ كان صحيحاً فهو من باب الإبدال، والأصل السَدَل.
سدن (الصَحَاح في اللغة) السادِنُ: خادم الكعبة وبيت الأصنام، والجمع السَدَنةُ.
عول (لسان العرب) والعوْل: المُستعان به، وقد عوّل به وعليه. وأعْوَل عليه وعوّل، كلاهما: أدلّ وحَمل. ويقال: عوّلْ عليه أي اسْتعِنْ به. وعوّل عليه: اتّكل واعْتمد؛ وعيالُ الرّجُلِ وعيّلُه: الذين يتكفلُ بهم، وقد يكون العيّلُ واحداً والجمع عالةٌ؛ وعال عياله عوْلاً وعُؤولاً وعيالةً وأعالهم وعيّلَهم، كلّه: كفاهم ومانهم وقاتهم وأنفق عليهم.
عيل (لسان العرب) وعيالُ الرجل وعيّله: الذين يتكفّل بهم ويعولهم؛
أهل (لسان العرب) الأهْلُ: أهل الرجل وأهْلُ الدار، وكذلك الأهْلةُ؛ المازني: لا يجوز أن تقول أنت مُستأْهل هذا الأمر ولا مستأْهل لهذا الأمر لأنك إنما تريد أنت مستوجب لهذا الأمر، ولا يدل مستأْهل على ما أردت، وإنما معنى الكلام أنت تطلب أن تكون من أهل هذا المعنى ولم تُردْ ذلك، ولكن تقول أنت أهْلٌ لهذا الأمر، وروى أبو حاتم في كتاب المزال والمفسد عن الأصمعي: يقال استوجب ذلك واستحقه ولا يقال استأْهله ولا أنت تسْتأْهل ولكن تقول هو أهل ذاك وأهل لذاك، ويقال هو أهْلةُ ذلك. وأهّله لذلك الأمر تأْهيلاً وآهله: رآه له أهْلاً. واسْتأْهله استوجبه، وكرهها بعضهم، ومن قال وَهِلْتُه ذهب به إلي لغة من يقول وامرْتُ وواكَلْت. وأهْلُ المذهب: منْ يدين به. وأهْلُ الأمر: وُلاتُه. وأهْلُ البيت: سُكّانه. وأهل الرجل: أخصُّ الناس به. وآلُ الرجل: أهْلُه.
ألل (لسان العرب) والإلّ: القرابة. والإلُّ: الجار. وقيل: الإلُّ النّسب والقرابة والإلّ: الربوبية. والألُّ، بالضم: الأول في بعض اللغات وليس من لفظ الأوّل؛ من أعْراب قيس وتميم: أيلة الرجل بنو عمه الأدْنون.
وأل (لسان العرب) وقال بعضهم: مَن أطاف بالرجل وحلّ معه من قرابته وعشيرته فهو إيلتُه. وقال العكلي: هو من إيلتنا أي من عشيرتنا.
لتهذيب: وأيلة قرية عربيّة كأنها سميت أيلة لأن أهلها يؤولون إليها، وأمّا إلْيةُ الرجل فقراباته، وكذلك لِيَتُه.

§ 40.—XII, 39-48

ePSD: ahu
a [ARM] wr. a_2 "arm; labor; wing; horn; side; strength; wage; power" Akk. ahu; idu
gu [NECK] wr. gu_2 "bank, side; neck" Akk. ahu; kišādu; tikku
pap [RELATION] wr. pap "first and foremost, pre-eminent; father; male, virile; brother" Akk. abu; ahu; ašarēdu; zikaru
šeš [BROTHER] wr. šeš "brother; junior worker, assistant" Akk. ahu
zag [SIDE] wr. zag "arm; shoulder; side; border, boundary, district; limit; right side, the right" Akk. ahu; idu; imittu; ishu; mişru; pāţu

هوا (لسان العرب) والإهْواء: التَّناوُل باليد والضَّرْبُ، والإراغةُ: أن يَذْهب الصَّيدُ هكذا وهكذا والعُقاب تتْبَعُه. ابن سيده: والإهْواء والاهْتِواء الضَّرب باليد والتناوُلُ. وهوت يدي للشيء وأهْوتْ: امْتَدَّت وارْتفعت. وقال ابن الأعرابي: هَوى إليه من بُعْدٍ، وأهْوى إليه من قُرْبٍ، وأهْوَيْت له بالسيف وغيره، وأهْوَيْت بالشيء إذا أوْمأْت به، وأهْوى إليه بيده ليأخذه. وفي الحديث: فأهْوى بيده إليه أي مَدَّها نحْوه وأمالها إليه. يقال: أهْوى يده وبيده إلى الشيء ليأْخذه. قال: وتقول أهْوى فأخذ؛ معناه أهْوى إليه يده، وتقول: أهْوى إليه بيده. وهَوٌّ من الأرض: جانبٌ منها.
أهه (لسان العرب) الأهَةُ: التَحزُّنُ. وقد أَهَ أهاً وأهَةً. وقد تردُ بمعنى التَّوجُّع، وقيل: التوجعُ يقال فيه آهاً،
أخخ (لسان العرب) أخٌ: كلمةُ توجع وتأوه من غيظ أو حزن؛ قال ابن دريد: وأحسبها مُحْدَثة. والأخُّ والأخَّةُ: لغة في الأخ والأُخْتِ، حكاه ابن الكلبي؛ قال ابن دُرَيْد: ولا أدري ما صحة ذلك.
أخا (لسان العرب) الأخ من النسَب: معروف، وقد يكون الصديق والصاحِبَ، والأخا، مقصور، والأخْوُ لغتان فيه حكاهما ابن الأعرابي؛ الجوهري: الأخُ أصله أخَوٌ، وقال بعضُ النحويِّين: سُمِّي الأخُ أخاً لأنَّ قصْده قصْد أخيه، وأصله من وَخَى أي قصَد
حوا (لسان العرب) والحُوَاءة الرجل اللازم بيته، وحَوّة الوادي: جانبه.

§ 41.—XII, 49-62

ePSD: nipiltu
nambura [PAYMENT] wr. nam-bur_2-a "payment" Akk. nipiltu
ePSD: niplu
henbur [STALK] wr. ^{gi}henbur; $^{gi}henbur_2$; $henbur_x$(|IGI.KAK|) "stalk; growth of rushes" Akk. habburu; niplu; udittu
ligima [SHOOT] wr. ^{ĝeš}ligima "shoot, sapling" Akk. ligimû; niplu; ziqpu
AALD: bahû (v.) يُضعف، يُفزع، يجعله ينْحل

النَفْلُ (القاموس المحيط) ج: أنفالٌ ونفالٌ، ونَبتٌ من أحْرار البُقول، نَوْره أصْفرُ طيِّبُ الرائحة، تَسْمَنُ عليه الخَيْلُ. ونفلهُ النَّفَل ونفَلهُ وأنْفلهُ: أعْطاهُ إياهُ.
ونفَل: حلَف، وأعْطى نَافلةً من المعروف. والتَّنْفيلُ: التَّحليفُ، والدَّفْعُ عن صاحبِك.
نفل (الصَّحاح في اللغة) النفْلُ والنافلةُ: عطيَّةُ التطوُّع من حيث لا تجِبُ، والنفلُ أيضاً: نَبتٌ.
بوخ (لسان العرب) باخَتِ النارُ والحربُ تَبُوخُ بَوْخاً وبُو وخاً وبَوَخاناً: سكنتْ وفترت، وكذلك الحرُّ والغضب والحُمّى؛ قال رؤبة: حتى يَبُوخ الغضَبُ الحميتُ وأباخَها الذي يُخْمِدُها، وأبخْتُ الحَرْب إباخة. وباخ الرجلُ يبوخُ: سكن غضَبُه. وباخ الحَرُّ يبوخُ إذا فتر؛ وقيل: باخ الحرَ إذا سكن فَوْرُه. وأبخْ عنك من الظهيرة أي أقم حتى يسكن حر النهار ويبْرُد. وعدا حتى باخَ أي أعيا وانْبهرَ. وهم في بُوخٍ من أمرهم أي في اختلاط.

§ 42.—XII, 63- XIII, 5

ePSD: erēšu
al dug [DESIRE] wr. al dug_4 "to desire" Akk. erēšu
uru [SOW] wr. uru_4; uru_{11}^{ru}; i-ru "to sow; to cultivate" Akk. erēšu
AALD: šūşû (adj.) protruding?, turned out? (see aşû)
ePSD: aşû
e [LEAVE] wr. e_3; i; e "to leave, to go out; to thread, hang on a string; to remove, take away; to bring out; to enter; to bring in; to raise, rear (a child); to sow; to rave; to winnow; to measure (grain) roughly (with a stick); to rent" Akk. aşû; erēbu; mahû; rubbû; zarû; šakāku
ePSD: šammu
u [PLANTS] wr. u_2 "bread, loaf; food; grass, herb; pasture; plant(s)" Akk. akalu; rîtu; šammu
ePSD: šipru
gašam [WISE] wr. gašam "(to be) knowing, wise; sending, mission; work; craftsman, specialist" Akk. mūdū; ummiānu; šipru
ePSD: epēšu
ak [DO] wr. ak; a "to do; to make; to act, perform; to proceed, proceeding (math.)" Akk. epēšu
du [BUILD] wr. du_3 "to build, make; to do, perform" Akk. banû; epēšu

<u>dug</u> <u>[SPEAK]</u> wr. dug_4 "to speak, talk, say; to order; to do, perform; to negotiate" Akk. atwû; dabābu; epēšu; qabû

ePSD: itti

<u>ki</u> <u>[WITH]</u> wr. ki "with (math.)" Akk. itti

أرث (لسان العرب) والأُرْثُ والأُرَفُ: الحُدودُ بين الأَرضين، واحدتها أُرْثة وأُرْفة. ابن سيده: والأُرْثة الحدّ بين الأَرْضين، وأَرَّثَ الأَرْضَيْن: جعل بينهما أُرْثة؛

العَرْثُ (القاموس المحيط) العَرْثُ: الانْتِزاعُ، والدَّلْكُ.

حرث (مقاييس اللغة) الحاء والراء والثاء أصلان متفاوتان: أحدهما الجمع والكَسْب، والآخر أنْ يُهزَل الشيء.فالأول الحَرْث، وهو الكَسْب والجمع، وبه سمِّي الرجل حارثاً. وفي الحديث: "احْرُثْ لدُنْياك كأنّك تعيش أبداً، واعملْ لآخرتك كأنك تموت غداً".ومن هذا الباب حرث الزَّرع.

حرث (لسان العرب) الحَرْثُ والحِراثةُ: العَمل في الأَرض زرْعاً كان أو غرْساً، وقد يكون الحرْثُ نفسَ الزَّرْع، وبه فسَّر الزجاجُ قوله تعالى: أَصابت حرْثَ قوم ظلَمُوا أَنفسَهم فأَهلكته. حرَث يحْرُثُ حرْثاً. الأَزهري: الحرْثُ قذْفُك الحبَّ في الأَرض لازْدِراع، والحرْثُ: الزَّرْع. والحَرَّاثُ: الزَّرَّاعُ. وقد حرَث واحترَث، مثْل زرَع وازْدرَع. والحرْثُ الكسْبُ، والفعلُ كالفعل، والمصدر كالمصدر، وهو أَيضاً الاحتراثُ.

أرس (لسان العرب) الإِرْس: الأَصل، والأَريس: الأَكَّارُ؛ عن ثعلب. ابن الأَعرابي: أَرس يأْرِسُ أَرْساً إِذا صار أَريساً، وأَرَّسَ يُؤَرِّسُ تأْريساً إِذا صار أَكَّاراً، وجمع الأَريس أَريسون، وجمع الإِرِّيس إِرِّيسُونَ وأَرارسة وأَرارِسُ، وأَرارِسةٌ ينصرف، وأَرارِسُ لا ينصرف، وقيل: إِنما قال ذلك لأَن الأَكَّارِينَ كانوا عندهم من الفُرْسِ، وهم عَبَدَة النار، فجعل عليه إِثمهم. قال الأَزهري: أَحسب الأَريس والإِرِّيس بمعنى الأَكَّار من كلام أَهل الشام، قال: وكان أَهل السَّواد ومن هو على دين كِسْرى أَهلَ فلاحة وإِثارة للأَرض، وكان أَهل الروم أَهلَ أَثاثٍ وصنعة، فكانوا يقولون للمجوسي: أَريسيٌّ، نسبوهم إِلى الأَريس وهو الأَكَّارُ، وكانت العرب تسميهم الفلاحين، فأَعلمهم النبي، صلى الله عليه وسلم، أَنهم، وإِن كانوا أَهل كتاب، فإِن عليهم من الإِثم إِن لم يؤْمنوا بنبوته مثل إِثم المجوس وفلاَّحي السَّواد الذين لا كتاب لهم،

شصا (لسان العرب) وأَشْصاه صاحِبُه: رفعه. وكلُّ ما ارْتَفعَ فقد شصا.

أص \ أصص \ أسأص (تاج العروس) وعن ابن عبَّادٍ: الأَصُوصُ: اللِّصُّ، يُقال: أَصُوصٌ عليْها أَصُوصٌ، الجمع: أُصُصٌ، بضمَّتَيْن. والأَصِيصُ الذُّعْرُ، يُقال: أَفْلتَ ولَهُ أَصِيصٌ؛ أي رِعْدَةٌ، ويُقال: ذُعْرٌ وانْقِباضٌ. والأَصِيصُ: البِناءُ المُحْكَمُ، كالرَّصيص. والتَّأْصِيصُ: الإيثاقُ، كالتَّأْسيس. ويُقال: جِئْ بِهِ من إصِّكَ، أَيْ من حَيْثُ كان. وأَنه لأَصِيصٌ كَصِيصٌ، أَيْ مُنْقَبِضٌ. ولهُ أَصِيصٌ، أَيْ تَحرُّكٌ والْتِواءٌ من الجَهْدِ. والتَّأْصِيصُ: التَّشْدِيدُ والإحْكامُ، وإلْزاقُ بَعْضٍ ببَعْضٍ. وعن ابن عبَّاد: يُقال: أَصَّصُوا، إذا اجْتمَعُوا وتزاحَمُوا، كائْتَصُّوا ائْتِصاصًا.

أصا (القاموس المحيط) أصا النَّبْتُ يأْصُو: اتصَل، وكثُر.

أصا (لسان العرب) الأَصاةُ: الرَّزانة كالحصاة. وقالوا: ما له حَصاةٌ ولا أَصاةٌ أي رأْيٌ يرجع إليه. ابن الأَعرابي: أَصى الرجلُ إذا عقَل بعد رُعُونة. والشَّاصِيةُ: التي ترْفع رجليها،

أصَّهُ (القاموس المحيط) والتَّأْصِيصُ: الإيثاقُ، والتشديدُ، وإلْزاقُ بعضٍ ببعضٍ.

وثق (لسان العرب) والوَثاق اسم الإيثاق؛ تقول: أَوثَقْتُه إيثاقاً ووَثاقاً،

أسب (لسان العرب) وقد أَوْسَبَتِ الأَرض إذا أَعْشَبَتْ، فهي مُوسِبةٌ.

الإسْبُ (القاموس المحيط) وآسبتِ الأرضُ: أعْشبَتْ.

سبر (لسان العرب) السَّبْرُ: التَّجْرِبةُ. وسبر الشيء سبْراً: حَزره وخَبرهُ. واسْبُرْ لي ما عنده أي اعْلَمْه. والسَّبْر اسْتِخْراجُ كُنْه الأمر. والسَّبْر مَصْدَرُ سَبَر الجُرْح يسْبُرُه ويَسْبِرُه سَبْراً نَظر مِقْداره وقاسه ليعْرف غوْره، ومسْبُرَتُه: نهايَتُه. وفي حديث الغار: قال له أبو بكر: لا تَدْخُلْه حتى أَسْبُرَه قبْلك أي أَخْتبره وأَعْتبره وأنظر هل فيه أَحد أو شيء يؤذي. والمِسْبارُ والسِّبارُ: ما سُبِرَ به وقُدِّرَ به غوْرُ الجراحات؛ والسِّبْرُ والسَّبْرُ: الأَصلُ واللَّوْنُ والهيْئةُ والمَنْظرُ. وفي الحديث: يَخْرج رجل من النار وقد ذَهبَ حِبْرُه وسِبْرُه؛ أي هيْئَتُه.

سفر (مقاييس اللغة) ومن الباب، وهو الأصل: سفرتُ البيت كنستُه. ومنه الحديث: "لو أمَرْتَ بهذا البيت فسُفِر. يسمَّى ما يسقُطُ من ورق الشّجر السَّفير.

سفر (لسان العرب) وفي الحديث: مَثَلُ الماهِر بالقرآن مَثَلُ السَّفَرةِ؛ هم الملائكة جمع سافر، والسافِرُ في الأَصل الكاتب، سمي به لأَنه يبين الشيء ويوضحه. قال الزجاج: قيل للكاتب سافر، وللكتاب سِفْرٌ لأَن معناه أَنه يبين الشيء ويوضحه.

عفش (لسان العرب) عَفَشَه يَعْفِشُه عَفْشاً: جمعه.

عفس (مقاييس اللغة) العين والفاء والسين أصل صحيح يدلُّ على ممارسة ومعالجة. يقولون: هو يعافس الشّيء، إذا عالَجه.

عفس (تاج العروس) والعَفْسُ: الابْتِذالُ للشَّيْءِ والامْتِهانُ، يقال: عَفَسْتُ ثوْبي؛ أي ابْتَذَلْتُه. وتعافسوا: تَعالجوا في الصِّراع ونحوه، وقد عفسه، إذا صَرَعه. والمُعافسةُ: المُعالجةُ بالأُمور والمُمارسة بها، يقال: باتَ فُلانٌ يُعافِس الأُمورَ. العفْس: الرَّدُّ والكَدُّ والإتْعاب والإذالةُ والاستِعمال والضَّباطة في الصِّراع، والدَّوْس، وأن يُرَدِّدَ الرَّاعِي غنَمه يثْنِيها ولا يدَعُها تَمْضي على جِهاتِها. وعفَسَه: أَلْزقَه بالتُّراب ووطِئه. والعِفاس: العِلاجُ والمُمارسةُ.

أبش (مقاييس اللغة) الهمزة والباء والشين ليس بأصل، لأنَّ الهمزة فيه مبدلة من هاء. قال ابن دريد: أَبَشْتُ الشيء وهبَشْتُه إذا جمعته.

أبس (تاج العروس) أَبَسَه يأْبِسُه أَبْساً: وبَّخه وروَّعه وغاظَه، قالهُ الخليلُ. وقيل: صَغَّره وحقَّره، نقله الأَصْمَعِيُّ، كأَبَّسه تأْبِيسًا. التَّأْبيسُ: التَّعْييرُ. وقيل: الإرْغامُ. وقيل: الإغْضابُ. وقيل: حَمْلُ الرَّجُلِ على إغلاظِ القوْل له.

أبس (العين) الأبسُ: يكون توبيخا، ويكون ترويعًا. أبستُه بما صنع آبِسُهُ أبْسًا، قال: ولا تأبِسَنْهُ بالذي، كان، فاعلُه أي: لا تلمْهُ، واعفُ عنه.

العَبْشُ (القاموس المحيط) العَبْشُ والعَمْشُ: الصَّلاحُ في كلِّ شيءٍ،

هبش (مقاييس اللغة) الهاء والباء والشين: كلمةٌ واحدة. يقال هو يتهَبَّش، أيْ يتكسَّب.

حبش (لسان العرب) وحَبَشْت لعيالي وهَبَشْت أي كسبْتُ وجمعْتُ، وهي الحُباشة والهُباشة؛ وحبش الشيءَ يَحْبشُه حَبْشاً وحبَّشه وتحَبَّشه واحْتبَشه: جمعه؛ والحَبَشِيّ: ضرْب من الشعير سُنْبُلة حرفان وهو حَرِش لا يؤكل لخشونته ولكنه يصلح للعلف.

أتي (لسان العرب) الإتيان: المجيء. وفي حديث اللُّقطة: ما وجَدْتَ في طريق ميتاءٍ فعرِّفه سنةً، أي طريق مَسلوكٍ، وهو مفْعال من الإتيان، والميم زائدة. وداري بِميتاء دار فلان وميداءَ دارِ فلان أي تلْقاءَ داره. وقوله عز وجل: أتى أمْرُ اللهِ فلا تَستَعْجِلوه؛ أي قرُب ودنا إتيانُه. ويقال للرجل إذا دنا منه عدوُّه: أُتيتَ أيُّها الرجلُ.

§ 43.—XIII, 6-16

ePSD: marru
mar [SHOVEL] wr. ^{ĝeš}mar; ^{urud}mar "shovel" Akk. marru
mun [SALT] wr. mun; mun_4; $munu_3$ "(to be) brackish; salt" Akk. marru; ţabtu
ses [BITTER] wr. ses "(to be) bitter, brackish" Akk. marru
ePSD: mahāşu
sag [BEAT] wr. sag_3; sag_2 "to strike, beat; weave" Akk. mahāşu
šu rah [BEAT] wr. šu rah_2 "to beat; to knead" Akk. mahāşu
tu [BEAT] wr. tu_{14} "to beat; to weave" Akk. mahāşu; ţurru
tuku [BEAT] wr. $tuku_5$ "to beat, strike of cloth; to weave" Akk. mahāşu
ePSD: mahāşu ša [...]
tug tag [PLOW?] wr. tug_2 tag "to plow, to apply a certain type of plow?" Akk. mahāşu ša [...]
ePSD: šakāku
e [LEAVE] wr. e_3; i; e "to leave, to go out; to thread, hang on a string; to remove, take away; to bring out; to enter; to bring in; to raise, rear (a child); to sow; to rave; to winnow; to measure (grain) roughly (with a stick); to rent" Akk. aşû; erēbu; mahû; rubbû; zarû; šakāku
ĝeš ur [HARROW] wr. ĝeš ur_3 "to harrow" Akk. šakāku

أدي (مقاييس اللغة) الهمزة والدال والياء أصلٌ واحد، وهو إيصال الشيء إلى الشيء أو وصوله إليه من تلقاء نفسه.
معر (لسان العرب) وتمَعَّر رأْسه إذا تمعَّط. وأرض معِرةٌ إذا انْجرد نبْتها. وأرض معِرةٌ: قليلةُ النبات. وأمْعرتِ الأرض: لم يك فيها نباتٌ.
وأمْعرتِ المواشي الأرضَ إذا رعتْ شجرها فلم تدعْ شيئًا يُرْعى؛ والمعِرُ الكثيرُ اللّمْس للأرض. وغضب فلان فتمعّر لونُه ووجهُه: تغير وعلَتْه صُفْرةٌ. وفي الحديث: فتمعّرَ وجهُه أي تغير، وأصلُه قلةُ النَّضارة وعدمُ إشْراقِ اللون، من قولهم: مكان أمْعرُ وهو الجدْبُ الذي لا خِصْب فيه.
ومعَّر وجهه: غيَّرهُ.
معر (مقاييس اللغة) الميم والعين والراء أصلٌ يدلُّ على مَلاسة وحَصٍّ وانجراد.
محص (لسان العرب) ومَحص به الأرضَ محْصاً: ضرب. الجوهري: محصَ المذبوحُ برجْله مثل دَحص.
دحص (لسان العرب) دَحص يدْحصُ: أسرع. الأزهري: ودحصتِ الذبيحةُ برجْليها عند الذّبح إذا فَحصتْ وارْتكضتْ؛ والدَّحْصُ إثارةُ الأرض.
وفي حديث إسمعيل، عليه السلام: فجعل يدْحصُ الأرضَ بعقبيه أي يفْحص ويبْحث ويُحرّك التراب.
شكك (لسان العرب) وشككْته بالرمح إذا خزقته وانتظمته؛ وكل شيء أدخلته في شيء، فقد شككْته. والشَّكّةُ خشبة عريضة تجعل في خُرْت الفأس ونحوه يُضيَّقُ بها.

§ 44.—XIII, 17-34

ePSD: KI.KAL
KIKAL [BOTTOM] wr. KI.KAL "chariot platform; bottom of a leather bag; sole of a shoe" Akk. sassu
KIKAL [GRASSES] wr. KI.KAL "a writing for different types of grasses"
KIKAL [LAND] wr. KI.KAL "a writing for different types of land"
AALD: teptītu (s.) (taptītu, taptētu, teptētu) See petû فتح الارض، الحراثة الاولى، تنضيف الارض للحراثة
ePSD: petû
bad [OPEN] wr. bad; ba; be_2 "(to be) remote; to open, undo; to thresh grain with a threshing sledge" Akk. be'ēšû; nesû; petû
ĝal taka [OPEN] wr. $ĝal_2$ $taka_4$; $ĝal_2$ $taka_x$(BALAG) "to open" Akk. petû
ĝal [OPEN] wr. $ĝal_2$ "to open" Akk. petû
hal [DIVIDE] wr. hal-ha; ha-la; hal "to divide, deal out, distribute; to perform an extispicy; to open; a secret; to pour away; to sieve; to slink, crawl away; a qualification of grain" Akk. barû; halālu; nazālu; petû; pirištu; zâzu; šahālu
AALD: GAN
ganum [STAND] wr. gan; ga-an-nu; ^{ĝeš}gan-nu-um "(vessel-)stand; a large vessel" Akk. Kannu
ePSD: GAN_2
ašag [FIELD] wr. a-$šag_4$; ašag; $^{a\text{-}šag}{}_4$ašag "field; surface (math.)" Akk. eqlu
gana [FIELD] wr. $gana_2$; gan_2-ne_2 "field; area (of a geometric figure)" Akk. eqlu
iku [UNIT] wr. iku "a unit of area; a unit of volume" Akk. ikû

ePSD: gan$_2$-ne$_2$
gana [FIELD] wr. gana$_2$; gan$_2$-ne$_2$ "field; area (of a geometric figure)" Akk. eqlu
ePSD: GUR
gur [UNIT] wr. gur; gur$_9$ "unit of capacity; a measuring vessel" Akk. kurru; namandu
ePSD: ŠE
še [BARLEY] wr. še "barley; grain; a unit of length; a unit of area; a unit of volume; a unit of weight" Akk. uţţatu; û; uţţatu
AALD: kurru (s.) مقياس للحجم والسعة
AALD: pānu (s.) GUR السلة، الحاوية، مقياس الخُمس الـ
ePSD: madādu
aĝ [MEASURE] wr. aĝ$_2$ "to measure" Akk. madādu

كعل (لسان العرب) الكَعَل من الرجال: القصير الأسود؛ قال جندل: وأصبحتْ ليلى لها زَوْج قذرْ، كَعْلٌ تغشّاه سوادٌ وقِصَرْ والكَعَل: الرَّجيع من كل شيء حين يضعه؛ عن ابن الأعرابي. والكعَل ما يتعلق بخُصى الكِباش من الوَذَح.

كهل (لسان العرب) واكْتَهَل النبتُ: طال وانتهى منتهاه، واكْتَهَلت الروضة إذا عَمَّها نبتُها

كهل (مقاييس اللغة) الكاف والهاء واللام أصلٌ يدلُّ على قُوَّة في الشَّيء أو اجتماع جبلَّة.

قحل (مقاييس اللغة) القاف والحاء واللام أصلٌ صحيحٌ يدلُّ على يُبْس في الشيء وجفاف. فالقحل: اليُبْس.

قَحلَ (القاموس المحيط) والمُتقحِّلُ: الرجُلُ اليابسُ الجلْدِ، السَّيِّئُ الحالِ.

جنأ (مقاييس اللغة) الجيم والنون والهمزة أصلٌ واحد، وهو العطف على الشيء والحُنُوّ عليه. يقال جَنِئَ عليه يَجْنأُ جنأً، إذا احْدَوْدَب، ورجل أدنأ وأجنأ بمعنىً واحد.

جَنأ (القاموس المحيط) جَنأَ عليه، كجَعلَ وفرِحَ، وجُنوءاً وجَناً: أكبَّ، كأَجْنأَ وجانأَ وتَجانأَ.

جنأ (لسان العرب) جَنأَ عليه يَجْنأُ جُنوءاً وجانأَ عليه وتجانأَ عليه: أكبَّ. وفي التهذيب: جَنأَ في عَدْوه: إذا ألحَّ وأكبَّ، وأنشد: وكأَنّه فوت الحوالِب، جانِئاً، * ريمٌ، تُضايِقُه كِلابٌ، أَخْضَعُ تُضايِقُه: تلجئه، ريمٌ أخْضعُ. وأَجْنأَ الرَّجُلُ على الشيء: أكبَّ؛

قنع (لسان العرب) قنعَ بنفسه قنعا وقناعةً: رَضيَ؛ والقَنْعُ مُستدارُ الرمل، وقيل: أَسفَلُه وأَعلاه، وقيل: القَنْعُ أرض سَهْلَةٌ بين رمال تُنْبتُ الشجر، وقيل: هو خَفْضٌ من الأرض له حواجبُ يَحْتقِنُ فيه الماءُ ويُعْشِبُ؛ قال ذو الرمة ووصف ظُعُناً: فلمّا رأَين القَنْعَ أَسْفى وأَخْلقَتْ، من العَقْرِبيّاتِ، والهَجْيُوجُ الأَواخِرُ والجمع أَقْناعٌ. والقنْعةُ من القِنْعان: ما جرى بين القُفّ والسهْلِ من التراب الكثير فإذا نضبَ عنه الماءُ صار فراشاً يابساً، والجمع قِنْعٌ وقِنعةٌ، والأَقْيَسُ أن يكون قِنعةٌ جَمْع قِنْع. والقِنْعانُ، بالكسر: من القِنْع وهو المستوى بين أكمَتين سهْلَتين؛ قال ذو الرمة يصف الحُمُرَ: وأَبْصرْنَ أَنّ القِنْعَ صارتْ نطافُه فراشاً، وأَنّ البَقْلَ ذاوٍ ويابسُ وأَقْنعَ الرجلُ إذا صادف القِنْع وهو الرمل المجتمع. والقِنْعُ مُتَسعُ الحَزْنِ حيث يَسْهُلُ، ويجمع القِنْعُ قِنَعةً وقِنْعاناً. والقَنَعةُ من الرَّمْل: ما اسْتوى أسفلُه من الأرض إلى جَنْبه، وهو اللَّبَبُ، وما اسْترقَّ من الرمل.

قنا (لسان العرب) وأقناه الله أيضاً أي رَضّاه. وأغناه الله وأقْناه أي أعطاه ما يسكُن إليه. وفي التنزيل: وأنه هو أغْنى وأقْنى؛ ويقال: قَنيت به أي رَضيت به. واقْتَنَيْت لنفسي مالاً أي جعلته قِنية ارْتَضَيْته؛

الجَوْرُ (القاموس المحيط) و~ المَتاعَ: جَعلَهُ في الوِعاءِ، والجارُ: المُجاوِرُ، والشَّريكُ في التِّجارةِ، كالجارةِ، والمُقاسِمُ، والحَليفُ، والنَّاصِرُ،

جرر (الصَّحاح في اللغة) الجرَّةُ من الخزف، والجمع جرٌّ وجِرارٌ.

جرر (لسان العرب) ابن الأعرابي: الجُرُّ جمع الجُرَّة، وهو المَكُّوكُ الذي يثقب أسفله، يكون فيه البَذْرُ ويمشي به الأَكّارُ والفدّان وهو ينْهالُ في الأرض. والجرَّةُ: إناء من خَزَفٍ كالفَخّار، وجمعها جرٌّ وجِرارٌ.

جأن (لسان العرب) الجُؤْنة: سَلَّة مُسْتديرة مُغشّاة أدماً يجعل فيها الطِّيبُ والثِّياب.

جون (لسان العرب) والجُونةُ: جُونةُ العطّار، وربما هُمِزَ، والجمع جُوَنٌ، بفتح الواو؛ وقال ابن بري: الهمز في جؤْنة وجُؤَن هو الأَصل، والواوُ فيها منقلبةٌ عن الهمزة في لغة من خفَّفها، قال: والجُون أيضاً جمعُ جُونةٍ للآكام؛ والجُونةُ: سُلَيلَةٌ مُسْتديرةٌ مُغشّاة أدماً تكون مع العطّارين، والجمع جُوَن، وهي مذكورة في الهمزة، وكان الفارسيُّ يَسْتحسن تَرْكَ الهمزة؛ وكان يقول في قول الأعشى يَصِف نساءً تَصدَّين للرجال حالياتٍ: إذا هُنَّ نازَلْنَ أَقْرانَهُنَّ، وكان المِصاعُ بما في الجُوَنْ. ما قاله إلاّ بطالع سعد، قال: ولذلك ذكرته هنا. وفي حديثه، صلى الله عليه وسلم: فوجدتُ لِيَده بَرْداً وريحاً كأَنما أَخْرَجها من جُونة عطّار؛ الجُونة، بالضم: التي يُعدُّ فيها الطيبُ ويُحْرز. ابن الأعرابي: الجَوْنةُ الفَحْمةُ. غيره: الجَوْنةُ الخابيةُ مطليَّة بالقار: قال الأعشى: فقُمْنا، ولمّا يَصِحْ ديكُنا، إلى جَوْنةٍ عند حَدّادِها. ويقال: لا أفعله حتى تَبْيضَّ جُونةُ القار؛ هذا إذا أَردت سواده، وجَوْنةُ القار إذا أردت الخابية، ويقال للخابية جَوْنة، وللدَّلْو إذا اسودَّت جَوْنة، وللعرَق جَوْنٌ؛

كَرَّ (القاموس المحيط) ج: أكْرارٌ وكُرُورٌ، وبالضم: مِكْيالٌ للعراقِ،

كرر (لسان العرب) والكُرّ: ستة أوقار حمار، وهو عند أهل العراق ستون قفيزاً. ابن سيده: يكون بالمصري أربعين إرْدَبّاً؛ قال أَبو منصور: الكُرّ ستُّون قَفيزاً، والقَفيز ثمانية مَكاكِيكَ، والمَكُّوكُ صاع ونصف، وهو ثلاثُ كَيْلجاتٍ؛ قال الأزهري: والكُرُّ من هذا الحساب اثنا عشر وَسْقاً، كل وَسْقٍ ستون صاعاً.

قفر (لسان العرب) والقَفير: الزَّبيل؛ يمانية. أبو عمرو: القَفير القَليفُ والنجوية (* قوله« والنجوية» كذا بالأصل ولم نجدها بهذا المعنى فيما بأيدينا من كتب اللغة بل لم نجد بعد التصحيف والتحريف الا البحونة بموحدة مفتوحة وحاء مهملة ساكنة، وهي القربة الواسعة؛ والبحنانة بهذا الضبط الجلة العظيمة.) الجُلَّة العظيمة البَحْرانية التي يُحْمَلُ فيها القَبابُ، وهو الكَنْعَدُ المالِحُ.

فتَحَ (القاموس المحيط) فتَح، كمَنَعَ: ضِدُّ أغْلَقَ، كفَتَّح وافْتَتَح. والفَتْحُ: الماءُ الجاري،

فتت (لسان العرب) فتَ الشيء يفُتّه فتَاً، وفتّته: دقّه. وقيل: فتّه كسره؛ والفتُ والتَتُّ: الشَقّ في الصَخْرة، وهي الفُتوتُ والتُّتوتُ. والتفَتُّتُ: التَكسُّر. والانْفِتاتُ: الانكسار.

الفتاءُ (القاموس المحيط) وأفْتاهُ في الأمْر: أبانهُ له.

الفتُّ (القاموس المحيط) الفتُّ: الدَقّ والكسرُ بالأصابع، والشَقُّ في الصَخرَة.

فت (مقاييس اللغة) الفاء والتاء كلمةٌ تدلّ على تكسير شيء ورفته. يقال: فتتُّ الشيءَ أفتُّ فتّاً، فهو مفتوتٌ وفتيت.

بتت (لسان العرب) البتُّ: القطْعُ المُستأْصِل. وسكرانُ ما يَبُتُّ كلاماً أي ما يُبيِّنه. والبَتّةُ اشتقاقُها من القطْع، غير أنه يُستعمل في كل أمْرٍ يَمضي لا رَجْعَة فيه، ولا الْتواء.

بتَ (مقاييس اللغة) وكلُّ شيءٍ أنفذْته وأمْضيته فقد بتَتّهُ.

بتع (لسان العرب) ويقال: بتَع فلان عليَّ بأمْر لم يُؤامِرْني فيه إذا قطعه دُونك؛ قال أبو وجْزة السَعْدي: بانَ الخَليطُ، وكان البيْنُ بائجةً، ولم نخفْهُم على الأمْر الذي بتِعُوا بتَعُوا أي قطعوا دُوننا. أبو محجن: الانْبتاع والانْبتال الانْقطاع.

بتأ (القاموس المحيط) بتأ بالمكان، كمنَع: أقام، كبثأ.

مدى (لسان العرب) والمُدْيُ من المكاييل معروف؛ قال ابن الأعرابي: هو مكيال ضَخْم لأهل الشام وأهل مصر، والجمع أمْداءٌ. التهذيب: والمُدْيُ مكيال يأخذ جريباً. وفي الحديث: أن علياً، رضي الله عنه، أجْرى للناس المُدْيَيْن والقِسْطيْن؛ فالمُدْيان الجريبان، والقِسطان قِسطان من زيت كل يرْزُقهما الناس؛ قال ابن الأثير: يريد مُدْيَيْن من الطعام وقِسْطيْن من الزيت، والقِسط نصف صاع. الجوهري: المُدْيُ القفيز الشامي وهو غير المُد. قال ابن بري: المُدْيُ مكيال لأهل الشام يقال له الجريب، يسع خمسة وأربعين رطلاً، والقفيزُ ثمانية مكاكيك، والمَكُوك صاع ونصف. وفي الحديث: البُرُّ بالبُرّ مُدْيٌ بمُدْيٍ أي مكيال بمكيال.

المدُّ (القاموس المحيط) والمُدُّ، بالضم: مِكْيالٌ، وهو رِطْلان، أو رِطلٌ وثُلُثٌ، أو مِلْءُ كفَّي الإنسان المُعتَدلِ إذا ملأهُما ومدَّ يدهُ بهما، وبه

مدد (الصَحاح في اللغة) مَددْتُ الشيء فامتد. والمادّةُ: الزيادة المتَصلة. سُمّي مُدّاً، وقد جرّبْتُ ذلك فوجدْتُهُ صحيحاً، وأمْدَدْتُ الجيشَ بمَدَدٍ. والاستمدادُ طلب المَدد. قال أبو زيد: مددْنا القوم، أي صرنا مَدداً لهم. وأمددْناهم بغيرنا. وأمْددْناهُم بفاكهة.

مدد (لسان العرب) المدُّ: الجَذْب والمطْلُ. وتمدّد الرجل أي تمطّى. مدّه يمُدُّه مدّاً ومدَّ به فامتدّ ومدّده فتمدّد، وتمددناه بيننا: مددْناه. وفلان يُمادُّ فلاناً أي يُماطِلُه ويُجاذبه. وماددْتُ الرجل مُمادّةً ومداداً: مددْتُه ومدّني؛ والتَمدُّد كتمدُّدِ السِقاء، وكذلك كل شيء تبقى فيه سعةُ المَدّ. ويقال مددْت الأرض مدّاً إذا زدت فيها تراباً أو سماداً من غيرها ليكون أعمر لها وأكثر ريْعاً لزرعها، وكذلك الرمال، والسَمادُ مِداد لها؛ وقول الفرزدق: رأتْ كمراً مثْل الجَلاميد فتّحتْ أحاليلها، لمّا اتْمأدّتْ جُذورُها قيل في تفسيره: اتمأدّتْ. والمادّةُ: كل شيء يكون مدداً لغيره. وتقول: قد أمْددْتُك بألف فمَدّ. والمَديدُ: ما يُخْلط به سَويقٌ أو سِمْسمٌ أو دقيق أو شعير جَشٌّ؛ وقال في موضع آخر: المديدُ شعير يُجَشُّ ثم يُبلُّ فيُضفَرُ البعير. ومددْتُ الإبل وأمْددْتُها بمعنى، وهو أن تنْثرَ لها على الماء شيئاً من الدقيق ونحوه فتسْقيها، والاسم المديدُ. ومدّه مداداً وأمدّه: أعطاه؛ وقول الشاعر: نمُدُّ لهم بالماء من غير هُونه، ولكنْ إذا ما ضاق أمرٌ يُوسَعُ يعني نزيد الماء لتكثر المرقة. والمُدُّ: ضرْبٌ من المكاييل وهو رُبْع صاع، وهو قدْرُ مُدّ النبي، صلى الله عليه وسلم، والصاعُ: خمسة أرطال؛ قال: لم يَغْذُها مُدٌّ ولا نصيفُ، ولا تُميْراتٌ ولا تَعْجيفُ والجمع أمدادٌ ومِددٌ ومِدادٌ كثيرة ومِددةٌ؛ قال: كأنّما يبْرُدْن بالغَبُوق كيْلَ مِداد، من فحاً مَدْقوق الجوهري: المُدُّ، بالضم، مكيال وهو رطل وثلث عند أهل الحجاز والشافعي، ورطلان عند أهل العراق وأبي حنيفة، والصاع أربعة أمداد.

§ 45.—XIII, 35-46

ePSD: rahāşu

a ĝar [IRRIGATE] wr. a ĝar "to irrigate" Akk. rahāşu

ĝiri ĝar [TRAMPLE] wr. ĝiri$_3$ ĝar "to trample" Akk. rahāşu

rah [BEAT] wr. rah$_2$; ra-ah "to beat, kill; to break, crush; to flood; to thresh (grain with a flail)" Akk. dâku; diāšu; hepû; rahāşu; rapāsu

ePSD: biblu

niĝdea [GIFT] wr. niĝ$_2$-de$_2$-a "marriage gift" Akk. biblu

AALD: biblu (s.) See abālu الفيضان المدمر، شهية، امنية، هدية، يقدم

ePSD: patāqu

budug [MOLD] wr. bu-du-ug "to mold bricks" Akk. patāqu

de [SHAPE] wr. de$_2$ "to shape, create" Akk. patāqu

ePSD: batāqu

šu dag [ABANDON] wr. šu dag "to cut off, abandon" Akk. batāqu

AALD: batāqu (v.) يفتق

AALD: bitqu (s.) See batāqu الفتحة، الخسائر

رهص (مقاييس اللغة) الراء والهاء والصاد أصلٌ يدلّ على ضَغْط وعصر وثباتٍ. فالرَهْص، فيما رواه الخليل: شِدّة العصْر

فتق (مقاييس اللغة) الفاء والتاء والقاف أصلٌ صحيح يدلّ على فتح في شيء. من ذلك: فتَقت الشَيء فتْقاً. والفَتْق شقُّ عصا الجماعة.

فتق (لسان العرب) الفَتْق: خلاف الرَتْق. فتَقَهُ يفْتُقُه ويفْتِقُه فتْقاً: شقّه؛ وأفْتق الرجل إذا ألحت عليه الفُتُوق، وهي الآفات من جوع وفقر ودَيْن. والفتقُ الخصب، سمّي بذلك لانشقاق الأرض بالنبات؛

الفتْكُ (القاموس المحيط) وتَفتّك بأمره: مَضى عليه لا يُؤامرُ أحداً.

فتك (مقاييس اللغة) الفاء والتاء والكاف كلمةٌ تدلّ على خلاف النُسك والصَلاح. من ذلك الفتْك، وهو الغدْر، وهو الفِتْك أيضاً.

بول (لسان العرب) والبَوْلُ الولَد. ابن الأعرابي عن المفضل قال: الرجل يَبُول بَوْلاً شَرِيفاً فاخِراً إذا وُلِد له ولَدٌ يشبهه. والبالُ: الحال والشأن؛ قال الشاعر: فبِتْنا عَلى ما خَيَّلَتْ ناعِمِيْ بال وفي الحديث: كل أمر ذي بال لا يُبدأ فيه بحمد الله فهو أبتر؛ البال: الحال والشأن. وأمر ذو بالٍ أي شريفٌ يُحتفل له ويُهتَمُّ به. وقال أبو سعيد: البالة الرائحة والشَّمَّة، وهو من قولهم بلوته إذا شممته واختبرته،

البَوْلُ (القاموس المحيط) الوِلْدُ، والعدَدُ الكثيرُ، والانْفِجارُ، والبالُ: الحالُ، والخاطِرُ، والقلبُ، والحوتُ العظيمُ، والمَرُّ الذي يُعْتَمَلُ به في أرض الزَّرْع، ورخاءُ العَيْش،

مرر (لسان العرب) والمُرَّةُ شجرة أو بقلة، وجمعها مُرٌّ وأَمْرارٌ؛ والمَرُّ المِسْحاةُ، وقيل: مَقْبِضُها، وكذلك هو من المِحراث.

§ 46.—XIII, 47-57

ePSD: mišlu

ba [HALF] wr. ba_3; ba_7 "half; thirty" Akk. bāmtu; mišlu; šalāšā

niĝsura [~TABLET] wr. $niĝ_2$-sur-ra "a section of a tablet" Akk. mišlu

sa [HALF] wr. sa_9 "half; middle, center; to reach the middle" Akk. mišlu

sur [HALF] wr. sur; sur_3 "half" Akk. šinnû; mišlu

ePSD: mašālu

sa [EQUAL] wr. sa_2; sa_x(ZAG); se_3 "to equal, compare, compete, be equal to, rival" Akk. kašādu; mašālu; šanānu

sig [EQUAL] wr. sig_{10} "to equal" Akk. mašālu

ePSD: izuzzu

gub [STAND] wr. gub "to stand; (to be) assigned (to a task)" Akk. izuzzu

ePSD: zâzu

ba [ALLOT] wr. ba "to divide into shares, share, halve; to allot" Akk. qiāšu; zâzu

hal [DIVIDE] wr. hal-ha; ha-la; hal "to divide, deal out, distribute; to perform an extispicy; to open; a secret; to pour away; to sieve; to slink, crawl away; a qualification of grain" Akk. barû; halālu; nazālu; petû; pirištu; zâzu; šahālu

مثل (الصَحاح في اللغة) مِثْلَ: كلمة تسوية. يقال: هذا مِثْلُهُ ومَثَلُهُ كما يقال شِبْهُهُ وشَبَهُهُ بمعنًى.

مثل (لسان العرب) مثل: كلمةُ تَسْوِيَةٍ. يقال: هذا مِثْله ومَثَله كما يقال شِبْهه وشَبَهُه بمعنى؛ قال ابن بري: الفرق بين المُماثَلة والمُساواة أن المُساواة تكون بين المختلفين في الجِنْس والمتَّفقين، لأن التَساوِي هو التكافُؤُ في المِقْدار لا يزيد ولا ينقُص، وأما المُماثَلة فلا تكون إلا في المتفقين،

عزز (لسان العرب) والعَزَزُ والعَزازُ: المكان الصُّلْب السريع السيل. وتعَزَّزَ الشيءُ: اشتدَّ؛ ويقال للعَنْز إذا زُجِرت: عَزْعَزْ، وقد عَزْعَزْتُ بها فلم تعزْعَزْ أي لم تتنحَّ،

أزز (لسان العرب) وأزَّ الشيءَ يؤُزُّه إذا ضم بعضه إلى بعض. أبو عمرو: أزَّ الكتائبَ إذا أضاف بعضها إلى بعض؛ قال الأخطل: ونَقْضُ العُهُودِ بإِثْرِ العُهود يؤُزُّ الكتائبَ حتى حَمِينا الأصمعي: أززْتُ الشيءَ أؤُزُّه أزّاً إذا ضممت بعضه إلى بعض.

أزَبَ (القاموس المحيط) وتأزَّبوا المالَ بينهُمْ: اقْتَسَمُوه.

زأز (لسان العرب) تَزَأْزَ منه: هابه وتصاغر له وزَأْزَأَهُ الخوف. وتزأْزأَ منه: اخْتَبأَ. الليث: تزأْزأَ عني فلان إذا هابك وفرِقَك، وتزأْزأَت المرأةُ إذا اختبأت؛

زوي (لسان العرب) الزَّيُّ: مصدر زوى الشيءَ يزْويه زَيّاً وزُوِيّاً فانْزوى، نَحّاه فتنَحَّى. وزواهُ: قبضه. وزَوَيْتُ الشيءَ: جمعته وقبضته. قال شمر: لم أسمعْ زَوَأْت بالهمز، والصواب لَيُزْوَيَنَّ أي لَيُجْمعَنَّ ولَيُضمَّنَّ، من زَوَيت الشيء إذا جمعته، وكذلك ليأرِزَنَّ أي ليَنْضمَّنَّ. ابن الأعرابي: زوى إذا عدَلَ كقولك زوى عنه كذا أي عدَله وصرَفه عنه، وزوى إذا قبض، وزوَى جمَعَ، ومصدَرُه كلُّه الزَّيُّ. وقال: الزُّوِيُّ العدولُ من شيء إلى شيء، والزَّيُّ في حالِ التَّنْحية وفي حال القَبْض. أبو تراب: زَوَّرْتُ الكلامَ وزوَّيْتُه أي هيَّأْته في نفسي. ويقال: الزِّيُّ الشارَةُ والهَيْئَةُ؛

§ 47.—XIII, 58-70

AALD: aššum (conj.) (aššu) بسبب، بالرغم من، لذلك، ذلك

AALD: aššum (prep.) (aššu, ašši, aššumi, aššumma) بخصوص، بالاضافة الى، بسبب كذا، فيما يتعلق

ePSD: manahtu

akuš [TOIL] wr. a_2-$kuš_2$ "toil, labor" Akk. manahtu

AALD: anāẖu (v.) ينوح، يكدح؛ متعب، منهك؛ اكتفى؛ يتسكع، يتألم؛ في غم، مكتئب؛ يغني، يخرج صوت عويل

ePSD: ebûru

buru [HARVEST] wr. $buru_{14}$; gur_7; gur_{16} "harvest, summer" Akk. ebûru

ePSD: habburu

henbur [STALK] wr. ^{gi}henbur; ${}^{gi}henbur_2$; $henbur_x$(|IGI.KAK|) "stalk; growth of rushes" Akk. habburu; niplu; udittu

مَخَرَت (القاموس المحيط) مَخَرَت السفينةُ، كمنَعَ مَخْراً ومُخوراً: جَرَتْ، أو اسْتَقْبلتِ الريحَ في جَرْيِها، وفي لَفْظ: "اسْتَمْخِروا الريحَ"، أي: اجْعَلوا ظُهورَكُم إلى الريحِ، كأنَّه إذا وَلاَّها، شَقَّها بِظَهْرِهِ، فأَخَذَتْ عن يَمينه ويَسارِهِ، وقد يكونُ اسْتِقْبالُها تَمَخُّراً، غيرَ أنَّهُ في الحديثِ اسْتِدْبارٌ.

نوح (لسان العرب) النَّوْحُ: مصدر ناحَ يَنُوحُ نَوحاً.ويقال نائحة ذات نِياحة. ونَوَّاحةٌ ذات مَناحةٍ. والنَّوْحةُ القوة، وهي النَّيْحة أيضاً. والتَّناوُحُ: التَّقابُلُ؛
أنه (لسان العرب) الأَنِيهُ: مثْل الزَّفير، والآنَهُ كالآنح. وأَنَه يأْنِهُ أَنْهاً وأُنُوهاً: مثل أَنح يأْنِحُ إذا تَزَحَّرَ من ثِقَلٍ يجِدْه، والجمع أُنَّهٌ مثل أُنَّح؛
قبع (لسان العرب) والقَبْعُ الصِّياحُ.
الحَبْرُ (القاموس المحيط) وأرضٌ مِحْبارٌ: سَريعةُ النَّبات. وحَبِرتْ، كفرِحَ: كثُر نَباتُها، كأَحْبَرتْ، وسُورةُ الأَحْبار: سورةُ المائدَة.
حبر (لسان العرب) وفي الحديث: يخرج رجل من أهل البهاء قد ذهب حِبْرُه وسِبْرُه؛ أي لونه وهيئته، وقيل: هيئته وسَحْناؤه، من قولهم جاءت الإبل حسنَةَ الأَحْبارِ والأَسْبار، وقيل: هو الجمال والبهاء وأَثَرُ النِّعمَة. والحِبْرُ والحَبرُ والحَبْرة والحُبُور، كله: السُّرور؛ قال العجاج: الحمدُ لله الذي أَعْطى الحَبَرْ ويروى الشَّبَرْ من قولهم حبَرَني هذا الأَمْرُ حَبْراً أي سرني، وقد حرك الباء فيهما وأَصله التسكين؛ والحَبْرُ والحَبْرَةُ: النَّعْمَةُ، وقد حُبِرَ حَبْراً. وفي الحديث في ذكر أَهل الجنة: فرأَى ما فيها من الحَبْرَة والسرور؛ الحَبْرَةُ، بالفتح: النَّعْمةُ وسعةُ العَيْش، وكذلك الحُبُورُ؛ ومنه حديث عبدالله: آل عِمْرانَ غِنًى والنِّساءُ مَحْبَرَة أي مَظِنَّةٌ للحُبُور والسرور. وقال الزجاج في قوله تعالى: أَنتم وأَزواجكم تُحْبَرُون؛ معناه تكرمون إكراماً يبالغ فيه. وأَرض مِحْبارٌ: سريعة النبات حسنَتُهُ كثيرة الكلإِ؛ والحُبْرةُ السَّلْعَةُ تخرج في الشجر أَي العُقْدَةُ تقطع ويُخْرطُ منها الآنية.

§ 48.—XIII, 71-XIV, 17

ePSD: hubullu
urra [LOAN] wr. ur_5-ra; ur_5 "interest-bearing loan; debt; requital, favour" Akk. gimillu; hubullu
ePSD: şibtu
maš [INTEREST] wr. maš; $maš_2$ "interest (on a loan); an irrigation tax" Akk. şibtu
ePSD: mû
a [WATER] wr. a "water; semen; progeny" Akk. mû; rihûtu
eš [WATER] wr. $eš_{10}$ "water" Akk. mû
illu [WATER] wr. illu "water; source, spring; waterlogging?; flood waters" Akk. mû; mīlu; namba'u; zâbu
me [BEING] wr. me "Being, divine properties enabling cosmic activity; office; (cultic) ordinance" Akk. mû; parşu

حبل (لسان العرب) والحَبْل العَهْد والذِّمَّة والأَمان وهو مثل الجِوار؛ قال أَبو عبيد: وأَصل الحَبْل في كلام العرب ينصرف على وجوه منها العهد وهو الأَمان. والحَبْل العهد والميثاق.
الرَّدْبُ (القاموس المحيط) الرَّدْبُ: الطريقُ الذي لا يَنْفُذُ.
ردب (لسان العرب) ويقال للبالُوعةِ من الخزف الواسِعةِ: إِرْدَبَّة؛ شُبِّهتْ بالإِرْدَبِّ المكيالِ، وجمع الإِرْدَبِّ: أَرادِبُ. والإِرْدَبُّ القَناةُ التي يَجْري فيها الماءُ على وجهِ الأَرضِ.
الضبُّ (القاموس المحيط) و~ فلاناً: لَزِمه فلم يُفارِقْهُ، و~ عليه: أمْسَكه،
ضبط (لسان العرب) وقال الليث: الضَّبْطُ لزومُ شيء لا يفارقه في كل شيء، وضَبْطُ الشيء حفْظه بالحزم، والرجل ضابطٌ أَي حازِمٌ.
ضبط (مقاييس اللغة) الضاد والباء والطاء أصلٌ صحيحٌ. ضَبَط الشّيء ضَبْطاً.
ضبث (مقاييس اللغة) الضاد والباء والثاء أصل صحيحٌ يدلُّ على قَبْض.
ضبث (لسان العرب) وقال شمر: ضَبَث به إذا قَبَضَ عليه وأخذه.
الماءُ (القاموس المحيط) الماءُ والمهُ والماءَةُ، وهمزَةُ الماءِ مُنْقَلِبةٌ عن هاءٍ: م، وسُمِعَ: اسْقِني ماً، بالقَصْرِ ج: أمْواهٌ ومِياهٌ، وعِندي مُوَيْهٌ ومُوَيْهَةٌ.
موه (لسان العرب) الماءُ والماهُ والماءَةُ: معروف.

§ 49.—XIV, 18-44

ePSD: esēpu
šab [TRIM] wr. šab "to inspect exta; to incise; to draw, design; to gather together, collect, scrape up; to break off, deduct; to trim, peel off; to dig, hollow out; to have a grooved shape; to cut, fell (of trees); to become loose, fall out; to disintegrate; to disappear; to make clear" Akk. barû ša uzu; esēpu; harāru; harāşu; harāşu; eşēru; harāşu; šarāmu; nakāsu; šahāhu
šu sub [GATHER UP] wr. šu su-ub "to gather up, to collect, to scrape together" Akk. esēpu
AALD: esēpu (v.) (eşēpu) يجمع، يحك، يكشط
AALD: eşēpu (v.) (aşābu) يجمع، يضيف
ePSD: aşābu
tah [ADD] wr. tah "to add, increase" Akk. aşābu
ePSD: ešēbu; uššubu
lam [FLOURISH] wr. lam; lam_x(LUM) "to flourish; to make grow luxuriantly" Akk. ešēbu; uššubu

أسب (لسان العرب) وقد أوْسبتِ الأرض إذا أعْشبتْ، فهي مُوسبةٌ.
الإسْبُ (القاموس المحيط) وآسبَت الأرضُ: أعْشبتْ.
عشب (مقاييس اللغة) وأرضٌ عشِبةٌ: مُعْشبة، وأعْشبتْ إذا كثُر عُشْبُها. وأعْشب الرَّجُل: أصابَ العُشْب.
عشب (لسان العرب) وأعْشبَ القومُ، واعْشَوْشبُوا: أصابُوا عُشْباً. وبعيرٌ عاشبٌ، وإبلٌ عاشبةٌ: ترْعى العُشْب. وتعشّبتِ الإبلُ: رعتْه، وسمِنتْ، كأعْشبتْ.
وصب (الصِّحَاح في اللغة) وأوصب القومُ على الشيء، إذا ثابروا عليه.
وصب (لسان العرب) وأوْصَبه الداءُ وأوْبرَ عليه: ثابرَ. والوُصُوبُ: ديمومةُ الشيء. ووَصَبَ يصِبُ وُصُوباً، وأوْصَبَ: دامَ. ويقال: واظب على الشيء، وواصَبَ عليه إذا ثابرَ عليه. يقال: وَصَبَ الرجلُ على الأمْرِ إذا واظب عليه؛ وأوْصَبَ القومُ على الشيء إذا ثابروا عليه؛
صوب (لسان العرب) الصَّوْبُ: نُزولُ الـمَطرِ. صابَ الـمَطرُ صَوْباً، وانْصابَ: كلاهما انْصَبَّ. قال أصابَ الإنسانُ من المال وغيره أي أخذ وتناول؛ وفي الحديث: يُصِيبُون ما أصابَ الناسُ أي ينالون ما نالوا. وأصابَ الشيءَ: وَجده. وأصابه أيضاً: أراده.
عسف (لسان العرب) العَسُوف: التي تمرّ على غيرِ هداية فتركب رأسها في السير ولا يَثْنِيها شيء. وكم أعْسِفُ عليك أي كم أعْمَل لك، وقيل: كل خادم عَسِيف.
عسف (العباب الزاخر) العَسْفُ: الأخذ على غير الطريق. وعسفْتُه: إذا استخدمته.
عَسف (القاموس المحيط) وعَسَفَهُ تَعْسِيفاً: أتْعبَهُ.
أسف (مقاييس اللغة) الهمزة والسين والفاء أصلٌ واحد يدلّ على الفوت والتلهُّف وما أشبه ذلك. يقال أسف على الشيء يأسَفُ أسفاً مثل تلهف.
أسف (لسان العرب) والأسِيفُ: العبد والأجيرُ ونحو ذلك لذُلّهم وبُعْدهم، والجمع كالجمع، والأُنثى أسيفةٌ، وقيل: العسِيفُ الأجير. وتأسّفتْ يدُه: تشعّثتْ.
وسف (لسان العرب) الوَسْف: تشقُّقٌ يبْدو في اليد وجِلْدة: صُلْبة. لم توَسَّفَ: لم تُقشّر. وتوسّفت أيوبار الإبل: تطايرت عنها وافترقت. الفراء: وسَفْته إذا قشرته. والتوسُّف التقشّر؛
وسف (مقاييس اللغة) الواو والسين والفاء كلمةٌ واحدة. يقال توسّفتِ الإبلُ: أخْصبت وسَمِنت وسقط وبرُها الأول ونبت الجديد.

§ 51.—XIV, 56-66

AALD: pû (s.) (pā'u, pī'u) الفم، الامر، القرار، الحكم، التوجيه

AALD: şimdu (s.) الضماد، العِصابة ، القانون، التنظيم

AALD: şimdātu (s.) (şindātu) مرسوم ملكي، قانون ملكي

فيأ (لسان العرب) وفاءَ إلى الأمْرِ يَفِيءُ وفاءه فيْئاً وفُيُوءاً: رَجع إليه. وأفاءَهُ غيرُه: رجعه. ويقال: فِئْتُ إلى الأمر فيْئاً إذا رجَعْت إليه النظر.
الفاهُ (القاموس المحيط) الفاهُ والفُوهُ، بالضم، والفيهُ، بالكسر، والفُوهةُ والفمُ: سواءٌ وتفاوهوا: تكلّمُوا.
فوه (لسان العرب) الليث: الفُوهُ أصلُ بناء تأسيس الفم. قال أبو منصور: ومما يَدُلُّك على أن الأصل في فم وفُو وفا وفي هاءٌ حُذفت من آخرها قولُهم للرجل الكثير الأكل فِيَهٌ، وامرأة فِيَهةٌ. وقالوا: فُوك وفُو زيد، في حدّ الإضافة وذلك في حد الرفع، وفا زيدٍ وفي زيد في حدّ النصب والجر، لأن التنوين قد أمِنَ ههنا بلزوم الإضافة، وصارت كأنها من تمامه؛ والفَيِهُ: المُفَوَّهُ المِنْطيقُ أيضاً. ابن الأعرابي: رجل فَيِهٌ ومُفَوَّهٌ إذا كان حسَن الكلام بليغا في كلامه.
الصَّمْدُ (القاموس المحيط) وما يَلُفُّهُ الإنْسانُ على رأسِهِ من خِرْقةٍ أو مِنْديلٍ دونَ العِمامةِ.
صمد (مقاييس اللغة) الصاد والميم والدال أصلان: أحدهما القصْد، والآخر الصَّلابة في الشَّيء. فالأوّل: الصَّمْد: القصد. يقال صَمَدْتُه صَمْداً. وفلان مُصَمَّدٌ، إذا كان سيِّداً يُقصَدُ إليه في الأمور.
صمد (لسان العرب) صَمَده يَصْمِدُه صَمْداً وصمد إليه كلاهما: قصده. وصمد صَمْدَ الأمْرِ: قصَدَ قصْدَه واعتمده. وأصْمَد إليه الأمر: أسْنَده.
والصَّمَد، بالتحريك: السَّيِّدُ المُطاع الذي لا يُقْضى دونه أمر، وقيل: الذي يُصْمَدُ إليه في الحوائج أي يُقْصَدُ؛ وقيل: الصمد الدائم الباقي بعد فناء خلقه؛ وقيل: هو الذي يُصمد إليه الأمر فلا يُقْضَى دونه، وهو من الرجال الذي ليس فوقه أحد، وقيل: الصمد الذي صَمد إليه كل شيء أي الذي خَلق الأشياءَ كلها لا يَسْتغْني عنه شيء وكلها دالّ على وحدانيته. والصمد الرَّفيعُ من كل شيء.
ضمد (الصِّحَاح في اللغة) ضَمَدَ الجُرحَ يَضْمِدُهُ ضَمْداً بالإسكان، أي شدَّهُ بالضِماد، وهي العِصابةُ. وأنا على ضمادةٍ من الأمر، أي أشرفْت عليه.
ضمد (لسان العرب) والضَّامِدُ: اللازم؛ عن أبي حنيفة.

§ 52.—XV, 1-6

ePSD: nu [NOT] (785x: ED IIIb, Old Akkadian, Lagash II, Ur III, Early Old Babylonian, Old Babylonian, unknown) wr. nu "(to be) not, no; without, un-" Akk. lā; ula

نأي (لسان العرب) النَّأْيُ: البُعْدُ. نأى ينْأى: بعُد، بوزن نعى ينْعى. ونأَوْتُ: بعُدت، لغة في نأيْتُ. والنَّأْيُ المُفارقةُ؛ قال المنذري: أنشدني المبرد:
أعاذِلَ، إنْ يُصْبحْ صَدايَ بقَفْرةٍ بعيداً، نآني زائري وقريبي قال المبرد: قوله نآني فيه وجهان: أحدهما أنه بمعنى أبعدني كقولك زدْته فزاد ونقصته فنقص، والوجه الآخر في نآني أنه بمعنى نأى عني، والنُّوْيُ والنُّئِيُ والنَّأْيُ والنُّوَى، بفتح الهمزة على مثال النُّفَى؛
نهاهُ (القاموس المحيط) نهاهُ يَنْهاهُ نهْياً: ضِدُّ أمَرَهُ، فانْتَهى وتَناهى، وهو نَهُوٌّ عن المُنْكر أمُورٌ بالمَعْرُوفِ. والنُّهْيَةُ، بالضم: الاسمُ منه وغايةُ الشيءِ، وآخِرُهُ، كالنِّهايةِ والنِّهاءِ، مكسورتيْنِ. وانْتهى الشيءُ، وتناهى ونَهّى تنْهيةً: بلَغ نهايته. وطَلَبَ حاجةً حتى نَهِيَ عنها، أو أنْهى، أي: تركها، ظفر بها أو لم يَظْفرْ.

§ 53.—XV, 7-20

ePSD: ugāru

agar [MEADOW] wr. a-gar$_3$; agar$_4$; agar$_2$; agar$_3$; a-da-ar "meadow" Akk. ugāru

ePSD: magāru
<u>šeg</u> [<u>AGREE</u>] wr. še "to agree, be in agreement; to obey" Akk. magāru
ePSD: kâru
<u>udi</u> [<u>DAZED</u>] wr. u$_3$-di "(to be) dazed; sleep" Akk. kâru; šittu

كور (لسان العرب) وكُرْت الأرض كَوْراً: حفرتها. والكُوارات: الخلايا الأهْلِيَة؛
الكِيرُ (القاموس المحيط) الكيرُ، بالكسر: زِقٌ يَنفُخ فيه الحَدّادُ، وأما المَبْنيّ من الطين، فكُورٌ
وجر (مقاييس اللغة) الواو والجيم* والراء كلمةٌ تدلُّ على جنسٍ من السَّقْي.
الوَجُورُ (القاموس المحيط) و~ الماءَ: شربَهُ كارِهاً.
وقر (مقاييس اللغة) الواو والقاف والراء: أصلٌ يدلُّ على ثِقَل في الشَّيء. ويقال نخلةٌ مُوقرةٌ ومُوقِرٌ، أي ذات حملٍ كثير.
أُقُرٌ (القاموس المحيط) أُقُرٌ، بضمَّتين: وادٍ واسعٌ، مَمْلوءٌ حَمْضاً ومِياهاً.
عقر (لسان العرب) وعُقْرُ كلِّ شيء: أصله. وعُقْرُ الدار: أَصلُها، وقيل: وسطها، وهو محلَّة للقوم. وفي الحديث: ما غُزِيَ قومٌ في عُقْرِ دارهم إلاَّ ذَلُّوا؛ عقْر الدار؛ بالفتح والضم: أَصلُها؛ ومنه الحديث: عُقْرُ دار الإسلام الشامُ أي أصله وموضعه، كأنه أشار به إلى وقت الفِتَن أي يكون الشأم يومئذٍ آمِناً منها وأهلُ الإسلام به أَسْلَمُ. قال الأصمعي: عُقْرُ الدار أَصلُها في لغة الحجاز، فأما أهل نجد فيقولون عَقْر، ومنه قيل: العَقارُ وهو المنزل والأرض والضِّياع. وعُقارُ الكلإِ أي خيارُ ما يُرعى من نبات الأرض ويُعْتَمد عليه بمنزلة الدار. والعَقْرُ والعَقارُ: المنزل والضَّيْعةُ؛ يقال: ما له دارٌ ولا عَقارٌ، وخص بعضهم بالعقار النخل. يقال للنخل خاصة من بين المال: عَقارٌ. وفي الحديث: من باع داراً أو عَقاراً؛ قال: العَقارُ، بالفتح، الضَّيْعة والنخل والأرض ونحو ذلك. وعقارُ كل شيء: خياره. ومنه قيل للبُهْمَى: عُقْرُ الدار أي خيرُ ما رَعت الإبل؛ والعَقار والعَقِيرُ: ما يُتَداوى به من النبات والشجر.

§ 55.—XV, 31-38

ePSD: šaqû ša eqli
<u>a de</u> [<u>IRRIGATE</u>] wr. a de$_2$ "to irrigate (by flooding)" Akk. šaqû ša eqli
<u>a dug</u> [<u>IRRIGATE</u>] wr. a dug$_4$ "to irrigate (from canal water)" Akk. šaqû ša eqli
ePSD: šaqûm
<u>iri</u> [<u>HIGH</u>] wr. i-ri "(to be) high" Akk. šaqûm
ePSD: šikkatu
<u>saman</u> [<u>VESSEL</u>] wr. saman$_x$(|A.PA.BI.SI.A.GA|) "flask; a vessel" Akk. rakību; šikkatu
<u>šaĝan</u> [<u>FLASK</u>] wr. šaĝan; ^{dug}šaĝan "a flask" Akk. šikkatu
ePSD: atappu
<u>par</u> [<u>CANAL</u>] wr. pa$_5$; pa$_6$ "(small) canal, irrigation ditch" Akk. atappu; palgu; pattu

سكك (لسان العرب) وطريق سُكٌّ: ضَيِّق مُنسَدّ؛ عن اللحياني. وبئر سُكٌّ وسُكٌّ: ضيقة الخرق، وقيل: الضيقة المَحْفر من أولها إلى آخرها؛ والسُّكُّ، بالضم: البئر الضيقة من أعلاها إلى أسفلها؛ والسُّكُّ: جُحْر العقرب وجُحْرُ العنكبوت لضيقه. والسِّكَّةُ والسِّنَّةُ: المأنُ الذي تحرث به الأرض. وقال أبو حنيفة: كان الأصمعي يذهب في السِّكَّةِ المأبورة إلى الزرع ويجعل السكة هنا سكة الحرّاث كأنه كنى بالسكة عن الأرض المحروثة، ومعنى هذا الكلام خير المال نتاج أو زرع، والسِّكَّة أوسع من الزُّقاق، سميت بذلك لاصطفاف الدور فيها على التشبيه بالسِّكَّةِ من النخل.
عتف (العباب الزاخر) ابن الأعرابي: العُتُوفُ: النُّتُفُ. وقال ابن دريد: مضى عَتْفٌ من الليل وعَدْفٌ -بالكسر-: أي قطعة منه.
عطف (لسان العرب) ومُنْعطَفُ الوادي: مُنْعرَجُه ومُنْحناه؛ وعِطْفا كل شيء: جانباه. ابن الأعرابي: يقال تَنَحَّ عن عِطْفِ الطَّريق وعَطْفِه وعِلْبِه ودَعْسِه وقَرْيِه وقارِعَتِه.

§ 57.—XV, 46-64

ePSD: rē'û
<u>munsub</u> [<u>SHEPHERD</u>] wr. mu$_6$-sub$_3$; munsub$_x$(|PA.GU$_2$@g|) "shepherd, herdsman; an official" Akk. rē'û
<u>sipad</u> [<u>SHEPHERD</u>] wr. sipad; su$_8$-ba; $^{lu}{}_2$sipad; šuba "shepherd; herder" Akk. rē'û
<u>u</u> [<u>SHEPHERD</u>] wr. u$_5$ "shepherd" Akk. rē'û
ePSD: re'û
<u>rig</u> [<u>EAT</u>] wr. rig$_7$ "to eat; to do something to barley; to pasture, tend; to drink; to sup" Akk. akālu; haţāpu; re'û; šatû; sarāpu
ePSD: akālu
<u>gu</u> [<u>EAT</u>] wr. gu$_7$ "to eat, consume" Akk. akālu
<u>rig</u> [<u>EAT</u>] wr. rig$_7$ "to eat; to do something to barley; to pasture, tend; to drink; to sup" Akk. akālu; haţāpu; re'û; šatû; sarāpu

ePSD: eşēdu
gur [REAP] wr. gur_x(|ŠE.KIN|); gur_{10}; gur_x(|ŠE.KIN.KIN|) "to reap" Akk. eşēdu
ur [PLUCK] wr. ur_4; ur_5 "to pluck; to gather, collect; to harvest" Akk. baqāmu; eşēdu; hamāmu; kapātu
رعي (مقاييس اللغة) الراء والعين والحرف المعتل أصلان: أحدهما المراقبة والحِفظ، والآخر الرجوع.فالأوّل رعيْتُ الشَّيء، رقبته؛ ورَعَيْته، إذا لاحظته.
أكل (لسان العرب) أكلْت الطعام أكْلاً ومأْكلاً. والرجل يَستأْكِل قوماً أي يأْكل أموالهم من الإسْنات. وفلان يستأْكِل الضَّعفاء أي يأْخذ أموالهم؛ واستأْكله الشيءَ: طلب إليه أن يجعله له أكْلة. وأكل الشيءُ وأْتكل وتأَكّل: أكل بعضُه بعضاً، والاسم الأُكال والإكال؛ وقال أبو نصر في قوله: أبا ثُبيتٍ، أما تَنْفَكُّ تأْتكل معناه تأْكل لحومنا وتغتابنا، وهو تفْتَعِل من الأكل.
حصد (مقاييس اللغة) الحاء والصاد والدال أصلان: [أحدهما] قطْع الشيء، والآخر إحكامه. وهما متفاوتان.فالأول حصدتُ الزّرع وغيرَه حصْدا. وهذا زمنُ الحَصاد والحِصاد. والأصل الآخر قولهم حبْلٌ مُحْصَدٌ، أي مُمَرٌّ مفتول.ومن الباب شجرةٌ حَصْداء، أي كثيرة الورق؛ ودرْع حصداء: مُحْكمة؛ واستحصدَ القومُ، إذا اجتمعوا.
حصد (لسان العرب) والحِصادُ والحَصِيدُ والحَصَد: الزرع والبر المحصود بعدما يحصد؛ والحَصَدُ ما أَحصَدَ من النبات وجف؛ والحَصَادُ: نبات ينبت في البرّاق على نَبْتَة الخافورِ يُخْبط للغنم.

§ 58.—XV, 65- XVI, 3

AALD: ištu (prep.) (uštu, ultu, ilti) منذ، بعد
AALD: ištu (conj.) (eštu, uštu, ultu, issu) من، نقطة مكان او زمان خارج، منذ، بعد
AALD: ištu See išdu and išti
AALD: gamāru (v.) يُبيد، ينهي، يهلك، يستنفذ، يطوق، يسيطر، يقود للنهاية، يدفع او يسلّم بالكامل، يحمل سوية، يركز، يستعمل كل قوته
ePSD: gamāru
til [COMPLETE] wr. til; til_3 "(to be) complete(d); (to be) old, long-lasting; to end" Akk. gamāru; labāru; qatû
ePSD: halālu
hal [DIVIDE] wr. hal-ha; ha-la; hal "to divide, deal out, distribute; to perform an extispicy; to open; a secret; to pour away; to sieve; to slink, crawl away; a qualification of grain" Akk. barû; halālu; nazālu; petû; pirištu; zâzu; šahālu
أسْتُ (القاموس المحيط) أسْتُ الدَّهْر: قِدَمُه.
سته (لسان العرب) السَّتَهُ والسَّتَهُ والاسْتُ: معروفة، وهو من المحذوف المُجْتَلبَةِ له أَلفُ الوصل، وقد يستعار ذلك للدهر؛ الجوهري: والاسْتُ العَجُزُ، وقد يُرادُ بها حَلْقة الدبر، واسْتُ الدهر: أَوَلُ الدهر. أبو عبيدة: يقال كان ذلك على اسْتِ الدَّهْرِ وعلى أُسِّ الدهر أَي على قِدَم الدهر؛
جمر (مقاييس اللغة) الجيم والميم والراء أصلٌ واحدٌ يدلُّ على التجمُّع. ويقال جَمَّرَ فلانٌ جيشه إذا حَبَسَهم في الغَزْو ولم يُقْفِلْهُمْ إلى بلادهم. وهذا جميرُ القوم أي مجتمِعُهم. وقد أجْمَرَ القوم على الأمر اجتَمَعُوا.
جمر (الصَّحاح في اللغة) وتجمَّرُوا هُمْ، أي تحبَّسُوا.
جمر (لسان العرب) وغيره: جَمَّرَ الأَميرُ الجيْشَ إِذا أَطال حبسهم بالثغر ولم يأْذن لهم في القَفْلِ إِلى أَهليهم، وهو التَّجْمِيرُ؛
خلل (لسان العرب) الخَلُّ: معروف؛ قال ابن سيده: الخَلُّ ما حَمُضَ من عَصير العنب وغيره؛ قال ابن دريد: هو عربي صحيح. وخُلَّلُ الأَرض: التي لا حَمْض بها، قال: ولا يقال للشجر خُلَّة ولا يذكر؛ وهي الأَرض التي لا حَمْضَ بها، وربما كان بها عِضاهٌ، وربما لم يكن، ولو أَتيت أَرضاً ليس بها شيء من الشجر وهي جُرُز من الأَرض قلت: إنها لَخُلَّة؛ وهو خَلَلَهم وخِلالَهم أَي بينهم. وخِلالُ الدار: ما حوالَيْ جُدُرها وما بين بيوتها. وتخلَّلْتُ ديارهم: مَشيت خلالها. وتَخلَّلتُ الرملَ أَي مَضيت فيه. وقال اللحياني: جَلَسْنا خِلالَ الحيِّ وخِلال دُور القوم أَي جلسنا بين البيوت ووسط الدور، قال: وكذلك يقال سِرْنا خِلَلَ العدُوّ وخِلالَهم أَي بينهم. وتخَلَّل الشيءُ أَي نفذ، وقيل: الخَلُّ الطريق بين الرملتين، وقيل: هو طريق في الرمل أَياً كان؛ وخلَّل، بالتشديد، أَي خَصَّص؛ والخِلال والمُخالَّة: المُصادَقة؛

§ 59.—XVI, 4-9

ePSD: işu
ĝeš [TREE] wr. ĝeš; mu; u_5 "tree; wood; a description of animals" Akk. işu
ePSD: kaşāşu
gaz [KILL] wr. gaz; gaz_2; kaz_8 "to kill, slaughter; to grind, grate; to beat; to thresh (grain); to execute, impose a death sentence; to break" Akk. dâku; habātu; hašālu; kaşāşu; pa'āşu; šagāšu
guru [GRIND] wr. gur_5 "to grind, grate; to cut up, chop; (to be) trimmed, pruned" Akk. kasāmu; kaşāşu; urrû
ePSD: kasāsu
tukur [CHEW] wr. $tukur_2$; tukur; $tukur_3$ "to chew, gnaw; to shear, pluck wool" Akk. gaşaşu; kasāsu; sepû siki
عصا (لسان العرب) العَصا: العُودُ، أُنثى. واعْتصى الشجرة: قطع منها عَصاً؛ وفي الحديث: أَنه حرم شجرَ المدينة إلاَّ عَصا حَديدةٍ أَي عصاً تصلح أَن تكون نِصاباً لآلة من الحديد. وأَعْصى الكَرْمُ: خرَجت عِيدانُه أَو عِصِيُّه ولم يُثْمِرْ.

كسس (لسان العرب) وكسَّ الشيءَ يَكُسُّه كسّاً: دَقَّه دقّاً شديداً. وخبز كسيسٌ ومكْسوس ومُكسكسٌ: مكسُور. وكسَّ الشيء يَكُسُّه كسّاً: دقّه دقّاً شديداً.
كسس (العباب الزاخر) قال: وكسَسْتُ الخُبزَ: إذا كسرْته. والكسْكاسُ: الرجل القصير الغليظ؛
كصص (لسان العرب) والكَصيصُ من الرجال: القصيرُ التارّ.

§ 60.—XVI, 10-26

ePSD: zaqāpu
du [PLANT] wr. du$_3$ "to plant; to fix upright, erect; to impregnate; to drive in, fix; a designation of grain" Akk. retû; zaqāpu
ePSD: NU
nu [MAN] wr. nu "man" Akk. Awīlu
ePSD: zittu
hala [SHARE] wr. ha-la; hal "inheritance share" Akk. zittu
AALD: nazāqu (v.) يقلق، يترنح، يستهجن، يكون فضا، يسبب القلق
ePSD: nasāqu
igi saĝ [CHOOSE] wr. igi saĝ$_5$; igi saĝ; igi zag; igi sig$_5$? "to choose; to sort" Akk. bêru; nasāqu
igi suh [CHOOSE] wr. igi suh "to choose" Akk. nasāqu
ePSD: hā'iru
ĝidlam [SPOUSE] wr. ĝidlam; ĝidlam$_2$; ĝidlam$_3$ "(equal ranking) spouse" Akk. hā'iru; hīrtu
mahāru
BU'I [FACE] wr. BU-I "to face" Akk. mahāru

زجب (لسان العرب) ما سَمِعْت له زُجْبة أي كلمة.
ثقف (لسان العرب) ثَقِفَ الشيءَ ثَقْفاً وثِقافاً وثُقُوفةً: حَذَقه. وثَقِفَ الرجلَ: ظَفِرَ به. وقال: فإمّا تَثْقَفُوني فاقتُلوني، فإن أَثْقَفْ فسَوْفَ تَرَوْن بالي وثَقِفْنا فلاناً في موضع كذا أي أَخَذْناه، ومصدره الثَّقْفُ.
لقف (لسان العرب) ورجل ثَقْفٌ لَقْفٌ وثَقِفٌ لَقِفٌ أي خفيف حاذق، وقيل: سريعُ الفَهْم لما يُرمى إليه من كلام باللسان وسريع الأَخذ لما يرمى إليه باليد،
زقف (العباب الزاخر) ابن عباد: الزَّقْفُ: التَّلَقُّفُ.
الزُّقْفَةُ (القاموس المحيط) الزُّقْفَةُ، بالضم: اللُّقْمَةُ. وما ازْدَقَفْتها بيدِك، أي: أَخَذْتها. وتَزَقَّفَه: اسْتلبه بسُرْعةٍ،
صقف (لسان العرب) التهذيب عن ابن الأعرابي: الصُّقوفُ المظالُّ؛ قال الأزهري: والأَصل فيه السُّقوف.
سقف (مقاييس اللغة) السين والقاف والفاء أصل يدلُّ على ارتفاع في إطلال وانحناء. من ذلك السقف سقف البيت، لأنه عالٍ مُطلٌ.
صقب (لسان العرب) الصَّقْب والصَّقَب، لغتان: الطَّويلُ التارُّ من كل شيء، ويقال للْغُصْن الرَّيَّان الغَلِيظ الطَّويل. والصَّقْبُ عمودٌ يُعْمَدُ به البَيْتُ؛ وقيل: هُو العَمُودُ الأَطولُ في وَسَطِ البَيْت والجمع صُقُوبٌ. وصَقَبَ البناءَ وغَيْرَه رفعه.
صقب (مقاييس اللغة) الصاد والقاف والباء لا يكاد يكون أصلاً؛ لأنّ الصَّاد يكون مرّةً فيه السين، والبابان متداخلان، مرّةً يقال بالسين ومرّةً بالصاد، إلاّ أنّه يدلُّ على القرب ومع الامتداد مع الدِّقّة. والرّجُلان يتصاقبان في المحلّة، إذا تقاربا. وأما الآخر فالصَّقْب: العمودُ يُعمَد به البيت، وجمعه صقوب.
سقب (لسان العرب) والسَّقْبُ: الطَّويلُ من كلِّ شيء، مع ترارة. الأزهري في ترجمة صقب: يقال للْغُصْن الرَّيَّان الغَلِيظ الطَّويل سَقْبٌ؛
زقب (لسان العرب) وانْزَقَب في جُحْره: دخل، وزَقَبه هو. التهذيب: ويقال انْزَبَق وانزقب إذا دخل في الشيء. والزَّقَبُ الطُّرُقُ الضَّيِّقَةُ، واحدتها زَقَبةٌ؛
ثقب (لسان العرب) الليث الثَّقْبُ مصدر ثَقَبْتُ الشيءَ أَثْقُبُه ثَقْباً. والثاقِبُ أيضاً: الذي ارتفع على النجوم، والعرب تقول للطائر إذا لحِق ببطن السماء: فقد ثَقَبَ، وكلُّ ذلك قد جاء في التفسير.
نوأ (العباب الزاخر) ناء يَنُوْءُ نَوْءاً: نهض بجهْد ومشقّة،
زتت (لسان العرب) وتزتّت للسَفَر: تهيَّأَ له. وأخذ زَتَّته للسَفَر أي جهازه؛
صتت (لسان العرب) والصَّتِيتُ: الفِرْقة من الناس في جَلَبة ونحوها؛ وتركتهم صَتِيتَيْن أي فِرْقتَيْن.
ثتت (لسان العرب) الأزهري: استعمل منه أبو العباس الثَّتُّ: الشقّ في الصَّخْرة؛ وقال أبو عمرو: في الصخرة ثَتٌّ، وفتٌّ، وشَرْمٌ، وشَرْنٌ، وخَقٌّ، ولَقٌّ، وشيقٌ، وشِرْيان.
نزق (القاموس المحيط) نزق الفرسُ، كسمع ونصر وضرب، نَزْقاً ونُزوقاً: نزا، أو تقدّم خفّةً ووثب. وأنزقه ونزّقه غيرُه. وتنازقا: تشاتما.
نزك (لسان العرب) ونَزَكه نَزْكاً: طعنه بالنَّيْزَك، وكذلك إذا نزعه وطعن فيه بالقول. والنَّيْزَكُ: ذو سنان وزُجٍّ، والعُكاز زُجٌّ ولا سنان له. والنَّزْكُ سُوءُ القول في الإنسان ورَمْيُك الإنسان بغير الحق. وتقول: نزكه بغير ما رأى منه. ورجل نُزَكٌ: طعّان في الناس، وفي الصحاح: ورجل نزّاك أي عيّاب.
نسق (القاموس المحيط) نَسَق الكلامَ: عَطَفَ بعضه على بعض. والنَّسَقُ، محرّكةً: ما جاء من الكلام على نظام واحد، والتَّنسيقُ: التَّنظيم.
نسك (مقاييس اللغة) وزعم ناسٌ أنّ المنسك: المكان يألفه.
النَّسْكُ (القاموس المحيط) والنَّسْكُ: المكانُ المَأْلوفُ،
نسك (لسان العرب) وقال الفراء: المَنْسَكُ المَنْسِكُ في كلام العرب الموضع المعتاد الذي تعتاده.

محر (لسان العرب) الليث: المَحارةُ دابة في الصَدَفَيْن وروي عن الأصمعي قال: المحارةُ الصَدَفةُ. قال الأزهري: ذكر الأصمعي وغيره هذا الحرف أعني المحارة في باب حار يحور، فدل ذلك على أنه مَفْعَلةٌ وأن الميم ليست بأصلية،
حير (لسان العرب) وتحَيَّر السحابُ: لم يتجه جهةً. الأزهري: قال شمر والعرب تقول لكل شيء ثابت دائم لا يكاد ينقطع: مُسْتحيرٌ ومُتحَيِّرٌ؛ ابن الأثير: المحارةُ والحائر الذي يجتمع فيه الماء، وأصل المَحارة الصدفة، والميم زائدة.
الحَوْرُ (القاموس المحيط) الحَوْرُ: الرُّجوعُ، والتَّحاوُرُ: التَّجاوُبُ.
مخر (مقاييس اللغة) الميم والخاء والراء أصلٌ يدل على شقّ وفتح. يقال مَخرت السَفينةُ الماءَ مخراً: شقّته. ويقال استمخَرْتُ الرّيحَ، إذا استقبلتها بأنفِك.

§ 61.—XVI, 27-33

ePSD: gamāru

til [COMPLETE] wr. til; til_3 "(to be) complete(d); (to be) old, long-lasting; to end" Akk. gamāru; labāru; qatû

ePSD: ezēbu

pag [LEAVE] wr. pag "to leave behind" Akk. ezēbu

taka [ABANDON] wr. tak_4 "to set aside, leave behind; to save, keep back, hold back" Akk. ezēbu; uhhuru; šêtu

ePSD: nidûtu

kislah [LAND] wr. kislah; $kislah_2$; $kislah_3$ "threshing floor; uncultivated, uninhabited, cleared land; empty house lot" Akk. maškanu; nidûtu; terīqtu; turbalû

sur [LOCUS] wr. su_7 "threshing floor; abandonment" Akk. maškanu; nidûtu

جمر (لسان العرب) وأَجْمَرُوا على الأمر وتجَمَّرُوا: تجمَّعُوا عليه وانضموا. وجَمَّرَهُمُ الأمر: أحوجهم إلى ذلك. وجَمَّرَ الشَيءَ: جَمَعَهُ. وفي حديث أبي إدريس: دخلت المسجد والناسُ أَجْمَرُ ما كانوا أي أجمع ما كانوا. وجمَرتِ المرأةُ شعرها وأَجْمَرتْهُ: جمعته وعقدته في قفاها ولم ترسله. وجاء القومُ جُمارَى وجَماراً أي بأجمعهم؛ حكى الأخيرة ثعلب؛ وقال: الجَمارُ المجتمعون؛
عزب (مقاييس اللغة) يقال: عَزَبَ حِلْمُ فلان، أي ذهب، وأعْزَبَ اللهُ حِلْمَه، أي أذهبه. قال الأعشى: والعازب من الكلأ: البعيد المطْلب. قال أبو النجم: وكلُّ شيء يفوتُك لا تقْدر عليه فقد عَزَب عنك.
ندي (لسان العرب) والنَّادياتُ من النخل: البعيدةُ الماء. ونَدا فلان يَنْدُو نُدُوّاً إذا اعْتزل وتنحّى.
يندا (القاموس المحيط) ونَخْلٌ نادِيَةٌ: بعيدةٌ عن الماءِ.

§ 62.—XVI, 34-47

ePSD: abšinnu

absin [FURROW] wr. $absin_3$; ab-sin_2; absin "furrow" Akk. abšinnu; šer'u

AALD: abšu (s.) (apšu) Pl. **:** abšena عشب، كلأ، بذور

أبش (لسان العرب) وقد أبشه وأبش لأهله يأْبِشُ أَبْشاً: كَسَب.
هبش (مقاييس اللغة) الهاء والباء والشين: كلمةٌ واحدة. يقال هو يَتهَبّش، أيْ يتكسّب. والهُباشة: الكسْب.
حبش (لسان العرب) وحَبَشْت لعيالي وهبشت أي كسبْتُ وجمعْتُ، وهي الحُباشة والهُباشة؛ والحَبَشِيّ: ضَرْب من العنب. قال أبو حنيفة: لم يُنعت لنا. والحَبَشِيّ: ضَرْب من الشعير سُنْبُلة حرفان وهو حَرِش لا يؤكل لخشونته ولكنه يصلح للعلف.
الوَبْشُ (القاموس المحيط) و~ الأرضُ: أنبتتْ، أو اخْتلَط نباتُها.

§ 64.—XVI, 58-70

ePSD: rakābu

u [RIDE] wr. u_5 "to ride; attatchment to a plow; upper pivot of a door; ship's cabin; to gain control" Akk. hinnu; kašāšu; rakābu; rikbu; šagammu

ePSD: adi

enna [UNTIL] wr. en-na; an-ma; en; en_7 Akk. adi

AALD: *adi (prep.) (hadi, hadu, qadi, qadu) حتى، طالما، مع الاعداد والوقت ومضاعفاتهما

ركب (لسان العرب) ورَكِبَ فلانٌ فُلاناً بأَمْرٍ، وارْتَكَبه، وكلُّ شيءٍ علا شيئاً: فقد رَكِبَه؛ ورَكِبَه الدَّيْنُ، ورَكِبَ الـهَوْلَ واللَّيْلَ ونحوَهما مثلاً بذلك. وركب منه أمْراً قبيحاً، وارْتَكَبه، وكذلك رَكِبَ الذَّنْبَ، وارْتَكبه، كلُّه على الـمَثَل. وارْتكابُ الذُّنوب: إتْيانُها. وفي الحديث: سيأْتيكم رُكَيْبٌ مُبْغَضُون، فإذا جاؤوكم فرَحِّبُوا بهم؛ يريدُ عُمَّالَ الزكاة، وجَعلهم مُبْغَضِين، لـما في نفوسِ أربابِ الأَمْوال من حُبِّها وكراهةِ فِراقِها. ورَكَّبَ الشيءَ: وَضَعَ بعضَه على بعضٍ، وقد تركَّبَ وتراكَبَ. والرَّكِيبُ: الـمَشارَةُ؛ وقيل: الجدول بين الدَّبْرَتَيْن؛ وقيل: هي ما بين الحائطين من الكَرْم والنَّخْل؛ وقيل: هي ما بين النَّهْرَين من الكرم، وهو الظَّهْرُ الذي بين النَّهْرَيْن؛ وقيل: هي الـمَزْرعة. التهذيب: وقد يقال للقَراح الذي يُزْرَعُ فيه: رَكِيبٌ؛ ومنه قول تأَبط شرّاً: فيوماً على أَهْلِ الـمَواشـي، وتارة * لأَهْلِ رَكِيبٍ ذي ثَمِيلٍ، وسُنْبُلِ الثَّمِيلُ: بقيَّةُ ماءٍ تبقى بعد نُضُوب المياه؛ قال: وأَهل الرَّكِيب هم الـحُضَّار، والجمعُ رُكُبٌ.
رقب (مقاييس اللغة) الراء والقاف والباء أصلٌ واحدٌ مطرِد، يدلّ على انتصاب لمراعاة شيء. من ذلك الرّقيب، وهو الحافظ. يقال منه رقَبْتُ أرْقب رِقْبة ورِقْباناً. والمَرْقب المكان العالي يقفُ عليه النّاظر.

الرَقيبُ (القاموس المحيط) وارْتقَب: أشرف وعلا.
عدا (القاموس المحيط) عدا عَدْواً وعُدُوًّا وعدواناً، محركَة، وتَعْداءً و~ عنه: جاوزَهُ، وتركَهُ، كتعَدّاهُ. وأعْدى الأمْرَ: جاوزَ غيْرَهُ إليه، وعدا: فِعْلٌ يُسْتَثْنى به، مع ما وبدُونه.
حتا (لسان العرب) حَتَا حَتْواً: عدا عَدْواً شديداً.
حتت (لسان العرب) قال ابن سيده: وحتّى حرف من حروف الجرّ كإلى، ومعناه الغاية، كقولك: سِرْتُ اليوم حتى الليلِ أي إلى الليل، وتدخل على الأفعال الآتية فتنصبها بإضمار أن، وتكون عاطفة؛ وقال الأزهري: قال النحويون حتى تجيء لوقت مُنْتظر، وتجيء بمعنى إلى، وأجمعوا أنَّ الإمالة فيها غير مستقيمة، وكذلك في على؛ ولحتى في الأسماء والأفعال أعمالٌ مختلفة، ولم يفسرها في هذا المكان؛
حدي (القاموس المحيط) حدِيَ بالمكان، كرَضِيَ، حدًى: لَزِمَه فلم يَبْرَحْ. ولا أفْعَلُهُ حدا الدَهْرِ: أبداً.
مدى (لسان العرب) أمْدى الرجلُ إذا أسنّ؛ قال أبو منصور: هو من مدى الغاية. ومَدى الأجل: منتهاه. والمَديُّ أيضاً: جدول صغير يسيل فيه ما هُريقَ من ماء البئر. والمدِيُّ والمَدْيُ: ما سال. قال أبو حنيفة: المدِيُّ الماء الذي يسيل من الحوض ويَخْبُثُ فلا يُقْرَبُ.

§ 65

ePSD: madādu

<u>aĝ</u> <u>[MEASURE]</u> wr. $aĝ_2$ "to measure" Akk. madādu

AALD: maṭû (v.) تكون الكمية غير كافية، يكون مفقودا، يقلل العدد، يصبح صغيرا، يضعف في القوة، يسبب تقليل الكمية، يخفض، يضعف

مدد (لسان العرب) المَدُّ: الجَذب والمَطْلُ. وتمَدّد الرجل أي تمطّى.
المُدّ (القاموس المحيط) والمُدُّ، بالضم: مِكْيالٌ، وهو رِطْلانِ، أو رِطْلٌ وثُلُثٌ، أو مِلْءُ كفَّي الإنسان المُعْتدِلِ إذا ملأهُما ومَدَّ يدهُ بهما، وبه
مطط (لسان العرب) وتمطَّط أي تمدَّد. والتمطي التَّمدُّد وهو من محوّل التضعيف، وأصله التمطط، وقيل: هو من المَطْواء، فإن كان ذلك فليس هذا بابه.
بدد (لسان العرب) التبديد: التفريق؛ وفي الدعاء: اللهم أحصهم عدداً واقتلهم بدداً؛ قال ابن الأثير: يروى بكسر الباء، جمع بِدّة وهي الحصة والنصيب، أي اقتلهم حصصاً مقسمة لكل واحد حصته ونصيبه، ويروى بالفتح، أي متفرقين في القتل واحداً بعد واحد من التبديد.وفي حديث خالد بن سنان: أنه انتهى إلى النار وعليه مدرعة صوف فجعل يفرّقها بعصاه ويقول: بَدّاً بَدّاً أي تبدّدي وتفرّقي؛ يقال: بَددْتُ بدّاً وبدّدْتُ تبديداً؛ وهذا خالد هو الذي قال فيه النبيّ، صلى الله عليه وسلم: نبيّ ضيعه قومه. يقال: شملٌ مُبَدَّد. وبدّد الرجلُ: أعيا وكلَّ؛ عن ابن الأعرابي؛ وأنشد: لما رأيت مِحْجما قد بدَّدا، وأوّلَ الإبلِ دنا فاسْتوردا، دعوتُ عَوْني، وأخذتُ المَسدا وبيني وبينك بُدّة أي غاية ومُدّة. ويقال: أبدَّ فلانٌ نظره إذا مدّه، وأبْدَدْتُه بصري. وأبددت يدي إلى الأرض فأخذت منها شيئاً أي مددتها.
بدد (تاج العروس) وبدَّه؛ أي بدَّ صاحبَه عن الشيْء: أبعده وكفّه، وأنا أبُدُّ بك عن ذلك الأمر؛ أي أدْفعه عنك. وبدَّ الشيْءَ يَبُدُّه بدًّا :تجافى به.
معط (مقاييس اللغة) الميم والعين والطاء أصلٌ يدلُّ على تجرُّد الشَيء وتجريده ومعِط تمرَّط شعره. ومعطْت السَيفَ من قِرابه: جرّدْتُه. ويكون من الباب معط في القوس: نزع.
بد (مقاييس اللّغة) الْباءُ وَالدَّالُ فِي الْمُضاعفِ أصْلٌ واحدٌ، وهُوَ التَفرُّقُ وَتباعُدُ ما بيْن الشَيْئيْن.
معط (العباب الزاخر) الليثُ: المعْطُ: مد الشيء. والمعطُ ضربٌ من النكاح، يقال معطها: إذا نكحها وقال ابن الأعرابي: المعطاءُ: السوءة. وأمعط وأمغط: إذا طال وامتد. والتركيبُ يدلُ على تجرد الشيء وتجريده.
معط (تاج العروس) مَعطَهُ، كمَنَعه، يمْعطُه مَعْطا: مدّهُ، نقلهُ اللَيْثُ، لُغةٌ في مغط، بالغيْن. ومنه: معَط السَيْف من قِرابه، إذا سلّهُ ومدّهُ، كامْتعطَهُ، نقله الصّاغانيُّ. ومنه أيضا :معط في القوس، إذا نزع وأغْرق. وامْتعط النّهارُ: ارْتفع وامْتدّ، مثل امْتغط، بالْغيْن، كانْمعط كانْفعل. وامّعط الحبْلُ، كافْتعل، أصْلهُ امْتعط، زاد في الصّحاح وغيْره: انْجرد، وعليْه اقْتصر الجوْهريُّ.
وقال أبو تُراب: امّعط على انْفعل: إذا طال وامْتدّ، مثْلُ امّغط، بالْغيْن، ومنه المُمّعطُ بتشْديد الميم الثّانيةِ المفْتوحةِ للبائن الطُولِ. وقال ابنُ الأعْرابيّ: المَعْطاءُ، والشّعْراء، والدّفْراءُ: من أسْماءِ السّوْأة.
معط (لسان العرب) مَعطَ الشيءَ يمْعطُه معطاً. مدّه. وتمعّطَ وامّعط، وهو افْتعل (* قوله «افتعل» كذا في الأصل والقاموس بالتاء، وفي الصحاح انفعل بالنون.): تمرّط وسقط من داء يعْرِضُ له. وتمعّطت أوبار الإبل: تطايرت وتفرّقت، ومن أسماء السّوءةِ المَعْطاء والشّعْراء والدّفْراء.

§ 66

AALD: watāru See atāru (v.)

ePSD: atru

<u>dirig</u> <u>[EXCEED]</u> wr. diri; RI "(to be) very great, supreme, excellent; more than; (to be) powerful, competent; (to be) big, huge; (to be) abundant; on, over, above; against; radiance; to project, stick up, build high; (to be) surplus" Akk. atru; eli; rabû; kapāšu; zaqāru; šarūru; šūturu; lē'û

AALD: tarkibtu (s.) (tarkubtu) See rakābu التركيب، التلقيح (الاشجار، النخيل، القصب)

وتر (لسان العرب) الوِتْرُ والوَتْرُ: الفرْدُ أو ما لم يتشفّعْ من العددِ. وأوْترَهُ أي أفذّهُ. وكلُّ من أدركته بمكروه، فقد وَترْته. ووترهُ حقّه وماله: نقصه إياه. وقال الجوهري: أي لن ينْتقِصكم في أعمالكم، كما تقول: دخلت البيت، وأنت تريد في البيت، وتقول: قد وَترْتُه حقّه إذا نقصْته، وأحد القولين قريب من الآخر. وفي الحديث: اعمل من وراء البحر فإن الله لن يترَك من عملك شيئاً أي لن ينْقُصك.
ذحل (مقاييس اللغة) الذال والحاء واللام أصلٌ واحد يدلُّ على مقابلةٍ بمثْل الجناية،
ركب (مقاييس اللغة) الراء والكاف والباء أصلٌ واحد مطّرد منقاس، وهو علُوُّ شيءٍ شيئاً. يقال ركب رُكوباً يرْكب. والرَكّابة: شبه فسيلةٍ من أعلى النخلة عند قِمّتها، ربّما حملتْ مع أمّها.

ركب (لسان العرب) ورَكِبَ فلانٌ فُلاناً بأمْر، وارْتَكبه، وكلُّ شيءٍ علا شيئاً: فقد رَكِبه؛ ورَكِب فلانٌ فُلاناً بأمْر، وارْتَكبه، وكلُّ شيءٍ علا شيئاً: فقد رَكِبه؛ ورَكِبه الدَّيْنُ، ورَكِبَ الـهَوْلَ واللَّيلَ ونحوهما مثلاً بذلك. ورَكِب منه أمْراً قبيحاً، وارْتكبه، وكذلك رَكِب الذَّنْبَ، وارْتكبه، كلُّه على الـمَثَل. وارْتِكابُ الذُّنوب: إتْيانُها. وفي الحديث: سيأتِيكم رُكَيْبٌ مُبْغَضُون، فإذا جاؤُوكم فرحِّبُوا بهم؛ يريدُ عُمَّال الزكاة، وجعَلهم مُبْغَضِين، لـما في نُفوس أربابِ الأموالِ من حُبِّها وكَراهةِ فِراقِها. ورَكِّب الشيءَ: وضَع بعضَه على بعضٍ، وقد تركَّب وتَراكَب. والرَّكِيبُ: الـمَشارةُ؛ وقيل: الجدولُ بين الدَّبْرتَيْنِ؛ وقيل: هي ما بين الحائطين من الكرْم والنَّخْل؛ وقيل: هي ما بين النَهْرين من الكرم، وهو الظَّهْرُ الذي بين النَّهْرَيْن؛ وقيل: هي الـمَزرعة. التهذيب: وقد يقال للقَراح الذي يُزْرَعُ فيه: رَكِيبٌ؛ ومنه قول تأبَّط شرّاً: فيوماً على أهْلِ الـمواشـي، وتارةً * لأهْلِ رَكِيبٍ ذي ثَمِيلٍ، وسُنْبُل الثَّمِيلُ: بَقِيَّةُ ماءٍ تَبْقى بعد نُضُوب المياه؛ قال: وأهلُ الرَّكِيب هُم الـحُضَّار، والجمعُ رُكُبٌ. وقال أبو حنيفة: الرَّكَابة الفَسِيلةُ، وقيل: شِبْهُ فَسِيلةٍ تخرُجُ في أعْلى النَّخْلة عند قِمَّتِها، ورُبَّما حملَتْ مع أمِّها، وإذا قُلِعت كان أفضل للأمِّ، فأثْبتَ ما نفى غيرُه من الرَّكابة، وقال أبو عبيد: سمعت الأصمعي يقول: إذا كانت الفَسِيلة في الجِذْع ولم تكن مُسْتأْرِضةً، فهي من خَسِيس النَّخْل، والعرب تُسَمِّيها الرَّاكِب؛ وقيل فيها الراكُوبُ، وجمْعُها الرَّواكِيبُ. ورَكَّب الشيءَ: وضَع بعضَه على بعضٍ، وقد تركَّب وتَراكَب. والراكِبُ: النخلُ الصِّغارُ تخرُج في أُصُول النخل الكِبار.

§ 66

ePSD: nabalkutu

bala [TURN] wr. bal; bil$_2$ "to rotate, turn over, cross; to pour out, libate, make a libation; reign, rotation, turn, term of office; to revolt; to hoist, draw (water); to transfer (boats over weirs etc. blocking a stream); to carry; to boil (meat in water); to change, transgress (the terms of an agreement); conversion (math.)" Akk. elû; nabalkutu; nakāru; naqû; palû; tabāku

ePSD: ballukku

mug [AROMATIC] wr. ^{šim}mug "an aromatic substance" Akk. ballukku

šembulug [RESIN] wr. šembulug$_2$; šembulug$_3$; šembulug$_5$; šembulug$_x$(|ŠIM.BAL|); šembulug$_x$(|ŠIM×KUŠU$_2$|) "a resin; a tree" Akk. ballukku

ePSD: nidûtu

kislah [LAND] wr. kislah; kislah$_2$; kislah$_3$ "threshing floor; uncultivated, uninhabited, cleared land; empty house lot" Akk. maškanu; nidûtu; terīqtu; turbalû

sur [LOCUS] wr. su$_7$ "threshing floor; abandonment" Akk. maškanu; nidûtu

ePSD: palāšu; šapālu

burud [PERFORATE] wr. burud$_x$(U) "breach, hole; depression, low-lying area, depth; to perforate; (to be) deep" Akk. palāšu; šapālu; pilšu; šupālu; šuplu

نبل (مقاييس اللغة) النون والباء واللام أصلٌ صحيح يدلُّ على فضْل وكِبر، ثم يستعار منه الحِذْق في العمل، فيقال للفضْل في الإنسان نُبْل. والنَّبَل عظام المَدَر والحِجارة. ويقال: نبلٌ ونُبلٌ. وفي الحديث: "أعِدُّوا النَّبَل. إنَّ النَّبَل هاهنا الصِّغار، وإنَّها من الأضداد، ونبِّلْني أحجاراً للاستنجاء: أعْطِنيها. ونبِّلْني عرْقاً: أعطِنيه.

نبل (الصِّحَاح في اللغة) والنابل: الحاذقُ بالأمر. يقال فلانٌ نابلٌ وابن نابل، أي حاذقٌ وابن حاذق. ويقال: ما انتبَل نبْله إلا بأخرةٍ، أي ما انتبَه له وما بالى به. قال يعقوب: وفيها أربعُ لغات: نبْله، ونباله، ونَبالَتَه، ونُبالَتَهُ. والنُّبْلة بالضم: العَطيَّة. والنُّبْل النَبالة والفضل.

نبل (لسان العرب) والنَّبل عِظام الحجارة والمَدَر ونحوهما وصغارها ضدّ، واحدتها نَبلة، وقيل: النَّبل العِظام والصِّغار من الحجارة والإبل والناس وغيرهم. والنَّبَلُ الحجارة التي يُسْتنجى بها؛ ومنه الحديث: اتَّقُوا المَلاعِنَ وأَعِدُّوا النَّبَل؛ قال أبو عبيد: وبعضهم يقول النُّبَل؛ قال ابن الأثير: واحدتها نُبْلة كغُرْفة وغُرَف، والمحدثون يفتحون النون والباء كأنه جمع نبيل في التقدير؛ والنَّبل، بالفتح، في غير هذا الكِبار من الإبل والصغار، وهو من الأضداد.

بَلكهُ (القاموس المحيط) بَلكَهُ: لَبكَهُ.

لبك (لسان العرب) اللَّبْكُ: الخَلْطُ، لبَكْتُ الأمْرَ ألْبُكه لبْكاً. اللَّبْكُ واللَّبْكَةُ: الشيء المخلوط. ولَبَكْتُ السَّوِيقَ بالعسل: خلطته؛

اللام والباء والكاف أصلٌ صحيح يدلُّ على خَلْط شيء بشيء.

فلك (مقاييس اللغة) الفاء واللام والكاف أصلٌ صحيح يدلُّ على استدارةٍ في شيء.

فلس (صحاح العربية) ويحوز أن يراد به أنه صار إلى حال يقال فيها: ليس معه فلس. كما يقال: أقهر الرجل إذا صار إلى حال يقهر عليها. وأذل الرجل: صار إلى حال يذل فيها. وقد فَلَّسَهُ القاضي تَفْليسًا: نادى عليه أنه أفلس.

ندي (لسان العرب) وقال ابن جني: أَما قولهم في فلان تَكرُّمٌ ونَدًى، فالإمالة فيه تدل على أن لام النُّدْوَة ياء، وقولهم النَداوة، الواو فيه بدل من ياء، وأَصله نَدايةٌ لما ذكرناه من الإمالة في النَّدى، ولكن الواو قلبت ياء لضرب من التوسع. وفي حديث عذاب القَبْر: وجَريدَتي النَّخْل لنْ يَزال يُخفِّفُ عنهما ما كان فيهما نُدُوٌّ، يريد نداوةً؛ قال ابن الأثير: كذا جاء في مسند أحمد بن حنبل ، وهو غريب، إنما يقال نَدِيَ الشيءُ فهو نَدٍ، وأَرضٌ نَدِيَةٌ وفيها نَداوةٌ. وأَرض نَدِيَةٌ، على فعِلة بكسر العين ، ولا تقل نَدِيَّةٌ ، وشجر نَدْيانٌ. والنَّدى: الكلأ؛ وأَنْدى الرَّجلُ: كثر نداه أي عَطاؤه، وأَنْدى إذا تَسَخَّى ، وأَنْدى الرجلُ إذا كثر نَداه على إخوانه، وكذلك انْتدى وتَنَدَّى. وفلان يَتَنَدَّى على أَصحابه: كما تقول هو يَتسخَّى على أَصحابه، ولا تقل يُنْدِي على أَصحابِه. وفلان نَدِي الكَفِّ إذا كان سَخِيًّا. ونَدوتُ من الجُود. ويقال سَنَّ للناس النَّدى فنَدَوْا. والنَّدى: الجُود.

§ 69

ePSD: kişru
zukešed [RENT] wr. zu$_2$-keš$_2$ "rent" Akk. kişru
zukešed [TROOP] wr. zu$_2$-keš$_2$; zu$_2$-keš$_2$-ra$_2$ "troop" Akk. kişru

كصر (لسان العرب) أبو زيد: الكصيرُ لغة في القَصِير لبعض العرب.

قصر (مقاييس اللغة) القاف والصاد والراء أصلان صحيحان، أحدهما يدلُّ على ألا يبلُغ الشَيءُ مداه ونهايته، والآخر على الحبْس. والمقاصر: جمع مقصورة، وكلُّ ناحيةٍ من الدار الكبيرة إذا أحيط عليها فهي مقصورة. وهذا جائزٌ أن يكون من القياس الأوّل.

قصر (لسان العرب) القَصْرُ والقِصَرُ في كل شيء: خلافُ الطُولِ؛ والقَصْرُ الغاية؛ قاله أبو زيد وغيره؛ وفي حديث معاذ: فإنَ له ما قصَرَ في بيته أي ما حبَسه. وقَصَرَ عني الوجعُ والغضَبُ يقْصُر قُصُوراً وقصَّر: سكن، وقصَرْتُ أنا عنه، وقصَرْتُ له من قيده أقْصُر قصْراً: قاربت. وقصَرْتُ الشَيء على كذا إذا لن تجاوز به غيره. يقال: قصَرْتُ اللِّقحة على فرسي إذا جعلت درَّها له. وامرأة قاصِرةُ الطَرْف: لا تمُدّه إلى غير بعلها. وفي حديث إسلام ثُمامة: فأبى أن يُسْلِم قصْراً فأعتقه، يعني حبساً عليه وإجباراً. يقال: قصَرْتُ نفسي على الشيء إذا حبستها عليه وألزمتها إياه، وقيل: أراد قهراً وغلبةً، من القسْر، فأبدل السين صاداً، وهما يتبادلان في كثير من الكلام، ومن الأول الحديث: ولتَقْصُرنَّه على الحق قصْراً. وقصَرَ الشيءَ يَقْصُره قصْراً: حبسه؛ والقصْرُ من البناء: معروف، وقال اللحياني: هو المنزل، وقيل: كل بيت من حجَر، قُرَشيّةٌ، سمي بذلك لأنه تُقصَرُ فيه الحُرَمُ أي تُحْبس، وجمعه قُصُور. وفي التنزيل العزيز: ويجْعل لك قُصُوراً. والمَقْصُورة: الدار الواسعة المُحصَّنَة،وقيل: هي أصغر من الدار، وهو من ذلك أيضاً.

§ 70

AALD: pānu (s.) GUR السلة، الحاوية، مقياس الخُمس الـ
AALD: kurru (s.) مقياس للحجم والسعة
AALD: uțțatu (s.f) (ețțetu, uțțetu) الحنطة (للأكل)، البذور، حبة الحنطة (كوحدة قياس)، الخال (الشامة)، البثرة
ePSD: sūtu
ban [UNIT] wr. ba-an; ban$_2$; ban$_3$; ba-an-AŠ; ^{dug}ban$_3$ "unit of capacity" Akk. sūtu

كَرَ (القاموس المحيط) ج: أكْرارٌ وكُرُورٌ، وبالضم: مِكْيالٌ للعراق،

كرر (لسان العرب) والكُرّ: ستة أوقار حمار، وهو عند أهل العراق ستون قفيزاً. ابن سيده: يكون بالمصري أربعين إرْدَبًا؛ قال أبو منصور: الكُرّ ستّون قفيزاً، والقفيز ثمانية مكاكيك، والمكّوكُ صاع ونصف، وهو ثلاثُ كَيْلَجاتٍ؛ قال الأزهري: والكُرّ من هذا الحساب اثنا عشر وَسْقاً، كل وَسْقٍ ستون صاعاً.

قفر (لسان العرب) والقَفير: الزَبيل؛ يمانية. أبو عمرو: القفير القليفُ والنجوية (* قوله« والنجوية» كذا بالأصل ولم نجدها بهذا المعنى فيما بأيدينا من كتب اللغة بل لم نجد بعد التصحيف والتحريف الا البحونة بموحدة مفتوحة وحاء مهملة ساكنة، وهي القربة الواسعة؛ والبحنانة بهذا الضبط الجلة العظيمة.) الجُلّة العظيمة البَحْرانية التي يُحْملُ فيها القِبابُ، وهو الكَنْعَدُ المالحُ.

حط (مقاييس اللغة) الحاء والطاء أصلٌ واحد، وهو إنزال الشيء من عُلوّ. يقال حططْت الشيءَ أحُطّه حطّاً. ومما شذَ عن هذا القياس الحَطاط: بثْرَةٌ تكون بالوجْه.

حطط (لسان العرب) الحطّ: الوَضْعُ، حطّه يَحُطُّه حطّاً فانْحط. وحطّ الحِمْل عن البعير يحُطّه حطّاً: أنزله. وكلُّ ما أنزله عن ظهر، فقد حطه. الجوهريّ: حطّ الرحلَ والسرْجَ والقوْسَ وحطّ أي نزل. والمَحطّ: المنْزلُ. واستحطّه وِزْره: سأله أن يحُطّه عنه، والاسم الحِطّةُ. وحكي أنَّ بني إسرائيل إنما قيل لهم: وقولوا حِطّة، ليسْتحطّوا بذلك أوْزارَهم فتُحطّ عنهم. وسأله الحِطّيطى أي الحِطّة. قال أبو إسحق في قوله تعالى: وقولوا حِطّة، قال: معناه قولوا مسألتنا حِطّة أي حطّ ذنوبنا عنا، وكذلك القراءة، وارتفعت على معنى مسألتنا حِطّة أو أمْرنا حِطّةٌ، قال: ولو قرئت حِطّةً كان وجها في العربية كأنه قيل لهم: قولوا احْطُط عنّا ذنوبنا حِطّةً، فحرّفوا هذا القول وقالوا لفظة غير هذه اللفظة التي أُمروا بها، وجملة ما قالوا أنه أمر عظيم سماهم الله به فاسقين، وقال الفراء في قوله تعالى: وقولوا حطة، يقال، والله أعلم: قولوا ما أُمرتم به حِطّةٌ أي هي حطة، فخالفُوا إلى كلام بالنَبطيّة، فذلك قوله تعالى: فبدّل الذين ظلموا قولاً غير الذي قيل لهم. وروى سعيد بن جبير عن ابن عباس في قوله تعالى: وادْخُلوا الباب سُجّداً، قال: رُكّعاً، وقولوا حِطّةٌ مغفرة، قالوا: حِنْطةٌ ودخلوا على أسْتاهِهم، فذلك قوله تعالى: فبدّل الذين ظلموا قولاً غير الذي قيل لهم؛ وقال الليث: بلغنا أن بني إسرائيل حين قيل لهم قولوا حِطّةٌ إنما قيل لهم كي يستحِطّوا بها أوزارهم فتُحطّ عنهم. وقال ابن الأعرابي: قيل لهم قولوا حطة فقالوا حنطة شمقايا أي حنطة جيدة، قال: وقوله عزّ وجلّ حطة أي كلمة تحُطّ عنكم خطاياكم وهي: لا إله إلا الله. ويقال: هي كلمة أُمِر بها بنو إسرائيل لو قالوها لحُطّت أوزارهم. والحطاطةُ والحُطائطُ والحطيطُ: الصغير وهو من هذا لأن الصغير محْطوط؛ أبو عمرو: الحُطائطُ الصغير من الناس وغيرهم؛ والحُطائطة: بَثْرةٌ صغيرة حمراء. والحَطاطةُ: بثْرة تخرج بالوجه صغيرة تَقيحُ ولا تُقرِحُ، والجمع حَطاطٌ؛ والحُطْطُ الأبدان النّاعمة. والحُطْطُ أيضاً: مراتبُ السّفل، واحدتها حِطّةٌ، والحِطّةُ: نُقْصانُ المرْتبة. وحطّ الجِلد بالمِحطّ يحُطّه حطّاً: سطره وصقله ونقشه. والمِحطّ والمِحطّةُ: حديدة أو خشبة يُصْقلُ بها الجلد حتى يلين ويبْرُق.

حنط (مقاييس اللغة) الحاء والنون والطاء ليس بذلك الأصل الذي يقاس منه أو عليه، وفيه أنَه حبٌّ أو شبيهٌ به. فالحنطة معروفة.

§ 72

ePSD: ţehû
teĝ [APPROACH] wr. teĝ$_3$; teĝ$_4$ "(to be) near to; to approach" Akk. ţehû
tehi [APPROACH] wr. tehi$_2$; tehi "to approach" Akk. ţehû
ePSD: qaqqadu
saĝ [HEAD] wr. saĝ "head; person; capital" Akk. qaqqadu; rēšu

saĝdu [HEAD] wr. saĝ-du; saĝdu "head" Akk. qaqqadu
ugu [SKULL] wr. ugu$_2$; ugu; ugu$_3$; ugu$_x$(|U.SAG|); ugu$_x$(|A.U.KA|); ugu$_x$(SAG@n@g) "skull, pate; first section of a balanced account, capital; on, over, above; against; more than; top" Akk. eli; muhhu; qaqqadu
ePSD: eššu
eš [SHRINE] wr. eš$_3$ "shrine; an establishment" Akk. bītu; eššu
AALD: eššūtu (s.) (iššūtu, edēšu) الجديد، الحداثة

طحا (القاموس المحيط) طحا، كسَعَى: بَسَط، وانْبسَط، واضْطجع، وذهَبَ في الأرض،

طحح (لسان العرب) الطَّحُّ: البَسْطُ. طَحَه يطُحُه طَحًا إذا بسطه فانْطحَّ؛ قال: قد ركِبتْ مُنبسِطاً مُنطَحًا، تَحْسَبُه تحت السَّرابِ المِلْحا يصف خرْقاً قد علاه السراب. والطَّحُّ أيضاً: أن تَضعَ عقبَك على شيء ثم تَسحَجه؛ قال الكسائي: طَحَانُ فَعلانُ من الطَّحِّ، ملحق بباب فَعلانَ وفعْلى، وهو السَّحْجُ. ابن الأعرابي: الطُّحُحُ المَساحِجُ، والمِطَحَة من الشاة مُؤخَّرُ ظِلْفها، وتحت الظِّلْف في موضع المِطَحَةِ عُظيم كالفلكة؛ وقال أحمد بن يحيى: يقال لهَنةٍ مثل الفلكَة تكون في رِجْل الشاة تَسْحجُ بها: المِطحَةُ.

وطَحْطَحَ الشَّيءَ فتطَحْطَحَ: فرّقه وكسره إهلاكاً. وطَحْطَح بهم طَحْطَحةً وطِحْطاحاً، بكسر الطاء، إذا بَدَّدهم. الليث: الطَّحْطحةُ تفريق الشيء إهلاكاً؛ وأطَحَّه، بتشديد الطاءِ: أسْقطه ورماهُ. وانْطحَ الشَّيْءُ: انْبسط. وقد طَحَّه طحاً.

فوق (لسان العرب) الفُوقُ والقاقُ، غيْرُ مَهْمُوز، والفُوَاق: الطَّوِيلُ، وقيلَ: هُو القَبيحُ الطُّولِ. والفُوقةُ: الصَّلعةُ. ورجل مُفوَّق: عظيم الصَّلعة.

فوق (شمس العلوم) رجل فوق: أي طويل قبيح الطول.

قد (تهذيب اللغة) والقَيْدُودُ: الناقةُ الطَّويلةُ الظَّهْر على الأرض. وصار القَوْمُ قِددًا: أي تفرَّقتْ أهواؤهم وأحوالهم. والقِدَةُ: الطَّرِيقة. والرجُلُ يَقْتدُّ الأمور: إذا دبّرها وميزها بعِلْم وإتْقان. قد: قال الليث: قد مثْلُ قط بمعنى حسب، تقول: قَدي وقَدْني.

قدد (منتخب الصحاح) والانْقِدادُ: الانشقاقُ.

قدد (لسان العرب) القَدُّ: الْقَطْعُ المستأصلُ والشَقُّ طوْلاً. والقَدُّ: قَدرُ الشَيْءِ وتَقْطِيعُهُ، وَالْجَمْعُ أَقُدٌّ وقُدُود، وَفِي حَدِيثِ جابر:«أُتِيَ بالْعَبَّاس يومَ بَدْرٍ أسيرًا ولَمْ يكُنْ عليْهِ ثوْبٌ فنَظرَ لَهُ النَّبيُّ» صلَّى اللهُ عليْهِ وسلَّمَ قميصًا فوجَدُوا قميص عبد اللهِ بْنُ أبيٍّ يُقَدَّدُ عليهِ فكساهُ إياه أي كان الثوبُ على قدره وطولهِ. والقَيْدُودُ: النَاقةُ الطويلةُ الظَّهر. وقَدْ، مُخففٌ: كلمةٌ مَعناها التَوقّع. وتكُونَ قدْ مثْل قط بمنْزلَة حسَبُ، يقُولُون: مَا لَكَ عِندي إلا هَذا فقَدْ أي فقطْ. قالَ الْجَوْهريُّ: وأما قَوْلُهُمْ قَدْك بمَعْنى حسْبُك فهُو اسْمٌ، تَقُولُ قَدي وقَدْني أيضًا، بالنُّون على غَيْر قِياس لأن هذِهِ النُّونَ إنما تُزادُ في الأفعال وقايَةً لَها، مِثْل ضَرَبني وشتَمني. ومنْهُ حديثُ التَّلْبيَةِ: فيقُولُ قَدْ قَدْ بِمَعْنى حسْبُ، وتكرارُها لتأْكيد الأمر، ويقُولُ المُتكلِّمُ: قَدِي أي حسْبي، والمخاطِب: قَدْكَ أي حسْبُك

عسس (الصحاح في اللغة) والمعس المطلبُ. والعسوس الطالبُ للصيد.

عسس (مقاييس اللغة) تاعين والسيم أصلان متقاربان: أحدهما الدنوُّ من الشّيء وطلبُه.

العشَةُ (القاموس المحيط) والمَعشُ: المطْلبُ

عش (العين) والمَعشُ: المطلب، والمَعسُ بالسين لغة فيه،

عش\ عشش\عشعس (تاج العروس) والعَشُ: الطَّلبُ، لُغةٌ في السِّين. الإعْشاشُ: الكِبرُ؛ أي عَزفْتَ بكِبرك عمّنْ تُحبَ وهذه عن الصّاغانيَ. والعشْعشُ، بالفتْح، كما ضَبطه الصّاغانيَ، ويُضمُّ، كما ضَبطهُ الجوْهريُّ، وحكاه عن ابن الأعْرابيَ كالعصْعص والعُصْعُص، قال: هُو العُشُّ المُتراكِبُ بعْضُه فِي بعْضٍ أيْ على بعْضٍ. والمعشُّ: المطْلبُ، قالهُ الخَليلُ، وقال ابنُ سيده نقْلا عن غيْرِ الخَليل: هُو المعشُّ، بالسِّين، وقد تقدّم. وبهاءٍ: الأرْضُ الغليظةُ، كالعشَّةِ، عن الأزْهرِيَ. وقال أبو زَيْد: جاءَ بهِ أيْ بالمالِ من عشِّهِ وبِشِّه، وعسِّهِ وبسِّه، أيْ منْ حيْثُ شاء، لُغةٌ فِي السِّينِ المُهْملَة، وقدْ تقدّم.

§ 73

AALD: maṭitu (s.) See maṭû الحد الأدنى، خلل، عيب
AALD: maṭû (v.) تكون الكمية غير كافية، يكون مفقودا، يقلل العدد، يصبح صغيرا، يضعف في القوة، يسبب تقليل الكمية، يخفض، يضعف
AALD: šūt (pron.) (šūtu) هو:مذكر مفرد، ذلك: كما وردآنفا، مذكر مفرد؛ هم: جمع مذكر

مطط (لسان العرب) وتمطَّط أي تمدّد. والتمطّي التَمدُّد وهو من محوّل التضعيف، وأصله التمطط، وقيل: هو من المَطْواء، فإن كان ذلك فليس هذا بابه.

معط (مقاييس اللغة) الميم والعين والطاء أصلٌ يدلّ على تجرُّد الشّيء وتجريده ومَعِط تمرَّط شعره. ومَعطْت السَيفَ من قرابه: جرَّدتُه. ويكون من الباب معَط في القَوس: نزع.

معط (العباب الزاخر) الليثُ: المعْطُ: مد الشيء. والمعْطُ ضربٌ من النكاح، يقال معطها: إذا نكحها وقال ابن الأعرابي: المَعطاءُ: السوءةُ. وأمعط وأمغط: إذا طال وامتد. والتركيبُ يدلُ على تجردِ الشيء وتجريدِه.

معط (تاج العروس) معْطَهُ، كمنَعه، يمْعطُه مَعْطا: مدّهُ، نقَلهُ اللّيْثُ، لُغةٌ في مغَط، بالغيْن. ومنه: مَعطَ السَّيْف من قِرابه، إذا سلّهُ ومدَّهُ، كامْتعطهُ، نقله الصّاغانيُّ. ومنه أيْضا :معَط في القوْس، إذا نزَع وأغْرق. وامْتَعط النّهارُ: ارْتفعَ وامْتدَّ، مثل امْتغط، بالْغيْن، كانْمعط كانْفعَل. وامَعط الحبْلُ، كافْتعل، أصلُهُ امْتعط، زادَ في الصّحاح وغيْره: انْجرد، وعليْه اقْتصرَ الجوْهريُّ.

وقال أبو تُراب: امَّعطَ على انْفعَل: إذا طالَ وامتَدَّ، مثلُ امَغط، بالْغيْن، ومنه المُمعطُ بتشْديدِ الميمِ الثّانيةِ المفْتُوحةِ للْبائنِ الطُّولِ. وقال ابنُ الأعْرابيَ: المعْطاءُ، والشّعْراء، والدّفْراءُ: من أسْماءِ السّوْأة.

معط (لسان العرب) مَعط الشيءَ يَمْعطُه معطاً. مدّه. وتمعَط وامَّعط، وهو افْتعل (* قوله «افتعل» كذا في الأصل والقاموس بالتاء، وفي الصحاح انفعل بالنون.): تمرّط وسقط من داء يَعْرِضُ له. وتمعّطت أوْبار الإبل: تطايرت وتفرّقت، ومن أسماء السّوءةِ المَعْطاء والشّعْراء والدّفْراء.

§ 77

ePSD: tappû

man [COMPANION] wr. man "companion, partner" Akk. tappû

sadu [COMPANION] wr. sa-du$_3$ "companion" Akk. tappû

tab [DOUBLE] wr. tab; tab$_4$ "to double; to repeat; companion, partner" Akk. eşēpu; tappû

taba [COMPANION] wr. $^{lu}{}_2$tab-ba "companion" Akk. tappû

تفا (لسان العرب) التُّفةُ: عناقُ الأرض، وهُو سبُع لا يقْتاتُ التِّبنَ إنَّما يقْتاتُ اللَّحم؛ قال ابنُ سيدهْ: وهُو من الْواو لأنا وجدْنا ت وف، وهُو قولُهمْ: ما في أمرهم تويفة. ولمْ نجدْ ت ي ف، فإنْ أبا عليّ يستدلُّ على المقلوب بالمقلوب، ألا تراهُ استدلَّ على أن لام أثفيَة واوٌ بقولهمْ وثف، والْواوُ في وثْف فاءٌ.

التوافي (شمس العلوم) توافوا: إذا وافى بعضهم بعضًا: أي أتاه. وتوافوا: أي تتامُّوا.

تفأ (الصّحاح في اللغة) تفيء تفأ، إذا غضب واحتدّ.

تفأ (العباب الزاخر) يُقال: تفئ -بالكسْر- تفأ -بالتّحريك-: إذا احْتدّ وغضب.

الأفى (القاموس المحيط) وآفى: أوْفى.

وفي (تاج العروس) ي وفى بالعهْد، كوعى، يفي وفاء، بالمدّ، فهو وافٍ: ضدُّ غدرٍ؛ كما في الصّحاح. وقال غيرهُ: الوفاءُ ملازمةُ طريقِ المواساة ومحافظة عهود الخلطاء؛ كأوْفى؛ وأوْفى عليه: أشْرف واطّلع؛

تبع (مقاييس اللغة) التاء والباء والعين أصل واحد لا يشذ عنه من الباب شيءٌ، وهو التُّلوُ والقفْو. والتبيع النصير، لأنه يتْبعه نصرهُ.

تبع (الصّحاح في اللغة) تبعْتُ القومَ تبعاً وتباعة بالفتح، إذا مشيت خلفهم، أو مرُّوا بك فمضيت معهم؛ وكذلك اتّبعْتهم. والتّباعُ: الولاءُ.

تبع (لسان العرب) تبعَ الشيءَ تبعاً وتباعاً في الأفعال وتبعْتُ الشيءَتبوعاً: سرْت في إثْره؛ والتّبيعُ: النّصير.

§ 100.—XVII, 1-6

ePSD: aplu

eduru [HEIR] wr. eduru "heir" Akk. aplu

esaĝ [HEIR] wr. a-sag; esaĝ; asag "heir" Akk. aplu

hibiz [HEIR] wr. hibiz$_2$ "heir" Akk. aplu

ibila [HEIR] wr. ibila; i$_3$-bi$_2$-la; ibila$_2$; i$_3$-bi-lu "heir" Akk. aplu

أفل (القاموس المحيط) وسبْعةٌ آفلٌ وآفلةٌ: حاملٌ. وأفْلهُ تأفيلاً: وقرهُ.

وقر (لسان العرب) ومنه الحديث: لعله أوقرَ راحلته ذهباً أي حمَلها وقراً. وأوْقرتِ النخلةُ أي كثُر حمْلُها؛ وتُعزّروه وتُوقّروه؛ والتوقير: التعظيم والتّرْزينُ. ووقّرْتُ الرجل إذا عظمته. وفي التنزيل العزيز: وتعزروه وتوقروه. والوقار السكينة والوداعةُ.

§ 101.—XVII, 7-14

ePSD: šamallû

šaĝan [MERCHANT] wr. šaĝan-la$_2$; šaĝan "an apprentice merchant" Akk. šamallû

ePSD: tarāşu

la [STRETCH] wr. la$_2$ "to stretch out; to be in order" Akk. tarāşu

AALD: tarāşu (v.) يمُد، يجهز، يرسلُ بدلا، سارا، مرضيا للعدل، للحق، يكون مشرفا، يكون مرضيا بالتبادل، ينجح، يزدهر، يلائم، يكون صحيحا، مناسبا

AALD: ašru (s. m. and f.) (ašaru, išru) الاشارة، المكان، الموقع، المنطقة، البلاد، المدينة، المكان المقدس

AALD: nēmelu (s.) (nēmalu) الأمل، الفائدة، النفع، الكسب، الفائض، الربح

سمل (مقاييس اللغة) السين والميم واللام أصلٌ يدلُّ على ضعفٍ وقلّة.

سمل (لسان العرب) والسّاملُ: الساعي لإصلاح المعيشة، وفي الصحاح: في إصلاح معاشه.

الطّرْسُ (القاموس المحيط) الطّرْسُ، بالكسر: الصّحيفةُ، أو التي مُحيتْ ثم كُتبتْ. وطرسهُ كضربهُ: محاهُ. والتّطْريسُ: تسْويدُ الباب، وإعادةُ الكتابةِ على المكْتوب. والتّطرُّسُ: أن لا تطْعمَ ولا تشْربَ إلا طيّباً، و~ عن الشيءِ: التّكرُّمُ عنه، والتّجنُّبُ. والمُتطرّسُ: المُتأنّقُ المُختارُ.

طرس (لسان العرب) الطِّرْسُ: الصحيفة، ويقال هي التي مُحيت ثم كتبت، وكذلك الطِّلْسُ. ابن سيده: الطِّرسُ الكتاب الذي محي ثم كتب، والجمع أطْراس وطُروس، والصاد لغة. الليث: الطِّرس الكتاب الممْحُوُّ الذي يستطاع أن تعاد عليه الكتابة، وفعْلُك به التّطْريسُ. وطرّسه أفسده.

ترص (مقاييس اللغة) التاء والراء والصاد أصلٌ واحد، وهو الإحكام. يقال ترُص الشّيءُ، وأتْرصْتُه أحكمْته فهو مُترصٌ. وكلُّ ما أحكمْت صنْعتهُ فقد أتْرصْته.

ترص (الصّحاح في اللغة) أتْرصْتُ الشيءَ وترّصْتُهُ، أي أحكمته وقوّمته، فهو مترصٌ وتريصٌ. وميزانٌ تريصٌ، أي مُقوّمٌ، وقيل محكمٌ. وقد ترُص تراصةً.

ترُصَ (القاموس المحيط) ترُص، ككرُم، تراصةً، فهو تريصٌ: مُحْكمٌ شديدٌ، وأتْرصْتُهُ. وفرسٌ تارصٌ: مُحْكمُ الخلْق. وميزانٌ مُترصٌ وتريصٌ: مُسْتوٍ عدْلٌ مُحْكمٌ، لا يَحيفُ. واتْرصهُ وترّصهُ: سوّاهُ وعدّله.

شارَ (القاموس المحيط) و~ إليه: أوْمأ، كأشار، ويكونُ بالكفّ والعيْنِ والحاجِب. وأشارَ عليه بكذا: أمرهُ، وهي: الشُّوْرى.

شور (لسان العرب) وأشار إليه وشَوَر: أومأ، يكون ذلك بالكفّ والعين والحاجب؛ وأشار الرجل يُشير إشارةً إذا أومأ بيديه. ويقال: شَوَّرت إليه بيدي وأشرت إليه أي لَوَّحت إليه وألَحْتُ أيضاً. وأشارَ إليه باليد: أَوْمأ، وأشارَ عليه بالرَّأي.
نيل (الصَّحاح في اللغة) نالَ خيراً يَنالُ نَيْلاً، أي أصاب.
نول (لسان العرب) الليث: النائل ما نِلْت من معروف إنسان، وكذلك النَوال. وأنالَهُ معروفه ونَوَّله: أعطاه معروفه؛ قال الشاعر: إنْ تُنولْهُ فقد تَمْنَعُه، وتُريه النَّجم يَجْري بالظُّهُرْ والنَالُ والمَنالةُ والمَنالُ: مصدر نلت أنال. ويقال: نُلْت له بشيء أي جُدت، وما نُلْته شيئاً أي ما أعطيته. وما أَصَبْتُ منه نَوْلةً أي نَيْلاً. وشيء مُنَوَّل ومَنيل؛ عن سيبويه.
نمل (لسان العرب) ورجل نمل أي حاذق. ابن سيده: ورجل نَمِل خفيف الأصابع لا يرى شيئاً إلا عمله. يقال: رجل نَمِل الأصابع أي خفيفها في العمل.
النَّمِلُ (القاموس المحيط) والمُنْمولُ: اللسانُ..والناملةُ: السابلةُ.
سبل (لسان العرب) وسَبيلٌ سابلةٌ: مَسلوكة. وفي حديث الاستسقاء: اسْقِنا غيْثاً سابلاً أي هاطلاً غزيراً.

§ 102.—XVII, 15-23

ePSD: damāqu
sag [GOOD] wr. sag_8; sag_9; sag_{10}; $šeg_{10}$; sag_{12} "(to be) good, sweet, beautiful; goodness, good (thing)" Akk. banû; damāqu; dumqu; ţābu
zil [GOOD] wr. zil_2 "(to be) good; (to be) benificent" Akk. damāqu

دمج (لسان العرب) دَمَجَ الأَمْرُ يَدْمُجُ دُمُوجاً: استقام. وأَمْرٌ دُماج ودِماج: مستقيم. وصُلْح دِماجٌ ودُماجٌ مُحْكَمٌ قويٌّ. وتدامَجوا على الشَّيء: اجْتَمَعوا. وأَدْمَجَ الحَبْلَ: أجاد فتْلَه؛ ورجل مُدْمَجٌ ومُنْدمِجٌ: مُداخل كالحبْلِ المُحْكَم الفتْلِ؛ ونسوة مُدْمَجاتُ الخَلْقِ ودُمَّجٌ: كالحبل المُدْمج؛ عن ابن الأعرابي؛
دَمَجَ (القاموس المحيط) دَمج دُموجاً: دخَلَ في الشيء، واسْتَحكم فيه، كانْدمج وادَّمج وادْرمَّجَ،
دمق (مقاييس اللغة) الدال والميم والقاف ليس أصلاً، وإن كانوا قد قالوا دمق في البيت واندمق، إذا دخل، وإنَّما القاف فيما يُرى مبدلةٌ من جيم، والأصل دَمج، وقد مضى ذكْرُه.
دمق (لسان العرب) والانْدِماقُ: الانخراط. ومَعْنى قولِه دمَقوا في الْخَمَرِ أَيْ دَخَلُوا واتّسعوا؛
جدا (لسان العرب) والجَدا، مقصور: الجَدْوَى وهما العطية، وهو من ذلك، وتثنيته جَدَوان وجَديان؛ قال ابن سيده: كلاهما عن اللحياني، فجَدوان على القياس، وجديان على المُعاقبة. وخَيْرُه جداً على الناس: واسع. والجَدْوَى: العطية كالجَدا، وقد جَدا عليه يَجْدُو جداً. وأَجْدَى فلان أي أعطى. وأَجْداه أي أعطاه الجَدْوَى.
جدد (لسان العرب) والجَدُّ: الحظ والرزق؛
وجد (لسان العرب) وأوجده إياه: جَعله يجِدُه؛ عن اللحياني؛ ووجدَتني فعلْتُ كذا وكذا، ووَجد المال وغيره يَجِدُه وَجْداً ووُجْداً وجِدة. التهذيب: يقال وجَدْتُ في المالِ وُجْداً ووَجْداً ووِجْداً ووِجداناً وجِدةً أي صرْتُ ذا مال؛ الواجِدُ: الغنيُّ؛ قال الشاعر: الحمدُ لله الغَنيِّ الواجد وأوجده الله أي أغناه.

§ 103.—XVII, 24-31

ePSD: nakru
lukur [STRANGER] wr. lu_2-kur_2 "stranger, foreigner" Akk. nakru
ePSD: mašā'u
gu gid [ROB] wr. gu_2 gid_2 "to rob" Akk. mašā'u
kar [FLEE] wr. kar "to flee; to take away (by force), remove; to deprive; to save" Akk. ekēmu; eţēru; mašā'u; nērubu

مكر (الصَّحاح في اللغة) المكْرُ: الاحتيالُ والخديعةُ. وقد مكر به يمْكُرُ فهو ماكرٌ ومكّارٌ.
مكر (لسان العرب) الليث: المَكْرُ احتيال في خُفية، ابن سيده: المَكْرُ الخديعة والاحتيال، مكر يَمْكُرُ مكْراً ومكر به. والمكْوَرَى: اللئيم؛ عن أَبي العمَيْثِل الأعرابي. قال ابن سيده: ولا أُنكر أن يكون من المكر الذي هو الخديعة.
النّكْرُ (القاموس المحيط) النُّكْرُ والنَّكارةُ والنَّكْراءُ والنُّكُرُ، بالضم: الدَّهاءُ، والفِطْنةُ. والنَّكرةُ: خِلافُ المَعْرِفة، وتناكرَ: تجاهلَ، و~ القومُ: تعادَوْا.
نكر (لسان العرب) والمُناكَرةُ: المُحاربةُ. وناكرَهُ أي قاتلَه لأن كل واحد من المتحاربين يُناكِرُ الآخر أي يُداهيه ويُخادِعُه. يقال: فلان يُناكرُ فلاناً. وبينهما مُناكَرةٌ أي مُعاداة وقتالٌ. وقال أبو سفيان بن حرب: إن محمداً لم يُناكرْ أحداً إلا كانت معه الأهوالُ أي لم يحارب إلا كان منصوراً بالرُّعب.
مشَعَ (القاموس المحيط) مشَع، كمنع: خلَس. وذئبٌ مَشُوعٌ: خلاَّسٌ، وتَمْشيعُ القَصْعة: أكلُ كلِّ ما فيها. وتمَشَّعَ الرجُلُ: أزال الأذى عن نفسه، أو هو الاسْتِنْجاءُ بالحجارة خاصَّةً. وامْتَشع ما في الضَّرْعِ: أخَذَهُ كلَّه، و~ ثَوبَهُ: اخْتَلسهُ،
مشع (لسان العرب) وامتشع السف من غِمْده وامْتَلخه إذا امْتَعده وسلّه مُسْرعاً. ويقال: امْتَشِعْ من فلان ما مَشع لك أي خُذ منه ما وجَدت. قال ابن الأعرابي: امْتَشَع الرجل ثوب صاحبه أي اخْتلسه.
أداهُ (القاموس المحيط) واسْتأدى عليه: اسْتَعدى، و~ فلانا مالاً: صادرهُ، وأخذه منه. وأديتُ له: خَتلْتُه. وتأَدَّيتُ له من حقِّه: قضيْتُه.

§ 104.—XVII, 32-45

ePSD: šīpātu
siki [HAIR] wr. siki "wool, fleece; hair; (animal's) pelt" Akk. šārtu; šīpātu
ePSD: pašāru
bur [SPREAD] wr. bur_2; bur "to release, free; to reveal; to spread out, cover" Akk. pašāru; šuparruru
u'en [RELEASE] wr. u_3-en; u_3-en_3 "to release" Akk. pašāru
AALD: kanku (s.) (kangu) See kanāku الختم، وثيقة مختومة
AALD: kânu (s.) (kuānu) يثبت، يبقى، يحافظ ويبقي، يشهد، شاهد، يصدق، يثبت

فسر (مقاييس اللغة) الفاء والسين والراء كلمة واحدة تدلُّ على بيانِ شيءٍ وإيضاحه. من ذلك الفَسْرُ، يقال: فَسَرْتُ الشَّيءَ وفسَّرته.

فشا (لسان العرب) فشا خَبَرُه يَفْشُو فُشُوّا وفُشِيّا: انتشر وذاع، كذلك فشا فضْلُه وعُرْفُه وأَفْشاه هو؛ قال: إنَّ ابن زَيْدٍ لا زالَ مُسْتَعْملاً بالخَيْرِ يُفْشي في مِصْرِه العُرْفا وفشا الشيءُ يَفْشُو فُشُوّا إذا ظهر، وهو عامّ في كل شيء، ومنه إفْشاء السر. والفَشاء، ممدود: تَناسل المال وكثرته، سمي بذلك لكثرته حينئذ وانتشاره.

ذيع (لسان العرب) الذَّيْعُ: أن يَشِيع الأَمرُ. يقال أَذَعْناه فذاع وأَذَعْت الأَمر وأَذَعْتُ به وأَذَعْتُ السِّرَّ إذاعة إذا أَفْشَيْته وأَظهرته. وذاع الشيءُ والخبر يَذيع ذَيْعاً وذَيَعاناً وذُيوعاً وذَيْعوعةً: فشا وانتشر. وأَذاعه وأَذاع به أي أَفشاه.

شعف (مقاييس اللغة) الشين والعين والفاء يدلُّ على أعالي الشيء ورأسه.

شعف (العباب الزاخر) ورجلٌ صُهْبُ الشِّعَاف: يراد بذلك شعر رأسه. وما على رأسه إلا شُعَيْفاتٌ: أي شُعيرات من الذؤابة. وفي حديث النبي - صلى الله عليه وسلم-: أنه ذكر في خطبته ياجوج وماجوج فقال :عِراضُ الوجوه صِغارُ العيون صُهْبُ الشِّعافِ ومن كل حدب ينسلون، قوله صهب الشِّعاف يريد شعور رؤوسهم، واحدتها شَعَفة، وهي أَعْلى الشعر. والشَّعْفَةُ خصلة في أعلى الرأس. وقال الليث :الشَّعفُ داء يُصيب الناقة فيتمعط شَعَر عينيها، يقال :شَعِفتْ وهي تَشْعَفُ؛

كنن (لسان العرب) الكِنُّ والكِنَّةُ والكِنانُ: وقاء كل شيءٍ وسِتْرُه. واسْتكنَ الشيءُ: استتر؛ وقال أَبو زيد: كَنَنْته وأَكْنَنْته بمعنى في الكِنّ وفي النَّفس جمعاً، تقول: كَنَنْتُ العلم وأَكْنَنْتُه، فهو مَكْنونٌ ومُكَنٌّ.

كين (لسان العرب) والكِينة الكَفالة، والمُكْتانُ الكفيلُ.

كان (القاموس المحيط) كان يكِينُ: خضَع. والمُكْتانُ: الكفيلُ.

كنع (لسان العرب) والتكَنُّع التحصن. وكَنع الشيءُ كَنعاً: لَزِمَ ودام. والكَنِعُ اللازمُ؛

§ 105.—XVII, 46-54

ePSD: egû, baţlu
daranšub [NEGLIGENT] wr. da-ra-an-šub "negligent" Akk. egû, baţlu
AALD: egû (v.) يهمل، لا يبالي للواجب
ePSD: nikkassu
niĝŠID [ACCOUNT] wr. $ni\hat{g}_2$-ŠID; $ni\hat{g}_2$-ŠID-ma "account" Akk. nikkassu

هجأ (القاموس المحيط) والهجأُ، مُحرَكَةً: كُلُّ ما كُنتَ فيه فانْقطع عنْك.

عجَه (القاموس المحيط) عجَهَ بينهما تَعْجِيها: عانهُما ففرَق بينهما. وتعجَه: تجاهل، والعُنْجهِيُّ، بالضم: المُتكبِّرُ، وبهاء: الجهْلُ، والحُمْقُ، والكِبْرُ، والعَظَمَةُ، كالعُنْجهانيَةِ، وتَخففُ.

عجه (لسان العرب) تعجَّه الرجلُ: تجاهل، وزعم بعضهم أنه بدل من التاء في تعتَه. قال ابن سيده: وإنما هي لغة على حدتها، إذ لا تبدل الجيم من التاء. قال أَبو منصور: رأَيت في كتاب الجيم لابن شميل: عَجَهْتُ بين فلان وفلان، معناه أنه أَصابهما بعينه حتى وقعتِ الفُرْقة بينهما، قال: وقال أَعرابي أَنْدرَ الله عيْن فلانٍ لقد عجَه بيْن ناقتي وولدها. ويقال: العُنْجهِيَّة الجهلُ والحُمْقُ؛ الأزهري: العُنْجُهُ الجافي من الرجالِ. يقال: إنَّ فيه لَعُنْجهِيَّةً أي جفْوَةً في خُشونةِ مطْعمه وأُموره؛

نكز (لسان العرب) نكزَتِ البئرُ تَنْكُزُ نكْزاً ونُكوزاً وهي بئر نكِزٌ وناكِزٌ ونكُوز: قلَّ ماؤها، وقيل: فنيَ ماؤها؛ ونكز ونكِز البحرُ: نقص.

عجي (مقاييس اللغة) العين والجيم والحرف المعتل أصلٌ صحيحٌ يدلُّ على وَهْن في شيءٍ، إما حادثاً وإمّا خِلقة.من ذلك العُجاية، وهو عصبٌ مركَّب فيه فُصوصٌ من عظام، يكونُ عند رُسْغ الدابَّة، ويكون رِخواً، وزعموا أنَّ أحدَهم يجوع فيدُقُّ تلك العُجاية بيْن فِهْرين فيأكلُها. ومما يدلُّ على صِحَّة هذا القياسِ قولهم للأمّ: هي تعجُو ولدَها، وذلك أن يُؤخِّر رَضاعَه عن مَواقيته، ويُورِث ذلك وَهْناً في جِسْمه.

النَّقْصُ (القاموس المحيط) النَّقصُ: الخُسْرانُ في الحظِّ، كالتَّنْقاص والنُّقْصانِ. والنُّقْصانُ أيضاً: اسْمٌ للقدْرِ الذَّاهِبِ من المنْقُوص. ونقصَ لازِمٌ مُتعدٍّ.

§ 106.—XVII, 55-67

ePSD: karāru (v.) يرمي، يهيّئ، يشكّل
ePSD: karāru (v.) معنى غير اكيد

ePSD: mala
mala [AS MUCH AS] wr. ma-la "as much as there is" Akk. mala
كرر (لسان العرب) الكَرُّ: الرجوع. وكَرَّ عنه: رجع، وكرَّ على العدوّ يَكُرُّ؛ والكَرُّ: الرجوع على الشيء، ومنه التَّكرار. وتَكَرْكَرَ الرجلُ في أمره أي تَرَدَّد. وتكَرْكَرَ الماءُ: تراجع في مسيله. وكَرْكَره عن الشيء: دَفعه ورَدَّه وحبسه. وفي حديث عمر، رضي الله عنه: لما قدمَ الشامَ وكان بها الطاعونُ تكَرْكَرَ عن ذلك أي رجع، من كَرْكَرْتُه عنّي إذا دفعْته ورَدَدْتُه. وفي حديث كناية: تَكَرْكَرَ الناسُ عنه. وفرس مِكَرٌّ مِفَرٌّ إذا كان مؤَدَّباً طَيِّعاً خفيفاً، إذا كُرَّ كَرَّ، وإذا أراد راكبه الفرارَ عليه فَرَّ به. الجوهري: وفرس مِكَرٌّ يصلح للكَرِّ والحملة. ابن الأعرابي: كَرْكَرَ إذا انهزم، ورَكْرَكَ إذا جَبُنَ.
كَرَّ (القاموس المحيط) كَرَّ عليه كَرًّا وكُرُوراً وتكْراراً: عَطَفَ، و~ عنه: رَجَعَ، فهو كَرَّارٌ ومِكَرٌّ، بكسر الميم. و~ الشيءَ: جَمَعَهُ، و~ عنه: دَفَعَهُ، وحَبَسَهُ، و~ الرَّحى: أدارها.
ملأ (العباب الزاخر) المَلْءُ -بالفتح-: مصدر ملأتُ الإناء، وكوزٌ ملآنُ، ودلو مَلأى، والعامة تقول: كُوزٌ مَلاَ ماءً؛ والصواب مَلآنُ ماءً، وقال ابن الأعرابي في نوادره: جعبةٌ مَلآنَةٌ وامرأة ثَكلانةٌ. والمِلءُ -بالكسر-: اسم ما يأخذه الإناء إذا امتلأ، يُقال: أعطني مِلأهُ ومِلْئَيه وثلاثة أمْلائه. والمُلأةُ -بالضم مثال المُلْعَة-: الزكام.
مَلأهُ (القاموس المحيط) والمِلْءُ، بالكسر: اسمُ ما يأخُذُهُ الإناءُ إذا امتلأ، أعْطِهِ مِلأهُ ومِلأيْهِ وثلاثةَ أملائِهِ. وبهاءٍ هَيْئَةُ الامْتلاءِ، ومصدرُ مَلأهُ، والكِظَّةُ من الطعام.

§ 107.—XVII, 68-XVII, 14

ePSD: qâpu
dirig [FALL] wr. dirig "to become loose, fall out; to disintegrate; to disappear; to fall down, collapse" Akk. qâpu; šahāhu
ĝiškim til [TRUST] wr. ĝiškim til$_3$ "to trust" Akk. qâpu
šu la$_2$ [TO ENTRUST] wr. šu la$_2$ "to entrust" Akk. qâpu
AALD: qâpu (v.) (qiāpu) يؤمن، يَثِق، يعطي الامان، يأتمن شخصا بمهمة، يأتمن شخصا الى شخص
AALD: qapû (v.) ينهض، يقف على رجليه
وقف (لسان العرب) الوُقوف خلاف الجُلوس، وقف بالمكان وقْفاً ووُقوفاً، فهو واقف، والجمع وُقْف ووُقوف، ويقال: وقفتِ الدابةُ تَقِفُ وُقوفاً، ووَقَفْتها أنا وَقْفاً. وفي كتابه لأَهل نجْران: وأَن لا يُغَيَّر واقف من وقِّيفاه؛ الواقف: خادم البيعة لأَنه وقف نفسه على خِدْمتها، والوِقِّيفى، بالكسر والتشديد والقصر: الخدمة، وهي مصدر كالخِصِّيصى والخِلِّيفى. ورجل وَقّاف: مُتَأَنٍّ غير عَجِل؛
قفا (لسان العرب) الأزهري: القفا ، مقصور ، مؤخر العُنق ، ألفها واو والعرب تؤنثها ، والتذكير أعم. وقيل: القَفِيَّةُ المختار. واقْتفاه إذا اختاره. وهو القِفْوةُ: كالصِّفْوة من اصْطفى، وقد تكرر ذلك القَفْو والاقْتفاء في الحديث اسماً وفعلاً ومصدراً. ابن سيده: وفلان قَفِيٌّ أَهله وقَفِيَّتُهم أي الخلف منهم لأَنه يَقْفُو آثارهم في الخير. وأَنا قَفِيٌّ به أي حَفِيٌّ، وقد تَقَفَّى به. والقَفِيُّ: الضَّيْف المُكْرَم. وأَقفاه به: اخْتصّه. واقْتفى الشيءَ وتَقَفّاه: اختاره، وهي القِفْوةُ، والقُفْوةُ: ما اخترت من شيء. وقد اقْتَفَيْت أي اخترت. وفلان قِفْوتي أي خيرتي ممن أُوثره.

§ 108.—XVIII, 15-25

ePSD: šakāru
si [DRUNK] wr. si$_3$ "(to be) drunk" Akk. šakāru
ePSD: šikaru
kaš [BEER] wr. kaš; kaš$_2$ "beer; alcoholic drink" Akk. šikaru
AALD: šikāru (s.) (šikru) المُسكِر، الشراب الكحولي
ePSD: ki-la$_2$
kalak [TRENCH] wr. gala$_3$; gala$_4$; gala$_5$; kala$_3$; ki-la$_2$ "excavation, trench; storeroom" Akk. kalakku
kila [WEIGHT] wr. ki-la$_2$ "weight" Akk. šuqultu
ePSD: ki la
ki la [DIG] wr. ki la$_2$ "to dig" Akk. ?
ki la [FALL TO THE GROUND] wr. ki la$_2$ "to fall to the ground" Akk. napalsuhu
ePSD: GEŠTIN
ĝeštin [VINE] wr. ĝeštin; ^{ĝeš}ĝeštin; mu-tin; mu-ti-in "vine; wine" Akk. karānu
ePSD: GEŠTIN.LUL.A
ĝeštinka'a [GRAPE] wr. ĝeštin-ka$_5$-a "a grape" Akk. karān šēlebi
ePSD: abnu
na [STONE] wr. na$_4$; na; $^{na}{}_4$na "stone; stone weight" Akk. abnu
niĝkiluha [STONE] wr. ^{ĝeš}niĝ$_2$-ki-luh-ha "stone or seed of a plant" Akk. abnu
za [BEAD] wr. za; za$_2$ "bead, gem" Akk. abnu

ePSD: rabû; kapāšu

<u>dirig</u> <u>[EXCEED]</u> wr. diri; RI "(to be) very great, supreme, excellent; more than; (to be) powerful, competent; (to be) big, huge; (to be) abundant; on, over, above; against; radiance; to project, stick up, build high; (to be) surplus" Akk. atru; eli; rabû; kapāšu; zaqāru; šarūru; šūturu; lē'û

كيل (مقاييس اللغة) الكاف والياء واللام ثلاث كلماتٍ لا يُشْبِهُ بعضُها بعضاً. فالأولى: الكيل: كيل الطعام. يقال: كِلْتُ فلاناً أعطيته. واكتلْتُ عليه: أخذْتُ منه. قال الله سبحانه: وَيْلٌ لِلْمُطَفِّفِين. الَّذين إذا اكتالُوا على النّاس يَسْتَوْفُون. وإذا كالوهُمْ أَوْ وزنُوهُمْ يُخْسِرُون [المطففين 1، 2، 3].والكلمة الثانية: كال الزَّنْدُ يَكِيلُ؛ إذا لم يُخرِجْ ناراً.والكلمة الثالثة: الكَيُّول: مُؤَخَّر الصَّفِّ في الحرب.

الشَّهْلُ (القاموس المحيط) والشَّهْلَةُ: العجوزُ، والنَّصفُ العاقِلَةُ، خاصٌّ بالنِساءِ.

شهل (لسان العرب) وقيل: الشَّهْلَة النَّصَفُ العاقلةُ، وذلك اسم لها خاصةً لا يوصف به الرجل. وامرأة شَهْلة كَهْلة، ولا يقال رجل شَهْلٌ كَهْلٌ، والشَّهْلَةُ: العَجوزُ؛ قال: باتَتْ تُنَزِّي دلوَها تَنْزِيًا، كما تُنَزِّي شَهْلَةٌ صَبِيًا (* قوله «باتت تنزي دلوها» هكذا في الأصل والمحكم، وهو الموجود في الاشموني. وفي الصحاح والتهذيب: بات ينزي دلوه، فعلى هذا فيه روايتان).

سعل (مقاييس اللغة) السين والعين واللام أصل يدل على صخب وعلوّ صوت.يقال للمرأة الصَخَابة قد استسعَلتْ، وذلك مشبّه بالسَّعلاة. والسُّعال، مشتقّ من ذلك أيضاً؛ لأنه شيءٌ عالٍ.

سعل (لسان العرب) والسِّعْلاةُ والسِّعْلا: الغُولُ، وقيل: هي ساحرة الجنّ. واسْتَسْعَلتِ المرأةُ: صارت كالسِّعْلاة خُبْثاً وسلاطةً، يقال ذلك للمرأة الصَّخَّابة البَذِيَّة؛ قال أبو عدنان: إذا كانت المرأة قبيحة الوجه سيِّئة الخُلُق شُبِّهت بالسِّعْلاة، وقيل: السِّعْلاة أخبث الغِيلان، وكذلك السِّعْلا، يمد ويقصر، والجمع سَعالى وسَعالٍ وسِعْلياتٌ، وقيل: هي الأُنثى من الغِيلان. قال الأعشى: ونساءٍ كأَنَهنّ السَّعالي قال أبو حاتم: يريد في سوءِ حالهن حين أَسرْنَ؛ وقال لبيد يصف الخَيل: عَلَيهِنّ وِلْدانُ الرِّجالِ كأَنّها سَعالى وعِقْبانٌ، عليها الرَّحائلُ وقال جِرانُ العَوْد: هِيَ الغُولُ والسِّعْلاةُ خَلْقي مِنْهما مُخَدَّشٌ ما بَيْن التَّراقي مُكَدَّحُ وقال بعض العرب: لم يَصِف العربُ بالسِّعْلاة إلا العَجائزَ والخيلَ؛

جعا (لسان العرب) والجِعْوُ: الجِعَةُ: والفتح أكثر، نبيذ الشعير. وفي الحديث عن علي، رضي الله عنه: نَهى رسولُ الله، صلى الله عليه وسلم، عن الجِعَةِ. وفي الحديث: الجِعةُ شرابٌ يتخذ من الشعير والحنطة حتى يُسكِر. وقال أبو عبيد: الجِعةُ من الأَشربة وهو نبيذ الشعير. وجَعوْتُ جِعَةً: نَبذْتُها.

الجَعْوُ (القاموس المحيط) الجَعْوُ: ما جمَعْته بيدك من بعَرٍ ونحوه تَجعلُه كُثْبَةً.

سَكِرَ (القاموس المحيط) والسَكَرُ، محركةً: الخَمْرُ، ونبيذٌ يُتَّخَذُ من التمرِ والكَشُوث، وكلُّ ما يُسْكِرُ،

سكر (مقاييس اللغة) السين والكاف والراء أصلٌ واحدٌ يدلُّ على حَيرة. من ذلك السُّكر من الشراب. يقال سكر سُكْراً، ورجلٌ سِكِّير، أي كثير السُّكر. والسَكَر الشَّراب.

ربا (القاموس المحيط) رَبَا رَبْوَاً، كعُلُوٍّ، ورِباءً: زاد، ونما، وارْتَبَيْتُه، و~ الرابيةَ: علاها، والرابيةُ والرَّباةُ: ما ارْتَفَع من الأرضِ.

ربي/أ (مقاييس اللغة) الراء والباء والحرف المعتل وكذلك المهموز منه يدلُّ على أصلٍ واحد، وهو الزِّيادة والنَّماء والعُلُوّ.

رب (مقاييس اللغة) الراء والباء يدلُّ على أُصولٍ. فالأول إصلاح الشيءِ والقيامُ عليه. فالرَّبُّ: المالكُ، والخالقُ، والصَّاحب.

والرّبُّ: المُصْلِح للشّيء. يقال رَبَّ فلانٌ ضيعته، إذا قام على إصلاحها. والرَّابُّ: الذي يقوم على أمر الرَّبيب.

ربب (الصِّحاح في اللغة) رَبُّ كلِّ شيءٍ: مالكُهُ. والربُّ: اسم من أسماء الله عزَّ وجلَّ، ولا يقال في غيره إلا بالإضافة، وقد قالوه في الجاهلية للملك.

ربب (لسان العرب) وكُلُّ مَنْ مَلك شيئاً، فهو ربُّه. يقال: هو رَبُّ الدابةِ، وربُّ الدار، وفلانٌ رَبُّ البيتِ، وهُنَّ رَبَّاتُ الـحِجالِ؛ ويقال: رَبٌّ، مُشَدَّد؛ ورَبَبْتُ القومَ: سُسْتُهم أي كنتُ فوْقَهم.

أبن (مقاييس اللغة) الهمزة والباء والنون يدلّ على الذِّكْر، وعلى العُقَد، وقفْو الشّيء. وهذا إبَانُ ذلك أي حينُه.

أبن (لسان العرب) أَبَن الرجلَ يأْبِنُه ويأْبُنه أَبْناً: اتَّهمه وعابه، وقال اللحياني: أَبَنْتُه بخير وبشرٍّ آبُنه وآبِنُه أَبْناً، وهو مأْبون بخير أو بشرٍّ؛ والأُبْنة، بالضم: العُقْدة في العُود أو في العَصا، وجمْعُها أُبَنٌ؛ والأُبْنةُ العُقْدةُ، وعنى بها ههنا الغَلْصمة، وإبَّانُ كلِّ شيءٍ، بالكسر والتشديد: وقْتُه وحِينُه الذي يكون فيه. يقال: جِئْتُه على إبَّانِ ذلك أي على زمنه. وأَبْنُ الأَرض: نبتٌ يخرُج في رؤُوس الإكام، له أَصل ولا يطول، وكأَنه شعَر يُؤْكل وهو سريع الخُروج سريع الهَيْج؛ عن أَبي حنيفة. قال ابن جني: وأَما قولهم للجبلين المُتَقابلين أَبانان،

أفن (لسان العرب) وأَخذ الشيءَ بإِفّانه أَي بزمانه وأَوّله، وقد يكون فِعْلاناً. وجاءه على إِفّان ذلك أَي إِبّانه وعلى حِينه.

§ 110.—XVIII, 36-44

ePSD: nin

<u>nin</u> <u>[LADY]</u> wr. nin; ga-ša-an; ga-ša$_2$-an; ka-ša-an "lady; mistress, owner; lord" Akk. bēltu; bēlu

ePSD: nin-dingir

<u>erešdiĝir</u> <u>[PRIESTESS]</u> wr. ereš-diĝir "a priestess" Akk. ēntu

ePSD: ašābu

<u>dur</u> <u>[SIT]</u> wr. dur$_2$ "imperfect singular stem of tuš[to sit (down)]" Akk. ašābu

<u>durun</u> [<u>SIT</u>] wr. $durun_x$(|KU.KU|); durun; dur_2-ru-un "plural stem of tuš[to sit (down)]" Akk. ašābu
<u>til</u> [<u>LIVE</u>] wr. til_3 "to live; to sit (down); to dwell" Akk. ašābu; balāţu
<u>tuš</u> [<u>SIT</u>] wr. tuš "to sit (down); to dwell" Akk. ašābu
ePSD: wāšipu
<u>kamuĝal</u> [<u>INCANTATION</u>] wr. ka-mu_7-$ĝal_2$ "incantation priest" Akk. wāšipu
ePSD: erēbu
<u>e</u> [<u>LEAVE</u>] wr. e_3; i; e "to leave, to go out; to thread, hang on a string; to remove, take away; to bring out; to enter; to bring in; to raise, rear (a child); to sow; to rave; to winnow; to measure (grain) roughly (with a stick); to rent" Akk. aşû; erēbu; mahû; rubbû; zarû; šakāku
<u>kur</u> [<u>ENTER</u>] wr. kur_9; kur_x(DU); kur_x(LIL) "to enter" Akk. erēbu
ePSD: qalû
<u>bil</u> [<u>BURN</u>] wr. bil_2; bil_3; bil "to burn" Akk. qalû
<u>niĝsasa</u> [<u>BURNING</u>] wr. $niĝ_2$-sa-sa "burning; brazier, oven" Akk. qalqallu; maqlû; qalû
<u>sa</u> [<u>ROAST</u>] wr. sa "to roast; to parch" Akk. qalû

الوثْبُ (القاموس المحيط) الوثْبُ: الظفْرُ، وثَبَ يثِبُ وثْبا ووثَبانا ووُثُوبا ووِثابا ووثِيباً، والقُعودُ بلُغةِ حمْيَرَ. والوِثابُ، ككِتابٍ: السَّريرُ، والفِراشُ، أو المَقاعدُ. والمَوْثَبانُ: المَلِكُ إذا قعد ولم يغْزُ.

وثب (مقاييس اللغة) الواو والثاء والباء يدلُّ في لُغة العرب على الظَّفْر، إلاّ في لغاتٍ من لُغات حمْير فإنَّه بخلاف هذا. ووَثب من مكانه: طَفر. وفي لغة حمير يقولون لمن قعد: قد وثب.

وثب (لسان العرب) الوَثْبُ: الطَّفْرُ. والوَثْبُ القُعود، بلغة حِمْير. يقال: ثِبْ أي اقْعُدْ. ودَخَلَ رَجُل من العَرب على مَلِكٍ من ملوك حِمْير، فقال له المَلِكُ: ثِبْ أي اقْعُدْ، فوَثَبَ فتكسَّر، فقال الملك: ليس عندنا عَرَبِيَّتْ؛ مَنْ دَخَلَ ظَفار حَمَّرَ أي تكلَّم بالـحِمْيَرية؛ وقوله: عَرَبِيَّت، يُريد العربيةَ، فوقف على الهاءِ بالتاءِ. وكذلك لغتهم، ورواه بعضُهم: ليس عندنا عَرَبِيَّة كعَرَبِيَّتِكم. قال ابن سيده: وهو الصواب عندي، لأَنَّ الملك لم يكن لِـيُخْرِجَ نَفْسَه من العرب، والفعل كالفعل. والوِثابُ: الفِراشُ، بلغتهم. والوُثوبُ، في غير لغة حِمْيَرَ: النُّهوضُ والقيامُ. والـمِيثَبُ: الأَرضُ السَّهْلةُ؛

الإِرْبُ (القاموس المحيط) الإِرْبُ، بالكسر: الدَّهاءُ، ومن هذا الباب أَرِبْتُ بكذا أي استعنتُ. ومن هذا الباب الأُرْبى، وهي الدّاهية المستنكَرة. وقالوا: سمِّيت لتأريب عقْدِها كأنَّه لا يُقدر على حلِّها

أرب (الصِّحَاح في اللغة) وقد أَرِبَ يَأْرَبُ إرِباً، وأرابة أيضاً. وفلان يؤارِبُ صاحبَه، إذا داهاه، والأَريبُ: العاقِلُ. والأَرَبُ أيضاً: الحاجَةُ، وفيه لُغاتٌ: إرْبٌ وإرْبةٌ، وأَرَبٌ، ومَأْرَبَةٌ. وأرِبَ بالشيءِ أيضاً: درِبَ به وصار بصيراً فيه، فهو أرِبٌ. والأُرْبةُ بالضم: العُقْدةُ. وَتأْريبُ العُقْدَةِ: إحْكامُها، يقالك أرِّبْ عُقْدتَك، وهي التي لا تَنْحلُّ حتى تُحلَّ حلاَ. وتأريبُ الشيءِ أيضاً: توْفيرُهُ.

أرب (لسان العرب) وأَرِبَ الدَّهْرُ: اشْتَدَّ. وأَرَّبها عقدها وشَدَّها. واستأْرَبَ الوتَرُ: اشْتَدَّ. وتَأَرَّبْتُ في حاجتي: تَشَدَّدْت. وتأَرَّب علينا: تَأَبَّى وتعسَّرَ وتَشَدَّد. وتَأَرَّبَ عليَّ إذا تعدَّى. الإِرْبةُ والإِرْبُ: الحاجة. وقد أَرِبَ الرجلُ، إذا احتاج إلى الشيءِ وطلَبه، يَأْرَبُ أَرَباً. وفي خبر ابن مسعود، رضي الله عنه: أَنَّ رجلاً اعترض النبي، صلى الله عليه وسلم، ليَسْأَله، فصاح به الناسُ، فقال عليه السلام: دَعُوا الرَّجل أرِب ما لَه؟ قال ابن الأَعرابي: احْتاج فسأَلَ ما لَه. وتَأْرِيبُ الشيءِ: تَوْفيرُه، وقيل: كلُّ ما وُفِّرَ فقد أُرِّبَ، وكلُّ مُوفَّر مُؤَرَّبٌ. وآرَبَ على القوم: فازَ عليهم وفَلَجَ. قال لبيد: قَضَيْتُ لُبانات، وسَلَّيْتُ حاجةً، * ونَفْسُ الفتى رَهْنٌ بقَمْرةِ مُؤْرِب أي نَفْسُ الفتى رَهْنٌ بقَمْرةِ غالب يَسْلُبُها. وأَرِبَ عليه: قَوِيَ. والأَرْبانُ لغة في العُرْبانِ.

الغَرْبُ (القاموس المحيط) الغَرْبُ: المَغْربُ، والذَّهابُ، والتَّنحّي، وأوَّلُ الشَّيء، وحَدُّهُ، و= يومُ السَّقْي، والفرسُ الكثيرُ الجرْي، ومُقَدمُ العَيْنِ، ومُؤْخرُها، والنَّوى والبُعْدُ، كالغَرْبَةِ وقد تغرَّب. وبالضم النُّزُوحُ عن الوطَنِ، كالغُرْبة والاغْتراب والتَّغرُّب، وغَرُبَ: غابَ، كغَرَّب، وبَعُدَ.

غرب (لسان العرب) وغَرَبه وغَرَّبَ عليه: تركه بُعْداً. وأَغْرَبَ الرجلُ إذا اشْتدَّ وجَعُه من مرضٍ أو غيره. فقال: إني أخافُ عليك غَرْبَ الشَّباب أي حِدَّته. والغَرْبُ النَّشاط والتَّمادِي. وأُغْرِبَ الرجلُ إذا اشْتَدَّ وَجَعُه؛ عن الأَصمعي.

العُرْبُ (القاموس المحيط) وعَرِبَ، كفَرِحَ: نَشِط،

هرب (الصِّحَاح في اللغة) الهرب: الفرار. وقد هرب.

لجأ (القاموس المحيط) واللَّجأ، مُحرَّكَةً: المعْقلُ والملاذُ، كالمَلْجأ،

لجأ (مقاييس اللغة) اللام والجيم والهمزة كلمة واحدة، وهي اللَّجأ والملجأ: المكان يُلتجأ إليه.

لجأ (لسان العرب) والمَلْجأُ واللَّجأُ: الـمَعْقِلُ، والجمع أَلْجاءٌ.

قلو (مقاييس اللغة) القاف واللام والحرف المعتلّ أصلٌ صحيحٌ يدلُّ على خفَةٍ وسرعة. يقال: قَلَيْت وقَلَوت. [و] القَلاَّءُ: الذي يَقْلي. وهو القياس، لأن الحَبَّة تُستَخَفُّ بالقَلْي وتَخِفُّ أيضاً.

قلا (لسان العرب) وقَلَى الشيءَ قَلْياً: أَنْضَجه على المِقْلاة. يقال: قَلَيْت اللحم على المِقْلَى أَقْليه قَلْياً إذا شويته حتى تُنْضِجه، وكذلك الحبّ يُقْلَى على المِقلى. وقلا الشيءَ في المِقْلى قَلْواً، وهذه الكلمة يائية وواوية. وقَلَوْت الرجل: شَنَئْتُه لغة في قَلَيْتُه.

§ 111.—XVIII, 45-49

ePSD: qû
gu [CORD] wr. gu "cord, net; unretted flax stalks" Akk. qû
gunu [FLAX] wr. gu-nu "flax" Akk. qû
sila [UNIT] wr. sila$_3$ "a unit of capacity; a vessel" Akk. mīšertu; qû
zabar [BRONZE] wr. zabar; zabar$_3$ "(to be) bright, pure; arrowhead; weapon; metal mirror; (to be) shiny; measuring vessel made of bronze; a metal bowl; bronze" Akk. ebbu; hutpu; kakku; mušālu; namru; qû; sappu; siparru

قوا (لسان العرب) الليث: القوّة من تأْليف ق و ي، ولكنها حملت على فُعْلة فأُدغمت الياء في الواو كراهية تغير الضمة، والفِعالةُ منها قِوايةٌ، وقال الأسدي: القاوي الآخذ، يقال: قاوه أي أَعْطِه نصيبه؛ التهذيب: والعرب تقول للسُّقاة إذا كَرَعوا في دَلْو ملآن ماء فشربوا ماءه قد تقاوَوْه، وقد تقاوينا الدَّلْو تقاوِياً. الأَصمعي: من أَمثالهم انقطع قُوِيٌّ من قاويةٍ إذا انقطع ما بين الرجلين أَو وجَبت بَيْعَةٌ لا تُستقال؛ قال أَبو منصور: والقاويةُ هي البيضة، سميت قاويةً لأَنها قوِيتْ عن فرْخها.

§ 112.—XVIII, 50-74

ePSD: šūbultu
niĝšutaka'a [GIFT] wr. niĝ$_2$-šu-taka$_4$-a; ŠU+TAG$_4$ "gift; shipment, consignment" Akk. šūbultu
ePSD: šābulu
ah [DRY] wr. ah$_3$ "(to be) dried (out), dry; to dry" Akk. abālu; šābulu
lah [DRY] wr. lah$_2$ "to dry" Akk. šābulu
ePSD: hurāşu
KU'UDKI [GOLD] wr. KU$_3$.UD.KI "gold" Akk. hurāşu
kugsig [GOLD] wr. kug-sig$_{17}$ "gold" Akk. hurāşu

سبل (مقاييس اللغة) السين والباء واللام أصلٌ واحد يدلُّ على إرسال شيءٍ من عُلو إلى سُفل، وعلى امتداد شيء. والممتدُّ طولاً: السَّبيل، وهو الطَّريق، سمِّي بذلك لامتداده.
السَّبيلُ (القاموس المحيط) السَّبيلُ والسَّبيلَةُ: الطَّريقُ، والسابلةُ من الطُّرُقِ: المَسْلوكَةُ، والقومُ المُخْتَلِفَةُ عليها. وأسْبَلَتِ الطَّريقُ: كثُرتْ سابِلَتُها،
سبل (لسان العرب) وسَبَّلت الشيء إذا أَبحْته كأَنك جعلت إليه طرِيقاً مطروقة. وسبيلٌ سابِلةٌ: مَسْلوكة. والسابِلَة: أَبناء السَّبيل المختلفون على الطُّرُقات في حوائجهم، والجمع السوابل؛
خرص (لسان العرب) والخُرْص والخِرْص: القُرْط بحَبّة واحدةٍ، وقيل: هي الحلْقة من الذهب والفضة، والجمعُ خِرصةٌ، والخُرْصة لغة فيها. وفي الحديث: أَن النبي، صلّى الله عليه وسلم، وعَظ النّساءَ وحثّهنّ على الصدقة فجعلت المرأَة تُلْقي الخُرْص والخاتَم. قال شمر: الخُرْص الحلْقة الصغيرة من الحَلْي كهيئة القُرْط وغيرها، والجمع الخِرْصان؛ قال الشاعر: عليهنّ لعسٌ من ظِباء تبالةٍ، مُذَبْذَبة الخِرْصان بادٍ نُحورُها وفي الحديث: أَيّما امرأَة جعَلتْ في أُذُنها خُرْصاً من ذهب جُعِل في أُذُنها مثْلُه خُرْصاً من النار؛ الخُرص والخِرص، بالضم والكسر: حلْقة صغيرة من الحلْي وهي من حَلْي الأُذُن، قيل: كان هذا قبل النسخ فإِنه قد ثبت إِباحةُ الذهب للنساء، وقيل هو خاصٌّ بمن لم تؤدّ زكاةَ حلْيها.

§ 113.—XVIII, 75-XIX, 16

ePSD: našpaku
arah [STOREHOUSE] wr. arah$_4$; arah$_3$; arah$_x$(|UŠ.BU.DA|) "storehouse, granary, storeroom; storage vessel" Akk. arahhu; našpaku
idub [GRANARY] wr. i$_3$-dub "granary" Akk. našpaku
ePSD: šapāku
de [POUR] wr. de$_2$ "to pour; to winnow" Akk. šapāku; šaqû
dub [HEAP] wr. dub "to strew; to heap up, pile, pour; to whirl up (a duststorm)" Akk. sarāqu; šapāku
sig [CAST] wr. sig$_{10}$ "to cast; to fashion" Akk. šapāku
ePSD: maškanu
kiĝal [LAND] wr. ki-ĝal$_2$; kankal "threshing floor; uncultivated land" Akk. maškanu
kislah [LAND] wr. kislah; kislah$_2$; kislah$_3$ "threshing floor; uncultivated, uninhabited, cleared land; empty house lot" Akk. maškanu; nidûtu; terīqtu; turbalû
kisur [LOCUS] wr. ki-su$_7$; ki-|LAGAR@g| "threshing floor" Akk. maškanu
lugud [LOCUS] wr. lugud$_4$ "threshing floor" Akk. maškanu; rahīşu
mašgana [SETTLEMENT] wr. maš-gana$_2$ "settlement; threshing floor" Akk. maškanu
sur [LOCUS] wr. su$_7$ "threshing floor; abandonment" Akk. maškanu; nidûtu

نسف (القاموس المحيط) كمَنْسِفٍ، كمَنْزِلٍ. وإناءٌ نَسْفانُ: مَلآنُ يَفيضُ،
نسف (لسان العرب) والنَّسْف تَنْقِية الجيِّد من الرَّديء، ويقال لمُنْخُل مُطوَّل المِنْسف. والمِنْسفة الغِرْبال. وانتسفوا الكلام بينهم: أَخْفوه وقلَّلوه. ونسَف الإِناءُ يَنْسِفُ: فاض.
سفك (لسان العرب) السَّفْكُ: صَبُّ الدم ونَثْرُ الكلام.

سبك (لسان العرب) سَبَكَ الذهبَ والفضة ونحوه من الذائب يسبُكهُ ويسبكُه سَبْكاً وسَبَكه: ذَوبه وأفرغه في قالبٍ.
سكن (لسان العرب) والسَّكَنُ والمَسْكَنُ والمَسْكِن: المنزل والبيت؛ الأخيرة نادرة، وأهل الحجاز يقولون مَسْكَنٌ، بالفتح.

§ 114.—XIX, 17-25

ePSD: nabû
<u>gu de</u> <u>[SAY]</u> wr. gu_3 de_2 "to say (addressing someone); to call; to read out" Akk. ?; nabû; šasû
<u>pad</u> <u>[FIND]</u> wr. pad_3 "to find, discover; to name, nominate" Akk. atû; nabû
<u>še</u> <u>[CALL]</u> wr. $še_{21}$ "to call by name" Akk. nabû
ePSD: bâ'u
<u>dib</u> <u>[PASS]</u> wr. dib; dib_2; di-ib "to pass, go along; to go past; to go through; to cross over; to audit; to transfer" Akk. bâ'u; etēqu
<u>ri</u> <u>[IMPOSE]</u> wr. RI; ru "to lay down, cast, place; to set in place, imbue; to lean on; to impose; to throw down; to release, let go; to walk along; to pour out; to lead away" Akk. bâ'u; emēdu; nadû; nasāku; ramû; rehû; tarû; wašaru
<u>ur</u> <u>[DRAG]</u> wr. ur_3 "to go along; to wipe clean; to beat, sweep away; to drag; to raise a boat" Akk. bâ'u; kapāru; šabāţu

بَاءَ (القاموس المحيط) بِفُلانٍ: قُتِل به فقاومَه، كأباءَهُ وباوأه. وتَباوآ: تَعادلا.
بوأ (العباب الزاخر) والبَواءُ: السَّواء، يُقال: دم فلان بواءٌ لدم فلان: إذا كان كُفْوًا له، وأبَأْتُ القاتِلَ بالقتيل واستَبأْتُه أيضاً: إذا قتَلْته به. وأباءتِ المرأةُ أديمها: جعلته في الدِّباغ. والتَّركيبُ يدلُّ على الرُّجوع إلى الشيء وعلى تساوي الشَّيْئين.
بوأ (لسان العرب) باءَ إلى الشَّيءِ يَبُوءُ بَوْءاً: رجَع. وبُؤْت إليه وأبأْتُه، عن ثعلب، وبُؤْته، عن الكسائي، كأبأْتُه، وهي قليلة. والباءة، مثل الباعة، والباء: النِّكاح. وسُمي النكاحُ باءةً وباءً من المَباءة لأن الرجل يتبوَّأ من أهله أي يَستمكنُ من أهله، كما يتبوَّأ من داره. ويقال: الجماعُ نفسُه باءةٌ، والأصلُ في الباءةِ المَنْزل ثم قيل لِعقْدِ التزويج باءةٌ لأَنَّ من تزوج امرأةً بَوَّأها منزلاً. وبُؤت إليه وأبأْتُه، عن ثعلب، وبُؤته، عن الكسائي، كأبأْتُه، وهي قليلة. وباءَ فُلانٌ بِفُلانٍ بَواءً، ممدود، وأباءه وباوأه: إذا قُتِل به وصار دَمُه بدمه. قال عبدُالله بنُ الزُّبير: قضَى اللهُ أنَّ النَّفْسَ بالنَّفْسِ بيْننا، * ولَـمْ نـكُ نَرْضَى أنْ نُباوئَكُمْ قَبْلُ والبَواء: السَّواء. وفُلانٌ بواءُ فُلانٍ: أي كُفْؤهُ ان قُتِلَ به، وكذلك الاثنان والجَميعُ. وقُسِمَ المال بينهم على بَواءٍ: أي على سواءٍ. وأبأْتُ فُلاناً بفُلانٍ: قتلْتُه به. ويقال: هم بواءٌ في هذا الأمر: أي أكْفاءٌ نُظَراء، وإذا أَقَصَّ السلطانُ رجلاً برجل قِيل: أباءَ فلاناً بفلان.
وباءَ بذَنْبِه وبإثْمه يَبُوءُ بَوْءاً وبَواءً: احتمله وصار المُذْنِبُ مأْوى الذَّنب، وقيل اعْترف به. وأصل البَواءِ اللزومُ. وفي الحديث: فقد باءَ به أحدُهما أي التزمه ورجع به. وباءَ بدم فلان وبحقِّه: أقَرَّ، وذا يكون أبداً بما عليه لا له. قال لبيد: أنْكَرْت باطِلَها، وبُؤْت بحقِّها * عِنْدي، ولم تَفْخَرْ عَلَيَّ كِرامُها وأبأْتُه: قرَّرْتُه وباءَ دَمُه بدَمِه بَوْءاً وبَواءً: عدَله. وبَوَّأَ الرُّمحَ نحوه: قابله به، وسَدَّده نحْوَه. وفي الحديث: أنَّ رجلاً بَوَّأَ رجلاً برُمحه، أي سَدَّده قبله وهَيَّأه. وبَوَّأَهُم منْزِلاً: نَزَلَ بهم إلى سَنَدِ جبَل. وأبأْتُ الإبل مباءةً: أنَخْتُ بعضَها إلى بعض. وأباءَ عليه مالَه: أراحَه. تقول: أبأْتُ على فلان مالَه: إذا ارحْتَ عليه إبلَه وغنمَه، وأباءَ منه. وتقول العرب: كلَّمناهم، فأجابونا عن بَواءٍ واحدٍ: أي جوابٍ واحد. وأبأْتُ بالمَكان: أقَمْتُ به.وبَوَّأْتُك بيتاً: اتَّخَذْتُ لك بيتاً.
نبا (لسان العرب) وأَنْبَيْتُه أنا أي دفعته عن نفسي. وفي المثل: الصِّدْقُ يُنْبي عنك لا الوعيدُ أي أنَّ الصِّدقَ يدفع عنك الغائلة في الحَرب دون التَّهْديد. قال أبو عبيد: هو يُنْبي، بغير همز؛ نبا بصره عن الشيء نُبُوًّا ونُبيًا؛ قال أبو نخيلة: لمَّا نبا بي صاحبي نُبيًا ونبْوة مرة واحدة. وفي حديث الأَحنف: قدِمْنا على عُمر مع وفْد فنبَتْ عيناه عنهم ووقعتا عليَّ؛ يقال: نَبا عنه بصرهُ يَنْبو أي تجافى ولم ينظر إليه، كأنه حقَرهم ولم يَرْفع بهم رأساً. والنَّبْوةُ: الإقامة.
نبأ (لسان العرب) ونبأْتُ من أرض إلى أرض إذا خرَجْتَ منها إلى أخرى. وسَيْلٌ نابئٌ: جاء من بلد آخَر. ورجل نا بِئٌ. ونبأَ عليْهِمْ يَنْبأُ نبْأً ونُبُوءًا: هجم وطَلع، وكذلك نبَه ونبع، كِلاهُما على البَدل.
نبأ (مقاييس اللغة) النُّونُ وَالْبَاءُ وَالْهَمْزَةُ قِيَاسُهُ الْإِتْيَانُ مِنْ مَكَانٍ إِلَى مَكَانٍ. يُقَالُ لِلَّذِي يَنْبَأُ مِنْ أَرْضٍ إِلَى أَرْضٍ نَابِئٌ.
نبا (الصِّحاح في اللغة) نَبا الشَّيء عنِّي يَنْبو، أي تجافى وتباعد. وأنْبَيْتُهُ أنا، أي دفعته عن نفسي. نَبا بصري عن الشيء. ونَبا بفلانٍ منزِلُه، إذا لم يوافقه.
نبو (المصباح المنير) وَنَبأَ يَنْبأُ مَهْمُوزٌ أَيْضًا بِفَتْحَتَيْنِ خَرَجَ مِنْ أَرْضٍ إلَى أَرْضٍ وَأَنْبَأَهُ غَيْرُهُ أَخْرَجَهُ فَهُوَ نَبِيءٌ عَلَى فَعِيلٍ.
نبو (مقاييس اللغة) النون والباء والحرف المعتلّ أصلٌ صحيح يدلُّ على ارتفاعٍ في الشيء عن غيره أو تنحٍّ عنه. [نبا بصرُه عن الشيء] ينبو.

§ 116.—XIX, 38-53

ePSD: māhāzu

kišupeš [LOCUS] wr. ki-šu-peš; ki-šu-peš$_5$ "a cultic place" Akk. māhāzu

zig [TOWN] wr. zig$_x$(|PA.GI|) "town, center" Akk. māhāzu

ePSD: ašāšu

azad [SHELTER] wr. azad$_2$; azad$_x$(|A.LAGAB×HAL.ŠU$_2$|) "reed shelter" Akk. ašāšu

zi ir [FEEL TROUBLED] wr. zi ir "to feel troubled" Akk. ašāšu

zir [BREAK] wr. zi; zi-ir; ze$_2$-er "to tear out; to break, destroy; to be troubled; to erase" Akk. ašāšu; pasāsu

AALD: uššušu (adj.) See ašāšu v. قلق، مشوش

حوز (مقاييس اللغة) الحاء والواو والزاء أصلٌ واحد، وهو الجمع والتجمع، يقال لكلّ مجْمعٍ وناحيةٍ حوْزٌ وحوْزة. وحمى فلانٌ الحوْزة، أي المَجْمع والناحية.

الحوْزُ (القاموس المحيط) الحوْزُ: الجمعُ، وضمُّ الشيء، كالحيازة والاحتياز، والسَّوقُ اللَّيِّنُ، والشديدُ، ضدٌّ، والسيرُ اللَّيِّنُ، والموْضعُ تُتَّخذُ حواليْه مُسنَّاةٌ، والملْكُ، والنّكاحُ، و~ القومُ: تركوا مركزهم إلى آخر. وتحاوزَ الفريقان: انحاز كلُّ واحدٍ عن الآخر. و"حوّازُ القُلوب" في حديث ابن مسعود: ما يحُوزُها ويغْلِبُها، حتى تركَب ما لا يُحبُّ. ويُروى: حوازٌ: جمعُ حازّةٍ، وهي الأمورُ التي تحُزُّ في القُلوب، وتحُكُّ، وتؤثّرُ، ويتخالَجُ فيها أن تكون معاصيَ، لفقْد الطمأنينة إليها. وتحوّزَ: تلوّى، كتحيّزَ، وتنحّى. والحوْزاءُ: الحرْبُ التي تحُوزُ القوم.

حوز (لسان العرب) الحوْزُ السير الشديد والرُّويد، وحوْزُ الإبل: ساقها إلى الماء؛ وتحوّز عنه وتحيّز إذا تنحّى، وهي تفيْعل، أصلها تحيْوز فقلبت الواو ياء لمجاورة الياء وأدغمت فيها. وتحوّز له عن فراشه: تنحّى. وفي الحديث: كما تحوّز له عن فراشه. قال أبو عبيدة: التَّحوُّز هو التنحي، وفيه لغتان: التّحوّز والتّحيّز. والحوْزاءُ الحرب تحوز القوم، حكاها أبو رياش في شرح أشعار الحماسة في وقول جابر بن الثعلب: فهلاّ على أخْلاق نعْليْ معْصبٍ شغبْت، وذو الحوْزاء يحفِزُه الوتْر الوتْر ههنا: الغضب. والتّحوُّز التلبُّث والتمكُّث. والحوْز الجمع. وكل من ضمّ شيئاً إلى نفسه من مال أو غير ذلك، فقد حازه حوْزاً وحيازة وحازه إليه واحْتازه إليه؛ وفي الحديث: أن رجلاً من المشركين جميع اللأْمة كان يحوز المسلمين أي يجمعهم؛ حازه يجُوزه إذا قبضه وملكه واستبدّ به. قال شمر: حُزْت الشيء جمعْته أو نحّيته؛ وفي الحديث: فحمى حوْزة الإسلام أي حدوده ونواحيه. وفلان مانع لحوْزته أي لما في حيّزه. والحوْزة، فعْلة، منه سميت بها الناحية. وحاز المرأة حوْزاً: نكحها؛ وحوْز الرجل: طبيعته من خير أو شر.

محص (لسان العرب) ومحص به الأرض محْصاً: ضرب. الجوهري: محص المذبوحُ برجْله مثل دحص.

محص (الصّحاح في اللغة) والتمْحيصُ: الابتِلاءُ والاختبارُ.

محص (لسان العرب) والمحْصُ شدة الخلق. والممْحوصُ والمحْص والمحيصُ والممحّصُ: الشديدُ الخلق، وقيل: هو الشديد من الإبل. والمحيصُ: الشديد الفتْل؛

محزَ (القاموس المحيط) محز الجارية، كمنع، محْزاً ومِحازاً: نكحها، و~ فلاناً: لهزهُ، أو محزهُ ونحزهُ وبحزهُ ونهزهُ ولهزهُ ومهزهُ وبهزهُ ولكزهُ ووكزهُ ووهزهُ ولقزهُ ولعزهُ: أخواتٌ.

محز (لسان العرب) وفي الحديث: فلم نزلْ مُفْطرين حتى بلغنا ماحُوزنا؛ قيل: هو موضعهم الذي أرادوه، وأهل الشام يُسمُّون المكان الذي بينهم وبين العدوّ وفيه أساميهم ومكاتبهم: ماحُوزاً، وقيل: هو من حُزْتُ الشيء أحْرزْته، وتكون الميم زائدة. قال ابن الأثير: قال الأزهري لو كان منه لقيل محازنا ومحُوزنا؛ قال: وأحسبه بلغة غير عربية.

حزز (لسان العرب) والحزيزُ والحزازُ من الرجال: الشديدُ على السّوق والقتال والعمل؛

لهز (مقاييس اللغة) اللام والهاء والزاء أصلٌ صحيح يدلُّ على دفْع بيدٍ أو غيرها أو رمي بوتر. قالوا: لهزْتُ فلاناً: دفعتُه.

ويقولون: اللّهْز: الضرْب بجُمْع اليد في الصّدر. ويقولون: لهزهُ القتير: فشا فيه. ولهزْتُه بالرُّمح في صدره: طعنتُه.

نهز (لسان العرب) نهزه نهْزاً: دفعه وضربه مثل نكزه ووكزه.

أشش (لسان العرب) الأشُّ والأشاش والهشاشُ: النشاط والارْتياح، وقيل: هو الإقبال على الشيء بنشاط، أشه يؤُشُّه أشّاً؛ بن الأعرابي: الأشُّ الخبز اليابس الهشّ؛ وأنشد شمر: ربَّ فتاةٍ من بني العناز، حيّاكةٍ ذاتِ هنٍ كناز ذي عضُديْنِ مُكْلئزٍّ نازي، تأشُّ للقُبْلة والمحاز. شمر عن بعض الكلابيين: أشّت الشّحمة ونشّت، قال: أشّت إذا أخذت تحلّب، ونشّت إذا قطرت.

§ 117.—XIX, 54-67

ePSD: kasû

a la [BIND] wr. a_2 la_2 "'to bind the arm'" Akk. kamû; kasû

gazi [CONDIMENT] wr. gazi; gazi$_2$ "mustard seed or licorice" Akk. kasû

šu la [PARALYZE] wr. šu la_2 "to paralyze" Akk. eşēlu; kasû

ePSD: kašāšu

u [RIDE] wr. u_5 "to ride; attatchment to a plow; upper pivot of a door; ship's cabin; to gain control" Akk. hinnu; kašāšu; rakābu; rikbu; šagammu

AALD: kašāšu (v.) See kašāšu القوة، القدرة، القوة الجسدية

AALD: kiššātu (s. pl.) See kašāšu مركز الشخص المعطى كحجز لدين، تعويض (لشيء مفقود)، تبديل (للشخص المحجوز)

AALD: kiššūtu (s.) See kāšišu, kaššu (adj.) يتطلب، يبتز خدمات مقابل دين، يتسلط، يُسيطر على، يجعله يؤدي خدمات مقابل دين، يُخضع

ePSD: anduraāru

amargi [REVERSION] wr. ama-ar-gi$_4$; ama-gi$_4$ "reversion to a previous state" Akk. anduraāru

AALD: andurāru (s.) (durāru, addurāru, andarāru) See durāru v. تحرير، عتق، الغاء خدمات فرضت بغير شرعية

كسا (لسان العرب) ابن الأعرابي: كاساهُ إذا فاخره، وساكاه إذا ضُيِّقَ عليه في المُطالبة، وسَكا إذا صغر جسمه.

كسأ (لسان العرب) كُسْءُ كل شيءٍ وكُسُوءُهُ: مُؤخَّره. وكَسأَ القومَ يَكْسَؤُهم كَسأً: غَلَبهم في خُصُومة ونحوها. وكَسأْتُه تبعْتُه. ومَرَّ يَكْسَؤُهم أي يَتْبعُهم، عن ابن الأعرابي. ويقال للرجل إذا هَزم القومَ فمَرَّ وهو يَطْرُدُهُم: مرَّ فلان يَكْسَؤُهم ويَكْسَعُهم أي يَتْبعُهم.

كسأ (العباب الزاخر) وكَسأْتُ وسطه بالسيف وكَشأْتُه: ضربْتُه.

كسع (مقاييس اللغة) الكاف والسين والعين أصلٌ صحيح يدلُّ على نوع من الضَرب. يقال: كسعه، إذا ضَرب برِجله على مؤخَرِه أو بيده.

كسع (لسان العرب) يقال: كَسَعه بكذا وكذا إذا جعله تابعاً له ومُذْهباً به؛

درر (لسان العرب) دَرَّ اللبنُ والدمع ونحوهما يدِرُّ ويَدُرُّ دَرّاً ودُرُوراً؛ والدِّرَّةُ، بالكسر: كثْرة اللبن وسيلانه. وفي حديث خزيمة: غاضت لها الدِّرَّةُ، وهي اللبن إذا كثر وسال؛ والدَّرُّ: اللبن ما كان؛ ابن الأعرابي: الدَّرُّ العمل من خير أو شر؛ ومنه قولهم: لله دَرُّكَ، يكون مدحاً ويكون ذمّاً، والريحُ تُدِرُّ السَّحاب وتَسْتَدِرُّه أي تَسْتَحْلِبه؛ ودَرَّ الشيء: لانَ؛ ومَرَّ على دِرَّتِه أي لا يثنيه شيء. سيف: تلألُؤُه وإشراقُه، إما أن يكون منسوباً إلى الدُّرِّ بصفائه ونقائه، وإما أن يكون مشبهاً بالكوكب الدريّ؛ ودَرَرُ الطريق: قصده ومتنه، ويقال: هو على دَرَر الطريق أي على مَدْرَجَتِه، وفي الصحاح: أي على قصده. ودَرَرُ الريح: مَهَبُّها؛ وهو دَرَرُك أي حِذاؤك وقُبالَتُك. ويقال: دَرَرك أي قُبالَتك؛ والدَّرُّ: النَّفْسُ، ودفع الله عن دَرِّه أي عن نَفْسه؛ حكاه اللحياني.

در (مقاييس اللغة) الدال والراء في المضاعف يدلُّ على أصلين: أحدهما تولُّد شيء عن شيء، والثاني اضطرابٌ في شيء. ودَرَرُ الطَّريق: قَصْدُهُ؛ لأنَه لا يخلو من جاءٍ وذاهب.

§ 118.—XIX, 68-73

ePSD: etēqu

dib [PASS] wr. dib; dib$_2$; di-ib "to pass, go along; to go past; to go through; to cross over; to audit; to transfer" Akk. bâ'u; etēqu

ePSD: pagru

adda [CORPSE] wr. adda; adda$_2$; ad$_x$(|LU$_2$@s×BAD|); ad$_x$(|BAD.LU$_2$|); ad$_x$(|LU$_2$×GAM|); ad$_x$(|LU$_2$@s|); $^{a\text{-}da}$adda$_x$(|LU$_2$@g.UŠ$_2$|) "corpse; wreck (of a boat)" Akk. pagru; šalamtu

AALD: paqaru(v.) baqaru يطالب (بملكية)، يُطالب، ينازع (في شرعية)، يخاصم، يتحدّى، يهدد

وقي (لسان العرب) وقاهُ اللهُ وَقْياً ووِقايةً وواقِيةً: صانه؛ والتَّوْقِيةُ: الكلاءة والحِفْظ؛ قال: إنَّ المُوَقَّى مِثْلُ ما وُقِّيتُ وتوقَّى واتَّقى بمعنى. وقد توَقَّيْتُ واتَّقَيْتُ الشيء وتَقَيْتُه أَتْقِيه وأَتْقِيه تُقًى وتقِيَّةً وتِقاء: حَذِرْته؛ وروِي عن ابن السكيت قال: يقال اتَّقاه بحقه يَتَّقيه وتَقاه يَتْقيه، وتقول في الأمر: تَقِ، وللمرأة: تَقِي؛ اتَّقى كان في الأصل اوْتَقى، والتاء فيها تاء الافتعال فأُدغمت الواو في التاء وشددت فقيل اتَّقى، ثم حذفوا ألف الوصل والواو التي انقلبت تاء فقيل تَقى يَتْقي بمعنى استقبل الشيء وتَوَقَّاه، قال: والتَّقْوى اسم، وموضع التاء واو وأَصلها وَقْوى، وهي فَعْلى من وَقَيْتُ، وقال في موضع آخر: التَّقوى أَصلها وَقْوى من وَقَيْتُ، فلما فُتحت قُلبت الواو تاء، ثم تركت التاءُ في تصريف الفعل على حالها في التُّقَى والتَّقوى والتَّقِيَةِ والتَّقِيّ والاتِّقاءِ، قال: والتُّقاةُ جمع، ويجمع تُقِيّاً، كالأُباةِ وتُجْمع أُبِيّاً، وتَقِيٌّ كان في الأصل وَقُويٌ، على فَعُولٍ، فقلبت الواو الأُولى تاء كما قالوا تَوْلج وأَصله وَوْلَج، قالوا: والثانية قلبت ياء للياءِ الأخيرة، ثم أُدغمت في الثانية فقيل تَقِيٌّ، وقيل: تَقِيٌّ كان في الأَصل وَقِيّاً، كأَنه فَعِيل، ولذلك جمع على أَتْقِياء.

وقي (مقاييس اللغة) الواو والقاف والياء: كلمةٌ واحدة تدلُّ على دَفْع شيءٍ عن شيءٍ بغيره. ووقَيْتُه أَقيه وَقْياً. والوِقاية: ما يقي الشَّيء.

عتق (الصّحاح في اللغة) والعِتْقُ الحرِّيَةُ، وكذلك العَتاقُ بالفتح والعَتاقَةُ. تقول منه. عَتَقَ العبد يعتِق بالكسر عِتْقاً وعَتاقاً وعَتاقَةً، فهو عَتيقٌ وعاتِقٌ؛ وأَعْتَقْتُهُ أنا. وعَتَقَتْ فرسُ فلان تَعْتِقُ عِتقاً، أي سبقَتْ فنجتْ.

عتق (مقاييس اللغة) العين والتاء والقاف أصل صحيح *يجمع معنى الكرم خلْقةً وخُلُقاً، ومعنى القِدم. وقد عتق وعَتُق، إذا أتى عليه زمن. قال ابنُ الأعرابيَ: كلُّ شيء بلغ إناهُ فقد عتَق، وسمِّي العبدُ عتيقاً لأنَه بلغ غايته.

بجر (الصّحاح في اللغة) البُجْرُ بالضم: الشرُّ، والأمرُ العظيمُ.

بجر (لسان العرب) وأَبْجَرَ الرجلُ إذا استغنى غِنًى يكاد يطغيه بعد فقر كاد يكفره. وقال: هُجْراً وبُجْراً أي أمراً عجباً، والبُجْرُ: العَجبُ؛ وفي نوادر. الأعراب: ابْجارَرْتُ عن هذا الأمر وابْثارَرْتُ وبَجِرْتُ ومَجِرْتُ أي استرخيت وتثاقلت.

فجر (الصّحاح في اللغة) ومفاجِرُ الوادي: مرافضُهُ حيث يرفضُّ إليه السيل.

رفض (مقاييس اللغة) الراء والفاء والضاد أصلٌ واحد، وهو التَّرك، ثم يشتقّ منه. يقال رَفضْتُ الشيء: تركته. هذا هو الأصل، ثم يشتقَ منه ارفضَّ الدَّمْعُ من العين: سال، كأنه ترَكَ موضِعَه. وكلُّ متفرّق مرفَضّ. وقال بعضهم: مَرافِضُ الوادي: مَفاجِرُه، وذلك حيث يرفضُّ إليه السَيل.

فجر (لسان العرب) وفي حديث ابن الزبير: فَجَرْت بنفسك أي نسبتها إلى الفُجور كما يقال فَسَّقْته وكفَّرْته. وانْفجرَتْ عليهم الدواهي: أتتهم من كل وجه كثيرة بَغْتة؛ وانْفجر عليهم القومُ، وكله على التشبيه. ابن الأعرابي: أَفْجر الرجلُ إذا جاء بالفجر، وهو المال الكثير، وأَفْجر إذا كذب، وأَفْجر إذا عصى، وأَفْجَرَ إذا كفر. وفَجَرَ الإنسانُ يفْجُرُ فَجْراً وفُجوراً: انْبعَثَ في المعاصي. قال الأَزهري: فالفجْرُ أَصله الشق، ومنه أُخذ فَجْرُ السَّكْر، وهو بَثْقُه، ويسمى الفَجْرُ فَجْراً لانْفجاره، وهو انصداع الظلمة عن نور الصبح. والفُجورُ: أَصله الميل عن الحق؛ وقول الناس في الدعاء: ونَخْلَع ونترك مَنْ يَفْجُرْك؛ فسره ثعلب فقال: مَنْ يَفْجُرُك من يعصيك ومن يخالفك، وقيل: من يضع الشيء في غير موضعه. وفي حديث عمر، رضي الله

عنه: أن رجلاً استأذنه في الجهاد فمنعه لضعف بدنه، فقال له: إن أطلقتني وإلا فجرْتُك؛ قوله: وإلا فجرْتُك أي عصيتك وخالفتك ومضيت إلى الغزو، يقال: مال من حق إلى باطل. ابن الأعرابي: الفجُور والفاجرُ المائل والساقط عن الطريق. وفي حديث أبي بكر، رضي الله عنه: إياكم والكذب فإنه مع الفجُور، وهما في النار؛ يريد الميل عن الصدق وأعمال الخير. وأيامُ الفجار: أيامٌ كانت بين قيس وقريش. وفجر الراكبُ فُجوراً: مال عن سرجه.

بقر (الصَحاح في اللغة) وبقَرْتُ الشيء بَقْراً: فتحته ووسعته.

بقر (لسان العرب) وبَقِرَ الرجل، بالكسر، إذا أعيا وحسَر، وبَيْقَر مثله. ابن الأعرابي: بيقر إذا تحير. يقال: بقِرَ الكلب وبَيْقر إذا رأى البقر فتحير، كما يقال غزِلَ إذا رأى الغزال فلهي. وبيْقر: خرج من بلد إلى بلد. وبيْقر إذا شك،

فقر (لسان العرب) وروى مُجالدٌ عن عامر في قوله تعالى: وسلامٌ عليَّ يومَ وُلِدْتُ ويومَ أموت ويوم أُبعث حياً؛ قال الشعبي: فَقَرات ابن آدم ثلاثٌ: يوم ولد ويوم يموت ويوم يبعث حياً، هي التي ذكر عيسى « عليه السلام؛ قال: وقال أبو الهيثم الفَقَرات هي الأمور العظام جمع فُقْرة، بالضم، وأَفْقَرك الصيدُ: أمكنك من فقاره أي فارمه، وقيل: معناه قد قرُب منك. والفُقْر الجانب، والجمع فُقَر، نادر؛ عن كراع، وقد قيل: إن قولهم أفْقَرك الصيدُ أمكنك من جانبه. وفقَر الأرضَ وفقَرها: حفرها. وفقْر الخرز: ثقبه للنظم؛ وهو منك فُقْرة أي قريبٌ؛

§ 120.—XX, 4-23

ePSD: qarītu

<u>esaĝ</u> <u>[STORE]</u> wr. e$_2$-saĝ; esaĝ$_2$ "grain-store" Akk. qarītu

<u>usi</u> <u>[STOREROOM]</u> wr. usi "storeroom" Akk. qarītu

جري (مقاييس اللغة) الجيم والراء والياء أصلٌ واحدٌ، وهو انسياحُ الشيء. وأما الجِرِّيَة، وهي الحوْصلة فالأصل الذي يعوَّل عليه فيها أنَّ الجيم مبدلة من قاف، كأن أصلها قِرِّيَة، لأنها تقري الشيءَ أي تجمعه، ثم أبدلُوا القافَ جيما كما يفعلون ذلك فيهما.

جرا (لسان العرب) والجِرِّيَة الحَوْصلة، ومن جعلهما ثنائيين فهما فِعْليٌّ وفِعْليَة، وكل منهما مذكور في موضعه. الفراء: يقال أَلْقِه في جِرِّيَتِك، وهي الحَوْصلة. أبو زيد: هي القِرِّيَةُ والجِرِّيَةُ والنَّوْطةُ لحوصلة الطائر؛ هكذا رواه ثعلب عن ابن نجْدة بغير همز، وأما ابنُ هانئ: فإنه الجريئة، مهموز، لأبي زيد.

قري (مقاييس اللغة) القاف والراء والحرف المعتل أصلٌ صحيحٌ يدلُّ على جمع واجتماع.

قرا (لسان العرب) وقريْتُ في شدقي جَوْزةً: خبأْتها. وقرت الظبيةُ تقْري إذا جمعت في شدقها شيئاً، ويقال للإنسان إذا اشتكى شدقه: قرى يَقْري. والمدّةُ تقري في الجرح: تجتمع. وأقْرت الناقةُ تُقْري، وهي مُقْر: اجتمع الماء في رحمها واستقرّ. قرى فيه الضيف. والجفنةُ مِقْراة؛ وأنشد ابن بري لشاعر: حتى تَبول عَبورُ الشِّعْرَيَيْن دماً صَرداً، ويَبيضَ في مَقْراته القارُ والمقاري: القُدور؛

§ 122.—XX, 31-43

AALD: kalāmu = kullumu (v.) يُري، يُهدي

AALD: kullumu (v.) يُري، يكشف، يبين، يعرض، يؤشر، وثيقة، يقدم شخص او وثيقة، يرى

AALD: kalû (v.) kali'u يحجز، يؤخر، يحافظ، يحتفظ

AALD: kullu (v.) يحفظ ، يحافظ، يهدي، يقبض، يمسك

كلأ (العباب الزاخر) وكَلأَ الدَين: أي تأخر. والكلأ العُشب، وقد كلِئتِ الأرض فهي كَلِئَةٌ. وأكْلأْتُ بصري في الشيء: رددته فيه. واكْتَلأْتُ منه: احترسْتُ، قال كعب بن زهير -رضي الله عنه-: أنخْتُ قَلوصي واكْتَلأْتُ بعينها. وآمرتُ نفسي أي أمريَّ أفعل. ويقال: اكْتَلأَتْ عيني: إذا لم تنم وسهرت وحذرت أمراً. وتكلأْتُ واسْتكلأْتُ: أي اسْتنسأْتُ. وكلأْتُ إلى فلان: تقدمتُ إليه. وكلأْتُ فيه: نظرتُ إليه مُتأملاً فأعجبني.

كلأ (مقاييس اللغة) الكاف واللام والحرف المعتل أو الهمزة أصلٌ صحيح يدلُّ على مراقبة ونظر، وأصلٌ *آخر يدلُّ على نبات، والثالث عضوٌ من الأعضاء ثم يُستعار. فأمّا النظر والمراقبة فالكلاءة، وهي الحِفظ، تقول: كلأه الله، أي حفظه. قال الله عزّ وعلا: قُلْ مَنْ يَكْلَؤُكُمْ بِاللَّيْلِ وَالنَّهارِ مِنَ الرَّحْمنِ[الأنبياء 42]، أي يحفظكم منه، بمعنى لا يحميكم أحدٌ منه، وهو الباب الذي ذكرناه أنه المراقبة، لأنه إذا حفظه نظر إليه ورقبه.

§ 125.—XX, 66-XXI, 7

ePSD: egû

<u>šembizida</u> <u>[KOHL]</u> wr. šembi; šem-bi-zid; šembizi "kohl, eye makeup, antimony paste; to anoint, smear on" Akk. egû; eqû; šimbizidû

<u>ši</u> <u>[TIRE]</u> wr. ši "to become tired" Akk. egû

ePSD: egû, baţlu

<u>daranšub</u> <u>[NEGLIGENT]</u> wr. da-ra-an-šub "negligent" Akk. egû, baţlu

بطل (مقاييس اللغة) الباء والطاء واللام أصلٌ واحد، وهو ذهاب الشيء وقِلّة مُكثه ولُبثه. يقال بطَل الشيءُ يبطُل بُطلاً وبُطولاً. وسُمّي الشيطانُ الباطلَ لأنه لا حقيقة لأفعاله، وكلُّ شيء منه فلا مَرْجُوع لـه ولا مُعوَّل عليه.

بطَل (القاموس المحيط) بطَل بُطْلاً وبُطولاً وبُطلاناً، بضمهن: ذهب ضياعاً وخُسْراً، وأبطلَه. ~ في حديثه بطالةً: هزَل، ورجُلٌ بطَلٌ، محرّكةً، وكشدّاد، بَيِّنُ البطالة والبُطولة: شُجاعٌ، تبْطُلُ جراحَتُه فلا يكْترِثُ لها، أو تبْطُلُ عنده دماءُ الأقران،

أجأ (لسان العرب) ابن الأعرابي: أجأَ إذا فرّ.

أجأ (القاموس المحيط) وكجَعَل: هرب.

وجأ (لسان العرب) أبو زيد: يقال للفحل إذا رُضّتْ أُنْثياه قد وُجِئ وِجاءً، فأراد أنه يقْطَعُ النّكاح لأن الـمَوْجُوء لا يضْرِبُ. أراد أن الصوم يقْطَعُ النّكاح كما يقْطَعُه الوِجاءُ، ورووي وَجًى بوزن عصاً، يريد التّعب والحفى، وذلك بعيد، إلا أن يُراد فيه معنى الفُتُور لأن من وَجِيَ فتر عن الـمَشْي، فشبّه الصوم في باب النّكاح بالتّعب في باب الـمَشْي.

عجا (لسان العرب) الأُمّ تَعْجُو ولدها: تُؤخِّرُ رَضاعه عن مواقيته ويورثْ ذلك ولدها وَهْناً؛ وقيل: عَجتِ المرأة ابْنها عجْواً أخّرتْ رَضاعه عن وَقْته، وقيل: داوتْه بالغذاء حتى نهض.

هجع (مقاييس اللغة) الهاء والجيم والعين: كلمةٌ تدلُّ على نوم. ومما قيس على هذا: رجلٌ هجع، أي أحمقُ مُستَنيمٌ إلى كُلٍّ.

طنا (لسان العرب) وطنِيَ في الفُجور وأطْنَى: مضَى فيه. وفي حديث اليهوديَّة التي سمَّت النبي، صلى الله عليه وسلم: عَمدتُ إلى سَمٍّ لا يُطْني أي لا يَسْلم عليه أحدٌ. يقال: رماه الله بأفْعى لا تُطْني أي لا يُفْلت لديغُها.

تنأ (لسان العرب) تنأَ بالمكان يَتْنأُ: أقام وقطن. وتنأَ فهو تانئٌ: إذا أقامَ في البلد وغيره. وقالوا تنَا في المكان فأبدلوا فظنَّه قوم لغة، وهو خَطأ.

الازهري: تنَخ بالمكان وتنأ، فهو تانخٌ وتانِئٌ، أي مقيم.

تنا (لسان العرب) التّناوَةُ: ترك المذاكرة. قال ابن الأثير: التّناية الفِلاحة والزراعة؛ والأَتْناءُ الأقْدام. والأتْناءُ الأقران.

تنأَ (القاموس المحيط) تَنأ، كجَعَلَ، تُنُوءاً: أقام،

وتن (لسان العرب) ووَتَنَ بالمكان وتْناً ووُتُوناً: ثبت وأقام به. والمُواتنة: المُلازمة؛ والواتِنُ: الثابت. والماءُ الواتِن: الدائم أعني الذي لا يجري، وقيل: الذي لا ينقطع.

بلك (لسان العرب) ابن الأعرابي: البَلْك أصوات الأَشداق إذا حركتها الأصابع من الوَلع، وقد بَلك الشيء: كَلبكهُ، وسنذكره.

لبك (لسان العرب) اللَّبْكُ: الخَلْطُ، لَبكْتُ الأمْرَ ألْبكُه لَبْكاً. اللَّبْكُ واللَّبَكةُ: الشيء المخلوط. ويروى: بكلْتَ، والتبَك الأمْرُ: اختلط والتبس. وأمر مُلْتبكٌ: ملتبس، على النسب؛ واللَّبيكةُ من الغنَم: كالبكِيلة. ابن السكيت عن الكلابيّ قال: أقول لِبيكة من غنم، وقد لبكُوا بين الشاء أي خلطوا بينها، وهو مثل البَكِيلة. وقال عَرّام: رأيت لُباكة من الناس ولَبيكة أي جماعة.

اللَّبْكُ (القاموس المحيط) اللَّبْكُ: الخَلْطُ، وأمرٌ لبِكٌ، ككتِفٍ: مُلْتبسٌ مُخْتلِطٌ. والتبكَ الأمرُ: اخْتلَط. واللَّبيكةُ: البكيلَةُ، والجَماعةُ، وتلبَّك الأمرُ: تلبَّس.

§ 126.—XXI, 8-24

ePSD: ibbissû

ibiza [LOSS] wr. i$_{3}$-bi$_{2}$-za; i-bi$_{2}$-za "financial loss" Akk. ibbissû

ePSD: ragāmu

inim ĝar [SUE] wr. inim ĝar; inim ga$_{2}$-ga$_{2}$ "to sue, to make a legal claim" Akk. baqāru; ragāmu

ePSD: ebēru

asilala [JOY] wr. asila; asil-la$_{2}$; asil$_{3}$-la$_{2}$; asila$_{3}$; si$_{11}$-le$_{2}$; sila; asila$_{x}$(|EZEN×KASKAL|); asil$_{x}$(EZEN)-la$_{2}$; asil$_{x}$(EZEN)-le$_{2}$ "joy; to rejoice; decorative fancy work" Akk. ašilalû; ebēru; riāšu; rīšātu

AALD: ebēru (v.) (epēru, habāru) يعبر، يمتد الى ما وراء شيء،

بَبَ (مقاييس اللغة) قال الخليل: البَبّةُ: هدير الفحْل في ترجيعه. وقد قالوا رجل بَبٌّ أي سمين، وكان بعضهم* يُلقَب .بَبّة

ببب (لسان العرب) والببُّ الغلامُ السائلُ، وهو السَّمينُ، ويقال: تَببَّب إذا سمن. وبَبَّةُ صوتٌ من الأصوات، وبه سُمّيَ الرجل، وكانت أمه تُرقِّصه به. وفي الصحاح: بَبّةُ: اسم جارية، غيره: بَبّة لقب رجل من قريش، ويوصف به الأحْمقُ الثَّقيلُ. والبَبّةُ: السَّمينُ، وقيل: الشابُ الـمُمْتلئُ البدنِ نعْمةً، قال: ألسْتَ بَبّة؟ قال ابن الأثير: يقال للشابِّ الـمُمْتلئِ البدنِ نعْمةً وشباباً بَبّةٌ. والببُّ: الغلامُ السائلُ، وهو السَّمينُ، ويقال: تَببَّب إذا سمِنَ. وبَبّةُ: صَوتٌ من الأصْوات، وبه سُمّيَ الرجل، وكانت أمه تُرقِّصه به. وهم على بَبّانٍ واحد وببان (قوله «وهم على ببان إلخ» عبارة القاموس وهم ببان واحد وعلى ببانٍ واحد ويخفف ا هـ فيستفاد منه استعمالات أربعة.) أي على طَريقة. قال: وأرى ببانا محذوفاً من بَبّانٍ، لأنَّ فَعْلانَ أكثر من فعالٍ، وهم بَبّانٌ واحدٌ أي سَواءٌ، كما يقال بأْجٌ واحِدٌ. قال الأزهري: وبَبّانٌ كأنها لغة يمانيةٌ.

عبر (مقاييس اللغة) العين والباء والراء أصلٌ صحيح واحدٌ يدلُّ على النفوذ والمضيِّ في الشيء. يقال: عَبرت النَّهر عُبوراً.

عبر (الصَحاح في اللغة) العِبْرَةُ: الاسم من الاعتبار. وعَبَرت عن فلان أيضاً، إذا تكلمت عنه. واللسان يُعبِّرُ عما في الضمير.

عَبَرَ (القاموس المحيط) عبَرَ الرُّؤيا عبْراً وعِبارةً وعَبَّرها: فسَّرَها، وأخْبرَ بآخرِ ما يؤُولُ إليه أمْرُها. واسْتَعْبَره إيَاها: سَألَه عبْرَها. وعَبّرَ عما في نفسه: أعْرَبَ، وعَبّرَ عنه غيرُهُ فأعْرَبَ عنه، والاسم: العَبْرَةُ والعِبارَةُ.

عبر (لسان العرب) عَبرَ الرُّؤيا يَعْبُرُها عَبْر وعِبارةً وعبَّرها: فسَّرها وأخبر بما يؤول إليه أمرُها. العابر: الناظر في الشيء، والمُعْتَبرُ: المستدلّ بالشيء على الشيء. وعَبّر عن فلان: تكلّم عنه؛ واللسان يُعبِّر عما في الضمير. قال الأصمعي: يقال في الكلام لقد أسرعت اسْتِعبارَك للدراهم أي استخراجك إياها. وعَبرَ المتاع والدراهم يعبرها: نظر كمْ وزْنُها وما هي، وعبَّرها: وزنَها ديناراً ديناراً، وقيل عَبَر الشيءَ إذا لم يبالغ في وزنه أو كيله، وتعبير الدراهم وزنُها جملة بعد التفاريق.

§ 127.—XXI, 25-34

ePSD: ubānu

si [HORN] wr. si "horn; finger; fret" Akk. qarnu; ubānu

šusi [FINGER] wr. šu-si "finger; a unit of length" Akk. ubānu

u [FINGER] wr. u "finger; toe" Akk. ubānu

umbin [NAIL] wr. umbin "(finger/toe-)nail; claw; hoof; finger, toe" Akk. ubānu; ṣupru

ePSD: rīṣu

atah [HELPER] wr. a$_{2}$-tah "helper" Akk. rīṣu

ePSD: rēṣu

saĝtab [PROTECTION] wr. saĝ-tab; sag-tab-ba "helper, ally; protection" Akk. rēṣu; ṣulūlu

ePSD: muttatu

kiši [HALF] wr. $kiši_4$ "half" Akk. muttatu

AALD: muttatu (s.) (muttutu) النصف، نصف الحزمة، شريط الرأس

AALD: gallābu (s.); OAkk. on ; gallāpu in Assy. See gullubu الحلاق

AALD: gullubu

ePSD: gallābu

hursaĝ [BARBER] wr. hursaĝ "barber, hairdresser" Akk. gallābu

kinda [BARBER] wr. kinda "barber, hairdresser" Akk. gallābu

munsub [HAIR] wr. munsub; $munsub_2$; $munsub_x$(|KA×SUHUR|); ^{su}munsub; $^{su}munsub_2$; u_2-šu-p? "hair; barber" Akk. šārtu; šārat zumri; gallābu

بنن (لسان العرب) وأبنّت السحابةُ: دامتْ ولزمتْ. ويقال: رأيت حيّاً مُبِناً بمكان كذا أي مقيماً. والتبنينُ: التثبيت في الأمر. والبنينُ: المتثبّت العاقل. وفي حديث شريح: قال له أعرابيّ وأراد أن يعْجل عليه بالحكومة. تبنّن، أي تثبّتْ، من قولهم أبنّ بالمكان إذا أقام فيه؛ والبنان: الأصابع: وقيل: أطرافها، واحدتها بنانةٌ؛ وأنشد ابن بري لعباس بن مرداس: ألا ليتني قطعتُ منه بنانه، ولاقيْته يقْظان في البيتِ حادرا وفي حديث جابر وقتْل أبيه يومَ أُحُد: ما عرفْتُه إلا ببنانه. والبنانُ في قوله تعالى: بلى قادرين على أن نُسوّي بنانه؛ يعني شواهُ؛

البنامُ (القاموس المحيط) البنامُ: البنانُ. وهذا ابْنَمٌ، أي: ابنٌ، والميمُ زائدةٌ، وذُكِرَ في ب ن ي.

أبن (لسان العرب) أبَن الرجل يأْبُنه ويأْبِنه أبْناً: اتّهمه وعابه، يقال: أبَنْتُ الرجل آبُنُه إذا رَمَيْته بخلّة سَوْء، فهو مأبونٌ، وهو مأخوذ عن الأُبن، وهي العُقَد تكونُ في القِسيِّ تُفْسِدُها وتُعابُ بها. وقال ابن الأعرابي: أبَنْتُ الرجلَ آبِنُه وآبُنُه إذا رمَيْته بقبيح وقذفْته بسوء، فهو مأبونٌ، وقوله: لا تُؤْبَنُ فيه الحُرَمُ أي لا تُرْمى بسُوء ولا تُعابُ ولا يُذْكرُ منها القبيحُ وما لا ينْبغي مما يُسْتحى منه. الجوهري: أبَنه بشرٍّ يأْبُنه ويأْبِنه اتّهمه به. وفلانٌ يُؤْبَنُ بكذا أي يُذْكرُ بقبيح. وقوله: لا تُؤْبنُ فيه الحُرَمُ أي لا تُرْمى بسُوء ولا تُعابُ ولا يُذْكرُ منها القبيحُ وما لا ينْبغي مما يُستحى منه. والأبْنُ التهمةُ. والأُبْنة، بالضم: العُقْدة في العُود أو في العصا، وجمْعُها أُبَنٌ؛ والأُبْنةُ العيْبُ في الكلام، وقد تقدّم قولُ خالد بن صفْوانَ في الأُبْنة والوَصْمة؛ وأُبْنة البعير: غَلْصَمتُه؛ قال ذو الرُّمّة يصف عيْراً وسَحيله: تُغنّيه من بين الصَّبيَّيْن أُبْنةٌ نَهُومٌ، إذا ما ارتدَّ فيها سَحيلُها. تُغنّيه يعني العَيْر من بين الصَّبيَّيْن، وهما طرَفا اللَّحي.

عير (مقاييس اللغة) العين والياء والراء أصلانِ صحيحان، يدل أحدُهما على نتوّ الشيء وارتفاعه،

العيْرُ (القاموس المحيط) والعارُ: كلُّ شيءٍ لزِمَ به عيْبٌ، وعيّرهُ الأمرَ، ولا تَقُلْ بالأمر. وتعايَروا: عيّر بعضُهم بعضاً. وعيّرَ الدّنانيرَ: وزَنها واحداً بعد واحد،

ترص (مقاييس اللغة) التاء والراء والصاد أصلٌ واحد، وهو الإحكام. يقال ترُص الشّيءُ، وأترصْتُه أحكمْتُه فهو مُترَصٌ.

ترص (الصّحاح في اللغة) أترَصْتُ الشيءَ وترّصْتُه، أي أحكمته وقومته، فهو مُترَصٌ وتريصٌ. وميزانٌ تريصٌ، أي مُقوّمٌ، وقيل محكمٌ. وقد ترُص تراصةً.

ترُصَ (القاموس المحيط) ترُصَ، ككرُمَ، تَراصةً، فهو تريصٌ: مُحكَمٌ شديدٌ، وأترَصْتُه. وفرسٌ تارصٌ: مُحكَمُ الخَلْقِ. وميزانٌ مُترَصٌ وتريصٌ: مُسْتوٍ عدْلٌ مُحْكَمٌ، لا يحيفُ. واتّرصهُ وترّصهُ: سوّاهُ وعدّله.

ترص (لسان العرب) التّريصُ: المحكَمُ، ترُصَ الشيءُ تراصةً، فهو مُترَصٌ وتريص مثل ماء مُسْخَن وسَخين وحبْل مُبْرم وبَريم أي مُحْكم شديد؛ وأترَصَه هو وترصه وترّصه: أحْكمه وقوّمه؛ ويقال: أترِصْ ميزانك فإنه شائلٌ أي سوّه وأحْكِمْه.

رصا (لسان العرب) ابن الأعرابي: رصاه إذا أحكمَهُ

رصاهُ (القاموس المحيط) رصاهُ: أحْكمَهُ، وأتقنه. وأرْصى بالمكان: لزمه لا يبْرحُ.

رصص (لسان العرب) رصّ البُنْيان يرُصّه رصّاً، فهو مرْصُوصٌ ورصيصٌ، ورصّصه ورصْرصه: أحْكمه وجمعه وضمّ بعضَه إلى بعض. وكلُّ ما أُحْكِمَ وضُمَّ، فقد رُصّ. ورصّصْتُ الشيءَ أرُصّهُ رصّاً أي ألْصقْتُ بعضَه ببعض، ومنه: بُنْيان مرْصوصٌ، وكذلك التّرْصيصُ، وفي التنزيل: كأنهم بُنْيانٌ مرْصُوصٌ. وشيء مُرصّصٌ: مطْليٌّ به. والتّرْصيصُ: ترْصيصُك الكُوزَ وغيرَه بالرّصاص.

رهص (لسان العرب) ورهصه في الأمر رهْصاً: لامه: وقيل: استْعجله. والرّواهصُ: الصخورُ المُتراصفةُ الثابتة. والرّواهصُ من الحجارة: التي ترْهصُ الدابةَ إذا وطِئتْها، وقيل: هي الثابتة المُلْتزقةُ المُتراصفةُ، واحدتُها راهصةٌ. ورهصت الحائطَ بما يُقيمه إذا مالَ. ورُهِصَ الحائطُ: دُعِمَ. والرِّهْصُ الطين الذي يُجْعل بعضُه على بعض فيُبْنى به، والإرْهاصُ على الذّنب: الإصْرارُ عليه. وفي الحديث: وإنْ ذنْبه لم يكن عن إرْهاصٍ أي عن إصْرار وإرْصادٍ، وأصله من الرّهْص، وهو تأْسيسُ البُنْيان.

رهص (مقاييس اللغة) الراء والهاء والصاد أصلٌ يدلُّ على ضغْط وعصر وثبات. فالرّهْص، فيما رواه الخليل: شدّة العصْر.

الرّهْصُ (القاموس المحيط) وراهصَ غريمهُ: راصدهُ.

متت (لسان العرب) ومتّه: طلب إليه المتاتَ. ابن الأعرابي: متمَتَ الرجلُ إذا تقرّب بمودّةٍ أو قرابة. قال النّضْر: متتُّ إليه برحم أي مددْتُ إليه وتقرّبْتُ إليه؛ وبيننا رحِمٌ ماتّةٌ أي قريبة. ومتّ في السّير: كمدّ. والمتُّ: المدُّ، مدُّ الحبْل وغيره.يقال: متّ ومطّ، وقطَل (قوله «وقطل» كذا بالأصل والتهذيب، ولعله محرف عن معط، بالميم والعين المهملة.) والمتُّ: النّزْعُ على غير بكرةٍ.

متا (لسان العرب) متوْت في الأرض كمطوْت. ومتوْت الحبلَ وغيره متْواً ومتيْته: مددْته؛ قال امرؤ القيس: فأتته الوحْشُ واردةً، فتمتّى النّزْعَ من يسرهْ فكأنه في الأصل فتمتّت فقلبت إحدى التاءات ياء، والأصل فيه متّ بمعنى مطّ ومدّ بالدال. والتّمتّي في نزْع القوس: مدُّ الصُّلْب. ابن الأعرابي: أمْتى الرجلُ إذا امتدّ رزْقُه وكثُر.

مطط (لسان العرب) ومطّ الطائرُ جناحيه: مدّهما. وتكلم فمطّ حاجبيه أي مدّهما. ومطّ حاجبه مطّاً: مده في تكلمه. ومطّ حاجبيه أي مدّهما وتكبّر.

جلب (مقاييس اللغة) الجيم واللام والباء [أصلان]: أحدهما الإتيان بالشيء من موضع إلى موضع، والآخر شيءٌ يغشّي شيئاً. والأصل الثاني : الجُلبة، جلدةٌ تُجعل على القتب .والجُلبة القشرة على الجرح إذا برأ. يقال جلب الجرْحُ وأجلب.
جلب (الصَّحاح في اللغة) جلبَ الشيءَ يجلِبُه ويجلُبُه جلْباً وجلَباً.والجلوبةُ: ما يُجلبُ للبيع. وأجْلب عليه مثلُه. وأجلبَ قتبَه: غشّاه بالجُلْبَةِ، وهو أن يجعل عليه جلْدةً رطبة فطيراً ثم يتركها عليه حتى تيْبس. وأجْلبَه، أي أعانه. والجلبُ والأجلاب: الذين يجلُبون الإبل والغنم للبيع.
جلب (لسان العرب) وجلبَ الدَّمُ، وأجْلبَ: يبِسَ، عن ابن الأعرابي. والجُلْبةُ القِشْرةُ التي تعْلُو الجُرْحَ عند البُرْء. والجُلْبةُ جِلْدةٌ تُجعَلُ على القتَب، وقد أجْلبَ قتبه: غشّاه بالجُلْبةِ. وقيل هو أن يجعل عليه جلدة رطبة فطيرا ثم يتْركها عليه حتى تيْبسَ. التهذيب: الإجْلابُ أن تأْخذ قِطعةَ قِدٍّ، فتُلبسها رأْس القتَب، فتيْبس عليه، وهي الجُلْبةُ. قال النابغة الجعْدي: أمِرَّ، ونُحّي منْ صُلْبه، * كتنْحِية القتَبِ المُجْلَبِ والجُلْبةُ: حديدةٌ صغيرة يُرْقعُ بها القدحُ. والجُلْبةُ العُوذة تُخْرز عليها جِلْدةٌ، وجمعها الجُلبُ. والمُجْلِبُ الذي يجْعل العُوذةَ في جِلْدٍ ثم تُخاطُ على الفرس.
جلف (لسان العرب) الجَلْفُ: القشْر. جلف الشيءَ يجْلُفُه جلْفاً: قشره، وقيل: هو قشْرُ الجلد مع شيء من اللحم، والجُلْفةُ: ما جلفْت منه، والجلْفُ أجْفى من الجرْفِ وأشدُّ استِئصالاً. والجلْفُ مصدر جلفْت أي قشرْتُ. وجلف ظُفْره عن إصْبَعه: كشطه. والجالِفةُ: الشجّة التي تقْشِرُ الجلد مع اللحم وهي خلافُ الجائفة. وجلفْتُ الشيءَ: قطعْته واستأْصلْته: وجلف الطِينَ عن رأْس الدّنّ يجْلُفه، بالضم، جلْفاً: نزعه. والجِلْفُ الخبز اليابسُ الغليظُ بلا أدْم ولا لبن كالخشبِ ونحوه؛
جلف (العباب الزاخر) الجلف: القشر، يقال: جلفت الطين عن رأس الدن أجلفه -بالضم-. والجالفة: الشجة التي تقشر مع اللحم. قال: وأجلف الرجل: إذا نحى عن رأس الخنبجة. والمجلف الذي أخذ من جوانبه، والمجلف والمجرف أيضاً: الرجل الذي جلفته السنون: أي ذهبت بأمواله. ويقال: جلفت كحل: أي استأصلت السنة الأموال، والاجتلاف: الاستئصال. وجاء متجلفاً: أي مهزولاً. والتركيب يدل على القطع وعلى القشر.
جلف (مقاييس اللغة) الجيم واللام والفاء أصلٌ واحدٌ يدلّ على القطع وعلى القشْر. يقال جلفَ الشيءَ جلْفاً، إذا استأصله؛ وهو أشدُّ من الجرْف. والجلْفة: القِطعة من الشيء.
جفل (لسان العرب) جفَل اللحمَ عن العظم والشّحْمَ عن الجِلْد والطّيْرَ عن الأرض يَجْفِلُه جفْلاً وجفَله، كِلاهما: قشره؛ قال الأزهري: والمعروف بهذا المعنى جلفت وكأنّ الجفْل مقلوب.

§ 128.—XXI, 35-41

ePSD: ahāzu
deg [COLLECT] wr. deg_x(RI) "to take; to gather up, glean; to tear out; to collect, pick up" Akk. ahāzu; laqātu; leqû; nasāhu

حوز (لسان العرب) وكل من ضمَّ شيئاً إلى نفسه من مال أو غير ذلك، فقد حازه حوْزاً وحيازة وحازه إليه واحْتازهُ إليه؛
أخذ (مقاييس اللغة) الهمزة والخاء والذال أصل واحد تتفرّع منه فروعٌ متقاربة في المعنى. [أمّا] أخذ فالأصل حوْز الشيء وجبْيه وجمعه.

§ 129.—XXI, 42-53

ePSD: itūlu
šed [LIE] wr. $še_{21}$; $še_x$(NA_2) "to lie down (of animals); to rest, sleep (of animals)" Akk. itūlu; rabāşu
ePSD: zikaru
duri [MALE] wr. duri "male; (to be) virile" Akk. zikaru
ĝeš [PENIS] wr. $ĝeš_3$; mu "penis; male" Akk. išaru; zikaru
nita [MALE] wr. $nita_2$; nita; $nita_x$(|ARAD×KUR|) "male" Akk. zikaru
pap [RELATION] wr. pap "first and foremost, pre-eminent; father; male, virile; brother" Akk. abu; ahu; ašarēdu; **ePSD:** zikaru
pil [MALE] wr. pil_6 "male" Akk. zikaru
urum [MALE] wr. $urum_3$ "male" Akk. zikaru
ePSD: kasû
a la [BIND] wr. a_2 la_2 "'to bind the arm'" Akk. kamû; kasû
gazi [CONDIMENT] wr. gazi; $gazi_2$ "mustard seed or licorice" Akk. kasû
šu la [PARALYZE] wr. šu la_2 "to paralyze" Akk. eşēlu; kasû
AALD: balāţu (v.) يتحسن، يتماثل للشفاء 2) ينشط، بصحة تامة، يستمر، يدوم 3) يحيا، يبقى حيا، يهرب، يعيش، يحصل على طعام
See: balittu, balitti
AALD: balāţu (s.) الحياة، العيش، الصحة الجيدة 2) طول الحياة، مدى الحياة 3) السنوات القادمة 4) الاحتياط، التوفير
AALD: bulţu (s.) See balāţu (v.) الحياة، العمر، الصحة، الشباب (العنفوان)

أتل (مقاييس اللغة) الهمزة والتاء واللام يدلّ على أصل واحد، وهو البطءُ والتّثاقل. قال أبو عبيد: الأتلانُ تقارب الخطْو في غضَبٍ، يقال: أتَل يأْتِلُ، وأتن يأْتِنُ
أتل (لسان العرب) الفراء: أتَل الرجلُ يأْتِلُ أتولاً، وفي الصحاح: أتْلاً، وأتَن يأْتِنُ أُتوناً إذا قارب الخطْوَ في غضب؛ وقال في مصدره: الأَتَلان والأَتنان؛ تأْتالُ: تُصْلحُ، وأصله تأْتول ونصبه بإضمار أن.
أتن (لسان العرب) وأتن يأْتِنُ أتْناً: خطبَ في غضَب. وأتن الرجلُ يأْتِنُ أتناناً إذا قاربَ الخطْوَ في غضَب، وأتلَ كذلك، وقال في مصدره: الأتنانُ والأتلانُ. وأتن بالمكانِ يأْتِنُ أتْناً وأتوناً: ثبتَ وأقامَ به؛

تلَهُ (القاموس المحيط) تلَهُ فهو مَتْلولٌ وتليلٌ: صرَعهُ، أو ألقاهُ على عُنُقِه وخَدِّهِ، وذهب يَتالُ مُتالَةً: يطْلُبُ لفرسِه فحْلاً. والتَّلَّةُ: الصَبَّةُ، والضَجْعَةُ، وبالكسر: الضِجْعَةُ، (بالكسر)، والبلَلُ، والحالَةُ، والكسلُ. وأتلَ المائعَ: أقْطرهُ. والتَّللُ، محرَكَةً: البلَلُ. وكصبُورٍ: الذي لا يَنْقادُ إلاَ بَطيئاً. وأتلَهُ: ارْتبطهُ واقتادهُ.

تلل (لسان العرب) تلَه يَتُلُّه تلاً، فهو متلول وتليل: صرعه، وقيل: ألقاه على عُنقه وخدّه، والأول أعلى، وبه فسر قوله تعالى: فلما أسلما وتلّه للجبين؛ معنى تلّه صرَعه كما تقول كبَّه لوجهه. والتَّلَّة: الضَجْعة والكسل.

وتل (لسان العرب) التهذيب: ابن الأعربي الوَتْلُ (قوله «الوتل» قال في القاموس بضمتين وضبط في التكملة كقفل وهو القياس) من الرجال الذين ملَؤوا بطونهم من الشراب، الواحد أوْتل، والكُتّام، بالتاء: المالئوها من الطعام.

الذِّكْرُ (القاموس المحيط) الذِّكْرُ، بالكسر: الحِفْظُ للشيء، كالتَّذْكار، والشيءُ يَجْري على اللسان، والصِّيتُ، كالذُّكْرَة، بالضم، والثَّناءُ، والشرفُ، والصلاةُ لله تعالى، والدُّعاءُ، والكِتابُ فيه تفصيلُ الدِّين. ووضْعُ المِلَل، و~ من الرجال: القويُّ الشجاعُ الأبيُّ، ورجلٌ ذَكَرٌ وذَكَرٌ وذكيرٌ وذِكِّيرٌ: ذو ذُكْرٍ. والذَّكَرُ: خلافُ الأُنْثى ج: ذُكورٌ وذُكورةٌ وذِكارٌ وذِكارة وذُكْرانٌ وذِكَرَةٌ،

كسأ (العباب الزاخر) كسأْتُه: تبعته، يقال للرجل إذا هزم القوم فمرَّ وهو يطردهم: مرَّ فلان يكسؤهم ويكسعُهم: أي يتبعهم. والأكْساءُ الأدبار، قال المُثلم بن عمرو التنوخي؛

كسأ (لسان العرب) كُسْءُ كل شيءٍ وكُسوءُهُ: مُؤخَره. وكسأ الدابّة يكْسؤها كَسْأً: ساقها على إثْر أخرى. وكسأ القوم يكْسؤهم كسْأً: غلبهم في خُصُومة ونحوها. وكسأْته تبعْته. ومرَّ يكْسؤهم أي يتبعهم، عن ابن الأعرابي.

كسع (لسان العرب) الكسْعُ: أنْ تضْربَ بيدك أو برجلك بصدر قدمك على دبر إنسان أو شيء. قال الأزهري: سميت الحمر كُسْعةً لأنها تُكسَعُ في أدبارها إذا سيقتْ وعليها أحمالُها. قال أبو سعيد: والكُسْعةُ تقعُ على الإبل العوامل والبقر الحوامل والحمير والرَّقيق، وإنما كُسْعتُها أنها تُكْسعُ بالعصا إذا سيقت، والحمير ليست أولى بالكُسعة من غيرها، وقال ثعلب: هي الحمر والعبيد: وقال ابن الأعرابي: الكُسْعة الرقيق، سمي كسْعةً لأنك تكسَعه إلى حاجتك، قال: والنَّخَةُ الحمير، والجَبْهةُ الخيل. وفي نوادر الأعراب: كسَعَ فلان فلاناً وكسحه وثفنه ولظَه ولاظه يلُظّه ويلُوظه ويلأظُه إذا طرده. والكُسْعةُ وثَنٌ كان يُعْبَدُ، وتكسّع في ضلاله ذهب كتسكَّع؛ عن ثعلب.

كتا (لسان العرب) الكَتْوُ: مقاربة الخطو، وقد كتا. ابن الأعرابي: أكْتى إذا غلا (قوله« غلا» هو بالمعجمة كما في الأصل والتهذيب والتكملة وبعض نسخ القاموس.) على عدوَه. الليث. اكْتوتى الرجلُ فهو يكتوتي إذا بالغ في صفة نفسه من غير فعل ولا عمل، وعند العمل يكْتوتي أي كأنه ينْقمع. واكتوتى إذا تتعْتع.

يدي (لسان العرب) والعرب تقول لمن عمل شيئاً يُوبّخ به: يداك أوْ كتا وفُوك نفخ؛ قال الزجاج: يقال للرجل إذا وُبّخ ذلك بما كسبتْ يداك، وإن كانت اليدان لم تجْنيا شيئاً لأنه يقال لكل من عمِل عملاً كسبتْ يداه لأن اليديْن الأصل في التصرف؛

كتع (مقاييس اللغة) الكاف والتاء والعين كلماتٌ غير موضوعةٍ على قياس، وليست من الكلام الأصيل. يقولون الكُتع: الرَجُل اللّئيم. ويقولون كتع بالشيء: ذهب به. وجاء القومُ أجمعون أكتعُون على الإتباع.

كتع (لسان العرب) ورجل كُتَعٌ: مُشمِّرٌ في أمره، وقد كتعَ كتعاً وكتَع؛ وقيل كتَع تقبّض وانضمّ ككنع. وكاتَعه الله كقاتَعه أي قاتله، وزعم يعقوب أنّ كاف كاتعه بدل من قاف قاتعه. قال الفراء: ومن كلام العرب أن يقولوا قاتله الله ثم تُستَقْبح فيقولوا قاتعه الله وكاتعه، ومن ذلك قولهم وَيحك ووَيْسك بمعنى ويْلك، إلا أنها دونها. وحكى ابن الأعرابي: لا والذي أكْتعُ به أي أحْلِفُ. وكتَعَ أي هرب. والكُتَعُ الذليلُ.

قتع (لسان العرب) قتع يَقْتَعُ قُتُوعاً: انْقمعَ وذلَّ.

قتا (لسان العرب) القَتْوُ: الخِدمة.

§ 130.—XXI, 54-67

AALD: kabālu (v.) See kibiltu, kubultu يكبَل، يشل، يعيق الحركة

ePSD: zenû

šag dab [ANGRY] wr. šag$_4$ dab$_5$ "to feel hurt, to be angry, to be worried" Akk. zenû

ePSD: abu

abba [FATHER] wr. ab; ab-ba; abba$_2$ "old (person); witness; father; elder; an official" Akk. abu; šību

adda [FATHER] wr. ad-da; ad "father" Akk. abu

aya [FATHER] wr. a-a; aya$_2$; a-ia "father" Akk. abu

pabilga [RELATION] wr. pa-bil$_2$-ga; pa-bil$_3$-ga; pa$_4$-bil$_2$-ga; pa-bil-ga; pa$_4$-bil-ga; pa$_4$-bi-ga "a kinship term" Akk. abu

pap [RELATION] wr. pap "first and foremost, pre-eminent; father; male, virile; brother" Akk. abu; ahu; ašarēdu; zikaru

كبل (لسان العرب) الكَبْل: قَيد ضخم. ابن سيده: الكبْل والكِبْل القَيْد من أيّ شيء كان، وقيل: هو أعظم ما يكون من الأقْياد، وجمعهما كُبُول. يقال: كَبَلْت الأسير وكبَّلْته إذا قيدته، فهو مكْبول ومُكبّل. وكبله يكبِله كبْلاً وكبَله وكبله كبْلاً: (قوله «وكبله كبْلاً» تكرار لما سبق الكلام عليه) حبسه في سجن أو غيره، وأصله من الكبْل؛

زنأ (لسان العرب) زنأ إلى الشيء يَزْنأ زَنأً وزُنُوءاً: لجأ اليه. وأزْنأه إلى الأمْر: ألجأه. وزنأَ عليه إذا ضيّق عليه، مُثقّلةٌ مهموزة. والزَّناءُ: الضَّيّقُ والضّيّقُ جميعاً، وكلُّ شيءٍ ضيّقٍ زناءٌ. وفي الحديث: أنه كان لا يُحبُّ من الدنيا إلاَ أزْنأها أي أضيقها. وزنّأ عليه تزْنئةً أي ضيّق عليه. قال العفيفُ العبْديُّ: لا هُمَّ، إنَّ الحرث بن جبلَه، زنَا على أبيه ثمّ قتلَه وركِبَ الشّادخة المُحجّله، وكان في جاراته لا عهْد له وأيُّ أمْرٍ سيّءٍ لا فعلَه قال: وأصله زَنَأَ على أبيه، بالهمز. قال ابن السكيت: إنما ترك همزه ضرورةً. والحرِثُ هذا هو الحرث بن أبي شمر الغسّانيّ. يقال: إنه كان إذا

أعجبته امرأة من بني قَيس بَعثَ اليها اغْتصبها، ويقال منه: قد زنأَ بَوْله يَزْنأُ زَنأً وزُنوءاً: احْتقن، وأَزْناه هو إِزْناءً إذا حَقنه، وأصله الضّيقُ. قال: فكأن الحاقِن سُمّي زَناءً لأنّ البولَ حَتقنُ فيُضيّقُ عليه، والله أعلم.

زنأ (القاموس المحيط) زَنأَ إليه، كمَنَعَ زَنْئاً وزُنُوءاً: لجأَ، وأَزْنأَهُ: أَلْجأَهُ، وصَعَّدَهُ، وحَقنَهُ. وزنَأَ عليه تَزْنِئَةً: ضَيَّقَ.

زنن (لسان العرب) والزَّنَنُ والزَّنيُّ والزَّنَاءُ: الضَّيِّق. وفي الحديث: لا يقبل الله صلاة العبد الآبق ولا صلاة الزِّنّين؛ قال ابن الأعرابي: هو الحاقنُ. يقال: زَنَّ فذَنَّ أي حقَنَ فقطَر،

ذنن (لسان العرب) والذُّنانة، بالنون والضم: بقية الدَّيْن أو العدةِ لأن الذُّبانةَ، بالباء، بقية شيءٍ صحيح، والذُّنانةُ، بالنون، لا تكون إلا بقية شيء ضعيف هالك يَذِنُّها شيئاً بعد شيء.

زعن (لسان العرب) النهاية لابن الأَثير: في حديث عثمان وفي رواية في حديث عمرو بن العاص أردتَ أن تُبلّغ الناس عني مقالةً يَزْعَنون إليها أي يميلون؛ قال ابن الأثير: يقال زَعَن إلى الشيء إذا مال إليه؛ قال أبو موسى: أظنه يركنون إليها فصحف، قال ابن الأثير: الأقرب إلى التصحيف أن يكون يُذْعِنون من الإذعان، وهو الانقياد، فعداها بإلى بمعنى اللام، وأما يركنون فما أبعدها من يَزْعَنون.

ذعن (مقاييس اللغة) الذال والعين* والنون أصلٌ واحدٌ يدلُّ على الإصحاب والانقياد.

ذعن (لسان العرب) قال الله تعالى: وإن يكن لهم الحقُّ يأْتوا إليه مُذْعِنين؛ قال ابن الأعرابي: مُذْعِنين مقرِّين خاضعين، وقال أبو إسحق: جاء في التفسير مسرعين، قال: والإذعان في اللغة الإسراع مع الطاعة، تقول: أَذعَن لي بحقي، معناه طاوعني لما كنت أَلتمسه منه وصار يُسْرع إليه؛ وقال الفراء: مُذْعِنين مطيعين غير مستكرهين، وقيل: مذعنين منقادين.

زون (لسان العرب) قال جرير: يَمْشي بها البَقرُ المَوْشيُّ أَكْرُعُه، مَشْيَ الهَرابذِ تَبْغي بيعَةَ الزُّونِ وهو مثل الزُّور، قال: تَزُوننا وتَزِينُنا واحد. والزُّونةُ كالزِّينة في بعض اللغات.

الزَّوْرُ (القاموس المحيط) الزَّوْرُ: وسَطُ الصَّدْر، أو ما ارْتَفعَ منه إلى الكَتِفيْن، أو مُلْتقى أطْرافِ عِظام الصَّدْر حيثُ اجْتَمَعَتْ،

زور (مقاييس اللغة) الزاء والواو والراء أصلٌ واحدٌ يدلُّ على المَيْل والعدول. من ذلك الزُّور: الكذب؛ لأنه مائلٌ عن طريقةِ الحق. والزَّوْرُ القومُ الزُّوّار؛ يقال ذلك في الواحد والاثنين والجماعة والنِّساء. فأمَّا قولهم إن الزَّوْرَ القويّ الشديد، فإنما هو من الزَّوْر، وهو أعلى الصدر شاذٌّ عن الأصل الذي أصَّلْناه.

زور (لسان العرب) الزَّوْرُ: الصَّدْرُ، وقيل: وسط الصدر، وقيل: أَعلى الصدر، وقيل: مُلْتَقى أطراف عظام الصدر حيث اجتمعت، وقيل: هو جماعة الصَّدْر من الخُفّ، والجمع أزوار. والزَّوَرُ عِوَجُ الزَّوْر وقيل: هو إشراف أحد جانبيه على الآخر، زَوِرَ زَوَراً، فهو أَزْوَرُ. والزَّوَرُ، بالتحريك: المَيْلُ وهو مثل الصَّعَر. وعُنُقٌ أَزْوَرُ: مائل. والزُّورُ شهادة الباطل وقول الكذب، ولم يشتق من تزوير الكلام ولكنه اشتق من تَزْوِير الصَّدْر. والزُّورُ والزُّونُ جميعاً: كل شيء يتخذ رَبّاً ويعبد من دون الله تعالى؛ ومفازة زَوْراءُ: مائلة عن السَّمْتِ والقصدِ. وقَوْسٌ زَوْراءُ: معطوفة. والزِّيرُ: الذي يخالط النساء ويريد حديثهن لغير شرٍّ، والجمع أَزْوارٌ وأَزْيارٌ؛ وقيل: الزِّيرُ المُخالِطُ لهن في الباطل، الزِّيرُ من الرجال: الذي يحب محادثة النساء ومجالستهن، سمي بذلك لكثرة زيارته لهن، وأصله من الواو؛ والزُّورُ والزُّونُ جميعاً: كل شيء يتخذ رَبّاً ويعبد من دون الله تعالى؛

ذون (الصَّحاح في اللغة) الذانُ: العيبُ. قال ابن السكيت: سمعت أبا عمرو يقول: الذامُ، والذيمُ، والذانُ، والذابُ، بمعنىً واحد.

ذون (لسان العرب) الكسائي في الذَّآنين: منهم من لا يهمز فيقول ذُونُون وذَوانين للجمع، قال: والذُّونون في هيئة الهِلْيَوْن مسموع من العرب. ابن الأعرابي: التَّذَوُّن النَّعمة، والذَّانُ والذَّيْنُ العيب.

الذِينُ (القاموس المحيط) الذِينُ، بالكسر: العَيْبُ.

ذين (لسان العرب) الذَّيْنُ والذَّانُ: العيب. وذامه وذانه وذابه إذا عابه.

عيب (لسان العرب) ابن سيده: العَابُ والعَيْبُ والعَيْبَةُ: الوَصْمة. والعربُ تَكني عن الصُّدُور والقُلُوب التي تَحتوي على الضمائر المُخْفاةِ: بالعِياب. وذلك أن الرجلَ إنما يَضعُ في عَيْبته حُرَّ مَتاعِه، وصَوْنَ ثيابه، ويَكْتُم في صَدْره أَخصَّ أسراره التي لا يُحِبُّ شُيوعَها، فسُمّيت الصدور والقلوبُ عِياباً، تشبيهاً بعِيابِ الثياب؛ ومنه قول الشاعر: وكادتْ عِيابُ الوُدِّ منّا ومِنْكُمُ، * وإن قيلَ أبناءُ العُمومَةِ، تَصْفَرُ أرادَ بعِيابِ الوُدِّ: صُدُورَهم.

شرج (الصَّحاح في اللغة) شَرَجَ العَيْبَةِ بالتحريك: عُراها. وقد أشرجْتُ العَيبة، إذا داخلْت بين أشْراجِها.

أبى (القاموس المحيط) أَبى الشيءَ يَأْباهُ ويأْبِيه إباءً وإباءةً، بكسرهما: كرِهَهُ، وآبَيْتُه إيّاهُ. وأبو المرأةِ: زَوْجُها.

أبي (لسان العرب) وأَبو المرأَة: زوجُها؛ عن ابن حبيب.

§ 131.—XXI, 68-76

ePSD: mutu

dam [SPOUSE] wr. dam "spouse" Akk. aššatu; mutu

§ 133.—XXII, 7-17

ePSD: šalālu

ir [PLUNDER] wr. ir "to plunder" Akk. šalālu

sur [SPIN] wr. sur "to spin; to twist; to slither" Akk. ţawû; šalālu

ePSD: aklu

ugula [OVERSEER] wr. ugula "instructor; overseer, foreman" Akk. aklu; šāpiru

ePSD: akālu

gu [EAT] wr. gu_7 "to eat, consume" Akk. akālu

rig [EAT] wr. rig_7 "to eat; to do something to barley; to pasture, tend; to drink; to sup" Akk. akālu; haţāpu; re'û; šatû; sarāpu

AALD: naşāru (v.) ينصر، يحافظ، يراقب، ينتظر، يحمي

سلل (لسان العرب) السَّلُّ: انتزاعُ الشيء وإخراجُه في رِفق، سَلَّه يسُلُّه سَلاًّ واسْتَلّه فانسلَّ وسَلَّلْتُه أَسُلُّه سَلاًّ. والانسلالُ: المُضِيُّ والخروج من مَضيق أو زحام. وانسلَّ وتَسَلَّلَ: انطلق في استخفاء. الجوهري: وانسلَّ من بينهم أي خرج. والسَّلَّةُ: السَّرقة، وقيل السَّرقة الخَفيَّةُ. وقد أَسَلَّ يُسِلُّ إسلالاً أي سَرق، ويقال: في بَني فلان سَلَّةٌ، ويقال للسارق السَّلاّل. والأَسَلُّ: اللصُّ. ابن السكيت: أَسَلَّ الرجلُ إذا سرق، والمَسَلُّ اللطيف الحيلة في السَّرق. ابن سيده: الإسلال الرَّشوة والسرقة. ويقال انسلَّ وانْشَلَّ بمعنى واحد، يقال ذلك في السَّيل والناس: قاله شمر.

أصر (مقاييس اللغة) الهمزة والصاد والراء، أصلٌ واحدٌ يتفرع منه أشياء متقاربة. فالأصر الحبسُ والعَطف وما في معناهما. والعرب تقول: "ما تأصِرُني على فلان آصرةٌ"، أي ما تعطفني عليه قرابة.

أصر (لسان العرب) والعَهْدُ يقال له: إصْر. والأَصِيرُ المتقارب. والمآصِرُ هو مأْخوذ من آصرَة العهد إنما هو عَقْدٌ ليُحْبس به؛ ويقال للشيء الذي تعقد به الأشياء: الإصارُ، من هذا. والإصْرُ العَهْد الثَّقيل. وفي حديث ابن عمر: من حلف على يمين فيها إصْر فلا كفارة لها؛ يقال: إن الإصْر أن يَحْلف بطلاق أو عَتاق أو نَذْر. وأصل الإصْر: الثِّقْل والشَّدُّ لأَنها أَثْقل الأيمان وأَضْيَقُها مَخْرَجاً؛ يعني أنه يجب الوفاء بها ولا يُتَعوَّضُ عنها بالكفارة. والعَهْدُ يقال له: إصْر.

صرر (لسان العرب) قال: وهي مشتقة من أَصْرَرْت على الشيء إذا أقمت ودُمْت عليه؛

صَراهُ (القاموس المحيط) صَراهُ يَصْرِيه: قطعهُ، ودفعهُ، ومنعهُ، وحفظهُ، وكفاهُ، ووقاهُ، و~ ماءَهُ: حبَسهُ في ظَهْرِه بامتناعِه عن النِّكاح، وتقدَّم، وتأخَّر، وعلا، وسَفل، ضِدٌّ، وعَطف، وأَنْجى إنْساناً من هَلَكةٍ، و~ فُلاً في يد فُلان: بَقِي مَحْبوساً، و~ بينهم: فصَل.

صري (لسان العرب) والصاري: الحافِظ. وصَراهُ الله: وقاه، وقيل: حفظه، وقيل: نجّاه وكَفاهُ، وكلُّ ذلك قريبٌ بعضُه من بعض. ابن الأعرابي: صَرَى يَصْرِي إذا قطع، وصَرَى يَصْرِي إذا عَطفَ، وصَرَى يَصْرِي إذا تقدم، وصَرَى يَصْرِي إذا تأَخَّر، وصَرَى يَصْرِي إذا علا، وصَرَى يَصْرِي إذا سفل، وصَرَى يَصْرِي إذا أَنْجَى إنْساناً مِنْ هَلَكةٍ وأَغاثَه؛

§ 135.—XXII, 37-66

ePSD: hā'iru

ĝidlam [SPOUSE] wr. ĝidlam; $ĝidlam_2$; $ĝidlam_3$ "(equal ranking) spouse" Akk. hā'iru; hīrtu

خير (لسان العرب) وفلان خَيْرِيَّ من الناس أي صَفِيِّي.

الخَيْرُ (القاموس المحيط) وخارَ اللهُ لكَ في الأمرِ: جَعَلَ لكَ فيه الخَيْرَ. وهو أخْيَرُ منك، كخَيْرٍ، وإذا أرَدْتَ التَّفْضِيلَ، قلتَ: فلانٌ خَيْرَةُ الناس، بالهاء، وفلانةُ خَيْرُهُمْ، بتَرْكِها، أو فلانةُ الخَيْرَةُ من المرأتينِ، وهي الخَيْرَةُ والخِيرَةُ والخِيرَى والخُورَى. ورجلٌ خِيرَى وخُورَى وخِيرَى، كحِيْرَى وطوبَى وضِيزَى: كثيرُ الخَيْرِ.

§ 136.—XXII, 57-72

AALD: abātu (v.) na'butu (See abtāti, abtu; munnabtu) يخرب، يدمر، يقضي؛ يهرب، يفر

AALD: nepû (v.) napû See napītu, niputû (غالبا النساء، او الحيوانات) يسبب التعاسة لشخص ما

AALD: neptû (v.) naptû

AALD: neptû (v.) See petû v. الكسر، الصدع، الفتحة

ePSD: zêru

gu bar [DISLIKE] wr. gu_2 bar "to dislike" Akk. zêru

gu du [NEGLECT] wr. gu_2 du_3 "to neglect" Akk. zêru

hulu gig [HATE] wr. hul gig "to hate" Akk. zêru

AALD: zērāti (s. pl. only) (zērūtu) (see zerû) العداوة، البغضاء

AALD: zirītu (v.) (şirītu) OB Elam معنى غير مؤكد

AALD: zerû (v.) (ze'āru) يكره، يبغض، يتجنب، يكون مكروها

بتت (لسان العرب) البَتُّ: القطعُ المُستأْصل. يقال: بَتَتُّ الحبلَ فانْبَتَّ. ابن سيده: بَتَّ الشيءَ يَبُتُّه، ويبِتُّه بَتّاً، وأَبَتَّه: قطَعه قطعاً مُستأْصلاً؛ وأَبَتَّ يمينه: أَمْضاها. وبَتَّتْ هي: وجبتْ، تَبِتُّ بُتوتاً، وهي يمين باتَّةٌ. وحلَفَ على ذلك يميناً بَتّاً، وبَتَّةً، وبَتاتاً: وكلُّ ذلك من القَطْع؛ ويقال: أَعْطَيْتُه هذه القطيعة بَتّاً بَتْلاً. والبَتَّةُ اشْتقاقُها من القطْع، غير أَنه يُستعمل في كل أَمْرٍ يمضي لا رَجْعةَ فيه، ولا الْتِواءَ. وأَبَتَّ الرجلُ بعيره من شدَّة السَّير، ولا تُبِتَّه حتى يَمْطوه السَّيرُ؛ والمَطْوُ: الجِدُّ في السَّير. والانْبتاتُ: الانقطاعُ. ورجل مُنْبَتٌّ أَي مُنْقطِعٌ به. وأَبَتَّ بعيرَه: قطعه بالسير. والمُنْبَتُّ في حديث الذي أَتْعب دابَّته حتى عطِب ظَهْرُه، فبَقِي مُنْقطعاً به؛ ويقال للرجل إذا انْقطع في سفره، وعطِبتْ راحلتُه: صار مُنْبَتّاً؛ ومنه قول مُطرِّف: إنَّ المُنْبَتَّ لا أَرضاً قطع، ولا ظهْراً أَبقى. غيره: يقال للرجل إذا انْقَطع به في سفره، وعطِبتْ راحلتُه: قد انْبَتَّ من البتِّ القطْع، وهو مُطاوِعُ بَتَّ؛ يقال: بتَّه وأَبتَّه، يريد أَنه بقِي في طريقه عاجزاً عن مَقْصِده، ولم يقْضِ وطَره، وقد أَعْطب ظَهْره. الكسائي: انْبَتَّ الرجلُ انْبتاتاً إذا انْقَطع ماءُ ظَهْره؛ وأَنشد: لقد وجَدْتُ رَثْيةً من الكِبَرْ، عند القيام، وانْبتاتاً في السَّحَرْ وبتَّ عليه الشهادةَ، وأَبَتَّها: قطع عليه بها، وأَلزمه إياها. وقال الليث: يقال انقطع فلانٌ عن فلان، فانْبتَّ حبْلُه عنه أَي انقطع وِصالُه وانْقبض؛

نفي (لسان العرب) نَفَى الشيءُ يَنْفِي نفْياً: تنحَّى، ونفَيْتُه أنا نفْياً؛ ونفى الرجلُ عن الأَرض ونفَيْتُه عنها: طردته فانْتَفى؛ ونفَوْته: لغة في نفَيْته. وانْتفى منه: تبرأَ. ونفَى الشيءَ نفْياً: جَحده. ونفى ابنَه: جحده، وهو نَفِيٌّ منه، فعِيل بمعنى مفعول. ونُفايةُ الشيءِ: بقيته وأَردؤه، وكذلك نُفاوته ونفاته ونفايَتُه ونِفوته ونِفْيته ونفِيُه، وخص ابن الأعرابي به رديء الطعام. قال ابن سيده: وذكرنا النُّفْوة والنُّفاوة ههنا لأنها معاقبة، إذ ليس في الكلام ن ف و وضعاً. ابو زيد: النِّفْية والنِّفْوة وهما الاسم لنفيِ الشيء إذا نفَيْته. الجوهري: والنِّفوة، بالكسر، والنِّفْية أيضاً كل ما نفَيْت.

نبا (الصَحَاح في اللغة) نَبا الشيء عنّي ينْبو، أي تجافى وتباعد. وأنْبَيْتُه أنا، أي دفعته عن نفسي.

نبا (لسان العرب) وأنْبَيْتُه أنا أي دفعته عن نفسي. والنَّبوة: الجَفْوةُ.

جفو (مقاييس اللغة) الجيم والفاء والحرف المعتل يدلُّ على أصلٍ واحد: نبوَ الشيء عن الشيء. من ذلك جفوْتُ الرَجُلَ أجْفُوه، وهو ظاهر الجِفْوة أي الجَفَاء. وجَفَا السَّرْجُ عن ظهر الفرَس وأجفيته أنا. وكذلك كلُّ شيءٍ إذا لم يلْزم [شيئاً] يقال جفا عنه يَجفُو.

زعر (مقاييس اللغة) الزاء والعينِ والراء أُصَيلٌ يدلُّ على سُوء خُلُق وقلّةِ خير. فالزَّعارة: شراسَة الخُلُق.

زر (مقاييس اللغة) الزاء والراء أُصَيلٌ يدلُّ على شِدّة.

زري (لسان العرب) وازْدريْته أي حقَّرته. وفي الحديث: فهو أجْدَرُ أن لا تُزْدرَى نِعمةَ الله عليْكم؛ الازْدراء: الاحْتِقارُ والانْتقاصُ والعيْبُ، وهو افْتِعالٌ من زريْت عليه زِرايةً إذا عِبْتَه، قال: وأصل ازْدريْتُ ازْترَيْتُ، وهو افْتعلْتُ منه، فقُلِبت التاء دالاً لأجل الزاي، وأزْرَى بِعلْمِي وزرَى؛ قال ابن سيده: حكاه اللحياني ولم يفسره، قال: وعندي أنه قصَّرَ به.

زري (مقاييس اللغة) الزاء والراء والحرف المعتل يدلُّ على احتقارِ الشيء والتّهاون به. يقال زَريْت عليه، إذا عِبْتَ عليه. وأزْرَى به، بالألف، إزْراءً: قصَّرَ به وحقَّره وهوَّنه.

صري (لسان العرب) وقيل: صِرْتُ أصير كما قالوا عَثيت أعْثي وعِثْت أعيثُ بالعين، من قولك عِثْتُ في الأرض أي أفسدْت.

§ 137.—XXII, 73-XXIII, 13

AALD: šugītu (s.) See šugû طبقة من النساء

AALD: šugû (s.) See šugītu رجل كبير السن

ePSD: aplu

eduru [HEIR] wr. eduru "heir" Akk. aplu

esaĝ [HEIR] wr. a-sag; esaĝ; asag "heir" Akk. aplu

hibiz [HEIR] wr. hibiz$_2$ "heir" Akk. aplu

ibila [HEIR] wr. ibila; i$_3$-bi$_2$-la; ibila$_2$; i$_3$-bi-lu "heir" Akk. aplu

AALD: aplu See abru

ePSD: ş̄ītu

zig [RISE] wr. zig$_3$ "to issue; to levy, raise, muster; to swell; to expend; to rise" Akk. dekû; gapāšu; tebû; şītu

ziga [EXPENDITURE] wr. zi-ga "expenditure" Akk. şītu

ePSD: ezēbu

pag [LEAVE] wr. pag "to leave behind" Akk. ezēbu

taka [ABANDON] wr. tak$_4$ "to set aside, leave behind; to save, keep back, hold back" Akk. ezēbu; uhhuru; šêtu

ePSD: šarāku

a ru [DEDICATE] wr. a ru "to dedicate" Akk. šarāku

sag rig [BESTOW] wr. sag rig$_7$ "to bestow" Akk. šarāku

ePSD: šuršu

arina [ROOT] wr. e-ri$_2$-na; i$_3$-ri$_2$-na; erina$_8$; ^{ĝeš}arina; a-i$_3$-ri$_2$-na; ^{ĝeš}arina$_x$(|UR$_2$×A|)^{na}; a-ri$_2$-na; a-ri$_8$-na; e-ri$_8$-na; i-ri$_8$-na; ^{ĝeš}arina$_x$(|I.LU$_2$@s.NA|); ^{ĝeš}arina$_x$(|LU$_2$@s.NA|) "a root" Akk. šuršu

ePSD: šuršudu

ki us [SET ON THE GROUND] wr. ki us$_2$ "to set on the ground" Akk. šuršudu

ePSD: šerku

gir [GIFT] wr. ^{gi}gir "dowry; gift" Akk. šerku

šergu [STRING] wr. še-er-gu; šer$_7$-gu; ^{še}$_3$šer$_7$-gu; še$_3$-er-gu "a string of fruit" Akk. šerku

AALD: ištu (conj) (uštu, ultu, ilti) منذ، بعد، حالما، بقدر

سجا (لسان العرب) قال الله تعالى: والضُحى والليل إذا سجا؛ معناه سكن ودام؛ وامرأةٌ ساجيةٌ: فاترَة الطَرْفِ. الليث: عينٌ ساجيةٌ: فاترةُ النظر، يَعْتري الحُسْن في النساء (* قوله: يعتري الحسن في النساء؛ هكذا في الأصل). وامرأةٌ سَجْواءُ الطّرْفِ وساجيةُ الطرف: فاتِرة الطَرْفِ ساكِنته. وطرْفٌ ساج أي ساكِنٌ. وناقة سَجْواءُ: ساكنةٌ عند الحلْب؛

شجا (لسان العرب) الشَجْوُ: الهَمُّ والحُزْنُ، وقد شَجاني يَشْجُوني شجْواً إذا حزنه، وأشجاني، وقيل: شَجاني طرَبَني وهَيَّجني. وأشْجَيْتُ فلاناً عنّي: إمّا غريمٌ، وإما رجُلٌ سألك فأعطيته شيئاً أرْضَيْتَه به فذهب فقد أشْجَيْته. ويقال للغريم: شَجِي عنّي يَشْجَى أي ذهب. ومفازةٌ شَجْواءُ: صعبةُ المَسْلك مَهْمةٌ. أبو عمرو بن العلاء: جَمَشَ فتيً من العرب حَضريَّةً فتشاجَتْ عليه، فقال لها: واللهِ ما لكِ مُلأةُ الحُسْنِ ولا عَمودهُ ولا بُرْنُسهُ فما هذا الامتناعُ؟ قال: مُلأتُه بياضهُ، وعَمودهُ طُولُه، وبُرْنُسهُ شعَرهُ، تشاجَت أي تمنَّعت وتحازنت،

شوق (لسان العرب) الشَوْقُ والاشْتياقُ: نِزاعُ النفس إلى الشيء، والجمع أشْواقٌ، شاقَ إليه شَوْقاً وتَشوَّق واشتاق اشْتياقاً. والشَوْقُ حركة الهوى. والشُوق العُشّاق. وشاقني شَوْقاً وشوَّقنى: هاجني فتَشوَّقت إذا هَيَّجَ شوقك، ويقال منه: شاقني حُسْنُها وذكْرُها يَشُوقني أي هيَّج شَوْقي؛

الشّوقُ (القاموس المحيط) الشّوقُ: نزاعُ النفسِ، وحركةُ الهوى، ج: أشْواقٌ. وقد شاقني حُبُها: هاجني، كشوّقني، وبالضم: العُشّاقُ، وجمعُ الأشْوق.

عفل (لسان العرب) والعَفل شيءٌ مُدوّر يخرج بالفرج، قال: والعفل لا يكون في الأبكار ولا يُصيب المرأة إلا بعدما تلد؛

افل (لسان العرب) قال الليث: إذا استقر اللّقاح في قرار الرّحم قيل قد أفل، ثم يقال للحامل آفل.

أبل (لسان العرب) وأبَل الرجلَ: كأبَنه؛ عن ابن جني؛ اللحياني: أبَنْت الميت تأبيناً وأبّلته تأبيلاً إذا أثنيت عليه بعد وفاته.

أبن (لسان العرب) وأبَن الرجل تأبيناً وأبّله: مدحه بعد موته وبكاه؛

ضحي (مقاييس اللغة) الضاد والحاء والحرف المعتل أصلٌ صحيحٌ واحدٌ يدلُّ على بُروز الشيء. فالضَحاء: امتداد النَّهار، وذلك هو الوقت البارز المنكشف.

ضحا (لسان العرب) الضَحْوُ والضَحْوةُ والضَحِيّةُ على مثال العشيّة: ارْتفاعُ النهار. والضَحاءُ أيضاً: الغداءُ، وهو الطّعامُ الذي يُتغدّى به، سُمّي بذلك لأنه يُؤكلُ في الضَحاء، تقول: هم يتضحّوْن أي يتغدّوْن؛ وضحّيْتُ فلاناً أُضحّيه تضْحِيةً أي غدّيْتُه؛ وضحا الطريق يضْحو ضُحُوّاً: بدا وظهر وبرز. وضاحيةُ كلّ شيء: ما برزَ منه. وضحا الشّيءُ وأضحيْته أنا أي أظهرْته. وضحّى عن الأمر: بيّنه وأظهره؛ قال الأزهري: العربُ قد تضع التّضحِية موضِع الرِّفْق والتّأني في الأمر، ثم وضعُوا التّضحية موضِع الرِّفق لرفقهمْ بحمولتِهم ومالِهم في ضحائها وما لها من الرِّفق تضْحيتها وبُلوغها مثْواها وقد شبعتْ؛

ضحح (لسان العرب) الضِحّ: الشمس، وقيل: هو ضوؤها، وقيل: هو ضوؤها إذا استمكن من الأرض، وقيل: هو قرْنُها يصيبك، وقيل: كلُّ ما أصابته الشمس ضِحٌّ؛ وضحْضح الأمرُ إذا تبين؛ قال الأصمعي: هو مثْلُ الضحْضاح ينْتشر على وجه الأرض. وروى الأزهري عن أبي الهيثم أنه قال: الضِحُّ كان في الأصل الوضَحُ، وهو نور النهار وضوْءُ الشمس، فحذفت الواو وزيدت حاءٌ مع الحاء الأصلية فقيل: الضِحُّ؛ وجاء فلان بالضِحّ والريح إذا جاء بالمال الكثير؛ وإنما الضِيحُ عند أهل اللغة لغة الضِحّ الذي هو الضوء وسيذكر؛ والضِحُّ: ما برز من الأرض للشمس. والضِحُّ: البراز الظاهرُ من الأرض، ولا جمع لكل شيء من ذلك.

العضْبُ (القاموس المحيط) العضْبُ: القطْعُ، والشّتْمُ، والتّناوُلُ، والضّرْبُ، والطّعْنُ، والرُّجوعُ، والإزْمانُ، وجعْلُ النّاقةِ والشّاةِ عضْباء، والأعْضبُ: منْ لا ناصرَ له.

عضب (لسان العرب) العضْبُ: القطع. عضبه يعْضبه عضباً. قطعه. الداخل؛ والأعضبُ من الرجال: الذي ليس له أخٌ، ولا أحدٌ؛ وقيل: الأعْضبُ الذي مات أخوه؛ وقيل: الأعْضبُ من الرجال: الذي لا ناصرَ له. والمعضوبُ: الضعيفُ؛ تقول منه: عضبه؛

الحصْبةُ (القاموس المحيط) الحصْبةُ، ويُحرّكُ، وكفرحةٍ: بثْرٌ يخْرُجُ بالجسدِ، وتحصّب الحمامُ: خرج إلى الصّحْراء لِطلبِ الحبّ. و~ عن صاحبه: تولّى، كأحْصب.

حصب (مقاييس اللغة) فأمّا قولُهم حصّب القوم عن صاحبهم *يحصّبون، فذلك تولّيهمْ عنه مسرعين كالحاصب، وهي الريح الشديدة.

حصب (لسان العرب) وحصَب في الأرض: ذهب فيها.

الحضْبُ (القاموس المحيط) والحضَبُ، مُحرّكةً: الحصبُ، وقد يُسكّنْ.

حضب (لسان العرب) والحضبُ الحطبُ في لغة اليمن؛ وقيل: هو كلُّ ما أُلقى في النار مِن حطبٍ وغيره، يُهيّجها به. والحضبُ لغة في الحصب، ومنه قرأ ابن عباس: حضبُ جهنم، منقوطة. قال الفرّاءُ: يريد الحصَب.

عزب (مقاييس اللغة) العين والزاء والباء أصلٌ صحيحٌ يدلُّ على تباعدٍ وتنحٍّ. يقال: عزب يعزُبُ عُزوباً. والعزب الذي لا أهل لـه.

عزب (الصّحاح في اللغة) العُزّابُ: الذين لا أزواج لهم من الرجال والنساء. قال الكسائي: العزب: الذي لا أهل له، والعزَبة: التي لا زوج لها. وعزب طُهر المرأة، إذا غاب عنها زوجُها.

سرس (العباب الزاخر) السّرِسُ والسّرِيْس: الذي لا يأتي النساء، قال ذلك ابن الأعرابي، وقال أبو عمرو: السّرِيْس: الكيّس الحافظ لما في يديْه. وسرس إذا عُنّن عن امرأته.

سرس (الصّحاح في اللغة) السريسُ: الذي لا يأتي النساء. وقال أبو عبيدة: هو العنّينُ. وفحلٌ سرِيسٌ، بيِّن السّرس، إذا كان لا يُلقح.

سرس (العباب الزاخر) السّرِسُ والسّرِيْس: الذي لا يأتي النساء، قال ذلك ابن الأعرابي، وقال الأصمعي: السّرِيْسُ: الذي لا يولد لهُ، ويروى: "الشّرِيْسُ" بالإعجام؛ وهو الظالم المنيع السيِّء الخُلُق.

السّرِسُ (القاموس المحيط) السّرِسُ، ككتِفٍ وأميرٍ: العِنّينُ، أو الذي لا يأتي النّساء، أو من لا يولدُ له، والفحْلُ لا يُلْقِحُ، والضعيفُ،

سرس (لسان العرب) السّريس: الكيّسُ الحافظ لما في يده، وما أسْرسه، وقد سرِس إذا ساء خُلُقه وسرِس إذا عقل وحزم بعد جهْل. وقد سرِس إذا عُنّ، وقيل: السّريسُ هو الذي لا يولد له، والجمع سُرساءُ، وفي لغة طيء: السّريس الضعيف. وفحلٌ سرِسٌ وسرِيسٌ بيّنُ السّرس إذا كان لا يُلقحُ.

شرث (لسان العرب) والشّرْثةُ: النّعْلُ الخلق. ابن الأعرابي: الشّرْثُ الخلقُ من كل شيء.

خلق (لسان العرب) وخلق الشيءُ خُلوقاً وخُلوقة وخلُق خلاقةً وخلِق وأخْلق إخْلاقاً واخْلولق: بلي؛ وشيءٌ خلقٌ: بالٍ، الذكر والأنثى فيه سواء لأنه في الأصل مصدر الأخْلق وهو الأمْلس. يقال: ثوب خلق وملْحفة خلق ودار خلقٌ. وثوب خلقٌ: بالٍ؛ والخلْق في كلام العرب: ابتداع الشيء على مثال لم يُسبق إليه. ال أبو بكر بن الأنباري: الخلق في كلام العرب على وجهين: أحدهما الإنشاء على مثال أبدعه، والآخر التقدير؛ وأخلقه خلقاً: أعطاه إياها. وأخلق فلان فلاناً: أعطاه ثوباً خلقاً. وأخلقته ثوباً إذا كسوْته ثوباً خلقاً؛ وهو خليقٌ له أي شبيه. وما أخْلقه أي ما أشبهه.

شور (مقاييس اللغة) الشين والواو والراء أصلان مطّردان، الأوّل منهما إبداء شيء وإظْهارُهُ وعرْضه، والآخر أخْذ شيء. والباب الآخر: قولهم: شُرْت العسل أشُوره.

شور (لسان العرب) شار العسلَ يشُوره شوْراً وشِياراً وشِيارةً ومشاراً ومشارةً: استخرجه من الوقْبة واحتناه؛ أبو عبيد: شُرْت العسل واشْترْته اجْتنيْته وأخذته من موضعه؛

شنق (القاموس المحيط) وشانقه مُشانقةً وشِناقاً: خلط مالهُ بمالِه. والشِّناقُ: أخْذُ شيءٍ من الشّنق، ومنه الحديثُ: "لا شِناق".

شنق (الصّحاح في اللغة) الشّنْقُ في الصدقة: ما بين الفريضتين. وفي الحديث: "لا شِناقَ" أي لا يؤخذ من الشّنق حتّى يتم. والشّنقُ أيضاً: ما دون الديةِ، وذلك أن يسوقَ ذو الحمالةِ الدية كاملة، فإذا كانت معها دياتُ جراحاتٍ فتلك هي الأشْناقُ. كأنها متعلّقة بالدية العُظمى.

شنق (لسان العرب) وقال ابن الأعرابي والأصمعي والأثرم: كان السيد إذا أعطى الدية زاد عليها خمساً من الإبل ليبين بذلك فضله وكرمه، فالشَّنَقُ من الدية بمنزلة الشَّنَق في الفريضة إذا كان فيها لغواً، كما أنه في الدية لغو ليس بواجب إنما تكرُّمٌ من المعطي. والشِّناقُ: أن يكون على الرجل والرجلين أو الثلاثةِ أشْناقٌ إذا تفرّقت أموالهم، فيقول بعضهم لبعض: شانِقْني أي اخْلِطْ مالي ومالَك، فإنه إن تفرّق وجب علينا شَنَقانِ، فإن اختلط خفَّ علينا؛ فالشِّناقُ: المشاركة في الشَّنَق والشَّنَقين.

§ 138.—XXIII, 14-24

ePSD: terhātu

niĝmussa [GIFT] wr. nig_2-mi_2-us_2-sa_2; $ni\hat{g}_2$-mussa; $ni\hat{g}_2$-mi_2-us_2-sa "a betrothal gift" Akk. terhātu

AALD: terhātu (tirhatu, tarhatu) (s.f.) ثروة العروس، الجهاز، هدية العرس

ترح (لسان العرب) التَّرَحُ: نقيض الفرح. والتَّرِحُ القليل الخير؛ والتَّرَحُ الفقرُ؛

طرح (مقاييس اللغة) الطاء والراء والحاء أصلٌ صحيحٌ يدلُّ على نبْذ الشَّيء وإلقائه. يقال طرحَ الشَّيءَ يطرحُه طرحا.

طرح (لسان العرب) ابن سيده: طَرَح بالشيء وطَرَحه يَطْرَحُه طَرْحاً واطَّرَحه وطرَّحه: رمى به؛ وطَرَح عليه مسألةً: ألقاها، وهو مثل ما تقدم؛ قال ابن سيده: وأراه مولَّداً. والأُطْرُوحةُ: المسألة تطْرَحُها.

ضرح (لسان العرب) الضَّرْحُ: التنحيةُ. وقد ضَرَحه أي نحاه ودفعه، فهو مُضْطَرِحٌ أي رمى به في ناحية؛ قال الشاعر: فلما أن أتين على أُضاخ، ضَرَحْنَ حَصاه أشْتاتاً عِزِينا وضَرَحَ عنه شهادة القوم يَضْرَحُها ضَرْحاً: جَرَّحها وألقاها عنه لئلا يشهدوا عليه بباطل. والضَّرْحُ أن يؤخذ شيء فيرمى به في ناحية؛ قال الهذلي: تعلو السيوفُ بأيديهم جماجمَهُمْ، كما يُفَلِّقُ مَرْوَ الأَمْعَزِ الضَّرَحُ أراد الضَّرْحَ، فحرك للضرورة. واضْطَرَحُوا فلاناً: رَمَوْه في ناحية، والعامة تقول: اطَّرَحُوه، يظنونه من الطَّرْح، وإنما هو من الضَّرْح. قال الأزهري: وجائز أن يكون اطَّرَحُوه افتعالاً من الطَّرْح، قلبت التاء طاء ثم أُدغمت الضاد فيها فقيل اطَّرَح.

§ 141.—XXIII, 33-59

AALD: wāşû See āşû

AALD: āşû (adj.) عاص، خارج، متمرد، يذهب خارج

ePSD: aşû

e [LEAVE] wr. e_3; i; e "to leave, to go out; to thread, hang on a string; to remove, take away; to bring out; to enter; to bring in; to raise, rear (a child); to sow; to rave; to winnow; to measure (grain) roughly (with a stick); to rent" Akk. aşû; erēbu; mahû; rubbû; zarû; šakāku

AALD: zapāhu See sapāhu

ePSD: sapāhu

bir [SCATTER] wr. bir; bi-bi-re; bir_9 "to scatter, disperse" Akk. sapāhu

sag [SCATTER] wr. sag_2; sag_3; sag_7 "to throw (down); to scatter, disperse; to kill, to beat" Akk. dâku; nasāku; nêru; sapāhu

tar [CUT] wr. tar; tar^{ar} "to cut down; to untie, loosen; to cut; to scatter, disperse; to decide" Akk. harāşu; parāsu; paţāru; sapāhu

AALD: šamādu (v.) تضع (حلية، زينة، ترصيع)

وصم (لسان العرب) الوَصْمُ: الصَّدْعُ في العود من غير بينونة. يقال: بهذه القناة وَصْمٌ. وَصَمه وَصْماً: صدَعه.

هَصَا (القاموس المحيط) هَصَا هَصْواً: أسَنَّ، وكبِرَ. والأَهْصاءُ: الأشداءُ. وهاصاهُ: كسَرَ صُلْبَهُ.

وهص (لسان العرب) الوَهْصُ: كسْرُ الشيء الرِّخْو؛ وقد وَهَصه وَهْصاً فهو مَوْهوصٌ ووهيص: دقَّه وكسره، وقال ثعلب: فدغه، وهو كسْرُ الرطب، وقد اتَّهصَ هو؛ عنه أيضاً. ووَهَصه الدَّيْنُ: دقَّ عنقه. ووَهَصه: ضرب به الأرض. قال أبو عبيد: وهَصَه يعني كسره ودقه. يقال: وهَصْت الشيءَ وَهْصاً ووقَصْته وَقْصاً بمعنى واحد. وكذلك إذا وضع قدمه على شيء فشدخه تقول وَهَصه. ابن شميل: الوَهْصُ والوَهْسُ والوَهْزُ واحدٌ، وهو شدة الغمْز، وقيل: الوَهْصُ الغمْزُ؛

غمز (مقاييس اللغة) الغين والميم والزاء أصلٌ صحيح، وهو كالنَّخْس في الشيء بشيء، ثم يُستعار. من ذلك: غمَزْتُ الشَّيءَ بيدي غمزاً. ثم يقال: غمزَ، إذا عاب وذكر بغير الجميل.

هزم (لسان العرب) الهَزْمُ: غَمْزك الشيء تَهْزِمُه بيدك فينْهزِمُ في جوفه كما تَغْمِزُ القَناةَ فتنْهزم، وكذلك القِربةُ تَنْهزم في جوفها، وهَزَمَ الشيء يَهْزِمُه هَزْماً فانْهزَمَ: غمزه بيده فصارت فيه وَقْرةٌ كما يُفْعل بالقِثّاء ونحوه، وكلُّ موضع مُنْهزم منه هَزْمةً، والجمع هَزْمٌ وهُزومٌ. والهَزيمُ والمُتَهزِّمُ: الرعدُ الذي له صوتٌ شبيهٌ بالتكسُّر. وفرسٌ هزيمٌ: يتشقق بالجَرْي: والهَزيمُ: صوتُ جَرْي الفرس. والهَزيمةُ في القتال: الكسْرُ والفلُّ، هَزَمه يَهْزِمُه هزْماً فانْهزَمَ، وهُزِمَ القومُ في الحرب، والاسم الهَزيمة والهِزِّيمى، وهَزَمْتُ الجيشَ هزْماً وهزيمةً فانْهزَمُوا؛ والتَّهَزُّمُ: التكسُّرُ.

وهس (مقاييس اللغة) الواو والهاء والسين: كلمتان: إحداهما الشِّدة في الأمور، والثانية من السِّرار. فالأولى الوَهْس: شدَّة السَّير. والوَهْس شِدَّة الأكْل. والوَهْس شِدَّة الوَطْء. وقال حميد: فهذا من التَّوهُّس، وهو التشدُّدُ والتَّطاوُل على العشيرة.

وهز (الصِّحاح في اللغة) وَهَزْتُ فلاناً، إذا ضربته بثِقل يدك.

وهز (مقاييس اللغة) الواو والهاء والزاء. يقولون: الوَهْز: المُلَزَّز الخَلْق. ووَهَزْتُ دفعْت.

وهز (لسان العرب) الكسائي: وَهَزْتُه ولَهَزْتُه ونَهَزْتُه، بن سيده: وَهَزَه وَهْزاً دفعه وضربه.

وزي (لسان العرب) وزى الشيءُ يزي: اجتمع وتقبّض. والوزى: القَصيرُ من الرجال الشديد المُلزَزُ الخَلْق المقتدر؛ يقال: ما لي أَراكَ مُستوزياً أي مُنتصباً؛ وعيرٌ مُستوز: نافرٌ؛ ويقال: أَوزَيْته أشْخصتُه ونصبْتُه؛ يقال: وزى فلاناً الأمرُ أي غاظه، ووزاه الحسدُ؛ قال أبو البَخْتَريّ: فوازَيْنا العدُوّ وصافَفْناهُم؛ المُوازاةُ: المُقابلة والمُواجهةُ، قال: والأصل فيه الهمزة، يقال آزيْته إذا حاذيْته؛ ووزأ اللحم وزْءاً: أَيْبسه، ذكره في الهمزة، والله أعلم.

وزا (القاموس المحيط) وَزا، كوَعى: اجْتمع. وأوزى ظهرَهُ: أسندَهُ، والوزى، كفَتى: الحمارُ المصكُّ الشديدُ، والرَّجلُ القصيرُ المُلزَزُ الخَلْق. والمُستَوزي: المُنْتَصِبُ، والمُستَبِدُّ برأيه.

أزا (لسان العرب) الأزْوُ: الضيِّق؛ عن كراع. وأزَيْتُ إليه أزْيا وأُزِيّاً: انضممت. وآزاني هو: ضمَّني؛ قال رؤبة: تَغْرِفُ من ذي غيْثٍ وتُوزي وأزى يأْزي أَزْياً وأُزِيّاً: انقبض واجتمع. والإزاءُ: المُحاذاةُ والمُقابلة؛ قال: ويقال فيه وازَنا. وفي حديث صلاة الخوف: فوازَيْنا العدوّ أي قابلناهم، وأنكر الجوهري أن يقال وازَيْنا.

وصي (مقاييس اللغة) الواو والصاد والحرف المعتلّ: أصلٌ يدلّ على وَصلِ شيءٍ بشيء. ووَصَيْتُ الشَّيءَ: وصَلْتُه. ويقال: وطِئْنا أرضاً واصية، أي إنّ نبتَها متَّصلٌ قد امتلأتْ منه. ابن الأعرابي: الوَصيُّ النبات المُلْتفُّ، وأرض واصيةٌ: متصلة النبات إذا اتّصل نبْتها، وربما قالوا تواصى النبتُ إذا اتصل، وهو نبت واصٍ؛ ووصى الرجلَ وَصْياً: وصلَه. ووَصَى الشيءَ بغيره وَصْياً: وصلَه. أبو عبيد: وصَيْتُ الشيءَ ووصَلْته سواء؛

وصَى (القاموس المحيط) وَصَى، كوَعى: خسَّ بعد رِفْعة، واتّزنَ بعد خِفَّة، واتّصل، ووَصَل، و~ الأرضُ وَصْياً ووُصِيّاً ووَصاءً ووَصاءةً: اتّصلَ نباتُها.

وأص (لسان العرب) وأَصَتْ به الأرضَ ووأَص به الأرضَ وأْصاً: ضربها، ومَحص به الأرض مثله.

وأص (مقاييس اللغة) الواو والهمزة والصاد. يقولون: ما أدري أي الوئيصةِ هو، أيْ أيُّ الناس هو. والوئيصة: الجماعة.

أصا (القاموس المحيط) أصا النَّبتُ يأْصُو: اتَّصل، وكَثُر.

أصا (لسان العرب) وقالوا: ما له حَصاةٌ ولا أَصاةٌ أي رأْيٌ يرجع إليه. ابن الأعرابي: أَصى الرجلُ إذا عقَل بعد رُعُونة.

عصو/ي (مقاييس اللغة) العين والصاد والحرف المعتل أصلان صحيحان، إلاّ أنهما متباينان يدلُّ أحدهما على التجمُّع، ويدلُّ الآخر على الفُرقة.

عصص (لسان العرب) العَصُّ: هو الأصلُ الكريم وكذلك الأُصُّ. وعصَّ يعَصُّ عصّاً وعَصَصاً: صلُب واشْتدّ.

عصا (لسان العرب) ويقال: عصا إذا صلُب؛ واعْتصت النَّواةُ أي اشْتَدَّتْ.

العَصُّ (القاموس المحيط) العَصُّ: الأصْلُ. وعصَّ، كملَّ: صلُبَ، واشْتَدَّ.

زكل (مقاييس اللغة) الزاء والكاف واللام ليس بأصل، وقد جاءت فيه كلمة: الزَّونَكل من الرجال: القصير.

السَّكْلُ (القاموس المحيط) ج: أَسْكالٌ وسِكلةٌ، كقِرَدةٍ.

دكل (لسان العرب) وتدكَّل عليه: تدلَّل وانبسط. أبو زيد: تدكَّلت عليه تدكُّلاً أي تدلَّلت؛

شكل (لسان العرب) الشَّكْلُ، بالفتح: الشِّبه والمِثْل، والجمع أشكالٌ وشُكُول؛ وشَكْلُ الشيء: صورتُه المحسوسة والمُتوَهَّمة، والجمع كالجمع. وأشْكل الأمْرُ: الْتبس. وأمورٌ أشْكالٌ: ملتبسة، وبيْنهم أشْكلة أي لبْسٌ. والشَّكْل غُنْجُ المرأة وغزَلُها وحُسْن دلِّها؛ شَكِلتْ شكَلاً، فهي شَكِلةٌ؛ يقال: إنها شَكِلة مُشْكِلةٌ حسنة الشَّكْل؛ وفي تفسير المرأة العَرِبة أنها الشَّكِلة، بفتح الشين وكسر الكاف، وهي ذاتُ الدَّلّ. والشِّكْل، بالكسر: الدَّلُّ، ويجوز هذا في هذا وهذا في هذا. والشَّكْلُ للمرأة: ما تتحسَّن به من الغُنْج. يقال: امرأة ذات شِكْل.

دلل (لسان العرب) وهو الدَّلُّ الذي هو الدَّلال والشَّكْل والشِّكْل.

تكل (القاموس المحيط) تكِلَ عليه، كفرِح: لُغةٌ في اتَّكل، ذكرْتُه على اللَّفظ.

زقل (مقاييس اللغة) الزاء والقاف واللام ليس بشيء. على أنه حكِيَ عن بعض العرب: زَوْقل فلانٌ عمامتَه، إذا أرخى طرفَيها من ناحيتَيْ رأسه.

الزُّقْلُ (القاموس المحيط) الزُّقْلُ، بالضم، والزَّواقيلُ: اللُّصوصُ. وكسفينةٍ: السكّةُ الضَيِّقةُ. وزوْقل عِمامتَه: سَدل طرَفَيْها. وزواقيلُ العِمامةِ: أن تُخْرِجَ الشُّعورُ من تحتها.

سفح (مقاييس اللغة) السين والفاء والحاء أصلٌ واحدٌ يدلُّ على إراقة شيء.

سفح (الصَّحاح في اللغة) وسَفَحْتُ الماءَ: هرقْتُه. وسَفَحْتُ دمَه: سفكته.

سفح (لسان العرب) والتَّسافُحُ والسِّفاح والمُسافحة: الزنا والفجور؛ والمُسافِحة: الفاجرة؛ وقال تعالى: مُحْصَناتٍ غيرَ مُسافِحات؛ وقال أبو إسحق: المُسافِحة التي لا تمتنع عن الزنا؛ قال: وسمي الزنا سِفاحاً لأنه كان عن غير عقد، كأنه بمنزلة الماء المَسْفوح الذي لا يحبسه شيء؛ وقال غيره: سمي الزنا سفاحاً لأنه ليس ثَمّ حرمة نكاح ولا عقد تزويج. وكل واحد منهما سفح مَنْيته أي دفقها بلا حرمة أباحت دفْقها؛

سمد (الصَّحاح في اللغة) سَمَدَ سُموداً: رفع رأسه تكبُّراً. والسُّمودُ: اللهْوُ. والسامِدُ: اللاهي والمغنِّي.

سمد (لسان العرب) سَمَدَ يَسْمُد سُموداً: علا. ولا أفعل ذلك أبداً سمداً سرمداً.والسُّمود: اللهو. وسَمَد سُمُوداً: لها. وسمَّده ألهاه. ابن الأعرابي: السامِدُ اللاهي، والسامِدُ الغافِلُ، والسامد الساهي، والسامد المُتكبِّر، والسامد القائم، والسامد المُتحير بطراً وأشَراً، والسامد الغبيُّ. وسمَد سُموداً: رفع رأسه تكبُّراً. وكلُّ رافعٍ رأسَه، فهو سامد.

§ 142.—XXIII, 60-XXIV, 5

AALD: hādītu See hādû
AALD: hādû (s.) الشمَات (الذي يشمت بمصائب الآخرين)
AALD: hadû (v.) يكون سعيد، يكون حسن النيَة
AALD: hidātu (s.) hidi’ātu الفرح، الابتهاج
ePSD: hadû
lib [RICH] "(to be) rich, well-off; high quality; (to be) happy" Akk. hadû; hidiātu; râšu; rāšû; rīšātu
šag hul [HAPPY] wr. $šag_4$ hul_2 "to be happy" Akk. hadû

حد (مقاييس اللغة) الحاء والدال أصلان: الأوَل المنع، والثاني طَرف الشيء.فالحدَ الحاجز بيْن الشَيئين. وسمَي الحديدُ حديداً لامتناعه وصلابته وشدّته.

حد (مقاييس اللغة) ويقال حدَت المرأة على بعْلها وأحدَتْ، وذلك إذا منعتْ نفْسها الزّينة والخِضاب. والمحادَة: المخالَفة، فكأنه الممانعةُ. ويجوز أن يكون من الأصل الآخر. ويقال: مالي عن هذا الأمر حَدَدٌ ومُحْتَدٌ، أي مَعْدل ومُمتنع. ويقال حَدداً، بمعنى مَعاذ الله. وأصله من المَنْع. وحَدُّ العاصي سُمّي حَدّاً لأنّه يمنعه عن المعاوَدة. قال الدّريديَ: "يقال هذا أمر حَدَدٌ، أي منيع". وأمّا الأصل الآخر فقولهم: حدُّ السَّيف وهو حَرْفه، وحدُّ السّكّين. وحدُّ الشّراب: صلابته. قال الأعشى: وحَدُّ الرّجل: بأسُه. وهو تشبيه. ومن المحمول الحِدَة التي تعتري الإنسان من النّزق. تقول: حَددت على الرّجل أحِدُّ حِدَّةً.

حدأ (العباب الزاخر) الحِجأَةُ: الفأسُ ذات الرأسين، وجمْعُها حِداً مثل قصبةٍ وقصب، عن الأصمعي، قال: وحدِئْتُ عليه وإليه: إذا حَدِبْتَ عليه ونصرْته ومنَعْته من الظُّلْم. أبو عُبَيْد :حدأتُ الشَيء حَدْءً: صرفْتُه.

الحدُّ (القاموس المحيط) الحَدُّ: الحاجزُ بينَ شيْئيْن، ومُنْتَهى الشيءِ، و~ من كلّ شيءٍ: حِدّتُهُ، وحدّ عليه يحِدُّ حَدداً، وحَدَدَ، واحْتَدَ، واسْتَحدَ: غضِبَ. وحادّهُ: غاضَبهُ، وعاداهُ، وخالَفهُ. وحدادتُك: امرأتُك. والحادُ والمُحِدُّ: تاركةُ الزّينَةِ للعِدّة، حَدّتْ تحِدُّ وتَحُدُّ حدًا وحِداداً، وأحَدّتْ. وحدادُك أن تَفعَل كذا: قُصاراك.

حدأ (لسان العرب) وقيل: الحِدأَةُ: الفأسُ العظيمة؛ وقيل: الحِدأُ: رُؤوسُ الفُؤوس، والحِدأةُ: نَصْل السهم. وحَدِئَ بالمكان حَدأً بالتحريك: إذا لزِقَ به. وحَدِئَ اليه حَدأً: لجأ. وحَدِئَ عليه وإليه حَدأً: حَدب عليه وعطف عليه ونصره ومنعه من الظُّلم. وحَدِئَ عليه: غضِب. وحدأ الشيءَ حَدْءاً: صرفه.

الحَذْيَةُ (القاموس المحيط) وحذى اللبنُ وغيرُه لِسانهُ يَحْذيه: قرصه، و~ الإهاب: خرّقهُ فأكْثَر، و~ يده: قطعها، و~ فلاناً بلِسانه: وقعَ فيه، فهو مِحْذاءٌ: يَحْذِ الناس.

مجل (مقاييس اللغة) أنّ الماجل: مستنقعُ الماء، وهذا من باب أجل، وذكر أن المجلة: الصّحيفة، هو من جَل. وجُلّ الشيء: معظمه.

جلل (الصّحاح في اللغة) وجُلّ الشيء: معظمه. والجُلَى: الأمر العظيم؛ وجمعها جُلَلٌ، مثل كُبْرى وكُبَر. وجلالُ الله: عظمته.

جلل (لسان العرب) وناقة جُلالة: ضخْمة. وبَعير جُلال: مخرج من جليل. وما له دقيقة ولا جليلة أي ما له شاة ولا ناقة. وجُلُّ كل شيء: عُظْمه. ومنه حديث أنس: أُلقي إلينا مَجالٌ؛ هي جمع مَجلة يعني صُحُفاً قيل إنها معرّبة من العبرانية، وقيل: هي عربية، وقيل: مَفْعلة من الجلال كالمذلة من الذل.

§ 144.—XXIV, 13-27

ePSD: magāru

<u>šeg</u> <u>[AGREE]</u> wr. še "to agree, be in agreement; to obey" Akk. magāru

مجر (لسان العرب) وما له مَجْرٌ أَي ما له عقْلٌ.

مجر (الصّحاح في اللغة) وسئل ابنُ لسانِ الحُمَّرة عن الضأن فقال: مالُ صِدْق، قرْيةٌ لا حمى بها إذا أفلتتْ من مَجْرَتَيْها، يعني من المَجْرِ في الدهر الشديد وهو الهُزال، ومن النشر، وهو أن تنتشر بالليل فتأتي عليها السباع. فسمّاها مَجْرَتَيْنِ، كما يقال: القَمرانِ والعُمَرانِ.

§ 146.—XXIV, 43-59

وبت (لسان العرب) وَبتَ بالمكان وَبْتاً: أقام.

وبت (القاموس المحيط) وبَتَ بالمكان، كوعَد: أقامَ.

وعد (لسان العرب) ويوم واعِدٌ: يَعِدُ بالحرّ؛

أبت (مقاييس اللغة) الهمزة والباء والتاء أصلٌ واحد، وهو الحرّ وشدّته.

§ 148.—XXIV, 65-81

ePSD: la'ību

<u>dihi</u> <u>[ILLNESS]</u> wr. dih "an illness" Akk. la'ību

ePSD: šâmu

<u>sa</u> <u>[PAY FOR]</u> wr. sa_{10} "to pay for, buy; to be paid for, sell" Akk. šâmu

AALD: šâmu (v.) (šiāmu) يخصص، يثبت، يعين، يرسم او يقرر المصير، يقرّر، يقدّر

لعب (مقاييس اللغة) وقيل: إنّ أصل الباب هو الذّهاب على غير استقامة.

لعب (لسان العرب) اللّعِبُ واللّعْبُ: ضدُّ الجِدّ، لعب يلْعبُ لعِباً ولَعْباً، ولعّب، وتلاعب، وتَلعّب مرّة بعد أُخرى؛ سَمّى اضطراب المَوْج لَعِباً، لما لم يَسِرْ بهم إلى الوجْه الذي أرادوه.

اللّوْبُ (القاموس المحيط) اللّوْبُ واللُّوبُ واللُّوُوبُ واللُّوابُ: العطَشُ، أو اسْتِدارةُ الحائمِ حوْلَ الماءِ وهو عطْشانُ لا يَصِلُ إليه. واللُّوابُ، بالضمّ: اللُّعابُ.

لاب (مقاييس اللغة) اللام والألف والباء. اللاّبة: الحرّة، والجمع* لُوب. واللُّواب: العطش؛ لاب يلوب.

لوب (مقاييس اللغة) اللام والواو والباء كلمتانِ متباينتان، ويمكن أن يُحمل إحداهما على الأخرى. فالكلمة الأولى: اللّوْب واللُّواب: العطش، والفعل لابَ يلوب، وهو لائب.

شيم (لسان العرب) والانْشِيامُ في الشيء: الدخولُ فيه. وشامَ الشيءَ في الشيء: أدخله وخَبأَه؛ وانْشام الشيءُ في الشيء وتَشَيّم فيه وتشيّمه: دخل فيه؛ وشام إذا دخَل.

سيم (لسان العرب) قوم سُيُوم آمِنُونَ. وفي حديث هجرة الحَبَشَة: قال النجاشي لمن هاجر إلى أرضه امْكُثوا فأنتم سُيُوم بأرْضي أي آمنون؛

سوم (لسان العرب) السَّوْمُ: عَرْضُ السِّلْعة على البيع. وسامه الأمرَ سَوْماً: كَلَّفه إياه، وقال الزجاج: أولاه إياه، ويقال: سُمْتُه حاجة أي كلفته إياها وجَشَّمْتُه إياها،

سمم (لسان العرب) وسَمَّتِ النَّعْمَةُ أي خصت؛ ابن الأعرابي: المَسمَّةُ الخاصَّةُ، والمَعَمَّةُ العامَّةُ. سَمَّ إذا خصَّ.

§ 151.—XXV, 26-51

AALD: lamā (prep.) (lām) قبل

لم (الصِّحاح في اللغة) لمْ: حرفُ نفي لما مضى. تقول: لم يفعل ذاك، تريد أنه لم يكن ذلك الفعل منه فيما مضى من الزمان. وهي جازمةٌ. وحروف الجزم: لَمْ، ولَمَّا، وألَمْ، وألَمَّا.

لمم (لسان العرب) وتكون لَمّا بمعنى لم الجازمة؛ قال الله عز وجل: بل لَما يَذُوقوا عذاب؛ أي لم يذوقوه، وتكون بمعنى إلاَّ في قولك: سألتك لَمّا فعلت، بمعنى إلا فعلت، وهي لغة هذيل بمعنى إلا إذا أجيب بها إن التي هي جَحْد كقوله عز وجل: إنْ كلُّ نفس لَمّا عليها حافظ، فيمن قرأ به، معناه ما كل نفس إلا عليها حافظ؛ ومثله قوله تعالى: وإن كلٌّ لَمّا جميعٌ لَدينا مُحْضَرون؛ شدّدها عاصم، والمعنى ما كلٌّ إلا جميع لدينا. وقال الفراء: لما إذا وُضِعت في معنى إلا فكأنها لَمْ ضُمَّت إليها ما، فصارا جميعاً بمعنى إن التي تكون جَحداً، فضموا إليها لا فصارا جميعاً حرفاً واحداً وخرجا من حدّ الجحد، وكذلك لَمّا؛ قال: ومثل ذلك قولهم: لولا، إنما هي لَوْ ولا جُمعتا، فخرجت لَوْ من حدّها ولا من الجحد إذ جُمعتا فصُيِّرتا حرفاً؛ قال: وكان الكسائي يقول لا أعرفُ وَجْه لَمّا بالتشديد؛ قال أبو منصور: ومما يدلُّك على أن لَمّا تكون بمعنى إلا مع إن التي تكون جحداً قولُ الله عز وجل: إن كلٌّ إلا كذَّب الرُّسُلَ؛ وهي قراءة قُرّاء الأمْصار؛ وقال الفراء: وهي في قراءة عبد الله: إن كلُّهم لَمّا كَذَّب الرسل، قال: والمعنى واحد. وقال الخليل: لَمّا تكون انتِظاراً لشيء متوقَّع، وقد تكون انقطاعة لشيء قد مضى؛

§ 152.—XXV, 52-60

AALD: apālu (v.) uppulu;يسدد، يعطي، يرد، يُجيب على سؤال يحمل شخص مسؤلية

فلا (لسان العرب) وافْتَلَيْته: اتخذته؛ وقال آخر: أفْليه بالسيف إذا استَفلاني، أجيبُه: لَبَّيْك، إذ دَعاني وفلتِ الدابةَ فَلْوها وأفْلَتْه، وفلَتْ أحسن وأكثر؛ وفليت الشِّعر إذا تدبرته واستخرجت معانيه وغريبه؛ عن ابن السكيت. وفَلَيْت الأمر إذا تأملت وجوهه ونظرت إلى عاقبته. وفَلَوْتُ القومَ وفَلَيْتهم إذا تخللتهم. وفلاه في عَقْله فلياً: رازه. أبو زيد: يقال فليْت الرجل في عقله أفليه فلياً إذا نظرت ما عَقْلُه.

افل (لسان العرب) وسَبُعَةٌ آفِل وآفِلة: حامل. قال الليث: إذا استقر اللِّقاح في قرار الرَّحم قيل قد أفَل، ثم يقال للحامل آفِل.

§ 153.—XXV, 61-66

ePSD: dâku

gaz [KILL] wr. gaz; gaz_2; kaz_8 "to kill, slaughter; to grind, grate; to beat; to thresh (grain); to execute, impose a death sentence; to break" Akk. dâku; habātu; hašālu; kaşāşu; pa'āşu; šagāšu

gi [KILL] wr. gi_4 "kill" Akk. dâku

rah [BEAT] wr. rah_2; ra-ah "to beat, kill; to break, crush; to flood; to thresh (grain with a flail)" Akk. dâku; diāšu; hepû; rahāşu; rapāsu

sag [SCATTER] wr. sag_2; sag_3; sag_7 "to throw (down); to scatter, disperse; to kill, to beat" Akk. dâku; nasāku; nêru; sapāhu

ePSD: gašīšu

gazinbu [POLE] wr. ga-zi-in-bu; gazinbu; gu_4-zi-in-bu; ga-šim-bu "a pole, post; stick, club" Akk. gazamānu; gašīšu; nappaşu; timmu

سدك (مقاييس اللغة) السين والدال والكاف كلمةٌ واحدة لا يقاس عليها. تقول: سدك به، إذا لزِمَه.

سدك (لسان العرب) سَدِك به، بالكسر، سَدْكاً وسَدَكاً، فهو سَدِكٌ ولكِيَ به لكىً: لزمه. ورجل سَدِكٌ بالرُّمح: طعّان به رفيف سريع.

الدَّكُّ (القاموس المحيط) الدَّكُّ: الدَقُّ والهَدْمُ، وما اسْتوى من الرَّمْلِ،

دَقَّهُ (القاموس المحيط) دَقَّهُ: كسرَهُ، أو ضربَهُ فهشَمه فانْدَقَّ،

دقق (لسان العرب) الدَّقُّ: مصدر قولك دققت الدّواء أدُقُّه دقّاً، وهو الرَّضُّ. والدَّقُّ: الكسر والرَّضُّ في كل وجه، وقيل: هو أن تضرب الشيء بالشيء حتى تهْشِمَه، دَقّه يدُقّه دقّاً ودقّقته فاندقّ.

جسس (لسان العرب) الجَسُّ: اللَّمْسُ باليد. وتَجَسَّسْتُ الخبر وتحَسَّسْته بمعنى واحد. وفي الحديث: لا تَجَسَّسُوا؛ التَّجَسُّس، بالجيم: التفتيش عن بواطن الأمور، وأكثر ما يقال في الشر. والجاسُوسُ: العيْنُ يَتَجَسَّسُ الأخبار ثم يأْتي بها، وقيل: الجاسُوسُ الذي يتجَسَّس الأخبار. والعرب تقول: فلان ضَيِّقُ المَجَسِّ إذا لم يكن واسع السِّرْب ولم يكن رحيب الصدر. ويقال: في مَجَسِّك ضيقٌ. وجَسَّ إذا اختبر. والمَجَسَّةُ: الموضع الذي يَجُسُّه الطبيب. وجواسُّ الإنسان: معروفة، وهي خمس: اليدان والعينان والفم والشم والسمع، والواحدة جاسَّة، ويقال بالحاء؛ قال الخليل: الجَواسُّ الحواسُّ.

جسس (العباب الزاخر) جَسَّه بيده: أي مَسَّه. والمَجَسَّة -بالفتح-: الموضع الذي يَجُسُّه الطبيب.

قسس (لسان العرب) ويقال: تقَسَّسْت أصوات الناس بالليل تقَسُّساً أي تسمّعتها. والقَسْقَسَة: السّؤال عن أمر الناس. ورجل قَسْقاسٌ: يسأل عن أمور الناس؛ والقَسْقاسُ: العصا. وقوله، صلى الله عليه وسلم، لفاطمة بنت قيس حين خطبها أبو جَهْم ومعاوية: أَمّا أبو جَهْم فأخاف عليك قَسْقاسَته؛ القَسْقاسة: العصا؛ قيل في تفسيره قولان: أحدهما أنه أراد قَسْقَسته أي تحريكه إياها لضربك فأشبع الفتحة فجاءت ألفاً، والقول الآخر انه أراد

بقسقاسته عصاه، فالعصا على القول الأول (* قوله «العصا على القول الأول إلخ» هذا إنما يناسب الرواية الآتية.) مفعول به، وعلى القول الثاني بدل. أبو زيد: يقال للعصا هي القَسْقاسة؛

§ 154.—XXV, 67-71

ePSD: lamādu
zu [KNOW] wr. zu "to know; to learn" Akk. edû; lamādu
ePSD: šêtu
taka [ABANDON] wr. tak_4 "to set aside, leave behind; to save, keep back, hold back" Akk. ezēbu; uhhuru; šêtu

مدد (لسان العرب) ومدَّ بصرَه إلى الشيء: طمَح به إليه. وفي التنزيل العزيز: ولا تمُدَّنَّ عينيك إلى ما. وأمَدَّ له في الأجل: أنسأه فيه. والمدُّ: أن يمُدَّ الرجل الرجل في غيّه. وكل ما أعنت به قوماً في حرب أو غيره، فهو مادَّة لهم. ومَدَّه مِداداً وأمدَّه: أعطاه؛

لمس (لسان العرب) وقال ابن الأعرابي: لَمَسْتُه لَمْساً ولامَسْتُه مُلامَسَة، ويفرق بينهما فيقال: اللَّمْسُ قد يكون مَسَّ الشيء بالشيء ويكون مَعْرِفة الشيء وإن لم يكن ثَمَّ مَسٌّ لجَوْهَرٍ على جوهر، والمُلامَسَة أكثر ما جاءت من اثنين.

لمَذ (القاموس المحيط) لمَذ: لَمَجَ، لغةٌ فيه.

لمج (لسان العرب) ولَمَجَ المرأةَ: نكَحَها. وذكر أعرابي رجلاً، فقال: ما له لَمَجَ أُمَّه؟ فرفعوه إلى السلطان، فقال: إنما قلت: مَلَجَ أُمه، فخَلَّى سبيلَه.

قال أبو زيد: لا أعرف اللَّمْجَ إلاَّ في الحمير، قال: وهو مثل اللَّمْسِ أو فَوْقَه. واللَّميجُ: الكثير الجِماع. واللامِجُ: الكثير الجماع. وقد لَمَجْتُه ولَهَنْتُه، بمعنى واحد.

لمد (لسان العرب) أهمله الليث، وروى أبو عمرو: اللَّمْدُ التواضعُ بالذلّ.

اللَّمْدُ (القاموس المحيط) اللَّمْدُ: التَّواضُعُ بالذُّلّ. واللَّمْدانُ: الذَّليل. ولَمدَهُ: لَدمَهُ.

لدم (مقاييس اللغة) اللام والدال والميم أصلٌ يدلّ على إلصاق شيءٍ بشيءٍ، ضرباً أو غيره، فاللَّدْم: ضرب الحجَر بالحجَر. والْتَدم النساءُ: ضرَبْنَ وجوهَهنَّ وصُدورهنَّ في المَناحة.

اللَّدْمُ (القاموس المحيط) اللَّدْمُ: اللَّطْمُ، والضَّرْبُ بشيءٍ ثَقيلٍ يُسْمَعُ وقْعُه،

لدم (لسان العرب) ويقال: فلان فَدْمٌ ثَدْمٌ لَدْمٌ بمعنى واحد. ويُسمَّى الضَّرْبُ لَدْماً. ولدمْتُ ألْدِمُ لَدْماً، فأَنا لادِمٌ، وقوم لدَمٌ مثل خادم وخَدَم. واللَّدَمُ، بالتحريك: الحُرَمُ في القَرابات. ويقال: إنما سميت الحُرْمَةُ اللَّدَم لأَنها تَلْدِم القَرابة أي تُصْلِح وتَصِل؛ تقول العرب: اللَّدَمَ اللَّدَمَ إذاَ أرادت توكيد المُحالفة أي حُرْمَتُنا حُرْمَتُكم وبيتنا بيْتُكم لا فرق بيننا.

شئِزَ (القاموس المحيط) شئِزَ، كفرِحَ، شأزا وشُؤُوزاً، فهو شئِزٌ وشأْزٌ: غلُظ، وارْتفع، واشْتدّ، و~ الرَّجُلُ: قَلِق، وذُعِرَ، كشُئِزَ، كعُنِيَ، فهو مَشْؤُوزٌ ومَشْوزٌ، وأشْأزَهُ غيرُهُ. واشْتاز: نفر.

شأز (لسان العرب) وأَشْأَز الرجلُ عن كذا وكذا: ارتفع عنه؛

شوز (لسان العرب) الأَشْوَز: مثل الأَشْوس، وهو المتكبر.

الأَشْوزُ (القاموس المحيط) الأشْوَز: المُتكبِّرُ. وشِيز به شَوْزاً: شُغِف به. والمَشْوزُ: القلقُ.

شع (مقاييس اللغة) الشين والعين في المضاعف أصلٌ واحد يدلّ على التفرُّق والانتشار.

شَتَّ (القاموس المحيط) شَتَّ يَشِتُّ شَتّاً وشَتاتاً وشَتِيتاً: فرَّقَ، وافْترق، كانْشتَّ وتَشتَّت واسْتَشتَّ. وشَتَّته الله، وأَشَتَّهُ.

شتت (لسان العرب) الشَّتُّ: الافتراق والتَّفْريقُ. لأصمعي: شَتَّ بقلبي كذا وكذا أي فرّقه. ويقال: أَشَتَّ بي قومي أي فَرَّقوا أَمْري. ويقال: شَتُّوا أَمْرَهم أي فرّقوه. ويقال: إِني أَخافُ عليكم الشَّتاتَ أي الفُرْقة. والشَّتُّ: المُتفرّق،

§ 155.—XXV, 72-XXVI, 1

AALD: kallatu (s.) الكنَّة: زوجة الابن الذي يعيش مع ابيه، العروس

كلل (الصَحاح في اللغة) الكلُّ: العِيالُ والثِقْلُ. قال ابن الأعرابي: الكلالةُ: بنو العمَ الأباعدَ. والعرب تقول: هو ابن عمّ الكلالة، وابن عمّ كلالةٍ، إذا لم يكن لحًا وكان رجلاً من العشيرة. والكِلَّةُ: السِترُ الرَقيقُ يُخاطُ كالبيتِ يُتوقَّى فيه من البقّ.

كنن (لسان العرب) الكِنُّ والكِنَّةُ والكِنانُ: وقاء كل شيءٍ وسِتْره. والكَنَّةُ، بالفتح: امرأَة الابن أَو الأَخ، والجمع كَنائنُ، نادر كأَنهم توهموا فيه فَعِيلة ونحوها مما يكسر على فعائل.

خلل (لسان العرب) والخُلَّة الزوجة، قال جِران العَوْد: خُذا حَذراً يا خُلَّتيَّ، فإِنني رأَيت جِران العَوْد قد كاد يَصْلُح فثَنَّى وأَوقعه على الزوجتين لأَن التزوج خُلَّة أَيضاً. التهذيب: فلان خُلَّتي وفلانة خُلَّتي وخِلّي سواء في المذكر والمؤنث.

§ 158.—XXVI, 24-32

ePSD: nāsihu
gabzi [REMOVER] wr. ga-ab-zi "remover" Akk. nāsihu

ePSD: nasāhu
<u>bur</u> <u>[TEAR]</u> wr. bur$_{12}$; bu$_{7}$ "to tear out" Akk. nasāhu
<u>deg</u> <u>[COLLECT]</u> wr. deg$_{x}$(RI) "to take; to gather up, glean; to tear out; to collect, pick up" Akk. ahāzu; laqātu; leqû; nasāhu
<u>dirig</u> <u>[TEAR]</u> wr. dirig "to tear out" Akk. nasāhu
<u>suh</u> <u>[EXTRACT]</u> wr. suh$_{5}$; suh "to tear out; to extract; to choose" Akk. nasāhu
<u>zi</u> <u>[CUT]</u> wr. zi$_{2}$; zi; zi$_{x}$(|IGI@g|) "to cut, remove; to erase" Akk. baqāmu; barāšu; naţāpu; nasāhu

نسح (لسان العرب) الليث: النَسْحُ والنُساحُ ما تحاتَ عن التمر من قشره وفُتاتِ أقماعه ونحو ذلك مما يبقى في أسفل الوعاءِ.
والمنساحُ: شيء يُدْفعُ به الترابُ ويُذْرى به. الجوهري: نَسحَ الترابَ نَسْحاً أذراه، ونسحَ نسحاً: طمع.
نزح (مقاييس اللغة) النون والزاء والحاء كلمةٌ تدلُّ على بُعد.
نزح (لسان العرب) نَزَحَ الشيءُ يَنْزَحُ (* قوله «نزح الشيء ينزح إلخ» بابه منع وضرب كما في القاموس.) نَزْحاً ونُزوحا: بَعُدَ.وشيءٌ نُزُحٌ ونَزوحٌ: نازحٌ؛ أنشد ثعلب: إنَ المَذَلّةَ مَنْزِلٌ نُزُحٌ عن دار قَومِك، فاتْرُكي شَتْمي ونزحت الدارُ فهي تَنْزَحُ نُزوحاً إذا بَعُدتْ. وقد نُزِحَ بفلان إذا بَعُدَ عن دياره غيبَةً بعيدةً؛ وأنشد الأصمعي: ومن يُنْزَحْ به، لا بُدَّ يوماً يجيءُ به نَعيٌّ أو بَشيرُ وأنت بمُنْتَزِح من كذا أي ببعد منه؛ قال ابن هَرْمَةَ يَرْثي ابنه: فأنتَ، من الغوائلِ، حين تُرْمى، ومن ذَمِّ الرجالِ، بمُنْتَزاحِ إلا أنه أشبع فتحة الزاي فتولدت الألف.
نزه (مقاييس اللغة) النون والزاء والهاء كلمةٌ تدلُّ على بُعد في مكان وغيره.
نزه (لسان العرب) وقد نَزُه نزاهةً وتَنزَّهَ تنزُّهاً إذا بَعُدَ. ونزَّهَ نفْسَه عن القبيح: نحَاها. وهو بنُزْهةٍ عن الماء أي بُعْد. وفلان نزيهٌ أي بعيد. وتنزَّهُوا بحُرَمكُم عن القوم: تباعدوا.
نسخ (مقاييس اللغة) النون والسين والخاء أصلٌ واحد، إلاَ أنَه مختلفٌ في قياسِه. قال قوم: قياسُه رفْعُ شيءٍ وإثباتُ غيرِه مكانَه. وقال آخرون: قياسُه تحويلُ شيءٍ إلى شيءٍ.
نسخ (لسان العرب) والنسخ نقل الشيء من مكان إلى مكان وهو هو؛ ونسخ الشيء بالشيء ينسَخه وانتسخه: أَزاله به وأَداله؛ والشيء ينسخ الشيءَ نَسْخاً أي يزيله ويكون مكانه. الليث: النسْخ أن تزايل أمراً كان من قبلُ يُعْمل به ثم تنسخه بحادث غيره. والعرب تقول: نسَخَت الشمسُ الظلَ وانتسخته أزالته، والمعنى أذهبت الظلَ وحلَت محله؛
ربب (الصِحاح في اللغة) والرابُّ: زوج الأمِّ. والرابَّةُ: امرأة الأب. وربيبُ الرجلِ: ابنُ امرأته من غيره، وهو بمعنى مَرْبوبٍ؛ والأنثى ربيبَة. والربيبةُ الحاضنةُ.

§ 159.—XXVI, 33-46

AALD: palāsu (v.) يحدق، ينظر، يتفحص، يسبب الهم والقلق والاثارة، يواجه
فلس (العباب الزاخر) والفَلس -بالتحريك-: من قولهم في حُبِّها فلس: أي لا نَيْلَ معه؛ وأفْلَسْتُ فلاناً: إذا طَلَبْته فأخْطأت مَوْضِعَه،
الفَلَسُ (القاموس المحيط) وبالتحريك: عدمُ النَيْل،
بلس (لسان العرب) أَبْلَسَ الرجلُ: قَطِعَ به؛ عن ثعلب. وأَبْلَس سكت. والمُبْلِسُ اليائسُ، ولذلك قيل للذي يسكت عند انقطاع حجته ولا يكون عنده جواب: قد أَبْلَسَ؛ والمُبْلِسُ الساكت من الحزن أو الخوف. والإبْلاسُ: الحَيْرة؛ ومنه الحديث: أَلم تر الجنَ وإبلاسَها أي تحَيُّرها ودهَشَها.

§ 161.—XXVI, 60-77

AALD: garā'u See gerû
AALD: gerû (v.) (garû) يعادي، يخاصم، يبدأ قضية، يتعارك
ePSD: gerû
<u>gabal du</u> <u>[HOSTILE]</u> wr. ga-ba-al du$_{3}$ "to be hostile, to challenge" Akk. gerû
ePSD: gašru
<u>ir</u> <u>[MIGHTY]</u> wr. ir$_{9}$; ir$_{3}$ "mighty" Akk. gašru
ePSD: gašāru (v.) يُصبحُ قويا
guttaššuru; gittaššuru يبين انه الافضل، يتنافس احدهم مع الاخر

جرأ (العباب الزاخر) الجُرأةُ -مثال الجُرْعة- والجُرةُ - بتخفيفِ الهمْزِ وتليينه- مثالُ الشُبَة والكُرة كما يُقال للمرأة:المرةُ والجَراءةُ والجَرائيةُ -كالكراهةِ والكراهيةِ- :الشَجاعةُ. وتقول: جرَأتُك على فلان حتى اجْتَرأت عليه.
جرأ (لسان العرب) الجُرأةُ مثل الجُرْعة: الشجاعةُ، وقد جَرُؤَ يَجْرُؤُ جُرْأَةً وجراءةً، بالمدِّ، وجرايةً، بغير همز، نادر، وجَرائيةً على فعالية، واستَجْرأ وتَجرّأ وجرَّأه عليه حتى اجترأ عليه جُرْأةً، وهو جريءُ المُقْدَم: أي جريءٌ عند الاقدام. وفي حديث ابن الزبير وبناء الكعبة: تركها حتى إذا كان الموسِمُ وقدمَ الناسُ يريد أن يُجرِّئهم عل أهل الشام، هو من الجُرأة والإقدام على الشيء. أراد أن يَزِيد في جُرْأتهم عليهم ومُطالبتهم بإحراق الكعبة، ويروى بالحاء المهملة والباء، وهو مذ كور في موضعه.
جسر (مقاييس اللغة) الجيم والسين والراء يدلُّ على قوةٍ وجُرْأة. فالجَسْرة: الناقة القوية، ويقال هي الجريئة على السَير. وصُلْبٌ جَسْرٌ أي قويّ.
جسر (لسان العرب) جَسَرَ يَجْسُرُ جُسُورا وجَسارَةً: مضى ونفذ. وجَسَرَ على كذا يَجْسُر جسارةً وتجاسر عليه؛ أقدم. والجَسُورُ: المِقْدامُ. رجل جَسْرٌ وجَسُورٌ: ماضٍ شجاعٌ، والأُنثى جَسْرَةٌ وجَسُورٌ وجَسُورةٌ. ورجل جَسْرٌ: جسيمٌ جَسُورٌ شجاع. وإن فلاناً لَيُجَسِّرُ فلاناً أي يُشَجِّعُه.

§ 164.—XXVII, 24-32

ePSD: harāşu

kud [CUT] wr. kud; gur_5 "to break off, deduct; to separate, cut off; to cut; to incise; to decide; to make clear" Akk. harāşu; napādu; parāsu; harāşu; parāsu; harāşu

šab [TRIM] wr. šab "to inspect exta; to incise; to draw, design; to gather together, collect, scrape up; to break off, deduct; to trim, peel off; to dig, hollow out; to have a grooved shape; to cut, fell (of trees); to become loose, fall out; to disintegrate; to disappear; to make clear" Akk. barû ša uzu; esēpu; harāru; harāşu; harāşu; eşēru; harāşu; šarāmu; nakāsu; šahāhu

tar [CUT] wr. tar; tar^{ar} "to cut down; to untie, loosen; to cut; to scatter, disperse; to decide" Akk. harāşu; parāsu; paţāru; sapāhu

ePSD: karāşu

kid [BREAK] wr. kid_2; gir_8; kid_4; kid_7 "to break off, pinch off" Akk. karāşu

tuk [BREAK] wr. tuk_x(|IM.KAD_3|) "to break off, pinch off; to cut, fell; to demolish; to scratch; to soften, dissolve" Akk. karāşu; nakāsu; naqāru; narābu

حرص (مقاييس اللغة) الحاء والراء والصاد أصلان: أحدهما الشَق، والآخر الجشع.فالأول الحَرْصُ الشقُّ؛ يقال حَرص القصّار الثوبَ إذا شقَّه.

حرص (لسان العرب) والحَرْصُ الشقُّ.

هرض (لسان العرب) وهَرَضَ الثوبَ يَهْرِضُهُ هَرْضاً: مزّقه.

خرص (مقاييس اللغة) الخاء والراء والصاد أصولٌ متباينة جداً.فالأوّل الخَرْص، وهو حَزْرُ الشَيء، يقال خَرَصْتُ النَخْل، إذا حزَرْتَ ثمره.
والخرّاصُ: الكذاب، وهو من هذا، لأنَه يقول ما لا يعلم ولا يَحُقّ. وأصلٌ آخر، يقال للحلْقة من الذهب خُرْصٌ.وأصلٌ آخر، وهو كل ذي شُعبَةٍ من الشَيء ذي الشُعب. فالخريص من البحر: الخليجُ منه.

خرص (لسان العرب) وخَرَصَ العددَ يَخْرُصُه ويَخْرِصُه خَرْصاً وخِرْصاً: حزره، وقيل: الخَرْصُ المصدرُ والخِرْصُ، بالكسر، الاسمُ. يقال: كم خِرْصُ أرْضِك وكم خِرْصُ نَخْلِك؟ بكسر الخاء، وفاعلُ ذلك الخارِصُ. وكان النبي، صلّى الله عليه وسلّم، يبعث الخُرّاص على نخيل خَيْبَر عند إدراك ثمرها فيحزِرُونه رُطباً كذا وتمْراً كذا، ثم يأْخذهم بمكِيلة ذلك من التمر الذي يجب له وللمساكين، وإنما فعل ذلك، صلّى الله عليه وسلّم، لما فيه من الرِّفْق لأصحاب الثمار فيما يأْكلونه منه مع الاحتياط للفقراء في العُشْر ونصف العُشْر ولأَهل الفَيْءِ في نصيبهم. وجاء في الحديث عن النبي، صلّى الله عليه وسلّم: أنه أَمر بالخَرْص في النخل والكرْم خاصّةً دُون الزَّرْع القائم، وذلك أن ثِمارها ظاهرةٌ، والخَرْصُ يُطِيفُ بها فيُرَى ما ظهر من الثمار وذلك ليس كالحَبّ في أكْمامه. ابن شميل: الخِرْص، بكسر الخاء، الحزْر مثل عِلمت عِلْماً؛ قال الأزهري: هذا جائز لأن الاسم يوضع موضع المصدر.

الخَرْصُ (القاموس المحيط) وخارَصَهُ: عاوضه، وبادله.

أتَيْتُه (القاموس المحيط) أتَيْتُه أتْياً وإتْيانناً وإتْيانةً، بكسرهما، ومَأْتاةً وأُتِيًّا، كعُتِيٍّ ويُكسَرُ: جِئْتُه. وآتى إليه الشيءَ: ساقه، و~ فلاناً شيئاً: أعْطاهُ إيَّاهُ، و~ فلاناً: جازاهُ.

§ 165.—XXVII, 33-50

AALD: sidru (s.) (sadru) See sadāru السّطر، الصَف، خط المعركة، قرابين

سطر (مقاييس اللغة) السين والطاء والراء أصلٌ مطرد يدلُّ على اصطفافِ الشيء، كالكتاب والشجر، وكلّ شيء اصطفَّ.

سطر (لسان العرب) السَطْرُ والسَطَرُ: الصَفُّ من الكتاب والشجر والنخل ونحوها؛ والسَطْرُ الخطُّ والكتابة، وهو في الأَصل مصدر. وسَطَرَ يَسْطُرُ إذا كتب؛ قال أبو سعيد الضرير: سمعت أعرابيّاً فصيحاً يقول: أَسْطَرَ فلانٌ اسمي أي تجاوز السَطْرَ الذي فيه اسمي، فإذا كتبه قيل: سَطَرَهُ.

§ 168.—XXVIII, 9-24

AALD: kabātu (v.) (kabādu) يكبد، يُثْقِل، يضخم، يسمَن

ePSD: kabtu

alim [BISON] wr. alim; e-lum "bison; heavy; important" Akk. ditānu; kabtu; kusarikku

aratta [IMPORTANT] wr. aratta "heavy; important; praise, glory" Akk. kabtu; tanattu

dilmun [IMPORTANT] wr. dilmun "(to be) made manifest; (to be) heavy; (to be) important; ritually unclean, impure person; instruction" Akk. kabtu; musukku; têrtu; šûpû

dugud [HEAVY] wr. dugud "(to be) heavy; (to be) important" Akk. kabtu

idim [HEAVY] wr. idim "(to be) heavy; (to be) important" Akk. kabtu

mah [GREAT] wr. mah; mah_2 "(to be) great" Akk. kabtu; mādu; rabû; şīru

tukur [IMPORTANT] wr. $tukur_2$; tukur "important" Akk. kabtu

كبد (لسان العرب) وكَبِد كل شيءٍ: عِظَمُ وسطِه وغِلَظُه؛ كَبِدَ كَبَداً، وهو أكْبَدُ. ورملة كَبْداء: عظيمة الوسط؛ وناقة كَبْداء: كذلك؛ وفي حديث الخَنْدق: فعَرضَتْ كَبْدَةٌ شديدة؛ هي القِطْعة الصُلْبة من الأرض. وأرضٌ كَبْداءُ وقَوْسٌ كَبْداءُ أي شديدة؛ قال ابن الأثير: والمحفوظ في هذا الحديث كُدْيَةٌ، بالياء، وسيجيءُ. وتكَبَّد اللبنُ وغيرُه من الشراب: غَلُظ وخَثُر. قال أبو منصور: ومكابَدَةُ الأمر معاناة مشقته. وكابَدْت الأمر إذا قاسيت شدته. والكبَدُ الشدَّة والمشَقَّة.

كبت (لسان العرب) وقال الفراء: كُبِتُوا أي غِيظُوا وأُحزنُوا يوم الخندق، كما كُبِتَ مَن قاتَلَ الأنبياء قبلهم؛ قال الأزهري: وقال من احتجَّ للفراء: أصلُ الكَبْتِ الكَبْدُ، فقلبت الدال تاء، أُخذ من الكبد، وهو مَعْدِنُ الغَيْظ والأَحقاد، فكأَن الغَيْظ، لما بلَغ بهم مبلَغه، أصاب أَكبادهم فأَحرقها، ولهذا قيل للأَعداء: هم سُودُ الأَكباد.
كبب (لسان العرب) وكَبَّ إذا ثَقُل. وأَلقى عليه كُبّته أي ثِقْله.

§ 170.—XXVIII, 38-61

AALD: bulṭu (s.) See balāṭu (v.) (العنفوان) الحياة، العمر، الصحة، الشباب
AALD: baltu (see baštu)
AALD: baštu (s.) الوقار، الكبرياء، حسن المنظر، الجلال، الغرور
ePSD: TUR.SAG
dumusaĝ [FIRST-BORN] wr. dumu-saĝ "first-born"
ePSD: TUR.SAL
dumumunus [DAUGHTER] wr. dumu-munus "daughter" Akk. mārtu
ePSD: tur
tur [CHILD] wr. tur "(young) child" Akk. šerru
tur [SMALL] wr. tur; tu "(to be) small; to reduce, diminish; to subtract; (to be) young" Akk. ṣehērum

الطِّرْسُ (القاموس المحيط) والمُتطرِّسُ: المُتأنِّقُ المُختار.
طرس (العباب الزاخر) وقال ابن عباد: يقال هو يتطرَّس عن كذا: أي يتكرَّم عنه، وهو يتطرَّس عن فُلانة أن يتزَوَّجها: بأنه يرفَعُ نفسه عنها.
طرس (لسان العرب) ابن الأعرابي: المُتطرِّسُ والمُتنطِّسُ المُتنوِّقُ المختار؛ قال المَرَّار الفقعسي يصف جارية:بيضاءُ مُطْعَمةُ الملاحة، مِثْلُها لَهْو الجليس ونيقةُ المُتطرِّس وطرسُوسُ (* قوله «وطرسوس» كحلزون، واختار الأصمعي فيه ضم الطاء كعصفور اهـ. شارح القاموس.): بلد بالشام، ولا يخفف إلا في الشعر لأن فَعْلُولاً ليس من أبنيتهم، والله أعلم.
التَّوْرُ (القاموس المحيط) والتّارَةُ: الحينُ، والمرَّةُ، ج: تاراتٌ وتيرٌ. وأتارَهُ: أعادهُ مرَّةً بعد مرَّة.
تور (لسان العرب) والتّارَةُ: الحين والمرَّة، ألفها واو، جمْعُها تاراتٌ وتيرٌ؛
الطَّوْرُ (القاموس المحيط) الطَّوْرُ: التارة وبلغ في العلم أطْوريه، بفتحها وقد تكسرُ، أي: أوَّلَه وآخرَه.
طور (لسان العرب) الطَّوْرُ: التارة، تقول: طَوْراً بعْدَ طَوْر أي تارة بعد تارة؛
طَار (لسان العرب) ما بها طُوْرِيٌّ أي أحَدٌ.
طر (مقاييس اللغة) ومن الباب فتىً طارٌّ: طَرَّ شاربُه.
طرر (الصّحاح في اللغة) ومنه طَرَّ شاربُ الغلام فهو طارٌّ.
طرر (لسان العرب) ورجلٌ طَرِيرٌ: ذو طُرَّة وهيئة حسنة وجمال. وقيل: هو المُستقبل الشباب؛ ابن شميل: رجل جميلٌ طريرٌ. وما أطرَّه أي ما أجمله وما كان طريراً ولقد طَرَّ. ويقال: رأيت شيخاً جميلاً طريرا. وقوم طرارٌ بَيِّنُو الطَّرارة، والطَّريرُ: ذو الرُّواء والمَنْظر؛ ويقال: اسْتطَرَّ إتمام الشكير. . . (* هنا بياض بالأصل، وبهامشه مكتوبا بخط الناسخ: كذا وجدت وبإزائه مكتوبا ما نصه: العبارة صحيحة كتبه محمد مرتضى اهـ). الشعر أي أنبته حتى بلغ تمامه؛ وطَرَّ النبتُ والشاربُ والوبرُ يطُرُّ، بالضم، طرّاً وطُروراً: طلع ونبت؛ وكذلك شعرُ الوحشيِّ إذا نسله ثم نبت؛ ومنه طَرَّ شاربُ الغلام فهو طارٌّ. وغلام طارٌّ وطريرٌ: كما طَرَّ شاربُه. التهذيب: يقال طَرَّ شاربُه، وبعضهم يقول طُرَّ شاربُه، والأول أفصح. الليث: فتى طارٌّ إذا طَرَّ شاربُه.
ترر (لسان العرب) والتَّرارَةُ: السِّمَنُ والبضاضةُ؛ يقال منه: تَرِرْتَ، بالكسر، أي صرت تارّاً وهو الممتلئ والتَّرارة: امتلاء الجسم من اللحم وريُّ العظم؛ يقال للغلام الشاب الممتلئ: تارٌّ. وفي حديث ابن زِمْلٍ: رَبْعَةٌ من الرجال تارٌّ؛ التارُّ: الممتلئ البدن، وتَرَّ الرجلُ يَتِرُّ ويَتَرُّ تَرّاً وترارة وتروراً: امتلأ جسمه وتروّى عظمه؛ قال العجاج: بسلْهبٍ لَيْنٍ في تُرُورِ وقال: ونُصْبِحُ بالغداة أَتَرَّ شيءٍ، ونُمْسي بالعشيِّ طَلَنْفحينا ورجلٌ تارٌّ وتَرٌّ: طويل. قال ابن سيده: وأرى تَرّاً فعلا، وقد تَرَّ ترارة، وقصرةٌ تارةٌ. والتَّرَّةُ: الجارية الحسناء الرَّعْناءُ. ابن الأعرابي: التَّراتيرُ الجواري الرُّعْنُ. ابن شميل: الأُتْرُورُ الغلام الصغير.

§ 172.—XXIX, 6-26

زحم (لسان العرب) الزَّحْمُ: أن يزْحمَ القومُ بعضهم بعضاً من كثْرة الزحام إذا ازدحموا. والزَّحْمةُ الزِّحامُ. وزحم القومُ بعضهم بعضاً يزْحَمُونَهُمْ زَحْماً وزحاماً: ضايقوهم. وازْدحمُوا وَزاحموا: تضايقوا. وزحمتُه وزاحمتُه، والأمواج تزْدحمُ وتتزاحم: تلتطم. والزَّحْمُ المزْدحمُون؛ وزَحْمُ من أسماء مكة، شرفها الله تعالى وحرسها؛ حكاها ثعلب؛ قال ابن سيده: والمعروف رُحْم.
الزَّهْومَةُ (القاموس المحيط) والمُزاهمةُ: العداوةُ، والمُحاكَّةُ، والمُفارقةُ، والمُقاربةُ، ضدٌّ، والمُداناةُ في السير والبيع والشِّراءِ وغيرِها. و~ الرَّجُلَ: أَكْثَرَ الكلام عليه.

§ 175.—XXIX, 57-68

ePSD: qadum
gada [WITH] wr. ga-da "with" Akk. qadum

قدم (مقاييس اللغة) القاف والدال والميم أصلٌ صحيحٌ يدلُّ على سَبْق ورَعْف ثم يفرع منه ما يقاربه: يقولون: القِدَم: خلاف الحُدوث. ويقال: شيءٌ قديم، إذا كان زمانُه سالفاً. ولفلانٍ قَدمُ صِدقٍ، أي شيءٌ متقدِّم من أثَر حسَن. ومن الباب: قَدِمَ من سفره قُدوماً، وأَقْدم على الشيء إقداماً. قال ابن دريد: وقادمُ الإنسان: رأسُه، والجمع قوادم. قال: ولا يكادون يتكلَّمون بالواحد. ومُقدّمة الجيش: أوّلُه: وأَقْدمْ: زجرٌ للفرس، كأنّه يؤمر بالإقدام.

القدَم (القاموس المحيط) القدَم، محرَكة: السَابقةُ في الأمْرِ،
جدم (لسان العرب) وإجْدَمْ وهِجْدَم على البدل كلاهما: مَن زَجْر الخيل إذا زُجِرت لِتمْضيَ. ويقال للفرس: إجْدَمْ وأَقْدِمْ إذا هِيج ليمْضِيَ. وأَقْدِمْ
أَجْودها. وأجْدَم الفرسَ: قال له إجْدَمْ، وسنذكر ذلك مستوفى في هجدم.
قدو (مقاييس اللغة) القاف والدال والحرف المعتلّ أصلٌ صحيح يدلُّ على اقتباس بالشَيء واهتداء، ومُقادرة في الشيء حتى يأتي به مساوياً لغيره.
قدا (لسان العرب) والقُدوة والقِدوة: الأُسْوة. يقال: فلان قدوة يقتدى به. ابن الأَعرابي: القَدْوةُ التقدُّمْ. ابن الأعرابي: القَدْر القُدوم من السفر، والقَدْوُ
القُرْب.

§ 176.—XXIX, 69- XXX, 9

ePSD: emēdu

ri [IMPOSE] wr. RI; ru "to lay down, cast, place; to set in place, imbue; to lean on; to impose; to throw down; to release, let go; to walk along; to pour out; to lead away" Akk. bâ'u; emēdu; nadû; nasāku; ramû; rehû; tarû; wašaru

us [LEAN] wr. us$_2$ "to lean on, impose; to check" Akk. emēdu; sanāqu

AALD: emēdu (v.) يمد، يتكئ، يصل، يلتصق بـ، يتصل، يوصل، يوحّد، يربط، ينألف، يسند، يساعد، يسنند بعضهم الى بعض

مدد (لسان العرب) ومَدَدْنا القومَ: صِرْنا لهم أنصاراً ومدداً وأَمْدَدْناهم بغيرنا. وحكى اللحياني: أَمَدَّ الأمير جنده بالحبل والرجال وأعاثهم، وأَمَدَّهم
بمال كثير وأَغانهم. قال: وقال بعضهم أعطاهم، والأول أكثر. وفي التنزيل العزيز: وأَمْدَدْناهم بأموال وبنين. والمَدَدُ: ما مدَّهم به أو أَمَدَّهم؛ وقال:
وأَمْدَدْناكم بأموال وبنين، فالمَددُ ما أَمْدَدْت به قومك في حرْب أو غير ذلك من طعام أو أعوان.
عمد (مقاييس اللغة) العين والميم والدال أصلٌ كبير، فروعه كثيرة ترجع إلى معنىً، وهو الاستقامة في الشيء، منتصباً أو ممتدَاً، وكذلك في الرَأي
وإرادةِ الشيء.من ذلك عَمَدْتُ فلاناً وأنا أعْمِدُه عمْداً، إذا قصدتَ إليه. وعَمُود الأمر: قِوامه الذي لا يستقيم إلاّ به. وعَميد القوم: سيِّدهم ومُعْتَمَدُهم
الذي يعتمدونه إذا حَزبهم [أمرٌ] فزِعوا إليه. والعماد: الطُول.
عمد (الصَحاح في اللغة) وعَمَدْتُ الشيءَ فانْعَمَدَ، أي أقمته بعمادٍ يَعْتَمِد عليه. والعُمْدَةُ ما يُعتمد عليه. واعْتَمَدْتُ على الشيء: اتَكأتُ. واعْتَمَدْتُ
عليه في كذا، أي اتَكأتُ عليه.

§ 177.—XXX, 22-60

ePSD: NU.MU.SU

numunkuš [WIDOW] wr. nu-mu-un-kuš; nu-mu-kuš; nu-mu-un-kuš$_8$ "widow" Akk. almattu

ePSD: NU.MU.UN.SU

numunkuš [WIDOW] wr. nu-mu-un-kuš; nu-mu-kuš; nu-mu-un-kuš$_8$ "widow" Akk. almattu

ePSD: nu-kuš$_2$-u$_3$

nukušu [WIDOW] wr. nu-kuš$_2$-u$_3$ "widow" Akk. almattu

nukušu [~DOOR] wr. ^{ĝeš}nu-kuš$_2$-u$_3$ "a door fitting" Akk. nukušu

ePSD: paqādu

saĝ sig [ENTRUST] wr. saĝ sig$_{10}$ "to take care of; to entrust" Akk. paqādu

šu šum [ENTRUST] wr. šu šum$_2$ "to entrust" Akk. paqādu

ePSD: šūzubu

šu kar [SPARE] wr. šu kar "to spare" Akk. šūzubu

ePSD: unūtu

akar [IMPLEMENT] wr. ^{ĝeš}a$_2$-kar$_2$ "implement, tool, utensil" Akk. unūtu

niĝguna [UTENSILS] wr. niĝ$_2$-gu$_2$-na "utensils" Akk. unūtu

šukara [TOOL] wr. ^{ĝeš}šu-kara$_2$ "tool, implement, utensil" Akk. unūtu

AALD: unūtu (s.) (enūtu, anūtu) البضائع، العُدة، الادوات، الادوات المنزلية، الاثاث، الاواني، الامتعة

رمل (لسان العرب) وأَرْمَل القومُ: نَفِد زادُهم، وأَرْمَلوه أَنفدوه؛ ويقال للفقير الذي لا يقدر على شيء من رجل أو امرأة أَرْمَلة، ولا يقال للمرأة التي
لا زوج لها وهي مُوسِرة أَرْملة، والأَرامل: المساكين. والأَرْمَل الذي ماتت زوجته، والأَرْملة التي مات زوجُها، وسواء كانا غنيَيْن أو فقيرَين.
ويقال للذكر أَرْمَل إذا كان لا امرأة له، تقوله العرب، وكذلك رجل أَيِّم وامرأة أَيِّمة؛ وامرأة أَرْمَلة: لا زوج لها؛ ويقال: رُمِّل فلان بالدم وضُمِّخ
بالدم وضُرِّج بالدم كُلُّه إذا لُطِّخ به، وقد ترَمَّل بدمه. الجوهري: رَمَّله بالدم فترَمَّل وارْتمَلَ أي تلطَّخ؛
نقس (مقاييس اللغة) النون والقاف والسين أُصيلٌ يدلُّ على لَطْخ شيءٍ بشيءٍ غير حسَن.
نقس (لسان العرب) النِّقْسُ: الذي يكتب به، بالكسر. ابن سيده: النِّقْسُ المداد، والجمع أَنْقاسٌ وأَنْقُسٌ؛ قال المرار: عَفتِ المنازلُ غيرَ مِثْلِ الأَنْقُسِ،
بعْدَ الزَمانِ عرَفْته بالقِرْطسِ أي في القِرْطاسِ، تقول منه: نَقَس دواته تنقيساً. ورجل نَقِسٌ: يعيب الناس ويُلَقِّبهم، وقد نَقَسهم يَنْقُسُهم نَقْساً وناقَسهم،
وهي النَقاسة. الفراء: اللَّقْسُ والنَّقْسُ والنَّقْز كله العيب، وكذلك القَذْل، وهو أن يعيب القومَ ويَسْخَر منهم.
نقس (الصَحاح في اللغة) والنَقْسُ أيضاً: مثل اللَقْس، وهو أن تعيب القومَ وتسخر منهم.
النَقْصُ (القاموس المحيط) النَقْصُ: الخُسْرانُ في الحظِ، كالنُقْصانِ والنُقْصانِ. وأنْقصَهُ وانْتقصَهُ ونقَصَهُ: نَقصَهُ فانْتقص. والانْتقاصُ: الانتِقاصُ.
وهو يتَنقَصُهُ: يَقَعُ فيه، ويَذُمُّهُ. واسْتَنْقَصَ الثَمن: اسْتحطَهُ.

نكس (لسان العرب) وفي حديث أبي هريرة: تعس عبدُ الدِّينار وانتكس أي انقلب على رأسه وهو دعاء عليه بالخيبة لأن من انتكس في أمره فقد خاب وخسر. وقوله تعالى: ومن نُعَمِّرْهُ نُنَكِّسْه في الخَلْق؛ قال أبو إسحق: معناه من أطلنا عمره نكّسنا خلقه فصار بدل القوة ضعفاً وبدل الشباب هرماً. وقال الفراء: قرأ عاصم وحمزة: نُنَكِّسْه في الخلق، وقرأ أهل المدينة: نَنْكُسه في الخلق، بالتخفيف، وقال قتادة: هو الهَرَم، وقال شمر: يقال نُكِسَ الرجل إذا ضعف وعجز؛

خيب (لسان العرب) والخَيْبَة: الحِرْمانُ والخُسْران؛

نمس (لسان العرب) النَّمَسُ، بالتحريك: فساد السَّمْن والغالية وكلِّ طيبٍ ودُهْنٍ إذا تغير وفسد فساداً لَزِجاً. ونَمِسَ الدهن، بالكسر، يَنْمَسُ نَمَساً، فهو نَمِسٌ: تغير وفسد، وكذلك كل شيء طَيِّب تغير؛

فقد (لسان العرب) فَقَدَ الشيءَ يَفْقِدُه فَقْداً وفِقْداناً وفُقُوداً، فهو مَفْقُودٌ وفَقِيدٌ: عَدِمَه؛ ابن الأعرابي: الفَقْدَةُ: الكُشُوث.

كشث (الصّحاح في اللغة) الكشوثُ: نبت يتعلّق بأغصان الشجر من غير أن يضرب بعِرْقٍ في الأرض.

كشث (لسان العرب) بن الأعرابي: الكَشُوثاءُ الفَقْدُ

شزب (مقاييس اللغة) الشين والزاء والباء ليس بأصل، لأنَّه من باب الإبدال.

شزب (لسان العرب) التهذيب: الشَّوزَبُ والـمَئِنَةُ: العَلامةُ؛

شذب (لسان العرب) وشَذَبَ العُودَ، يَشْذِبُه شَذْباً: أَلقى ما عليه من الأَغْصانِ حتى يَبْدُوَ؛ وشَذَبَ عنه شَذْباً أي ذَبَّ. والشَّاذِبُ: الـمُتَنَحِّي عن وطنه. ورجل شَذْبُ العُروق أي ظاهِرُ العُرُوق.

عنن (لسان العرب) عَنَّ الشيءُ يَعِنُّ ويَعُنُّ عَنَناً وعُنُوناً: ظَهَرَ أَمامك؛ والعِنان: الحبل؛ والعُنَّة: الحَظِيرة من الخَشَبِ أو الشجر تجعل للإبل والغنم تُحْبَسُ فيها، وقيد في الصحاح فقال: لتتدرأ بها من بَرْدِ الشَّمال. قال ثعلب: العُنَّة الحَظِيرةُ تكون على باب الرجل فيكون فيها إبله وغنمه. ومن كلامهم: لا يجتمع اثنان في عُنَّةٍ، وجمعها عُنَنٌ؛ قال الأَعشى: ترى اللَّحمَ من ذابلٍ قد ذَوى، ورطْبٍ يُرفَّعُ فوقَ العُنَن. وقال البُشْتِيُّ: العُنَنُ في بيت الأعشى حبال تُشَدُّ ويُلْقى عليها القَديدُ. قال أبو منصور: الصواب في العُنَّة والعُنَن ما قاله الخليل وهو الحظيرة، وقال: ورأيت حُظُراتِ الإبل في البادية يسمونها عُنَناً لاعْتِنانها في مَهَبِّ الشَّمال مُعْتَرِضة لتقيها بَرْدَ الشَّمال، قال: ورأيتهم يشُرُّون اللحم المُقَدَّد فوقها إذا أرادوا تجفيفه؛ قال: ولست أدري عمن أخذ البُشْتِيُّ ما قال في العُنَّة إنه الحبل الذي يُمَدُّ، ومَدُّ الحبل من فعل الحاضرة، قال ابن بري: والعُنَّةُ، بالضم أيضاً، خَيْمة تجعل من ثُمام أو أغصان شجر يُسْتَظَلُّ بها. والعُنَّة: ما يجمعه الرجل من قصبٍ ونبت ليَعْلِفه غنمه. يقال: جاء بعُنَّةٍ عظيمة. والعَنَّة، بفتح العين: العَطْفَة؛ قال الشاعر: إذا انصرفتْ من عَنَّةٍ بعد عَنَّةٍ، وجَرْسٍ على آثارها كالمُؤلَّب والعُنَّةُ: ما تُنْصَبُ عليه القِدْرُ.وعُنَّةُ القِدْر: الدَّقْدانُ؛ وقال البُشْتِيُّ: العُنَنُ في بيت الأعشى حبال تُشَدُّ ويُلْقى عليها القَدِيدُ. قال أبو منصور: الصواب في العُنَّة والعُنَن ما قاله الخليل وهو الحظيرة،

العَيْنُ (القاموس المحيط) والعِيانُ أيضاً: حديدةٌ في مَتاعِ الفَدَانِ. والعِينةُ، بالكسر: السَّلَفُ، وخِيارُ المالِ، ومادَّةُ الحَرْبِ،

عين (الصّحاح في اللغة) والعَيْنُ الدينار. والعَيْنُ المالُ الناضُّ.

§ 178.—XXX, 61-XXXI, 19

AALD: zikru (s.) (siqaru) الذِّكر، الحديث، الاسم، الشهرة، القسم

AALD: ēma (conj. prep.) حيثما، اينما، فيما اذا

AALD: šamādu (v.) (حلية، زينة، ترصيع) تضع

ePSD: emqu

igiĝaltuku [WISE] wr. igi-ĝal$_2$-tuku "wise, clever" Akk. emqu

usandu [WISE] wr. usandu; usandu$_x$(|NUNUZ.AB$_2$×AŠGAB|) "wise, clever" Akk. emqu

ePSD: NI

i [OIL] wr. i$_3$; u$_5$; u$_2$ "oil; butter; container for oil" Akk. tallum; šamnu

li [OIL] wr. li$_2$ "oil; fat; cream" Akk. šamnu

li [PRESS] wr. li$_2$; li$_9$ "to press (oil)" Akk. ruqqû

suš [GREASE] wr. suš$_2$; suš "grease" Akk. šēmu

zaĝa [PRESS] wr. zaĝa(NI) "to press out oil; exudation (of oil)" Akk. za'u; şahātu ša šamni

ePSD: sig$_8$

sig [PLUCK] wr. sig$_7$; sig$_8$ "to pluck hair or wool; (to be) trimmed, pruned" Akk. sepû ša šarti; urrû

ذكر (لسان العرب) الذِّكْرُ: الحِفْظُ للشيء تَذْكُرُه. والذِّكْرُ أيضاً: الشيء يجري على اللسان. والذِّكْرُ جَرْيُ الشيء على لسانك، وقد تقدم أن الذِّكْرَ لغة في الذكر، ذَكَرَهُ يَذْكُرُه ذِكْراً وذُكْراً؛ الأخيرة عن سيبويه. وقوله تعالى: واذكروا ما فيه؛ قال أبو إسحق: معناه ادْرُسُوا ما فيه. قال أبو العباس: الذكر الصلاة والذكر قراءة القرآن والذكر التسبيح والذكر الدعاء والذكر الشكر والذكر الطاعة. والذِّكْرُ ذِكْرُ الشرف والصِّيت. ورجل ذَكِيرٌ: جَيِّدُ الذِّكْره والحِفْظ. والذِّكْرُ الشرف.

سمد (لسان العرب) سَمَدَ يَسْمُدُ سُموداً: علا. وسَمَدت الإبل وتَسْمُدُ سُموداً: لم تعرف الإعياء. ويقال للفحل إذا اغتلم. قد سمد. والسَّمْد من السَّيْر: الدأب. وسَمَدَ سُموداً: رفع رأْسه تكبُّراً. وكلُّ رافع رأْسه، فهو سامد. وسَمَدَ الرجلُ سُموداً: بُهِتَ، وسمده سَمْداً: قصده كصَمَده. وسَمَدَ الأَرض سَمْداً: سهلها.

صمد (مقاييس اللغة) الصاد والميم والدال أصلان: أحدهما القَصْد، والآخر الصَّلابة في الشَّيء.فالأوّل: الصَّمْد: القصد. يقال صَمَدْتُه صَمْداً. وفلان مُصَمَّدٌ، إذا كان سيِّداً يُقصَدُ إليه في الأمور.

صمد (الصّحاح في اللغة) وصَمَدَهُ يَصْمُدُه صَمْداً، أي قَصَدَهُ.

صمد (لسان العرب) وصَمَدَ صَمْدَ الأَمْر: قَصَدَ قَصْدَه واعتمده.

عمق (الصَحاح في اللغة) وعمَقَ النظرَ في الأمور تَعْميقاً. وتَعمَق في كلامه، أي تنطَع.
عمق (لسان العرب) العُمْق والعمْق: البعد إلي أسفل، ويقال لي في هذه الدار عَمقٌ أي حق، وما لي فيها عمق أي حق.
نحي (مقاييس اللغة) النون والحاء والياء كلمةٌ واحدة، هي النّحي: سِقاء السَمْن.
النَّحْيُ (القاموس المحيط) النِّحيُ، بالكسر: الزِقُّ، أو ما كان للسَمْن خاصةً، ونحا اللَّبن ينْحيهِ وينْحاهُ: مَخضَهُ، و~ الشيءَ: أزاله، كَنَحَّاهُ فتَنَحَّى،
وشج (لسان العرب) وَشَجتِ العُروقُ والأغصان: اشْتَبكتْ، وكلُّ شيء يشتبك. وَشَجَ يَشِجُ وَشْجاً ووَشيجاً، فهو واشِجٌ: تداخل وتَشابك والْتَفَ؛
سجا (لسان العرب) وقيل ناقةٌ سَجْواءُ مطمئنَة الوبَر. وشاةٌ سَجْواءُ: مطمئنة الصُوفِ. وسجى الميتَ: غطّاه. وسَجَّيْت الميت تسجيةً إذا مدَدْت عليه ثوباً.

§ 181.—XXXI, 60-75

ePSD: NU.BAR
nubar [PROFESSION] wr. nu-bar "a profession for women" Akk. kulmašītu
ePSD: qadištu
lukur [PRIESTESS] wr. lukur "a priestess; (junior) wife of a deified king" Akk. nadītu; qadištu
nugig [PRIESTESS] wr. nu-gig; nu-u_8-gig; mu-gi_{17}-ib; mu-gib_3 "a priestess; a divine epithet; a profession for women" Akk. qadištu
ePSD: I.GI
igi [EYE] wr. igi; i-bi_2; i-gi "eye; carved eye (for statues)" Akk. īnu
igi [FACE] wr. igi; i-bi_2; igi_3; i-gi "first, earlier; front; face" Akk. mahrum; pānû
ePSD: GAL
gal [BIG] wr. gal; gu-la; gu-ul; gal-gal; ku-ul "(to be) big, great; (to be) retired, former; (to be) mature (of male animals)" Akk. rabû

الوَجْهُ (القاموس المحيط) الوجْهُ: م، ومُسْتَقْبَلُ كلّ شيءٍ. ج: أوْجُهٌ ووُجُوهٌ وأُجوهٌ، ونَفْسُ الشيءِ، و~ من الدَهْرِ: أَوَّلُهُ،
وجه (لسان العرب) ووَجْهُ النهار: أَوّلُهُ. وجئتك بوَجْه نهار أي بأوّل نهار. وكان ذلك على وَجْهِ الدهرأي أوّله؛ وبه يفسره ابن الأعرابي. ويقال: أتيته بوَجْهِ نهارٍ وشبابِ نهار وصَدْرِ نهار أي في أوّله؛ ومنه قوله: مَنْ كان مَسْروراً بمَقْتَلِ مالكٍ، فلْيأْتِ نِسْوَتَنا بوَجْهِ نهار وقيل في قوله تعالى: وَجْهَ النهارِ واكْفُروا آخِرَهُ؛ صَلاة الصبح، وقيل: هو أَوّل النهار. ووَجَّهتِ الأرضَ المَطرَةُ: صَيَّرتها وَجْهاً واحداً، كما تقول: تركتِ الأرضَ قَرْواً واحداً.
جلل (الصَحاح في اللغة) وجَلَّ الشيءُ: معظمه. والجُلَى: الأمر العظيم؛ وجمعها جُلَلٌ، مثل كُبْرى وكُبَر. وجلالُ الله: عظمته.
جلل (لسان العرب) وناقة جُلالَة: ضَخْمة. وبعير جُلال: مخرج من جليل. وما له دقيقة ولا جليلة أي ما له شاة ولا ناقة. وجُلُّ كل شيء: عُظْمه.
جَلَّ (القاموس المحيط) وما أجَلَّني: ما أعْطانيها، وتَجَلَّله: علاهُ، وأخَذَ جُلَّهُ. والجَلَلُ، محرَكَةً: العظيمُ والصَغيرُ، ضِدٌّ.
قدس (الصَحاح في اللغة) القُدْسُ والقُدُسُ: الطُهْرُ، اسمٌ ومصدرٌ.
كلسم (لسان العرب) الكَلْسَمةُ: الذَهاب في سُرْعة، وهي الكَلْمسة أيضاً، تقول: كَلْمَسَ الرجلُ وكَلْسم إذا ذهب ابن الأعرابي: يقال كَلْسَمَ فلان إذا تمادى كسَلاً عن قضاء الحُقوق.
نفر (مقاييس اللغة) النون والفاء والراء: أصلٌ صحيح يدلُّ على تجافٍ وتباعد. منه نفر الدَابّةُ وغيرُه نفاراً، وذلك تَجافيه وتباعُدُه عن مكانه ومَقرِّه.
النَّفْرُ (القاموس المحيط) النَّفْرُ: التَفرُّقُ، وجَمْعُ نافِرٍ، والغَلَبةُ. نَفرتِ الدَابَّةُ تَنْفِرُ وتَنْفُرُ نُفوراً ونِفاراً، فهي نافِرٌ ونَفورٌ: جَزِعَتْ، وتَباعدَتْ، ونفر جلْدُه: وَرِمَ.
نبر (مقاييس اللغة) النون والباء والراء أصلٌ صحيح يدلُّ على رَفْع وعُلُوَ.

§ 182.—XXXI, 76-XXXII, 1

Ancient Mesopotamian Gods and Goddesses

(http://oracc.museum.upenn.edu/amgg/listofdeities/marduk/):

“The etymology of Marduk's name is controversial. It is difficult to determine whether the logographic writing of his name dAMAR.UD, Sumerian for "calf of the sun/sun-god," is in any way significant or not. The suggestion to translate this spelling as "calf of the storm" should probably be rejected as there is no evidence for Marduk originally having been a storm god nor is there evidence for his association with the storm god Iškur/Adad.”

“In gratitude the other gods then bestow 50 names upon Marduk and select him to be their head. The number 50 is significant, because it was previously associated with the god Enlil, the former head of the pantheon, who was now replaced by Marduk. This replacement of Enlil is already foreshadowed in the prologue to the famous Code of Hammurabi, a collection of "laws," issued by Hammurabi (r. 1792-1750 BCE), the most famous king of the first dynasty of Babylon. In the prologue, Hammurabi mentions that the gods Anu and Enlil determined for Marduk to receive the "Enlil-ship" (stewardship) of all the people, and with this elevated him into the highest echelons of the Mesopotamian pantheon.”

“The interpretation of líl as ‘wind’ is apparently a secondary development of the first millennium BCE, which has led to an interpretation of Enlil's name as ‘Lord Wind’ or ‘Lord Air’.”
Written Forms
Logographic spellings: AMAR.UD/UTU, ^{d}AMAR.UD/UTU, ^{d}AMAR.UD/UTU.KAM, ^{d}AMAR.UD/UTU.KÁM, ^{d}DUMU.Ú.TUK, ^{d}ŠÀ.ZU, ^{d}MES, ^{d}TUŠ.A(?), ^{d}ŠÚ, ^{d}KU, ^{d}EN
Syllabic spellings
ma-ru-tu-uk, ^{d}ma-ru-tu-uk-ku, ma-ru-tu-UD, ^{d}mar-duk
ePSD: AMAR
amar [YOUNG] wr. amar "calf; young, youngster, chick; son, descendant" Akk. būru; māru
ePSD: UD
ud [STORM] wr. ud "storm; storm demon" Akk. ūmu
ud [SUN] wr. ud "day; heat; a fever; summer; sun" Akk. immu; ummedu; umšu; šamšu; ūmu

أمر (الصَحَاح في اللغة) والإمَرُ أيضا: الصغيرُ من وَلَد الضأن؛ والأنثى إمَرَةٌ. يقال: ما له إمَرٌ ولا إمَرَةٌ، أي شيءٌ.
أمر (لسان العرب) وأمِرَ الشيءُ أمراً وأمَرةً، فهو أمِرٌ: كثُرَ وتمّ؛ قال: أمّ عِيالٍ ضنؤُها غيرُ أمِرْ والاسم: الإمْرُ. والأمَرةُ الزيادة والنماء والبركة. أمِرَ المالُ إذا كثُرَ. والإمَّرُ الصغيرُ من الحُمْلان أولادِ الضأن، والأنثى إمَّرةٌ، وقيل: هما الصغيران من أولاد المعز. والإمَّرُ الخروف. والإمَّرَةُ الرِّخْلُ، والخروف ذكر، والرِّخْلُ أنثى.
دوك (مقاييس اللغة) الدال والواو والكاف أصلٌ واحد يدلُّ على ضغْط وتزاحُم. فيقولون: دُكتُ الشيء دَوْكاً.
دوك (لسان العرب) وداكَ الطِّيبَ والشيءَ يَدُوكه دوْكاً ومَداكاً أي سحقه. الدَّوْكُ: دق الشيء وسحقه وطحنه كما يَدُوك البعيرُ الشيء بكَلْكلِه. وفي حديث خيبر: أن النبي، صلى الله عليه وسلم، قال: لأعطينَّ الراية غداً رجلا يفتح الله على يديه، فبات الناس يَدُوكون تلك الليلة فيمن يدفعها إليه؛ قوله يَدُوكون أي يخوضون ويموجون ويختلفون فيه. والدَّوْك الإختلاط. وباتوا يدوكون دَوْكاً إذا باتوا في اختلاط ودوران.
دوغ (لسان العرب) وقال أبو سعيد: في فلان دوغة ودَوكة أي حُمْقٌ.
توك (لسان العرب) أحمق تائكٌ: شديد الحمق، ولا فعل له؛ قال ابن سيده: لذلك لم أخص به الواو دون الياء ولا الياء دون الواو.
عود (لسان العرب) وكل من أتاك مرة بعد أخرى، فهو عائد، وأما قول أبي النجم: حتى إذا الليلُ تجلّى أصْحَمُه، وانْجابَ عن وجْهِ أغرَّ أدْهَمُه، وتبعَ الأحْمرَ عَوْدٌ يرْجُمُه فإنه أراد بالأحمر الصبح، وأراد بالعود الشمس. قال الأزهري: قال بعضهم: العَوْد تثنية الأمر عَوْداً بعد بَدْءٍ. يقال: بدأ ثم عاد، والعَوْدةُ عَوْدَةُ مرةٍ واحدة.
أود (لسان العرب) والتأَوّد التثني.

§ 185.—XXXII, 31-38

ePSD: tarbītu
nambuluĝ [UPBRINGING] wr. nam-buluĝ$_3$ "upbringing of an adopted child" Akk. tarbītu
ePSD: tarbûtu
a'e [CHILD] wr. a$_2$-e$_3$ "foster-child" Akk. tarbûtu
buluĝ [GROW] wr. buluĝ$_3$; buluĝ$_5$; bu-lu-ug; buluĝ "to grow up, rear, make grow; novice; foster child" Akk. rabû; tarbûtu
AALD: tarbītu (s.) التربية، تربية الاطفال، طفل موضوع للتربية
AALD: tarbûtu (s.) تربوية، مركز الطفل المُربى
ePSD: mû
a [WATER] wr. a "water; semen; progeny" Akk. mû; rihûtu

ربب (لسان العرب) وربَّ ولده والصَّبيَّ يَرُبُّه ربّاً، وربَّبه تَرْبيباً وتَربَّة، عن اللحياني: بمعنى ربَّاه. وفي الحديث: لك نعْمةٌ ترُبُّها، أي تَحْفظها وتُراعيها وتُربّيها، كما يُرَبّي الرَّجُلُ ولده؛ وفي حديث ابن ذي يزن: أسْدٌ تُرَبّبُ، في الغَيْضات، أشْبالا أي تُرَبّي، وهو أبْلَغ منه ومن تَرُبُّ، بالتكرير الذي فيه. وتَربَّبه، وارْتَبّه، وربّاه تَرْبية، على تَحْويلِ التَّضْعيف، وترَبّاه، على تحويل التضعيف أيضا: أحسَنَ القِيامَ عليه، ووَلِيَه حتى يُفارِقَ الطُّفُولِيَّة، كان ابْنَه أو لم يكن؛ وأنشد اللحياني: تُرَبِّبُه، من آلِ دُودان، شَلّةٌ * تربَةَ أمٍّ، لا تُضيعُ سِخالَها وزعم ابن دريد: أنَّ ربِبْتُه لغةٌ؛ والتَّرَبُّبُ الاجْتِماعُ. ومكانٌ مَرَبٌّ، بالفتح: مجْمَعٌ يَجْمعُ الناسَ؛ والرَّبِيبةُ: الحاضِنةُ؛ قال ثعلب: لأنها تُصْلِحُ الشيءَ، وتقُوم به، وتَجْمَعُه. والرَّبُوبُ والرَّبِيبُ: ابن امرأةِ الرجل من غيره، وهو بمعنى مَرْبُوب. ويقال لامرأةِ الرجل إذا كان له ولدٌ من غيرها: رَبيبةٌ، وذلك معنى رابّةٍ ورابٌّ. وفي الحديث: الرَّابُّ كافِلٌ؛ وهو زَوْجُ أمِّ اليتيم، وهو اسم فاعل، من رَبَّه يَرُبُّه أي إنه يَكْفُل بأمْرِه. والرَّابَّةُ: امرأةُ الأب.
موه (لسان العرب) الماءُ والماهُ والماءةُ: معروف. الليث: المُوهةُ لونُ الماء. يقال: ما أحسن مُوهةَ وجْهِه. قال ابن بري: يقال وَجْهٌ مُمَوَّهٌ أي مُزَيَّنٌ بماء الشَّباب؛ قال رؤبة: لمَّا رأتْني خلَقَ المُمَوَّهِ والمُوهةُ: تَرَقْرُقُ الماء في وجه المرأة الشابة. ومُوهةُ الشَّباب: حُسْنُه وصفاؤه. ويقال: عليه مُوهةٌ من حُسْنٍ ومُواهةٌ ومُوَّهةٌ إذا مُنِحه. وتَموَّه المالُ للسِّمَنِ إذا جرى في لُحُومه الربيعُ. وتموَّه العنبُ إذا جرى فيه اليَنْعُ وحَسُن لوْنُه. وكلامٌ عليه مُوهةٌ أي حُسْنٌ وحلاوةٌ، وفلانٌ مُوهةُ أهل بيته.

§ 186.—XXXII, 39-49

ePSD: hiţītu
luĝa [DAMAGE] wr. luĝa; luĝ$_2$ "damage; sin; shamelessness" Akk. hiţītu; šillatu

AALD: ẖaṭû (v.) يُخطئ، يفشل، يرتكب جريمة، يؤذي، يُضر

حطط (الصَحاح في اللغة) وحط، أي نزل. وحطَه، أي حدرَهُ.
خطأ (لسان العرب) الخطأُ والخَطاءُ: ضدُّ الصواب. وخَطِئَ الرجل يَخطأُ خِطْأً وخِطْأَةً على فِعْلة: أذنب. والخَطِيئةُ، على فَعيلة: الذَّنب،

§ 187.—XXXII, 50-53

AALD: muzzazu (v.) (munzizu) See uzuzzu الشاهد، الحاضر، المرافق
ePSD: uzuzzu
sug [STAND] wr. sug_2 "plural stem of gub[to stand]" Akk. uzuzzu

حرس (لسان العرب) حرَسَ الشيءَ يَحْرُسُه ويَحْرِسُه حَرْساً: حفظه؛ وهم الحُرَّاسُ والحَرَسُ والأَحْراسُ. والحَرَس وهم خَدَمُ السلطان المرتبون لحفظه وحراسته.
عرس (مقاييس اللغة) العين والراء والسين أصل واحد صحيح تعود فروعُه إليه ، وهو الملازمة. قال الخليل: عرس به، إذا لزمه.
عرس (العباب الزاخر) وأنكره الأزهري وقال: هذا حرْفٌ مُنْكر ولا أدري ما هو. وقال ابن عبّاد :تعرّس لامْرأتِه: تحبَبَ إليها. والتركيب يدل على المُلازمة.
عرس (لسان العرب) العَرَسُ، بالتحريك: الدَهَشُ. وعرس الرجل وعَرِشَ، بالكسر والسين والشين، عَرَساً، فهو عرِسٌ: بطِرَ، وقيل: أَعْيا ودَهِشَ؛ وعَرِسَ الشيءُ عَرَساً: اشتدَّ. وعَرِسَ الشَرُّ بينهم: لزِمَ ودامَ. وعَرِسَ به عَرَساً: لَزِمه. وعَرِسَ عَرَساً، فهو عَرِسٌ: لزم القتال فلم يَبْرَحْه. وعَرِسَ الصبي بأمه عَرَساً: أَلِفها ولزمها. والمُعْرِسُ الذي يغشى امرأته. يقال: هي عِرْسُه وطَلَّته وقعيدته؛وأَعْرَس بأَهله إذا بَنى بها وكذلك إذا غشيها، ولا تَقُلْ عَرَّسَ، والعامة تقوله؛ قال الراجز يصف حمارا: يُعْرِسُ أبكاراً بها وعُنَسا، أَكْرَمُ عِرْسٍ باءةً إذْ أَعْرَسا وفي حديث عمر: أنه نَهى عن مُتعة الحج، وقال: قد علمت أن النبي، صلى الله عليه وسلم، فعله ولكني كرهت أن يظلوا مُعْرسين بهن تحت الأَراك، ثم يَلُبُّونَ بالحج تَقْطُرُ رؤوسهم؛ قوله مُعْرسين أي مُلِمّين بنسائهم، وهو بالتخفيف، وهذا يدل على أن إلْمام الرجل بأهله يسمى إعراساً أيام بنائه عليها، وبعد ذلك، لأن تمتع الحاج بامرأته يكون بعد بنائه عليها. والمُعَرِّسُ السائق الحاذق بالسياق، فإذا نَشط القوم سار بهم، فإذا كسلوا عَرَّس بهم والمِعْرَسُ: الكثير التزويج.
عرص (مقاييس اللغة) العين والراء والصاد أصلان صحيحان: أحدهما يدلُّ على إظلال شيءٍ على شيء، والآخر يدلُّ على الاضطراب.
العَرْصُ (القاموس المحيط) العَرْصُ: العَرْسُ، والمحدِّثُون يلْحنون فيُعْجِمُون الصاد. وتعَرَّصَ: أقام.
حرص (لسان العرب) الحِرْصُ: شدّةُ الإرادة والشَّرَه إلى المطلوب. وقال الجوهري: الحِرْصُ الجَشَعُ، وقد حَرَصَ عليه يَحْرِصُ ويَحْرُصُ حِرْصا وحَرْصاً وحَرِص حَرَصا؛ وقول أبي ذؤيب: ولقد حَرِصْت بأَن أُدافِعَ عنهمُ، فإِذا المنيّةُ أَقبلَتْ لا تُدْفَعُ عدّاه بالباء لأنه في معنى هممْتُ، والمعروف حَرَصْتُ عليه. الأزهري: قول العرب حَرِيصٌ عليك معناه حَرِيصٌ على نَفْعِك، قال: واللغة العالية حَرَص يَحْرِصُ وأما حرِص يَحْرَصُ فلغة رديئة، قال: والقُراء مُجْمِعون على: ولو حَرَصْت بمؤمنين؛ ورجل حَرِيصٌ من قوم حُرصاءَ وحِراصٍ وامرأَة حَرِيصةٌ من نسوة حِراصٍ وحَرائص. والحَرْصةُ كالعَرْصة، زاد الأزهري: إلا أن الحَرْصةَ مُسْتقَرّ وسط كل شيء والعَرْصةُ الدارُ؛
أزز (لسان العرب) أزَّتِ القِدْرُ تؤُزُّ وتئِزُّ أزّاً وأزِيزاً وأزازاً وائتَزَّتِ ائْتِزازاً إذا اشتدّ غليانها،
عز (مقاييس اللغة) العين والزاء أصلٌ صحيح واحد، يدلُّ على شدّةٍ وقوّة وما ضاهاهما، من غلبةٍ وقهر.
عزز (الصَحاح في اللغة) ويقال: إنَكم معزَزٌ بكم، أي مشدّد بكم، غير مخفّف عنكم.
عزز (لسان العرب) قال: تَعزُّزاً أن لا يدخلها إلا من أرادوا أي تكبُراً وتشدُّداً على الناس، وجاء في بعض نسخ مسلم: تَعزُّراً، براء بعد زاي، من التَّعْزير والتوقير، فإما أن يريد توقير البيت وتعظيمه أو تعظيمَ أنفسهم وتكبُّرهم على الناس. والعِزُّ في الأَصل: القوة والشدة والغلبة. ورجل عَزيزٌ: مَنيع لا يُغْلب ولا يُقْهر. وتعزَّز تشرَّف. وفي حديث عمر، رضي الله عنه: اخْشَوْشِنوا وتمَعْزَزُوا أي تشددوا في الدين وتصلَّبوا، من العِزّ القوّة والشدة، والميم زائدة، كتَمَسْكَن من السكون، وقيل: هو من المَعَز وهو الشدة، وسيجيءُ في موضعه. وعززْتُ القومَ وأَعْزَزْتُهم وعَزَّزْتُهم: قَوَّيْتُهم وشدَّدْتُهم. والعَزّاءُ: الشّدَّةُ. وفي حديث ابن عمر، رضي الله عنه: أن قوماً مُحْرِمين اشتركوا في قتل صيد فقالوا: على كل رجل مِنّا جزاءٌ، فسأَلوا بعضَ الصحابة عما يجبُ عليهم فأمر لكل واحد منهم بكفَارة، ثم سأَلوا ابنَ عمر وأَخبروه بفُتْيا الذي أَفتاهم فقال: إنكم لَمُعَزَّزٌ بكم، على جميعكم شاةٌ، وفي لفظِ آخر: عليكم جزاءٌ واحدٌ، قوله لَمُعَزَّزٌ بكم أي مشدد بكم ومُثَقَّل عليكم الأَمرُ. وفلانٌ مِعْزازُ المرضِ أي شديده. ويقال له إذا مات أيضاً: قد اسْتُعِزَّ به. والعَزَّة، بالفتح: بنت الظَبْية؛ ويقال للعَنْز إذا زُجرت: عَزْعَزْ، وقد عَزْعَزْتُ بها فلم تَعَزْعَزْ أي لم تَتَنَحَّ، والله أعلم.

§ 188.—XXXII, 54-59

ePSD: ummānu
ugnim [ARMY] wr. ugnim "army, troops" Akk. ummānu
ummia [EXPERT] wr. um-mi-a; um-me-a "expert, master craftsman" Akk. ummānu

أمن (لسان العرب) ورجلٌ أَمينٌ وأُمّانٌ أي له دينٌ، وقيل: مأْمونٌ به ثِقَةٌ؛ قال الأعشى: ولَقَدْ شَهِدْتُ التّاجرَ الـ أُمّانَ مَوْروداً شرابُهُ التاجرُ الأُمّانُ، بالضم والتشديد: هو الأَمينُ، وقيل: هو ذو الدِّين والفضل، وقال بعضهم: الأُمّان الذي لا يكتب لأَنه أُمّيٌّ، وقال بعضهم: الأُمّان الزرّاع؛

§ 193.—XXXIII, 10-22

AALD: ṣirītu See zirītu
AALD: zirītu (v.) (ṣirītu) OB Elam معنى غير مؤكد
AALD: wēdu See ēdu
AALD: wedu See edu (adj.)
AALD: ēdu (s.) (wēdu, īdu) وحيد، منفرد
AALD: edû (v.) See idû يُهدي، يُعرَف
AALD: edû (adj.) (wedû) See idû معروف، مُلاحظ

ePSD: edû
zu [KNOW] wr. zu "to know; to learn" Akk. edû; lamādu

زعر (مقاييس اللغة) الزاء والعين والراء أُصيلٌ يدلُّ على سوء خُلُق وقلة خير. فالزَّعارة: شراسة الخُلُق.
زري (مقاييس اللغة) الزاء والراء والحرف المعتل يدلُّ على احتقار الشيء والتهاون به. يقال زريْت عليه، إذا عبْت عليه. وأزرى به، بالألف، إزراءً: قصَّر به وحقَّره وهوَّنه.
صري (لسان العرب) صرَى الشيءَ صرْياً: قطعَه ودفعه؛ ويقال: صرَى الله عنك شرَّ فلان أي دفعه؛ وأنشد ابن بري للطرماح: ولو أنَّ الظعائن عُجْنَ يوماً عليَّ ببطنِ ذي نفر، صراني (قوله «ذي نفر» هكذا في الأصل بهذا الضبط، ولعله ذي بقر). أي دفع عني ووقاني. وصرَيْتُه منعْته؛ قال ابن مقبل: ليس الفؤادُ براءٍ أرضها أبداً، وليس صاريةً منْ ذكرها صار وصرَيْتُ ما بينهم صرْياً أي فصلْتُ. يقال: اختصمنا إلى الحاكم فصرَى ما بيننا أي قطع ما بيننا وفصل. التهذيب في قوله تعالى: فصُرْهُنَّ إليك، قال: فسروه كلهم فصُرْهُنَّ أمِلْهُنَّ، قال: وأما فصِرْهُنَّ، بالكسر، فإنه فسِّر بمعنى قطِّعْهُنَّ، قال: ولم نجد قطِّعْهُنَّ معروفة، قال: وأراها إن كانت كذلك من صرَيْتُ أصْري أي قطعت، فقدِّمت ياؤها وقلب، وقيل: صِرْتُ أصير كما قالوا عثَيْت أعْثي وعِثْت أعيث بالعين، من قولك عِثْتُ في الأرض أي أفسدت.
ود (مقاييس اللغة) الواو والدال: كلمةٌ تدلُّ على محبَّة. وددتُه أحببته. وودِدتُ أنَّ ذاك كان، إذا تمنَّيته، أوَدُّ فيهما جميعاً.
أدي (مقاييس اللغة) الهمزة والدال والياء أصلٌ واحد، وهو إيصال الشيء إلى الشيء أو وصوله إليه من تلقاء نفسه.
هدي (مقاييس اللغة) الهاء والدال والحرف المعتلّ: أصلانِ [أحدهما] التقدُّمُ للإرشاد، والآخر بَعْثة لطف.فالأوّل قولهم: هديتُه الطَّريق هداية، أي تقدمته لأرشده.
هدى (الصّحاح في اللغة) الهُدى: الرشادُ والدلالةُ، يؤنث ويذكَّر. يقال: هداهُ الله للدين هُدى. وقوله تعالى: "أَوَ لَمْ يَهْدِ لَهُمْ"، قال أبو عمرو بن العلاء: أو لم يُبيِّنْ لهم. وهدَيْتُهُ الطريق والبيت هداية، أي عرَّفته، هذه لغة أهل الحجاز، وغيرهم يقول: هدَيْتُهُ إلى الطريق وإلى الدار. وهدى واهْتدى بمعنى.
أدا (لسان العرب) وأدَّى الشيءَ: أوْصله، والاسم الأداءُ. وتأدَّى إليه الخَبرُ أي انْتَهى. ويقال: استأْداه مالاً إذا صادره واستَخْرج منه.

§ 194.—XXXIII, 23-40

ePSD: mušēniqtu
eme [NURSE] wr. eme_2 "wet nurse" Akk. mušēniqtu
emegagu [NURSE] wr. eme_2-ga-gu_7 "wet nurse" Akk. mušēniqtu
emegala [NURSE] wr. eme_2-ga-la_2; |URU×GA|.ME-ga-la_2 "wet nurse" Akk. mušēniqtu
AALD: enēqu (v.) يرضع
AALD: ēniqu (adj.) رضاعة الطفل
ePSD: tulû
ubur [BREAST] wr. ubur; $ubur_2$; u_3-bur; u_2-bi-ur "breast" Akk. tulû
AALD: rikištu See rikistu
AALD: kaşāşu See gaşāşu
ePSD: kaşāşu
gaz [KILL] wr. gaz; gaz_2; kaz_8 "to kill, slaughter; to grind, grate; to beat; to thresh (grain); to execute, impose a death sentence; to break" Akk. dâku; habātu; hašālu; kaşāşu; pa'āşu; šagāšu
guru [GRIND] wr. gur_5 "to grind, grate; to cut up, chop; (to be) trimmed, pruned" Akk. kasāmu; kaşāşu; urrû

نقا (لسان العرب) ونقى العظم نقْياً: استخرج نقْيه. وانْتَقيْتُ العظم إذا استخرجت نِقْيَه أي مخه؛
نقت (الصّحاح في اللغة) نقتُّ المخَ أنْقُتُهُ نقتاً: لغة في نقوْتُه، إذا استخرجته. كأنَهم أبدلوا الواو تاء.
النَقْتُ (القاموس المحيط) النَقْتُ: اسْتِخْراجُ المُخ.
سنق (مقاييس اللغة) السين والنون والقاف فيه كلمةٌ واحدة، وهي السَنَق، وهو كالبَشَم. يقال شرب الفصيل حتى سَنِق. وهو كالتَّخم في الناس.
سنق (لسان العرب) السَنَقُ: البَشَمُ. والسُّنَيْقُ: البقرة؛
بشم (لسان العرب) البَشَم: تُخمةٌ على الدَسَم، وربما بَشِمَ الفَصيلُ من كثرة شُرْب اللبَن حتى يدْقى سَلْحاً فيهلك.
تلع (مقاييس اللغة) التاء واللام والعين أصلٌ واحد، وهو الامتداد والطُّول صُعُداً. والتَّلعة أرض مرتفعة غليظة، وربما كانت عريضة، يتردَّد فيها السَّيل ثم يدفع منها إلى تلعة أسفل منها. والأتلع: الطَّويل العُنُق.
تلع (لسان العرب) تلع النهارُ يَتْلَعُ تَلْعاً وتُلوعاً وأَتْلع: ارْتَفع.
تل (مقاييس اللغة) التاء واللام في المضاعف أصلٌ صحيح، وهو دليل الانتصاب وضدّ الانتصاب.فأمّا الانتصاب فالتلّ، معروف. والتَّليل العُنُق.
تلل (لسان العرب) والتَلُّ من التراب: معروف واحد التِّلال، ولم يفسر ابن دريد التَّل من التراب. ورجل متلٌّ: منتصب في الصلاة؛
الرَّكْسُ (القاموس المحيط) الرَّكْسُ: رَدُّ الشيءِ مَقْلوباً، وقَلْبُ أوله على آخره،

ركس (لسان العرب) الرِّكْسُ: الجماعة من الناس، وقيل: الكثير من الناس، والرِّكْسُ شبيه بالرَّجيع. يقال: رَكَسْتُ الشيء وأَرْكَسْتُه إذا رددْتَه ورَجَعْتَه، وفي رواية: إنه رَكِيس، فعيل بمعنى مفعول؛ ومنه الحديث: اللهم أرْكِسْهما في الفتنة رَكْساً؛ والرَّكْسُ: قلبُ الشيء على رأسه أو ردُّ أوله على آخره؛ وقال شمر: بلغني عن ابن الأعرابي أنه قال المَنْكُوس والمَرْكُوس المُدْبر عن حاله. والرَّكْسُ ردُّ الشيء مقلوباً.

جصص (لسان العرب) الجِصُّ والجَصُّ: معروف، الذي يُطْلى به، وهو معرب، قال ابن دريد: هو الجِصُّ ولم يُقل الجَصّ، وليس الجصّ بعربي وهو من كلام العجم، ولغةُ أهل الحجاز في الجصّ: القصّ.
قصص (الصّحاح في اللغة) وقَصَصْتُ الشَعرَ: قطعته.

§ 195.—XXXIII, 41-44

ePSD: rittu
kišib [HAND] wr. kišib-la$_2$; kišib "hand, wrist" Akk. rittu
silig [HAND] wr. silig$_2$; silig$_4$ "hand; (cupped) hand" Akk. lupnu; qātu; rittu
tibir [HAND] wr. tibir; tibir$_2$; tibir$_4$; tibir$_3$ "hand; fist" Akk. qātu; rittu; upnu

رتا (لسان العرب) رَتا الشيءَ يَرْتُوه رَتْواً: شدَّه وأَرْخاه، ضِدٌّ. ابن الأَعرابي: الرَّتْوُ يكون شدّاً ويكون إِرْخاءً؛ ورتوْتُه ضممْته. ورُتِيَ في ذرْعِه: كَفُتَّ في عَضُدِه. والرَّتْوة العُقْدة الشَدِيدة، والرَّتْوة العُقْدة المسْتَرْخية، ورَتَوْت رمَيْت.

§ 196.—XXXIII, 45-49

AALD: habātu (v.) يخبط، يخطف، يسرق

هبد (لسان العرب) وتَهَبَّد الرجلُ والظَّلِيمُ واهْتَبدا: أَخذاه من شجرته أو استخرجاه للأكل. الأزهري: اهْتبدَ الظليم إذا نقر الحنظل فأكل هَبيدَه؛ ويقال للظليم: هو يَتَهَبَّدُ إذا استخرج ذلك ليأكله. وفي حديث عمر وأَمّه: فَزَوّدَتْنا من الهبيد؛ الهَبيد: الحنظل يكسر ويستخرجُ حبّه ويُنْقَع لتذهب مَرارته ويُتّخذ منه طبيخ يؤكل عند الضرورة.

§ 197.—XXXIII, 50-53

ePSD: šebēru
haš [BREAK] wr. haš "to break off; to break; to divert (water)" Akk. haşābu; šebēru
ePSD: šebēru (v.) (šabāru) يكّسر، يحطم، يهدم، يؤذي

تبر (لسان العرب) والتَّبارُ الهلاك. وتبّره تَتْبيراً أَي كَسَّره وأَهلكه. وهؤلاء مُتَبَّرٌ ما هم فيه أَي مُكسَّرٌ مُهْلَكٌ. وفي حديث عليٍّ، كرّم الله وجهه: عَجْزٌ حاضر ورَأْيٌ مُتَبّر، أَي مهلك. وتَبَّرَهُ هو: كسره وأَذهبه.
رفد (لسان العرب) والتَّرفيدُ: التَّسويدُ. يقال: رُفِّدَ فلان أَي سُوِّد وعظم. والرِّفْدة العُصبة من الناس؛ والمِرْفد: العُظّامةُ تتعظّم بها المرأة الرَّسْحاء. والتَّرْفيدُ: العجيزة: اسم كالتَّمْتِين والتَّنْبيت؛ والرَّافدان: دجلة والفرات؛

§ 202.—XXXIII, 75-81

ePSD: lē'û
a ĝal [STRONG] wr. a$_2$ ĝal$_2$ "to be strong" Akk. lē'û
atuku [POWERFUL] wr. a$_2$-tuku "powerful, able-bodied" Akk. igigallu; lē'û
da [WRITING BOARD] wr. ^{ĝeš}da "writing board" Akk. lē'û
AALD: La'ītu See lītu
AALD: lītu (s.) (lētu) النصر، القوة، القُدرة
ePSD: lētu
te [CHEEK] wr. te "cheek" Akk. lētu
ePSD: mašku
kuš [SKIN] wr. kuš "skin; leather; body; person" Akk. mašku; zumru
ePSD: qinnāzu
usan [WHIP] wr. ^{kuš}usan$_3$; ^{ĝeš}usan$_3$; ^{kuš}u$_4$-za-an "whip" Akk. qinnāzu
ePSD: geštu [60] wr. ge-eš-tu "60"
ePSD: namĝeš [GROUP OF 60] (1x: Old Babylonian) wr. nam-ĝeš$_2$ "group of 60"
ePSD: šuššu
šuš [SIXTH] wr. šuš "one sixth" Akk. šuššu
AALD: šūššīšu (adv.) See šūšī ستون مرة
AALD: šūšī (num) (šūš, šūša, šuššu) ستون

اللَّعْوُ (القاموس المحيط) وذُو لَعْوَة: قَيْلٌ، ورجلٌ آخرُ.
لأو (مقاييس اللغة) اللام والهمزة والحرف المعتلّ كلمتان: إحداهما الشّدَّة، والأخرى حيوان.فالأُولى اللأْواء: الشّدة.
لتا (لسان العرب) ابن الأعرابي: لَتا إِذا نَقص. قال أبو منصور: كأنه مقلوب من لاتَ أو من أَلَتَ.

ليت (لسان العرب) لاته حقه يليته ليتاً، وألاته: نقصه، والأولى أعلى. قال: أليتَ الحقَ أحيله وأصرفُه، ولاته عن أمره ليتا وألاته: صرفه. ولاته ليتاً: أخبره بالشيء على غير وجهه؛ ولاتَه عن وجهه يليته ويلوته ليتاً أي حبسه عن وجهه وصرفه؛
ألت (لسان العرب) الألتُ: الحلفُ. وألته بيمينٍ ألتاً: شدد عليه. وألت عليه: طلب منه حلفاً أو شهادة، يقوم له بها. والألتُ: القسم؛ وألته ماله وحقه يألته ألتاً، وألاته، وآلته إياه: نقصه.
لاتَ (القاموس المحيط) لاتَ الرَجلُ: أخبرَ بغيرِ ما يُسألُ عنه،
لت (مقاييس اللغة) وذُكر عن ابن الأعرابيّ: لَتَّ فلانٌ بفلان، إذا قُرن به. فإن صح فهو من باب الإبدال، كأنَ التاء مبدلة من زاء.
لزز (لسان العرب) لَزَّ الشيءَ بالشيءِ يلُزُّه لزّا وألَزَّه: ألزمه إياه. واللَزَزُ الشدَّةُ. ولَزَّه يلُزُّه لزّا ولزازاً أي شدَّه وألصقه. الليث: اللَّزُّ لزوم الشيء بالشيءِ بمنزلة لزازِ البيت، وهي الخشبة التي يُلَزُّ بها البابُ. واللَزَزُ المترسُ. ولزازُ الباب: نطاقُه الذي يُشدّ به. وكل شيءٍ دُونيَ بين أجزائه أو قُرن، فقد لُزَّ.
ليت (القاموس المحيط) والليتُ، بالكسر: صفحةُ العُنق.
اللِّيتُ (شمس العلوم) اللِّيتان، بالتاء: صفحتا العنق حيث يقع أسفل القرطين، والجميع: اللِّيتة، مثل درص ودرصة.
ليت (تاج العروس) والليتُ، بالكسْر: صفْحةُ العُنق، وقيل: اللِّيتان: أدْنى صفْحتَي العُنق من الرَّأسِ، عليهما ينْحدرُ القُرْطان، وهما وراءَ لهْزمَتي اللَحْيين، وقيل: هما موضعُ المحْجمتين، وقيل: هما ما تحت القُرْط من العُنق، والجمع أليات وليتة، وفي الحديث: يُنْفخُ في الصُّور فلا يسْمعُه أحدٌ إلا أصْغى ليتًا. أي أمالَ صفْحة عُنقه. ولاتَه يليته ويلُوته ليْتا؛ أي حبسه عن وجْهِ وصرفه.
ليت (الصّحاح في اللغة) والليتُ بالكسر: صفْحة العنق، وهما ليتان. ولاتَهُ عن وجهه يلوتُهُ ويليتُه، أي حبسه عن وجهه وصرفه.
ليت (مقاييس اللغة) اللام والياء والتاء كلمتان لا تنقاسان: إحداهما: اللِّيت: صفْحة العُنق، وهما لِيتانِ. والأخرى اللَّيت، وهو النَّقص. يقال: لاته يليتُه: نقصه.
ليت (لسان العرب) واللِّيتُ، بالكسر: صفْحة العُنق؛ وقيل: اللِّيتان صفْحتا العُنق؛ وقيل: أدْنى صفْحتي العُنق من الرأس، عليهما ينْحدرُ القُرْطان، وهما وراء لِهْزمتي اللَّحْييْن؛ وقيل: هما موضع المحْجمتيْن؛ وقيل: هما ما تحْت القُرْطِ من العُنق، والجمع أليات وليتة. وفي الحديث: يُنْفخُ في الصور فلا يسمعُه أحدٌ إلا أصْغى ليتاً أي أمال صفْحة عُنقه.
مسك (لسان العرب) المَسْكُ، بالفتح وسكون السين: الجلد، وخصَّ بعضهم به جلد السَّخْلة، قال: ثم كثر حتى صار كل جلد مسْكاً، والجمع مُسُكٌ ومُسُوك؛ قال سلامة بن جنْدل: فاقْني لعلَّك أن تحْظيْ وتحْتبلي في سحْبلٍ، من مُسوك الضأن، منْجوب ومنه قولهم: أنا في مسْكك إن لم أفعل كذا وكذا. وفي حديث خيبر: أين مسْكُ حُييّ بن أخْطب كان فيه ذخيرة من صامتٍ وحُليّ قُومت بعشرة آلاف دينار، كانت أوّلاً في مسْك جمَلٍ ثم مسْك ثور ثم مسْك جمل. وفي حديث علي، رضي الله عنه: ما كان على فراشي إلاّ مسْكُ كبْشٍ أي جلده.
قنز (لسان العرب) القنْز: لغة في القنص،
قنص (لسان العرب) قنص الصيْد يقْنصُه قنْصاً وقنصاً واقْتنصه وتقنّصه. صاده كقولك صِدْت واصْطدت. وفي حديث علي: قمصتْ بأرْجُلها وقنصتْ بأحْبُلها أي اصطادت بحبائلها.
القنْسُ (القاموس المحيط) وقانسةُ الطَيْر: قانصتُهُ.
قنس (لسان العرب) القنْسُ والقنْس: الأصل؛ وقوْنسُ الفرس: ما بين أُذُنيْه، وقيل: عظم ناتئ بين أذنيه، وقيل: مقدّم رأْسه؛ قال الشاعر: اضْربَ عنك الهُمومَ طارقها، ضرْبك بالسَوْط قوْنس الفرس أراد: اضْربنْ فحذف النون؛ قال ابن بري: البيت لطرفة.

§ 205.—XXXIII, 92-XXXIV, 3

ePSD: uznu; nešmû
<u>ĝizzal</u> <u>[EAR]</u> wr. ĝizzal; $gizzal_2$ "wisdom; understanding; ear; hearing" Akk. hasīsu; uznu; uznu; nešmû
أذن (مقاييس اللغة) الهمزة والذال والنون أصلان متقاربان في المعنى، متباعدان في اللفظ، أحدهما أُذُنُ كلّ ذي أُذن، والآخر العِلْم؛

§ 206.—XXXIV, 4-13

AALD: tamû (v.) (tamā'u) يقسم
AALD: rasābu (v.) See rasibtu يضلّ، يُخطئ، يعمل بغير إتقان
AALD: rasibtu (s.) الخطأ، الاهمال
AALD: rasābu (v.) (rasāpu, raṣāpu, rašāpu) يلكم، يضرب، يصرع، يسحق، يحطم
AALD: risbatu (s.) الشّجار
ePSD: zīmu
<u>muš</u> <u>[FACE]</u> wr. $muš_3$; $muš_2$ "face, appearance" Akk. zīmu
<u>mušme</u> <u>[FACE]</u> wr. $muš_3$-me "face, appearance" Akk. zīmu; būnu
AALD: zīmu (s.) الوهج (للنجوم)، المظهر، الهيئة، الرونق، البهاء
ePSD: simmu
<u>sim</u> <u>[CARBUNCLE]</u> wr. sim_x "carbuncle, skin sore" Akk. simmu
ePSD: $A.ZU_5$
<u>azu</u> <u>[DOCTOR]</u> wr. a-zu; $a\text{-}zu_5$; azu "doctor" Akk. asû
تأم (الصّحاح في اللغة) أتأمت المرأةُ، إذا وضعت اثنين في بطنٍ، فهي مُتْئمٌ. فإذا كان ذلك عادتها فهي مِتْآمٌ، والولدان توْأمان. يقال: هذا توْأمُ هذا وهذه توْأمةُ هذه. والجمع توائمُ. والتوْأمُ: الثاني من سهام الميسر. ويقال: فرسٌ مُتائمٌ، للذي يأتي بجريٍ بعد جريٍ. وثوبٌ مِتْآمٌ، إذا كان سداه ولُحمته طاقين وقد تاءمْتُ مُتاءمةً، إذا نسجته على خيطين خيطين. وأتْأمها، أي أفضاها.

تأم (لسان العرب) وأتْأَمها أي أفضاها؛ وفرس مُتائم: تأتي بجَرْي بَعد جَرْي؛

فضا (لسان العرب) وأفْضى فلانٌ إلى فلانٍ أي وَصَل إليه، وأصله أنه صارَ في فُرْجته وفَضائه وحَيِّزه؛ وأَفْضى إليه الأَمْرُ كذلك.

زمم (الصَّحاح في اللغة) وقومٌ زُمَمٌ، أي شُمَّخٌ بأنوفهم من الكبْر. وداري من داره زَمَمٌ، أي قريبٌ. وقال أعرابيٌّ: لا والذي وجهي زَمَمَ بَيْتِهِ ما كان كذا وكذا، أي تِجاهه وتلقاءه.

زمم (لسان العرب) وزَمَّ برأْسه زَمّاً: رفعه.

سمم (لسان العرب) السَّمُّ والسِّمُّ والسُّمُّ: القاتلُ، وجمعها سِمامٌ. والسامَّةُ: الخاصَّة؛ يقال: كيف السَّامَّةُ والعامَّةُ. وأَهل المَسَمَّة: الخاصَّةُ والأَقارب، وأهلُ المَنْحاة: الذين ليسُوا بالأَقارب. ابن الأعرابي: المَسَمَّةُ الخاصَّةُ، والمَعَمَّةُ العامَّةُ. والسَّمُّ: الثَّقْبُ. وسمُّ كلِّ شيء وسُمُّه: خَرْتُه وثَقْبُه، والجمع سُمُومٌ، ومنه سَمُّ الخِياط. وقال الأصمعي: سُمَّةُ المرأة ثُقْبة فَرْجها. وسُمومُ الإنسانِ والدابة: مَشَقُّ جِلْده (قوله «مشق جلده» الذي في المحكم: مشاق). وسُمُوم الإنسانِ وسِمامُه: فَمُه ومَنْخِرُه وأُذنُه، الواحد سَمٌّ وسُمٌّ؛ وأَصاب سَمَّ حاجته أي مطلبه، وهو بصير بسَمِّ حاجته كذلك. وسَمَمْت سَمَك أي قصدت قصْدك. ويقال: أصبت سَمَّ حاجتك في وجهها. والسَّمُّ: كل شيء كالوَدَع يخرُج من البحر. وسَمَّ شيئاً: أَصلحه. وسَمَمْت الشيءَ أَسُمُّه: أَصلحته. وسَمَمْت بين القوم: أَصْلَحْت؛ وفلان يَسُمُّ ذلك الأمر، بالضم، أي يسبُره وينظر ما غَوْرُهُ. وسَمامةُ الرجُلِ وكلِّ شيء وسَماوتُه: شخصُه، وقيل: سَماوتُه أعلاه. والسَّمامةُ: الشخص؛ قال أبو ذؤيب:وعادية تُلْقِي الثِّياب كأَنَما تُزَعْزِعُها، تحت السَّمامةِ، ريحُ وقيل: السَّمامة الطَّلْعة.

رسب (لسان العرب) الرُّسُوبُ: الذَّهابُ في الماء سُفْلاً. ورَسَبتْ عَيْناه: غارتَا. وسَيْفٌ رَسبٌ ورَسُوبٌ: ماضٍ، يَغيبُ في الضَّريبةِ؛ والرَّسوبُ: الحليم. وفي النوادر: الرَّوْسَبُ والرَّوْسَمُ: الداهيةُ.

رسب (الصَّحاح في اللغة) رسب الشيء في الماء رُسوباً: سَفَلَ فيه.

ضرب (لسان العرب) وضَربَ الوَتدَ يضْرِبُه ضَرْباً: دَقَّه حتى رَسَب في الأرض.

سقط (القاموس المحيط) سَقَطَ سُقوطاً ومَسْقَطاً: وقَع، و~ في كلامه: أخْطأ، و~ القومُ إليَّ: نزلُوا.

سقط (لسان العرب) وسَقَطَ الحَرّ يَسْقُطُ سُقُوطاً: يكنى به عن النزول؛ والسَّقَطُ والسِّقاطُ: الخَطأُ في القولِ والحِساب والكِتاب. وأَسْقَطَ وسَقَطَ في كلامه وبكلامه سُقوطاً: أَخْطأَ. وقد سقَط من يدي وسُقِط في يد الرجلِ: زلَّ وأَخْطأَ، وقيل: ندِمَ. والسَّقَّاطُ: السيفُ يسقُط من وراء الضَّرِيبة يقطعها حتى يجوز إلى الأرض.وسِقْطُ السَّحاب: حيثُ يُرى طرفُه كأنه ساقِطٌ على الأرض في ناحية الأُفُق.

ربس (مقاييس اللغة) الراء والباء والسين أصلٌ واحد ذكره ابن دريد؛ قال: أصل الرَّبْس الضَّرْب باليدين. يقال أصل الرَّبْس الضَّرب؛ يقال ربسه بيديه. قال: ويقولون: داهيةٌ رَبْساء. أي شديدة.

ربس (العباب الزاخر) رَبَس قِرْبَتَهُ رَبْساً: إذا ملأها. وقال ابن دريد: أصْلُ الرَّبْسِ: الضَّرْبُ باليَدين، يقال: رَبَسَهُ بِيَدَيه: إذا ضَرَبَهُ بهما. وداهية رَبْساء: أي شديدة. والرَّبيْس والرَّبْس والرِّبْس: الداهية.

ربس (لسان العرب) الرَّبْسُ: الضرب باليدين. يقال: رَبَسه رَبْساً ضربه بيديه. وفي الحديث: أَ○ن رجلاً جاء إلى قريش فقال: إن أَهل خيبر أسروامحمداً ويريدون أن يرسلوا به إلى قومه ليقتلوه فجعل المشركون يُرْبِسُون به العباس؛ قال ابن الأثير: يحتمل أن يكون من الإِرْباس وهو المُراغمة، أي يُسْمِعُونه ما يُسْخطه ويَغيظُه، وارْبَسَ الرجلُ ارْبِساساً أي ذهب في الأرض. وقيل: ارْبَسَّ إذا غدا في الأرض. وارْبَسَّ أَمرُهم ارْبِساساً: لغة في ارْبَثَّ أي ضَعُفَ حتى تفرقوا. ابن الأعرابي: البِرْباسُ البئر العميقة.

أسو (الصَّحاح في اللغة) الإساءُ، مكسورٌ ممدودٌ: الدواءُ بعينه. والإساءُ: الأطِبَّةُ، جمع الآسي. قال الحطيئة: تواكَلها الأطِبَّةُ والإساءُ. والأَسْوُ: دواء تأسو به الجُرح. وقد أَسَوْتُ الجرحَ آسُوهُ أَسْواً، أي داويته، فهو مأْسوٌّ وأَسِيٌّ أيضاً.

أسو (مقاييس اللغة) الهمزة والسين والواو أصل واحد يدلّ على المداواة والإصلاح، يقال أسوْت الجُرْحَ إذا داويته، ولذلك يسمَّى الطبيب الآسي.

§ 215.—XXXIV, 55-66

ePSD: GIR$_2$.NI

ĝirizal [SCALPEL] wr. ĝiri$_2$-zal; ĝiri$_2$-KAK "scalpel"

ePSD: siparru

zabar [BRONZE] wr. zabar; zabar$_3$ "(to be) bright, pure; arrowhead; weapon; metal mirror; (to be) shiny; measuring vessel made of bronze; a metal bowl; bronze" Akk. ebbu; hutpu; kakku; mušālu; namru; qû; sappu; siparru

ePSD: nagbu

gu [ENTIRETY] wr. gu$_2$ "entirety, sum, total" Akk. nagbu; napharu

idim [SPRING] wr. idim "spring, underground water" Akk. nagbu

جرن (مقاييس اللغة) الجيم والراء والنون أصلٌ واحد، يدلُّ على اللين والسُّهولة. يقال للبَيْدَرِ جرينٌ؛ لأنه مكان قد أُصْلِحَ ومُلِّسَ. ومن الباب جِرَانُ البعير: مُقَدَّم عُنُقه من مَذْبَحِه، والجمع جُرُن. وذكرَ ناسٌ أنّ الجارنَ ولد الحيّة. فإن كان صحيحاً فهو من الباب، لأنه ليِّن المسّ أملس.

جرز (مقاييس اللغة) الجيم والراء والزاء أصلٌ واحد، وهو القطْع. يقال جرَزْتُ الشيءَ قطعتُه. وسيفٌ جُراز أي قطّاع. وأرضٌ جُرُزٌ لا نَبْت بها.

جرز (لسان العرب) والجُرْزُ من السلاح، والجمع الجِرَزَةُ والجُرَزُ. والجُرُزُ العمود من الحديد، معروف عربي، والجمع أَجْرازٌ وجِرَزَةٌ، ثلاثة جِرَزة مثل جُحْر وجِحَرَةٍ؛ قال يعقوب: ولا تقل أَجْرِزَةٌ؛ قال الراجز: والصَّقْعُ من خابطةٍ وجُرْزِ وجَرَزَهُ يَجْرُزُه جَرْزاً: قطعه. وسيف جُرازٌ، بالضم: قاطع، وكذلك مُدْيَةٌ جُرازٌ كما قالوا فيهما جميعاً هُذامٌ. ويقال: سيف جُرازٌ إذا كان مستأْصلاً. والجُرازُ من السيوف: الماضي النافذ.

صفر (مقاييس اللغة) قال الأصمعي: النُّحاس الطَّبيعة والأصل، والنُّحاس هو الصُّفر الذي تعمل منه الآنية، فقال "الصُّفْر"، بضم الصاد. قال أبو عبيدٍ مثلَه، إلاّ أنّه قال الصِّفْر، بكسر الصاد.

نجب (لسان العرب) وإناءٌ مَنْجُوبٌ: واسعُ الجوف، وقيل: واسع القَعْر، وهو مذكور بالفاءِ أيضاً؛ قال ابن سيده: وهو الصواب؛ وقال غيره: يجوز أن تكون الباء والفاء تعاقبتا، وسيأْتي ذكره في الفاءِ أيضاً.

نجف (مقاييس اللغة) النون والجيم والفاء أصلان صحيحان: أحدهما يدلّ على تبسُّطٍ في شيءٍ مكانٍ أو غيره، والآخر يدلّ على استخراج شيء.
النَّجَفُ (القاموس المحيط) والنُّجْفَةُ، بالضم: القليلُ من الشيءِ.
نجف (العباب الزاخر) وانْتِجافُ الشيءِ: استخراجه، يقال: انْتَجَفْتُ الغنم: إذا استخرجْت أقصى ما في الضَّرع من اللبن. وانْتَجفتِ الريح السَّحاب: إذا استفرغَتْه، وكذلك اسْتَنْجَفتْه. والتركيب يدل على تبسُّط في شيء مكان أو غيره؛ وعلى استخراج شيء.
نجف (لسان العرب) والنَّجَفَةُ شبه التلّ؛ النَّجَفة: أرض مُستديرة مشْرِفة، والجمع نَجَفٌ ونِجافٌ. ابن الأعرابي: النجفةُ المُسنَاةُ، والنجَف التلّ. قال الأزهري: والنجفة التي بظَهر الكوفة، وهي كالمُسنَاة تمنع ماء السيل أن يعلو منازل الكوفة ومقابرها.

§ 221.—XXXIV, 95-XXXV, 9

AALD: hāni (s.) in DIŠ-hani (always written DIŠ-ha-ni or DIŠ-ha-a-ni) (معنى غير اكيد) جزء من جسم الحيوان
ePSD: DIŠ
<u>diš</u> <u>[ONE]</u> wr. diš; de-eš-$šu_2$; di-id; di-t- "one" Akk. ištēn
<u>ge</u> <u>[BLOW]</u> wr. ge_{14}; ge_{15}; ge_3; ge_{22}; ge_{23} "blow; wound; stroke of the stylus; (piece of) writing, copy, exemplar, written" Akk. mihiştu; mihiştu; šaţāru
<u>ĝeš</u> <u>[SIXTY]</u> wr. $geš_2$; mu-uš "sixty"
<u>makkaš</u> <u>[LAMENTATION]</u> wr. $makkaš_2$; makkaš "lamentation; clamor, uproar" Akk. ikkillu
<u>saĝtak</u> <u>[TRIANGLE]</u> wr. saĝ-KAK; saĝtak; $santak_3$; $saĝtak_4$; $santak_2$ "triangle (math.); wedge" Akk. santakku
<u>tal</u> <u>[CLAMOR]</u> wr. tal_3; ti-il; tal; tal_4; tal_5; ta-il; til "cry, clamour; battle cry" Akk. ikkillu; tanūqātu; šīsu
ePSD: hamû
<u>dubul</u> <u>[PARALYZE?]</u> wr. du-bu-ul "to paralyse?" Akk. hamû
ePSD: hamû $ša_2$ zumri
<u>hum</u> <u>[PARALYZE]</u> wr. hum "to paralyze (bodies); a blood clot disease (stroke?)" Akk. hamû $ša_2$ zumri; hurpi gig
ePSD: marşu
<u>gig</u> <u>[SICK]</u> wr. gig "(to be) sick; (to be) troublesome" Akk. marāşu; marşu
AALD: şimmu (s.) See simmu المرض

حنن (لسان العرب) الحَنانُ: من أسماء الله عز وجل. قال ابن الأعرابي: الحَنّانُ، بتشديد النون، بمعنى الرحيم، والحَنانُ، بالتخفيف: الرحمة. تقول: حنّ عليه يَحِنُّ حَنانا؛ ويقال: حَنّ عليه أي عطف. وحنَّت القوسُ حنيناً: صوّتت، وأحنّها صاحِبُها. وقوسٌ حَنّانة: تحنّ عند الإنْباض؛ وما حَنَن عني أي ما انثنى ولا قصّرَ؛
حَناهُ (القاموس المحيط) حَناهُ حَنْواً وحنّاهُ: عطفهُ، والحِنْوُ، بالكسر والفتح: كُلُّ ما فيه اعْوجاجٌ من البدن، كعظْم الحَجاج واللَّحْي والضِّلَع والحِنى، ومن غيرهِ كالقَقَفِ والحِقْفِ، وكلُّ عودٍ مُعوجٌ. ج: أحْناءٌ وحنِيٌّ وحُنيٌّ. والحَواني: أطْولُ الأضْلاع كُلُّهنَّ. والحِنايةُ، بالكسر: الانْحناءُ.
حنا (لسان العرب) حَنا الشيءَ حَنْواً وحَنْيا وحنّاهُ: عَطفه؛ وفي حديث معاوية: وإذا ركع أحدُكم فليفرُشْ ذراعيه على فخذيه ولْيَحْنا (* قوله «وليحنا» هي في الأصل ونسخ النهاية المعتمدة مرسومة بالألف)؛ قال ابن الأثير: هكذا جاء في الحديث، فإن كانت بالحاء فهو من حنا ظهره إذا عطفه، وإن كانت بالجيم فهو من جنأ على الشيء أكبّ عليه، وهما متقاربان، قال: والذي قرأناه في كتاب مسلم بالجيم وفي كتاب الحميدي بالحاء. وفي حديث أبي هريرة: إياك والحَنْوةَ، والإقْعاء؛ يعني في الصلاة، وهو أن يُطأطئ رأسه ويُقَوّسَ ظهْره من حَنيْتُ الشيءَ إذا عطفته، وحديثه الآخر: فهل ينْتظِرُ أهْلُ بَضاضَة الشَّبابِ إلا حواني الهَرَم؟ هي جمع حانيَة وهي التي تَحني ظهْرَ الشيخ وتكُبّه. أبو زيد: يقال للمرأة التي تقيم على ولدها ولا تتزوّج قد حنت عليهم تَحْنو، فهي حانيَة، وإذا تزوجت بعده فليست بحانية؛ والحَنيَّةُ: القوس، والجمع حنِيٌّ وحَنايا، وقد حَنَوْتُها أحنوها حنْواً. وحِنْوُ كلّ شيءٍ: اعْوجاجُه. والحِنْوُ: كلّ شيءٍ فيه اعوجاج أو شبْهُ الاعوجاج، كعظْم الحجاج واللحْي والضِّلَع والقَفّ والحِقْفِ ومُنْعرَج الوادي، والجمع أحْناءٌ وحُنيٌّ وحنيٌّ. الأزهري: والحِنْوُ والحجاج العظْم الذي تحت الحاجب من الإنسان؛ وتحنّى الحِنْوُ: اعْوجّ؛ والحَواني: أطول الأضلاع كلّهن، في كل جانب من الإنسان ضِلعان من الحَواني، فهنّ أربعُ أضلُع من الجوانح يلين الواهِنَتين بَعدهما. وناقة حَنْواءُ: حدْباءُ. والحِنو: واحد الأحناء، وهي الجوانب مثل الأعْناء. وحَنوْت عليه أي عطفت عليه. وتَحنّى عليه أي تعطّف مثل تحنّن؛ وفلان أحْنى الناس ضُلوعاً عليك أي أشْفقُهم عليك.
سمم (لسان العرب) السَّمُّ والسُّمُّ والسِّمُّ: القاتلُ، وجمعها سِمامٌ. والسامَّةُ: الخاصّةُ؛ يقال: كيف السَّامَّةُ والعامَّةُ. وأهل المَسمَّةِ: الخاصّةُ والأَقارب، وأهلُ المَنْحاة: الذين ليسُوا بالأقارب. ابن الأعرابي: المَسمَّةُ الخاصّةُ، والمَعمَّةُ العامَّةُ. والسَّمُّ: الثَّقْبُ. وسمّ كلّ شيء وسُمُّه: خَرْتُه وثَقْبُه، والجمع سُمُومٌ، ومنه سَمُّ الخِياط. وقال الأصمعي: سَمَّةُ المرأة ثَقْبة فَرْجِها. وسُمومُ الإنسانِ والدابة: مَشقُّ جِلْده (قوله «مشق جلده» الذي في المحكم: مشاق). وسُمُوم الإنسانِ وسِمامُه: فمُه ومَنْخِرُه وأذنُه، الواحد سَمٌّ وسُمٌّ؛ وأصاب سَمَّ حاجته أي مطلبه، وهو بصير بِسَمّ حاجته كذلك. وسمَمْت سَمَك أي قصدت قصْدك. ويقال: أصبت سَمَّ حاجتك في وجهها. والسَّمُّ: كل شيء كالوَدع يخرُج من البحر. وسَمَّ شيئاً: أصلحه. وسمَمْت الشيءَ أسُمُّه: أصلحته. وسَمَمْت بين القوم: أصْلَحْت؛ وفلان يسُمُّ ذلك الأمر، بالضم، أي يسبُره وينظر ما غَوْرُهُ. وسَمامةُ الرجُلِ وكلّ شيء وسماوتُه: شخصُه، وقيل: سَماوتُه أعلاه. والسَّمامةُ: الشخص؛ قال أبو ذؤيب:وعاديَة تُلْقِي الثِّيابَ كأنّما تُزَعْزِعُها، تحت السَّمامةِ، ريحٌ وقيل: السَّمامة الطَّلْعة.
ضم (مقاييس اللغة) الضاد والميم أصلٌ واحدٌ يدلُّ على مُلاءمةٍ بين شيئين. يقال ضممت الشَّيءَ إلى الشيء فأنا أضُمُّه ضمّاً.
ضمم (الصّحاح في اللغة) ضَمَمْتُ الشيءَ إلى الشيء فانْضَمّ إليه، وضامَّهُ وتضامّ القومُ، إذا انْضمّ بعضهم إلى بعض. واضْطمَت عليه الضلوعُ، أي اشتملتْ. والإضمامة من الكتب: الإضبارة، والجمع الأضاميم، ويقال فلان بإضمامة من كتب والإضْمامَةُ: الجماعةُ.

ضمم (لسان العرب) الضَمُّ: ضَمُّكَ الشيءَ إلى الشيءِ، وقيل: قَبْضُ الشيءِ إلى الشيءِ، وضمَّه إليه يضُمُّه ضماً فانضمَ وتضامَ. تقول: ضممْتُ هذا إلى هذا، فأنا ضامٌ وهو مَضْموم. الجوهري: ضَمَمْتُ الشيءَ إلى الشيءِ فانْضمَ إليه وضامَّهُ. واضْطمَّتْ عليه الضُلُوعُ أي اشْتملت. والضُمامُ: كلُّ ما ضُمَّ به شيءٌ إلى شيءِ وأصْبحَ مُنْضماً أي ضامرا كأنه ضُمَّ بعضُه إلى بعض. وضامَمْتُ الرجلَ: أقمت معه في أمر واحد مُنْضماً إليه. وضَمَّ على المال وضَمْضَم: أخذه كُلَّه. الأُمويُّ: يقال للرجل البخيل الضَرِّزُ، بتشديد الزاي، والضُماضِمُ والعَضَمَّرُ كُلُّه من صفة البخيل، قال: وهو الصُوتنُ على فُعلن أيضاً. ابن الأعرابي: الضَمْضَمُ الجسيمُ الشُجاعُ، بالضاد، والصَمْصَمُ البخيل النهاية في البُخْل، بالصاد.
صم (مقاييس اللغة) الصاد والميم أصلٌ يدلُ على تضامِّ الشيءِ وزوالِ الخرْق والسَمّ. من ذلك الصَمَم في الأذن. يقال صَمِمْت، وأنت تَصَمُّ صمما. وربّما قالوا صُمَّ بمعنى صَمّ.
الصَمّمُ (القاموس المحيط) والصَميمُ: العظْمُ الذي به قِوامُ العُضْو، وبُنْك الشيءِ وخالِصُه،
صمم (لسان العرب) وصَمَّ رأْسَ القارورةَ يصُمُّه صَماً وأصمَّه: سَدَّه وشَدَّه، وصِمامُها: سِدادُها وشِدادُها. والصَمَمُ في الحجَر: الشِدَّةُ، وفي القَناة الاكتِناز. وحَجرٌ أصَمُّ: صُلْبٌ مُصْمَتٌ. والصَميمُ: العَظْمُ الذي به قِوامُ العُضْو كصَميم الوَظِيف وصَميم الرأْس؛

§ 227.— XXXV, 43-55

ePSD: dâşu
<u>a dar</u> [<u>CONFISCATE</u>] wr. a_2 dar "to confiscate, seize illegally; to sequester; to take hold of" Akk. dâşu
<u>a ĝar</u> [<u>DEFEAT</u>] wr. a_2 ĝar; a_2 $ĝa_2$-$ĝa_2$; a_2 $ĝal_2$ "to defeat" Akk. dâşu
<u>sig</u> [<u>FLATTEN</u>] wr. sig_{10} "to flatten, lay flat; to disrespect" Akk. dâşu; sapānu
AALD: dâşu (v.) (See dā'işu, dāştu) dâşu يهين، يعامل بدون عدالة، يخدع، يغش
دَوَّصَ (القاموس المحيط) دَوَّصَ تَدْويصاً: نزلَ من عُلْيا إلى سُفْلى.
ديص (الصّحّاح في اللغة) داصَ يَديصُ دَيَصاناً، أي راغَ وحادَ. ورجلٌ دَيّاصٌ، إذا كان لا يُقْدَرُ عليه. والدائِصُ: اللصُّ، الجمع الداصَةُ.
والانْدِياصُ: انْسِلالُ الشيءِ من اليد. ويقال: انْداصَ فلانٌ علينا بشرِّه، وإنَّه لَمُنْداصٌ بالشرِّ.
ديص (لسان العرب) وانْداصَ علينا فلانٌ بالشَرِّ: انْهجَمَ. وإنه لَمُنْداصٌ بالشرِّ أي مُفاجِئٌ به وقّاع فيه. والدَّيْصُ نَشاطُ السائس.
وداصَ الرجلُ إذا خَسَّ بعد رِفْعة. والداصةُ: السَفِلةُ لكثْرة حركتهم، واحدُهم دائصٌ؛ عن كراع. والدائصُ: اللّصُّ، والدَّيّاص: الشديدُ العضَل.
الأَصمعي: رجل دَيّاصٌ إذا كُنت لا تقدر أن تقبضَ عليه من شدة عَضَلِه. الجوهري: رجل دَيّاصٌ إذا كان لا يُقْدَرُ عليه؛ وأنشد ابن بري لأبي النجم: ولا بذاك العضَلِ الدَّيّاصِ.
راغَ (القاموس المحيط) راغَ الرجلُ والثَعلَبُ رَوْغاً ورَوَغاناً: مالَ وحادَ عن الشيءِ، وأخَذَتْني بالرُّوَيْغَة: بالحيلَة، من الرَوْغ. والمُراوَغَةُ: المصارعة،

§ 228.— XXXV, 56-63

AALD: šār (num.) (see šuššār) المجموع الكلي. (2 3600 (1
ePSD: šuklulu
<u>sub</u> [<u>COAT</u>] wr. sub_6 "to complete, perfect; to coat" Akk. šuklulu
<u>šu du</u> [<u>COMPLETE</u>] wr. šu du_7 "to complete, perfect; to be in working order (of tools)" Akk. šuklulu
<u>šudu</u> [<u>EQUIPPED</u>] wr. šu-du_7; $šita_4$ "fully equipped, in full working order" Akk. šuklulu
سأر (العين) السَأر من السُؤر، تقول: أسأر فلانٌ طعامه وشرابه، أي: أبْقى منه بقيّةً، وبقية كلّ شَيْءٍ: سؤْرُه، وأسأر الحاسب، أي: حسب فأفضل من حسابه شيئًا، وفي الشِعْر أجود لقلّة استعماله، قال: في هجمةٍ يَسأر منها الفائض أي: يفضلُ الفائض من حساب المائة، لأنّه إذا بلغ إلى تسعة وتسعين لم يقدر على قبض الفضل لتمام المائة.
السُورُ (مقاليد العلوم) السُورُ (في علم المنطق): اللَفظ الدَال على بيَان كُلية أَفْرَاد مَا عَلَيْه الحكم.
السور في القضية (تعريفات الجرجاني) هو اللفظ الدال على كمية أفراد الموضوع.
سور (تاج العروس) والسُورةُ مِن القُرآن: معروف أي مَعْرُوفَةٌ، لأَنها مَنْزِلَةٌ بعد مَنْزِلَة، مَقْطوعةٌ عن الأُخْرَى. وقال أبو الهَيْثَم: والسُورةُ من القُرْآنِ عِنْدنا: قِطْعَةٌ من القرآن سَبَقَ وُحْدانُها جَمْعَها، كما أنَ الغُرْفَةَ سابِقَةٌ للغُرَف، وأَنزلَ الله عزّ وجلَ القُرْآن على نَبيِّه صلى الله عليه وسلم شَيْئًا بعد شَيْءٍ، وجَعلَه مُفصّلاً، وبيَّن كلَّ سورة [منها] بخاتمتِها، وبادِئتِها، ومَيّزَها من التي تَلِيهَا. قال الأَزْهَرِيّ: وكأَنَّ أبا الهَيْثَم جعل السُورَةَ من سُوَر القرآن من أَسْأَرْتُ سُؤْرًا؛ أي أَفضَلْت فضْلاً، إلّا أنها لما كثُرت في الكلام وفي القُرآن تُرِك فيها الهَمْز، كما تُرِكَ في المَلَك. والسُور العَلامَةُ، عن ابن الأعرابيّ. وسُورةُ كُلّ شيْءٍ: حَدُّه، عن ابن الأَعْرابيّ.
سأر (لسان العرب) السُؤْرُ بَقِيَّة الشيء، وجمعه أسآرٌ، وسُؤْرُ الفأْرةِ وغيرها؛ وأَسْأَر منه شيئاً: أَبْقَى. والسَائِرُ: الباقي، وكأَنه من سَأَرَ يَسْأَرُ فهُو سائِر. والسائر، مهموز: الباقي؛
السُؤْرُ (القاموس المحيط) والسائِرُ: الباقي لا الجميعُ، كما تَوَهَّمَ جَماعاتٌ، أو قد يُسْتَعْمَلُ له.
سرر (لسان العرب) والمِسَرَّةُ: الآلَةُ التي يُسارُّ فيها كالطُومار.
طمر (لسان العرب) والمِطْمَرُ: الزِّيجُ الذي يكون مع البنَّائين. والمِطْمَرُ والمِطْمارُ: الخيط الذي يُقدَّر به البنَاء البناء، يقال له التَّرْقال بالفارسية. والطُومارُ واحدُ المطامِير (* قوله: «والطومار واحد المطامير» هكذا في الأصل والمناسب أن تقول والمطمار واحد المطامير أو يقول والطومار واحد الطوامير). ابن سيده: الطامُورُ والطُومارُ الصحيفةُ، قيل: هو دَخيل، قال: وأُراه عربيّاً محضاً لأن سيبويه قد اعتدّ به في الأبنية فقال: هو ملحق بفُسْطاط، وابن كانت الواو بعد الضمة، فإنما كان ذلك لأن موضع المدَ إنما هو قُبيل الطرَف مُجاوراً له، كألِف عِمادٍ وياء عَمِيدٍ وواو عَمُود، فأَما واوُ طُومار فليست للمدَ لأنها لم تُجاور الطرَف، فلما تقدمت الواو فيه ولم تجاور طرفه قال: إنه مُلْحق، فلو بَنَيْتَ على هذا من سأَلت مثْل طُومار ودِيماسٍ لَقُلْت سُوْآل وسِيْآل، فإن خَفَفْتَ الهمزة أَلقيت حركتها على الحرف الذي قبلها، ولم تخش ذلك فقلت سُوال وسِيال، ولم تُجْرِهما

مُجْرى واو مقْرُوءة وياء خطيئة في إبدالك الهمزة بعدهما إلى لفظهما وإدغامك إيَاهما فيهما، في نحو مقْرُوة وخطيَة، فلذلك لم يُقلْ سُوَال ولا سِيَال أعْني لتقدُمها وبُعْدها على الطَرفِ ومشابهةِ حرف المد.
زيج (لسان العرب) الزِيجُ: خَيْطُ البَنَاءِ وهو المِطْمَرُ، فارسي معرَب؛ قال الأصمعي: لست أدري أعربي هو أم معرَب؟
شكل (مقاييس اللغة) الشين والكاف واللام مُعظمُ بابه المُماثلة. تقول: هذا شَكل هذا، أي مِثله. ال الكسائيَ: أشكلَ النخْل، إذا طابَ رُطَبُه وأدرَك. وهذا أيضاً من الباب؛ لأنَه قد شاكل التَمر في حلاوته ورُطوبته وحُمرته. فأمَا قولُهم: شكلت الكتاب أشكُله شكْلاً، إذا قيدْته بعلامات الإعراب فلستُ أحْسبه من كلام العرب العاربة، وإنما هو شيءٌ ذكره أهلُ العربيَة، وهو من الألقاب المولَدة.
شكل (الصِحاح في اللغة) وتشكَلَ العنبُ: أينع بعضُه. وشكلْتُ الكتاب أيضاً، أي قيَدته بالإعراب. ويقال أيضاً: أشكلْتُ الكتاب بالألف، كأنَك أزلت به عنه الإشْكالَ والالتباسَ وهذا نقلته من غير سماع. والمُشاكلَةُ: الموافقةُ. والتَشاكُلُ مثله.
الشَكْلُ (القاموس المحيط) الشَكْلُ: الشَبهُ، والمِثْلُ، ويُكْسرُ، وما يُوافقُك ويصلُحُ لك، تقولُ: هذا من هواي ومن شَكْلي،
شكل (لسان العرب) الشَكْلُ، بالفتح: الشَبْه والمِثْل، والجمع أشكالٌ وشُكُول؛ وتَشَكَلَ العِنَبُ: أَيْنَع بعضُه. المحكم: شَكَّل (قوله «المحكم شكل إلخ» في القاموس: شكل العنب مخففاً ومشدداً وتشكل) العِنبُ وتَشَكَلَ اسْوَدَ وأَخَذَ في النُضج؛ وشكل الكِتابَ يشْكُله شكْلاً وأَشْكَله: أعجمه.

§ 229.— XXXV, 64-73

AALD: maqātu (v.) ينهار، يسقط، يسقط في معركة، يهاجم، يغزو، يدمر، يقلل، ينقص
ePSD: qatû
<u>til</u> <u>[COMPLETE]</u> wr. til; til_3 "(to be) complete(d); (to be) old, long-lasting; to end" Akk. gamāru; labāru; qatû
<u>zal</u> <u>[PASS]</u> wr. zal "to get up early; to finish, come to an end; to dissolve, melt, disintegrate, break down, collapse; to quake; to pass time" Akk. naharmumu; naharmuţu; qatû; râbu
بكت (لسان العرب) بكته يَبْكُته بَكْتاً، وبكَته: ضربه بالسيف والعصا ونحوهما.
بكته (القاموس المحيط) بكته: ضربه بالسَيف والعصا، واستقبله بما يكْرهُ، كبكَته. والتَبكيتُ: التَقْريعُ، والغلبةُ بالحُجَة.
بقط (لسان العرب) وبقطَ الشَيءَ: فرَقه. ابن الأعرابي: القَبْطُ الجمع، والبقْطُ التفْرقةُ. والبقْطُ ما سقط من التمر إذا قُطع يُخطِئُه المخْلبُ، والمِخلبُ المِنجلُ بلا أسنان.
كتت (لسان العرب) كَتَتِ القِدْرُ والجرَةُ ونحوُهما تكِتُ كَتِيتاً إذا غلَت، وهو صوتُ الغليان؛ والكَتيتُ: صوتُ البَكْر، وهو فوق الكشيش. وكتَ البَكْرُ يكِتُ كَتَاً وكتيتاً إذا صاح صياحاً لَيناً، وهو صوتٌ بين الكشيش والهدير. وقيل: الكتيتُ ارتفاع البكر عن الكشيش، وهو أَوَل هديره. وكتَ القوم يكُتُهم كتَاً: عدَهم وأحصاهم، وأكثرُ ما يستعملونه في النفي، يقال: أتانا في جيش ما يُكتُ أي ما يُعلَمُ عددُهم ولا يُحصَى؛ قال: إلاَ بجيْش، ما يُكتُ عديدُه، سُودِ الجُلودِ، من الحديد، غِضاب وفي المثل: لا تكُته أو تكُتَ النجومَ أي لا تعُدُه ولا تُحصيه. ابن الأعرابي: جيْشٌ لا يُكتُ أي لا يُحصَى، ولا يُسهَى أي لا يُحزَرُ، ولا يُنكفُ أي لا يُقطعُ. وفي حديث حُنين: قد جاء جيش لا يُكتُ، ولا يُنكفُ أي لا يُحصى، ولا يُبلَغُ آخرُه. والكتُ: الإحْصاءُ. وفعل به ما كَتَه أي ما ساءه. ورجل كتٌ: قليلُ اللحم؛ والكَتِيتُ والكَتْكتَةُ: المَشْيُ رُوَيْدا.
قتت (لسان العرب) وقولٌ مقْتُوتٌ: مكذوبٌ؛ قال رؤبة: قُلْتُ، وقولي عِنْدهُمْ مقْتُوتٌ أي كَذبٌ؛ وقيل: مقْتُوتٌ مُوَشًى به، منْقولٌ؛ وقتَ أثَرهُ يقُتُه قتَا: قصَه. وتقتَتَ الحديثَ: تتبَعه، وتسمَعه، وقيل: إن القتَ، الذي هو النميمةُ، مُشتقٌ منه. وقتَ الشَيءَ يقُتُه قتَا: هيَأه. وقتَه: قلَله. واقْتَتَهُ: استأصلَه؛
مقت (لسان العرب) ابن سيده: المقْتُ أشدُ الإبْغاض. مقُت مقاتَةً، ومقته مقْتاً: أبْغضه، فهو ممْقُوتٌ ومقيتٌ، ومقَته؛
القطُ (القاموس المحيط) القطُ: القطْعُ عامَةً أو عرْضاً، أو قطْعُ شيءٍ صُلْب كالحُقَة، وتقطْقطت الدَلْوُ: انْحدرت،
مقط (مقاييس اللغة) الميم والقاف والطاء كلماتٌ لا ترجع إلى قياسٍ واحد، بل هي متباينةٌ جدَاً. فالمِقاط: حبلٌ شديد الإغارة. والمَقْط ضرْبك بالكُرة على الأرض ثم تأخذها إذا نزلتْ. قال: ومقطْتُ صاحبي أمقُطه، إذا غظته.
مقط (القاموس المحيط) مقطَ عُنُقه يمقِطُها ويمقُطُها: كسرها، و~ فلاناً: غاظه، أو ملأه غيْظاً، وقد مقط مُقُوطاً: هُزِل شديداً، ومقطه تَمقيطاً: صرعه. وامْتقطه: اسْتخْرجه.
مقط (لسان العرب) مَقَط عُنُقه يمقُطها ويمْقطها مقْطاً: كسرها. ومقطْتُ عُنُقه بالعصا ومقرْته إذا ضربته بها حتى ينكسر عظم العنق والجلد صحيح. ومقط الرجل يمْقطه مقْطاً: غاظه، وقيل: ملأه غيْظاً. قال: مقطْت صاحبي مَقْطاً وهو أن تبْلغ إليه في الغيْظِ، ويروى بالعين، وقد تقدَم. قيل: والمقط الشَدَة، وهو ماقطٌ شديد، والهمطُ: الظُلْم. ومقط الرجلَ مقْطاً ومقط به: صرعه؛ الأخيرة عن كراع. ومقط الكرة يمْقُطها مقْطاً: ضرب بها الأرض ثم أخذها. والماقطُ: الضَارب بالحصى المُتكهِن الحازي. والماقِطُ من الإبل: مثل الرَازم، وقد مقط يمقُط مُقوطاً أي هُزِلَ هُزالاً شديداً.
الفراء: الماقِطُ البعير الذي لا يتحرَكُ هُزالاً.
مكت (تاج العروس) مَكتَ، أَهمله الجوهريَ، وقال ابنُ دريد: مكتَ بالمكان أقام، كمكَد به، وقيل: إنَها لُثْغة، وقيل: أُبدلت المُثنَاةُ من المُثَلَثة، قاله شيخُنا .ويُقال: اسْتمْكتتِ البثْرةُ، إذا امْتلأتْ قيْحاً، وهو قولُ ابن الأعرابيَ، نقله الأزهريَ في التهذيب في آخر ترجمة متك وهذا نصُه: يُقال: اسْتمْكت العُدُ فافْتحْهُ، والعُدُ: البثْرةُ، واستِمْكاتُها: أنْ تمْتلِيءَ قيْحاً، وفتْحُها: شقُها وكسْرُها. كذا في اللسان.
مكت (لسان العرب) مكَت بالمكان: أقام، كمكَد؛ الأزهري في آخر ترجمة مكت. ابن الأعرابي: يقال استَمْكت العُدُ فافتحْه؛ والعُدُ: البثْرة، واستِمْكاتُها: أن تَمْتلئَ قيحاً، وفتْحُها: شقُها وكسْرُها.

§ 233.— XXXV, 93-XXXVI, 3

ePSD: esēpu
<u>šab</u> <u>[TRIM]</u> wr. šab "to inspect exta; to incise; to draw, design; to gather together, collect, scrape up; to break off, deduct; to trim, peel off; to dig, hollow out; to have a grooved shape; to cut, fell (of trees); to become loose, fall out; to disintegrate; to disappear; to make clear" Akk. barû ša uzu; esēpu;

harāru; harāşu; harāşu; eşēru; harāşu; šarāmu; nakāsu; šahāhu
<u>šu sub</u> [GATHER UP] wr. šu su-ub "to gather up, to collect, to scrape together" Akk. esēpu
ePSD: eşēpu
<u>tab</u> [DOUBLE] wr. tab; tab_4 "to double; to repeat; companion, partner" Akk. eşēpu; tappû
ePSD: aşābu
<u>tah</u> [ADD] wr. tah "to add, increase" Akk. aşābu
AALD: eşēpu See esēpu
AALD: eşēpu (v.) See aşābu يجمع، يضيف
AALD: aşābu (v.) (aşāpu, waşābu, uşābu) يجمع، يضيف، يوسَع، يُضيف، يُزيد في الحجم والعدد، يُكبر
ePSD: qatāpu ša karāni
<u>šu gur</u> [PICK] wr. šu gur "to pick grapes" Akk. qatāpu ša karāni
AALD: qatāpu (v.) (qaţāpu) يقطف، يجني، ينتف، يقلّم خشب، يفكك
ePSD: igāru
<u>egar</u> [WALL] wr. e_2-gar_8; ba-ar; ba_9-ar_2 "wall" Akk. igāru
<u>izid</u> [WALL] wr. iz-zi; i-zi "wall; wave" Akk. agû; igāru
ePSD: egēru
<u>gilim</u> [CROSS] wr. gilim; $gilib_x$(|GI%GI|)^{ib}; gi_{16}-il; gil-gil^{il} "to lie across; to be entwined; to entwine, twist; to block; (to be) difficult to understand" Akk. egēru; parāku
AALD: igāriš (adv.) مثل حجارة، مثل جدار
AALD: igartu (s.) الحجارة، الجدار او السور
AALD: igāru (s.) الحجارة، جدار للبناء، السور الدائري، جانب السفينة

حسب (مقاييس اللغة) الحاء والسين والباء أصول أربعة:فالأول: العدّ. وفلان حسَنُ الحِسْبة بالأمر، إذا كان حسَن التدبير؛ وليس من احتساب الأجر. والأصل الثاني: الكِفاية. تقول شيء حِسَابٌ، أي كافٍ. ويقال: أحسَبْتُ فلاناً، إذا أعطيته ما يرضيه؛ وكذلك حسَّبْته. والأصل الثالث: الحُسْبَانُ، وهي جمع حُسبانةٍ، وهي الوسادة الصغيرة. ومن هذا الأصل الحُسْبان: سهامٌ صغار يُرْمى بها عن القسيّ الفارسية، الواحدة حُسبانة.
حسف (مقاييس اللغة) الحاء والسين والفاء أصلٌ واحد، وهو شيءٌ يتقشّر عن شيء ويسقط.
عسب (مقاييس اللغة) لعين والسين والباء كلماتٌ ثلاثٌ متفرّدة بمعناها، لا يكاد يتفرّع منها شيء. فالأولى: طَرْق الفرَسِ وغيرِه، والثانية عَسِيب الذَّنب، والثالثة نوعٌ من الأشياء التي تطير.
عسب (لسان العرب) والعَسْبةُ والعَسِبةُ والعسِيبُ: شقٌّ يكون في الجبل.
عصب (مقاييس اللغة) العين والصاد والباء أصلٌ صحيحٌ واحد يدلُّ على رَبْط شيءٍ بشيء، مستطيلاً أو مستديراً. ومن الباب: العَصّاب: الغزّال، وهو القياس لأنَ الخيط يُعصَب به. قال:والشجرة تُعْصَب أغصانُها لينتثِر ورقُها. وقال ابن أحمر: يا قوم ما قومي على نأيهمَ إذْ عَصَبَ النَّاس جَهامٌ وقَرّ أي جمَعهم وضمَّهم. واليوم العصيب: الشّديد. واعصوصَبَ اليومُ: اشتدّ. ويوم عصبْصَبٌ واعْصَوْصَبَتْ: تجمَّعتْ. قال أبو زيد: كلُّ شيءٍ بشيء فقد عَصَب به.
عصب (لسان العرب) وعَصَبَ الشيءَ يَعْصِبُه عَصْباً: طَواه ولَواه؛ وقيل: شدّه.
عظب (لسان العرب) عَظَبَ الطَّائرُ يَعْظِبُ عَظْباً: حرّكَ زِمِكّاهُ بسُرْعة. وقال مُبْتكرٌ الأعرابي: عَظَب فلانٌ على ماله، وهو عاظِبٌ، إذا كان قائماً عليه، وقد حَسُن عُظوبُه عليه. والـمُعَظَّبُ والـمُعْظَبُ: الـمُعَوَّدُ للرِّعْيَةِ والقيام على الإبل، الملازمُ لعمله، القويُّ عليه، وقيل: اللازم لكل صَنْعة.
الوصَبُ (القاموس المحيط) ووَصَبَ يصِبُ وُصوباً: دامَ، وثبتَ، كأوْصَبَ، و~ على الأمْرِ: واظَبَ، وأحْسَنَ القِيامَ عليه.
وظب (مقاييس اللغة) الواو والظاء والباء: كلمةٌ تدلُّ على مداومة. يقال: وَظَبَ يَظِبُ وَظْباً. ووَاظَبْتُ على الشّيءِ مُواظبةً، وهي المداومة.
وظف (مقاييس اللغة) الواو والظاء والفاء: كلمة تدلُّ على تقدير شيء. يقال: وظَّفْتُ له، إذا قدّرتَ له كلَّ حينٍ شيئاً من رزقٍ أو طعام.
ضيف (لسان العرب) وأضفت الشيء إلى الشيء أي أملْته، والنحويون يسمون الباء حرف الإضافة، وذلك أنك إذا قلت مررت بزيد فقد أضفت مرورك إلى زيد بالباء.
وصف (مقاييس اللغة) والصِّفَة الأمارة اللاّزِمةُ للشّيء، كما يقال وَزَنْتُه وَزْناً، والزِّنَة: قَدْرُ الشَّيء.
قطف (مقاييس اللغة) القاف والطاء والفاء أصلٌ صحيح يدلُّ على أخْذِ ثمرةٍ من شجرة،
قطف (لسان العرب) قطَف الشيءَ يَقْطِفُه قَطْفاً وقَطفاناً وقَطافاً وقِطافاً؛ عن اللحياني: قطعه. وأَقْطَف العِنَبُ: حان أن يُقْطَف. وأَقْطَفَ الكَرْمُ: دنا قِطافه. والقَطْف الخَدْشُ، وجمعه قُطوفٌ. قطفه يَقْطِفه قَطْفاً وقطَفه: خدشه؛ وقطَف الماءَ في الخَمْر: قطَره؛
قطب (لسان العرب) قطبَ الشيءَ يَقْطِبُهُ قَطْباً: جَمعه. وقطَّب ما بين عينيه أي جمعَ كذلك.
قتب (لسان العرب) القِتْبُ والقَتَبُ: إكافُ البعير، وقد يؤنث، والتذكير أعم، ولذلك أنثوا التصغير، فقالوا: قُتيبة. وأقْتب البعيرَ إقْتاباً إذا شَدَّ عليه القَتَبَ. والقَتوب: الرَّجل الـمُقْتَبُ. التهذيب: أَقْتَبْتُ زيداً يميناً إقتاباً إذا غَلَّظْتَ عليه اليمين، فهو مُقْتَبٌ عليه. ويقال: ارْفِقْ به، ولا تُقْتِبْ عليه في اليمين؛ قال الراجز: إليك أشْكو ثِقْل دينٍ أقتبا ظَهْري بأقْتابٍ تَركْن جُلبا ابن سيده: القِتْبُ والقَتَبُ: الـمِعَى، أُنثى، والجمع أقْتابٌ؛ وهي القِتْبةُ، بالهاء، وتصغيرها قُتَيبةٌ.
الأجُرُ (القاموس المحيط) والإجَارُ: السَّطْحُ، كالإنْجار، والأُجورُ واليأجُورُ والآجُرُون والأُجُرُّ والآجُرُ والآجُرُ: طبيخُ الطين، الواحدة، بالهاء، أُجُرَةٌ وآجُرَةٌ وآجرَةٌ؛ أبو عمرو: هو الآجُر، مخفف الراء، وهي الآجُرة. وقال غيره: آجرٌ وآجُورٌ، على فاعُول، وهو الذي يبنى به، فارسي معرّب. قال

الكسائي: العرب تقول آجَرَة وآجَرَ للجمع، وآجرة وجمعها آجَرٌ، وأجُرَةٌ وجمعها أجُرٌ، وآجُورةٌ وجمعها آجُورٌ. والإجَارُ: السَّطح، بلغة الشام والحجاز، وجمع الإجَار أجاجيرُ وأجاجرةٌ. ابن سيده: والإجَار والإجَارةُ سطح ليس عليه سُترةٌ. وفي الحديث: من بات على إجَار ليس حوله ما يرُدّ قدميه فقد برئتْ منه الذمّةُ. الإجَارُ، بالكسر والتشديد: السطحُ الذي ليس حوله ما يرُدّ الساقطَ عنه. وفي حديث محمد بن مسلمةَ: فإذا جارية من الأنصار على إجَار لهم؛ والأنجارُ، بالنون: لغة فيه، والجمع الإناجيرُ. وفي حديث الهجرة: فتلقى الناسُ رسولَ الله، صلى الله عليه وسلم، في السوق وعلى الأجاجير والأناجير؛ يعني السطوح، والصوابُ في ذلك الإجار. ابن السكيت: ما زال ذلك إجّيراهُ أي عادته.

حجر (مقاييس اللغة) والحَجَر معروف، وأحسَب أنّ البابَ كلَّه محمولٌ عليه ومأخوذ منه، لشدّته وصلابته. وقياسُ الجمْع في أدنى العدد أحجار، والحجارة أيضاً له قياس، كما يقال: جمل وجمالة، وهو قليل. والحاجِرُ: ما يُمسك الماءَ من مكانٍ منْهبط، وجمعه حُجْرانٌ.

الحَجْرُ (القاموس المحيط) ونشأ في حجْره وحِجْره، أي: في حفْظه وسِتْره.

حجر (الصّحاح في اللغة) والحَجْرةُ حظيرة الإبل؛ ومنه حُجرة الدار. تقول: احتجَرتُ حجرةً، أي اتخذتها. والجمع حُجَرٌ، وحُجَراتٌ. وكُلُّ ما حجَرتَه من حائط فهو حَجْرٌ.

حجر (لسان العرب) الحَجَرُ: الصَّخْرةُ، والجمع في القلة أحجارٌ، وفي الكثرة حجارٌ وحجارةٌ؛ واستَحجَر الطينُ: صار حَجَراً، والحُجْرُ ما يحيط بالظفر من اللحم. ومحْجِرُ العين: ما دار بها وبدا من البُرْقُع من جميع العين، وحجَر القمرُ: استدار بخط دقيق من غير أن يغلظ، وكذلك إذا صارت حوله دارة في الغيْم. ابن سيده: الحاجر ما يمسك الماء من شفة الوادي ويحيط به. والحِجْرُ حِجْرُ الكعبة. قال الأزهري: الحِجْرُ حَطيمُ مكة، كأنه حُجْرةٌ مما يلي المثْعب من البيت. قال الجوهري: الحِجْرُ حِجْرُ الكعبة، وهو ما حواه الحطيم المدار بالبيت جانبَ الشِّمالِ؛ وكُلُّ ما حجَرتَه من حائط، فهو حَجْرٌ.

§ 234.—XXXVI, 4-9

ePSD: malahhu

malah [SAILOR] wr. ma_2-lah_5; ma_2-lah_4; ma_2-lah_6; ${}^{lu}{}_2ma_2$-lah_5; ${}^{lu}{}_2ma_2$-lah_4; ${}^{lu}{}_2ma_2$-lah_6 "sailor" Akk. Malahhu

AALD: malāhu (s.) (malahhu) الملاّح، البلاّم، صانع المركب

ePSD: eleppu

ma [SHIP] wr. ma_2; ${}^{geš}ma_2$ "ship, boat" Akk. eleppu

ePSD: pehû

du [SPREAD] wr. du_8 "to bake; to spread out mud to make bricks; to caulk" Akk. epû; labānu; pehû

henzer [BLOCK] wr. henzir "to block" Akk. pehû

AALD: pehû (v.; adj.) يعيقُ، يسدّ، يغلف، يحجز، يخزن سرا، يطيّن، يغلق، يكسو، يلحمُ؛ مسدود، مغلق

ملع (مقاييس اللغة) الميم واللام والعين أصلٌ يدلُّ على سرعة وخفة. والمَلْع السُّرعة في المرور والاختطاف.

ملع (الصّحاح في اللغة) المَلْعُ: السيرُ السريعُ الخفيف.

ملع (لسان العرب)وأنشد الفراء: وتهْفو بهادٍ لها مَيلع، كما أقحم القادسَ الأرْدَمُونا قال: المَيْلعُ المُضطرِبُ ههنا وههنا. والمَيْلَعُ: الخفيفُ. والقادسُ: السفينةُ. والأرْدمُ: الملاّحُ. والمَليعُ: الفضاءُ الواسعُ؛

ملح (مقاييس اللغة) والمَلاّح: صاحبُ السفينة، قياسُه عندنا هذا، لأنّ ماء البحر ملحٌ وقال ناسٌ: اشتقاقُه من الملح: سُرعة خفقان الطَّير بجناحيه.

ملح (لسان العرب) والمَلْحُ سرعة (قوله «والملح سرعة إلخ» يقال ملح الطائر كمنع كثرت سرعة خفقانه كما في القاموس.) خفقان الطائر بجناحيه؛ قال: مَلْحَ الصُّقُور تحت دجْنٍ مُغْين قال أبو حاتم: قلت للأصمعي أتراه مقلوباً من اللَّمْح؟

ألف (مقاييس اللغة) الهمزة واللام والفاء أصلٌ واحد، يدلُّ على انضمام الشيء إلى الشيء، والأشياء الكثيرة أيضاً.

ألف (لسان العرب) وألَفْتُ الشيءَ أي وصَلْتُه.

علف (العباب الزاخر) وموضع العلف: مَعْلَفٌ. وقال ابن عبّاد: المَعْلَفُ: كواكب مستديرة متبددة؛

علب (لسان العرب) والعُلْبةُ قدحٌ ضخم من جلود الإبل. وقيل: العُلْبة من خشب، كالقدَح الضخْم يُحلَبُ فيها. وقيل: إنها كهيئة القَصْعة من جلد، ولها طوْق من خشب.

قصع (لسان العرب) القصْعة: الضخْمةُ تشبع العشرة، والجمع قِصاعٌ وقِصَعٌ. وقيل: القاصعاء والقُصَعةُ فم جحر اليربوع أول ما يبتدئ في حفره، ومأخذه من القصْع وهو ضم الشيء على الشيء.

العَلَبُ (القاموس المحيط) والعُلْبةُ، بالضم: النَّخْلةُ الطويلةُ، وقدحٌ ضخْمٌ من جُلود الإبل أو منْ خشب يُحْلَبُ فيها،

ألب (لسان العرب) وقد ألَبْتُها ألْباً، تقدير علبْتها عَلْباً.

ولب (القاموس المحيط) ولب يلِبُ وُلُوباً: دخَل وأسرَع، و~ الشيءَ، و~ إليه: وَصَلَهُ كائناً ما كان.

فيح (لسان العرب) وفاحت القِدْرُ وأفحْتُها أنا: غلتْ. وفاح الدمُ فَيْحاً وفيَحاناً، وهو فاحٍ: انْصبّ. وأفحْتُ الدم: أسلْتُه. والفَيْحُ والفيَحُ: السَّعةُ والانتشار. والأفْيحُ والفيّاحُ: كل موضع واسع. بحرٌ أفْيحُ بيِّنُ الفيَح: واسعٌ، وفيّاحٌ، أيضاً، بالتشديد. وأفاحه هراقه؛ وفاحت الغارةُ تَفيح: اتّسعتْ.

§ 235.—XXXVI, 10-26

ePSD: akālu

gu [EAT] wr. gu_7 "to eat, consume" Akk. akālu

rig [EAT] wr. rig_7 "to eat; to do something to barley; to pasture, tend; to drink; to sup" Akk. akālu; haţāpu; re'û; šatû; sarāpu

AALD: zabru (s.) (zapru, şaparu, şapru) معنى غير معروف

ePSD: id

<u>id</u> [<u>RIVER</u>] wr. id$_2$; id$_3$; id$_6$; id$_7$; id$_5$ "river, watercourse, canal" Akk. nāru

AALD: naqāru (v.) يهدم، يفلش، يهدم (تحضيرا لاعادة البناء)، يقطع بفأس، ينحت

تكلَ (القاموس المحيط) تَكِل عليه، كفرح: لُغةٌ في اتَّكل، ذكرْتُهُ على اللَّفظ.

وكل (لسان العرب) ويقال: قد اتَّكل عليك فلان وأوْكَل عليك فلان بمعنى واحد. ويقال: قد أوْكَلْت على أخيك العمل أي خلَّيته كلَّه. ورجل وُكَلَةٌ إذا كان يَكِلُ أمره إلى الناس. وواكلْت فلاناً مُواكلةً إذا اتَّكلْت عليه واتَّكل هو عليك.

أكل (لسان العرب) وآكَلْتُك فلاناً إذا أمكنته منه؛ ولما أنشد المُمزِّق قوله: فإنْ كنتُ مأكولاً، فكُنْ خيرَ آكلٍ، وإلاَّ فأدْركْني، ولمَّا أُمزَّق فقال النعمان: لا آكُلُك ولا أُوكِلُك غيري.

الزَّبْرُ (القاموس المحيط) الزَّبْرُ: القويُّ الشديدُ، والأزْبرُ: المُؤْذي.

زفر (مقاييس اللغة) الزاء والفاء والراء أصلان: أحدُهما يدلُّ على حِمْل، والآخر على صَوْتٍ من الأصوات. فالأول الزِّفْر: الحِمْل، والجمع أزفار. وازْدفَرَه، إذا حمله، وبذلك سمِّي الرجلِ زُفَر، لأنه يزدفِر بالأموال مطيقاً لها، ومن الباب الزَّافرة: عشيرةُ الرَّجُل؛ لأنهم قد يتحمَّلون بعضَ ما ينُوبُهُ. وزِفْر المسافر: جهازه. ويقال الزُّفَر: النَّهر الكبير، ويكون سمِّي بذلك لأنَّه كثير الحملِ للماء.

زَفَرَ (القاموس المحيط) والمُزْدفِرُ والمُزْفِرُ والزَّفْرةُ، ويضمُّ: التَّنفُّسُ كذلك، والمُتنفِّسُ.

زفر (لسان العرب) الزَّفْرُ والزَّفيرُ: أن يملأ الرجل صدره غماً ثم هو يزْفِرُ به، والشهيق. وزُفْرةُ كل شيء وزفْرتُه: وَسَطُه. والزَّفْرةُ والزُّفْرةُ: التنفُّسُ. الليث: وفي التنزيل العزيز: لهم فيها زفيرٌ وشهيقٌ؛ الزفير: أول نهيق الحمار وشبْهِه، والشَّهيقُ: آخِرُه، لأن الزفير إدخال النفس والشهيق إخراجه، والاسم الزَّفْرةُ، والجمع زَفَراتٌ، بالتحريك، لأنه اسم وليس بنعت؛ وربما سكنها الشاعر للضرورة، كما قال: فتَسْتَريح النَّفْسُ من زفْراتها وقال الزجاج: الزَّفْرُ من شِدَةِ الأنين وقبيحه، والشهيق الأنين الشديد المرتفع جداً، والزَّفير اغْتراقُ النَّفَسِ للشِّدَّة.

حادَ (القاموس المحيط) وحايَدَهُ مُحايَدَةً وحِياداً: جانَبَه.

حيد (الصّحاح في اللغة) وحايدَهُ مُحايدةً وحِياداً: جانَبَهُ.

حد (مقاييس اللغة) الحاء والدال أصلان: الأوّل المنع، والثاني طَرَف الشيء.فالحدّ: الحاجز بَيْن الشّيئين.

حدد (الصّحاح في اللغة) وفلان حَديدُ فلان: إذا كان أرضه إلى جنب أرضه.

الحَدُّ (القاموس المحيط) الحَدُّ: الحاجزُ بين شَيْئَيْنِ، ومُنْتَهى الشَّيء، و~ من كُلِّ شيءٍ: حِدَّتُه، وداري حَديدَةُ دارِه، ومُحادَّتُها: حَدُّها كحَدِّها. والحَدَّادُ: مُعالِجُهُ والسَّجَّانُ، والبَوَّابُ، والبَحْرُ، ونَهْرٌ.

نقر (مقاييس اللغة) النون والقاف والراء أصلٌ صحيح يدلُّ على قَرع شيءٍ حتَّى تُهْزَم فيه هزْمَةٌ، ثم يتوسَّع فيه.[منه] منقار الطَّائر، لأنه ينْقُر به الشَّيء حتَّى يؤثِّر فيه.

نقر (لسان العرب) ونقَرَهُ يَنْقُره نَقْراً: ضربه. والمِنْقارُ: حديدة كالفأس يُنْقَرُ بها، وفي غيره: حديدة كالفأس مُشَكَّكةٌ مستديرة لها خَلْفٌ يُقطع به الحجارة والأرض الصُّلْبَةُ. ونقَرتُ الشيءَ: ثَقَبْتُه بالمِنْقار. والمِنْقر، بكسر الميم: المِعْول؛ قال ذو الرمة: كأرْحاءِ رَقْدٍ زَلَّمَتْها المَناقِرُ ونقَرَ الطائرُ الشيءَ يَنْقُره نَقْراً: كذلك. والتَّنْقيرُ عن الأمر: البحث عنه. ورجل نقَّارٌ: مُنقِّرٌ عن الأمور والأخبار. ونقرت الرَّحى بالمنقار، وهي تلك الحديدة.ومن الباب نقَرتُ عن الأمر حتَّى علِمتُه، وذلك بَحْثُك عنه، كأنَّ عِلمك به نقْرٌ فيه. وانْتقَر القومَ: اختارهم.

§ 237.—XXXVI, 38-55

ePSD: suluppu

<u>zulum</u> [<u>DATE</u>] wr. zu$_2$-lum "the fruit of the date-palm" Akk. suluppu

الصَّلَفُ (القاموس المحيط) الصَّلَفُ: خَوافي قلْبِ النَّخْلَة، الواحِدَةُ: بهاءٍ،

سلف (العباب الزاخر) ومنه حديث عامر بن ربيعة -رضي الله عنه- كان رسول الله -صلى الله عليه وسلم- يبعثنا ومالنا طعام إلا السَّلَفُ من التمر فنقسمه قبضة قبضة حتى ننتهي إلى تمرة تمرة، فقال له عبد الله بن عامر: ما عسى أن تنفعكم تمرة تمرة؟، قال: لا تقل ذاك فوالله ما عدا أن فقدناها اختللناها. أي اختللنا إليها؛ فحذف الجار وأوصل الفعل، والمعنى: احتجنا إليها؛ من الخلة وهي الحاجة. والسُّلْفَةُ بالضم- ما يتعجله الرجل من الطعام قبل الغداء كاللُّهنَة. وقال الليث: تسمى غُرْلَةُ الصبي سُلْفَةَ. والسُّلْفَةُ جلد رقيق يجعل بطانة للخِفافِ، وربما كان أحمر وأصفر.

سلف (لسان العرب) سَلفَ يَسْلُفُ سَلَفاً وسُلُوفاً: تقدَم؛ وسُلافُ الخمرِ وسُلافَتُها: أَوَّل ما يُعْصَر منها، وقيل: هو ما سال من غير عصر، وقيل: هو أَوَّلُ ما ينزل منها، وقيل: السُلافةُ أَوَّلُ كل شيء عُصِر، وقيل: هو أَوَّل ما يُرفع من الزبيب، والنَّطْلُ ما أُعِيدَ عليه الماء. التهذيب: السُّلافةُ من الخمر أَخْلَصُها وأَفْضَلُها، وذلك إذا تَحلَّب من العنب بلا عَصْر ولا مَرْثٍ، وكذلك من التمر والزبيب ما لم يُعَدْ عليه الماء بعد تحلُّب أَوَّله.

والسلافُ: ما سال من عصير العنب قبل أن يعصر، ويسمى الخمر سُلافاً. وسُلافةُ كلِّ شيء عصرَتِه: أوَّله، وقيل: السلافُ والسلافةُ من كل شيء خالِصُه. والسلْفةُ، بالضمَ: الطعامُ الذي تَتعلَّلُ به قبل الغِذاء، وقد سلَّفَ القومَ تَسْليفاً وسلَّفَ لهم، وهي اللُّهنة يَتعجَّلها الرجلُ قبيل الغذاء. والسُّلفة ما تَدَّخِرُه المرأةُ لِتُتحف به مَن زارَها.

§ 240.—XXXVI, 67-80

AALD: muqqelpû See muqqalpû

AALD: muqqelpû (adj.) (f. muqqelpītu) إنجراف، السير مع التيار

AALD: muqqelpītu (s.) in sa muqqelpīti (s.) صاحب المركب الذي يسير مع مجرى النهر

ePSD: qalāpu

<u>bar</u> [<u>OUTSIDE</u>] wr. bar; ba-ra; bala; bur "outside, (other) side; behind; outer form, outer; fleece; outsider, strange; back, shoulder; liver; because of; to set aside; to cut open, slit, split" Akk. būdum;

kabattu; kawûm; ahû; warkatu; qalāpu; salātu; šalāqu
zil [BOIL] wr. zil "to boil; to peel" Akk. qalāpu; salāqu

قلف (مقاييس اللغة) القاف واللام والفاء أصلٌ صحيح يدلّ على كَشْط شيء عن شيء. يقال: قَلَفت الشَّجرة، إذا نحَّيْتَ عنها لحاءها.

قلف (الصّحاح في اللغة) وقلَفتُ السفينة، إذا خَرَزت ألواحها بالليف وجعلت في خللِها القار.

قلف (العباب الزاخر) وقلَفَها الخاتن قلْفاً: قطعها. وقلَفتُ السفينة: إذا خَرَزْتَ ألواحها بالليف وجعلت في خللها القار، والاسم القِلافة. وقال ابن عبّاد : قَلَفْتُ الجَزُور تقليفا: عضَّيْتُها. وقال غيره :قَلَفْتُ السفينة: مثل قلَفْتُها. والتَّقْليفُ من كلام أهل حضر موت، وهو تمر يُنزع نواه ويُكنز في قِرب وظروف من الخوص. واقْتَلَفْتُ من فلان أربع قلَفاتٍ وأربع مَقْلوفات: وهو أن تأتي الجُلَة عند الرجل فتأخذها بقوله منه ولا تَكيلها. والاقْتلافُ - أيضاً-: اقْتِلاعُ الظفر من أصله، والتّركيب يدل على كشط شيء عن شيء.

قلف (لسان العرب) وقلَف الشيءَ قلْفاً: كقلبه قلباً؛ عن كراع. والقَلَف لغة في القَنَف. قال أبو مالك: القَلَف والقَنَف واحد وهو الغِرْينُ واليَفَنُ إذا يبس، ويقال له غِرْيَنٌ إذا كان رَطْباً ونحو ذلك؛

قلب (مقاييس اللغة) القاف واللام والباء أصلان صحيحان: أحدهما يدلّ على خالص شَيءٍ وشريفه، والآخرُ على ردّ شيءٍ من جهةٍ إلى جهة. والقليب: البئرُ قبل أنْ تُطوى؛ وإنّماسمِّيت قليباً لأنّها كالشَّيء يقلب من جهةٍ إلى جهة، وكانت أرضاً فلما حُفرت صار ترابُها كأنّه قُلِب. فإذا طُويت فهي الطَّوِيّ.

قلب (لسان العرب) القَلْبُ: تحويلُ الشيء عن وجهه.

§ 242.—XXXVI, 85-88

ePSD: ur [DRAG] (53x: Old Akkadian, Ur III, Old Babylonian) wr. ur_3 "to go along; to wipe clean; to beat, sweep away; to drag; to raise a boat" Akk. bâ'u; kapāru; šabāţu

عرا (لسان العرب) عَراهُ عَرْواً واعْتَراه، كلاهما: غَشِيَه طالباً معروفه، وحكى ثعلب: أنه سمع ابن الأعرابي يقول إذا أتيت رجلا تَطْلُب منه حاجة قلت عَرَوْتُه وعَرَرْتُه واعْتَرَيْتُه واعْتَرَرْتُه؛ قال الجوهري: عَرَوْتُه أَعْرُوه إذا أَلْمَمْت به وأتيته طالباً، فهو مَعْرُوٌّ. وعُرْوَةُ الدَّلْو والكوز ونحوه: مَقْبِضُهُ. وعَرَّى الشَّيْءَ: اتَّخذ له عُرْوَة. وقوله تعالى: فقد اسْتَمْسَك بالعُرْوة الوُثْقى لا انْفِصامَ لها؛ شَبَّه بالعُرْوة التي يُتَمَسَّك بها. قال الزجاج: العُرْوة الوُثْقى قولُ لا إله إلا الله، وقيل: معناه فقد عقد لنفسه من الدِّين عَقْداً وثيقاً لا تَحُلُّه حُجَّة. وعُرْوتا الفرْج: لَحْمٌ ظاهِرٌ يدقُّ فيأْخُذُ يَمْنَةً ويَسْرَة مع أَسْفلِ البطْنِ، وفرْجٌ مُعرًى إذا كان كذلك. وعُرَى المَرْجان: قلائدُ المَرْجان. ويقال لطوق القلادة: عُرْوةٌ.

عرر (لسان العرب) وعَرَّ أَرْضه يعُرُّها أي سمَدَها، والتَّعْرِيرُ مثله. ومنه حديث ابن عمر: كان لا يَعُرُّ أَرْضه أي لا يُزَبِّلُها بالعُرَّة. وكلُّ شيءٍ باء بشيءٍ، فهو له عَرار؛ وأنشد للأعشى: فقد كان لهم عَرار وقيل: العَرارُ القوَدُ. وعَرار، مثل قطام: اسم بقرة. والعَرارةُ الشدة؛ وفي حديث طاووس: إذا اسْتَعَرَّ عليكم شيءٌ من الغنم أي نَدَّ واسْتَعْصَى، من العَرارة وهي الشدة وسوء الخلق، والعَرارةُ: الرِّفْعة والسُّودَدُ.

بوأ (لسان العرب) وأَصل البَواءِ اللُّزومُ. وفي الحديث: فقد باءَ به أَحدُهما أي التزمه ورجع به.

§ 243.—XXXVI, 89-91

ePSD: SAG
saĝ [CVVE] wr. $saĝ_5$; saĝ; zag "(compound verb verbal element)"
saĝ [FRONT] wr. saĝ "front side (math.)"
saĝ [HEAD] wr. saĝ "head; person; capital" Akk. qaqqadu; rēšu
saĝĝar [MILLSTONE] wr. $saĝĝar_2$; saĝĝar; $^{na}{}_4$saĝ-ĝar "upper millstone"

الساجُ (القاموس المحيط) والسَّوجانُ: الذَّهابُ والمَجيءُ.

سوج (لسان العرب) ساجَ سَوْجاً: ذهب وجاء؛

الوسيجُ (القاموس المحيط) الوَسيجُ: سَيْرٌ للإبِل، وسج، كوعَد، وسيجاً. وإبِلٌ وَسُوجٌ عَسُوجٌ، وجملٌ وسّاجٌ عسّاجٌ: سريعٌ. وأوسَجْتُهُ: حمَلْتُهُ على الوسيجِ.

§ 244.—XXXVII, 1-5

ePSD: urmahhu
urmah [LION] wr. ur-mah "lion" Akk. nēšu; urmahhu

عرم (لسان العرب) والعَرَمُ والعُرْمَةُ: لونٌ مختلطٌ بسوادٍ وبياضٍ في أيِّ شيء كان، وقيل: تَنْقيطٌ بهما من غير أن يتَّسع، كُلُّ نُقْطةٍ عُرْمَةٌ؛ عن السيرافي، الذكرُ أَعْرَمُ والأُنثى عَرْماءُ، وقد غَلَبتِ العَرْماءُ على الحية الرَّقْشاءِ؛ قال مَعْقِلٌ الهُذَليُّ: أبا مَعْقِل، لا تُوطِئَنْك بغاضتي رُؤُوسَ الأفاعي في مَراصِدِها العُرْمِ الأصمعي: الحَيَّةُ العَرْماءُ التي فيها نُقَطٌ سودٌ وبيضٌ، ويروى عن معاذ بن جبل: أنه ضَحَّى بكبشٍ أعْرَم، وهو الأبيض الذي فيه نُقَطٌ سُود. قال ثعلب: العَرِمُ من كل شيء ذُو لَوْنَيْن، قال: والنَّمِرُ ذو عَرَم. والعَرَمْرَمُ الشديدُ؛ والعَرِيمُ: الدَّاهِيَةُ.

هرم (مقاييس اللغة) ويقال: الهرِمَة: اللَّبُوَة.

§ 246.—XXXVII, 14-21

ePSD: šēpu
ĝiri [FOOT] wr. $ĝiri_3$; me-ri; $ĝiri_{16}$ "via, by means of, under the authority of someone; foot; path" Akk. šēpu
AALD: šēpu (s.) الموظَف
AALD: lubānu see lupānu

lapānu

lamgal [NUT] wr. ^{ĝeš}lam-gal; lam-gal; lam-gal-gal; ^{ĝeš}lam-hal; lam-hal "a nut" Akk. buţumtu; lapānu

labānu

du [SPREAD] wr. du$_8$ "to bake; to spread out mud to make bricks; to caulk" Akk. epû; labānu; pehû

سيف (مقاييس اللغة) السين والياء والفاء أصلٌ يدلُّ على امتدادٍ في شيء وطول. من ذلك السَيف، سمّي بذلك لامتداده. والسَّيْفُ، بفتح السين: سَيَبُ الفرَس.

وظف (مقاييس اللغة) الواو والظاء والفاء: كلمة تدلُّ على تقدير شيء. يقال: وظَفْتُ له، إذا قدَرت له كلَّ حينٍ شيئاً من رزقٍ أو طعام. ثمَّ استُعير ذلك في عَظْم السَّاق، كأنَّه شيءٌ مقدَّر، وهو ما فوق الرُّسْغ من قائمة الدّابَة إلى الساق.

وظف (الصّحاح في اللغة) الوَظيفُ: مُسْتَدَقُّ الذراع والساق من الخيل والإبل ونحوهما. والجمع الأَوْظِفَةُ.

وظف (لسان العرب) والوَظِيفُ لكل ذي أَربع: ما فوق الرُّسْغ إِلى مَفْصِل الساق. ووَظِيفا يدي الفرس: ما تحت رُكْبَتَيْه إِلى جنبيه، ووظِيفا رجليه: ما بين كعبيه إِلى جنبيه. وقال ابن الأَعرابي: الوظِيفُ من رُسْغَي البعير إِلى ركبتيه في يديه، وأَما في رجليه فمن رُسْغيه إِلى عُرقوبيه، والجمع من كل ذلك أَوْظِفة ووُظُف. ووظَفْت البعير أَظِفُه وظْفاً إِذا أَصبت وظِيفَه. الجوهري: الوظيف مُسْتَدَقُّ الذراع والساق من الخيل والإِبل ونحوهما، والجمع الأَوْظِفة.

ظفف (لسان العرب) الكسائي: ظَفَفْتُ قوائم البعير وغيره أَظُفُّها ظَفاً إِذا شَدَدْتَها كلَّها وجمعتها.

لبن (الصّحاح في اللغة) واللَبَنُ أيضاً: وجعٌ في العنق من الوسادة. واللبانُ بالفتح: ما جرى عليه اللببُ من الصدر.

اللَّبَنُ (القاموس المحيط) واللُّبانُ: الرَّضاعُ، وبالضم: الكُنْدُرُ، والصَّنَوْبَرُ، والحاجاتُ من غير فاقةٍ، بَلْ من هِمَّةٍ، جَمْعُ لُبانةٍ، وبالفتح: الصَّدْرُ، أو وَسَطُه، أو ما بين الثَّدْيَيْنِ، أو صَدْرُ ذي الحافِرِ. ولِبْنُ القَميصِ، ككَتِفٍ، ولَبِنَتُهُ ولِبْنَتُهُ، بالكسر: بَنِيقَتُه.

لبن (مقاييس اللغة) وكان ينبغي أن يقول: هو من اللَبن، ولكنَّه لا يقال بلبن أمِّه إنّما يقال بلبان أمّه. ومما يقارب هذا اللَّبان: الصدر، بفتح اللام.

لبن (لسان العرب) ابن سيده: ولِبْنَةُ القميص ولَبِنَتُه بَنِيقَتُه؛ البَنِيقة طَوْقُ الثوب الذي يَضُم النحر وما حوله، وهو الجُرُبّان؛ واللَّبانُ: الصدر، وقيل: وسَطُه، وقيل: ما بين الثَّدْيين، ويكون للإِنسان وغيره؛ وأَصلُ اللَّبان في الفرس موضعُ اللَّبَب، ثم استعير للناس؛ وفي قصيد كعب، رضي الله عنه: تَرْمي اللَّبانَ بكفَّيْها ومِدْرَعِها وفي بيت آخر منها: ويُزْلِقُه منها لبانٌ ولبنه يَلْبِنُه لَبْناً: ضَرَبَ لَبانَه. واللَّبَنُ وجَعُ العُنق من الوِسادة، وفي المحكم: وجَعُ العُنق حتى لا يقْدِرَ أَن يَلْتَفِت، وقد لَبِنَ، بالكسر، لَبَناً.

§ 248.—XXXVII, 28-35

AALD: garnu (s.) See qarnu قرن الحيوان

AALD: zibbatu (s.) (zimbatu, simbatu, sibbatu) ذيل الحيوان، الجزء الخلفي، الحرس الخلفي (لجيش)

ePSD: šārtu

munsub [HAIR] wr. munsub; munsub$_2$; munsub$_x$(|KA×SUHUR|); ^{su}munsub; ^{su}munsub$_2$; u$_2$-šu-p? "hair; barber" Akk. šārtu; šārat zumri; gallābu

siki [HAIR] wr. siki "wool, fleece; hair; (animal's) pelt" Akk. šārtu; šīpātu

AALD: pasuttu (s.) (pasuntu, pasumtu) pl. pasūmāti الشبكة

ePSD: sakku

idim [BLOCKED] wr. idim "(to be) blocked, stilted; (to be) obtuse, deaf; simple person, imbecile; weak, helpless (person)" Akk. sakku; saklu; ulālu

AALD: sâqu (v.) (siā qu) (See suqaqu) يضيق، يقلص

قرن (مقاييس اللغة) القاف والراء والنون* أصلان صحيحان، أحدهما يدلُّ على جمع شيءٍ إلى شيء، والآخر شيءٌ ينْتَأ بقوّة وشِدّة.

القَرْنُ (القاموس المحيط) القَرْنُ: الرَّوْقُ من الحَيوانِ، وموضِعُهُ من رأسِنا، أو الجانِبُ الأَعْلَى من الرأس

زب (مقاييس اللغة) الزاء والباء أصلان: أحدهما يدل على وُفُورٍ في شعرٍ، ثم يحمل عليه. فالزَّبَب: طُول الشَّعَر، وكثرتُه. ويقال بعيرٌ أزَبُّ.

الزَّبَبُ (القاموس المحيط) الزَّبَبُ، مُحرَّكَةً: الزَّغَبُ، و~ فينا: كثْرَةُ الشَّعَرِ، و~ في الإبلِ: كثْرَةُ شَعَرِ الوجْهِ والعُثْنون. والزَّبَّاءُ: الاسْتُ،

زبب (الصّحاح في اللغة) الزُّبُّ: الذكَرُ. والزُّبُّ: اللحية بلغة اليمن.

زبب (لسان العرب) الزَّبَبُ: مصدر الأَزَبِّ، وهو كثْرة شَعَر الذِّراعَيْن والحاجبين والعينين، والجمعُ الزُّبُّ. والزَّبَبُ طولُ الشعَر وكثرتُه؛

ذبب (لسان العرب) والذَّبْذَبةُ: تَرَدُّدُ الشيءِ المُعلَّق في الهواءِ . والذَّبْذَبُ: اللِّسانُ، وقيلَ الذكَر. والذَّباذِبُ: ذكر الرجل، لأَنـه يتَذَبْذَبُ أَي يتردَّد؛ وقيل الذَّباذِبُ: الخُصَى، واحِدتُها ذَبْذَبةٌ. ورجلٌ مُذَبْذَبٌ ومُتَذَبْذِبٌ: مُتَردِّدٌ بين أَمْرَين أَو بين رجُلين، ولا تَـثْبُتُ صُحْبَتُه لواحدٍ منهما. والتَّذَبْذُبُ: التَّحرُّكُ. والذَّبْذَبةُ: نَوسُ الشيءِ الـمُعلَّق في الهواءِ. وتَذَبْذَب الشيءُ: ناسَ واضْطرَبَ ، وذَبْذَبَه هو؛

ذنب (مقاييس اللغة) الذال والنون والباء أصول ثلاثة: أحدها الجُرم، والآخر مؤخَر الشيء، والثالث كالحظِّ والنَّصيب.فالأوّل الذَّنب والجُرم. يقال أَذْنَبَ يُذْنب. والذِّناب: عَقِبُ كلِّ شيء. والذّانب: التابع؛ وكذلك المستذْنِبُ: الذي يكون عند أذناب الإبل.

ذيل (لسان العرب) الذَّيْل: آخر كل شيء. وذَيْلُ الفرس والبعير ونحوهما: ما أَسْبَلَ من ذنبه فتعلَّق، وقيل: ذَيْلُه ذنبه.

شعر (لسان العرب) شَعَرَ به وشَعُرَ يَشْعُر شِعْراً وشَعْراً وشِعْرَةً ومَشْعُورَةً وشُعُوراً وشُعُورَةً وشِعْرَى ومَشْعُوراء ومَشْعُوراً؛ الأَخيرة عن اللحياني، كله: عَلِمَ. والشَّعْرُ والشَّعَرُ مذكران: نِبْتَةُ الجسم مما ليس بصوف ولا وبر للإِنسان وغيره، وجمعه أَشْعار وشُعُور، والشَّعْرَةُ الواحدة من الشَّعَر، وقد يكنى بالشَّعْرَة عن الجمع كما يكنى بالشَّيبة عن الجنس؛ يقال رأَى (* قوله: «يقال رأى إلخ» هذا كلام مستأنف وليس متعلقاً بما قبله ومعناه أنه يكنى بالشعرة عن الشيب: انظر الصحاح والاساس). فلان الشَّعْرَة إِذا رأَى الشيب في رأْسه. ورجل أَشْعَرُ وشَعِرٌ وشَعْرانِيَ: كثير شعر الرأْس

والجسد طويلَه، وقوم شُعْرٌ. والشَّعراءُ والشِّعْرَةُ، بالكسر: الشَّعَرُ النابت على عانة الرجل وركب المرأة وعلى ما وراءها؛ وفي الصحاح: والشِّعْرَةُ، بالكسر، شَعَرُ الرَّكَبِ للنساء خاصة. والشِّعْرَةُ منبت الشَّعر تحت السُّرَّة، وقيل: الشِّعْرَةُ العانة نفسها. وفي حديث المبعث: أتاني آتٍ فشقَّ من هذه إلى هذه، أي من ثُغْرَةِ نَحْرِه إلى شِعْرَتِه؛ قال: الشِّعْرَةُ، بالكسر، العانة؛ والشَّعْرَةُ من الغنم: التي ينبت بين ظِلْفَيها الشعر فيَدْمَيان، والشَّعْراءُ الفَرْوَة، سميت بذلك لكون الشعر عليها؛ حكي ذلك عن ثعلب. والمَشاعِرُ: الحواسُّ؛ وكل ما ألزقه بشيء، فقد أشْعَره به. وأشْعَرَ البَدَنَةَ: أعلمها، وهو أن يشق جلدها أو يطعنها في أَسْنِمَتِها في أحد الجانبين بمِبْضَعٍ أو نحوه، وقيل: طعن في سَنامها الأيمن حتى يظهر الدم ويعرف أنها هَدْيٌ، والأَشْعَرُ شيء يخرج بين ظِلْفَي الشاةِ كأنه ثُؤْلُولُ الحافر تكوى منه؛ هذه عن اللحياني. والأَشْعَرُ اللحم تحت الظفر.

بسّ (مقاييس اللغة) الباء والسين أصلان: أحدهما السَّوْق، والآخر فتُّ الشَّيء وخلطه. فالأول قولـه تعالى: وبُسَّتِ الجبالُ بسّاً [الواقعة 5]، يقال سِيقت سَوْقا. والأصل الآخر قولهم بُسَّت الحنطة وغيرها أي فُتّتْ. وفُسِّر قولـه تعالى: وبُسَّتْ الجِبالُ بَسّاً [الواقعة 5]، على هذا الوجه أيضاً.

البسُّ (القاموس المحيط) وجاء به من حسِّه وبسِّه، مُثَلَّثي الأول: مِنْ جَهْدِه وطاقته. ولأَطْلُبَنَّهُ من حَسِّي وبَسِّي: جَهْدي وطاقتي. البَسُّ: السَّوْقُ اللَّيِّنُ، والباسَّةُ والبَسَّاسَةُ: مكةُ شرَّفَها اللهُ تعالى. و{بُسَّتِ الجبال}: فُتِّتَتْ، فصارتْ أرْضاً،

بسس (لسان العرب) وبَسَّ الإبل بَسّاً: ساقها؛ وبَسَّ الرجلَ يَبُسُّه: طرده ونحاه. وانْبَسَّ: تنحَى. وبَسَّ عَقاربه: أرسل نمائمه وأذاه.

بَسْتٌ (القاموس المحيط) والبَسْتُ: السَّيْرُ، أو فوقَ العنق، أو السَّبقُ في العَدْوِ.

بست (لسان العرب) البَسْتُ من السَّير كالسَّبْت.

سبت (مقاييس اللغة) السين والباء والتاء أصلٌ واحد يدلُّ على راحةٍ وسكون. يقال للسَّير السهل اللَّين. سَبْتٌ.

سبط (العباب الزاخر) شَعر سَبَطٌ -بالتحريك- وسبِط -مثالُ كتف- وسبْط -بالفتح-: أي مُسْتَرسَلٌ غير جعدٍ لا حجنةَ فيه.

بسط (مقاييس اللغة) الباء والسين والطاء أصلٌ واحدٌ، وهو امتدادُ الشَّيء، في عرَض أو غير عرَض. فالبِساط ما يُبْسط. والبَساط الأرض، وهي البسيطة.

فسط (مقاييس اللغة) الفاء والسين والطاء كلمتانِ متباينتان. فالفسيط: ثُفْرُوق التَّمرة، ويقال قُلامة الظُّفر. والفُسطاط الجماعة.

فسط (الصّحاح في اللغة) الفُسْطاطُ: بيتٌ من شعرٍ، وفيه ثلاث لغات: فُسْطاطٌ وفُسْتاطٌ وفُسّاطٌ، وكسر الفاء لغةٌ فيهنَ. والفسيطُ: ثُفْروقُ التمرة، وقلامةُ الظفر.

فسط (العباب الزاخر) الليثُ: الفسيْطُ: علاقةُ ما بين القمع إلى النواة، وهو الثفروقُ، الواحدةَ: فَسِيْطةٌ. والفسيْطُ -أيضا-: قُلامةُ الظفر،

فسط (لسان العرب) الفسِيط: قُلامة الظُّفر، وفي التهذيب: ما يُقلم من الظُّفر إذا طال، واحدته فسيطة، وقيل: الفسيط واحد؛ ويقال لقُلامة الظُّفر أيضاً: الزِّنْقير والحِذْرِفوت. والفُسطاط بيت من شعَر، وفيه لغات: فُسْطاط وفُسْتاط وفُسّاط، وكسر التاء لغة فيهنَ. والفُسْتاط والفِسْتاط: لغة فيه التاء بدل من الطاء لقولهم في الجمع فساطيط، ولم يقولوا في الجمع فساتيط، فالطاء إذاً أعمّ تصرُّفا، وهذا يؤيد أن التاء في فُستاط إنما هي بدل من طاء فُسْطاط أو من سين فُسَاط، هذا قول ابن سيده، قال: فإن قلت فهلاّ اعتزَمْت أن تكون التاء في فُستاط بدلاً من طاء فُسْطاط لأن التاء أشبه بالطاء منها بالسين؟ قيل: بإزاء ذلك أيضاً أنك إذا حكمت بأنها بدل من سين فُسّاط ففيه شيئان جيّدان: أحدهما تغيير الثاني من المثلين وهو أقيس من تغيير الأول من المثلين لأن الاستكراه في الثاني يكون لا في الأول، والآخر أن السينين في فُسّاط ملتقيان والطاءان في فُسْطاط مُفترقتان منفصلتان بالألف بينهما، واستثقال المثلين ملتقيين أحْرَى من استثقالهما منفصلين، وفُسْطاط المِصر: مجتمع أهله حوْل جامِعه.

وسق (لسان العرب) وقد وَسق الليلُ واتَّسق؛ وكل ما انضم، فقد اتَّسق. ووَسقْت الشيءَ: جمعته وحملته. والوَسْق: ضم الشيء إلى الشيء. والوَسْقُ: الطرد؛ وفي حديث أُحُد: اسْتوسَقُوا كما يَسْتوسِق جُرْبُ الغنم أي استجمعوا وانضموا، ووَسيقهُ الحمار: عانته.

سقق (لسان العرب) ويقال: سَقَّ وزَقَّ وزَخَّ وترَّ وهكَ إذا حذف به.

السَّكُّ (القاموس المحيط) السَّكُّ: المِسْمارُ، كالسَّكِّيِّ، كالسُّكاك، والمُسْتبدُّ برأيه. والسَّكْسَكةُ: الضَّعفُ، والشَّجاعةُ. واسْتَكَّ النَّبتُ: الْتفَّ، و~ المَسامعُ: صمَّتْ وضاقتْ.

سكك (الصّحاح في اللغة) والأسكُّ: الأصمُّ، وفرسٌ لبعضِ بني عبدِ الله بن عَمْرو بنِ كُلْثوم. ويقال سَكَّهُ يَسُكُّهُ، إذا اصطلم أُذُنيه. واسْتكَّتْ مسامعه، أي صمَّتْ وضاقت. واستَكَّ النبتُ، أي التفَّ وانسدَّ خصاصُهُ. قال أبو عمرو: السِّكَّةُ: حديدة تحرث بها الأرض.

سكك (لسان العرب) السَّكَكُ: الصَّمَمُ، وقيل: السَّكك صِغَر الأُذن ولزوقها بالرأس وقِلَّة إشرافها، وقيل: قِصَرها ولصوقها بالخُشَشاء، وقيل: هو صِغَر فوق الأُذن وضيقُ الصِّماخ، وقد وصف به الصَّمَمُ، يكون ذلك في الآدميين وغيرهم، وقد سَكَّ سككاً وهو أسكُّ؛ ويقال: سَكَّهُ يَسُكُّه إذا اصطلم أذنيه. وفي الحديث: أنه مرَّ بجدي أَسَكَّ أي مُصْطلِم الأذنين مقطوعهما. والسِّكَّةُ والسِّنَّةُ: المِأنُ الذي تحرث به الأرض. ابن الأعرابي: السَّكُّ لُؤمُ الطبع. يقال: هو بسُكِّ طَبْعه يفعل ذلك. وسكَّ إذا ضُيِّق، وسكَّ إذا لُؤِمَ. والسُّكاكةُ من الرجال: المُسْتَبِدُّ برأيه وهو الذي يُمْضِي رأيه ولا يشاور أحداً ولايبالي كيف وقع رأيه، والجمع سُكاكاتٌ ولا يُكسَّر. وسَكَّ بسَلْحِه سَكّاً: رماه رقيقاً. يقال: سَكَّ بسَلْحه وسَجَّ وهكَّ إذا حذف به.

صك (مقاييس اللغة) الصاد والكاف أصلٌ يدلُّ على تلاقِي شيئين بقوّة وشِدَّة، حتَّى كأنَّ أحدهما يضربُ الآخر. من ذلك قولهم: صَكَكْتُ الشيء صكّا. والصَّكَك أن تَصْطَكَّ رُكبتا [الرَّجُل]. [وصَكَّ البابَ]: أغْلقه بعنفٍ وشِدَّة. ويقال بعير مَصَكّ، إذا كان اللَّحمُ قد صُكَّ فيه صكّاً. ورجلٌ مِصَكٌّ: شديد. ويقال ذلك في الخَيل والحُمُر وغيرها.

صكك (لسان العرب) الصَّكُّ: الضرب الشديد بالشيء العريض، وقيل: هو الضرب عامة بأيِّ شيء كان، صَكَّه يَصُكُّه صكّاً. وبعير مَصْكوك ومُصَكَّكٌ: مضروب باللحم (* قوله «مضروب باللحم» قال شارح القاموس: كأن اللحم صك فيه صكاً أي شك). وفي الحديث: مَرَّ بجَدْي أَصَكَّ ميِّت؛ الصَّكَكُ: أن تضرب إحدى الركبتين الأخرى عند العدو فتؤثر فيها أثراً، كأنه لما رآه ميتاً قد تقلَّصت ركبتاه وصفه بذلك، أو كأنَّ شعر ركبتيه قد ذهب من الاصطكاك وانْجرد فعرَّفه به، ويروى بالسين؛ ومنه كتاب عبد الملك إلى الحجاج: قاتلك الله، أُخَيْفِشَ العينين أصَكَّ وصُكُوكٌ وصِكاك؛ قال أبو منصور: والصك الذي يُكتبُ للعُهدة، معرَّب أصله جَكّ، ويُجمَعُ صِكاكاً وصُكوكاً، وكانت الأرزاق تسمى صِكاكاً لأنها كانت تُخْرَجُ مكتوبة؛ والصَّكيكُ: الضعيف؛ عن ابن الأنباري، حكاه الهرويّ في الغريبين. أبو عمرو: كان عبد الصمد بن عليّ قُعْدداً وكانت فيه خصْلة لم تكن في هاشميّ: كانت أسنانه وأضراسه كلها ملتصقة؛ قال: وهذا يسمى أصَكَّ، قال الأزهري: ويقال له الأَلَصُّ أيضاً.

§ 250.—XXXVII, 44-51

ePSD: nakāpu
<u>du [PUSH]</u> wr. du$_7$ "to push, thrust, gore; to make encounter (math.)" Akk. nakāpu
<u>saĝ sag [TREMBLE]</u> wr. saĝ sag$_3$ "to tremble" Akk. nakāpu
AALD: nakāpu (v.) naqāpu ينطح
ePSD: sūqu
<u>esir [STREET]</u> wr. e-sir$_2$; e-sir "street" Akk. sūqu
<u>sila [STREET]</u> wr. sila; sila$_3$ "street" Akk. sūqu
<u>tilla [STREET]</u> wr. tilla$_2$; tilla$_3$; tilla; tilla$_4$; tilla$_5$; tilla$_x$(|AN&AN|) "street" Akk. sūqu

نقب (لسان العرب) النَّقْبُ: الثَّقْبُ في أيِّ شيءٍ كان، نَقبه يَنْقُبه نَقْباً.

قبب (لسان العرب) وقَبه يَقُبُّه قَباً، واقْتبه: قطعه؛ والقبُّ: الثَّقْبُ الذي يجري فيه الـمحْورُ من الـمَحالَة؛ وقيل: القبُّ الخَرقُ الذي في وَسط البَكرة؛ وقبُ الدُّبُر: مَفْرجُ ما بين الأَلْيتَيْنِ. والقُبَّةُ من البناء: معروفة، وقيل هي البناء من الأدم خاصَّة، مشتقٌ من ذلك، والجمع قُبَبٌ وقِبابٌ. وقَبَّبها: عملَها. وتَقبَّبها: دخلَها.

النَّقْفُ (القاموس المحيط) النَّقْفُ: كَسْرُ الهامَةِ عن الدِّماغ، أو ضَرْبُها أشَدَّ ضَرْبٍ، أو برُمْحٍ أو عَصاً، وثَقْبُ البَيْضَةِ، وشَقُّ الحَنْظَلِ عن الهبيد، كالإِنْقافِ والانْتِقافِ، وهو مَنْقُوفٌ ونَقيفٌ، وبالكسر: الفَرْخُ حين يَخْرُجُ من البيضة، ويُفْتَحُ، وحينئذٍ يكونُ تَسْمِيَةً بالمَصْدَرِ، وبالضم: جمعُ النَّقيفِ من الجُذوعِ.

نقف (العباب الزاخر) النَّقْفُ: كسر الهامة عن الدماغ. ونَقَفْتُ الحنظل: أي شققته عن الهبيد، وقال الليث: المُنَاقَفَةُ: هي المُضاربة بالسيوف على الرؤوس،

نقف (لسان العرب) الليث: النَّقف كَسْر الهامة عن الدماغ ونحو ذلك كما يَنْقُف الظليم الحنْظل عن حبه. والمُناقَفة: المضاربة بالسيوف على الرُّؤوس. ونقف رأْسه يَنقُفه نَقْفاً ونقحه: ضربه على رأْسه حتى يخرج دماغه، وقيل: نقفه ضربه أيسر الضرب، وقيل: هو كسر الرأْس على الدماغ، وقيل: هو ضربك إياه برُمْح أَو عصا، وقد ناقفْت الرجل مُناقفة ونقافاً. يقال: اليوم قِحافٌ وغداً نِقافٌ أي اليوم خَمْر وغداً أَمْر، ومن رواه وغداً ثِقاف فقد صحَّف. وفي حديث عبد الله بن عمرو: اعْدُدْ اثني عشر من بني كعب بن لؤيّ ثم يكون النَّقْفُ والنِّقافُ أي القتْل والقِتال؛ والنَّقْفُ: هشْم الرأْس، وأي تَهيجُ الفتن والحروب بعدهم.

نقب (مقاييس اللغة) النون والقاف والباء أصلٌ صحيح يدلُّ على فتح في شيء. ونقب الحائطَ ينقُبه نَقْباً. والبَيطارُ ينقُبُ سُرَّةَ الدّابّة ليخرج منها ماء. وتلك الحديدة مِنْقَب. وكلبٌ نقيبٌ: نُقِبتْ غَلْصَمتُه ليضعُفَ صوته، يَفعلُه اللِّئامُ لئلاّ يسمعَ صوتَه الضَّيْف. والنّاقِبة: قَرْحةٌ تخرج بالجَنْب تهجم على الجَوف. ونَقِبَ خُفُّ البعير: تخرَّق نَقباً.

نقب (الصّحاح في اللغة) وأنقبَ الرجلُ، إذا نَقِبَ بعيره. ونَقِبَ الخُفُّ الملبوس، أي تَخرَّقَ.

كب (مقاييس اللغة) الكاف والباء أصلٌ صحيح يدلُّ على جَمع وتجمع، لا يَشِذُّ منه [شيء]. يقال لما تجمَّع من الرَّمل كُباب. قال:ومنه: كَبَبْتُ الشَّيءَ لوجهه أكُبُّه كبّاً.

كبب (الصّحاح في اللغة) كَبَّه الله لوجهه، أي صرعه، فأكبَّ على وجهه.

كبب (لسان العرب) كبَّ الشيءَ يَكُبُّه، وكَبْكَبه: قلبه. وكَبَبْتُ القَصْعَة: قَلَبْتُها على وجْهها، وطعنه فكَبَّه لوجْهه كذلك؛ قال أَبو النجم: فكَبَّه بالرُّمْح في دمائه. وفي حديث معاوية: إنكم لَتُقَلِّبون حُوَّلاً قُلَّباً إنْ وُقـي كَبَّةَ النار؛ الكَبَّة، بالفتح: شِدَّة الشيء ومُعْظَمُه. وكَبَّةُ النار: صَدْمَتُها. وكُبَّ إذا قُلِب. وكَبَّ إذا ثَقُل. وأَلْقى عليه كُبَّته أي ثِقْله.

سوق (مقاييس اللغة) السين والواو والقاف أصل واحد، وهو حَدْوُ الشَّيء. يقال ساقه يسوقه سَوقاً. والسَّيِّقة ما استيق من الدوابّ. ويقال سقتُ إلى امرأتي صَدَاقها، وأسَقْتُهُ. والسُّوق مشتقَّةٌ من هذا، لما يُساق إليها من كلِّ شيء، والجمع أسواق.

زجج (الصّحاح في اللغة) ابن السكيت: أَزْجَجْتُ الرمح فهو مُزَجٌّ، إذا عمِلت له زُجّاً. قال: وزَجَجْتُ الرجل أزُجُّهُ زجّاً فهو مزجوجٌ، إذا طعنته بالزُّجِّ.

زجج (لسان العرب) الزُّجُّ: زُجُّ الرُّمْح والسَّهم. وأَزَجَّ الرُّمْحَ وزَجَّجه وزجّاه، على البدل: ركَّب فيه الزُّجَّ وأَزْجَجْتُه، فهو مُزَجٌّ؛ ابن الأعرابي: زَجَّ إذا طعن بالعَجلَةِ. وزَجَّ بالشيء من يده يَزُجُّ زَجّاً: رمى به. والزَّجُّ: رميك بالشيء تَزُجُّ به عن نفسك. وزَجَّ الظليمُ برجله زَجّاً: عدا فرمى بها. وظليم أَزَجُّ: يَزُجُّ برجليه؛ ويقال للظليم إذا عدا: زجَ برجليه. والزَّجَجُ في النعامة: طولُ ساقيها وتباعد خطوها؛ يقال: ظَليم أَزَجٌّ ورجل أَزَجٌّ طويل الساقين. وظَليمٌ أَزَجُّ: بعيدُ الخَطْوِ. وأَزجُّ الخطو: واسعه.

زأج (لسان العرب) التهذيب: شمر: زأَجَ بين القوم وزمجَ إذا حَرَّشَ.

حرَش (القاموس المحيط) والحُرْشَةُ، بالضم: الخُشونةُ.

حرش (لسان العرب) ودراهِمُ حُرْشٌ: جيادٌ خَشِنٌ حديثة العهد بالسِّكة. وقيل: كلُّ شيء خشِنٍ أَحْرشُ وحَرِشٌ؛ الأَخيرة عن أَبي حنيفة، وأُراها على النسب لأَني لم أَسمع له فِعْلاً.

زجا (لسان العرب) زَجا الشَّيءُ يَزْجُو زَجْواً وزُجُوّاً وزجاءً: تيسَّر واستقام. والتَّزْجِيةُ: دفْعُ الشيء كما تُزَجّي البَقَرةُ ولدَها أي تَسُوقُه؛ وقال: تزَجَّ من دُنْياك بالبَلاغِ وزَجّى الشَّيءَ وأَزجاه: ساقه ودفعه.

سوق (لسان العرب) السَّوق: معروف. ساقَ الإبلَ وغيرَها يَسُوقها سَوْقاً وسِياقاً، وهو سائقٌ وسَوّاق، شدِّد للمبالغة؛

§ 251.—XXXVII, 51-65

AALD: mušēdû (adj.) See idû المُخبِر، المُستشار، الناصح
AALD: edû (v.) See idû يُهدي، يُعرِّف

ePSD: sanāqu
dim [CHECK] wr. dim_4 "to check; to approach" Akk. sanāqu
sir [CHECK] wr. sir_2 "to check; to approach" Akk. sanāqu
us [LEAN] wr. us_2 "to lean on, impose; to check" Akk. emēdu; sanāqu
AALD: šarāmu (v.) يشرم، يشق، يشذب، يقطع، يقلّم

أدي (مقاييس اللغة) الهمزة والدال والياء أصلٌ واحد، وهو إيصال الشيء إلى الشيء أو وصوله إليه من تلقاء نفسه.
هدي (مقاييس اللغة) الهاء والدال والحرف المعتلّ: أصلانِ [أحدهما] التقدُّمُ للإرشاد، والآخر بعثة لطَف.فالأوّل قولُهم: هديتُه الطَّريق هداية، أي تقدَّمته لأرشُدَه.
هدى (الصّحاح في اللغة) الهُدى: الرشادُ والدلالةُ، يؤنث ويذكر. يقال: هداهُ الله للدين هُدى. وقوله تعالى: "أو لَمْ يهْدِ لهم"، قال أبو عمرو بن العلاء: أو لم يُبيِّنْ لهم. وهَدَيْتُهُ الطريق والبيت هداية، أي عرَفته، هذه لغة أهل الحجاز، وغيرهم يقول: هدَيْتُهُ إلى الطريق وإلى الدار. وهَدى واهْتَدى بمعنًى.
أدا (لسان العرب) وأَدَّى الشيءَ: أَوْصَلَه، والاسم الأَداءُ. وتأَدَّى إليه الخَبرُ أَي انْتهى. ويقال: اسْتأْداه مالاً إذا صادرَه واسْتخْرج منه.
سهد (لسان العرب) وما رأَيتُ من فلان سَهْدَةً أَي أَمراً أَعْتَمِدُ عليه من خير أَو بركة أَو خبرٍ أَو كلام مُقْنِع. وفلان ذُو سَهْدَةٍ أَي ذُو يَقَظَةٍ. وهو أَسْهَدُ رأْياً منك. وفي باب الإِتباع: شيءٌ سَهْدٌ مَهْدٌ أَي حسَن.
سدد (لسان العرب) والتَّسْديدُ: التوفيقُ للسداد، وهو الصواب والقصد من القول والعمل. ورجل سَديدٌ وأَسَدُّ: من السداد وقصد الطريق، وسدّده الله: وفقه. وأمر سديد وأَسدُّ أَي قاصد. ابن الأَعرابي: يقال للناقة الهرِمة سادَّةٌ وسلِمةٌ وسَدِرةٌ وسَدِمةٌ. والسَّاد، بالفتح: الاستقامة والصواب؛
صنق (لسان العرب) وأَصْنَق الرجلُ في ماله إِصْناقاً إِذا أَحسن القيام عليه. ورجل مِصْنَاقٌ وميصابٌ إِذا لزم ماله وأَحسن القيام عليه. والصَّنَقُ الحلقة من الخشب تكون في طرف المرير، والجمع أَصْنَاقٌ؛ عن أَبي حنيفة؛ وأَنشد: أَمِرَّة اللِّيف وأَصْنَاق القُطفْ الأَمِرَّة: الحبالُ جمع مِرار، والأَصْنَاقُ جمع الصَّنَق وهو الحلقة من الخشبة تكون في طرف المرير، والقطفُ: ضَرْبٌ من الشجر متين القضبان تتخذ منه الأَصْنَاق.
زنق (مقاييس اللغة) الزاء والنون والقاف أصل يدلُّ على ضيق أو تضْييق. يقولون: زنَقْت الفرسَ، إذا شكَلْته في قوائمه الأربع.
الزَّنَقُ (القاموس المحيط) وزنَقَ على عيالِه يزْنِقُ: ضَيَّقَ بُخْلاً أو فقْراً، كأَزْنَقَ وزنّق، و~ فرسَهُ: جعَل تحْت حنَكِه الأسفَل حلْقَةً في الجُلَيْدة، ثمّ جعَل فيها خيْطاً، و~ البغْلَ: شكَلَهُ في قوائمِه، وكلُّ رباطٍ في الجِلْد تحْتَ الحنَكِ فهو: زِناقٌ، كغُراب.
زنق (لسان العرب) الزِّناقُ: جبل تحت حنك البعير يُجْذب به. والزِّناقة: حلقة تجعل في الجُليدة هناك تحت الحنك الأَسفل، ثم يجعل فيها خيط يشد في رأْس البغل الجَمُوح، زَنَقه يزْنُقه زَنْقاً؛ قال الشاعر: فإِن يظْهرْ حديثُك، يُؤْتَ عدواً برأْسك في زِناقٍ أَو عِران الزِّناقُ تحت الحنك. وكل رباط تحت الحنك في الجلد فهو زِناقٌ، وما كان في الأَنف مثقوبا فهو عِران؛ وبغل مَزْنوق. وفي حديث أَبي هريرة: وإِن جهنم يُقادُ بها مَزْنوقة؛
المَزْنوقُ: المربوط بالزِّناق وهو حلقة توضع تحت حنك الدابة ثم يجعل فيها خيط يشد برأْسه يمنع بها جماحه. وفي حديث عثمان: مَنْ يَشْتري هذه الزَّنقة فيزيدها في المسجد؟ وزنق الفرسَ يَزْنُقه ويزْنِقه: شكَله في أَربعة. وأَمر زَنيقٌ: وثيق. ابن الأَعرابي: الزُّنُق العقولُ التامَّة.
شرم (مقاييس اللغة) الشين والراء والميم أصلٌ واحدٌ لا يُخْلِف، وهو يدلُّ على خَرْق في الشيء ومَزْق. من ذلك قولُهم: تشرَّم الشَّيء، إذا تمزَّق.
شرم (الصّحاح في اللغة) والشَرْمُ مصدر شرَمه، أي شقَّهُ. والتَشْريمُ: التشقيق. وتَشَرَّم الشيء: تمزّق وتشقّق. ورجل أَشْرَمُ بيِّن الشَرَم، أي مَشْرومُ الأنف.
شرم (لسان العرب) الشَّرْمُ والتَّشْريمُ: قَطْعُ الأَرْنبة وثَفَر الناقة، قيل ذلك فيهما خاصة. ناقة شَرْماء وشَريمٌ ومَشْرومةٌ. ورجل أَشْرمُ بَيِّنُ الشَّرَم: مشْرُومُ الأَنف، ولذلك قيل لأَبرهة الأَشْرَمُ. وأُذُنٌ شَرْماءُ ومُشَرَّمَةٌ: قُطع من أَعلاها شيءٌ يسير.

§ 253.—XXXVII, 69-82

ePSD: zar
zar [SHEAF] wr. zar_3; zar "sheaf (of barley); stack of sheaves" Akk. zarru
ePSD: zēru
i'iz [SEED] wr. i-iz "seed" Akk. zēru
numun [SEED] wr. numun "seed" Akk. zēru
šenumun [SEED] wr. še-numun "seed" Akk. zēru

ولد (مقاييس اللغة) الواو واللام والدال: أصلٌ صحيح، وهو دليل النَّجْل والنسْل، ثمَّ يقاس عليه غيرُه. وتولَّد الشَّيءُ عن الشَّيء: حصَل عنه. واللِّدَة نُقصانُه الواو لأنّ أصله وِلْدة.
الوَلَدُ (القاموس المحيط) وولَدتْ تلِدُ وِلاداً ووِلادةً وإلادةً ولِدةً ومَوْلِداً. واللِّدَةُ: التِّرْبُ، والتَّوْليدُ: التَّرْبيةُ، ومنه قولُ اللهِ عزَّ وجلَّ لعيسى، صلى الله عليه وسلم: " أنتَ نبيِّي وأنا ولَدْتُك"، أي: ربَّيْتُك، فقالتِ النصارى: أنت بُنَيِّي وأنا ولدْتُك، تعالى اللهُ عن ذلك عُلُوّاً كبيراً.
هَلَدَ (القاموس المحيط) هلَدَ الوَعْكُ الناسَ: أخَذهم، وعمَّهم.
ذر (مقاييس اللغة) الذال والراء المشددة أصلٌ واحد يدلُّ على لطافة وانتشار. ومن ذلك الذَّرُّ: صِغار النَّمل، الواحدة ذرَّةٌ. وحكي عن أبي زيد: ذَرَّ البَقْلُ، إذا طلَعَ من الأرض. وهو من الباب؛ لأنّه يكون حينئذٍ صِغاراً منتشراً.
ذرر (الصّحاح في اللغة) وذَرَرْتُ الحبَّ والدواء والمِلحَ أَذُرُّهُ ذَرًّا: فرَّقْتُهُ.
ذرر (لسان العرب) ذَرَّ الشيءَ يَذُرُّه: أَخذه بأَطراف أَصابعه ثم نثره على الشيء. وذَرَّ الشيءَ يَذُرُّهُ إِذا بَدَّدَهُ.
زغر (مقاييس اللغة) الزاء والغين والراء أُصَيْلٌ. يقال زَغر الماءُ وزَخر. وليس هذا عندي من جهة الإبدال؛ لأن قياسَ زغر قياسٌ صحيح، وسيجيء *في الرباعيّ مايصحِّحه. وذكر ابن دُريد أنَّ الزَّغر الاغتصاب؛ يقال زَغَرْت الشيء زَغْراً. قال: والزغْر فعلٌ مُماتٌ.
زَغْرهُ (القاموس المحيط) وزَغْرُ كلِّ شيءٍ: كثْرتُه وإفراطُه.

زغر (لسان العرب) زَغَرَ الشيءَ يَزْغَرُه زَغْراً: اقْتَضَبهُ (قوله: «اقتضبه» في القاموس: اغتصبه. قال شارحه: في بعض النسخ اقتضبه. وهو غلط). الكَثْرةُ؛ قال الهذلي: بل قد أتاني ناصِحٌ عن كاشحٍ، بِعَداوةٍ ظَهرتْ، وزَغْرِ أقاولِ أراد أقاويل، حذف الياء للضرورة. وزَغْرُ كل شيء: كثرته والإفْراطُ فيه.
زغد (لسان العرب) ونهر زَغّاد: كثير الماءِ، وقد زغدَ وزخر وزغر بمعنى واحد؛
قضب (لسان العرب) القَضْبُ: القَطْعُ. قضَبه يقْضِبه قضْباً، واقْتَضبه، وقضَّبه، فانْقَضب وتقَضّب: انقطع؛ قَضبْت عقالَها، واقْتَضبْته: اقْتَطعْته من الشيء؛ والقَضْبُ: قَضْبُك القَضِيب ونحوه. ومنه قيل: اقْتَضبْتُ الحديثَ، إنما هو انْتَزَعْتُه واقْتَطَعْتُه، وقُضابةُ الشيءِ: ما اقْتُضِبَ منه؛ وخصَّ بعضُهم به ما سقط من أعالي العِيدان المُقْتَضبة. وقُضابةُ الشَّجر: ما يَتَساقطُ من أطراف عيدانها إذا قُضِبَت. والقَضِيبُ: الغُصْنُ. والقضِيبُ: كلُّ نبْتٍ من الأغصان يُقْضَبُ، والجمع قُضُبٌ وقُضْبٌ، وقُضْبانٌ وقِضْبانٌ. الأخيرة اسم للجمع.

§ 254.—XXXVII, 83-87

ePSD: marru
<u>mar</u> <u>[SHOVEL]</u> wr. ^{ĝeš}mar; ^{urud}mar "shovel" Akk. marru
<u>mun</u> <u>[SALT]</u> wr. mun; mun$_4$; munu$_3$ "(to be) brackish; salt" Akk. marru; ţabtu
<u>ses</u> <u>[BITTER]</u> wr. ses "(to be) bitter, brackish" Akk. marru
مَرّ (القاموس المحيط) مَرَّ مَرّا ومُروراً: جازَ، وذَهبَ، كاسْتَمَرَّ. مَرَّهُ، و~ به: جاز عليه. وامْتَرَّ به، و~ عليه: كمَرَّ. وقَولُ الله تعالى: {حَمَلَتْ حَمْلاً خَفيفاً فَمَرَّتْ بِه}، أي: اسْتَمَرّتْ به. وتمَرْمرَ الرَّمْلُ: مارَ. ومَرَّرَهُ: جعلَهُ مَرّا، ودحاهُ على وجهِ الأرض. وأمَرَّهُ على الجِسْرِ: سَلَكَهُ فيه. وأمَرَّهُ به: جعلَهُ يمُرُّ به. ومارَّهُ: مَرَّ مَعَهُ. واسْتَمَرَّ: مضَى على طريقةٍ واحدةٍ،
مرر (لسان العرب) مَرَّ عليه وبه يَمُرُّ مَرّا أي اجتاز. يقال: فلان يَصْنَعُ ذلك الأَمْرَ ذاتَ المرار أي يصنعه مراراً ويدعه مراراً. ولقيه ذاتَ المِرار أي مِراراً كثيرة. وذو المُرار: أرض، قال: ولعلها كثيرة هذا النبات فسمّيت بذلك؛ والتَمَرْمُرُ: الاهتزازُ. قال أبو منصور: وسمعت أعرابيّاً يقول لهمّ وذلّ وذلّ، يُمَرْمرُ مرْزةَ ويَلُوكُها؛ يُمرْمِرُ أصلُه يُمرّرُ أي يَدْحُوها على وجه الأرض. والمَرارةُ: ضِدُّ الحلاوة، والمُرُّ نَقِيضُ الخُلْو؛ مَرَّ الشيءُ يَمُرُّ؛
التِّنُّ (القاموس المحيط) والتِينانُ، بالكسر: الذِئبُ، ومِثالُ الشيء. وتانَّ بينهما: قايسَ.
تنن (لسان العرب) التِّنُّ، بالكسر: التِّرْبُ والحِتْنُ، وقيل: الشِّبْه، وقيل: الصاحب، والجمع أَتْنان. يقال: صِبْوةٌ أَتْنانٌ. ابن الأعرابي: هو سِنُّه وتِنُّه وحِتْنُه، وهم أَسنان وأَتنان وأتراب إذا كان سِنُّهم واحداً، وهما تِنّان، قال ابن السكيت: هما مستويان في عَقْلٍ أو ضَعْفٍ أو شِدّة أو مروءَة. قال ابن بري: جمع تِنّ أَتنان وتِنين؛ عن الفراء؛ وأنشد فقال: فأصبح مبصراً نهاره، وأقصر ما يعدّ له التّنينا (* قوله «فأصبح» كذا في النسخ). وفي حديث عمار: إنّ رسول الله، صلى الله عليه وسلم، تِنّي وتِرْبي؛ تِنُّ الرجل: مثله في السِّنّ. والتِّنُّ والتَّنُّ: الصبيّ الذي قصَعه المرضُ فلا يَشِبّ، وقد أَتَنّه المرضُ. أبو زيد: يقال أَتَنّه المرضُ إذا قصَعه فلم يلحقْ بأتنانِه أي بأقرانه، فهو لا يَشِبّ، قال: والتِّنُّ الشخصُ والمِثال.

§ 256.—XXXVII, 97-100

AALD: mašāru (v.) (يهجر) يمشط (الملابس)، ينسحب (على الارض)، يدفع حول، يسحب حول، يؤجل؟
AALD: wašāru (See ašāru)
AALD: ašāru (v.) يحرر
مسرهُ (القاموس المحيط) مَسرَهُ: سَلّهُ، واسْتخْرَجهُ من ضِيقٍ، و~ الناسَ: غَمزَ بهم، وسعَى، أو أغْراهمْ.
مسر (لسان العرب) مَسَرَ الشيءَ يَمْسُرُه مَسْراً: استخرجه من ضيق، والمَسْرُ فعل الماسِر. ومَسَرَ الناسَ يَمْسُرُهُمْ مَسْراً: غمزَ بهم. ويقال: هو يَمْسُرُ الناسَ أي يُغْرِيهِمْ. ومَسَرْتُ به ومَحَلْتُ به أي سَعَيْتُ به.
مشر (مقاييس اللغة) الميم والشين والراء أصلٌ صحيح يدلُّ على تشعُّبٍ في شيء وتفرُّق. ومَشَرتِ الأرض: أخرجَتْ نباتَها. ومَشَرْتُ الشَيء. فرَّقتُهُ.
مصر (الصّحاح في اللغة) المِصْرُ: واحد الأمْصار. والمِصْرُ أيضاً: الحدُّ والحاجز بين الشيئين. وأهل مِصْرَ يكتبون في شروطهم: اشترى فلان الدار بمُصورِها، أي بحدودها.
مصر (لسان العرب) ومَصَّر عليه العطاءَ تَمْصِيراً: قلّله وفرّقه قليلاً قليلاً. والمُصارةُ: الموضع الذي تُمْصَرُ فيه الخيل، قال: حكاه صاحب العين. والتمصر التتبع، وجاءت الإبل إلى الحوض مُتَمصِّرة ومُمْصِرة أي متفرقة. والمِصْرُ الحدّ في كل شيء، وقيل: المصر الحدُّ في الأرض خاصة.

§ 257.—XXXVII, 101-XXXVIII, 4

ePSD: AK
<u>ak</u> <u>[DO]</u> wr. ak; a "to do; to make; to act, perform; to proceed, proceeding (math.)" Akk. epēšu
<u>ša</u> <u>[SNAP]</u> wr. ša$_5$ "to snap off" Akk. haşāşu
ePSD: ŠU
<u>šu</u> <u>[HAND]</u> wr. šu; sum$_5$; šu-x "hand" Akk. qātu
<u>šuniĝin</u> <u>[TOTAL]</u> wr. šu-niĝin$_2$; šu-niĝin; |ŠU "total, sum" Akk. napharu
شوا (لسان العرب) والشَّوى: اليدانِ والرجلان.
عكا (الصّحاح في اللغة) والعَكِيُّ من ألبان الضأن: ما حُلب بعضه على بعض فاشتدّ وغلُظ. وعكتِ الناقة، أي سمنت وغلظت. ويقال: مائةٌ مِعْكاءٌ، أي سِمانٌ غلاظٌ.
عكا (لسان العرب) العُكْوة: أصلُ اللّسان، والأكثر العَكدة. وعُكْوةُ كلّ شيء: غِلَظُه ومُعْظَمُه. والعاكي: الشادُّ، وقد عكا إذا شدَّ، ومنه عَكْوُ الذَّنب وهو شدُّه. ويقال: عَكَوْتُه في الحديد والوَثاق عَكْواً إذا شدَدْته؛ وعكاهُ عَكْواً: شدَّه. وعكا بالمكان: أقام.
عكو (مقاييس اللغة) وهذا صحيح لأنَّه إذا عقد ثوبه فقد عكاه وجمعه.

عك (مقاييس اللغة) العين والكاف أصولٌ صحيحة ثلاثة: أحدها اشتداد الحرّ، والآخر الحبْس، والآخر جنْسٌ من الضرب.
عكك (الصّحاح في اللغة) ورجلٌ عكٌّ، أي صلْبٌ شديدٌ. وحكى أبو زيد: عككْتُهُ الحديث أعُكُّهُ عكًّا، إذا استعدته الحديث حتّى كرّره عليك مرتين.
عكك (لسان العرب) وعكّني بالأمر عكاً إذا ردّده عليك حتى يُتْعبك، وكذلك عكّه بالقول عكاً إذا ردّه عليه متعنتاً. وعكّ عليه: عطف كعاك. وفرس معكٌّ: يجري قليلاً ثم يحتاج إلى الضرب. وأما قول العجاج: عكٌّ شديدُ الأمْر قسْبرِيٌّ قال أبو زيد: العكّ الصلب الشديد المجتمع.
عفش (لسان العرب) عفشه يعْفشه عفشاً: جمعه.
أبش (مقاييس اللغة) الهمزة والباء والشين ليس بأصل، لأنّ الهمزة فيه مبدلة من هاء. قال ابن دريد: أبشْتُ الشيء وهبشْتُه إذا جمعته.
عفس (مقاييس اللغة) العين والفاء والسين أصل صحيح يدلّ على ممارسة ومعالجة. يقولون: هو يعافس الشّيء، إذا عالجه.
واعتفس القومُ: اصطرعوا. وعُفس، إذا سُجن.
العفْسُ (القاموس المحيط) العفْسُ، كالضّرْب: الحبْسُ، والابتذالُ، وشدّةُ سوْقِ الإبلِ، ودلْكُ الأديمِ، والضرْبُ على العجُزِ بالرِّجْل، والجذْبُ إلى الأرضِ في ضغْطٍ شديدٍ.
عكش (مقاييس اللغة) العين والكاف والشين أصلٌ صحيح يدلُّ على مثل ما دلّ عليه الذي تقدّم من التجمُّع. يقال عكش شعرُه إذا تلبّد.
عكش (القاموس المحيط) و~ الشيءَ: جمعهُ،
عكش (لسان العرب) عكش عليه: حمل. والعكْش جمْعك الشيء.

§ 259.—XXXVIII, 10-15

ePSD: GIŠ
ĝeš [TREE] wr. ĝeš; mu; u$_5$ "tree; wood; a description of animals" Akk. işu
ildag [POPLAR] wr. ^{ĝeš}ildag$_2$; ^{ĝeš}ildag$_4$; ildag$_2$; ^{ĝeš}ildag$_3$; ^{ĝeš}ildag; ^{ĝeš}ildag$_x$ "a poplar" Akk. adāru; ildakku
ePSD: AB.NAM
absin [FURROW] wr. absin$_3$; ab-sin$_2$; absin "furrow" Akk. abšinnu; šer'u
ePSD: apin
apin [PLOW] wr. apin; ^{ĝeš}apin "(seed) plow" Akk. epinnu
ePSD: APIN
absin [FURROW] wr. absin$_3$; ab-sin$_2$; absin "furrow" Akk. abšinnu; šer'u
apin [PLOW] wr. apin; ^{ĝeš}apin "(seed) plow" Akk. epinnu
ari [DISEASE] wr. ari$_2$; uru$_4$ "a disease" Akk. maškadu
engar [FARMER] wr. engar; mu-un-gar$_3$; mu-un-ga-ar "farmer; an official" Akk. ikkaru
ereš [CULTIVATOR] wr. ereš$_4$ "cultivator" Akk. errēšum
uru [SOW] wr. uru$_4$; uru$_{11}^{ru}$; i-ru "to sow; to cultivate" Akk. erēšu

جشش (لسان العرب) الجوهري: المجش الرحى التي يُطحن بها الجشيش. وقال أبو حنيفة: الجشّاء من القسيّ التي في صوتها جُشّة عند الرمْي؛ قال أبو ذؤيب: ونميمة من قانِص مُتلبِّب، في كفه جشْءٌ أجشُّ وأقطع قال: أجش فذكر وإن كان صفة للجشْء، وهو مؤنث، لأنه أراد العوْد. وقال في موضع آخر: والسّراءُ ضرْب من شجر القسيّ، الواحدة سراءةٌ. قال الجوهري: السّراءُ، بالفتح ممدود، شجر تُتّخذ منه القسيّ؛ وفي الحديث: أنه سمع تكْبيرة رجُلٍ أجشّ الصوت أي في صوته جُشّة، وهي شدّة وغلظ. والجُشّ أيضاً: مما ارتفع من الأرض ولم يبْلُغ أن يكون جبلاً. والجُشّ: النّجفة فيه غِلظ وارتفاع.
أفن (مقاييس اللغة) الهمزة والفاء والنون يدلّ على خلوّ الشيء وتفريغه. ويقال إنّ الجوز المأفونَ هو الذي لا شيء في جوفه.
أفن (القاموس المحيط) أفن الناقة يأفِنُها: حلبها في غير حينِها، فيفْسدُها ذلك، وأخذه بإفّانهِ، بالكسر مُشدّدةً: بإبّانه.
أفن (الصّحاح في اللغة) والأفْن النقْص. والمُتأفّنُ المُتنقّصُ.
أفن (لسان العرب) أفن الناقة والشاة يأفِنُها أفْناً: حلبها في غير حينها، وقيل: هو استخراجُ جميع ما في ضرعها. وفي حديث عليّ: إيّاك ومشاورة النساء فإن رأيهنّ إلى أفْن؛ الأفْنُ: النقصُ. ورجل أفِينٌ ومأفونٌ أي ناقصُ العقل.
أبن (لسان العرب) ويُقالُ: إنّهُ ليُوبرُ أثرًا إذا اقتصّه، وقيل لمادح الميّت مُؤبّنٌ لاتّباعه آثار فعاله وصنائعه. والتّأبينُ: اقتِفار الأثر. الجوهريّ: التأبينُ أن تقْفو أثر الشّيْء.

§ 260.—XXXVIII, 16-20

ePSD: TUG$_2$.KIN
tuggur [PLOW] wr. tug$_2$-gur$_{10}$; tug$_2$-gur$_x$(|ŠE.KIN|); ^{ĝeš}tug$_2$-gur$_{10}$; tug$_2$-gur; ^{ĝeš}tug$_2$-gur$_8$; tukur$_x$(|LAGAB×U|) "a plow; to plow, to apply a tuggur-plow"
tugsaga [PLOW] wr. tug$_2$-saga$_{11}$; ^{ĝeš}tug$_2$-sig$_{18}$; ^{ĝeš}tug$_2$-sa-ga; šu-saga$_{11}$; ^{ĝeš}tug$_2$-sig$_x$(|ŠE.KIN|); tug$_x$(LAK483)-sig$_9$ "a plow"
ePSD: GAN$_2$.UR$_4$
ganagur [PATH] wr. gana$_2$-gur$_4$; gana$_2$-gur$_{10}$; gana$_2$-gur$_{15}$ "a path" Akk. kanagurru
AALD: kanagurru (s.) (ganagurru) الممر الدائري، البيدر
ePSD: ĝeš-gana$_2$
ĝešgana [PESTLE] wr. ĝeš-gan-na; ĝeš-gin$_7$-na; ĝeš-gana$_2$; ĝeš-gi-na; ĝeš-gin$_7$; ĝeš-TAG "pestle"

Akk. bukānu

ĝešgana [TREE] wr. ĝeš-kin$_2$; ĝeš-gana$_2$ "a tree" Akk. kiškanû

تكك (الصَحَاح في اللغة) وقد تَكَّهُ النبيذُ، مثل هَكَّهُ وهَرَّجَهُ، إذا بلغ منه.

تكك (لسان العرب) تَكَّ الشَيءَ يَتُكُّه تكّاً: وطئه فشدخه، ولا يكون إلاَّ في شيء لين كالرطب والبطيخ ونحوهما. وتُكُك كبُزُل، وما كنت تاكّاً ولقد تَكَكْتَ، بالفتح، تُكُوكاً.

أنن (لسان العرب) وأَنَّ الماءَ يؤُنُّه أَنّاً إذا صبَّه. وفي كلام الأَوائل: أُنَّ ماءً ثم أَغْلِه أي صُبَّه وأَغْلِه؛

كنن (لسان العرب) الكِنُّ والكِنَّةُ والكِنانُ: وقاء كل شيءٍ وسِتْرُه. والكِنانة: جَعْبة السِهام تُتَّخذُ من جُلود لا خَشب فيها أَو من خشب لا جلود فيها.

الليث: الكِنانة كالجَعْبة غير أَنها صغيرة تتخذ للنَّبْل. ابن دريد: كِنانة النَّبْل إذا كانت من أَدم، فإِن كانت من خشب فهو جفير.

طجن (لسان العرب) الطاجِنُ: المِقْلى، وهو بالفارسية تابه. والطَّجْنُ قَلْوُك عليه، دَخيل. قال الليث: أُهملت الجيم والطاء في الثلاثي الصحيح، ووجدناها مستعملة بعضها عربية وبعضها معرَّبة، فمن المعرَّب قولهم طَجَنَةُ بلد معروف، وقولهم للطابقِ الذي يُقْلى عليه اللحم الطاجِنُ، وقَلِيَّةٌ مُطَجَّنة، والعامة تقول مُطَنْجنة. الجوهري: الطَّيْجَنُ والطاجِنُ يُقْلى فيه، وكلاهما معرَّب لأَن الطاء والجيم لا يجتمعان في أَصل كلام العرب.

تكن (تاج العروس) تِكِّينٌ، كسِكِّينٍ زِنَةً ومَعْنًى؛

قنر (مقاييس اللغة) القاف والنون والراء كلمة: القِنَوْر: الضَّخْم الرَّأْس.

قنر (العين) القِنَوَّرُ: الشديد الرأس، الضخم من كل شيء.

قنر (تاج العروس) القِنَوْر، كهِبَيَّخ: الشَديدُ الضَخْمُ الرأس من كلّ شيْءٍ وقيل: القِنَوْر: الشَرِسُ الصَعْبُ من كُلِّ شيْءٍ، والقِنَارُ، والقِنَارَةُ، بكسْرِهِما: الخَشَبَة يُعلَّق عليها القصّابُ اللَّحْمَ، يُقال: إِنّه ليس من كلام العرَب.

كنر (لسان العرب) قال ابن سيده: والكِنَّاراتُ يختلف فيها فيقال هي العيدان التي يضرب بها، ويقال هي الدُّفُوف؛ ومنه حديث عبد الله بن عمرو بن العاص، رضي الله عنهما: إن الله تبارك وتعالى أنزلَ الحقَّ ليُذْهِبَ به الباطل ويُبْطِلَ به اللَّعِبَ والزَّفْنَ والزَّمّارات والمَزاهِرَ والكِنّارات. وفي صفته، صلى الله عليه وسلم، في التوراة: بعثتك تمحو المَعازِفَ والكِنَّارات؛ هي، بالفتح والكسر، العيدان، وقيل البَرابِطُ، وقيل الطَّنْبُورُ، وقال الحَربي: كان ينبغي أن يقال الكِرانات، فقدّمت النون على الراء، قال: وأظن الكِرانَ فارسيّاً معرّباً. قال: وسمعت أبا نصر يقول: الكَرِينةُ الضاربة بالعُود، سميت به لضربها بالكِرانِ؛ وقال أبو سعيد الضرير: أحسبها بالباء، جمع كِبار، وكِبار جمع كَبَر، وهو الطبل كجَمَل وجمال وجمالات. ومنه حديث عليّ، عليه السلام: أمرنا بكسر الكُوبَة والكِنّارة والشِّياع. ابن الأعرابي: الكَنانيرُ واحدتها كِنّارة، قال قوم: هي العيدان، ويقال: هي الطنابير، ويقال الطُّبُول. التهذيب في ترجمة قنر: رجل مُقْنَوِرٌ ومُقَنَّرٌ ومُكْنَوِرٌ ومُكَنَّر إذا كان ضَخْماً سَمِجاً أَو مُعْتَمّاً عِمَّةً جافية.

جنارَةُ (القاموس المحيط) والجَنُّورُ، كتَنُّور: مَداسُ الحِنْطَة والشَعير.

جنر (تاج العروس) والجَنُّورُ، كتَنُّور: مَداسُ الحِنْطَةِ والشَعِير.

دوس (لسان العرب) وداسَ الناسُ الحَبَّ وأَداسُوه: دَرَسُوه؛ عن أَبي حنيفة. وفي حديث أُمِّ زَرْعٍ: ودائس ومنقٍّ: الدائس الذي يَدُوسُ الطعامَ ويَدُقُّه ليُخْرِجَ الحَبَّ منه، وهو الدِّياسُ، وقلبت الواو ياء لكسرة الدال.

وجن (لسان العرب) ووَجَنَ به الأَرضَ: ضربها به. والوَجْنُ: الدَقُّ. وفي حديث عليَ، كرم الله وجهه: ما شَبَّهْتُ وَقْعَ السيوف على الهامِ إلا بوَقْعِ البيازِرِ على المَواجِنِ؛ جمع مِيجَنةٍ وهي المِدقَّةُ. يقال: وَجَنَ القصّارُ الثوب يَجِنُه وَجْناً دقَّه، والميم زائدة، وهي مِفْعَلَةٌ، بالكسر.

§ 261.—XXXVIII, 21-27

ePSD: naqidu

nagada [HERDSMAN] wr. na-gada "herdsman" Akk. naqidu

نقد (العين) والإنسان ينقد بعينيه إلى الشيء وهو مداومته النظر واختلاسه حتى لا يفطن له.

نقد (مقاييس اللغة) النون والقاف والدال أصلٌ صحيح يدلُّ على إبراز شيءٍ وبُروزه. وتقول العرب: ما زالَ فلانٌ يَنْقُد الشَّيء، إذا لم يزَلْ ينظُر إليه.

نقد (لسان العرب) النَقْدُ: خلافُ النَّسيئة. ونقد أَرنبَته بإِصبعه إِذا ضربها؛ ونقد الرجلُ الشيءَ بنظره يَنْقُدُه نقْداً ونقَدَ إِليه: اختلَسَ النظر نحوه.

§ 264.—XXXVIII, 44-60

ePSD: mahāru

BU'I [FACE] wr. BU-I "to face" Akk. mahāru

šu gid [ACCEPT] wr. šu gid$_2$ "to accept" Akk. mahāru

šu teĝ [ACCEPT] wr. šu teĝ$_4$; šu teĝ$_3$ "to accept" Akk. leqû; mahāru

AALD: tālittu (s.) See alādu الذرية، الصغير، الناشئ

ePSD: alādu

peš [THICK] wr. peš; peš$_5$; peš$_4$; peš$_6$ "innards; to breathe; grandson; descendant; to give birth (to); (to be) pregnant; pregnancy; to gather; (to be) thick; (to be) wide" Akk. alādu; kabattu; līp līpi; mār māri; mērû; napāšu; šabāšu

ugu [BEAR] wr. ugu; ugu$_4$ "to give birth (to)" Akk. alādu

utud [BEAR] wr. tud; u$_3$-tu; tu-ud "to give birth (to), bear a child" Akk. alādu

مخر (مقاييس اللغة) الميم والخاء والراء أصلٌ يدل على شَقٍّ وفَتْح. يقال مَخَرت السَفينةُ الماءَ مخراً: شقَّته.

مخر (الصَحَاح في اللغة) وامْتَخَرْتُ القومَ: انتقيت خيارهم ونُخْبَتَهُم. والمِخْرَةُ والمُخْرَةُ: الشيء الذي تختاره. والماخورُ: مجلسُ الفُسّاقِ.

خرت (مقاييس اللغة) الخاء والراء والتاء أصلٌ يدلُ على تثقّبٍ وشِبْهه. فالخُرْت: ثَقب الإبرة والأخرات: الحلَق في رؤوس النَّسْوع. والخِرِّيتُ: الرجلُ الدَّليلُ الماهر بالدَّلالة. وسُمّي بذلك لشقّه المفازة، كأنّه يدخُل في أخْراتِها. ويقال خَرَتْنا الأرض، إذا عرفْناها فلم تخْفَ علينا طرقُها.
التَالِدُ (القاموس المحيط) التَّالِدُ، كصاحِبٍ، والتَّلْدُ، بالفتح والضم والتَّحْرِيكِ، والتِّلادُ والتَّليدُ والإتْلادُ والمُتْلَدُ: ما وُلِدَ عندك من مالِكَ أو نُتِجَ. تلد المالُ يَتْلُدُ ويتِلِدُ تُلوداً، وأتْلَدَهُ هو.
تلد (لسان العرب) التالد: المال القديم الأَصليُّ الذي وُلد عندك، وهو نقيض الطارف. ابن سيده: التَلْدُ والتُّلْدُ والتِّلادُ والتَّليدُ والإتْلادُ كالإِسْنام والمُتْلَدُ، الأخيرة عن ابن جني: ما وُلد عندك من مالك أو نُتج، ولذلك حكم يعقوب أن تاءه بدل من الواو، وهذا لا يقوى، لأنه لو كان ذلك لرُدَّ في بعض تصاريفه إلى الأصل. وجارية تليدة إذا ورثها الرجل فإذا وُلدتْ عنده فهي وَليدَة.

§ 265.—XXXVIII, 61-75

ePSD: sarāru

<u>ganTIR</u> <u>[LIAR?]</u> wr. ga-an-TIR "a liar?" Akk. sarāru

ePSD: sarru

<u>hulu</u> <u>[BAD]</u> wr. hul; hul_3 "to destroy; (to be) bad-smelling, maloderous; (to be) bad, evil; (to be) slight, lightweight; (to be) false; (to be) criminal, dishonest; enemy; to raid; to strike the eyes; blinker, winker, one with vision problems" Akk. abātu ša īni; bēšu; lapātu ša īni; şabru; lemnu; masku; qallu; sarru; zāmânû

<u>lu'IM</u> <u>[CRIMINAL]</u> wr. lu_2-IM "criminal; false, fraudulent" Akk. sarru

<u>lul</u> <u>[FALSE]</u> wr. lul "(to be) false; (to be) criminal" Akk. sarru

<u>lulul</u> <u>[LIAR]</u> wr. lu_2-lul "liar" Akk. sarru

AALD: šimtu (s.) عاقد العزم، الوصية، الميثاق

سرر (لسان العرب) السِّرُّ: من الأَسْرار التي تكتم. والسر: ما أَخْفَيْتَ، والجمع أَسرار. ورجل سِرِّيٌّ: يصنع الأَشياءَ سِراً من قوم سِرِّيِّين.
والسريرَةُ: كالسِّرِّ، والجمع السرائرُ. الليث: السِّرُّ ما أَسْرَرْتَ به. والسريرةُ: عمل السر من خير أَو شر. وأَسَرَّ الشيءَ: كتمه وأَظهره، وهو من الأَضداد، سَرَرْتُه: كتمته، وسررته: أَعْلَنْته، والوجهان جميعاً يفسران في قوله تعالى: وأَسَرُّوا الندامة؛

ذمم (لسان العرب) والذِّمَّة العهد والكفالة، وجمعها ذِمامٌ. وفلان له ذِمَّة أَي حق والذَّمامةُ والذِّمامةُ: الحق كالذِّمَّة؛ قال ذو الرمة: تكُنْ عَوْجةً يجزيكما الله عندها بها الأَجْرَ، أَو تُقضى ذِمامةُ صاحب ذِمامة: حُرْمةٌ وحق. وفي الحديث ذكر الذِّمَّة والذِّمام، وهما بمعنى العَهْد والأَمانِ والضَّمانِ والحُرْمَةِ والحق، وسُمّي أَهل الذِّمَّةِ ذِمَّةً لدخولهم في عهد المسلمين وأَمانهم.
سمت (لسان العرب) السَّمْتُ: حُسْنُ النَّحْو في مَذْهبِ الدِّينِ، والفعلُ سَمَتَ يَسْمُتُ سمْتاً، وإِنه لحَسَنُ السَّمْت أَي حَسَنُ القَصْد والمَذْهب في دينه ودُنْياه. والسَّمْتُ الطريقُ؛ يقال: الْزَمْ هذا السَّمْتَ؛ وسَمْتُ الطريق: قَصْدُه. والسَّمْتُ السَّيْرُ على الطَّريق بالظَّنِّ؛

§ 266.—XXXVIII, 76-81

ePSD: libbātu

<u>murgu</u> <u>[RAGE]</u> wr. $murgu_3$ "rage" Akk. libbātu

ePSD: rabāşu

<u>šed</u> <u>[LIE]</u> wr. $še_{21}$; $še_x(NA_2)$ "to lie down (of animals); to rest, sleep (of animals)" Akk. itūlu; rabāşu

ePSD: tarbaşu

<u>kisim</u> <u>[STALL]</u> wr. $kisim_2$ "animal stall" Akk. tarbaşu

<u>rig</u> <u>[SHEEPFOLD]</u> wr. rig_{10} "sheepfold, animal stall" Akk. isru; tarbaşu

<u>tur</u> <u>[STALL]</u> wr. tur_3; ${}^{e}{}_{2}tur_3$ "animal stall" Akk. tarbaşu

AALD: maqātu (s.) يسقط على، ينقض على، يسقط في معركة، يتحمل الهزيمة، يهاجم، يغزو، ينهار، ينقص، يقتطع، يدمر

لبت (لسان العرب) لَبَتَ يده لَبْتاً: لواها. واللَّبْتُ أَيضاً: ضَرْبُ الصَّدْرِ والبَطْنِ والأَقراب بالعصا.
لبت (تهذيب اللغة) سلمة عن الفراء في قول الله جلَ وعزَ: {مِنْ طينٍ لازبٍ} [الصافات: 11] وقال: اللازب واللاتِبُ واللاصقُ واحد، لَتَبَ عليه ثيابه ورتّبها إذا شدَّها عليه، ولَبَبَ على الفرس جُلَّه إذا شدَّه عليه، يعني فرسه، وقال الليث: اللَّبْتُ اللُّبسُ يقال: لبت عليه ثوبه، والتَّتَب، وهو لُبسٌ كأنّه لا يريد أن يَخْلعُه، وقال غيره :أَلْتَبَ فلانٌ عليه الأمر إلْتابا أي أوْجبه فهو مُلْتِبٌ.
لبت (تاج العروس) ولبتَ فُلانا لَبْتا: ضَرَبَ صَدْرَهُ وبطْنَهُ وأَقْرابَهُ أي خَواصره بالعَصا. وفي التهذيب في ترجمة ب أ س: إِذا قال الرَّجُلُ لعَدُوّه: لا بأْس عليك فقد أَمَّنَهُ، لأَنّهُ نفى البأْسَ عنه، وهو في لغة حِمْيَرَ: لَباتِ عليك؛ أَي لا بأْس،
ربض (مقاييس اللغة) الراء والباء والضاد أصلٌ يدلُّ على سكونٍ واستقرار.من ذلك رَبَضَتِ الشاة وغيرها تَرْبِض رَبْضا. والرَّبيض الجماعةُ من الغنم الرَّابضة رَبَض البطن: ما ولِيَ الأرضَ من البعير وغيره حين يَرْبِضُ. والرَّبَض ما حَولَ المدينة؛ ومسكن كلِّ قوم رَبَض. والرَّبْضة مَقتَل كلِّ قومٍ قُتلوا في بُقعةٍ واحدة.فأمّا قولُهم قِرْبَةٌ رَبوضٌ، للواسعة، فمن الباب، كأنّها تُملأُ فترْبِضُ، أو تُروِي فترْبِض. فأما الرَّبوض فهي الدَّوحة والشَّجرةُ العظيمة، وسميت بذلك لأنه يُؤوى إليها ويُرْبَض تحتها. ومأوى الغنم: رَبَضها؛ لأنها تربض [فيه]. وقال قوم: أَرْبَضَتِ الشمس، إذا اشتدَّ

حرَّها، حتى تُرْبض الشاةَ والظبي. ورَبْضُ الرَجُل ورُبْضُه: امرأته؛ والقياس مطَّرد، لأنها سَكَنُه. والدَليل على صحة هذا القياس أنَهم يُسمُّون المسكن كله ربضاً.

ربص (مقاييس اللغة) الراء والباء والصاد أصلٌ واحدٌ يدلُّ على الانتظار. من ذلك التربُّص. يقال تربَّصْت به.

رَبصَ (القاموس المحيط) رَبصَ بفلانٍ رَبْصاً: انْتظرَ به خيراً أو شرّاً يَحُلُّ به، كتربَّصَ، ويقالُ: رَبصَني أمرٌ، وأنا مَرْبُوصٌ.

ربص (لسان العرب) التَربُّصُ: الانْتظارُ. رَبص بالشيء رَبْصاً وترَبّصَ به: انتظر به خيراً أو شرّاً، وتربّصَ به الشيء: كذلك. الليث: التَربُّصُ بالشيء أن تَنْتَظِرَ به يوماً ما، والفعل تَربَّصْت به،

ربص (لسان العرب) التَربُّصُ: الانْتظارُ. رَبص بالشيء رَبْصاً وتَربّصَ به: انتظر به خيراً أو شرّاً، وتربّصَ به الشيء: كذلك. الليث: التَربُّصُ بالشيء أن تَنْتَظِرَ به يوماً ما، والفعل تَربَّصْت به، وفي التنزيل العزيز: هل تَربّصُون بنا إلاّ إحْدَى الحُسْنَيَيْن؛ أي إلا الظَّفَر وإلاّ الشَهادة، ونحن نَتربَّصُ بكم أَحَدَ الشرَّين: عذاباً من الله أو قَتْلاً بأيدينا، فبين ما نَنْتَظِرُه وتَنْتظِرونه فَرْقٌ كبير. وفي الحديث: إنما يُريدُ أن يَترَبّص بكم الدَوائِر؛ التربُّصُ: المُكْثُ والانتظارُ. ولي على هذا الأمر رُبْصةٌ أي تلبّثٌ. ابن السكيت: يقال أقامت المرأة رُبْصتَها في بيت زوجها وهو الوقت الذي جُعل لزوجها إذا عُنِّن عنها، قال: فإن أتاها وإلاّ فُرِّق بينهما. والمُترَبِّصُ المُحتَكِرُ. ولي في متاعي رُبْصةٌ أي لي فيه تَربّصٌ؛ قال ابن بري: تَربَّصَ فِعْلٌ يتعدى بإسقاط حرف الجر كقول الشاعر: ترَبّصْ بها رَيْبَ المَنُونِ لعلَّها تُطَلَّقُ يوماً، أو يَمُوتُ حليلُها.

مقت (مقاييس اللغة) الميم والقاف والتاء كلمةٌ واحدةٌ تدل على شناءةٍ وقُبْح.ومَقَته مَقْتاً فهو مَقيتٌ وممقوت.

مقت (الصَحّاح في اللغة) مَقَتَهُ مَقْتاً: أبغضه، فهو مَقيتٌ وممقوتٌ.

مقت (لسان العرب) المَقيتُ: الحافِظُ. الأزهري: المُقيتُ، الميم فيه مضمومة وليست بأَصلية، وهو في المعتلات. ابن سيده: المَقْتُ أَشدُّ الإبْغاض. مَقُتَ مَقاتَةً، ومَقَته مَقْتاً: أَبْغَضه، فهو مَمْقُوتٌ ومَقِيتٌ، ومَقَّته؛ قال: ومن يُكْثِر التَسْآلَ، يا حُرُّ، لا يَزَلْ يُمقَّتُ في عَينِ الصَدِيق، ويَصْفَحُ وما أَمْقَته عندي وأَمْقَتَني له. قال سيبويه هو على معنيين: إذا قلت ما أَمْقَته عندي، فإنما تُخبر أنه ممقوت؛ وإذا قلتَ ما أَمْقَتَني له، فإنما تُخبر أنك ماقِتٌ.

§ 267.—XXXVIII, 82-89

AALD: kasāsu (v.) (kizāzu) See kāsisu, kissatu يقضم، يمضغ؛ يؤذي ، يلسع، يلدغ، يستهلك؟

AALD: kāsisu (adj.) استهلاك بالنار

ePSD: kazazakku

kazazak [INSECT] wr. kazaza "a destructive insect" Akk. kazazakku

AALD: qaşû See kaşû

AALD: kissatu (s.) (kişşatu or kizzatu) See kasāsu المرض

AALD: kaşû (v.) See kaşatu, kuşşu يقصع، يبرُد، يدعه يبرد

قصص (الصَحّاح في اللغة)والمِقصُّ: المقراضُ، وهما مقصّان. قال الأصمعي: قُصاصُ الشَعْرِ حيث تنتهي نبتَتُهُ من مقدّمه ومؤخَّره.

قصص (لسان العرب) قصَّ الشعر والصوف والظفر يقُصُّه قصّاً وقَصَّصه وقصّاه على التحويل: قطعه. وقصَّصْتُ الشَعرَ: قطعته. وطائرٌ مَقْصوصُ الجناح. وما يَقِصُّ في يده شيء أي ما يَبْرُدُ ولا يثبت؛ عن ابن الأعرابي؛ وأنشد: لأُمِّكَ وَيلَةٌ وعليك أُخْرى، فلا شاةٌ تَقِصُ ولا بَعيرُ.

التهذيب: أما ما قاله الليث في القُصاقِص بمعنى صوت الأسد ونعت الحيّة الخبيثة فإني لم أجِدْه لغير الليث، قال: وهو شاذٌ إن صحَّ. ورُوي عن أبي مالك: أسد قُصاقِصٌ ومُصامِصٌ وفُرافِصٌ شديد. ورجل قُصاقِصٌ فُرافِصٌ: يُشَبَّه بالأسد. والقُصْقُصُ والقُصْقُصة، بالضم، والقُصاقِصُ من الرجال: الغليظُ الشديد مع قِصَر.

كسس (لسان العرب) الكَسَسُ: أن يقصُر الحنك الأَعْلى عن الأسفل. والكَسْكاسُ: الرجل القصير الغليظ؛

كصص (الصَحّاح في اللغة) الكَصيصُ: الرعدةُ، ويقال الحركةُ والالتواءُ من الجهد. وقيل: الكَصيصُ الانقباض من الفرَق،

كصص (لسان العرب) كَصَّ يَكِصُّ كَصّاً وكَصِيصاً وكَصْكَص؛ عن ابن الأعرابي؛ وأنشد: جَدَّ به الكَصِيصُ ثم كَصْكَصا ويقال: له من فَرَقِه أَصِيصٌ وكَصِيصٌ أي انقباض.

كز (مقاييس اللغة) الكاف والزاء أصلٌ صحيحٌ يدلُّ على قبضٍ وتقبُّض. من ذلك الكَزازة: الانقباض واليُبْس. رجلٌ كَزٌّ، أي بخيل. ويقال: كَزَزْتُ الشَّيءَ، إذا ضيَّقته، فهو مكزوز. والكُزاز داءٌ يأخذه من شِدَة البَرْد. وأحسبه من تقبُّضِ الأطراف.

كزز (لسان العرب) الكَزُّ: الذي لا ينبسط. ووجْه كَزٌّ: قبيح، كَزَّ يَكَزُّ كَزازةً. وجَملٌ كَزٌّ: صُلْب شديد. وذَهبٌ كَزٌّ: صلب جدّاً. والكُزازُ داء يأْخُذُ من شِدَةِ البَرْدِ وتَعْتَري منه رِعْدَةٌ، وهو مَكْزُوزٌ. وقد كُزَّ الرجلُ، على صيغة ما لم يسمَّ فاعله: زُكِم. وأَكَزَّه الله، فهو مَكْزُوزٌ: مثل أَحَمَّه، فهو محموم، وهو تَشَنُّج يصيب الإنسان من البرد الشديد أو من خروج دمٍ كثير. ابن الأَعرابي: الكُزازُ الرِّعْدةُ من البرْد، والعامة تقول الكُزاز، وقد كُزَّ: انْقَبض من البرد. وفي البحديث: أن رجلاً اغتسل فكُزَّ فمات؛ الكُزازُ: داء يتولد من شدة البرد، وقيل: هو نفس البرد. واكْلأَزَّ اكْلِئْزازاً: انقبض، واللام زائدة.

§ 268.—XXXVIII, 90-92

ePSD: diāšu

rah [BEAT] wr. rah_2; ra-ah "to beat, kill; to break, crush; to flood; to thresh (grain with a flail)"
Akk. dâku; diāšu; hepû; rahāşu; rapāsu

<u>us</u> <u>[FOLLOW]</u> wr. us$_2$ "(to be) of a lesser quality; to drag; to stretch; to accompany, follow; a qualification of grain; to thresh (grain) by treading; to coagulate?" Akk. diāšu; redû; šadādu

الدَّيْسُ (القاموس المحيط) الدَّيْسُ: الثَّدْيُ، عِراقِيَّةٌ لا عربيَّةٌ.

دوس (مقاييس اللغة) الدال والواو والسين أُصَيْلٌ، وهو دَوْس الشَّيء. تقول دُسْتُه؛ والذي يُداسُ به مِدْوَسٌ. وحُمِل عليه قولُهم لما يَسُنُّ به الصَّيقلُ السَّيفَ مِدوسٌ، كأنَّه عند اتِّكائه عليه كالذي يَدُوس الشَّيء.

لَدَوْسُ (القاموس المحيط) الدَّوْسُ: الوطْءُ بالرِّجلِ، كالدِّياسِ والدِّياسة، والجِماعُ بمُبالغةٍ، والذُّلُّ، وابنُ عُدْنان بن عبد الله، أبو قبيلةٍ، وصَقْلُ السَّيفِ ونحوِه، وبالضم: الصَّقْلةُ. والمِدْوَسُ: المِصْقَلةُ، وما يُداسُ به الطَّعامُ، كالمِدْواس.

دوس (لسان العرب) والدَّوائس: البقر العوامل في الدَّوس؛ يقال: قد أَلْقَوا الدَّوائسَ في بَيْدرهم. والدَّوْسُ شدة وَطْءِ الشيء بالأَقدام. وقولهم الدَّوابَ حتى يتفتَّت كما يتفتت قصبُ السَّنابل فيصير تبناً، ومن هذا يقال: طريق مَدُوسٌ.

§ 270.—XXXVIII, 96-98

AALD: lilu (s.) Mari نوع من الاغنام

علل (لسان العرب) والعَلُّ التَّيس الضَّخْم العظيم؛ قال: وعَلْهباً من التُّيوس علاً والعَلُّ: القُراد الضَّخْم، وجمعها عِلالٌ (* قوله «وجمعها علال» كذا في الأصل وشرح القاموس، وفي التهذيب: أعلال) ، وقيل: هو القُراد المَهْزول، وقيل: هو الصغير الجسم. والعَلُّ الكبير المُسِنّ. ورَجُلٌ عَلٌّ: مُسِنٌّ نحيف ضعيف صغير الجُثَّة، شُبِّه بالقُراد فيقال: كأنه عَلٌّ؛ قال المُتنخِّل الهذلي: لَيسَ بعَلٍّ كبيرٍ لا شبابَ له، لكنْ أُثَيْلَةُ صافي الوَجْهِ مُقْتَبِل أي مُستأنِف الشَّباب، وقيل: العَلُّ المُسِنُّ الدقيق الجسم من كل شيء.

لَعَلَّ (مختار الصحاح) كلِمةُ شكٍّ وأَصْلُها عَلَّ واللَّامُ في أَوَّلِها زائدةٌ.

التَّيْسُ (القاموس المحيط) التَّيْسُ: الذَّكَرُ من الظِّباء والمَعَز والوُعُول، أو إذا أَتَى عليه سَنَةٌ

تيس (الصّحاح في اللغة) التَّيسُ من المَعْز، والجمع تُيوسٌ وأَتياسٌ. والتَّيَاسُ: الذي يمسكه. يقال للذكر من الظباء أيضاً: تَيسٌ، وللأنثى: عنزٌ. والمَتْيُوساءُ: التُّيوسُ. ويقال: اسْتَتْيَسَتِ العنزُ، كما يقال: استَنْوَقَ الجمل.

§ 271.—XXXVIII, 99-XXXIX, 2

AALD: şumbu (s.) şubbu عجلة العربة، العربة، الكراجة: عربة اثقال واطئة

ePSD: redû

<u>us</u> <u>[FOLLOW]</u> wr. us$_2$ "(to be) of a lesser quality; to drag; to stretch; to accompany, follow; a qualification of grain; to thresh (grain) by treading; to coagulate?" Akk. diāšu; redû; šadādu

صفف (لسان العرب) وصُفَّةُ الرَّحْل والسَّرْج: التي تضُمّ العَرْقُوتَين والبدادين من أَعْلاهما وأَسفلهما، والجمع صُفَفٌ على القياس. وحكى سيبويه: وصَفَ الدابة وصفَ لها عمل لها صُفَّة. وصَفَفْتُ لها صُفَّة أي عمِلْتُها لها. وصَفَفْتُ السرْجَ: جعلت له صُفَّة. وفي الحديث: نَهى عن صُفَفِ النُّمورِ؛ هي جمع صُفَّة وهي للسرج بمنزلة المِيثَرة من الرَّحل؛ قال ابن الأثير: وهذا كحديثه الآخر: نهى عن رُكوب جلود النُّمور. والصُّفَّةُ: الظُّلَّة. وصَفَّتِ الطيرُ في السماء تَصُفُّ: صَفَّتْ أجنحتها ولم تحركها. وقوله تعالى: والطيرُ صافَّاتٍ؛ باسطاتٍ أَجْنِحَتَها.

صف (العين) والصُّفَّةُ من البُنْيانِ والسَّرج ايضًا.

§ 273.—XXXIX, 8-19

AALD: šeššet (num.) (šiššet, šiššat) See šudušu ستة

ePSD: rēšu

<u>sağ</u> <u>[HEAD]</u> wr. sağ "head; person; capital" Akk. qaqqadu; rēšu

AALD: taqtītu See qatû النهاية، نهاية الوقت، نهاية العصر

ePSD: qatû

<u>til</u> <u>[COMPLETE]</u> wr. til; til$_3$ "(to be) complete(d); (to be) old, long-lasting; to end" Akk. gamāru; labāru; qatû

<u>zal</u> <u>[PASS]</u> wr. zal "to get up early; to finish, come to an end; to dissolve, melt, disintegrate, break down, collapse; to quake; to pass time" Akk. naharmumu; naharmuţu; qatû; râbu

ستت (لسان العرب) التهذيب، الليث: السِّتُّ والسِّتَّة في التأسيس على غير لفظيهما، وهما في الأصل سِدْسٌ وسِدْسَةٌ، ولكنهم أرادوا إدغام الدال في السين، فالتقيا عند مَخْرَج التاء، فغلَبَتْ عليها كما غلَبَتِ الحاءُ على الغين في لغة سَعْد، فيقولون: كنتُ محهم، في معنى معَهُم. وبيان ذلك: أنك تصغر ستة سُدَيْسة، وجميع تصغيرها على ذلك، وكذلك الأسداس. ابن السكيت: يقال جاء فلان خامساً وخامياً، وسادساً وسادياً وساتّاً؛ وأنشد:إذا ما عَدَّ أربعةٌ فِسالٌ، فزَوْجُكِ خامسٌ، وأبوكِ سادي قال: فمن قال سادساً، بناه على السُّدْسِ، ومَن قال ساتّاً بناه على لفظ سِتَّة وسِتٍّ، والأَصْلُ سِدْسة، فأدغموا الدال في السين، فصارت تاء مشددة؛ ومن قال سادياً وخامياً، أبدل من السين ياء؛

سدس (مقاييس اللغة) السين والدال والسين أصلٌ في العدد، وهو قولهم السُّدْس: جزءٌ من ستّة أجزاء. وإزارٌ سَدِيس، أي سُداسيّ. والسِّدْس من الورد في أظماء الإبل: أن تنقطع الإبل عن الورد خمسةَ أيام وترِد السّادس. وأسدسَ البعير، إذا ألقى السِّنّ بعد الرَّباعية، وذلك في السنة الثامنة. فأمّا الستة فمن هذا أيضاً غير أنّها مُدْغمة، كأنّها سِدْسة.

رأس (مقاييس اللغة) الراء والهمزة والسين أصلٌ يدل على تجمُّع وارتفاع.فالرَّأس رأسُ الإنسان وغيره.

رأس (الصّحاح في اللغة) وتقول: أَعِدْ عليَّ كلامك من رأسٍ، ولا تقل من الرأس، والعامة تقوله. وقولهم: أنت على رِياس أمرِك، أي أوّله. والعامة تقول: على رأسِ أمرك.

كتت (لسان العرب) كَتَّتِ القِدْرُ والجرَّةُ ونحوُهما تَكِتُّ كَتِيتاً إذا غلَتْ، وهو صوتُ الغَلَيان؛ والكَتيتُ: صوتُ البكْر، وهو فوق الكَشِيش. وكتَّ البَكْرُ يكِتُّ كَتّاً وكَتِيتاً إذا صاح صِياحاً لَيِّناً، وهو صَوتٌ بين الكَشِيش والهَدير. وقيل: الكَتيتُ ارتفاع البَكْر عن الكَشِيش، وهو أَوَّل هديره. وكتَّ القومَ يَكُتُّهم كَتّاً: عدَّهم وأَحْصاهم، وأَكثرُ ما يستعملونه في النفي، يقال: أَتانا في جيش ما يُكتُّ أَي ما يُعلَمُ عددُهم ولا يُحْصَى؛ قال: إلاَّ بجَيْش، ما يُكتُّ عديدُه، سُودِ الجُلُودِ، من الحديد، غِضابِ وفي المثل: لا تَكُتُّه أَو تَكُتُّ النجومَ أَي لا تَعُدُّه ولا تُحْصِيه. ابن الأَعرابي: جَيْشٌ لا يُكتُّ أَي لا يُحصَى، ولا يُسْهَى أَي لا يُحْزَرُ، ولا يُنْكَفُ أَي لا يُقْطَعُ. وفي حديث حُنَين: قد جاء جيش لا يُكَتُّ، ولا يُنْكَفُ أَي لا يُحْصَى، ولا يُبْلَغُ آخِرُه. والكَتُّ: الإِحْصاءُ. وفعل به ما كَتَّه أَي ما ساءَه. ورجل كَتٌّ: قليلُ اللحم؛ والكَتِيتُ والكَتْكَتةُ: المَشْيُ رُوَيْدا.

كتد (لسان العرب) وفي نوادرِ الأَعراب: يقال خرجوا علينا أَكْتاداً وأَكْداداً أَي فِرَقاً وأَرْسالاً.

قتت (لسان العرب) واقْتَتَّه اسْتَأْصَلَه؛

§ 274.—XXXIX, 20-44

ePSD: GABA

du [HEAP] wr. du$_8$ "to heap up, pile up" Akk. kamāru

du [SPREAD] wr. du$_8$ "to bake; to spread out mud to make bricks; to caulk" Akk. epû; labānu; pehû

duh [BRAN] wr. duh; dah-hu "bran" Akk. tuhhu

duh [LOOSEN] wr. duh; ze$_2$-eb "to loosen, release; to open" Akk. paţāru

gaba [CHEST] wr. gaba "breast, chest; frontier" Akk. irtu

ePSD: KAD$_4$

kad [TIE] wr. kad$_5$; kad$_4$; kad$_6$; kad$_8$ "to tie, gather; to itch, scratch; to weave a mat?" Akk. harādu; harāsu; kaşāru

ePSD: GUL

gul [DESTROY] wr. gul; gu-ul "to destroy; to break; to flatten; to carve, cut; to engrave" Akk. abātu; hepû; naqāru; sapānu

isin [STALK] wr. išin; i$_3$-si-na; e-si-na; isin$_x$(|ŠE.IGI.TUR|); isim$_2$; isim$_3$ "culm, grain stalk, stem" Akk. išīnu

si [UNMNG] wr. si$_{23}$; si$_5$ ""

sumun [COW] wr. sumun$_2$; u$_3$-sumun$_2$ "wild cow" Akk. rīmtu

sumun [VESSEL] wr. sumun$_2$; u$_3$-sun$_2$ "soaking vessel; beer mash" Akk. narţabu

ePSD: SA

sa [BUNDLE] wr. sa; ^{gi}sa "reed-bundle" Akk. kiššu

sa [ENTRY] wr. sa "lexical entry"

sa [JEWELRY] wr. sa "jewelry" Akk. šukuttu

sa [NET] wr. sa "net" Akk. šētu

sa [ROAST] wr. sa "to roast; to parch" Akk. qalû

sa [SINEW] wr. sa "gut; sinew, tendon; string (of a bow, musical instrument); catgut string" Akk. dāmu; erru; matnu; pitnu

عمل (لسان العرب) امِلٌ: هو الذي يتولَّى أُمور الرجل في ماله ومِلْكِه وعمَلِه، ومنه قيل للذي يَسْتَخْرِج الزكاةَ: عامِل. والعمَل: المِهْنة والفِعْل، والجمع أَعمال، عَمِلَ عمَلاً، وأَعْمَلَه غيرُهُ واسْتَعْمَله، واعْتَمَل الرجلُ: عَمِلَ بنفسه؛ ورجل عَمِلٌ: ذو عمَل؛

أمل (لسان العرب) الأَمَل والأَمْل والإِمْل: الرَّجاء؛ ابن الأَعرابي: الأَمَلة أَعوان الرجل، واحدهم آمِل.

جأب (الصَّحاح في اللغة) أبو زيد: الجَأْبُ: الغليظ من حُمُرِ الوحش، يهمز ولا يهمز. ويقال: فلان شَخْتُ الآل جأْبُ الصبْرِ، أي دقيق الشَخْصِ غليظ الصبرِ في الأمور. والجَأْبُ الكَسْبُ، تقول منه: جأَبْتُ أَجْأَبُ.

جأب (لسان العرب) والجَأْبُ الكَسْبُ. وجأَب يَجْأَبُ جَأْباً: كَسَبَ.

جوب (لسان العرب) وجابَ الشيءَ جَوْباً واجْتابَه: خرقه. وكلُّ مُجَوَّفٍ قطَعْتَ وسَطه فقد جُبْتَه. وجابَ الصخرة جَوْباً: نقبها. وفي التنزيل العزيز: وثَمُودَ الذين جابُوا الصَّخْرَ بالواد. قال الفرّاءُ: جابُوا خَرقُوا الصَّخْرَ فاتَّخَذُوه بُيُوتاً. ونحو ذلك قال الزجاجُ واعتبره بقوله: وتَنْحِتُون من الجبال بُيُوتاً فارِهين. وجاب يَجُوبُ جَوْباً: قطَعَ وخَرَقَ. وفلان جوّابٌ جَأْبٌ أي يَجُوبُ البلاد ويَكْسِبُ المالَ. وجابَ النعلَ جَوْباً: قَدَّها. والمِجْوَبُ: الذي يُجابُ به، وهي حديدةٌ يُجابُ بها أي يُقْطَعُ. وجابَ المفَازةَ والظُّلْمة جَوْباً واجْتابها: قطَعها. وجابَ البِلادَ يَجُوبُها جَوْباً: قَطَعها سَيْراً.وجُبْتُ البَلَدَ واجْتَبْتُه: قطَعْتُه. وانْجابَتِ الأَرضُ: انْخَرقَتْ. والجَوْبة: فَجْوةٌ ما بين البُيُوت. والجَوْبةُ: الحُفْرةُ.

جب (مقاييس اللغة) الجيم والباء في المضاعف أصلان: أحدهما القطْع، والثّاني تجمُّع الشيء.فأمّا الأول فالجبُّ القطع، يقال جبَبْتُه أَجُبُّه جَبّاً. والجُبّ: البئر.

جبب (لسان العرب) الجَبُّ: القَطْعُ. جَبَّه يَجُبُّه جَبّاً وجِباباً واجْتَبَّه وجَبَّ خُصاه جَبّاً: اسْتَأْصله. والجِبابُ تلقيح النخل. وجَبَّ النَخْلَ: لَقَّحه. ابن شميل: الجِبابُ الركايا تُحْفَر يُنْصَب فيها العنب أي يُغْرس فيها، كما يُحْفر للفَسِيلة من النخل، والجُبُّ الواحد. والشَّرَبَةُ الطَّرِيقةُ من شجر العنب على طَرِيقة شربه. والجَبُوبُ: وَجْهُ الأَرضِ. وقيل: هي الأَرضُ الغَلِيظةُ. وقيل: هي الأَرضُ الغليظةُ من الصَخْر لا من الطِّينِ. وقيل: هي الأَرض عامة، لا تجمع.

جبي (لسان العرب) والجَبا شَفة البئر؛ عن أبي ليلى. قال ابن بري: الجبا، بالفتح، الحوض والجبا، بالكسر، الماء؛

قعد (لسان العرب) والمَقْعَدُ والمَقْعَدَةُ: مكان القُعود. والمَقاعِدُ: موضِعُ قُعودِ الناس في الأسواق وغيرها. والمُقْعَدةُ الدَّوْخَلَةُ من الخُوص.

كعد (مقاييس اللغة) الكاف والعين والدال. يقولون: الكَعْد. الجُوالِق.

الجوالِقُ (القاموس المحيط) الجوالِقُ، بكسر الجيم واللامِ، وبضمِّ الجيم، وفتح اللامِ وكسرِها: وِعاءٌ م، ج: جَوالِقُ، كصَحائف، وجَواليقُ وجُوالِقاتٌ. وجِلِقٌّ، كحِمِّص بكسْرَتَيْن مُشَدَّدَة اللامِ، وكقِنَّب: دمشْقُ، أو غُوطَتُها.

جول (لسان العرب) جالَ في الحَرْب جَوْلة، وجالَ في التَّطْواف يَجول جَوْلاً وجَوَلاناً وجُؤولاً؛ والجُول والجالُ والجِيلُ؛ الأَخيرة عن كراع: ناحيةُ البئرِ والقبرِ والبحرِ وجانبُها. والجُول، بالضم: جدار البئر؛ قال أَبو عبيد: وهو كل ناحية من نواحي البئر إلى أَعلاها من أَسفلها؛ ابن الأَعرابي: الجُول الصَّخْرة التي في الماء يكون عليها الطَّيُّ، فإن زالت تلك الصخرة تهَوَّر البئر، فهذا أَصل الجُول؛

صيا (لسان العرب) والصَّيَاصِي: شَوْكُ النَّسَّاجين، واحدتُه صِيصِيةٌ، وقيل: صِيصِيةُ الحائك الذي يَخُطُّ به الثَّوْبَ وتُدْعى المِخَطّ. أَبو الهيثم: الصِّيصِيَةُ حَفٌّ صَغيرٌ من قُرُون الظِّباء تَنْسِجُ به المَرْأَةُ؛ قال دُرَيْدُ ابنُ الصِّمَّة: فجئْتُ إليه، والرِّماحُ تَنُوشُه كوَقْعِ الصَّياصي في النَّسِيج المُمَدَّد ومنه الحديث حين ذكر الفِتْنَة فقال: كأَنَّها صَياصِي البقر؛ قال أَبو بكر: شَبَّه الفِتْنة بقُرون البقر لشِدَّتها وصُعوبةِ الأَمْر فيها.

سيا (لسان العرب) سِيَةُ القَوْس، طَرَفُ قابها، وقيل: رأْسُها، وقيل: ما اعْوَجَّ من رأْسها، وهو بعد الطائف، والنَّسبُ إليه سِيَوِيٌّ. الأَصمعي: سِيَةُ القَوْس ما عُطِف من طرَفَيها، ولها سِيَتان، وفي السِّية الكُظْرُ وهو الفرْضُ الذي فيه الوتَرُ، وكان رؤْبة ابن العجاج يهمز سِئَةَ القَوْس وسائرُ العرب لا يهمزونها، والجمع سِياتٌ، والهاء عوضٌمن الواو المحذوفة كعِدةٍ، وفي الحديث: وفي يده قوسٌ آخذٌ بسيتها؛ ومنه حديث أبي سفيان: فانْثَنَتْ عليَّ سِيَتاها، يعني سِيَتي القَوْس.

الصِّيصُ (القاموس المحيط) الصِّيصُ، بالكسر: الشِّيصُ، والصِّيصَةُ، بالكسر: شَوْكَةُ الحائكِ يُسَوِّي بها السَّدى واللُّحمَةَ، وشَوْكَةُ الدِّيك، وقَرْنُ البَقرِ والظِّباء، والحِصْنُ، وكُلُّ ما امْتُنِعَ به

صيص (لسان العرب) والصِّيصِيةُ: شَوْكةُ الحائك التي يُسَوِّي بها السَّداة واللُّحْمة؛ قال دريد بن الصمة: فجئتُ إليه، والرِّماحُ تَنُوشُه، كوَقْعِ الصَّياصي في النَّسيج المُمَدَّد ومنه صِيصِيةُ الدِّيك التي في رِجْله. قال ابن بري: حق صيصية شوكة الحائك أن تُذكر في المعتل لأن لامَها ياءٌ وليس لامُها صاداً. وصَياصِي البقر: قُرونها وربما كانت تُرَكَّبُ في الرِّماح مكان الأَسِنَّة؛ وكلُّ شيء امْتُنِع به وتُحُصِّن به، فهو صِيصةٌ، ومنه قيل للحصون: الصَّياصِي؛ قيل: شَبَه الرماح التي تُشْرَع في الفتنة وما يشبهها من سائر السلاح بقرون بقر مجتمعة؛ والصِّيصَة أَيضاً: الوَتِدُ الذي يقْلع به التَّمر، والصِّنَّارةُ التي يُغْزَل بها ويُنْسَج.

سها (لسان العرب) وقَوْسٌ سَهْوَةٌ: مُواتِيَةٌ؛ قال ذو الرمة: قليل نصاب المالِ إلاَّ سِهامَه، وإلاَّ زَجُوماً سَهْوَةً في الأَصابع التهذيب: المُعَرَّسُ الذي عُمِلَ له عَرْسٌ، وهو الحائطُ يُجْعَل بين حائطي البيت لا يُبلَغ به أَقصاهُ، ثم يُجْعَل الجائز من طرَف العَرْس الداخل إلى أَقصى البيت، ويُسَقَّفُ البيت كلُّه، فما كان بين الحائطين فهو السَّهوة، وما كان تحت الجائز فهو المُخْدع؛ قال ابن سيده: السَّهْوةُ حائطٌ صغيرٌ يُبنى بين حائطي البيت ويُجعَلُ السقفُ على الجميع، فما كان وسطَ البيت فهو سَهْوةٌ، وما كان داخله فهو المُخْدَع، وقيل: هي صُفَّةٌ بين بيتين أَو مُخْدَع بين بيتين تَسْتَتِرُ بها سُقاةُ الإبل من الحرِّ، وقيل: هي كالصُّفَّة بين يدي البيت، وقيل: هي شبيهٌ بالرَّفِّ والطاق يوضع فيه الشيءُ، وقيل: هي بيت صغيرٌ منحدرٌ في الأَرض سَمْكه موتَفِعٌ في السماء شبيهٌ بالخزانة الصغيرة يكون فيها المتاعُ، وذكر أَبو عبيد أَنه سمعه من غير واحد من أَهل اليمن، وقيل: هي أَربعةُ أَعواد أَو ثلاثةٌ يعارَضُ بعضُها على بعض، ثم يوضَعُ عليه شيء من الأَمتعة. والسَّهْوَةُ: الكُنْدوجُ. والسَّهْوَة: الرَّوْشَنُ. والسَّهْوَة: الكَوَّةُ بيْن الدارَيْن. ابْنُ الأَعرابي: السَّهوة الحَجلةُ أَو مِثْلُ الحجلةِ. والسَّهْوَةُ: بيتٌ على الماءِ يستظِلُّون بهِ تَنْصبه الأَعراب. أَبو لَيلى: السَّهْوة سُتْرَةٌ تكُونُ قُدامَ فناءِ البيتِ، رُبَّما أَحاطت بالْبَيْتِ شبه سور حوْل الْبَيْت. وفي الْحديث:« أَنه دَخَل على عائشةَ وفي الْبَيْت سهْوةٌ عليْها سترٌ »، هُو منْ ذلِك، وقيل: هُو شبِيهٌ بالرَّفِّ أَو الطاق يُوضَعُ فيه الشَّيءُ. والسَّهْوَة: الصخرةُ، طائيَّةٌ، لا يُسمُّون بذلك غيْر الصَّخْرة، وخصَّصهُ في التَّهْذيب فقال: الصَّخْرةُ الَّتي يقُوم عليْها السَّاقي، وجَمْعُ ذلك كلِّه سِهاءٌ.

سها (تهذيب اللغة) والسَّهوة: الكُنْدوخ والسَّهوة: الرَّوشَنْ، والسَّهْوة: الغفْلة، والسَّهوة: الكُوّة بين الدارين. وروى الخرّاز عن ابن الأعرابيّ أنه قال: السَّهْوة: الحَجلة أو مثْل الحَجلة، والسهوة: بيتٌ على الماء يستظلّون به تنصبه الأعراب. وقال أبو الهيثم: قال أبو ليلَى: السَّهْوة: سُترة تكون قُدّام فناء البيت، ربما أحاطت بالبيت شِبْه سُور حول البيت.

أتي (لسان العرب) الإتْيان: المَجيء. أَتيْته أَتْيا وأُتِيا وإتْيا وإتْيانا وإتْيانةً ومَأْتاةً: جِئْته؛

قوت (مقاييس اللغة) والقُوت: العَوْل. يقال: قُتُّه قَوتاً، والاسم القُوت. ويقال: اقْتَتْ لنارك قِيتةً، أي أطعِمْها الحطَب.

قطط (العباب الزاخر) قَطَطْتُ الشيء أقُطُّه -بالضم-: إذا قطعته عرضاً، وقطَّ السِّعْرُ يقِطُّ، بالْكسر، قطّا وقُطُوطا، فهُو قاطٌّ ومقْطُوطٌ بمعْنى فاعل: غلا. ويُقالُ: وردْنا أرضا قطّا سعْرُها؛ قال أبو وجْزة السَّعديّ: >أشكو إلى الله العزيز الجبّار، ***ثُمّ إليْك اليوم بُعْد المُسْتار، وحاجة الحيّ وقطّ الأسْعار وقال شمرٌ: قطّ السّعْرُ، إذا غلا، خطأٌ عنْدي إنما هو بمعْنى فتر، وقال الأزهري: وهم شمرٌ فيما قال. ورُوي عن الفرّاء أنه قال: حطّ السّعْرُ حُطوطا وانْحطّ انحطاطا وكسر وانْكسر إذا فتر، وقال :سعْرٌ مقْطوطٌ وقد قطّ إذا غلا، وقدْ قطّه اللهُ.

قطط (تاج العروس) وقطّ السّعْرُ يقطّ، بالكسْر، ورُوِي عن الفراء: قُطّ السّعْرُ، بالضّمّ؛ أي على ما لمْ يُسمّ فاعلُه، قطّا وقُطُوطا، بالضّمّ، فهو قاطٌّ، وقطٌّ، ومقْطوطٌ، الأخيرُ بمعنى فاعِل: غلا، وقال شمرٌ: وقطّ السّعْرُ بمعْنى غلا خطأٌ عنْدي، وإنّما هو بمعْنى فتر، قال الأزْهريُّ: وهمَ شمرٌ فيما قال. ويُقال: وردْنا أرْضا قطّا سعْرُها، قال أبو وجْزة السّعْديُّ: أشْكو إلى الله العزيز الجبّار *** ثمّ إليْك اليوم بُعْد المُسْتار وحاجة الحيّ وقطّ الأسْعار ورُوي عن الفرّاء أنّه قال: حطّ السّعْرُ حُطوطا، وانْحطّ انحطاطا، وكُسر وانْكسر، إذا فتر.

§ 278.—XXXIX, 58-66

AALD: bennu (s.) نوع من الصرع

بين (مجمل اللغة) البين: الفراق. وبان الشيء: (أنفصل) يبين بينونة.

البيْنُ (القاموس المحيط) البيْنُ: يكونُ فُرْقة ووصْلا، واسماً، وظرْفاً مُتمكناً، والبُعْدُ، وبالكسر: الناحيةُ، والفصْلُ بين الأرْضيْن، وارتفاعٌ في غلظ، وقدْرُ مدِّ البصر، وبانُوا بيْناً وبيْنونةً: فارقوا، و~ الشيءُ بيْناً بُيوناً وبيْنونةً: انْقطع،

§ 281.—XXXIX, 88-96

AALD: abāku (v.) يُرسل، يبعث، يقود، يجلب، يُحضر (حيوان او عبد)
ePSD: abāku
<u>šu us</u> <u>[SEND]</u> wr. šu us_2 "to send; to lead away; to fetch" Akk. abāku
ePSD: baqqu
<u>nu</u> <u>[FLY]</u> wr. nu "(small) fly, mosquito" Akk. baqqu

بقق (لسان العرب) البَقُّ: البعُوض، واحدته بقَّة. وأبقَ: كثر بقُّه. وأبقَ الوادي إذا أخرج نباته؛ وبقَ الرجلُ يبق ويَبُقُ بقّاً وبققاً وبقيقاً وأبقَ وبقْبق: كثَرَ كلامُه. وبقَ علينا كلامَه: أكثره، وبقَ كلاماً وبقَ به. ورجل مِبقّ وبقاق وبقْباقٌ: كثير الكلام، أخطأ أو أصاب، وقيل: كثير الكلام مُخلّط.
ويقال: بقْبقَ علينا الكلام أي فرّقه. وبقّت السماءُ بقّاً وأبقّت: كثر مطرها وتتابع وجاءت بمطر شديد. وبقَ يَبُقُ بقّاً: أوسع من العطيّة. وبقَ لنا العطاءَ: أوسعه؛ ويقال للكثير الكلام: بقْباقٌ. ابن الأعرابي: البقَقةُ الثّرْثارُون. وبقَ الخبرَ بقّاً: نشره وأرسله. والبقْبقةُ: حكاية صوت كما يُبقْبِق الكوزُ في الماء. يقال: بقْبقَ الكوزُ بالماءِ أي صوّت. وبقْبقتِ القِدر: غلت.
فقق (لسان العرب) والفقاقة والفقْفاق: الكثير الكلام الذي لا غناءَ عنده. والفقْفقة في الكلام: كالفيْهقَة، وقيل: هو التخليط فيه. وفقّقْت الشيء إذا فتحته.
أبق (مقاييس اللغة) الهمزة والباء والقاف يدلُّ على إباق العبد، والتشدُّد في الأمر. أبق العبد يأبق أبْقاً وأبقاً. ويقال عبدٌ أبُوقٌ وأبّاق. قال أبو زيد: تأبّقَ الرجل استتر. قال بعضهم: يقال للرّجل إنّ فيك كذا، فيقول: "أمَا والله ما أتأبّق"، أي ما أنكِر.
أبق (لسان العرب) الإباقُ: هرَبُ العبيد وذهابهم من غير خوف ولا كدِّ عمل، قال: وهذا الحكم فيه أن يُردَّ، فإذا كان من كدّ عمل أو خوف لم يردَّ.
وفي حديث شريح: كان يَرُدُّ العبدَ من الإباق الباتِّ أي القاطع الذي لا شُبهة فيه. وقد أبق أي هرب. وتأبّق استتر، ويقال احتبس؛ وروى ثعلب أنَّ ابن الأعرابي أنشده: ألا قالتْ بهانِ ولم تأبّقْ: كبرْتَ ولا يليقُ بك النَّعيمُ قال: لم تأبّق إذا لم تأثّم من مقالتها، وقيل: لم تأبّق لم تأنَف؛
وفي الحديث: أن عبداً لابن عمر، رضي الله عنهما، أبق فلحِق بالروم. ابن سيده: أبق يأبِق ويأبُق أبْقاً وإباقاً، فهو آبق، وجمعه أُبّاق. وأبق وتأبّق: استخفى ثم ذهب؛ قال الأعشى:فذاك ولم يَعجِزْ من الموتِ ربُّه، ولكنْ أتاه الموتُ لا يتأبّقُ الأزهري: الإباقُ هرَبُ العبد من سيده. قال الله تعالى في يونس، عليه السلام، حين ندَّ في الأرضِ مُغاضِباً لقومه: إذ أبَقَ إلى الفُلْك المَشْحُون.
أفق (لسان العرب) وأَفق يأْفِق: ركب رأْسه في الآفاق. وأفق على أصحابه يأْفِق أفْقاً: أفضلَ عليهم؛ ويقال: أَفق فلان إذا ذهب في الأَرض، وأفق في العطاء أي فضّل وأعطى بعضاً أكثر من بعض. الأصمعي: بعير آفِق وفرس آفق إذا كان رائعاً كريماً والبعير عتيقاً كريماً.
عفق (مقاييس اللغة) العين والفاء والقاف أصل صحيح، يدلُّ على مجيءٍ وذهاب، وربما يدلُّ على صوت من الأصوات. قال الخليل: عفق الرَّجل يَعْفِق عفْقاً، إذا ركب رأسَه فمضَى. تقول: لا يزال يعفق العفقة ثم يرجع، أي يغيب الغيبة. من الباب: عفقه عن حاجته، أي ردّه وصرَفه عنها. قال ابن الأعرابيّ: تعفّقَ بالشيء، إذا رجع إليه مرّةً بعد أخرى. ومن الباب: عفقت الرِّيحُ التُّراب، إذا ضربتْه وفرّقته.
عفق (الصّحاح في اللغة) وعفَق بها، أي حبَق. والعفَاقةُ: الاستُ؛ يقال كذبتْ عفَاقَتُك، إذا حبَق. والعفْقُ سرعة الإيراد وكثرتهُ. وعفقتِ الإبلُ تَعْفق عفْقاً إذا كانت ترجع إلى الماء كلَّ يوم.
عفق (لسان العرب) عفقَ: الرجلُ يَعْفِقُ عفْقاً: ركب رأسه فمضى. وعفقت الإبل تعْفِقُ عفْقاً وعُفوقاً: أُرْسلت في المرعى فمرَّت على وجوهها، وعَفقتْ عن المرْعى إلى الماء: رجعت. والعُفُوق والعِفاق: شبه الخُنوس، عفَق يعْفِقُ أي خنس وارتدّ ورجع؛ ومنه قول لقمان في حديث فيه طُول: خُذِي مني أخي ذا العِفاق، صَفّاقٌ أفّاقٌ يعْملُ البكْرة والساق؛ يصفه بالسير في آفاق الأرض راكباً وماشياً على ساقه. وعفَق الشيءَ يعْفِقُه عفْقاً: جمعه أو ضمه إليه. وعافقَهُ معافقةً وعِفاقاً: عالجه وخادعه؛

www.ingramcontent.com/pod-product-compliance
Ingram Content Group UK Ltd.
Pitfield, Milton Keynes, MK11 3LW, UK
UKHW051029041026
15470UKWH00015B/1745

9 780998 172705